ENFORCING CONSUMER AND CAPITAL MARKETS LAW

Co-funded by the
Erasmus+ Programme
of the European Union

The European Commission's support for the production of this publication does not constitute an endorsement of the contents, which reflect the views only of the authors, and the Commission cannot be held responsible for any use which may be made of the information contained therein.

ENFORCING CONSUMER AND CAPITAL MARKETS LAW

The Diesel Emissions Scandal

Edited by
Beate Gsell
Thomas M.J. Möllers

INTERSENTIA
Cambridge – Antwerp – Chicago

Intersentia Ltd
8 Wellington Mews
Wellington Street | Cambridge
CB1 1HW | United Kingdom
Tel: +44 1223 736 170
Email: mail@intersentia.co.uk
www.intersentia.com | www.intersentia.co.uk

Distribution for the UK and
Rest of the World (incl. Eastern Europe)
NBN International
1 Deltic Avenue, Rooksley
Milton Keynes MK13 8LD
United Kingdom
Tel: +44 1752 202 301 | Fax: +44 1752 202 331
Email: orders@nbninternational.com

Distribution for Europe
Intersentia Publishing nv
Groenstraat 31
2640 Mortsel
Belgium
Tel: +32 3 680 15 50
Email: mail@intersentia.be

Distribution for the USA and Canada
Independent Publishers Group
Order Department
814 North Franklin Street
Chicago, IL 60610
USA
Tel: +1 800 888 4741 (toll free) | Fax: +1 312 337 5985
Email: orders@ipgbook.com

Enforcing Consumer and Capital Markets Law. The Diesel Emissions Scandal

Artwork on cover: Seb Antoniou / sebantoniou.com

ISBN 978-1-78068-964-7
D/2020/7849/87
NUR 820

British Library Cataloguing in Publication Data. A catalogue record for this book is available from the British Library.

ACKNOWLEDGEMENTS

The editors would like to warmly thank Dominic Merk for organising and managing the INspiRE conference that resulted in this publication and for the editing work on this book. He was supported by Benita Bentlage, Michael Biesinger, Tristan Eickholt, Laura Kögel, Jan Längle, Laura Mähle, Alexander Mathis, Dr. Sebastian Meyer, Johanna Obermaier, Sandra Paulson, Antonia Ruck, Matthias Veicht and Lea Wolf. Many thanks also to all of them.

We owe further thanks to Ahmed Hegazi at Intersentia, as well as Lisa Cornish, for carrying out the linguistic revision of the manuscript.

We are also indebted to Ann-Christin Maak-Scherpe for her support and patience throughout the project.

Finally, we would like to thank in particular the authors of the individual chapters for their reliable work and the constant updating with regard to the developments of the diesel emissions scandal in the individual countries.

CONTENTS

PART V. INTRADISCIPLINARY ANALYSIS AND REFORM RECOMMENDATIONS

LIST OF CASES

AUSTRALIA

AUSTRIA

BRAZIL

CANADA

CHINA

DENMARK

EUROPEAN UNION AND SUPRANATIONAL COURTS

FRANCE

GERMANY

ITALY

LITHUANIA

NETHERLANDS

PORTUGAL

SWITZERLAND

UNITED KINGDOM

USA

LIST OF ABBREVIATIONS

ABGB	Allgemeines bürgerliches Gesetzbuch (*Austrian Civil Code*)
AC	Appeal Cases, Law Reports
ACCC	Australian Competition and Consumer Commission
ACM	Netherlands Authority for Consumers and Markets
ACPR	Autorité de contrôle prudentiel et de resolution (*French Prudential Control Authority*)
ACSR	Australian Corporations and Securities Reports
ADR	Alternative Dispute Resolution
ADRs	American Depositary Receipts
AFM	Netherlands Authority for the Financial Markets
AG	Aktiengesellschaft (*German stock corporation*)
AG	Die Aktiengesellschaft (Journal)
AGCM	Autorita' Garante della Concorrenza e del Mercato
AJA	Danish Administration of Justice Act (2018) (*retsplejeloven*)
AJP	Aktuelle Juristische Praxis (Journal)
AK Wien	Arbeiterkammer Wien (*Chambers of Labour Vienna*)
AktG	Aktiengesetz (*Austrian/German Stock Corporation Act*)
ALJ	Australian Law Journal
ALR	Australian Law Reports
ALRC	Australian Law Reform Commission
AMAG	Automobil und Motoren AG
AMF	Financial Markets Regulator
AnwBl	Anwaltsblatt (Journal)
APRA	Australian Prudential Regulation Authority
ARCEP	Autorité de régulation des communications électroniques et des postes (*French Regulatory Authority for Electronic Communications*)
art/arts	article/articles

ASADIP	Asociación Americana de Derecho Internacional Privado (*American Association for International Private Law*)
ASIC	Australian Securities and Investments Commission
ATM	Automated Teller Machine
AVIFA	Association of International Victims of Motor Vehicle Fraud
B2B	Business-to-Business
B2C	Business-to-Consumer
BaFin	Bundesanstalt für Finanzdienstleistungsaufsicht (*German Federal Financial Supervisory Authority*)
BB	Betriebs-Berater (Journal)
BeckRS	beck-online.RECHTSPRECHUNG
BGB	Bürgerliches Gesetzbuch (*German Civil Code*)
BGBl	Bundesgesetzblatt (*Austrian/German Federal Law Gazette*)
BGer	Bundesgericht (*Swiss Federal Court*)
BGH	Bundesgerichtshof (*German Federal Court of Justice*)
BGHZ	Entscheidungen des Bundesgerichtshofes in Zivilsachen (*Case Reporter German Federal Court of Justice, Civil Section*)
BIICL	British Institute of International and Comparative Law
BImSchG	Bundesimmissionsschutzgesetz (*German Federal Emission Protection Act*)
BL	Bannister Law
BörseG 2018	Börsegesetz 2018 (*Austrian Stock Exchange Act 2018*)
BRS	Boston Retirement System
BT-Drucks	Bundestagsdrucksache (*Official Document of the German Bundestag*)
BVerfG	Bundesverfassungsgericht (*German Federal Constitutional Court*)
BVerfGE	Entscheidungen des Bundesverfassungsgerichts (*Case Reporter German Federal Constitutional Court*)
C2C	Consumer-to-Consumer
CanLII	Canadian Legal Information Institute
CARB	California Air Resources Board
CASA	Centro de Arbitragem do Sector Automóvel

CBP	Customs and Border Protection
CC	Danish Act on Consumer Complaints (2015)
CCA	China Consumers' Association
CDC	Consumer Defense Code
CEDEP	Centro de Estudios de Derecho, Economía y Política (*Research Center for Law, Economy and Politics*)
CEO	Chief Executive Officer
CFI	Court of First Instance (EU)
CFPB	Consumer Financial Protection Bureau
CFR	Charter of Fundamental Rights of the European Union
Ch	Chancery Division
ch	chapter
ChD	Chancery Division, Law Reports
CJEU	Court of Justice of the European Union
CLCV	La Confédération du Logement et du Cadre de Vie
CLR	Commonwealth Law Reports
CMA	Capital Market Act (2018) (*kapitalmarkedsloven*)
CMA	Competition and Markets Authority
CMC	Computer-mediated-communication
CMLR	Common Market Law Review
CN¥	Chinesischer Yuan
Colum L Rev	Columbia Law Review
COM	Danish Consumer Ombudsman (*Forbrugerombudsmanden*)
CPC	Civil Procedure Code
CPC	Consumer Protection Cooperation
CPR	Canadian Patent Reporter
CPR	Civil Procedure Rules
CPS	Crown Prosecution Service
CRA	Credit Rating Agencies
DAR	Deutsches Autorecht (Journal)
DCC	Dutch Civil Code
DCCP	Dutch Code of Civil Procedure
DGCCRF	General Directorate for Competition Policy, Consumer Affairs and Fraud Control
DJT	Deutscher Juristentag

DPA	Deferred Prosecution Agreement
DPDC	Department of Consumer Protection and Defense
EBLR	European Business Law Review
EC	European Commission
ECFR	European Company and Financial Law Review
ECHR	European Convention on Human Rights
ECJ	European Court of Justice
ECR	European Court Reports
ECtHR	European Court of Human Rights
edn	edition
EEA	European Economic Area
EGR	Exhaust Gas Recirculation System
EGZPO	Einführungsgesetz zur Zivilprozessordnung
EP	European Parliament
EPA	United States Environmental Protection Agency
ERPL	European Review of Private Law
ESF	Ecologie Sans Frontière
ESMA	European Securities and Markets Authority
EU	European Union
EuR	Europarecht (Journal)
EvBl	Evidenzblatt
EWHC	England and Wales High Court
EWiR	Entscheidungen zum Wirtschaftsrecht (Journal)
EWS	Europäisches Wirtschafts- und Steuerrecht (Journal)
f/ff	et sequens/et sequentia
FAA	Federal Arbitration Act
FAW-Volkswagen	FAW-Volkswagen Automotive Co., Ltd.
FBI	Federal Bureau of Investigation
FCA	Federal Court of Australia
FCA	Fiat Chrysler Automobiles
FCA	Financial Conduct Authority
FCAFC	Federal Court of Australia Full Court
FCR	Federal Court Reports
FI	Il Foro Italiano
FLR	Federal Law Reports
FRCP	Federal Rules of Civil Procedure

FRD	Federal Rules Decisions Articles
FSA	Danish Financial Supervisory Authority (*Finanstilsynet*)
FSMA	Financial Services and Markets Act
FTC	Federal Trade Commission
GDPR	General Data Protection Regulation
GesRZ	Zeitschrift für Gesellschafts- und Unternehmensrecht (Journal)
GG	Grundgesetz (*German Basic Law*)
GLO	Group Litigation Order
GmbH	Gesellschaft mit beschränkter Haftung (*Limited Liability Company*)
GRUR	Gewerblicher Rechtsschutz und Urheberrecht (Journal)
GVG	Gerichtsverfassungsgesetz (*German Court Constitution Act*)
GWB	Gesetz gegen Wettbewerbsbeschränkungen (*German Act Against Restraints of Competition*)
Harv L Rev	Harvard Law Review
HCA	High Court of Australia
HGB	Handelsgesetzbuch (*German Commercial Code*)
IA	Danish Interest Act (2014) (*renteloven*)
IBAMA	Instituto Brasileiro do Meio Ambiente e dos Recursos Naturais Renováveis (*Brazilian Institute for the Environment and Natural Ressources*)
ICCT	International Council on Clean Transportation
IFG	Gesetz zur Regelung des Zugangs zu Informationen des Bundes (*German Freedom of Information Act*)
IGE	Intergovernmental Group of Experts
Ind LJ	Indiana Law Journal
INspiRE	Jean-Monnet Centre of Excellence 'European Integration – Rule of Law and Enforcement' at the University of Augsburg
IOSCO	International Organisation of Securities Commissions
JBl	Juristische Blätter (Journal)
JFin	Journal of Finance
JPML	Judicial Panel on Multidistrict Litigation

JZ	JuristenZeitung (Journal)
KapMuG	Kapitalanleger-Musterverfahrensgesetz (*German Capital Markets Model Case Act*)
KartG	Kartellgesetz (*Austrian Cartel Act*)
KB	King's Bench Division, Law Reports
KBA	Kraftfahrt-Bundesamt (*German Federal Motor Transport Authority*)
KMG	Kapitalmarktgesetz (*Austrian Capital Market Act*)
KSchG	Konsumentenschutzgesetz (*Austrian Consumer Protection Act*)
L&Soc'y Rev	Law and Society Review
LA	Danish Limitation Act (2015) (*forældelsesloven*)
LG	Landgericht (*Austrian/German Regional Court*)
MA	Danish Marketing Practices Act (2017) (*markedsføringsloven*)
MAR	Market Abuse Regulation (EU) No 596/2014 of the European Parliament and the Council of 16 April 2014
MB	Maurice Blackburn
mn	marginal number
n	number/footnote
NCA	National Competent Authorities
NEDC	New European Driving Cycle
NGO	Non-Governmental Organisation
NJW	Neue Juristische Wochenschrift (Journal)
No	number
NOx	nitrogen oxides
NSW	New South Wales
NSWCA	New South Wales Court of Appeal
NZV	Neue Zeitschrift für Verkehrsrecht (Journal)
ÖBl	Österreichische Blätter für Gewerblichen Rechtsschutz und Urheberrecht (Journal)
OCLAESP	Office Central de Lutte contre les Violations à l'Environnement et à la Santé Publique
ODR	Online Dispute Resolution
OeNB	Austrian National Bank
OGH	Oberster Gerichtshof (*Supreme Court of Austria*)

OJ	Official Journal
OLG	Oberlandesgericht (*Austrian/German Higher Regional Court*)
ONSC	Ontario Superior Court of Justice, Canada
OWiG	Gesetz über Ordnungswidrigkeiten (*German Act on Regulatory Offences*)
OZW	Zeitschrift für Wirtschaftsrecht (Journal)
PR	Prospectus Regulation
PROCON	Proteção e Defesa do Consumidor
PSA	Peugeot Société Anonyme
Pty Ltd.	Proprietary Limited
QB	Queen's Bench Division, Law Reports
QCCS	Québec Superior Court, Canada
RDG	Rechtsdienstleistungsgesetz (*German Act on Out-of-Court Legal Services*)
RDP	Revista di Diritto Processuale (Journal)
RdW	Österreichisches Recht der Wirtschaft (Journal)
RIW	Recht der Internationalen Wirtschaft (Journal)
RTR	Rundfunk und Telekom Regulierungs-GmbH (*Austrian Regulatory Authority for Broadcasting and Telecommunications*)
s	section
SAIC Volkswagen	SAIC Volkswagen Automotive Co., Ltd.
SCR	Selective Catalytic Reduction
SEC	Securities & Exchange Commission
SENACON	Secretaria Nacional do Consumidor
SFO	Serious Fraud Office
SGA	Danish Sale of Goods Act (2014) (*købeloven*)
Sim & St.	Simons & Stuart's Vice Chancellor's Reports
SINDEC	Sistema Nacional de Informações de Defesa do Consumidor
SNDC	National Consumer Defense System
SPSEIC	Danish State Prosecutor for Serious Economic and International Crime (*Statsadvokaten for Særlig Økonomisk og International Kriminalitet*)
StGB	Strafgesetzbuch (*Austrian/German Criminal Code*)
STJ	Brazilian Supreme Court of Justice

StPO	Strafprozeßordnung (*Austrian/German Code of Criminal Procedure*)
TAR	technical assisted review
TD	Transparency Directive
TDI	Turbocharged direct injection
TEU	Treaty on European Union
TFEU	Treaty on the Functioning of the European Union
TGI	Public Health Unit of the Paris Court of First Instance
TKG	Telekommunikationsgesetz (*Austrian Telecommunications Act*)
TPA	Trade Practices Act
TTIP	Transatlantic Trade and Investment Partnership
U.S.C.	United States Code
UCPD	Unfair Commercial Practices Directive
UFC Que Choisir	Union fédérale des consommateurs
UKlaG	Unterlassungsklagengesetz (*German Injunctions Act*)
UKSC	United Kingdom Supreme Court
UN	United Nations
UNCITRAL	United Nations Commission on International Trade Law
UNCTAD	UN Conference on Trade and Development
UNGCP	UN Guidelines on Consumer Protection
US/USA	United States of America
UTAC	United Test and Assembly Center Ltd.
UWG	Gesetz gegen den unlauteren Wettbewerb (*Austrian Act Against Unfair Competition*)
VbR	Zeitschrift für Verbraucherrecht (Journal)
VbVG	Verbandsverantwortlichkeitsgesetz (*Austrian Associations Liability Act*)
VCA	Vehicle Certification Agency
VEB	Vereniging van Effectenbezitters (*Association of Stockholders*)
VGI	Volkswagen Group Italia
VIP	very important person
VLRC	Victorian Law Reform Commission
VuR	Verbraucher und Recht (Journal)

VW	Volkswagen
VwGoA	Volkswagen Group of America, Inc.
vzbv	Verbraucherzentrale Bundesverband (*Federation of German Consumer Organisations*)
WAMCA	Wet Afwikkeling Massaschade in Collectieve Actie (*Collective Redress of Mass Damages Act*)
WASC	Western Australia Supreme Court
wbl	Wirtschaftsrechtliche Blätter (Journal)
WCAM	Wet Collectieve Afwikkeling Massaschade (*Collective Settlement of Mass Damage Act*)
WLR	Weekly Law Reports
WM	Zeitschrift für Wirtschafts- und Bankrecht (Journal)
WpHG	Wertpapierhandelsgesetz (*German Securities Trading Act*)
WuB	Entscheidungsanmerkungen zum Wirtschafts- und Bankrecht (Journal)
WuW	Wirtschaft und Wettbewerb (Journal)
ZBB	Zeitschrift für Bankrecht und Bankwirtschaft (Journal)
ZEuP	Zeitschrift für europäisches Privatrecht (Journal)
ZfPW	Zeitschrift für die gesamte Privatrechtswissenschaft (Journal)
ZGR	Zeitschrift für Unternehmens- und Gesellschaftsrecht (Journal)
ZHR	Zeitschrift für das gesamte Handelsrecht und Wirtschaftsrecht (Journal)
ZIP	Zeitschrift für Wirtschaftsrecht (Journal)
ZPO	Zivilprozessordnung (*Austrian/German Code of Civil Procedure*)
ZVglRWiss	Zeitschrift für Vergleichende Rechtswissenschaft (Journal)
ZZP	Zeitschrift für Zivilprozess (Journal)
ZZPInt	Zeitschrift für Zivilprozess International (Journal)

LIST OF CONTRIBUTORS

Prof. Dr. Willem H. van Boom
University of Leiden

Prof. Peter Cashman
LL.B, Dip. Crim. (Melbourne), LL.M, PhD (London), Barrister, Adjunct Professor, University of New South Wales

Prof. Dr. Tanja Domej
University of Zurich

Assistant Prof. Dr. Marcello Gaboardi
Bocconi University of Milan

Prof. Dr. Beate Gsell
Ludwig-Maximilians-Universität Munich; Judge at Munich Higher Regional Court (OLG München)

Jutta Gurkmann
Verbraucherzentrale Bundesverband e.V.

Patrick Honegger-Müntener
MLaw, University of Zurich

Prof. Dr. Emmanuel Jeuland
Director of the Sorbonne Institute of Legal Research, Paris

Remigijus Jokubauskas
Court of Appeal of Lithuania (Adviser of the Division of Court Practice)

Prof. Dr. Georg E. Kodek
LL.M (Northwestern), Vienna University of Economics and Business, Judge at the Supreme Court of Justice of Austria

Dr. Lene Kohl
Rechtsanwältin (German Attorney), Osborne Clarke, Berlin

Dr. Petra Leupold
LL.M. (UCLA), Johannes Kepler University Linz, Director of VKI-Academy, Verein für Konsumenteninformation

Prof. Dr. (Heidelberg) Claudia Lima Marques
LL.M (Tübingen), Federal University of Rio Grande do Sul, UFRGS, Porto Alegre

Prof. Dr. Caroline Meller-Hannich
Martin-Luther-University of Halle-Wittenberg

Prof. Dr. Thomas M.J. Möllers
University of Augsburg

Prof. Dr. Charlotte M.D.S. Pavillon
University of Groningen

Anders Schäfer
University of Copenhagen; Attorney-at-law, Kammeradvokaten/Poul Schmidt, Copenhagen

Prof. Amy J. Schmitz
Elwood L. Thomas Missouri Endowed Professor of Law, School of Law, University of Missouri, U.S.A.

Dr. John Sorabji
MA (Oxon), MPhil, LL.M, Barrister, University College London

Associate Prof. Dr. Henrique Sousa Antunes
Catholic University of Portugal, Lisbon

Prof. Dr. Egidija Tamošiūnienė
Vilnius University, Judge at the Court of Appeal of Lithuania

Prof. Dr. Rüdiger Veil
Ludwig-Maximilians-University of Munich

Maximilian Weiss
LL.M. (Northwestern), Rechtsanwalt (German Attorney), TILP Litigation, Kirchentellinsfurt

Prof. Dr. Tong Zhang
LL.M. (Frankfurt am Main), China University of Political Science and Law

PART I
INTRODUCTION

INTRODUCTION

Beate GSELL* and Thomas M.J. MÖLLERS**

I. THE DIESEL EMISSIONS SCANDAL AT VOLKSWAGEN AG: THE FACTS

If one wishes to analyse the enforcement of consumer protection law and capital markets law worldwide, the diesel scandal appears to present a perfect opportunity. The car manufacturer Volkswagen – and perhaps also other car manufacturers – allegedly manipulated their diesel engines in order to comply with emission requirements. As the largest car manufacturer in the world, Volkswagen sold its cars in almost every country. Volkswagen and its subsidiaries, such as Audi, had installed a 'defeat device' in their diesel engines in order to make emissions

* Beate Gsell, Dr., Professor, Ludwig-Maximilians-Universität Munich, Chair of Civil Law, Civil Procedure, European Private Law and Procedure; Judge at Munich Higher Regional Court (OLG München).

** Thomas M.J. Möllers, Dr., Professor, University of Augsburg, Chair of Civil Law, Commercial Law, European Law, International Private Law and Comparative Law, Jean-Monnet-Chair *ad personam*.

appear lower during emissions testing than they actually are in everyday use of the vehicles.[1] Even if the permissible emission limits in the individual countries differ to some extent, the facts of the cases – namely the manipulated diesel engines – remain the same.

II. THE BOOK INSPIRED BY THE JEAN-MONNET CENTRE OF EXCELLENCE INSPIRE: PEOPLE

The Jean-Monnet Centre of Excellence INspiRE (European Integration – Rule of Law and Enforcement)[2] at the University of Augsburg aims to bring together several legal spheres and to collaborate across the various areas of the law, as similar questions arise in multiple Member States of the European Union. Its mission is to conduct research on European law from the perspective of legal enforcement ('law in action'). The people behind INspiRE are Thomas MJ Möllers, Ferdinand Wollenschläger, Wolfgang Wurmnest (all Augsburg), Tong Zhan (Beijing), Frédérique Ferrand (Lyon), Beate Gsell (Munich) and Enrico Camilleri (Palermo). It is funded by the Erasmus+ Programme of the European Union.

III. INSPIRE'S LEGAL METHODOLOGY: THE INTRADISCIPLINARY AND INTERNATIONAL APPROACH

A. LEGAL METHOLOLOGY: THE THREE PILLARS

INspiRE is based on three pillars. The first 'intra-disciplinary-pillar' is particularly characteristic of the project – through this approach general topics are examined from the perspective of different fields of law. This allows for an in-depth depiction of the underlying difficulties within the framework of legal enforcement, and it enriches research with synergistic effects vis-à-vis innovative solutions existing at the macro level. Thus, the first INspiRE conference in November 2018 discussed the issue of private enforcement of EU competition

---

1 On the facts from the US perspective, see United States Department of Justice, 'Volkswagen AG Pleads Guilty in Connection with Conspiracy to Cheat U.S. Emissions Tests' (*Press Release*, 10 March 2017) <http://www.justice.gov/opa/pr/volkswagen-ag-pleads-guilty-connection-conspiracy-cheat-us-emissions-tests>, and Amy J Schmitz, 'Enforcing Consumer and Capital Markets Law in the United States' in this book, Section II.A.

2 <http://www.caplaw.eu/en/inspire>.

and state aid law;[3] the second conference in May 2019 – the results of which are published in this book[4] – dealt with issues surrounding the enforcement of consumer and capital markets law.

The second pillar is the transnational perspective. In Europe, a purely national perspective is too narrow because, on the one hand, it ignores the wealth of different – sometimes competing – national solutions and, on the other hand, it neglects the manifold supranational influences on the legal systems of the Member States as well as the harmonisation and innovation potential of European legislation. Therefore, the Centre of Excellence involves the participation of researchers from larger and smaller Member States of the European Union in order to generate a broader perspective. A horizontal comparison of law can serve to optimally depict the strengths and weaknesses of an individual solution, and thus mutually enrich the legal systems involved. The results of such a comparison can furthermore be exploited in the supranational Union law perspective. Various non-European legal systems – including those of the US, Australia, Brazil and China – are also taken into account as reference systems.

Finally, the research is based on a (primarily) inductive approach. The idea is to start with the specifics of different legal areas (consumer law, capital markets law, competition law, state aid law etc) and to progress to general principles. Which instruments and mechanisms of legal enforcement exist in which legal field? Are there requirements that can be generalised according to a standard of comparison, the *tertium comparationis*? Subsequently, it might be possible to draw conclusions deductively, moving from the general (back) to the specific.

B. THE PROJECT IN CONTEXT

Apart from the two international academic conferences previously mentioned, the project seeks to reach a broader public by organising panel discussions on the enforcement of EU law. The objective is to increase insight among citizens regarding the relationships between national and European law. In 2015, an event about TTIP, the planned free trade agreement between the EU and the US,

3 Ferdinand Wollenschläger, Wolfgang Wurmnest and Thomas MJ Möllers (eds), *Private Enforcement of European Competition and State Aid Law: Current Challenges and the Way Forward* (Wolters Kluwer 2020).

4 The conference on 'Enforcing Consumer and Capital Markets Law in Europe' was held at the University of Augsburg on 23–24 May 2019 within the framework of the EU-funded project INspiRE.

attracted several hundred citizens.[5] Another event organised in the summer of 2017, in cooperation with the Europa Union Augsburg and the city of Augsburg, dealt with mechanisms of collective redress.[6] Furthermore, a panel discussion on the issue of data protection was held in November 2018.[7]

Moreover, INspiRE aims to ameliorate access to law. The established 'CAPLAW'[8] database on German and European Economic Law is constantly being expanded with national court decisions relating to European law. Decisions of national courts that have been enacted after a preliminary ruling procedure before the European Court of Justice are translated into English and published online in the database. These judgments provide information on how the national judges methodologically adapt and apply the rulings of the European Court of Justice to national law. Until now, such judgments existed only in the respective national language, not in other languages of other Member States. Decisions collected in the CAPLAW database can also be those that – despite European relevance – have not led to preliminary rulings. The collection of such important national decisions will allow other scholars, judges, lawyers and the interested public (including journalists) to make horizontal legal comparisons, and it will thus ultimately serve the enforcement of European law.

IV. ENFORCEMENT OF CONSUMER AND CAPITAL MARKETS LAW

The diesel emissions scandal ('Dieselgate') serves as a current Mass Damage Event on which all chapters are based. The diesel scandal has implications for a consumer who purchased a faulty product. At the same time, the investor who was not informed about the scandal in a timely manner might also feel deceived. Based on adjudicated and pending cases, this book demonstrates how authorities – but also private claimants – can take steps and seek redress against the infringement of the law or of their rights without provoking an abuse of the respective instruments. In doing this, three areas are examined: legal enforcement by public institutions, legal enforcement by private individuals, and overlaps and interconnections between these two tracks of legal enforcement

---

5 Panel discussion on 5 May 2015: 'TTIP Chance oder Risiko? – Transatlantic Trade and Investment Partnership' (*TTIP a chance or a risk?*).

6 Panel discussion on 18 July 2018: 'Sammelklagen in der EU – Fluch oder Segen für den Verbraucherschutz?' (*Class actions in the EU – A curse or blessing for consumer protection?*).

7 Panel discussion on 13 November 2018: 'Google, Amazon, Facebook – Wer hat ein Recht auf meine Daten?' (*Google, Amazon, Facebook – Who has a right to my data?*).

8 <http://www.caplaw.eu/en/>. The database is (partly) available in several languages, including German, English, French and Chinese. The database is publicly accessible and generates around two million hits annually.

as well as hybrid instruments and mechanisms. There is a particular focus on collective redress by way of representative actions (class and group actions) and model case proceedings.

A. THE NATIONAL ANALYSIS: A SELECTION OF COUNTRY CHAPTERS

At the core of this book there is a collection of national contributions from Australia (Peter Cashman), Austria (Petra Leupold and Georg E. Kodek), Brazil (Claudia Lima Marques), China (Tong Zhang), Denmark (Anders Schäfer), England and Wales (John Sorabji), France (Emmanuel Jeuland), Germany (Caroline Meller-Hannich), Italy (Marcello Gaboardi), Lithuania (Egidija Tamošiūnienė and Remigijus Jokubauskas), the Netherlands (Charlotte M.D.S. Pavillon and Willem H. van Boom), Portugal (Henrique Sousa Antunes) and the US (Amy J. Schmitz). These national contributions analyse the current situation in the different countries, and specify which approach has an intended effective – or even efficient – impact, and which models have not been proven.

The reports have a similar structure, which allows for better cross-referencing, improved interaction, and comparability of results. Even so, the reporters were free to adapt the structure to their individual needs. Thus, each country report addresses two case studies concerning the diesel emissions scandal: the enforcement of the rights of consumers who bought a manipulated car; and the enforcement of the rights of investors who were informed too late about the impending scandal. Therefore, the authors of the national reports were given the following facts mirroring the current diesel scandal:

> Case 1: Automobile manufacturer A produces motor vehicles whose emission values are manipulated. It is assumed that this is a material defect of the vehicle and that consumers who have bought such vehicles have suffered a loss of the vehicle's value as a result of the manipulation being revealed.
>
> Case 2: Automobile manufacturer A produces motor vehicles whose emission values are manipulated. The stock market is informed about this situation far too late. A member of the management board, who has found out about the facts internally before publication of the information, sold his own shares before the ad hoc announcement. After A informs the stock exchange about the manipulated emission values, the company's share price falls by 50 per cent.

Various aspects are addressed within this structure: the elimination of the continuing effects of legal infringements through granting compensation of damages, skimming of profits, and penalties; the possible interlinking of public law-enforcement instruments and – individual as well as collective – civil actions; the possible binding effects of administrative and court decisions with regard to possible future proceedings; the suspension of the statute of limitations or regarding claims for disclosure against authorities or courts; parallel proceedings; settlements etc.

The great merit of this uniform structure of the country chapters – and in particular the reference to the concrete and worldwide similar diesel emissions cases – is that the legal solutions of the individual legal systems (most of which have been generally and theoretically well known) are subjected to a concrete practical test. In this way, it is possible to compare the various approaches much more precisely and specifically with regard to their effectiveness and efficiency.

B. THE SUPRANATIONAL ANALYSIS AND REFORM PERSPECTIVE

The country chapters serve as a basis for a comparative analysis focussing on the supranational perspective of the European Union level which is provided by Tanja Domej and Patrick Honegger-Müntener for consumer law, and by Rüdiger Veil for capital markets law. In particular, the contributions examine what conclusions can be drawn from the findings, merits and shortcomings of the various national solutions in the individual countries regarding the need for intervention by the European legislature. In doing so, the form and content of such an intervention and its chances of realisation are discussed. Despite the recent EU proposal on representative actions for the protection of the collective interests of consumers,[9] the assessment in consumer law is rather sceptical about the chances of decisive impulses for an effective system of collective litigation emerging from the EU level.[10] As regards capital markets law, it is proposed to follow the example of competition law and to harmonise private liability by way of enacting a directive.[11]

C. INSIGHT INTO PRACTICE

The country reports and the supranational analysis are complemented by comments of practitioners. Renowned lawyers share their extensive practical experience in the capital markets (Maximilian Weiss) and consumer law

---

9 Proposal for a Directive of the European Parliament and of the Council on representative actions for the protection of the collective interests of consumers, and repealing Directive 2009/22/EC [11 April 2018] COM(2018) 184 final, 2018/0089(COD).

10 See Tanja Domej and Patrick Honegger-Müntener, 'Enforcing Consumer Law in Europe and Beyond: Similarities and Differences' in this book, Section IV.

11 See Rüdiger Veil, 'Private Enforcement in European Capital Markets Law: Perspectives for Reform – the Example of the Obligation to Disclose Inside Information' in this book, Section V.

enforcement (Jutta Gurkmann and Lene Kohl) regarding the diesel emissions scandal in Europe – especially in Germany, Austria and France. The comments exploit the pool of relevant reference cases and illustrate the individual pitfalls and difficulties as well as the cost-benefit relationship between individual enforcement options.

D. THE INTRADISCIPLINARY ANALYSIS AND REFORM PERSPECTIVE

On the basis of the national and supranational analysis, Beate Gsell and Thomas MJ Möllers conduct an intradisciplinary analysis, including further areas of law (such as European competition, company and state-aid law). Thus cross-connections are drawn between the previously elaborated analyses and findings, and the deficits and benefits of the respective solutions are highlighted. The overarching perspective is that differences in the development of law enforcement become apparent not only between European countries and non-European countries, but also between different areas of law. This serves to outline what the general way forward could and should be and leads to several recommendations de lege ferenda. In particular, it will be shown that some mechanisms which promote legal enforcement in European competition law could and should be transferred by the European legislature to the enforcement of consumer law and capital markets law.

PART II

EUROPE

ENFORCING CONSUMER LAW IN AUSTRIA

Petra LEUPOLD*

I. INTRODUCTION

The European Union as well as Austria provides a relatively high level of consumer protection when it comes to substantive law and consumer rights. The greatest deficit that European as well as Austrian consumers are facing today consists in the lack of effective enforcement. A vast majority of consumers do not pursue their rights in court. Litigation is expensive, often (especially in typical consumer cases with relatively small amounts of dispute) economically

* Petra Leupold, Dr., LL.M. (UCLA), Director of VKI-Academy and Head of the Department of Knowledge Management at the Austrian Consumer Information Association (Verein für Konsumenteninformation) and Lecturer for Consumer Law and Capital Market Law at the Universities of Vienna and Liechtenstein.
Most of the cited cases and statutes can be found in The Austrian Legal Information System (Rechtsinformationssystem): <http://www.ris.bka.gv.at>.

irrational and time-consuming, even more so in cross-border cases. Most consumers simply lack the resources to enforce their rights in court individually.

A striking and painful reminder that access to justice is all too often limited to a small proportion of affected consumers, is the recent diesel emissions scandal. In the US, Volkswagen settled to compensate consumers (car buyers) only months after the scandal broke in September 2015 and weeks after dozens of class actions filed nationwide were centralised in the San Francisco federal court. More than four years later and despite a fairly evident violation of harmonised EU law, the difference to the situation in Europe could hardly be more extreme: Unfortunately, most EU Member States do not have a well-working system of collective redress. According to the Collective Redress Report, published by the European Commission in January 2018 following an extensive evaluation of the status quo, there are only five European countries which provide efficient collective redress procedures.[1] As a result, most European consumers have not received compensation yet and consumer organisations struggle with different legal systems, different approaches to enforcement and insufficient enforcement tools and mechanisms. In Austria, Volkswagen has not even bothered to come to the table so far; cases are settled behind closed doors on an individual level as soon as and only if they offer the chance to reach the Supreme Courts in order to prevent precedent.

However, politically the scandal has had severe repercussions: following years of stagnation after the European Commission had issued its non-binding Recommendation on collective redress,[2] it forcefully brought back the debate on collective redress in Europe. Most recent legislative developments triggered by the diesel emissions case relate to Germany and the Netherlands. While the Netherlands passed a new law on group actions that allows collective compensation claims,[3] Germany introduced an opt-in-based Model case declaratory procedure,[4] that does not allow performance claims but (only)

---

1 Those countries are Belgium, Italy, Portugal, Spain and Sweden.

2 Commission Recommendation 2013/396/EU of 11 June 2013 on common principles for injunctive and compensatory collective redress mechanisms in the Member States concerning violations of rights granted under Union Law [2013] OJ L201/60.

3 The new law applies to cases that took place on or after 15 November 2016. Previously, the Dutch law did not allow collective compensation, but only offered a voluntary collective settlement procedure (WCAM); when a ruling established liability and a settlement failed, consumers could only litigate individually. See Willem H van Boom and Charlotte MDS Pavillon, 'The Netherlands takes collective redress to a next level' [2019] Zeitschrift für Verbraucherrecht 133ff.

4 Gesetz zur Einführung einer zivilprozessualen Musterfeststellungsklage, BGBl I 2018/26: ss 606ff of the German Code of Civil Procedure. See – also regarding possible implications for non-German consumers and cross border-litigation – Thomas Klicka and Petra Leupold, 'Deutsche Musterfeststellungsklage und grenzüberschreitende Rechtsdurchsetzung' [2018] Zeitschrift für Verbraucherrecht 208ff (hereafter Klicka and Leupold, 'Musterfeststellungsklage').

offers a declaratory judgment.[5] More ambitious legislative steps that include compensation claims were initiated by the European Commission, launching the so-called 'New Deal for Consumers' in April 2018. The proposal on representative actions[6] was strongly welcomed by consumer organisations and was confirmed by the European Parliament in March 2019. Despite harsh resistance of business groups, a political agreement within the Council was reached in November 2019. In Austria, after more than a decade of working groups on collective redress conducted by the Ministry of Justice since 2006 and several expert proposals,[7] political initiatives to introduce a modern class action framework have not succeeded so far. The most recent proposals put forward by the Social Democratic party in 2017 and the Liste Pilz in 2018 did not pass the Parliament. Reforms unrelated to European mandatory provisions are unlikely to take place in the near future.

---

5 The new law came into force on 1 November 2018. The first action was filed the very same day by Verbraucherzentrale Bundesverband (vzbv) in the diesel emissions scandal. Though the new procedure avoids some of the flaws of its role model, the German KapMuG (Kapitalanlegermusterverfahrensgesetz), that is limited to investors' claims, the disillusioning experiences with this procedure in terms of efficiency and effectiveness do not warrant a particularly enthusiastic outlook for the new proceeding from a consumer's point of view. Its effectiveness remains to be seen. In the VW case, the settlement reached between VW and vzbv in February 2020 was designed to circumvent the safeguarding mechanism of judicial approval provided for by the law. It also significantly limited the beneficiaries of the settlement in comparison to the number of participating consumers. Critical e.g. Astrid Stadler, 'Pyrrhussieg für den Verbraucherschutz – vzbv umgeht durch Vereinbarung mit VW gesetzliche Sicherungsmechanismen' (2020) Verbraucher und Recht 163.

6 Proposal for a Directive on representative actions for the protection of the collective interests of consumers, and repealing Directive 2009/22/EC [11 April 2018] COM(2018) 184 final. See Axel Halfmeier and Peter Rott, 'New Deal für Verbandskläger?' [2018] Zeitschrift für Verbraucherrecht 136; Petra Leupold, 'Tauwetter im kollektiven Rechtsschutz' [2018] VuR 201 (hereafter Leupold, 'Tauwetter'); Petra Leupold, 'New Deal for Consumers' [2018] Zeitschrift für Verbraucherrecht 45.

7 See, e.g. Georg Kodek, 'Gesetzliche Möglichkeiten zur Regelung von Massenverfahren' in Tamara Gabriel and Beate Pirker-Hörmann (eds), *Massenverfahren – Reformbedarf für die ZPO* (Verlag Österreich 2005) 311; Georg Kodek, 'Möglichkeiten zur gesetzlichen Regelung von Massenverfahren im Zivilprozess' [2005] ecolex 751; Georg Kodek, 'Massenverfahren – Reformbedarf für die ZPO' [2006] AnwBl 72; Georg Kodek, 'Groß- und Massenverfahren de lege lata und de lege ferenda' in Matthias Neumayr (ed), *Beschleunigung von Zivil- und Strafverfahren – Zwischen Richtigkeitsgewähr, Fairness und Effizienz* (Manz 2014) 1; Georg Kodek, 'Die Gruppenklage nach der ZVN 2007' [2007] RdW 711; Paul Oberhammer, 'Kollektiver Rechtsschutz bei Anlegerklagen' in Susanne Kalss and Paul Oberhammer (eds), *Anlegeransprüche – kapitalmarktrechtliche und prozessuale Fragen* (Manz 2015) 73, 160; Paul Oberhammer, 'Empfehlungen zum kollektiven Rechtsschutz bei Anlegerklagen' [2015] Zeitschrift für Verbraucherrecht 42; Michael Bydlinski, 'Gedanken zum kollektiven Rechtsschutz in Anlegersachen' [2015] Zeitschrift für Verbraucherrecht 105; Alexander Klauser, 'Alpine, VW und noch immer keine echte österreichische Sammelklage' [2015] Zeitschrift für Verbraucherrecht 182; Georg Kodek, 'Kollektiver Rechtsschutz in Europa – Diskussionsstand und Perspektiven' in Walter Blocher, Martin Gelter and Michael Pucher (eds), *Festschrift Christian Nowotny* (Manz 2015) 127 (hereafter Kodek, 'Kollektiver Rechtsschutz').

This chapter will provide an overview of collective redress mechanisms in Austria and analyse the deficits of the status quo using the Volkswagen case (hypo 1) as an example (Sections II. and III.). It will address legal issues in the Volkswagen case under Austrian procedural and substantive law and present recent developments and experiences as well as actions taken so far (Section IV.). The final chapter concludes with a brief assessment of the proposal on representative actions by the European Commission from an Austrian perspective (Section V.).

II. COLLECTIVE REDRESS INSTRUMENTS IN AUSTRIA

The instruments currently available confirm urgent need for action. The Austrian Civil Procedure Code does not provide effective tools to address the challenges of mass harm-situations. Special rules regarding collective redress are lacking.

A. REPRESENTATIVE INJUNCTIVE ACTIONS

Representative actions brought by certain associations enumerated in the Austrian Consumer Protection Act (section 29 of the KSchG[8]) and the Unfair Competition Act (section 14 of the UWG) play an important role in preventing future infringements of consumer law. Those actions are widely used und have shown themselves to be effective instruments of preventive market surveillance. They are, however, limited to injunctive relief. Individual claims of consumers cannot be pursued.

Moreover, representative actions and judgments have effect only *inter partes*, thus only serve to prevent a certain unlawful practice of a particular trader in the future. If a trader is, for example, barred from using certain contract terms in the future and to raise claims based on these terms in existing contracts,[9] individual

[8] So far, only the association for consumer information (VKI) and the Austrian Chamber of Labour (Bundesarbeitskammer) used their standing and have brought forth actions under ss 28, 28a of the KSchG.

[9] The ECJ has added a real value for consumers through its case law on the effects of unfair terms, starting with its ruling in the *Banesto* leading case, according to which an unfair term is invalid, meaning (not just avoidable or subject to amendments/modification but) void under all circumstances: ECJ, C-618/10 *Banco Español de Crédito SA v Joaquín Calderón Camino* [14 June 2012] ECLI:EU:C:2012:349. Follow-up decisions are ECJ, C-488/11 *Dirk Frederik Asbeek Brusse, Katarina de Man Garabito v Jahani BV* [30 May 2013] ECLI:EU:C:2013:341; ECJ, C-26/13 *Árpád Kásler, Hajnalka Káslerné Rábai v OTP Jelzálogbank Zrt* [30 April 2014] ECLI:EU:C:2014:282; ECJ, C-482/13, C-484/13, C-485/13 and C-487/13, *Unicaja Banco, SA v José Hidalgo Rueda and Others, Caixabank SA v Manuel María Rueda Ledesma and others* [21 January 2015] ECLI:EU:C:2015:21, case note by Kurz, [2015] Zeitschrift für Verbraucherrecht 30; ECJ, C-118/17 *Zsuzsanna Dunai v ERSTE Bank Hungary Zrt* [14 March 2019] ECLI:EU:C:2019:207; See Petra Leupold and Martin Ramharter, 'Die ergänzende Auslegung von Verbraucherverträgen im Lichte des Europarechts' [2015] Bank Archiv 16.

consumers do not benefit directly and cannot invoke the ruling in subsequent proceedings. Also, claims of individual consumers that result from an unlawful behaviour are at risk to expire by limitation; the representative action has no time-barring effect on individual claims.[10]

Remedies for skimming off profits,[11] damages or eliminating the effects of an unlawful practice are not available. Unlike in Germany (section 2 of the UKlaG), the Austrian law does not explicitly govern a collective claim or representative action for removal of the unlawful consequences of a practice, thus does not enable consumer associations to demand direct repayments to consumers. Such an action is only provided for in section 15 of the UWG in the context of unfair commercial practices and has so far not been used in the context of a representative action.

Another obstacle Austrian consumer organisations are facing is their limited standing under section 28a of the KSchG regarding unlawful practices. The infringements that can be targeted with a representative action are restricted to certain sectors, that for example do not include core consumer areas as data protection,[12] insurance, financial services or telecommunications.[13] Consumer associations have standing to challenge violations in these areas only if they happen to be linked to unfair contract terms (such as the requirement of unambiguous consent under article 7 of the GDPR[14]) and are therefore covered

---

10 In order to strengthen enforcement, it would be crucial to create a (better) link between successful injunctions and redress possibilities for individuals, as well as the suspension of limitation periods. Both are now addressed accordingly in art 10 and art 11 of the Proposal for a Directive on representative actions.

11 Section 111 of the Austrian Telecommunications Act (TKG) provides for disgorgement of profits only in the very limited area of telecommunications. The Austrian antitrust court, following a motion by the Austrian Regulatory Authority for Broadcasting and Telecommunications (RTR), can skim off profits of up to 10 per cent of the annual turnover. If the proof of the actual amount of profit is not or only possible with disproportionate effort, the antitrust court can determine the amount at its own discretion. The skimmed-off profit flows to the Regulatory Authority for Telecommunications.

12 Unfortunately, the situation did not change with the entry into force of GDPR, since its art 80 does not grant not-for-profit organisations a right to take action independently of a data subject's mandate, but leaves that to the discretion of the Member States. Austria did not implement a representative action in its national law. Critical, e.g. Petra Leupold and Max Schrems, in Knyrim (ed), *DatKomm* (Manz 2018) art 80 GDPR mn 3, 37ff; Alexander Klauser, 'Rechtsdurchsetzung im Datenschutz nach der DSGVO und dem DSG 2018 idF des DS-DeregulierungsG 2018' [2018] Zeitschrift für Verbraucherrecht 89; Susanne Augenhofer, 'Datenschutz neu: Individuelle und kollektive Rechtsdurchsetzung' [2019] Zeitschrift für Verbraucherrecht 8.

13 Art 2 para 1 in conjunction with Annex I of the Proposal for a Directive on representative actions extends the scope of the current Injunctions Directive from 15 to 59 legislative acts, including among others core consumer regulations such as GDPR, Universal Services Directive, IDD, Solvency II, MiFID II.

14 In this case, unfair contract terms law comes into play as well. See the recent ruling OGH, 31 August 2018, 6 Ob 140/18h. Still disputed and not clear is whether 'data protection policies' represent contract terms or are simply informing consumers. If unfair contract terms law does not apply, consumer organisations do not have standing under s 28 of the KSchG to pursue infringements of data protection law even when they are notorious.

by section 28 of the KSchG. The effectiveness of representative actions as enforcement tools thus is seriously hindered. That is especially true for Austria, which – like Germany – heavily relies on complementing public enforcement with a longstanding tradition of private enforcement and, so far, has not established a special public authority to enforce consumer law.

B. TEST CLAIM PROCEEDING

The associations listed in section 29 of the KSchG can lodge a test claim, which may be heard by the Austrian Supreme Court regardless of the amount in dispute, i.e. also when it does not exceed the minimum requirement of €5,000 (section 502 paragraph 5 no 3 of the Austrian Civil Procedure Code). The Austrian legislator hereby recognised the value of strategic litigation by consumer organisations and the importance of leading cases for legal development and a coherent construction of consumer law. With this action, unlike the German Model case declaratory procedure, it is also possible to obtain a performance judgment. However, the procedure is based upon the assignment of a specific consumer claim; therefore, its scope is limited to performance claims and does not allow to seek declaratory judgments just for the purpose of clarifying legal issues. More importantly the test claim procedure is not designed to accomplish collective redress: the model case has no time-barring effect on the claims which are not part of the test proceeding; if the defendant does not voluntarily agree to suspend the limitation period of similar claims, consumers cannot wait for a final judgment in the model case to enforce their rights in court. Also, the judgment does not create binding legal precedent for other consumers; after a final ruling in the test case, the defendant can still delay other proceedings by contesting each claim.

C. AUSTRIAN-TYPE CLASS ACTION

These flaws of the test-case system and the lack of a 'real' instrument of collective redress led to the development of the third instrument currently available in Austria, that has been largely shaped by case law: the Austrian-type class action.[15] It is based on a combination of assignment of claims to an association or person,[16] that acts as plaintiff, and claim bundling via objective joinder of claims.[17] In order

[15] Georg Kodek, 'Die „Sammelklage" nach österreichischem Recht – Ein neues prozeßrechtliches Institut auf dem Prüfstand' [2004] Bank Archiv 615; for reform plans see Georg Kodek, 'Die Verbesserung des Schutzes kollektiver Interessen im Privat-und Verfahrensrecht' in Maria Reiffenstein and Beate Pirker-Hörmann (eds), *Defizite kollektiver Rechtsdurchsetzung* (Verlag Österreich 2009) 131; Kodek, 'Kollektiver Rechtsschutz' (n 7) 127.

[16] Ss 1392ff of the Civil Code (ABGB).

[17] S 227 para 1 of the Code of Civil Procedure (ZPO).

to be admissible, the assigned claims need to be based on a 'substantially similar' set of legal and factual issues.[18] By assembling large numbers of claimants, it is possible to use commercial litigation funding which is an essential part of the Austrian-style class action[19] because consumer associations typically cannot bear the high-cost risk. The fee for commercial litigation funding is usually between 10 and 40 per cent of the overall amount paid by the trader in case of a settlement or affirmative ruling. In 2016 the Austrian Supreme Court[20] held that a defendant does not have standing to dispute a contingency fee arrangement between a claimant and a litigation funding company. The prohibition of *quota litis* arrangements under section 879 paragraph 2 no 2 of the Austrian Civil Code only intends to protect the client, not – as the defendant argued – his adversary, that invokes the invalidity of the assignment.

III. DEFICITS OF THE STATUS QUO

A. GENERAL DEFICIENCIES

The Austrian-style class action has been used successfully in a number of cases, for example against banks for charging excessive interest rates on consumer loans (the so-called *Zinsenstreit*) or, more recently, against issuers of shares in a fund and financial intermediaries concerning poor investment advice. However, the Austrian-style class action entails costly and time-consuming interim disputes about admissibility and requires significant if not excessive resources on behalf of the plaintiff organisation.[21] Though the Austrian-style class action is cheaper in the beginning because the cost of legal fees is degressive and therefore lower in cases with high aggregate claim value than if the individual claims were pursued separately (economies of scale). However, the cost explodes at a later stage. For example, in the WEB proceedings with an amount in dispute of €54 million, according to LG Salzburg each day in court would have cost €400,000 with the proceeding taking several years on a district court level alone.

---

18 OGH, 12 July 2005, 4 Ob 116/05w.

19 Art 7 para 2 of the Proposal, according to which any influence of the commercial funding company over decisions regarding the proceeding or a settlement is prohibited, could be detrimental to the collective redress activities of Austrian consumer organisations. See also the limits the German Supreme Court has recently put on the cooperation of consumer organisations and commercial litigation funders in context of disgorgement claims under s 10 of the German UWG: BGH, Judgment of 13 September 2019, I ZR 26/17; to the contrary OLG Schleswig-Holstein, Judgment of 14 February 2019, 2 U 4/18.

20 OGH, 27 February 2013, 6 Ob 224/12b.

21 Art 15 no 2 of the proposal provides that the cost related to the representative action may be recovered from the trader if the action is successful and therefore – unlike now – opens the path to integrate administrative/organisational cost of consumer organisations in the loser-pays rule of the Austrian Civil Procedure Code.

Another major deficiency is that the action only provides for an opt-in mechanism since it is assignment-based. This is not just reducing the effectiveness of private enforcement,[22] but has shown to incentivise a strategic delay of proceedings on the part of the defendant at an early stage until other claims that are not part of the group action are time-barred. From a defendant's point of view, a settlement or affirmative judgment in the absence of an opt-out feature poses the risk of developing exemplary function, thus attracting more lawsuits.

Last but not least, the Austrian-style class action fails in cases of small damages claims, where the rational disregard of consumers is preventing them from even actively joining a class action. The Austrian law unlike Germany (section 10 of the German Unfair Competition Act) does not provide for a procedure of skimming off profits, hence does not ensure an adequate level of enforcement with regard to small claims.

B. CROSS-BORDER CASES

While class actions at the domestic level are already a challenge under the current legal framework, it proves even more difficult for consumer organisations to take cross-border cases and protect consumers against foreign traders. For individual consumers as well as consumer organisations, litigation in a foreign (mostly: the trader's) member state is burdensome and unattractive, as they face language barriers, have to investigate the procedural law of a foreign court and hire a foreign lawyer.[23] Apart from the question of which law applies, the foremost and most crucial issue at stake therefore is which courts have jurisdiction. The ECJ held that a consumer organisation does not have jurisdiction over consumer contracts under article 17 of the Brussels Ia Regulation. As clarified in subsequent rulings[24] that applies not only to injunctive actions but also to the assignment of performance claims, regardless of whether the plaintiff as assignee is a trader, consumer organisation or a consumer himself.[25] With regard to the assignment-based Austrian-style class action the loss of jurisdiction in the place of domicile of the consumer/the plaintiff association is probably the most significant drawback in cross-border-cases.

---

22 According to experiences from past class actions, even with broad media coverage only a small fraction of affected consumers, at the maximum 5 per cent, pursue their claims by actively joining a class action.

23 See for cross border litigation in data protection law Peter Rott, 'Data protection law as consumer law – How consumer organisations can contribute to the enforcement of data protection law' [2017] Journal of European Consumer and Market Law 113.

24 ECJ, C-89/91 *Shearson v TVB* [19 January 1993] ECR 1993 I-00139.

25 See regarding assignments C2C ECJ, C-498/16 *Schrems v Facebook* [25 January 2018] ECLI:EU:C:2018:37; follow up-ruling: OGH, Order of 28 February 2018, 6 Ob 23/18b; See Petra Leupold, 'Facebook-Klage: Verbrauchergerichtsstand bei Zession' [2015] Zeitschrift für Verbraucherrecht 166.

However, with regard to representative actions, the opportunity to litigate in the country where the consumer organisation is domiciled, is intact: the ECJ[26] established that representative injunctive actions of consumer organisations have jurisdiction in matters relating to tort, delict or quasi-delict under article 7 no 2 of the Brussels Ia Regulation,[27] according to which a person may be sued in another member state in the courts for the place where the harmful event occurred or may occur. This ruling is not limited to injunctive actions; article 7 no 2 applies to representative actions as such, regardless of whether they seek an injunctive or performance order or just a declaratory decision and whether the infringement relates to contractual or non-contractual obligations.[28] The relevant place regarding representative actions of Austrian consumer organisations against foreign traders under sections 28, 28a of the KSchG as well as section 14 of the UWG therefore is the member state in which consumers have suffered or may suffer harm from an unlawful practice (i.e. in Austria).

In the absence of special rules on jurisdiction in the Proposal on representative actions (recital (9), article 2 no 3 COM(2018) 184 final), this *Henkel* case law *de lege ferenda* also applies to representative actions seeking not just injunctive but compensatory redress orders and declaratory decisions establishing the trader's liability under articles 5 and 6 leg cit.[29] In the author's opinion, this is valid regardless of whether the member states decide for a system of registration (opt-in): according to the *Henkel* case the action as such relates to delict, regardless of the types of measures it is seeking.[30] Also, the definition of

26 ECJ, C-167/00 *VKI v Henkel* [1 October 2002] ECR I–08111.

27 Regulation (EU) 1215/2012 of the European Parliament and of the Council of 12 December 2012 on jurisdiction and the recognition and enforcements of judgments in civil and commercial matters [2012] OJ L351/1.

28 In the leading case (ECJ, C-167/00 *VKI v Henkel* [1 October 2002] ECR I–08111), VKI had filed for an injunction regarding the use of unlawful contract terms in consumer contracts under s 28 of the KSchG, which is a contractual matter. The European Court of Justice (ECJ, C-191/15 *VKI v Amazon* [28 July 2016] ECLI:EU:C:2016:612) recently held in a similar case that the law applicable to the injunction claim of a consumer organisation as such (re standing) is governed by the rules of Rome II Regulation, thus – in line with its *Henkel* judgment – under art 6 (1) leg cit this is usually the law of the member state where the consumer organisation is domiciled. The law applicable to the infringement is governed separately and in accordance with the rules in an individual case; in the *Amazon* case the unfairness of the contract terms therefore has to be determined under art 6 of the Rome I Regulation (No 593/2008), which regulates the law that is applicable to contractual obligations. See also Astrid Stadler, 'Die AGB-Kontrolle von Rechtswahlklauseln – Der Fall Amazon' [2016] Zeitschrift für Verbraucherrecht 168; Astrid Stadler, 'Grenzüberschreitende Rechtsdurchsetzung – Verbrauchergerichtsstand und AGB-Verbandsklagen' in Petra Leupold (ed), *Forum Verbraucherrecht* (Manz 2016) 109; Peter Rott, 'Das IPR der Verbraucherverbandsklage' [2016] EuZW 733.

29 Leupold, 'Tauwetter' (n 6) 201, 202.

30 This is in line with the general line of opinions of the ECJ and OGH, that an action has jurisdiction under art 7 no 2 regardless of whether it seeks an injunctive or performance order or just a declaratory decision: See, e.g. Dietmar Czernich in Dietmar Czernich,

representative actions (meaning under this Directive, i.e. including all types of measures) according to article 3 no 4 explicitly states that the consumers concerned are not parties to the proceeding and that (only) the qualified entity – not the consumers – acts as plaintiff; this is emphasised also by Recital (15).[31] Therefore, the *Henkel* ruling also applies when an action for compensatory redress of particular consumers is filed under the new Directive.[32] Considering the loss of jurisdiction under article 17 of the Brussels Ia Regulation and the current deficiency to concentrate litigation before a single court under the *locus damni* rule of article 7 no 2 leg cit with the assignment-based Austrian-type class action (see under Section IV.), this would be a crucial improvement to strengthen enforcement in cross-border cases.

IV. THE DIESEL EMISSIONS CASE

A. FACTS, FIGURES AND ACTIONS TAKEN SO FAR

The Austrian consumer organisation VKI (Verein für Konsumenteninformation) has filed 16 Austrian-style class actions against VW as the manufacturer (not: seller) of the cars in September 2018, bringing forth the claims of 10,000 consumers. Still, the number of harmed Austrian consumers in the diesel emissions scandal amounts to approximately 360,000, which makes for a proportion of only 2.77 per cent of consumers who participate in the class actions. The value of claims totals €60 million (€6,000 per consumer on average). The actions filed aim for compensation (€55 million) and seek a declaratory judgment (€5 million) regarding liability for consequential damages, e.g. further depreciation due to diesel bans, negative results of the software update or the necessity of hardware updates. The damages brought forward consist of the decrease in value of the cars due to the manipulation and an inflated purchase price, which according to expert opinions estimating the impact on the Austrian car sales market amounts to at least 30 per cent of the purchase price. The actions cover new as well as used cars, regardless of whether they are still in possession or have already been re-sold or were subjected to the software update or not.

Georg Kodek and Peter Mayr (eds), *Europäisches Gerichtsstands- und Vollstreckungsrecht* (4th edn, LexisNexis 2015) art 7 notes 122; OGH, Ruling of 8 July 2003, 4 Ob 122/03z; OGH, Judgment of 21 February 2017, 4 Ob 137/16z; OGH, Ruling of 20 December 2018, 4 Ob 181/18y.

31 In the General Approach, adopted by the European Council on 28 November 2019 (2018/0089(COD), 14600/19, ST 14600 2019 INIT), art 3 no 4 defines a 'representative action' as 'an action for the protection of the collective interests of consumers brought by a qualified entity aiming at an injunction measure or a redress measure, or both.'

32 Nevertheless, for clarifying purposes, an amendment to Recital (9) should be considered, according to which the ECJ rulings in the *Henkel* and *Amazon* cases regarding representative injunctive actions under the current Directive also apply to representative actions under art 3 no 4 of the new Directive (injunctive, compensatory, declarative orders/decisions).

Due to the deficiencies of the Austrian procedural framework handling mass damages cases, in addition to organising class actions to pursue claims of harmed consumers in civil court proceedings, criminal proceedings are often used as an alternative route in order to pursue civil claims that are likely to result from criminal conduct. Apart from the strategic value of increasing pressure on a defendant who is exposed for engaging in potentially criminally relevant conduct, initiating these so-called annex proceedings under s 67 of the Austrian Criminal Procedure Code has two major benefits for claimants: joining a criminal investigation is cheaper than a civil proceeding, risk-free for the injured party, requires no commercial litigation funding and less resources in terms of organisation and cost: if the claim is not successful, the injured party is not obliged to pay the defendant's attorney's fees and the official investigation of a case by prosecution and police can lead to a more efficient gathering of and discovery of evidence that can be used by the claimants. The major advantage for injured parties, however, is that their claims are safeguarded against becoming time-barred: Filing in the criminal proceeding suspends the statute of limitations period for the claims of the parties joining. Since the Austrian criminal law provides for corporate liability since its reform in 2006,[33] this applies to claims against corporate entities as well as natural persons.

In the diesel emissions case, VKI filed charges for criminal fraud (section 146 of the Austrian Criminal Code) against VW in 2016 and subsequently organised statements for claims of 13,000 consumers that were filed in order to join the ongoing criminal investigations. In August 2018, the Austrian prosecutor extended the scope of its investigations to cover not just the VW corporation but also potential criminal conduct of some of its employees.

Most recently, VKI also launched a representative injunctive action under section 14 of the UWG that aims to prevent VW from misleading consumers with regard to the consequences of the software update (i.e. by denying negative impacts on consumption, emissions, noises, engine power and turning moment). The case is currently pending at district court level. The claim could also be extended to the removal of the unlawful status quo under section 15 of the UWG.

Representative actions as well as test case proceedings are often strategically used by consumer organisations in mass damages cases in order to supplement class actions because they typically allow legal issues common to each case to be clarified faster and are not at risk to be settled and therefore silenced by the defendant before a final judgment is delivered. Affirmative rulings by the Austrian Supreme Court in these cases furthermore tend to – though not legally, but at least factually – function as precedent, steering the defendant towards considering a general settlement.

---

33 Sections 1ff of the Verbandsverantwortlichkeitsgesetz (VbVG).

B. SPECIAL PROBLEM: JURISDICTION

As a matter of tort law under article 7 no 2 of the Brussels Ia Regulation, the opportunity for litigation in the member state where the harmed consumer (as well as the consumer organisation) is domiciled, is intact in the diesel emissions case. However, article 7 no 2 leg cit governs jurisdiction not just regarding the courts of the respective member state, but also determines the jurisdiction of the specific local court, where the damage of the individual consumer occurred. This place does not change through the assignment of the claim to another plaintiff as is an element of the Austrian-style class action. Therefore, filing one single class action, that assembles all claims of Austrian consumers in one proceeding, which would be cost-efficient and ensure consistency through one uniform final ruling, is not possible in the diesel emissions case. Instead, VKI had to file 16 class actions in 16 different courts at a state-court level, that have jurisdiction for the different places, where the respective cars have been turned over to the consumers or where the consumers have entered the contracts.

The jurisdiction of Austrian courts under article 7 no 2 as such was – in line with the general opinion of academic writers[34] – already established in dozens of district and state court decisions throughout the last years.[35] However, in the context of collective redress jurisdiction got into dispute recently. Oberhammer[36] argued that only German courts have jurisdiction over the claims of Austrian consumers who purchased their cars in Austria from Austrian traders, entered

---

34 Judith Schacherreiter, 'Die internationale Zuständigkeit für Klagen aus der VW-Abgasmanipulation' [2018] Zeitschrift für Verbraucherrecht 178 (hereafter Schacherreiter, 'Internationale Zuständigkeit'); Judith Schacherreiter, 'VW Dieselgate – Rechtsdurchsetzung betroffener Fahrzeughalter in Österreich gegen den Hersteller' in Petra Leupold (ed), *Forum Verbraucherrecht 2018* (Facultas 2019) 37; Benedikt Wallner, 'Nur ein bisschen schmutzig?' [2017] Zeitschrift für Verbraucherrecht 89; Christian Krachler and Martin Rzehorska, 'Überschreitung von Abgasgrenzwerten: Nichterfüllung der Zulassungsvoraussetzungen' [2016] ZVR 148; Thomas Klicka, 'Die Anwendung des Deliktsgerichtsstands nach Art 7 Nr 2 EuGVVO auf reine Vermögensschäden eines Fahrzeugkäufers – Eine Replik auf *Oberhammer*, J Bl 2018, 750' [2019] J Bl 337 (hereafter Klicka, 'Die Anwendung des Deliktsgerichtsstands nach Art 7 Nr 2 EuGVVO').

35 Most recently OLG Wien, 4 March 2019, 1 R 15/19m; see also OLG Wien, 9 February 2017, 2 R 199/16y; OLG Wien, 27 April 2018, 2 R 17/18m; OLG Wien, 14 June 2018, 4 R 65/18k; OLG Wien, 18 June 2018, 13 R 68/18t; OLG Wien, 24 May 2018, 1 R 60/18b; OLG Wien, 5 June 2018, 5 R 65/18t; OLG Wien, 24 July 2018, 11 R 96/18w; OLG Graz, 16 May 2018, 5 R 84/18i; OLG Graz, 25 April 2018, 5 R 72/18z; OLG Graz, 7 March 2018, 5 R 24/18s; OLG Graz, 2 May 2018, 5 R 78/18p; OLG Graz, 16 May 2018, 5 R 85/18m; OLG Graz, 24 May 2018, 5 R 92/18s; OLG Linz, 6 October 2016, 3 R 123/16b; OLG Linz, 24 November 2016, 1 R 158/16k; OLG Linz, 24 November 2016, 1 R 159/16g; OLG Linz, 23 December 2016, 6 R 223/16f; OLG Linz, 13 March 2017, 1 R 34/17a; OLG Innsbruck, 22 March 2018, 3 R 37/18t. On state-court level to the contrary only (regarding the purchase of a used car) OLG, Wien 26 February 2018, 4 R 15/18g.

36 Paul Oberhammer, 'Deliktsgerichtsstand am Erfolgsort reiner Vermögensschäden' [2018] J Bl 750.

the contracts in Austria, wired the purchase price from their Austrian bank account to the Austrian bank account of the trader and use the cars in Austria. Three district-court decisions[37] followed his reasoning and rejected three class action lawsuits last year, pointing to the civil-law nature of the damages as 'pure or mere' financial losses and the difficulties to locate the place where the harm occurs in investment fraud and prospectus liability cases.[38] In the beginning of April 2019 the district court in Klagenfurt referred the issue to the ECJ, requesting a preliminary ruling (article 267 TFEU).[39] With reference to this pending case, the Austrian Supreme Court recently suspended a proceeding in order to wait for a decision by the ECJ.[40]

In the author's opinion,[41] the doctrine according to which in investment fraud cases the domicile of the investor in a certain member state as such (as the centre of his financial assets) does not suffice to constitute jurisdiction in this member state under article 7 no 2,[42] is not applicable in cases like the diesel emissions scandal, where the damage of the individual consumer has a strong physical reference point, manifesting in the purchased car and not just in virtual account transactions. The fact that according to (Austrian) civil law doctrine both cases involve mere financial losses (i.e. entering the contract, respectively the inflated purchase price) does not constitute a relevant, much less conclusive, argument for the purpose of determining jurisdiction in matters of international civil procedure. Moreover, applying the rulings in investment fraud cases would result in attributing jurisdiction to Austrian courts anyway: they meet the

---

37 LG Korneuburg, 29 January 2019, 4 Cg 77/18s; LG Wr Neustadt, 12 February 2019, 26 Cg 109/18m and LG Wels, 18 March 2019, 5 Cg 98/18p. All decisions were appealed against and are not final. The decisions of LG Korneuburg and LG Wels were overturned by OLG Wien, 9 May 2019, 2 R 31/19x and OLG Linz, 2 May 2019, 6 R 51/19s.

38 ECJ, C-375/13 *Kolassa v Barclays Bank Plc* [28 January 2015] ECLI:EU:C:2015:37; OGH, 24 October 2018, 8 Ob 75/18i; OGH, 23 October 2018, 4 Ob 185/18m. See for antitrust claims ECJ, C-352/13 *CDC Hydrogen Peroxide v Akzo Nobel et al* [21 May 2015] ECLI:EU:C:2015:335 and OGH, 30 August 2016, 4 Ob 120/16z; for unfair commercial practices OGH, 20 December 2018, 4 Ob 181/18y.

39 LG Klagenfurt, 17 April 2019, 21 Cg 74/18v, decision pending (case C-343/19, VKI/VW). On 2 April 2020, Advocate General Sánchez-Bordona delivered his opinion, according to which the damage occurred in the place where the victim purchased the product, provided that the other circumstances confirm the attribution of jurisdiction to the courts of that State. Those circumstances must include, at all events, one or more factors which enabled the defendant reasonably to foresee that an action to establish civil liability as a result of his or her actions might be brought against him or her by future purchasers who acquire the product in that place. Moreover, art 7(2) of Regulation No 1215/2012 does not authorise the court to determine that it does or does not have jurisdiction based on an appraisal of the other circumstances of the case, aimed at identifying which court is best placed, in terms of proximity and foreseeability, to decide on the dispute.

40 OGH, Order of 5 July 2019, 4 Ob 119/19g.

41 Petra Leupold, 'Enforcing Consumer Rights' [2019] Journal of European Consumer and Market Law 121.

42 ECJ, C-168/02 *Rudolf Kronhofer v Marianne Maier and Others* [2004] ECR I-06009.

objectives of article 7 no 2 like in no other case, i.e. a close link between the court and the action as well as foreseeability for the defendant.[43]

It cannot be stressed enough though, that the outcome of the preliminary proceeding in the *VW* case is of utmost political significance for the effectiveness of enforcement. If the ECJ denied jurisdiction in the consumer's home country as the place where the damage occurred, consumers as well as consumer organisations from all over Europe would have to litigate in Germany[44] – with much less hope of being compensated any time soon, considering the German courts would have to research and apply the law of 27 countries under article 4 of the Rome II Regulation and are stuck with a *lex fori* that is poorly equipped for mass-harm cases because it does not provide for a collective performance claim procedure.[45]

C. PRIVATE LAW

Due to the lack of a contractual relationship between VW as the manufacturer of the cars and the consumers, who bought their cars from Austrian VW subsidiaries, licensed dealers and other sellers, the basis for their claims against VW is tort law.[46] So far, the Austrian Supreme Court has not had the chance to deliver an opinion, but the lower courts predominantly confirm the claimants' case for liability resulting from malicious intent (section 1295 paragraph 2 ABGB, section 874 of the ABGB) and fraudulent behaviour (section 146 of the StGB, section 1311 of the ABGB). A similar stance was taken by the German Federal Supreme Court (BGH) recently, which issued its first seminal decision on May 25, 2020 (VI ZR 252/19); the court held that VW acted unconscionably under section 826 BGB and awarded damages to a used car buyer. Since the bases of and requirements for claims under

---

43 Schacherreiter, 'Internationale Zuständigkeit' (n 34) 96; Klicka, 'Die Anwendung des Deliktsgerichtsstands nach Art 7 Nr 2 EuGVVO' (n 34) 337; Lukas Aigner, 'ECJ, C-304/17 *Löber v Barclays Bank plc*' [2018] Zeitschrift für Verbraucherrecht 135 (note); OGH, 24 February 1998, 8 Ob 75/18i; OGH, Order of 23 October 2018, 4 Ob 185/18m – in all cases jurisdiction of the courts where the investor is domiciled, was confirmed.

44 This does not extend to actions that are not solely directed against VW as manufacturer, but also against the seller. If the seller is domiciled in the member state of the consumer, the jurisdiction for the claims against VW is secured under art 8 no 1 Brussels Ia Regulation (passive joinder of parties): OGH, 16 December 2019, 8 Ob 126/19s.

45 Regarding the implications of the German Model case declaratory procedure in cross-border cases, especially the issues of international private law in the context of the statute of limitations and recognition of the declaratory judgment under Brussels Ia Regulation see Klicka and Leupold, 'Musterfeststellungsklage' (n 4) 208.

46 See Gregor Maderbacher, 'Käuferrechte im Fall der Manipulation von Kfz-Emissionswerten (NOx)' [2019] Zeitschrift für Verbraucherrecht 51 (hereafter Maderbacher, 'Käuferrechte'); regarding similar considerations under German law Axel Halfmeier, 'Schadensersatzansprüche gegen Fahrzeughersteller im Abgasskandal' in Petra Leupold (ed), *Forum Verbraucherrecht 2018* (Facultas 2019) 13ff (hereafter Halfmeier, 'Schadensersatzansprüche').

Austrian and German law regarding fraudulent behaviour are analogous for the most part, this opinion is of significance for Austria as well. Whether individually harmed consumers additionally have direct remedies based on the infringement of section 2 of the Unfair Commercial Practices Act is highly controversial.[47] The same is true for the alleged violation of the EU regulation concerning type-approval requirements.[48] With regard to both laws, the violation as such seems evident and is hardly disputed; the issue is whether their provisions can – in general – be considered to be 'protective statutes' with respect to the damages of consumers resulting from the infringement and therefore provide affected consumers with a remedy[49] (section 1311 of the ABGB).

The limitation period of compensation claims under section 1489 of the Austrian Civil Code amounts to three years and starts when the injured party gains knowledge of the damages and the liable party. In the *VW* case, claims of affected consumers therefore did not expire until at the earliest three years after the scandal broke in September 2015, which was in the fall of 2018. However, the limitation period for damages caused by certain severe, intentional and criminally relevant conduct (like fraud, section 146 of the StGB) amounts to 30 years after the damage occurred.

V. THE NEW DEAL FOR CONSUMERS

The Proposal on 'representative actions for the protection of the collective interests of consumers'[50] launched by the European Commission on 11 April 2018 aims at ensuring better redress options for consumers than under the current

47 Petra Leupold, 'Schadenersatzansprüche der Marktgegenseite nach UWG' [2010] Österreichische Blätter für gewerblichen Rechtsschutz 164; Henriette Duursma-Kepplinger, 'Verbraucherschutz durch Wettbewerbsrecht' [2015] Zeitschrift für Verbraucherrecht 107; Georg Kodek and Petra Leupold in Andreas Wiebe and Georg Kodek (eds), *UWG* (2nd edn, Manz 2012) §16 notes 8ff.

48 See Maderbacher, 'Käuferrechte' (n 46) 51; regarding similar considerations under German law Halfmeier, 'Schadensersatzansprüche' (n 46) 13ff.

49 The European legislator by amendments of the Unfair Commercial Practices Directive recently introduced individual remedies for consumers against unfair commercial practices (art 3 of the Directive (EU) 2019/2161 as regards the better enforcement and modernisation of Union consumer protection rules [27 November 2019]): Under art 11a of the UCPD contractual remedies must include, as a minimum, the possibility for the consumer to unilaterally terminate the contract, non-contractual remedies must include the right to compensation. The latter addresses situations such as the VW emissions scandal, where consumers of some member states saw themselves unable to bring a claim against the manufacturer, who is not the contractual counterpart. The respective redress provisions enacted by the national legislators will be applicable starting 28 May 2022. See Christoph Schmon, 'Reform of EU Consumer Law 2018: a good deal?' [2018] Zeitschrift für Verbraucherrecht 141, 142.

50 See in more detail Peter Rott and Axel Halfmeier, 'New Deal für Verbandskläger?' [2018] Zeitschrift für Verbraucherrecht 136.

2009 Injunctions Directive, which provides qualified entities with the possibility to file representative injunctive actions only. From an Austrian perspective, this so-called 'New Deal for Consumers' addresses the following key deficits of the status quo:

- The proposal extends the scope of application of the Directive from currently 15 to 59 legislative acts, including core consumer regulations such as GDPR, Universal Services Directive, IDD, Solvency II, MiFID II (article 2, Annex I).
- The proposal establishes a close link between a representative action and redress possibilities for individual consumers by providing a binding (*erga omnes*) effect of the judgment that goes beyond the parties of the proceeding and by suspending the limitation periods for claims of affected consumers (articles 10 and 11).
- Representative actions can seek not just injunctive relief, but also declaratory judgments establishing the liability of a trader and performance orders, demanding direct repayments to harmed consumers (article 5ff).
- The proposal provides a solution for ensuring private enforcement in cases with small damages claims, that is based on a mandatory opt-out mechanism (article 6).
- The asymmetry in information available to consumers and consumer organisations and traders is addressed accordingly by providing access to evidence not through a pre-trial discovery, but through an obligation to disclose certain pieces of evidence in the possession of the defendant during the trial, which is especially important with regard to the number and identity of harmed consumers as well as the quantification of damages (article 13).

VI. CONCLUSIONS

The greatest deficits in Austrian consumer law as well as from a European angle relate to poor enforcement of consumer rights. On a market scale the lack of proper collective redress mechanisms not just harms (access to justice for) a large majority of Austrian consumers but also hinders further advancement of cross-border transactions within the European Single Market by impairing consumer trust as well as fair competition and has a market-distorting effect that benefits the notion of efficient breach of law.

The recent proposal of the EU Commission on representative actions builds on the longstanding tradition of private enforcement in Austrian consumer law. In light of past experiences with mass litigation cases in Austria it appears suited to address the biggest deficits of the current instruments. However, given the uncertainty of further progress and final outcomes on the European level, an equally if not more urgent call for action – from the Austrian consumers' point of view – has to be addressed to the Austrian legislator.

ENFORCING CAPITAL MARKETS LAW IN AUSTRIA

Georg E. Kodek*

* Georg E. Kodek, Dr., LLM (Northwestern), Professor, Vienna University of Economics and Business, Head of Department of Private Law; Judge at the Supreme Court of Justice of Austria.
Most of the cited cases and statutes can be found in The Austrian Legal Information System (Rechtsinformationssystem): <http://www.ris.bka.gv.at>.

I. INTRODUCTION

While it would be fascinating to discuss some fundamental questions of capital market law such as fraud-on-the-market theory or the distinction between transaction causation and loss causation[1] from the perspective of Austrian law,[2] the aim of this chapter is more modest. Its purpose is simply to analyse remedies available in Austria for violations of capital market law in Case 2[3] provided by the editors. Obviously, capital market law is an ideal example for a discussion of collective redress since violations of the law in this area typically affect numerous investors. While this paper will focus on the facts of hypo 2, this chapter will also briefly discuss some other aspects of violations of capital market law not covered by the hypo.[4]

This chapter will first provide a brief overview of substantive Austrian private law (Section II.). Then, an overview of procedural devices available under Austrian civil procedure for collective redress will be provided (Section III.). Subsequently, the chapter moves on to discuss public enforcement both from a perspective of administrative law and criminal law (Section IV). The chapter (Section V) will then discuss a number of general questions such as parallel proceedings, *res judicata*, the standard of proof, the statute of limitations and, last, but not least, costs. Some facts and figures will be presented in the chapter (Section VI). Then it will briefly address the discussion about a reform, in particular the various suggestions for the introduction of group proceedings (Section VII). The final chapter (Section VIII) will try to draw some conclusions.

II. PRIVATE LAW

A. INTRODUCTION

Claims for damages can be based on a violation of the respective provisions of capital market law, i.e. the duty to make an ad hoc announcement (article 16 of the MAR, §155 of the *BörseG 2018*) and the prohibition against insider dealings

1 On this, see *Dura Pharm, Inc v Broudo* 544 US 336 (2005), and the subsequent discussion this decision has triggered.

2 See Alexander Schopper and Benedikt Wallner, 'Aktuelle Fragen des Anlegerschutzes im österreichischen Kapitalmarktrecht' [2015] RdW 763 (hereafter Schopper and Wallner, 'Fragen des Anlegerschutzes').

3 See Introduction Section IV.A.

4 For a general overview see Martin Gelter, 'General Report' in Pierre-Henri Conac and Martin Gelter (eds), *Global Securities Litigation and Enforcement* (Cambridge University Press 2019) 3 (hereafter Gelter, 'General Report') and the country report on Austria by Martin Gelter and Michael Pucher in the same volume at 261ff.

(§§154, 163 of the *BörseG*).[5] While the losses incurred by investors obviously are pure economic losses (which generally can be recovered only in special circumstances), the Austrian Supreme Court has held that the respective provisions of the Stock Exchange Act (*BörseG*) are 'protective statutes' (*Schutzgesetze*) designed to protect also individual investors from financial losses.[6] Indeed, the Austrian Supreme Court has long recognised the importance of private enforcement in capital market law. Thus, it has held that the prospectus requirement, which was so important for the functioning of the capital market, was meaningless if the liability of the issuer, against the wording of §11 of the *KMG* (Capital Market Act) would not lead to a liability of the issuer.[7]

Under Austrian substantive civil law, damages are available, disgorgement of profits is not. Also, there are no punitive damages. The recoverable losses include actual losses as well as lost profits. Recovery of lost profits, however, is available only if the tortfeasor acted with gross negligence or intentionally. However, under Austrian law loss of future profits is regarded as actual loss if it is highly likely that the profits would have been made.[8]

In Case 2, investors could sue for losses they suffered because of the company's failure to make a timely ad hoc announcement.[9] This, arguably, will only serve as

5 The chapter notes that Austria, in light of the MAD and MAR, substantially amended its stock exchange law in 2017, replacing the former *BörseG* 1989 with the *BörseG* 2018, BGBl I 2017/149. While the provisions of the old Act may still be applicable (especially as to sanctions that can be imposed) on facts that occurred before the entry into force of the new law, this chapter only deals with the current law.

6 See Martin Gelter and Michael Pucher, 'Austria: Securities Litigation and Enforcement' in Pierre-Henri Conac and Martin Gelter (eds), *Global Securities Litigation and Enforcement* (Cambridge University Press 2019) 261, 289 (hereafter Gelter and Pucher, 'Austria'); Friedrich Rüffler, 'Kapitalmarktrechtliche Informations- und Verhaltenspflichten als Schutzgesetze?' [2010] Zeitschrift für Gesellschaftsrecht 113 (citing further authority); Susanne Kalss, Martin Oppitz and Johannes Zollner, *Kapitalmarktrecht* (2nd edn, Linde 2015) §20 mn 16, §22 mn 72; OGH, 15 March 2012, 6 Ob 28/12d, case notes by: Schuhmacher, [2012] GesRZ 252; Csoklich, [2012] EvBl 763; OGH, 24 January 2013, 8 Ob 104/12w; OGH, 14 January 2016, 6 Ob 98/15p, case notes by: Kronthaler and Schwangler, [2016] BankArchiv 834; RIS-Justiz RS0127724; RS0128527. This position is not affected by the entry into force of the MAD. See Florian Schuhmacher, 'Haftungsfragen im Spannungsfeld zwischen Kapitalmarktrecht und Kartellrecht' in Petra Leupold (ed), *Forum Verbraucherrecht 2015* (Manz 2015) 59, 62ff; Philipp Fidler, 'Private Enforcement – Rechtstheorie und Rechtswirklichkeit im Wettbewerbs- und Kapitalmarktrecht' [2018] JBl 81 and 152 (hereafter Fidler, 'Private Enforcement').

7 OGH, 15 March 2012, 6 Ob 28/12d; case notes by Schuhmacher, [2012] GesRZ 252; Csoklich, [2012] EvBl 763, citing Friedrich Rüffler, 'Gesellschaftsrecht und Kapitalmarktrecht – Über eine schwierige Beziehung' [2011] BankArchiv 699, 703. In this case, the Court dealt with the relationship between capital market law on the one hand and capital maintenance requirements under company law on the other hand, holding that in case of a conflict between these two principles the former should prevail.

8 Georg Kodek in Andreas Kletečka and Martin Schauer (eds), *ABGB-ON* (Manz 2018) §1293 mn 16.

9 Obviously, the effect of the manipulation on emission values itself arguably also brought about losses for the investors (including investors already owning stock at the time of

a basis for claims of new investors who bought stock after the manipulation of the emission value and suffered a loss because of the purchase.[10] It is not entirely clear whether an investor is only entitled to damages if he suffered a loss because of the capital market violation while buying or selling stock, i.e. the loss has to be transaction-related.[11] Academic authors have argued, in this author's view convincingly, that in principle Austrian law also allows for the compensation of investors who refrained from buying or selling because of false information. Here, the loss is the difference between not buying or selling and the profit gained in the alternative scenario where the investor did trade.[12] On the other hand, certainly all cases that have been decided so far concerned transaction-related losses. Thus, it remains to be seen whether an investor who claims that he would have bought or sold stock and only did not do so because of a violation of capital market law would also be awarded damages.

B. PERSONS LIABLE FOR FAILURE TO MAKE A TIMELY AD HOC ANNOUNCEMENT

The claim discussed above is a claim against the company. It is an open question whether the claim could also be raised against the management on the theory that the directors violated their duties vis-à-vis investors.[13] The Austrian Supreme

---

the manipulation). This, however, was not a violation of capital market law. Here it is noted that 'old' investors, i.e. shareholders who already owned stock at the time when the manipulation occurred, do not have a claim in this context. Rather, under Austrian civil law, only the company is entitled to damages (e.g. against the directors). A minority of 10 per cent of the shareholders can claim damages on behalf of the company (§135 of the AktG). Apart from this minority right, there are no shareholder derivative suits in Austrian law.

10 This excludes, for example, investors who bought and sold their stock while the prices were inflated. See Gelter, 'General Report' (n 4) 54 n 306; Allen Ferrell and Atanu Saha, 'Forward-Casting 10b-5 Damages: A Comparison to Other Methods' (2012) 37 Journal of Corporation Law 365, 370.

11 For an American perspective on this, see Thomas J Molony, 'Making a Solid Connection: A New Look at Rule 10B-5's Transactional Nexus Requirement' (2014) 53 Santa Clara L Rev 767.

12 Gelter and Pucher, 'Austria' (n 6) 285. See also Gelter in the same volume at 54 and Susanne Kalss and Martin Oppitz, 'Prospekt- und Kaptitalmarktinformationshaftung in Österreich' in Klaus J Hopt and Hans-Christoph Voigt (eds), *Prospekt- und Kapitalmarktinformationshaftung* (Mohr Siebeck 2005) 811, 859.

13 See Klaus J Hopt, 'Die Haftung für Kapitalmarktinformation – Rechtsvergleichende, rechtsdogmatische und rechtspolitische Überlegungen' [2013] WM 101, 109ff; for applicable causes of action see Friedrich Rüffler, 'Organaußenhaftung für Anlegerschäden' [2011] JBl 69; for market manipulation see Susanne Kalss, 'Die Außenhaftung der Leitungsorgane gegenüber Gesellschaftern und Dritten' in Eveline Artmann, Friedrich Rüffler and Ulrich Torggler (eds), *Die Organhaftung zwischen Ermessensentscheidung und Haftungsfalle* (Manz 2013) 73, 84ff. On the duties of directors in this respect in general, see Johannes Reich-Rohrwig and others in Eveline Artmann and Martin Karollus (eds), *Kommentar zum Aktiengesetz II* (6th edn, Manz 2018) Anhang zu §84.

Court has held that directors can be personally liable in case of violations of competition law (unfair trade practices)[14] and in case of violation of cartel law.[15] In one case the Austrian Supreme Court has expressed doubts as to whether a director can be personally liable in a capital market case.[16] This, however, was a mere *obiter dictum*, the thrust of the decision being that the particular corporate defendant was liable. On the other hand, a more recent decision did not find any particular difficulty in holding a director liable for violations of capital market law.[17] This decision, however, only dealt with the question of international jurisdiction. In this case, all corporate defendants were domiciled in Jersey (and, thus, outside the EU). In order to overcome this jurisdictional obstacle, plaintiffs had joined a director as a defendant who at that time lived in Vienna. The purpose of joining the director simply was to use him as 'anchor defendant' in order to enable the plaintiff to avail himself of the jurisdiction of Austrian courts. Only in this context the Austrian Supreme Court ruled that the director can be personally liable for violations of capital market law. The case was settled subsequently, so no decision on the merits was rendered by Austrian courts.

C. PERSONAL LIABILITY FOR INSIDER DEALINGS

In addition to bringing a claim against the company, new investors could also argue that they suffered a loss because of the board member's insider dealings. This loss is identical with the loss suffered from A's violation of its duty to make an ad hoc announcement. To this extent, the board member and A are jointly and severally liable. A pursuit of claims of individual investors against the board member would, in effect, result in a disgorgement of this person's profits. However, in light of the relatively low loss each shareholder suffered from the board member's insider dealings (as opposed to the losses suffered from A's violation of its duty to make an ad hoc announcement), a pursuit of these

14 OGH, 21 April 1998, 4 Ob 99/98g and the cases reported in the Austrian Legal Information System (*Rechtsinformationssystem*): RIS-Justiz RS0079491; RS0079521; RS0079743. The Court derived this liability from the directors' duty to prevent violations of the law. This approach was subsequently extended by the Court to trademark law. See OGH, 24 April 2007, 17 Ob 8/07m; OGH, 24 March 2009, 17 Ob 40/08v.

15 OGH, 14 February 2012, 5 Ob 39/11p.

16 OGH, 15 March 2012, 6 Ob 28/12d. The sceptical attitude of the Court was in large measure based on the fact that recent reforms providing for liability of directors for wrong capital market information had failed; on these reform proposals see Michael Gruber, 'Organaußenhaftung für Kapitalmarktinformationen?' [2006] wbl 445ff; Matthias Göschke, 'Drastische Verschärfung der Vorstandshaftung in Sicht' [2004] ecolex 617, 617ff; Clemens Völkl, 'Überlegungen zum Entwurf eines §82a BörseG – „Haftung für unrichtige oder unterlassene Finanzinformationen"' [2005] RdW 71ff.

17 OGH, 28 February 2012, 8 Ob 17/12a.

claims will not be regarded worthwhile by investors. There is no procedure available to collectively disgorge the board member's profits from the insider dealings.

III. CIVIL PROCEDURE

A. TRADITIONAL MULTI-PARTY PRACTICE

As to the availability of collective redress, there are no special rules for violations of capital market law. While the Austrian Code of Civil Procedure does not contain specific provisions on group actions, there are a number of procedural devices which, at least to a certain extent, can be utilised to handle mass litigation.[18] Joinder allows several plaintiffs to join their forces against one or more defendants. Also, the courts have discretion to consolidate cases if this is in the interest of justice. These traditional devices are based on the Austrian Code of Civil Procedure (§§11 f, 187 of the *ZPO*).

Every now and then potential litigants agree to file solely one case designed to resolve a number of similar controversies between the parties or to await the outcome of an already pending case (test case). Further, several statutes authorise the appointment of a curator in mass proceedings. Whereas in most cases this is for the purposes of service only, an 1874 statute authorises the appointment of a curator representing investors in court in cases involving '*Teilschuldverschreibungen*' (partial debentures).

B. THE 'AUSTRIAN MODEL OF GROUP LITIGATION'

In addition to these traditional devices, Austrian practice has developed a form of group litigation based on a combination of joinder of claims and litigation finance ('Austrian model of group litigation').[19] Under this scheme potential claimants assign their claims to an association (typically a consumer association)

18 Walter Rechberger, 'Verbandsklagen, Musterprozesse und "Sammelklagen". Möglichkeiten kollektiven Rechtsschutzes im österreichischen Zivilprozess' in Constanze Fischer-Czermak and others (eds), *Festschrift Rudolf Welser* (Manz 2004) 871.

19 Georg Kodek, 'Die „Sammelklage" nach österreichischem Recht – Ein neues prozeßrechtliches Institut auf dem Prüfstand' [2004] BankArchiv 615 (hereafter Kodek, 'Die „Sammelklage"'); Peter Kolba, 'Gemeinsam statt einsam – Von der Sammelklage zur Gruppenklage' [2009] ecolex 664; Peter Kolba, 'Gemeinsam statt einsam. Erfahrungen mit Sammelklagen in Österreich' in Maria Reiffenstein and Beate Blaschek (eds), *Konsumentenpolitisches Jahrbuch 2007–2008* (Verlag Österreich 2009) 119; Christian Koller, 'Effektive Rechtsdurchsetzung durch Sammelklagen!?' [2012] Zivilrecht aktuell 63.

which then files a complaint on its own behalf. Assembling a large number of claimants in this fashion enables the association to avail itself of commercial litigation finance. This enables the claimant to pursue his or her claim without any risk. This procedure has been successfully used in a number of mass cases, particularly in cases against banks for charging excessive interest rates and in lawsuits for poor investment advice. This model is primarily used by the *Verein für Konsumenteninformation* (Association for Consumer Information) and by the Chambers of Labour (*Arbeiterkammer*), but would also work with other legal entities, e.g. a limited liability company or an association specifically founded for such a proceeding.

For this procedure, the Austrian Supreme Court requires 'an essentially identical cause of action' and 'essentially identical questions of law or fact'.[20] From a theoretical point of view, most observers agree that this standard is too strict.[21] The practical problem with this standard is not so much that it prevents claimant associations from pursuing wholly unconnected claims (which they do not want to do anyway), but that it gives rise to litigation whether the respective criteria are met. Obviously, the requirements under substantive law and under the law of evidence have a bearing on whether or not these requirements can be met. In principle, in cases for violations of capital market law it should not be too difficult to pass the Austrian Supreme Court's test.[22] This is true in particular for cases based on wrong information vis-à-vis the general public in a prospectus, in a report or in an ad hoc announcement where the issuer violates his duties vis-à-vis all investors in an identical fashion. The same holds true for cases based on misappropriation of funds or mis-management of funds. On the other hand, the test may be more difficult to meet in cases for wrong investment advice because such advice has to be given on a personalised basis. Yet, even in these cases a group action may be possible if the adviser used standardised wrong or misleading information.

There are no special procedures for collective settlements.

C. PRACTICAL EXPERIENCE

So far, most cases decided by Austrian courts concerned claims for damages for wrong investment advice. There are also a number of cases based on an alleged violation of capital market law. Most of these cases probably concern

---

20 OGH, 12 July 2005, 4 Ob 116/05w.

21 Kodek, 'Die „Sammelklage"' (n 19) 620; Paul Oberhammer, '„Österreichische Sammelklage" und §227 ZPO' in Robert Fucik and others (eds), *Jahrbuch Zivilverfahrensrecht 2010* (NWV 2010) 247, 251ff.

22 For a distinction between types of cases in this field see Susanne Kalss, 'Massenverfahren im Kapitalmarktrecht' [2005] BankArchiv 322.

Meinl European Land (MEL), since renamed Atrium. The allegation is that MEL manipulated the market and/or violated its duty to make ad hoc announcements in connection with a capital increase. Claimants in essence allege that, contrary to the company's announcements, a large portion of the issued stock was bought by the issuing company (or affiliated companies) itself. In this context, a criminal proceeding is also pending. In the civil proceedings, it seems that so far all appellate decisions only dealt with preliminary questions such as jurisdiction[23] or the admissibility of certain documentary evidence.[24] In some civil cases against the issuing company the director had been joined as a defendant; these cases appear to have been settled.

A case by individual shareholders was brought against VW in Austria, but was dismissed for lack of jurisdiction.[25] The Austrian Supreme Court held that article 17 of the Brussels I bis Regulation was not available because there was no direct contractual relationship between the shareholders and the company, nor could the case based on article 7 paragraph 2 of the Brussels I bis on the ground that the locus of the tort was Germany where the act/omission took place and where the shares were listed on the stock exchange.

IV. PUBLIC LAW/PUBLIC ENFORCEMENT

A. ADMINISTRATIVE SANCTIONS

Insider dealings and market manipulations carry administrative sanctions (§154 of the *BörseG 2018*).[26] A fine of up to €5 million or three times the unlawful gain derived from the violation can be imposed. A fine can also be imposed against a company for acts of its directors and officers (§156 of the *BörseG*). In this case, the fine can be up to €15 million or 15 per cent of the annual turnover or three times the benefit derived from the violation, including avoidance of a loss which would have been occurred but for the violation.

A failure to make a timely ad hoc announcement carries an administrative fine of up to €500,000 (§155 of the *BörseG*). In this case, there is no express provision linking the amount of the fine to unlawful gains.

In addition to the fines described above, the Financial Market Authority (*Finanzmarktaufsicht*, FMA) can, *inter alia*, issue an injunction ordering to

---

23 See n 17 above.

24 See Section V.E. below.

25 OGH, 7 July 2017, 6 Ob 18/17s.

26 Most publications deal with the law before the 2017 reform, but can still be used. See Susanne Kalss and Martin Oppitz, 'Insiderhandel und Kursmanipulation – Sanktionen' [2011] RdW 575; Christian Thaler, *Sanktionen bei Marktmissbrauch: Marktmanipulation, Insiderhandel und Ad-hoc-Publizität* (Manz 2014).

discontinue certain behaviour, and can also declare that profits gained from the violation or losses avoided by the violation are forfeited if these can be determined accurately (§157 paragraph 2 subparagraph 2 of the *BörseG*). In this case, the FMA can also estimate the amount of profits (or losses avoided). This is important because practical experience gained from cartel law shows that it is often difficult in practice to accurately determine the amount of profits. Under the old Austrian Cartel Act the court could order disgorgement of profits.[27] Yet, this sanction apparently was never actually imposed. The reason for this was that it was found difficult to determine the exact amount of the unlawful profits.[28] So far, disgorgement of profits has not played a significant role in the enforcement of capital market law.

B. CRIMINAL SANCTIONS

Above certain thresholds, market manipulation and insider dealings are criminal offences.[29] Insider dealings constitute a criminal offence if financial instruments for more than €1 million are bought or sold (§163 of the *BörseG*). This offence carries a sentence of six months to five years' imprisonment. Similarly, market manipulation is a criminal offence if it involves dealings of more than €1 million (§164 of the *BörseG*). This offence also carries a sentence of six months to five years' imprisonment.

Before the 2017 reform, market manipulation arguably could also be regarded as fraud (which would have carried a sentence of up to 10 years' imprisonment in certain cases). One particular egregious case of market manipulation has been investigated by the public prosecutor in Vienna for many years, but no charges seem to have been brought.

Under criminal law, applicable sanctions, in addition to imprisonment, include a disgorgement of profits (§20 of the *StGB*). Skimmed profits and fines go to the federal government, not to victims.

---

27 Under the current Austrian Cartel Act of 2005, there is no provision on the disgorgement of profits. Rather, the illicit profits are one of several factors to be taken into account for the determination of the fine (§30 of the KartG 2005).

28 For suggestions on how to determine the amount of illicit profits, see Rüdiger Veil, 'Gewinnabschöpfung im Kapitalmarktrecht' [2005] ZGR 155, 196ff, for unlawful directors' dealings.

29 Most of the available literature deals with the law before the 2017 reform. See, e.g. Hubert Hinterhofer in Frank Höpfel and Eckart Ratz (eds), *Wiener Kommentar StGB* (2nd edn, Manz 2014) §48b BörseG; Hubert Hinterhofer, 'Aktuelle Entwicklungen bei der strafrechtlichen Sanktionierung des Marktmissbrauchs' [2015] OZW 151; Christopher Schrank, 'Kapitalmarktstrafrecht' in Robert Kert and Georg Kodek (eds), *Das große Handbuch Wirtschaftsstrafrecht* (Manz 2016) 679; Fritz Zeder, 'Neue Strafbestimmungen gegen Marktmissbrauch: MAR und MAD' [2017] Journal für Strafrecht 137.

Under §§163, 164 of the *BörseG*, normally only the individual engaging in insider dealings or market manipulation can be punished. The company is only liable under criminal law if the dealings or manipulations were made for its benefit or constituted a violation of duties of the company itself (§3 of the *Verbandsverantwortlichkeitsgesetz – VbVG*). In this case, a fine can be imposed against the company. Criminal proceedings against companies under this Act are extremely rare.

There are no criminal sanctions (only administrative fines) for the mere omission to make a timely ad hoc disclosure.

C. PROCEDURE

The procedure before the Financial Market Authority is an administrative procedure. The decision by the FMA can be challenged before the Federal Administrative Tribunal (*Bundesverwaltungsgericht*).[30] Under certain circumstances, the decision of this court can be appealed to the Court of Administrative Review (*Verwaltungsgerichtshof*), the court of last resort for administrative matters.

Decisions imposing an administrative fine have to be published on the Financial Market Authority's website. This information has to include the type of violation and the identity of the person responsible (§161 of the *BörseG*). Only in minor cases can the Financial Market Authority refrain from such publication if it determines that this measure would be excessive.

In criminal cases, the Code of Criminal Procedure (*StPO*) applies. The Criminal Court in Vienna (*Landesgericht für Strafsachen*) has jurisdiction for all crimes under §§163, 164 of the *BörseG*, regardless of where the offence was committed (§166 of the *BörseG*). The prosecutor can also use the FMA to investigate the case (§168 of the *BörseG*). If it is not entrusted with the investigation, the FMA has the same rights as the public prosecutor and victims. In particular, it can make applications and can appeal decisions of the court (§169 of the *BörseG*).

D. CIVIL CLAIMS IN CRIMINAL PROCEEDINGS

Occasionally criminal proceedings are used in mass damages cases as a vehicle to bring civil claims. Austrian criminal procedure law allows the victim of a

30 It should be noted that the *Bundesverwaltungsgericht* in Austria, unlike in Germany, is not a court of last resort, but an intermediate appellate court the decisions of which are subject to an appeal to the *Verwaltungsgerichtshof*.

crime to pursue his or her claims in the criminal proceeding (§67 of the *StPO*, so-called 'annex proceedings', *Adhäsionsverfahren*). It should be noted that this only works against the defendant in the criminal proceeding, not against his company (unless the proceeding includes the company as a defendant). The court can award damages or grant other remedies if the defendant is convicted. In case of an acquittal, damages can only be obtained by way of a separate civil proceeding. One advantage of the annex proceeding is that it allows the victim to pursue his claims without risk because, unlike in civil proceedings, the victim is not required to pay the defendant's attorney's fees if the claim is not successful. Also, sometimes this proceeding is used as a discovery device because in a criminal proceeding the gathering of evidence is done by the prosecutor and the police who also have more means at their disposal to investigate a case, including searches and seizures and wiretapping, all of which is not available in a civil case. While criminal courts in the past may have been reluctant to decide on civil claims (referring the victims to civil proceedings instead), this seems to have changed in recent years. Obviously, this avenue is available only if the damages claimed are the result of the criminal conduct of the defendant.

This 'annex' procedure is available regardless of the number of claimants and is cheaper than initiating a separate civil litigation. In a case against directors and officers of an Austrian bank, some 7,000 investors have filed their claims in the criminal proceeding.[31]

There is no equivalent to this procedure in administrative proceedings. Individual victims do not have standing in the administrative proceeding.

V. GENERAL PROCEDURAL LAW

A. ADMISSIBILITY OF PARALLEL PROCEEDINGS

Criminal or administrative proceedings and civil proceedings can be initiated simultaneously. Also, an investor can pursue his claims simultaneously by way of civil and criminal proceedings.[32] Unlike, e.g. in French law,[33] there is no maxim *electa una via non datur recursus ad alteram*.

---

31 See, e.g. OGH, 30 January 2018, 1 Ob 183/17v (holding that a CD-ROM with the particulars of some 7,000 private claimants filed in the criminal proceeding was sufficient to stall the limitation period).

32 Georg Kodek, 'Privatbeteiligtenanschluss' in Robert Kert and Georg Kodek (eds), *Das große Handbuch Wirtschaftsstrafrecht* (Manz 2016) 763, mn 20.33ff (citing further authority).

33 See art 5 of the Code de Procédure Pénale.

B. FOLLOW-ON CASES

A criminal conviction binds the defendant in all subsequent civil proceedings, whereas an acquittal would not be binding.[34] An administrative decision imposing a fine on an individual or a company does not have a similar binding effect on subsequent civil proceedings.[35]

A judgment in a civil case generally does not have binding effects beyond the particular lawsuit. This also holds true in case of group proceedings. There, technically only the consumer organisation and the defendant are parties to the proceeding. As a practical matter, the judgment binds all claimants who have assigned their claims to the consumer organisation. Claimants whose claims have not been decided by the court (e.g. because they did not assign their claims or because their claims, in spite of the assignment, were not brought by the consumer organisation) are not bound by the outcome.

However, the Austrian Supreme Court has recently held that a number of decisions arriving at the same factual conclusions may justify that the courts, in future proceedings, take judicial notice of these facts, with the burden then being on the other party to challenge these facts.[36] The effects of this new line of decisions remains yet to be ascertained. This may constitute a significant departure from the traditional concept under which facts had to be determined individually on a case-by-case basis on the basis of evidence introduced in the respective proceedings.

C. STATUTE OF LIMITATION

The Austrian Civil Code provides for a three-year period of limitation for claims for damages (§1489 of the *ABGB*). This period is calculated subjectively, i.e. it runs from the time the victim learns about the loss and the culpability of the tortfeasor. This period is extended to 30 years if the loss was inflicted

---

34 The binding effect of a conviction was 'invented' by the Austrian Supreme Court (OGH, 17 October 1995, 1 Ob 612/95 = SZ 68/195) after a statutory provision to this effect (§268 of the *ZPO*) was declared unconstitutional by the Austrian Constitutional Court. Unlike the old statutory provision, however, the binding effect under the judicially created rule only extends to the defendant himself, not to other parties who do not have standing in the criminal proceeding.

35 The only exception from this rule are cases for damages for violation of competition law. There, Austrian law, transposing the Private Enforcement Directive (Directive 2014/104/EU of the European Parliament and of the Council of 26 November 2014 on certain rules governing actions for damages under national law for infringements of the competition law provisions of the Member States and of the European Union [2014] OJ L349/1), provides for a binding effect of decisions of cartel authorities (see §37 para 2 of the KartG 2005).

36 OGH, 23 February 2016, 6 Ob 229/15t; OGH, 25 April 2017, 10 Ob 57/16d.

by an act which can only be committed intentionally, and which is punishable by imprisonment of at least one year. This is determined on the basis of the abstract sanctions provided for in the statute and does not depend on the actual sanction imposed in the specific case. As a result, all criminal offences for violations of capital market law (all of which carry a sanction of up to five years' imprisonment) trigger the long limitation period for claims for damages under civil law. For purposes of this provision, it is not necessary that the tortfeasor was actually convicted. Rather, the prerequisites of the extension of the limitation period could also be established in a civil proceeding.

The traditional view was that the extension of the limitation period works only against the individual acting culpably, not against the company. A more modern view would extend the extension of the limitation period to claims against the company if the company is liable for the individual's acts pursuant to the Corporation Liability Act (*Verbandsverantwortlichkeitsgesetz*) which provides for criminal sanctions against companies and other bodies corporate for certain acts committed by its directors and officers.[37]

On the other hand, if a capital market law violation only carries an administrative sanction, only the three-year period applies. The most important case falling into this category arguably is a violation of the duty to make an ad hoc announcement. The duration of the limitation period is important because often market participants, due to poor access to information, have to wait for the outcome of the administrative proceeding. In this case, the relative shortness of the limitation period often forces claimants to file their suit early, thus triggering the need for mass proceedings.

The statute of limitations for damages is interrupted by the filing of a civil action or of a 'joinder' as a civil party in a criminal proceeding.[38] If the court does not award damages in the criminal proceeding, the victim has to start civil proceedings without undue delay. The latter works regardless of whether the proceeding results in a conviction, but works only against the defendant, not against other perpetrators or against the company.

D. STANDARD OF PROOF

The standard of proof under Austrian civil procedure law is quite high. §272 of the *ZPO* requires that the judge be convinced that a fact is true. This is generally interpreted as requiring a high probability to be established by the party that

---

37 See Peter Vollmaier in Attila Fenyves, Ferdinand Kerschner and Andreas Vonkilch (eds), *Klang ABGB* (3rd edn, Verlag Österreich 2012) §1489 para 47 (citing further authority).

38 §1497 of the ABGB. For the effects of filing a civil claim in a criminal proceeding on the limitation period, see OGH, 16 May 2001, 2 Ob 180/00k; RIS-Justiz RS0115181, RS0115182, RS0041512, RS0034631.

has the burden of proof.[39] There are no particular facilitations of proof in capital market cases. While occasionally *prima facie* evidence may be sufficient, this does not apply if individual decisions and the reasons for them have to be proven.[40] There is no relaxation of evidentiary requirements for the connection between the acts of the tortfeasor and the loss.[41] In a decision concerning the alleged manipulation of LIBOR, the Court held that the plaintiff had to allege how the LIBOR increased because of the manipulations and how this effected the interest rate he had to pay because this constitutes his loss.[42]

Also, an investor claiming damages for incorrect advice has to prove that, if he had been advised correctly, he had not bought the securities in question and also what other investment he had made if he had been advised correctly.[43] Similarly, the Austrian Supreme Court has repeatedly held that a *prima facie* case is not sufficient in case of deficient information in a prospectus.[44] Rather, the investor has to prove that he made his decision in reliance on the certification of the prospectus and that this was the basis of his decision.[45] In order to establish this, it is sufficient if the investor proves that he relied on an adviser and the adviser knew about the certification of the prospectus.[46]

In a decision of 2015, the Austrian Supreme Court extensively dealt with the required nexus between an ad hoc announcement and the decision of an investor.[47] The Court held there was no room for a relaxation of the standard of proof as to whether the investor had made a different investment decision if he had had the information required to be provided in the ad hoc announcement. However, the claimant had only to establish by a preponderance of the evidence that he had learned about the information provided in the ad hoc announcement if such an announcement had been made. This, according to the Court, was a hypothetical course of events for which a reduced standard of proof applied.

---

39 RIS-Justiz RS0110701.

40 OGH, 25 January 1984, 1 Ob 502/84 = SZ 57/20 = EvBl 1984/129; expressly for the decision of an investor OGH, 14 January 2016, 6 Ob 98/15b; see also the cases reported in RIS-Justiz RS0040288.

41 OGH, 7 May 2014, 7 Ob 62/14i.

42 OGH, 10 February 2017, 1 Ob 157/16v.

43 OGH, 30 March 2011, 7 Ob 77/10i. In this decision, and even more so in subsequent decisions, however, the Austrian Supreme Court stressed that the required standard of proof is less strict when a hypothetical course of events has to be proven. See also OGH, 28 February 2012, 4 Ob 145/11v.

44 OGH, 11 September 1997, 6 Ob 2100/96h; OGH, 28 October 2013, 8 Ob 105/13v; OGH, 17 December 2013, 10 Ob 48/13a; OGH, 21 October 2014, 4 Ob 90/14k; OGH, 30 April 2018, 1 Ob 35/18f. See the cases documented in the Austrian Legal Information System (*Rechtsinformationssystem*) RIS-Justiz RS0108627.

45 OGH, 28 October 2013, 8 Ob 105/13v.

46 OGH, 17 December 2013, 10 Ob 48/13a.

47 OGH, 20 March 2015, 9 Ob 26/14k. On the consequences of this decisions (and some questions left open by the Supreme Court), see Schopper and Wallner, 'Fragen des Anlegerschutzes' (n 2) 763.

The Court held that the claimant, even if he had not read the ad hoc announcement himself, would have learned about its contents by way of advisers or other intermediaries.[48]

Particularly when it comes to the reconstruction of a hypothetical course of events the Austrian Supreme Court is quite ready to reduce the required standard of proof. Thus, in a case for wrong investment advice the Court held that an investor only had to make it 'plausible' that he suffered a loss because of the advice.[49]

E. ACCESS TO EVIDENCE

There is no equivalent to discovery proceedings in Austria. A 2017 reform, implementing the cartel damages directive, introduced a limited form of discovery only for cartel damages cases.[50] In all other cases, therefore, a plaintiff faces considerable difficulty to obtain the necessary information.

In order to compensate this, at least in part, the Austrian Supreme Court has held that a plaintiff can use the investigatory report (which was drawn up in preparation of measures to be taken by the Austrian Financial Market Authority) of the Austrian National Bank (*OeNB*) as evidence, even though this was a form of 'indirect' evidence.[51] Under this line of decisions this does not constitute a violation of the principle of 'immediateness' of taking evidence (*Unmittelbarkeitsgrundsatz*). This decision is particularly important for capital market claims of investors, due to the fact that internal processes within the defendant party (e.g. market manipulations) are usually not easy to prove. Defendants, however, are entitled to ask the court that direct evidence be heard by the court. It remains to be seen how courts will deal with such requests if this would result in duplicative taking of evidence.

Also, the files of a criminal proceeding are routinely used as evidence in civil proceedings. In the future, the files of the Financial Market Authority will also be used as evidence in civil proceedings.[52] The publication of the imposition of

48 A similar argument is expressed by OGH, 17 December 2013, 10 Ob 46/13g and OGH, 19 February 2016, 8 Ob 98/15t = SZ 2016/10.

49 OGH, 29 November 2017, 8 Ob 2/17b.

50 See §37j of the KartG 2005.

51 OGH, 22 October 2015, 1 Ob 39/15i; OGH, 12 November 2015, 9 Ob 27/15h; OGH, 21 December 2015, 6 Ob 111/15i; OGH, 14 January 2016, 6 Ob 98/15b; OGH, 19 February 2016, 8 Ob 98/15t.

52 See OGH, 22 October 2015, 1 Ob 39/15i; OGH, 12 November 2015, 9 Ob 27/15h; OGH, 21 December 2015, 6 Ob 111/15i; OGH, 14 January 2016, 6 Ob 98/15b; OGH, 19 February 2016, 8 Ob 98/15t concerning a report of the Austrian National Bank (*OeNB*) which was drawn up in preparation for measures to be taken by the Financial Market Authority.

administrative fines discussed above (see Section IV.C.) also serves to inform the general public. Unfortunately, there is no similar information requirement for criminal cases.

F. COSTS

Austrian civil procedure law has a 'loser pays' rule.[53] One purpose of this rule is to exercise a 'steering function' and to prevent abusive litigation. Due to the presence of a 'loser pays' rule, claimants refrain from bringing suits without any legal cause. On the other hand, this rule results in that the filing of a civil claim entails considerable risks. This is often alleviated by use of commercial litigation finance companies which cover the plaintiff's costs and the defendant's costs (in case plaintiff loses) but charge a contingency fee of 30 to 40 per cent of the award. Also, litigation finance is only available for higher claims. Usually the required threshold is about €400,000.

The Austrian Supreme Court has ruled that the defendant does not have standing to dispute a contingency fee arrangement between a claimant and a litigation finance company.[54] Claimants are, therefore, neither required to declare to the court the origins of their funds, nor is there a specific rule that would allow the court to stay the proceedings in case the criteria stated in the Recommendation on collective redress[55] are not met.[56]

VI. SOME FACTS AND FIGURES

A 2006 study stresses the importance of public enforcement of capital market law. It compares various jurisdictions and examine possible correlations to the development of capital markets there.[57] Indicators used to assess the efficiency of national authorities include independence of the authority from the government, competence for rule-making, competence for investigation and competence

53 Marianne Roth, 'Cost and Fee Allocation in Austrian Civil Procedure Law' in Bea Verschraegen (ed), *Austrian Law – An International Perspective* (Jan Sramek 2010) 133.

54 OGH, 27 February 2013, 6 Ob 224/12b. See Alexander Klauser, 'Prozessfinanzierung, Rechtsfreunde, quota litis und Sammelklage: Offene Fragen nach 6 Ob 224/12b' [2013] VbR 12.

55 Commission Recommendation 2013/396/EU of 11 June 2013 on common principles for injunctive and compensatory collective redress mechanisms in the Member States concerning violations of rights granted under Union Law [2013] OJ L201/60.

56 On these requirements, see arts 14 and 15 of the Recommendation.

57 Rafael La Porta, Florencio Lopez-de-Silanes and Andrei Shleifer, 'What works in Securities Laws?' (2006) 61 JFin 1.

for imposing sanctions (including criminal sanctions). These indicators form the basis for what the authors of the study call Public Enforcement Index. In this study, Austria fares poorly, getting a meagre 0.17, one of the lowest scores among all Western industrialised countries; the average figure is 0.52. It has to be pointed out that the study only used formal criteria, looking to the legal rules on financial market authorities on paper which do not necessarily reflect how the system works in practice.

A more recent study[58] compares the resources available to financial market authorities in relation to GDP. According to this study, in Austria the financial market authority has 9.97 employees per million inhabitants (compared to an average figure of 19.33) and a budget of $34,464 per million $ GDP compared to an average of $81,730.

While it is always difficult to compare figures from different national legal systems, in light of a wide range of differences both as to responsibilities of authorities, their structure and their way of working,[59] the Austrian figures may be substantially higher than those given in the two reports cited above. According to the FMA's annual report of 2008,[60] in 2007 the Financial Market Authority had 220 employees which equals 27.5 employees per million inhabitants, a budget of €15 million for personnel and some 6 million for non-staff expenses. This would place Austria well above average. Admittedly, though, not all of these staff and expenses relate to the capital market.[61] In 2018 (the latest figures available), the FMA had the equivalent of 379.34 employees (full-time equivalents) and a budget of €43.7 million for personnel and €23.9 million for non-staff expenses.[62]

---

58 Howell E Jackson and Mark J Roe, 'Public and private enforcement of securities laws: Resource-based evidence' (2009) 93 JFin Economics 207.

59 Of the 392 employees indicated in the Austrian Financial Market Authority's 2018 annual report, 28 are listed as 'management, procedure & law, internal auditing', 77.5 for 'bank supervision', 58 for 'insurance and pension funds supervision', 83.15 for 'securities supervision', 71.25 for 'integrated supervision', 50.10 for 'services' and 24 for 'winding-up of banks'. Clearly, only taking into account the personnel working in the securities supervision section would not be adequate since this does not take into account other staff in the areas of 'management, procedure & law, internal auditing', 'integrated supervision' and 'services'. If one assumes that the number of staff employed in these fields assists the 'securities supervision' proportionately to the numbers of staff of the respective fields (admittedly, a somewhat bold assumption), one would arrive at an additional 41.81 employees (which equals 28 per cent of the personnel of the aggregate of staff listed for 'management, procedure & law, internal auditing', 'integrated supervision' and 'services'). This would place Austria roughly in the centre-field of all countries examined in the reports.

60 FMA's annual reports are available at <http://www.fma.gv.at/publikationen/fma-jahresberichte/>.

61 See n 57 above.

62 See the FMA's annual report for 2018, available at <http://www.fma.gv.at/publikationen/fma-jahresberichte/>.

VII. REFORM PROPOSALS

In light of an increase in mass litigation, from about 2000 several reform proposals were made. In 2005, this author suggested introduction of a group proceeding which enabled claims to be 'bundled' by a group representative.[63] The proposal recommended a multi-tier approach consisting of a new group proceeding, disgorgement of profits and a number of technical reforms. In the proposed group proceeding, the determination of all common questions of fact and questions of law would be binding for all potential claimants (regardless of whether or not they join the group proceeding). In order to be awarded compensation, however, a claimant would have to join the group proceeding.

In 2007, a draft for a group procedure was worked out by the Austrian Ministry of Justice which was to be enacted as the 2007 Civil Procedure Reform.[64] Under the draft, a new group proceeding would be introduced for cases involving three or more claimants and a large number (probably more than 50) claims and similar questions of law and fact. However, a claimant would always be free to pursue his claims as by way of an individual action instead of participating in the group proceeding. The court would decide on all common questions of fact and law by judgment. Any questions not resolved in the group proceeding would have to be determined in individual lawsuits. The draft was met with severe resistance by the Chamber of Commerce and, consequently, the Conservative Party. As a result, the draft was not enacted. However, the introduction of group proceedings was listed on the official government's agenda (*Regierungsprogramm*).[65] In 2014 the Green Party introduced a bill for introduction of group proceedings.[66] In 2018, the Socialist Democrats followed suit with a similar proposal.[67] Both proposals were not adopted by Parliament.

---

63 Georg Kodek, 'Gesetzliche Möglichkeiten zur Regelung von Massenverfahren' in Tamara Gabriel and Beate Pirker-Hörmann (eds), *Massenverfahren – Reformbedarf für die ZPO* (Verlag Österreich 2005) 311; Georg Kodek, 'Möglichkeiten zur gesetzlichen Regelung von Massenverfahren im Zivilprozess' [2005] ecolex 751; Georg Kodek, 'Massenverfahren – Reformbedarf für die ZPO' [2006] AnwBl 72; Georg Kodek, 'Massenverfahren und Verfahrensmassen: Einige Gedanken zur aktuellen Diskussion' [2012] Zivilrecht aktuell 66; Georg Kodek, 'Groß- und Massenverfahren de lege lata und de lege ferenda' in Matthias Neumayr (ed), *Beschleunigung von Zivil- und Strafverfahren – Zwischen Richtigkeitsgewähr, Fairness und Effizienz* (Manz 2014) 1 (hereafter Kodek, 'Groß- und Massenverfahren').

64 This author was a member of the drafting committee. On the draft, see Georg Kodek, 'Die Gruppenklage nach der ZVN 2007' [2007] RdW 711.

65 'Regierungsprogramm für die XXIV. Gesetzgebungsperiode (2008–2013)' 122 (B.11. Gruppenklage) <http://www.konvent.gv.at/K/DE/INST-K/INST-K_00179/imfname_164994.pdf>; 'Arbeitsprogramm der österreichischen Bundesregierung 2013–2018'.

66 NR 25 GP S 277, 21–23 May 2014 Member of Parliament Aygül B Aslan (Grüne).

67 See <http://www.parlament.gv.at/PAKT/PR/JAHR_2018/PK0060/> and <http://www.parlament.gv.at/PAKT/VHG/XXVI/A/A_00096/fname_679852.pdf>.

In 2015, collective redress and its potential reform was discussed at the 19th Austrian *Juristentag*,[68] but did not eventually lead to respective legislative action.[69] In 2017, the president of the Viennese bar association publicly and firmly called for respective legislative action.[70] Under the coalition government of the Conservative Party and the 'Liberal' Party in 2018 and 2019, unlike in previous governments, the introduction of collective redress proceedings was not even mentioned in the government's official agenda. With the fall of the coalition government following a no-confidence vote and the institution of an interim government in May 2019, chances for the introduction of a collective redress mechanism (or, indeed, any other substantial reform) seem extremely remote.

Several authors have also suggested a disgorgement of profits similar to German law.[71] These suggestions have not been taken up by the legislature so far.

VIII. ANALYSIS[72]

The enforcement of capital market law is characterised by a policy mix of public and private enforcement.[73] Occasionally one can also identify hybrid elements of enforcement, a term which describes the use of private individuals for public

---

68 Paul Oberhammer, 'Kollektiver Rechtsschutz bei Anlegerklagen' in Susanne Kalss and Paul Oberhammer, *Anlegeransprüche – kapitalmarktrechtliche und prozessuale Fragen* (Manz 2015) 73, 160; Paul Oberhammer, 'Empfehlungen zum kollektiven Rechtsschutz bei Anlegerklagen' [2015] VbR 42; Michael Bydlinski, 'Gedanken zum kollektiven Rechtsschutz in Anlegersachen' [2015] VbR 105.

69 See also Alexander Klauser, 'Alpine, VW und noch immer keine echte österreichische Sammelklage' [2015] VbR 182; Kodek, 'Groß- und Massenverfahren' (n 63); Georg Kodek, 'Keine Angst vor Verfahrensrationalisierungen – sie sind ein Gebot der Stunde' in Hannes Jarolim (ed), *Beschleunigung von Verfahren als Gebot der Stunde – Sammel-, Musterklagen und andere Möglichkeiten. Dialog im Parlament Band 8* (LexisNexis 2016) 19; Georg Kodek, 'Kollektiver Rechtsschutz in Europa – Diskussionsstand und Perspektiven' in Walter Blocher, Martin Gelter and Michael Pucher (eds), *Festschrift Christian Nowotny* (Manz 2015) 127; Georg Kodek, 'Class Actions – Some Reflections from a European Perspective' in Eva Lein and others (eds), *Collective Redress in Europe – Why and How?* (BIICL 2015) 117.

70 *Die Presse* (Vienna, 25 April 2017).

71 See Georg Kodek, 'Die Verbesserung des Schutzes kollektiver Interessen im Privat- und Prozessrecht' in Maria Reiffenstein and Beate Pirker-Hörmann (eds), *Defizite kollektiver Rechtsdurchsetzung* (Verlag Österreich 2009) 131, 137; Martin Winner and Clemens Appl, *Wettbewerbsvollzug in Österreich im Vergleich zu ausgewählten Ländern: Die einvernehmliche Beendigung von Kartellverfahren durch „Settlement" unter Berücksichtigung der Anforderungen an die Verfahrenstransparenz und Bußgeldbemessung* (AK Wien 2013) 50ff.

72 For a more thorough discussion of the following observations, see the insightful article by Fidler, 'Private Enforcement' (n 6), in particular 162ff.

73 On this in general, see Gerhard Wagner, 'Rechtsdurchsetzung im Kapitalmarktrecht: Public vs Private Enforcement' in Matthias Casper and others (eds), *Festschrift für Johannes Köndgen* (RWS 2016) 650.

enforcement, e.g. by means of whistleblowing (§160 of the *BörseG*).[74] Clearly, compared to competition law, there is greater emphasis on private enforcement. This is due to a number of factors. Apparently, the seriousness of violations of competition law and their effect on the common market led to more emphasis being placed on public enforcement. On the other hand, the losses of market participants, while wide-spread, still seem to be high enough to provide an incentive for the participants to try to recover their losses by way of civil lawsuits, thus potentially rendering private enforcement more efficient than in competition law.[75]

Another important difference to competition law is that public enforcement of capital market law is mainly regulated by EU law, whereas private enforcement is still primarily left to the national law of the member states. Also, unfortunately there is little coordination between public and private enforcement.[76] As a result, the question of the relationship between the payment of damages and the imposition of sanctions remains, in large measure, unanswered.

From a substantive law viewpoint, Austrian law provides adequate tools for private enforcement. In particular the Austrian courts' position that capital market laws are provisions designed to protect not just the capital market as an institution, but also to protect individual investors (thereby enabling them to recover pure economic losses) significantly strengthens the position of investors and contributes to the coordination of public and private enforcement.

What is lacking, however, are procedural tools to allow for efficient enforcement of the claims available under substantive law. Substantive capital market law has to be supplemented by a functioning procedural law.[77] Perhaps the most important aspect is the absence of an institutionalised mechanism for collective redress. Such a mechanism is particularly important in capital market law because frequently violations of capital market law bring about spread-out effects which affect a large number of market participants. Effective collective redress mechanisms can contribute to the efficiency of capital markets in general.[78] 'Bundling' of individual claims can contribute to procedural efficiency, but also to justice in that they make sure that like cases are decided alike.

---

74 Fidler, 'Private Enforcement' (n 6) 152, 159.

75 Therefore, 'atomised' losses and the often observed 'rational apathy' of claimants in this regard is not an issue in capital market law. On this, see Georg Kodek, 'Atomised Losses in Tort Law: Conceptual Difficulties and Modern Developments' [2015] Journal of European Tort Law 109.

76 Fidler, 'Private Enforcement' (n 6) 152, 158.

77 Susanne Kalss, 'Zeit für gebündelte Verfahren am Kapitalmarkt' [2011] GesRZ 133; Fidler, 'Private Enforcement' (n 6) 152, 158.

78 Harald Koch, 'Sammelklage und Justizstandorte im internationalen Wettbewerb' [2011] JZ 438, 442ff ('*Effizienzfunktion*'); see also Axel Halfmeier and Philip Wimalasena, 'Rechtsstaatliche Anforderungen an Opt-out-Sammelverfahren: Anerkennung ausländischer Titel und rechtspolitischer Gestaltungsspielraum' [2012] JZ 649, 651ff.

It alleviates the burden not only on courts, but also on parties and witnesses. An efficient collective redress mechanism not only reduces the costs and risks for the plaintiff, but can also be in the interest of the defendant because it makes settlement of claims which concern a large number of market participants easier.[79] The ECtHR has recognised that such a procedure is in line with article 6 of the ECHR[80] and has held that collective representation is permissible if individual lawsuits were 'unworkable'.

Another obstacle to private enforcement is the poor access to information for investors. The publication of decisions of the Financial Market Authority (§161 of the *BörseG*) may help in the future, but without a binding effect of their decisions clearly will not be sufficient. What is needed is access to and admissibility of evidence gathered by the regulatory authority for parties of civil proceedings. In the absence of clear legislative rules, the courts have stepped in and have begun, by way of judicial 'self-help', to shape their own rules, trying to employ the concept of judicial notice in order to redress this problem.[81] In the absence of better access to information and collective redress mechanism (which can reduce risk and costs for claimants), potential claimants will often decide to either abandon their claims or to wait for the outcome of a public enforcement proceeding.[82]

Shifting responsibility for compensation of private losses to regulatory authorities[83] is not a convincing solution. At present, the Financial Market Authority is not equipped to handle these claims. Unlike in cartel law, civil lawsuits are not primarily follow-on actions after a finding of a violation by the regulatory authority. Rather, investors themselves are often the driving force. Perhaps more importantly, if regulatory authorities were to decide on claims under civil law, the procedure would have to comply with the requirements under article 6 of the ECHR which requires that the determination of civil rights and obligations be made by impartial 'tribunals'.

Attempting to provide 'compensation' or 'redress' in mass tort cases may often approach, and probably transgress, the traditional boundaries of tort law,

---

79 Tomas Arons and Willem H Van Boom, 'Beyond Tulips and Cheese: Exporting Mass Securities Claim Settlements from the Netherlands' (2010) 21 European Business Law Review 85; Xandra E Kramer, 'Enforcing Mass Settlements in the European Judicial Area: EU Policy and the Strange Case of Dutch Collective Settlements' in Christopher Hodges and Astrid Stadler (eds), *Resolving Mass Disputes* (Edward Elgar 2013) 63.

80 ECtHR, *Lithgow and others v United Kingdom*, App no 9006/80, 9262/81, 9263/81, 9265/81, 9266/81, 9313/81, 9405/81, 8 July 1986; ECtHR, *Wendenburg et al v Germany*, App no 71630/01, 6 February 2003.

81 See Section V.E. above.

82 Johannes Zollner, 'Kursmanipulation – Einblick in das österreichische Sanktionssystem' in Holger Fleischer, Susanne Kalss and Hans-Ueli Vogt (eds), *Gesellschafts- und Kapitalmarktrecht in Deutschland, Österreich und der Schweiz 2013* (Mohr Siebeck 2014) 251, 264.

83 This is the approach favoured by Christopher Hodges and Stefaan Voet, *Delivering Collective Redress: New Technologies* (Hart/Beck/Nomos 2017).

maybe even of private law itself. Indeed, the very number of people affected, and the loss inflicted to society as a whole elevates this problem from an individual level to one of public interest. Thus, Jolowicz,[84] when commenting on *Dyson v Attorney General*,[85] a case in which the plaintiff contested the lawfulness of a certain form sent out by the Inland Revenue authorities, asked: what real difference is there between a public interest, on the one hand, and the identical private interest of eight million individuals on the other? At least from a civil law perspective, the protection of interests of the general public is primarily a task of public, rather than private law. On the other hand, one is talking about civil rights and obligations in the sense of article 6 of the ECHR. Yet one has to bear in mind the inherent limits of private enforcement. 'Collectivisation' is just a form of 'bundled' individual claims; causation and quantum necessarily have to be determined for each individual claimant; this, after all, is the concept of substantive law.[86] The exercise of what in essence is a 'police' function is still essentially a public function which cannot be fulfilled by private litigants. Rather, private enforcement can supplement, but not replace public enforcement. Therefore, these two ways of enforcement have to be coordinated in order to function effectively, thereby contributing to the well-functioning of the capital market itself.

---

[84] John A Jolowicz, *On Civil Procedure* (Cambridge University Press 2000) 141.

[85] *Dyson v Attorney General* [1911] 1 King's Bench (KB) 410.

[86] Martin Spitzer, 'Kollektivinteressen im Zivilprozess' in Christoph Kietaibl, Rudolf Mosler and Harun Pačić (eds), *Gedenkschrift Robert Rebhahn* (Manz 2019) 581.

ENFORCING CONSUMER AND CAPITAL MARKETS LAW IN DENMARK

Anders SCHÄFER*

* Anders Schäfer, PhD student, University of Copenhagen, School of Law, Centre for Market and Economic Law (CME), attorney-at-law at the law firm Kammeradvokaten/Poul Schmidt.
Statutes – free access at <http://www.retsinformation.dk>.

This chapter describes and discusses public and private enforcement of consumer and capital market law in Denmark.[1] The chapter is divided into four sections. The first section focuses on enforcement of consumer law in light of Case 1.[2] The second section focuses on enforcement of capital market law in light of Case 2. The third section includes some remarks on general procedural law in Denmark. The fourth and final section includes a conclusion and some reflections on enforcement of consumer and capital market regarding compensation for damages and skimming of profits.

I. CONSUMER LAW

A. INTRODUCTION

No consumer cases (neither public nor private) have been filed in Denmark in the aftermath of the diesel emissions scandal. The reason seems to be a combination

1 The distinction between public and private enforcement is not always clear and at a closer look, the distinction is – in some situations – difficult to uphold in Denmark. Here 'public enforcement' relates to enforcement undertaken by a public authority with powers to secure compliance independent from private parties' rights and remedies. 'Private enforcement' relates to civil action by private parties taken against others for addressing rights and remedies. As one may notice, public authorities, who – as a part of their public duty – are enforcing private rights and remedies, including damages, on behalf of private parties, falls outside the scope of both definitions. Such a situation is here termed 'hybrid enforcement'.

2 See Introduction Section IV.A.

of insufficient resource and uncertainty of whether Danish consumers have suffered a loss due to the manipulation.[3]

The fact in Case 1 may, however, trigger different provisions in Danish consumer regulation. Firstly, one may argue that the sale of A's manipulated motor vehicles includes false advertisement.[4] In that case, both public sanctions and private remedies may come into play. Secondly, since the vehicles suffers from a material defect it is not in conformity with manufacturer A's obligations,[5] which may activate different private remedies.

Below enforcement of consumer law is viewed from a public and private enforcement perspective in light of the provisions just identified and the facts in Case 1 (Sections B and C). Thereafter, the relationship between public and private enforcement is discussed (Section D).

B. PUBLIC ENFORCEMENT

1. *Public Enforcers*

The Danish Consumer Ombudsman ('COM') is the main public enforcer of consumer law in Denmark. COM is an independent public body, with a large toolbox of different public sanctions and private remedies, which may be used to ensure compliance of consumer regulation. COM will as a starting point try to solve a case by negotiation. If that is not possible, a number of different legal tools, which (fully or partially) may eliminate the consequences of the violation, may come into play. The specific sanction and remedy depends on the provisions in question.

2. *Sanctions*

False advertisement is a criminal offence subject to a *fine*.[6] The fine may be issued administratively, but only if the prosecuted accepts the fine (*bødeforelæg*). If not, the fine has to be ordered by the court. That is because a fine – according to the Danish legal tradition – is always a criminal sanction and therefore has

3 In Denmark Volkswagen has offered consumers a software update which – apparently – removes the negative consequences of the manipulation. It is therefore currently the opinion of Danish Association of Car Owners (FDM), that Danish car owners have not suffered any economic loss due to the manipulation.

4 S 5(1) of the Danish Marketing Practices Act (2017) (hereafter MA (2017)) states that '(a) trader's commercial practice must not contain false information or in any other way, including overall presentation, deceive or be likely to deceive the average consumer'.

5 Danish Sale of Goods Act (2014) (hereafter SGA (2014)).

6 S 37(3) of the MA (2017) (n 4).

to be ordered by the court, if it is not accepted. It is the prosecution that decides whether to file charges, but COM may request to conduct the case before the court.[7]

Fines for violation of the MA (2017) are – as a general rule – calculated based on the gravity of the infringement, its extent and the intended financial profit.[8] In practice it is, however, often difficult to prove the intended profit. Instead, the court may use the size of the marketing costs as a benchmark.[9]

COM may also – as a part of the criminal procedure – ask the court to confiscate unjustified enrichment due to the violation. The proceeds of a criminal act, or a corresponding amount, may be confiscated in full or in part. Where the basis for determining the size of such amount is insufficient, an amount deemed equivalent to the proceeds made may be confiscated.[10] In recent years, COM has asked for confiscation in a number of cases, including cases regarding false/deceptive advertisement. So far with success. However, the amounts confiscated seems to be – relatively – small amounts (DKK 10,000–45,000).

Under Danish criminal procedure, the victims or the prosecutor may also ask the court for damages to cover the victim's loss due to the violation.[11] If the case does not raise questions of prison, it is the victim who may ask the court to order damages (the so-called 'partie civil' technique).[12] If the accused may face prison, the prosecutor may claim damages on behalf of the victims.[13] However, in both situations the court has wide power to exclude the question of damages from the criminal procedure and postpone the question to a subsequent civil action.[14] That will typically be the case if the question of damages are likely to complicate the case. In cases concerning mass consumer claims this technique is, therefore, not often used (if ever). Since false advertisement only raises questions of fines, it is the victim itself who has to ask the court for damages, but such a claim is – as already mentioned – likely to be postponed to a subsequent civil procedure.

The relation between confiscation, fines and damages is regulated in section 77 of the CA (2018). If a confiscation order is made and someone has a claim for compensation due to the offence, the property subject to confiscation may be used to settle the claim for compensation.[15] On the other side, where the

---

7 S 32(6) of the MA (2017) (n 4).

8 Caroline Heide-Jørgensen, *Lærebog i konkurrence- og markedsføringsret* (3rd edn, Jurist- og Økonomiforbundets Forlag 2017) 77–78 (hereafter Heide-Jørgensen, *Lærebog i konkurrence- og markedsføringsre*); Frank Bøggild, 'Markedsføringsret, erhvervshemmeligheder og industrispionage' in Jon Iversen (ed), *Erhvervsstrafferet* (Karnov Group 2016).

9 U.2003.827, H.D., 21 January 2003, i sag 466/2002 (1. afd.), Rigsadvokaten mod Dansk Præmieinvest ApS.

10 S 75(1) of the (2018) Danish Criminal Act (hereafter CA (2018)).

11 Chapter 89 of the Danish Administration of Justice Act (2018) (hereafter AJA (2018)).

12 Pursuant to s 991(1) of the AJA (2018) (n 11).

13 Pursuant to s 991(2) of the AJA (2018) (n 11).

14 Pursuant to s 991(4) of the AJA (2018) (n 11).

15 S 77(1) of the CA (2018) (n 10).

convicted person has paid compensation to the victim following the judgment, the amount subject to confiscation will be reduced correspondingly.[16] This author is not aware of any consumer cases where a confiscated amount has been used to compensate consumers.

C. PRIVATE ENFORCEMENT

1. *Enforcers*

COM does not just act as a traditionally public enforcer using a public law sanction. COM may also – as a public attorney general – claim damages on behalf of consumers and thus act as one may call a 'hybrid-enforcer'. Consumer associations also play a vital role in private enforcement of consumer claims and may file civil claims on behalf of consumers, including action for damages and injunctions. Finally, consumers themselves – either individually or collectively – play an important role as enforcers by filing civil claims to the courts or complaints to a consumer complaints tribunal.

2. *Remedies*

Case 1 may trigger different private remedies. To begin with, false advertisement may entitle consumers to damages.[17] Furthermore, the material defect of the vehicle, may also allow the buyer to, *inter alia*, cancel the purchase, if A's act is considered fraudulently. A buyer may also choose not to cancel the purchase and instead demand a proportional discount in the purchase price.[18] In both situations, a buyer may in addition claim damages for any loss.[19]

Despite the possibility to enforce damages collectively (see below), the calculation of damages is based on the individual loss. Skimming of the violator's profit without grounds in an individual loss is therefore – as a starting point – not possible as a private remedy. Calculating the loss can be difficult and in some commercial cases – especially regarding intellectual property rights – the violator's gain may be taken into account when calculating the damages.[20] However, in consumer cases such an approach has – according to the author's knowledge – not (yet) been used.

16 S 77(2) of the CA (2018) (n 10).
17 S 24(1) and (2) of the MA (2017) (n 4).
18 S 43(1) and (2) of the SGA (2014) (n 5).
19 S 43(3) of the SGA (2014) (n 5).
20 U.2012.107 U, H.D., 3 October 2011, i sag 218/2009 (1. afd.), VN Legetøj A/S mod Hasbro Europe, filial af Hasbro International Inc. og Hasbro Scandinavia A/S.

Punitive damages are not a possibility under Danish law. That being said, it is important to notice that the Danish regulation of interest may have a punitive effect. Interest is calculated (at the latest) from the day the legal proceeding is initiated.[21] The interest rate corresponds to a fixed reference rate with an addition of 8 per cent.[22] The reference rate is the official lending interest rate set by the Danish National Bank. The addition of 8 per cent applies even though it – depending on the time that has passed – may lead to a substantial amount above the consumer's actual loss.

3. *Collective Redress*

There are a number of different collective redress mechanisms available in Denmark, including (a) class action, (b) joinder of claims and test case, (c) small claim procedure (d) alternative dispute resolution, including complaints boards and tribunals (hereafter 'ADR') and (e) collective settlement.

In case of a public proceeding concerning the same matter as a civil litigation, the civil litigation will typically await the outcome of the public proceeding.

a) Class Actions

In 2008 the Danish class action scheme (*gruppesøgsmål*) was introduced.[23] The scheme is generic and applies accordingly to all civil cases as a starting point.[24] It is an in-court procedure based on private as well as public initiative and includes both the Opt-In and – to a limited extent – the Opt-Out model.

i) Group Representative

A class action is initiated by a potential group representative, who acts as the plaintiff on behalf of the individual group members and is appointed by the court. The following three physical or legal persons may act as a group representative: (1) a member of the group, (2) an association or (3) a public body authorised by law to act as a group representative.

In most of the class actions brought so far, a group representative has been an ad hoc association created with the specific purpose of litigating the claim. Quite often – but not always – is it a law firm who is administrating the ad hoc

21 S 3(4) of the Danish Interest Act (2014) (hereafter IA (2014)).

22 S 5 of the IA (2014) (n 21).

23 Chapter 23a of the AJA (2018) (n 11). The regulation is based on the Standing Committee on Procedural Law recommendations from 2015, Recommendation no 1468/2005 on class action lawsuits (Retsplejerådets betænkning nr. 1468/2005 om gruppesøgsmål).

24 However, some civil cases – such as matrimonial and paternity – are excluded. See s 254a(2) of the AJA (2018) (n 11).

association and the lawyer of the group representative may also be a member of its board.[25]

Until now, the only public body authorised to act as a group representative is COM, within specific (consumer) areas.[26] Even though, the regulation has been in force for more than ten years, the Consumer Ombudsman has not yet filed any class actions. However, the mere fact that the possibility exists has – according to COM – been sufficient to reach a settlement on compensation to consumers in a number of cases.[27]

The group representative does not have access to enforce a settlement or a judgment.[28] Only the group members have.

ii) Opt-Out and Opt-In

The Danish class action scheme includes those who have joined the group,[29] unless the court decides that the class action should include those who have not left the group.[30] However, only a public body may bring an opt-out class action and only if the court finds that the claim of each potential group member is so small that it is unlikely to be pursued individually (maximum DKK 2,000 (2008-level)) and a group action based on the opt-in model is not a suitable way to pursue the claims. So far, no opt-out class action has been filed in Denmark.

iii) Certification

A class action needs to be certified. Certification of the case corresponds with the appointment of the group representative. One – and probably the most

25 One may argue that this is an unfortunate constellation, because the lawyer may end up acting as a lawyer for himself instead of the group. The risk exists when the lawyer has a high influence on the group representative (e.g. the total board of the association are lawyers at the law firm representing the group representative), and there is nobody to monitor it. That may be case where the consumers' individual claim is limited, and one therefore cannot expect the group members to monitor the work of the lawyer and the group representative intensely. In that case, it may raise the risk of the so-called agent-dilemma. A group representative may here be tempted to agree to a 'sweetheart settlement' with the defendant. That could be a low-value settlement to the group against a high-value fee to the group representative's lawyer, since only the settlement but not the lawyer's fee, is subject to the court's approval pursuant to s 254h of the AJA (2018) (n 11). However, the author is not aware of any cases where that has been a real – and not just a theoretical – dilemma.

26 E.g. s 35 of the MA (2017) (n 4).

27 See Christopher Hodges and Stefaan Voet, *Delivering Collective Redress – New Technologies* (Hart 2018) 161–66; see also the Danish Department of Justice evaluation of the Danish Class action scheme from 3 March 2014, 'Redegørelse om erfaringerne med reglerne om gruppesøgsmål, fra justitsministeren' Retsudvalget (REU) (2013–14) Alm. del Bilag 159, 4 <http://www.ft.dk/samling/20131/almdel/REU/bilag/159/index.htm>.

28 Egil Lego Andersen, *Gruppesøgsmål* (Forlaget Thomson 2008) 189.

29 S 254e(5) of the AJA (2018) (n 11).

30 S 254e(8) of the AJA (2018) (n 11).

important – condition is that the claims need to have commonality. The required uniformity pertains to the factual and legal basis of the claims, but the claims do not have to be identical. This condition often raises difficulties and the certification stage therefore also has a tendency to be time consuming and may take up to a year and sometimes longer.

iv) Limitation Period

Class actions, which are certified, interrupt the limitation from the filing of the application with respect to the group members, who are subject to the group action. This also applies to group members who, with the court's permission, register after the expiry of the ordinary registration deadline. A class action does not interrupt the limitation period for class members, who do not register. A class action that is not approved has the same effect as an individual action that is rejected, i.e. the lawsuit will typically interrupt the limitation period, but in order to preserve the limitation period, a (new) legal action must be initiated to pursue the claim.

b) Joinder of Claims and Test Cases

If a number of cases regarding the same issue is pending at the same court, it is possible to join the different cases into one proceeding handled by the same judge(s).[31] At the request of a party, the court may also refer a case before the court to another court, if, after obtaining the opinion of the second court, the case is most appropriate to be considered with another case or other cases pending before the second court.[32] As an alternative (or sometimes in conjunction with joinder of claims), it is possible to run a test case. The court may then postpone the consideration of the other (possible joint) claims pending, while the test case is proceeded.[33] The test case will then work as a guiding star. That may very well be a faster way to resolve a large number of cases than a class action procedure, since the latter needs to be certified. However, a judgment in a test case does not have binding effect to anyone other than the parties, but it does – depending on the ranking of court of the judgment – have precedent in similar future cases. Therefore, proper use of a test case requires that the defendant agree to the procedure.

An approach which has been used a couple of times is a combination of a test case and a class action. Here a class action and a test case are filed simultaneously. The class action ensures that as many as possible of the potential group members

31 S 254(1) of the AJA (2018) (n 11).
32 S 254(2) of the AJA (2018) (n 11).
33 S 345 of the AJA (2018) (n 11).

join the case in a cheap way and do not have to file individual suits to suspend limitation. The test case ensures that the question is resolved as fast as possible, without having to await certification of the class action. That approach seems to be successful, and the class actions seem to settle in light of the outcome of the test case.

Furthermore, if a majority of consumers have a uniform claim for damages, COM may, if requested, choose to litigate those claims on behalf of the consumers.[34]

c) Small Claims Procedure

Denmark has a small claims procedure. It applies to claims that do not exceed DKK 50,000 (excluding interests) or if agreed by the parties.[35] The small claims procedure is a simplified procedure where the court is in charge of preparing the case for trial.[36] If the dispute raises particularly complicated issues or has general importance for one of the parties, the court may decide that the small claim procedure shall not apply. The procedure is therefore not suited for test cases in matters which may have an impact on a large number of consumers, such as in the situation described in Case 1.

d) Alternative Disputes Resolution (ADR)

As a more simplified and cheaper procedure than civil litigation, consumers may file a complaint to one of the many ADR under the Danish Act on Consumer Complaints (2015) (hereafter CC (2015), including the Consumer Complaints Board (*Forbrugerklagenævnet*)). Before a case is sent to a complaints board, the Complaint Resolution (Center for *Klageløsning*) tries to mediate a settlement.

Most often, a company will choose to follow a decision from the Consumer Complaints Board, but its decisions are not binding if the company declares within 30 days that it is not going to follow it. That may very well be the case if a large number of consumers have a similar claim. If that is the case, the consumer (or the Consumer Ombudsman) will have to file a civil claim with the court.

Purely private-based models dealing with consumers' damages claims have also emerged. Most notable are private-based models who handle compensation to consumers due to delay or cancellation of flights, but development seems to be under way to extend the approach to data protection.

---

34 S 34 of the MA (2017) (n 4).

35 Ss 400 and 401 of the AJA (2018) (n 11).

36 Ss 406 and 407 of the AJA (2018) (n 11).

e) Collective Settlement

In Denmark, overall there are two ways to enter into a collective settlement: out-of-court or in-court.

An out-of-court collective settlement will most likely be one negotiated by COM. The consumer can then afterward choose to join the settlement or proceed the claim on its own. An in-court collective settlement is a bit more cumbersome, since it needs to be under the class actions scheme. Therefore, a class action has to be certified before a settlement will have collective binding effect. The settlement will have binding effect on those who opt-in, unless the consumer ombudsman act as the group representative and the class action is certified under the opt-out model. If the latest is the case, it is possible to enter into a settlement, which will be binding for everybody expect those who opt-out. A collective settlement under the Danish class scheme is not valid unless approved by the court. The court approves the settlement unless there is unlawful discrimination by group members or the settlement otherwise is manifestly unreasonable.[37]

D. THE RELATIONSHIP BETWEEN PUBLIC AND PRIVATE ENFORCEMENT

COM is an active enforcer of consumer law using primarily public law tools. However, must consumer claims are enforced by consumers themselves through ADR, including complain boards and or private digital platforms. The consumers and consumer associations also play an important role in the public enforcement by informing COM of potential violations of consumer law.

II. CAPITAL MARKET LAW

A. INTRODUCTION

In Denmark no capital market cases (neither public nor private) have – according to the author's knowledge – been filed in the aftermath of the diesel emissions scandal, but the Danish Shareholder Association (*Dansk Aktionærforening*) has invited Danish shareholders to participate in the German lawsuit Stichting Volkswagen Investors Claim.

The fact in Case 2 may, however, violate different provisions in Danish capital market law. First, one may argue, that the board member of A may have

37 S 254h of the AJA (2018) (n 11).

committed insider trading.[38] Second, A may have failed to disclose information to the public.[39] Both situations may trigger both public sanction and private remedies.

Below enforcement of capital market law is viewed from a public and private enforcement perspective in light of the provisions just identified and the facts of Case 2 (Sections B and C). Finally, the relationship between public and private enforcement within capital market law is discussed (Section D).

Enforcement of consumer and capital market law is to some extent based on the same procedural rules. To avoid repetition, the reader is referred to Section I for a more in-depth description and discussion, when there is overlap.

B. PUBLIC ENFORCEMENT

1. *Enforcers*

Public enforcement of capital market law is divided between the Danish Financial Supervisory Authority (*Finanstilsynet*) (hereafter 'FSA') and the Danish State Prosecutor for Serious Economic and International Crime (*Statsadvokaten for Særlig Økonomisk og International Kriminalitet*) (hereafter 'SPSEIC').

FSA is an independent public body with its own board. It is the main enforcer of capital market and handles the administrative enforcement. It also notifies SPSEIC of potential criminal offences. SPSEIC handles the criminal part of the enforcement, including whether to bring charges.

2. *Sanctions*

Criminal enforcement of capital market law includes a number of different sanctions, which may (fully or partially) eliminate the consequences of the violation. The specific sanction depends on the violation.

Insider trading is prohibited in Denmark.[40] It is considered a criminal offence and is subject to fine and prison.[41] An issuer is also obligated to disclose information to the public,[42] and failure to do so is a criminal offence and subject to fine.[43]

---

38 Council Regulation (EU) No 596/2014 of 16 April 2014 on market abuse (market abuse regulation) and repealing Directive 2003/6/EC of the European Parliament and of the Council and Commission Directives 2003/124/EC, 2003/125/EC and 2004/72/EC [2014] OJ L173/12, art 17(1) (hereafter MAR).

39 Art 17 of the MAR (n 38).

40 Art 14 of the MAR (n 38).

41 S 249(2) of the Market Act (2018) (hereafter CMA (2018)).

42 Art 14 of the MAR (n 38).

43 S 249(1) of the CMA (2018) (n 41).

SPSEIC may – as a part of a criminal procedure – ask the court to issue a fine and confiscate unjustified enrichment due to the violation. SPSEIC and – to a certain extent – FSA may (instead) issue administrative fines, if the prosecuted accepts the fine (*bødeforelæg*). If not, a fine has to be ordered by the court. As also stated above, that is due to a fine – according to the Danish legal tradition – always being a criminal sanction and therefore has to be ordered by the court, if not accepted. The question of jail always has to be handled by the court.

Obtained financial advances following from a breach of CMA are subject to confiscation according to the general rules for confiscation of ill-gotten profit in s 75(1) CA (2018).[44] Therefore, the board member of A's financial advantage from insider trading may be subject to confiscation. However, if a fine is based on the financial advantage from the violation, there is no ground (also) to order confiscation.[45] If it is not possible to confiscate financial advantage obtained from the violation, account of that fact needs to be taken individually when a fine is calculated.[46] The purpose is to make sure that a violation does not pay off.

Depending on the case, victims or the SPSEIC may ask the court for damages to cover the victim's loss due to the violation under the criminal procedure.[47] If the case does not raise questions of prison, a victim may claim damages under the criminal procedure.[48] If the accused may face prison, the prosecutor may claim damages on the behalf of the victims.[49] Therefore, potential victims may claim damages under the criminal procedure against A. Since the criminal procedure against the board member of A may include prison, a request for damages needs to be made by SPSEIC on behalf of the victims. However, in both situations it is likely that the court will postpone the question of damages to a subsequent independent civil action.[50]

The questions regarding the relationship between confiscation, damage and fines are the same under enforcement of capital market law as under consumer law (see above Section I.B.).

---

44 S 255(5) of the CMA (2018) (n 41).

45 U. 1995.905 H, H.D., 31 August 1995, case no I 176/1995, Anklagemyndigheden mod T. In that case a CFO of a company was convicted for inside trading. He was sentenced to prison and the court ordered an additional fine of DKK 50,000 based on the minimum financial gains from the violation.

46 S 255(6) of the CMA (2018) (n 41).

47 See Chapter 89 of the AJA (2018) (n 11).

48 S 991(1) of the AJA (2018) (n 47).

49 S 991(2) of the AJA (2018) (n 47).

50 S 991(4) of the AJA (2018) (n 11); see – as an example – U.1999.513Ø, 1999 Ø.L.D., 14 December 1998, Case number S-1655-98.

C. PRIVATE ENFORCEMENT

1. *Enforcers*

Private enforcers of capital market law are shareholder associations and individual shareholders.

2. *Remedies*

Both A and the board member of A may be subject to civil collective litigation in the situation described in Case 2. A because of failure to disclose information in due time, which may stipulate the claim for damages from shareholders who has brought shares after the information should have been disclosed. The board member of A may be subject to civil litigation from the buyers of the shares due to a number of reasons.[51] Firstly, one may argue that the sale of the shares may lack conformity with the board member's duties as a seller. In that case, a buyer of the shares may cancel the purchase and claim money back or damages if A has acted fraudulently.[52] Instead of cancelling the purchase, a buyer of shares may demand a proportional discount in the purchase price.[53] Secondly, one may argue that the board member is subject to liability due to inside trading.[54]

3. *Collective Redress*

There is – as described above – a number of different collective redress mechanisms available in Denmark. Most relevant in the situation described in Case 2 is (a) class action or (b) joinder of claims and test cases. In case of a public proceeding concerning the same matter as a civil litigation, the civil litigation will typically await the outcome of the public proceeding.

a) Class Actions

As described in more detail above, class action is a possibility under Danish law.[55] Since the scheme is generic, it does also apply to situations as described in Case 2.

---

51 Recommendation no 1261/1991 on insider trading (Betænkning 1261/1991 om Insider-handel) 68–69.

52 S 43(3) of the SGA (2014) (n 5).

53 S 43(1) and (2) of the SGA (2014) (n 5).

54 Art 14 of the MAR (n 38).

55 Recommendation no 1468/2005 on class action lawsuits (Retsplejerådets betænkning nr. 1468/2005 om gruppesøgsmål).

A group representative initiates the class action. The group representative may be a member of the group, an association or a public body. For the latter to be the case, a public body needs to be given specific access to act as a group representative. No public body has access to initiate a class action due to any of the identified provisions in Case 2.[56] Thus, only group members or associations can initiate a class action in that situation and only as an Opt-In class action. That makes building up and joining the case more cumbersome. However, in capital market cases it does seem to be real barrier, since the individual claim normally has a certain size.

In Denmark, there has been a number of class actions initiated by ad hoc associations acting as a group representative on behalf of shareholders (group members). Sometimes the ad hoc association is associated to the Danish Shareholders' Association (*Dansk Aktionærforening*). That may ensure competent monitoring of the group representative and the lawyer's work. Other times the association is associated to a law firm and the lawyer, who also represents the group representative.[57]

Currently a couple of potential class actions is pending (none have been certified yet) regarding Danske Bank's (one of the major banks in Denmark) failure to disclose information in due time. The background of the cases is a significant decrease in the value of the bank's stocks, after it was disclosed that (a part of) the bank had been involved in extensive money laundering. The issue of the case is new legal territory in Denmark, and it is still uncertain whether the court will consider the different group members' claim common, since they have brought shares at a different time. If not, the class actions may be limited to liability. Thus, the calculation of a possible compensation must be subject to an independent civil trial.

Another pending class action is the *OW Bunker* case. The association OW Bunker-Investor, has brought proceeding against, *inter alia*, members of the executive Board in the former OW Bunker A/S (now bankrupt). The association is claiming that the defendants are liable for the loss suffered by subscribing for shares in the company in connection with the public listing and/or had suffered in connection with the acquisition of shares in the company. The case has been certified, but – in light of the criteria of commonality (see above Section I) – limited. The High Court stated that claims based on allegations of deficiencies

---

56 In relation to the board member of A, one may argue that an agreement declared void under the Danish Contracts Act (2016) and a sale that lacks conformity under the Danish Sale of Goods Act (2014) is also covered by the general provision regarding good marketing practice in s 3 Danish Marketing Act. In relation to A, one may argue the same in relation to A's lack of disclosure. In that case, in both situations it would stipulate legal ground for the Consumer Ombudsman to initiate a class action pursuant to s 35. However, the author considers such a result doubtful and has therefore chosen to disregard this.

57 As discussed more in depth in Section I that may – at least theoretically – raise the risk of the agent-dilemma.

in the prospectus, which formed the basis for the listing of the company, had the necessary commonality. However, claims based on a buyer liability defect would require the individual evaluation, *inter alia*, on information about the individual trades, who were the buyers of the quoted shares, their prerequisites, and who were the sellers of the shares.[58]

A class action from shareholders in Case 2 is – based on the current jurisprudence in Denmark – likely to limited to the question of liability.

b) Other Civil Collective Procedures

As described in more details in Section II, a number of alternative collective mechanisms are available in Denmark, including joinder of claims and test cases. An approach which has been used a couple of times in capital market class actions is the combination of test case and class actions.[59] That approach seems to be successful and the class actions typically settle in light of the outcome of the test case. The approach may be useful to get some guidance regarding calculation of damages in different situation, which may be used to settle a case.

D. THE RELATIONSHIP BETWEEN PUBLIC AND PRIVATE ENFORCEMENT

Private enforcement of capital market law is often based on prior public enforcement stating a violation of capital market law. A robust private enforcement is therefore – to a certain extent – depending on robust public enforcement. The Danish Government has just announced a political agreement aimed at significantly strengthening FSA.[60] The agreement is a direct consequence of

58 U.2019.962, Østre Landsrets kendelse af 14. afd. nr. B-407-17: Foreningen OW Bunker-Investor mod bl.a. OW Lux S.á.r.l. Invest.

59 U.2013.1107H, H.D., 18 January 2013, Case number 141/2012, Foreningen af Minoritetsaktionærer i bankTrelleborg som mandatar for Jørgen Ib Martin Jensen, Susanne Laugesen og Kasper Rich Kjærsgaard mod Sydbank A/S (free access: <http://www.hoejesteret.dk/hoejesteret/Pages/default.aspx>). The ruling clarified that shareholders who subscribe for new shares (or specifically in the case: converted guarantee capital for newly issued shares) may raise a claim against the issuing company, if there are deficiencies in the prospectus which are of significant importance for the assessment of the share and which can be blamed on the company. The judgment also introduced a presumption rule that when a subscription has been made on the basis of a prospectus with deficiencies that are of material importance for the assessment of the company, there is a presumption that the share subscription had not taken place if the prospectus had contained correct and complete information. Pending class actions were settled in light of the ruling.

60 Aftale mellem og Socialdemokratiet, Dansk Folkeparti, Radikale Venstre og Socialistisk Folkeparti, 'Styrkelse af indsatsen mod finansiel kriminalitet' (27 March 2019) <http://www.regeringen.dk/media/6607/aftale-om-styrkelse-af-indsatsen-mod-finansiel-kriminalitet-270319_endelig.pdf>.

the Danske Bank Scandal (see above). If that leads to more public infringement decision, that is also likely to lead to more private enforcement.

III. GENERAL PROCEDURAL LAW

A. LITIGATION COST AND FUNDING

1. Cost

Cost are divided into court fees, legal representation and other cost, including fees paid to experts (for expert reports and expert witness statements) and compensation to witnesses. In case of a class action, there may also be costs associated with building up the case, including announcement to group members.

In Denmark, the so-called English Rule applies to litigation costs. Thus, the looser of the case will – as a starting point – have to pay the cost of the litigation to the other party.[61] Expenses for legal assistance are reimbursed by an appropriate amount, and other expenses are fully compensated.[62] Since the actual legal expenses are not necessarily reimbursed, it is very likely that the winner of the case is not going to get all of its costs associated with the litigation covered.[63]

In a class action, it is, as a starting point, the group representative who bears the litigation cost. If the case is lost, the group representative will therefore have to pay the defendant's cost. Nevertheless, the court may order group members to pay costs to the other party and/or the group representative in an Opt-In class action. Such an order may – at most – equal any security order by the court and provided by the group members when the member joined the case with the addition of amounts that benefit the group member through the trial.[64] Hence, the group member knows what the maximum risk is when they join the case. The group representative – on the other hand – runs a higher risk.

2. Litigation Funding

It is possible to divide litigation funding into public and private funding.

---

61 S 312 of the AJA (2018) (n 11).

62 S 316 of the AJA (2018) (n 11).

63 Clement Salung Petersen, 'Access to the Danish Civil Justice System: Recent Reforms and Current Challenges' in Laura Ervo and Anna Nylund (eds), *The Future of Civil Litigation: Access to Courts and Court-annexed Mediation in the Nordic Countries* (Springer 2004) 298 (hereafter Petersen, 'Access').

64 S 254f(3) of the AJA (2018) (n 11).

a) Public Funding

Free legal aid is one way to fund a collective consumer claim.[65] In that case, that the consumers do not have to pay court fee and the cost of the proceeding, including the attorney's fee, is paid by the state. If the case is lost, the state will also pay the defendant's cost according to the order of the court.

Generally, free legal aid in civil proceedings is possible in two situations. First, an individual with a low income and no insurance coverage can get free legal aid if there is a reasonable cause to litigate (income based free legal aid).[66] Second, any individual, who – as a general rule – acts outside his or her commercial interest, can get free legal aid in certain special cases, including in cases of general public importance and in cases that are important to the individual's social or commercial situation (non-income-based free legal aid).[67]

Non-income-based free legal aid has so far funded most of the class actions which have been initiated under the Danish class action scheme, and it is not unlikely that a class action is abandoned, if free legal aid in civil proceedings is denied. However, if free legal aid is accepted, the court does not request security from the group members when they join the case. Therefore, there is no financial risk for the group members in that case. That plays a substantial role. The latest experience shows that it is possible to get a very large amount of people (approximately 280,000 people) to sign up for a class action, if it is easy and without financial risk to join.[68] The experience may very well also apply in a potential consumer class action against car manufacturer A.

b) Private Funding

Collective litigation, including class action, is expensive and risky. In Denmark – as in most of the European countries – lawyers are not able to enter into the contingency fee agreement with their clients. The same limitation does not apply to other players, who may enter into similar agreements (third-party funders).

Third-party litigation funding is still a relatively new phenomenon in Denmark but seems to be on the rise also as a way to fund class actions. So far, there seems to be no experience with funding consumer cases. However, information regarding this issue is not easy to get, since it is not mandatory to disclose to the court whether a case is funded by third party.

In Denmark, most households have a legal expenses insurance, which may cover up to DKK 175,000 in legal expenses. In case of a class action the

65 Petersen, 'Access' (n 63) 287–288.
66 Ss 325, 327 and 328 of the AJA (2018) (n 11).
67 S 329 of the AJA (2018) (n 11).
68 The case is against the Danish state and about repayment of overpaid licences (each group member may have a claim of up to approximately DKK 4,000).

general rule is that the insurance companies involved will cover 5 × 175,000. The insurance company will usually set an excess on 10 per cent and a minimum of DKK 2,500.

D. BURDEN OF PROOF AND ACCESS TO EVIDENCE

The burden of proof in Danish civil proceedings generally lies on the party asserting the affirmative of an issue. Access to evidence therefore plays a vital role.

If a claim is brought by private parties, the general procedural rules applies. Accordingly, the parties are free to put questions to each other and call in witnesses under the main hearing. A party or a third party is furthermore obligated to produce written evidence in his or her possession, which may be presumed to have evidentiary value, unless there will be information on matters which he or she would be excluded from or exempted from explaining as a witness.[69] To obtain a court order, the applicant will have to identify the document with sufficient clarity. The condition is to prevent fishing expeditions. If the other party does not obey the order, the court may decide that it will have a negative procedural impact when the court is evaluating the evidence.[70] If the third party does not obey the order, the court may, *inter alia*, issue a fine.

If a claim is brought by COM, the institution can (probably) use its power to require disclosure from anyone of all details considered necessary for COM's activities.[71] A party who omits to disclose information required by the Consumer Ombudsman shall be liable to a fine.[72]

C. BINDING EFFECT

A final judgment which states that a company or a person has violated public regulation, is not – unless otherwise explicitly stated (as it is the case in competition cases) – binding in a subsequent civil litigation.[73] However, a judgment will be a (substantial) proof of a violation in a subsequent civil litigation.

---

69 Ss 298 and 299 of the AJA (2018) (n 11).

70 S 344(2) of the AJA (2018) (n 11).

71 S 25(2) of the MA (2017) (n 4).

72 S 37(2) of the MA (2017) (n 4).

73 Stephan Hurwitz, *Den Danske Strafferetspleje* (3rd edn, Gad 1959) 562–65; Mogens Koktvedgaard and Hans Gammeltoft-Hansen, *Lærebog i Strafferetspleje* (2nd edn, Jurist- og Økonomforbundet 1978) 359–60; Hans Gammeltoft-Hansen, *Strafferetspleje III* (Jurist- og Økonomforbundet 1996) 194–95.

D. SUSPENSION OF THE LIMITATION PERIOD

The normal limitation period in Denmark is three years.[74] Nevertheless, the expiry of the limitation period does not prevent the defendant from being liable to pay compensation for the injured party in connection with the criminal offence, during a criminal case where the accused is found guilty. Such a claim may also be invoked under a separate action brought within one year of a final decision in a criminal case where the accused is found guilty or within one year of the adoption of a fine or other criminal penalties.[75]

IV. CONCLUSION AND REFLECTIONS

Public enforcement of consumer and capital market law may result in skimming off profit either by confiscation of unjustified profit, or calculation of a fine in light of an unjustified profit. Damages due to criminal violation may be included in the criminal procedure, but in practice it is typically postponed to a subsequent civil litigation.

Private enforcement may also remove the consequences of a violation, but it is not possible to calculate damages in light of the violator's unjustified profit. Calculation of damages is based on the claimant's loss.[76] Since focus is on the individual claimant's position, private enforcement may only remove the total profit from the violator, if every claim is included. Thus, punitive damages are not possible but the (very) high procedural interest rate in Denmark may result in a substantial higher amount of damages then the actual loos.

Denmark has had a class actions scheme for more than 10 years. After a slow start, it seems to have increased in speed, especially when it comes to cases within capital markets and the financial sector. It is based on the Opt-In model but does – to a limited extent – allow the COM to use the Opt-Out model. Most of the Opt-In cases have – a bit ironically – been publicly funded through free legal aid. Class action does therefore not (financially) supplement public enforcement much. If a class action does not get free legal aid, it is often abandoned. Some – but not many – have been funded through joint membership payment from the group members. That seems only possible where each group member has a substantial individual claim.

That leaves a gap for cases regarding small individual claims without general public importance. Such cases may also include large collective amounts, but

74 S 3 of the Danish Limitation Act (2015) (hereafter LA (2015)).
75 S13 of the LA (2015) (n 74).
76 Recommendation no 1468/2005 on class action lawsuits (Retsplejerådets betænkning nr. 1468/2005 om gruppesøgsmål) 237.

since contingency fee agreements are prohibited, and third-party litigation funding is still in a very early stage, they are not easy to fund. COM may – as a hybrid enforcer – fil in that gap, but the institution has limited resources and has to prioritise its enforcement. So far, the Consumer Ombudsman has not initiated a single class action, but the threat of doing so has occasionally secured a settlement to the benefit of the consumers. However, the lack of activity from the Consumer Ombudsman's side in the diesel emissions scandal seems to underscore that there is still a gap. Despite its advance, it is hard to get around that a fundamental problem with the hybrid enforcement model is funding. Especially because of the high cost involved in class actions. Unlike a lawyer working on a contingency fee agreement, there is no potential financial win for the Consumer Ombudsman in litigating a class action – only a very high financial risk. Third-party litigation funding may be a possible alternative solution, but it is still too early to say.

The *lega ferenda* it would improve enforcement of especially consumer claims, if not just a public body but also (special) private parties (it could be one or more consumer associations) get access to use the Opt-Out model. Furthermore, it should be possible to claim collective (but not punitive) damages without undertaking an assessment of the amount of damages recoverable in respect of the claim of each represented person but calculated on an aggregated level. It is also important that the group representative is able to enforce a settlement or a judgment on its own. If not, an Opt-Out class action may – by the end of day – prove to be waste of time, since only a fraction of the consumers are going to enforce their right if the individual claim is small. They simply do not bother! It should also be possible to distribute unclaimed damages to alternative receivers (e.g. cý-press distribution or similar instrument), when the Opt-Out model is used.

ENFORCING CONSUMER AND CAPITAL MARKETS LAW IN FRANCE

Emmanuel JEULAND*

In France, diesel technology has been favoured for decades until very recently. The price of diesel was actually much lower than any other products. Then, for many reasons, especially to promote environmental protection, diesel began

* Emmanuel Jeuland, Dr., LLM (King's College London), Professor, University Paris 1 Panthéon-Sorbonne, School of Law, Director of the Sorbonne Institute of Legal Research. Caselaw, Acts and Regulations may be found freely accessible on <http://www.legifrance.gouv.fr>.

to be criticised and its price increased. The yellow vests' demonstrations were triggered by such increases as when people living at the periphery of big towns started spending a lot of money on of their diesel cars. The Dieselgate scandal has also certainly had its part in the change of mind concerning diesel in France.[1] The role of the French State is very important as well.

As far as consumer protection and capital market are concerned, France is mainly a centralised system of administration. The General Directorate for Competition Policy, Consumer Affairs and Fraud Control (DGCCRF) is very powerful and plays the role of a consumer police, which serves as either an administrative or a judicial police. It can initiate administrative investigations and impose administrative sanctions. In the field of capital market, the Financial Markets Regulator (AMF) has administrative powers to investigate and sanction, and even potentially bring criminal charges. Hence, the French State is modelled upon the interventionist system, not upon the German ordo-liberalist system.

Criminal proceedings are available for consumer protection and capital market litigations. However, the Public Prosecutor is not an independent body from the executive power since its head is the Minister of Justice. Judges are in principle independent, but they are dependent on the Public Prosecutor for the pace of a case.

Private enforcement is not very developed, as it is in Competition Law (a consequence of the 2014 Directive). Many procedural tools have actually been implemented but are not often used (representative action, injunction to do something, collective redress action, collective interest action, etc.) since consumer associations, the ones that are able to bring actions, are not numerous and do not have the financial and human resources to do so. There is a lack of evidence tools as well (such as cross-examination or discovery, yet to be found in antitrust private enforcement or in front of the Paris International Chambers). Evidence brought by public authorities cannot always be easily used in criminal or civil proceedings. In a way, the possibilities of private enforcement may be seen as an alibi to hide the lack of political will to condemn manufacturers. This is a way of saying to consumers: 'Go ahead and bring your own action', knowing that this kind of private or collective actions involves many impediments.

---

1 Laurent Posocco, 'French Report' in Marco Frigessi di Rattalma (ed), *The Dieselgate, A Legal Perspective* (Springer 2017) 3–26; Julie de la Brosse, 'Dieselgate: la justice française déboute des clients de Volkswagen' *L'Express* (Paris, 27 April 2016) <http://lexpansion.lexpress.fr/actualite-economique/dieselgate-la-justice-francaise-deboute-des-clients-volkswagen_1786835.html>; Laure-Emmanuelle Husson, 'Une nuée de procédures judiciaires s'abat sur VW' *Challenges* (Paris, 6 October 2015) <http://automobile.challenges.fr/actu-auto/20151005.CHA0137/une-nuee-de-procedures-judiciaires-s-abat-sur-volkswagen.html>.

These remarks may explain why car manufacturers (which include two French companies) have not been condemned yet for having manipulated emission values.

I. CASE 1: CONSUMER PROTECTION[2]

In France, the Ministry of Economy is competent to enforce consumer protection via the DGCCRF (the General Directorate for Competition Policy, Consumer Affairs and Fraud Control), the administrative and judicial police based on Consumer Law (except for certain sectors such as the financial one, see Case 2). Sectorial agencies also intervene, namely: the Competition Authority *(Autorité de la concurrence)*, the Energy Regulatory Board (*Commission de la régulation de l'énergie*), the Regulatory Authority for Electronic Communications (*ARCEP; Autorité de régulation des communications électroniques et des postes*), the Financial Markets Regulator (*Autorité des marchés financiers*, see Case 2) and the Prudential Control Authority (*ACPR; Autorité de contrôle prudentiel et de résolution*), etc. However, for Case 1, there are no special agencies if UTAC is excepted (a French private company) which acts as a technical expert and the OCLAESP (*Office Central de Lutte contre les Violations à l'Environnement et à la Santé Publique*). Administrative, criminal and civil procedure are all available.

A. ADMINISTRATIVE PROCEEDINGS

In the field of motor vehicles emission values, a decree (Décret no. 91-102, 4 October 1991) has nominated a French private company, the Union technique de l'automobile, du motocycle et du cycle (UTAC) to act as a technical expert. The DGCCRF is competent (article L. 511-3 and L. 511-4 of the Consumer Code) to launch administrative investigations in case Consumer Law is violated. In Case 1, the infringement should be classified as unfair commercial practices and deception (article L. 120-1 of the Consumer Code). Case 1 might be answered by referring by analogy to the *VW* case.

In 2015, at the time of the Volkswagen case, the French Minister of Ecology, Sustainable Development and Energy, Mrs Royal, asked UTAC to carry out a protocol analysing the French market. UTAC was in charge of proposing an investigation protocol in order to identify vehicles which would be potentially equipped with cheating software affecting anti-pollution systems. Once established, this protocol was submitted to an independent commission and

---

2 See Introduction Section IV.A.

100 diesel vehicles of different brands, representing the market, were tested according to this protocol.

In parallel, the Direction Générale de la Concurrence, de la Consommation et de la Répression des Fraudes (DGCCRF) launched a survey among Volkswagen France managers to determine whether the updated practices had also been implemented in France. The survey is still being carried out among the main manufacturers marketing vehicles in France.

The first checks carried out on about ten vehicles (all brands combined) confirmed Volkswagen's 'cheating' (Intervention by the Minister, Mrs Royal, on France Info, on 6 November 2015). Indeed, in the case of Volkswagen, the regulation in nitrogen oxides exceeded 5 times the limit value, while other vehicles overrun was only by 1.5 to 2.

This administrative investigation led to a criminal investigation after several associations and VW vehicles owners brought an action (see Section II). In Case 1, such an administrative track was bound not to produce great effects. Actually, if administrative sanctions are provided for in relation to certain types of offences, the amount of the fine is low (i.e. €3,000 for a natural person, €15,000 for a legal person in case of tourism infringement (Code tourisme, article L. 211-23-III.[3]).

The DGCCRF could have proposed a settlement after stating the offence. The proposal would have been sent to the Public Prosecutor within three months of the statement of facts (articles R. 523-2, R. 141-3, II and R. 216-3, II of the Consumer Code) and the amount reached by the settlement would have been transferred to the Public Treasury.

It seems that the trend is to decriminalise consumer protection. In France, according to Act no. 2014-344 of 17 March 2014 (known as the 'Hamon Statute'), consumer infringements are no longer subject to criminal sanctions but fall under the administrative order.

B. CRIMINAL PROCEEDINGS

Therefore, after the administrative investigations relative to Consumer Law violations have been carried out, the DGCCRF may refer the case to the Public Prosecutor, who in turn may bring an action against automobile manufacturer A if the information of an infringement is provided.

In addition, victims may claim damages from the defendant in criminal proceedings, the infringer. If a victim does not initiate his or her civil case before

---

3 See Jacques Ranc, 'Instruments de mesure réglementés' in *Répertoire de droit commercial* (Dalloz January 2012).

a criminal court but before a civil court, he or she cannot piggyback. Consumer associations may intervene in criminal proceedings along with consumers.[4]

The Public Prosecutor can actively search for Consumer Law violations. He can also act when a complaint has been made. If he is of the opinion that an offence has been committed, he can ask the Court to impose sanctions. The Court cannot however apply sanctions *ex officio*.

These criminal procedures, if successful, can result in the punishment of the perpetrator of the deception (manufacturer A) by a prison sentence and the payment of a fine. Under no circumstances can these procedures lead to the cancellation of the sale. Only an action before civil courts would allow it.

Actions currently underway in the *VW* case in France: the consumer association 'La Confédération du Logement et du Cadre de Vie' (CLCV) has decided to file a complaint for unfair commercial practices and deception against VW. The NGO 'Ecologie Sans Frontière (E.S.F)' filed a complaint for aggravated deception and endangering the lives of others. The association also filed a complaint against the inaction of public authorities in the fight against air pollution, which is interesting in the line of our own general remarks (see Introduction).

The Paris Bar Association has set up an 'Avocats-Actions-Conjoint' platform allowing individuals to group around a lawyer in order to launch a joint action (a grouping of individual complaints within the same trial). Among the actions currently proposed, one of them concerns Volkswagen. The lawyer filed a complaint with the Public Prosecutor on the basis of the offences of deception, misleading commercial practice and fraud. On the web site, consumers' damages have already been estimated to be between 10 per cent to 20 per cent of the vehicle purchase value, which seems premature in the absence of concrete evidence. The consumer wishing to join this action should keep in mind that the compensation announced is not guaranteed. Registration took place before 31 December 2015 and the lawyer's fee was set at €600.

In France, investigations against Volkswagen, Renault, Fiat Chrysler and PSA are underway. After the start of the Volkswagen scandal, a collective movement of owners driving vehicles distributed by the German brand in France – where 948,064 cars have been affected by the massive scandal of pollution test rigging – has decided to take legal action. In total, the association brings together about 50 owners who consider themselves aggrieved by the German manufacturer's practices. Under the name of the Association of International Victims of Motor Vehicle Fraud (AVIFA), the movement claims to bring an action before the courts for 'misleading commercial practice, false advertising,

4 Not often used, see Coralie Ambroise-Castérot, 'Consommation' in *Repertoire de droit pénal et de procédure pénale* (Dalloz July 2016).

deception, fraud, endangering the lives of others, complicity, forgery and use of forgery'. The complaint was filed against X.[5] The lawyer, Mr Canoy, explains the French approach: 'About sixty individual approaches grouped in a single file before the Court'.

Similarly, Vice-President of the Ile-de-France Region in charge of Transport, Pierre Serne, referred the scandal of fake software designed to mask the polluting emissions of Volkswagen diesel vehicles to the Paris Public Prosecutor's Office, according to article 40 of the Code of Criminal Procedure, which requires any authority to report a crime of which it is aware.

On 2 October 2015, the Paris Public Prosecutor's Office opened a preliminary investigation for aggravated deception.[6]

Three judges from the 'Public Health' Unit of the Paris Court of First Instance are in charge of the case. The investigations are conducted by the DGCCRF and the OCLAESP (Office Central de Lutte contre les Violations à l'Environnement et à la Santé Publique). According to the court documents, investigators asked Volkswagen the source code of the offending software but were unable to obtain it. However, they were able to use the results of the Commission's tests.

The French investigation has not yet given rise to any indictment, but the DGCCRF has clearly designated 'Volkswagen AG, in the person of its legal representative: Matthias Müller, Director General', as 'presumed responsible'.

The French investigation was opened on the possibility of 'deception of a product that could endanger human and animal health'. A judicial inquiry has also been opened against Renault, PSA and FCA (2017).

As part of the investigation opened in April 2017 on the French manufacturer PSA, the General Directorate for Competition Policy, Consumer Affairs and Fraud Control (DGCCRF) sent a report to the courts, highlighting the existence of a fraudulent 'global strategy'. PSA is suspected of having manipulated, during the certification tests, its diesel engines so as to emit less nitrogen oxide – a polluting gas – than during real driving. The car manufacturer, which is at great risk, 'denies any fraudulent strategy' and has filed a complaint for violation of the secrecy of the investigation.

In the document sent to the courts by the DGCCRF, i.e. the consumer police, the manufacturer PSA is accused of having rigged the engines of its diesel vehicles to pass the approval tests. The method is the same as for Volkswagen: the engines are modified to emit fewer polluting gases during laboratory tests. But once on the road, nitrogen oxide emissions skyrocket. This is both fraud and deception for consumers.

---

5 A complaint against X is a legal complaint without naming the defendant so that the public prosecutor may investigate.

6 'Scandale Volkswagen: enquête en France pour « tromperie aggravée »' *Le Monde* (Paris, 2 October 2015) <http://www.lemonde.fr/automobile/article/2015/10/02/scandale-volkswagen-enquete-en-france-pour-tromperie-aggravee_4781214_1654940.html>.

The DGCCRF explained that the group-nine models tested by UTAC, the vehicle certification body, had nitrogen oxide (NOx) emission rates below the authorised limit (180 mg/km), under the specific conditions of the certification test.

Unlike Volkswagen, PSA did not use software but rather a device that modified the engine behaviour according to the moment, a technique the DGCCRF refers to as 'fraudulent calibrations'. In other words, the device ensured that the pollution control system was much more active during the tests than in real driving.

During their investigations at PSA headquarters, investigators found a document with a rather explicit name: 'Technical file on diesel emissions strategy Euro 5'. This is how investigators discovered the explanation of the fraud.

According to the DGCCRF, the sale of such cars brought PSA '€33.86 billion' at the very least between 2009 and 2015. Investigators estimated that Volkswagen sold 946,097 vehicles in France equipped with its fake software, with a turnover of more than €22 billion. As for Renault, they sold 898,557 cars, for nearly €17 billion.

The inquiry, entrusted to three judges of the Public Health Unit from the Paris Court of First Instance, directly targeted PSA as a legal entity, through its CEO Carlos Tavares and the previous managers as natural persons. An internal document submitted by the DGCCRF, revealed by *Le Monde*, led the newspaper to affirm that the management was aware of this, as the objective of the rigging scheme had been presented to it 'as early as November 2010'. As a result, the fraudulent 'global strategy' put in place by PSA led the court to open an investigation on 7 April 2017 for 'aggravated deception'. And the bill could be high. According to the DGCCRF minutes, PSA faces a fine of up to €5 billion, equivalent to 10 per cent of the average turnover for the years 2013, 2014 and 2015.

However, the case is still pending and no car manufacturer has been condemned in France so far.

C. CIVIL PROCEDURE, COLLECTIVE REDRESS ACTION

In civil procedure, individual actions are available, as well as interventions of consumer associations in civil or criminal proceedings (Section 3: Joint Action and Court Intervention chapter on consumer action, Consumer code), representative action, collective interest action, action for cessation of unlawful acts (article L621-7 of the Consumer Code) and collective redress action. However, individual actions may not a good track here, since the sale did not involve a specific level of emission values within the terms of the contractual provisions. An action made in the collective interest of the various owners may be brought by a representative association, but this kind of action may not bring in a high amount of damages. It actually does not take into account the owners' individual damage. Representative actions are available under Consumer Law but have almost never been used. Associations need to obtain at least two mandates from consumers but cannot use public means to get such mandates. About 15 associations may bring collective redress actions. However such a tool has not been used in the Dieselgate case.

1. *Individual Actions*

Two types of classic civil actions may be brought against car dealers by individual motorists, in the event of inaccurate information on CO2 emissions:

a) Non-compliant delivery (article 1604 of the Civil Code). If the vehicle does not correspond to the characteristics communicated by the seller, the buyer may, in theory, request the cancellation of the sale for non-compliant delivery. Judges have a sovereign discretion to determine the modalities of compensation for damages resulting from a lack of conformity; the statute of limitation is five years. This breach of delivery obligation obliges the seller to deliver something in accordance with the contract. The objective is to obtain damages or the resolution of the sale. In this case, motorists must prove that their vehicles do not comply with the sales contracts. However, information on nitrogen dioxide or CO2 emissions seems to be missing from the manufacturer's technical or advertising documents, as this information is not mandatory. As no contractual obligation has been entered into, the buyer will therefore not be able to request the resolution of the sale or claim damages.
b) Legal guarantee of conformity (article L. 217-4 of the Consumer Code). Such ground allows the buyer to request the repair or replacement of the non-conforming good delivered. It is up to the seller to decide on the most economically appropriate solution. It must be brought within two years of the purchase of the vehicle.
c) In both cases, for damages to be awarded, the buyer must be able to prove that he has suffered damage. In addition, the software does not affect the performance, consumption or safety of the vehicle. In addition, these two types of actions place the burden of proof on the claimant. Some lawyers advise the motorists concerned to enter into the recall procedure proposed by the car manufacturer.

Nine owners of Volkswagen vehicles decided to sue Volkswagen France to demand the delivery of a vehicle in accordance with the contract since the car they received did not match the one they bought when they signed the order form.

Soissons High Court dismissed the complaint of four of these manufacturers' customers who were seeking an interim injunction to exchange their vehicles after Dieselgate. The Court simply ruled that the importer of the vehicles, in this case the French subsidiary, could not be held liable in place of the manufacturer based in Europe. This validates www.weclaim.com's strategy in its class action engaging Volkswagen AG's liability in Germany. The consumer association UFC Que Choisir explains: 'There is no proven financial prejudice for the consumer since the recognised cheating concerns above all NOx, information that does not seem to have been communicated to consumers. For the time being, it is therefore difficult to argue that the consumer has suffered harm that could be the subject of real compensation.' In France, Germany, Italy and Spain, Volkswagen customers' attempts to obtain a replacement vehicle through civil proceedings have all failed so far. A firm working with several claimants would consider filing a civil suit with the Paris Public Prosecutor's Office as part of the judicial investigation for aggravated deception, in the hope that it would be referred to the court. But the deadlines are counted in years. Legislation seems to have been circumvented skilfully enough by Volkswagen (at least in France) to make it very difficult to make claims for compensation in France.

In the meantime, each claimant must therefore undertake this legal battle on an individual basis. 'This is done through what is called joint legal action,' says the lawyer. There are as many legal actions as there are claimants, concludes the lawyer. A dispersion that probably does not allow for pressure that would be similar to the ones Volkswagen experienced in the US.

2. *Collective Interest Actions and Interventions*

In proceedings before civil courts for compensation for damage suffered by one or more consumers for acts which do not constitute a criminal offence, consumer associations may act jointly or intervene to obtain compensation for any event causing direct or indirect damage to the collective interest of consumers (Section 3: Joint Action and Court Intervention chapter on consumer action, Consumer code).

3. *Action in Joint Representation*

(Article L622-1 of the Consumer Code): where several identified consumers have suffered individual damage caused by the same trader, and which have a common origin, an association, approved and recognised as nationally representative if it has been mandated by at least two of the consumers concerned, may initiate proceedings for damages before any court on their behalf. However (article L622-2 of the Consumer Code), the mandate mentioned in article L. 622-1 may not be requested by means of public television or radio call, or by means of posters, leaflets or personalised letters. This explains why this representative action is very rarely used under Consumer Law (less than ten cases in decades).

4. *Collective Redress Actions (since 2014 'Hamon Statute')*

Collective redress actions allow a group of consumers in a similar situation, victims of a breach by one or more professionals of their legal or contractual obligations, causing them harm, to obtain compensation through a single legal action. Only authorised national consumer associations are entitled to take legal actions before the courts to claim compensation for the damage suffered by consumers. Only economic damage is taken into account in the group action. In the current state of evidence in this case, it is not possible to quantify economic damage. Therefore, collective redress action does not seem appropriate. Moreover, lawyers or ad hoc associations (specially formed for the case and bringing together owners of disputed vehicles in order to obtain compensation) are not entitled to bring a collective redress action. These associations can, against payment of a fee, claim their large number of memberships, in order to put pressure on the manufacturer and possibly obtain an out-of-court agreement or encourage their members to take legal action individually. Some of these associations have been confusing and suggest that they will allow their members to obtain compensation, through a collective redress action, which is not the case.

According to article L623-1 of the Consumer Code, a consumer protection association, representative at the national level and approved pursuant to article L. 811-1, may bring proceedings before a civil court in order to obtain compensation for individual damage suffered by consumers placed in a similar or identical situation and having as their common cause a failure by the same professional or professionals to fulfil their legal or contractual obligations on the occasion of the sale of goods or the provision of services or when such damage results from anti-competitive practices.

In Case 1, there may not be a breach of contractual obligations, or at least there is an evidence issue. According to article L623-2, a collective redress action can only concern compensation for property damage resulting from material damage suffered by consumers. The French collective redress action procedure implies two stages: a judgment of liability, and then the notice of the judgment to the potential group members who can adhere to the group. According to article L623-4, the judge rules on the professional's liability in light of the individual cases presented by the applicant association, shall define the group of consumers to whom the professional's liability is incurred and lay down the criteria for their connection. The judge determines the damage that may be compensated for each consumer or each of the categories of consumers constituting the group he has defined, as well as their amount or all the elements allowing the assessment of these damages.

If the court considers that the trader is liable, the court orders appropriate measures to inform the consumers who may belong to the group concerned by that decision (article L623-7). The professional shall be responsible for the measures to advertise the decision. Such measures may only be implemented once the decision on liability is no longer subject to ordinary appeals or appeals in cassation. In the same decision declaring the trader liable, the court shall set the period within which consumers may join the group in order to obtain compensation for their loss (article L623-8). This period may not be less than two months or more than six months after the completion of the advertising measures ordered by him. The court determines the terms and conditions of such membership and specify whether consumers apply directly to the manufacturer or through the association qualified as the claimant. The victims involved do not become parties to the proceedings but to the group (article L623-9).

The sum (article L623-10) received as compensation for injured persons who are members of the group is immediately placed on an account opened with the Caisse des dépôts et consignations. The court sets the time limit within which compensation must be paid for the damage suffered by aggrieved consumers, as well as the time limit within which claims for compensation to which the trader has not been entitled may be brought before it on that date (article L623-11).

There is a simplified collective redress action (article L623-14) when the identity and number of injured consumers are known and where those consumers have suffered damage of the same amount, of the same amount per service rendered or of the same amount by reference to a period or duration. In this situation, the court, after deciding on the trader's liability, may order the trader to compensate them directly and individually, within a period and in accordance with procedures which it shall determine. It is an opt-out procedure, which might be used in Case 1 since the loss could be identical and the name of injured consumers known, by type of cars (they are registered in the manufacturer's accountability). This decision gives rise to individual information measures for the consumers concerned, at the trader's expense, in order to enable them to accept compensation under the terms of the decision. In any case (article L623-20), the qualified association shall represent consumers who are members of the group and who have not been compensated by the trader within the prescribed time limits for the purpose of the enforcement of the judgment on claims to which the trader has not been entitled.

Mediation and collective settlement. Only a qualified association may participate in mediation (article L623-22) in order to obtain compensation for individual losses. Any agreement negotiated on behalf of the group is subject to approval by the judge, who checks whether it is in the interests of those to whom it is intended to apply and gives it enforceability (article L623-23). This agreement specifies the advertising measures necessary to inform the consumers concerned of the possibility of joining it, as well as the deadlines and procedures for such membership. In Case 1, the collective redress action does not seem to be the good track.[7]

Motorists cannot claim, on the basis of moral prejudice or loss of opportunity, any prejudice whatsoever, insofar as no information on NOx performance was provided to them in the sales contract. As for the economic damage, everything will depend on the judicial expertise that will evaluate the technical capacities of the vehicles in terms of fuel consumption, power, etc. The Hamon Statute requires that the professional" breach to have been committed 'in connection with the sale of the property', which remains to be demonstrated. In addition, the heterogeneity of the situations of the motorists concerned could hinder the admissibility of such an action. Finally, it excludes compensation for moral damage. The only compensable loss is the financial loss, which shows the limits of French-style collective redress actions. And quantifying the damage resulting from a loss in value of the vehicle is not a simple matter. Many factors are taken into account in determining the resale price of a vehicle, and the financial loss resulting from the discount therefore seems very difficult to assess.

Since the entry into force of French collective actions in 2014, nine actions have been filed in different areas: telecommunications, financial services, housing and touristic accommodation. This procedure has made it possible to compensate nearly 100,000 consumers through the settlement concluded in one of these cases. However, such collective redress action is not considered to be successful. One of the reasons is the lack of financial and human resources of consumer associations (limited in number, only 14 associations are authorised to bring such an action, and an association may bring only one action at a time).

A collective action, initiated by the mass litigation platform www.weclaim.com, aims to allow consumers to return their vehicles in exchange for the purchase price. Unlike other actions, victims do not have to pay anything because the action is funded by Weclaim.

An association created by lawyers specialising in road litigation proposes to pool motorists' requests through the website https://vpourverdict.com/action-collective-dieselgate/.[8] There will be as many requests as there are applicants. But it is conceivable to group all the complaints filed in the different places

7 See Laurence Neuer, 'Scandale Volkswagen: faut-il engager une action de groupe?' *Le Point* (Paris, 12 November 2015) <http://www.lepoint.fr/editos-du-point/laurence-neuer/scandale-volkswagen-faut-il-engager-une-action-de-groupe-12-11-2015-1980911_56.php>.

8 On 23 January 2020 the Fondation Diesel Emissions Justice (FDEJ) initiated a class action in the Netherlands against Volkswagen. Affected car owners can register in France at the foundation website <http://www.emissionsjustice.com/en_fr/>. See Stéphane Mandard, '« Dieselgate »: première action collective en France contre Volkswagen' *Le Monde* (Paris, 23 January 2020), available at: <http://www.lemonde.fr/planete/article/2020/01/23/dieselgate-une-action-collective-europeenne-lancee-contre-volkswagen_6026899_3244.html>.

in France in one and the same place. For the time being, it will be necessary to launch 'pilot' actions to demonstrate the existence and seriousness of the damage. One could consider that there is deception on the goods as soon as it is demonstrated that the car does not have the technical specificities presented at the time of sale, and moreover, the cheating is recognised by the manufacturer himself. However, victims have to pay the fees.

Unfair commercial practices are prohibited by article L. 121-1 of the Consumer Code. According to article L. 121-1 of the Consumer Code a commercial practice is misleading

> … when it is based, in particular, on false claims, indications or representations … relating to … the essential characteristics of the good or service, namely: its substantial qualities, composition, accessories, origin, quantity, method and date of manufacture, the conditions of its use and its fitness for use, its properties and the results expected from its use, as well as the results and main characteristics of the tests and controls carried out on the good or service ….

Misleading commercial practices are punishable by two years' imprisonment and a fine of €300,000 (article L. 121-6 of the Consumer Code). The fact of misleading the contractor, by any means or process whatsoever, on the suitability for use, the risks inherent in the use of the product, the controls carried out, the instructions for use and the precautions to be taken is punishable under article L. 132-2 of the Consumer Code by a prison sentence of two years at most and a fine of €300,000 which may be increased in proportion to the benefits of the breach, up to 10 per cent of the average annual turnover calculated on the last three annual turnover figures. In the event of aggravated deception, prison sentences are increased to five years and the fine to €600,000 (article L. 213-2 of the Consumer Code).

The burden of proof rests on the claimant (whether an individual or a group claimant). There is no facilitation to give proof (except in discrimination cases which is not the case here).

In France, Renault, PSA and Fiat-Chrysler are the target of judicial investigations for 'aggravated deception'. The investigation has been entrusted to the judges of the Public Health Unit of the Paris Court of First Instance (TGI). The Parisian judges are still waiting for the return of an expert report in the case of Renault, PSA and Fiat-Chrysler and have ordered a 'complementary expertise' concerning Volkswagen. 'We can only be surprised at the slowness of the investigation of this case,' deplores François Lafforgue, the lawyer for ESF and Générations futures, another claimant. The two associations initiated the first complaint against X for endangering others due to air pollution. That was in March 2014. After its closure without further action by the Public Prosecutor, they filed a new complaint, with civil action (triggering public action), in July 2015, completed on 30 September of the same year on the ground of 'aggravated deception' after the Volkswagen boss confessed to the fraud. Three years later, Me Lafforgue received the order of inadmissibility of the civil party constitution of the two associations. 'We regret that the criminal justice system seeks to exclude civil parties, who are often the originators of the investigations,' said the lawyer, who appealed.[9]

> If the prosecutor's office had done its job by investigating our complaint in 2014, it could have verified that the vehicles did not meet the standards and that the air pollution was therefore increased by the manufacturers' fraud,' said Nadir Saïfi, vice-president of ESF and a key figure in the 2015 Senate inquiry committee on the cost of air pollution. 'On the one hand, people are dying and, on the other hand, criminal justice is silent. It's unbearable.

'We cannot let it be said that we are doing nothing,' said Jean-Michel Hayat, President of Paris TGI. 'Judges are neither in the spotlight nor in the spectacular. They work in a very methodical way, without rushing as others have done before them with cases that are collapsing and indictments cancelled.'

'In the case of rigged engines, judges have found themselves with tens of thousands of victims. We are faced with an extreme complexity of procedural tools,' continues the President of the TGI. 'In France, we are haunted by criminal negligence. Therefore, in order not to keep victims waiting, perhaps we should think, in terms of public health, about disconnecting compensation from criminal liability,' the high-ranking judge suggests.

This point exposes the limitations of the French judicial system: the lack of independence of the Public Prosecutor. As well as ESF and future Generations, environmental associations are calling for 'an independent Prosecutor's Office', considering 'overall overwhelming' the balance sheet of the Prosecutor's Office within the Public Health Unit. 'Very few cases are referred to Correctional Courts,' they note.

'The problem of French justice is its slowness,' acknowledges Jean-Michel Hayat, President of the Paris Civil High Court. Is judicial inquiry the most appropriate way to handle these cases? That is the real question. The senior judge advocates for other and more rapid forms of criminal responses, such as the CRPC 'appearance on a plea of guilty'. The President of the Paris TGI supports environmental associations on another point: the independence of the Public Prosecutor's Office. 'I hope that the reform of the Constitution will make it possible to make progress in this direction.'

---

9 See Stéphane Mandard, 'Dieselgate: D'un côté les gens meurent, et de l'autre, la justice pénale est silencieuse' *Le Monde* (Paris, 17 September 2018) <http://www.lemonde.fr/pollution/article/2018/09/17/dieselgate-d-un-cote-les-gens-meurent-et-de-l-autre-la-justice-penale-est-silencieuse_5356187_1652666.html>.

According to associations the investigations are very slow. These remarks show that the Public Prosecutor is not independent from the executive power. So, public enforcement is not stronger than private enforcement.

D. GENERAL PROCEDURAL LAW

All actions, individuals and collective, may coexist. If victims join a collective redress action, they cannot thereafter bring their individual actions for the same damage. Criminal proceedings may coexist with civil proceedings (victims may choose to bring their request in front of the criminal court) but the latter has to be suspended until the former is over.

Decisions issued from collective redress actions have the force of *res judicata* with regard to each of the members of the group whose damage has been remedied at the end of the proceedings (article L623-28). Membership of the group does not prevent the right from acting in accordance with ordinary law to obtain compensation for damages not falling within the scope defined by the decision of the court. The collective redress action shall not be admissible where it is based on the same facts, the same breaches and compensation for the same damage as those that are already the subject of the judgment of liability (article L623-30). Suspension of limitation period. Collective redress actions suspend the limitation period of individual actions for damages resulting from breaches established by the judgment (article L623-27). The limitation period shall begin to run again, for a period of not less than six months, from the date on which the judgment of liability is no longer subject to ordinary appeal or appeal in cassation.

The claimant, whether a natural person or a legal person, bears the litigation risks. In the case adjudicated by the Soissons Court, the Court also ordered the four claimants to pay Volkswagen €1,800 each for the reimbursement of the legal costs. A consumer association may have to reimburse, at least partially, the legal costs to the winning trader.

Victims receive damages in individual and collective redress action, an association in a collective interest action. The fines are received by the Public Treasury. Skimmed profits? According to article L621-6, penalty payments are recovered by the competent public accountant as a criminal fine. Volkswagen could risk a fine of nearly €20 billion in France for its faked TDIs.

There are no punitive damages in France. The preliminary draft to reform Tort Law under the *aegis* of Pierre Catala proposed to enshrine the notion of punitive damages (article 1371). The current draft reform proposal, dated 13 March 2017, is more oriented towards a civil fine.[10] Information obligations

---

10 See Jean-Sébastien Borghetti, 'Un pas de plus vers la réforme de la responsabilité civile: présentation du projet de réforme rendu public le 13 mars 2017' [2017] Recueil Dalloz 770.

in this regard are heavily punished, with article L. 131-4 of the Consumer Code providing for an administrative fine of up to €75,000 for a natural person and €375,000 for a legal person.[11]

Launched in February 2016 following the outbreak of the rigged diesel scandal that led to the opening of an investigation in October 2015, French judicial information on Volkswagen is still ongoing. According to *Le Monde*, that claims to have been able to consult the 24-page minutes of this ongoing investigation, the German group risks a fine of up to €19.73 billion in France.

According to the current rule, this is a ceiling corresponding to 10 per cent of Volkswagen's average turnovers in 2012, 2013 and 2014. According to the investigators, the amount of the fine will be set 'in proportion to the benefits derived from the fraud'. And for the EA189 type 2L TDI engines alone, the DGCCRF (fraud prevention) estimates that the 'fraudulent turnover' generated by the sale of the 94,087 vehicles concerned in France (approximately 600,000 Volkswagen, 192,000 Audi, 93,000 Seat and 65,000 Skoda) amounts to €22.78 billion. The DGCCRF also mentions an average annual saving of €1.52 billion between 2012 and 2014 on pollution control systems, representing 35 per cent of the company's investment in research and development.

For its part, the regulation of unfair commercial practices aims in particular to punish misleading advertising. It must be proven that Volkswagen (in the Case manufacturer 1) has reported NOx emissions from its cars for commercial purposes.

The General Directorate for Competition Policy, Consumer Affairs and Fraud Control (DGCCRF) has transmitted its conclusions to the courts following its investigations into possible deceptions committed by the FIAT Chrysler Automobile Group regarding diesel vehicles.

A report presenting the detailed results of these investigations has just been sent to the Paris Public Prosecutor's Office. It will be up to him whether or not to open a judicial investigation for deception.

In France, the survey targeting manufacturers is skidding, environmental associations deplore. The President of the Paris High Court pleads for 'other forms of response'. According to associations, investigations are very slow and call for an independent Public Prosecutor's Office. It is important to know that the French state is the owner of 15 per cent of Renault and indirectly of 12 per cent of Peugeot. There is no evidence of partiality, but not only must justice be done but also must it be seen to be done.

11 See Gilles Paisant, *Défense et illustration du droit de la consommation* (Lexis Nexis 2015) n 212, questioning the advisability of introducing punitive damages under French law. See in this sense Jean Calais-Auloy and Henri Temple, *Droit de la consommation* (9th edn, Dalloz 2015) n 688, affirming, with regard to the damages that a consumer protection association may obtain in the context of a civil action, that 'one may wonder whether the sums allocated to them are not, in essence, private penalties masked in the form of compensation'.

II. CASE 2: CAPITAL MARKET LAW[12]

A. PUBLIC LAW

In France, the elimination of consequences, damages and skimming of profits (by fines) are provided for through fines: the penalty shall be a five-year imprisonment and a fine of €100 million, which may be increased up to ten times the amount of the benefits derived from the offence, provided that the fine may not be less than that benefit.

Public enforcement might be stronger as long as there is a political will to be efficient since Public Prosecutors are under the supervision of the Minister of Justice. The Financial Market Regulator is a public body independent from the executive and judicial powers. This authority may investigate insider trading. The composition of this authority does not have the reputation to transform it in a place of contestation.

B. PRIVATE LAW/CIVIL PROCEDURE

There is no collective redress in France in this field. In the VW case, lawyers have discussed with stockholders but the author has not heard of any action in France. Concerning insider trading, the penalty shall be five years of imprisonment and a fine of €100 million, which may be increased up to ten times the amount of the benefits derived from the offence, provided that the fine may not be less than that benefit,

C. GENERAL PROCEDURAL LAW

In France, different procedures are available against insider trading. Article L465-1 (Amended by Law No 2016-819 of 21 June 2016 – article 1) provides that:

> The penalty shall be five years of imprisonment and a fine of €100 million, which may be increased up to ten times the amount of the benefit derived from the offence, provided that the fine may not be less than that benefit, if the Chief Executive Officer, the President, a member of the Management Board, the Manager, a member of the Board of Directors or a member of the Supervisory Board of an issuer concerned by inside information or a person exercising an equivalent function, a person holding inside information concerning an issuer in which he holds a participation, by a

12 See Introduction Section IV.A.

person possessing inside information in connection with his profession or duties or in connection with his participation in the commission of a crime or misdemeanour, or by any other person possessing inside information with full knowledge of the facts, to make use of such inside information by carrying out, for himself or for others, either directly or indirectly, one or more transactions or by cancelling or amending one or more orders placed by the same person before he holds the inside information, on the financial instruments issued by this issuer or on the financial instruments concerned by this inside information.

1. *Public Enforcement*

Two public bodies may have competence to investigate and initiate proceedings against manufacturer A and the member of the management board who sold his share: the Financial Public Prosecutor and the Financial Market Regulator (AMF). To avoid the issues raised by the *non bis in idem* principle, a 2016 statute (L. no 2016-819 of 21 June 2016) sets up a system to direct a case. The first body which initiates the proceedings notifies the other so that the latter is barred from starting its own proceedings. It is the French consequence of the landmark case 'Grande Stevens' (ECtHR, 2nd section, *Grande Stevens v Italy*, 18640/10, 18647/10, 18663/10, 18668/10 and 18698/10 [4 March 2014]). Only the AMF has the competence and the human resources to make a quick investigation, its goal is to defend market credibility; criminal proceedings take much longer, having to respect scrupulously the rights of the defence (and less human resources).

According to article L. 465-3-6 (L. no 2016-819 of 21 June 2016, article 2):

I. – The Public Prosecutor of the Financial Republic may not initiate public proceedings for the enforcement of the penalties where the Financial Market Regulator has notified the Public Prosecutor of grievances for the same facts and against the same person pursuant to Article L. 621-15. The Financial Market Regulator may not notify a person against whom a public action has been initiated by the Public Prosecutor of the Financial Republic for the same acts in relation to the application of the penalties provided for in this section.

II. – Before any public action is taken to enforce the penalties provided for in this section, the Financial Public Prosecutor shall inform the Financial Market Regulator of his intention. The latter has two months to inform him of its intention to notify the same person of the grievances for the same facts. If the Financial Market Regulator does not announce, within the time limit set, its intention to notify the grievances or if it indicates that it does not wish to do so, the Public Prosecutor may initiate a public action. If the Financial Market Regulator announces its intention to proceed with the notification of grievances, the Financial Public Prosecutor has a period of fifteen days to confirm his intention to initiate the public action and refer the matter to the Public

Prosecutor at the Paris Court of Appeal. Failing this, the Financial Market Regulator may proceed with the notification of grievances.

According to article 85 of the Code of Criminal Procedure, a complaint with civil action is admissible and will trigger a public action. In the context of financial market offence, the Public Prosecutor may not have the opportunity to prosecute when the Financial Market Regulator has the intention to initiate the proceedings. This is why the victim may bring a civil action only if the Public Prosecutor has the possibility to prosecute.

2. *Private Enforcement*

a) Individual Actions

Smallholders may take action against the professional who markets securities to obtain damages; it is not possible however to do the same against the managers of the issuers of the securities themselves, for example in case of insider trading, price manipulation or any behaviour that undermines the transparency of the markets. So, in Case 2, consumers may individually sue the company in front of a civil or a criminal court.

b) Collective Interest Action

French legislators authorised in 1989 the creation of accredited investor's protection associations, entitled to act before any court, even by way of civil actions. This was far from the American-style class action as they could only obtain compensation for the damage done to the investors' collective interest. In Case 2, this action would not allow to compensate the damage made to the stockholder.

c) Joint Representation Action

In 1994, legislators extended the rights of these associations by allowing them to seek compensation in front of any court for individual losses incurred by identified individual investors whose individual losses were caused by the same person and had a common origin. However, they could only act on behalf of the investors who had given them a written mandate and if they had not been solicited by 'public call, television or radio, or by means of posters, leaflets or personalized letters'. In addition, these associations had to be approved. Indeed, in practice, investors who complain of false information use ordinary associations under the 1901 Act. So, this track is not very useful.

d) 'Hamon Statute'

Finally, Statute no 2014-344 of 17 March 2014 on Consumption, known as the 'Hamon Statute' (see Case 1), has organised collective consumer protection. However, the financial sector had been excluded from the scope of the law. It would now be appropriate to consider setting up a genuine collective redress action in the stock market field (in particular for stock market offences that undermine market transparency) in which the seized court may request the expertise of the Financial Market Regulator to establish the reality and extent of any damage suffered. It is true that breaches of financial legislation can cause a large number of identical damages, the individual amount of which remains too small to justify the institution of a liability action in France. For example, savers were discouraged from acting in the *Benefic* case (marketing by La Poste of a structured fund to more than 300,000 investors, only 94 civil and two criminal proceedings;[13] Such action would have an indispensable deterrent effect and avoid class actions in the US against French companies (i.e. the *Vivendi* case, class action in the US by investors). It would therefore be all the more effective, as this action would probably not deprive consumer associations of their actions when investors are also consumers.[14]

III. CONCLUSION

France would need to improve the procedural system within the consumer and capital market fields:

- A non-sectorial collective redress action for all damages, comprising financial market infringement and damages for loss of profit and moral prejudice.
- The possibility to use the investigative power of the DGCCRF and AMF for collective redress actions.
- A special fund to help consumer associations and investors' protection associations to have human and financial resources to bring collective redress actions (maybe a special fund receiving a part of the damages awarded in previous collective redress actions and/or cy-près damages).

---

13 See Laurent Béteille and Richard Yung, 'Rapport d'information n° 499 (2009–2010) sur l'action de groupe' (Sénat, 26 May 2010) <http://www.senat.fr/rap/r09-499/r09-4991.pdf>.

14 See Cass. Com. 18 October 2017, no 16-10.271, Frank Martin Laprade, [2018] Revue des Sociétés 114 (note), Hugo Barbier, [2018] Recueil Dalloz 47 (note); Pierre-Henri Conac, 'Vers des class actions en matière boursière en Europe et en France?' [2018] Revue des Sociétés 472; Benoit Le Bars and Karine Rodriguès, 'Association d'actionnaires et de défense des investisseurs' in *Répertoire des sociétés* (Dalloz January 2019) n 32, 33.

- To have an independent Public Prosecutor, which supposes a constitutional reform.
- A punitive damages tool to deter companies from infringing Consumer Law (however this tool is discussed in France).

In a very general approach (and acknowledged naivety), consumers should not be an alibi for the lack of political will and should be seen as a European citizen exercising their political rights with a strong possibility of private enforcement, helped by public authority to take evidence.

ENFORCING CONSUMER AND CAPITAL MARKETS LAW IN GERMANY

Caroline MELLER-HANNICH*

* Caroline Meller-Hannich, Dr., Professor, Martin-Luther-University of Halle-Wittenberg, Law School, Chair for Civil Law, Civil Procedure and Commercial Law.

I. PRIVATE LAW/CIVIL PROCEDURE

A. ARE REMEDIES SUCH AS ELIMINATIONS OF CONSEQUENCES, DAMAGES AND SKIMMING OF PROFITS AVAILABLE?

1. *Eliminations of Consequences*

The elimination of the consequences of a breach of law is provided by German law only in a few regulations. As a rule, these regulations serve not only individual interests, but at least the interests of the general public as well. Moreover, these are all rules that combine omission duties and disposal obligations.

Elimination claims are provided for in the Injunctive Relief Act (UKlaG), in the Unfair Competition Act (UWG) and in the Law against Restraints of Competition (GWB).[1]

a) Injunctive Relief Act (Unterlassungsklagengesetz, UKlaG)

The UKlaG allows certain consumer and business associations to claim that an entrepreneur has been using or recommending unlawful terms and conditions or engaging in anti-consumer law practices.

In the case of anti-consumer law practices, section 2 of the UKlaG[2] expressly orders for the elimination of consequences. But there is also a duty of disposal according to the case law in cases where unlawful terms and conditions have been used (section 1 of the UKlaG[3]).[4]

Both Case 1 and Case 2 may in principle impose elimination actions, since they are anti-consumer law practices.

The problem, however, is that in Case 1 and Case 2 there is no danger of repetition, which in any case omits the injunctive relief claims. In addition, a right of action will only be available to special associations, but not to private buyers or investors. Moreover, the practical consequences of an elimination of consequences based on an injunction remain difficult to determine.[5]

---

1 German Federal Statutes are available at <http://www.gesetze-im-internet.de> and Cases of the German Federal Court (Bundesgerichtshof – BGH) are available at <http://www.bundesgerichtshof.de>.

2 S 2 of the UKlaG Claims in anti-consumer practices (Translation: author): (1) Anyone who fails to comply with regulations that otherwise serve the purpose of protecting consumers (consumer protection laws) other than by using or recommending general terms and conditions of business can be claimed for injunctive relief and disposal in the interests of consumer protection. (…) (2) Consumer protection laws within the meaning of this provision are in particular 1. the provisions of civil law applicable to (…) c) sales of consumer goods, (…) between an entrepreneur and a consumer, (…) 6. S 126 of the Investment Act or s 305 of the Capital Investment Code, 7. the provisions of Section 11 of the Securities Trading Act, which govern the relationship between an investment services enterprise and a client, (…).

3 S 1 of the UKlaG Injunctive relief and withdrawal in case of terms and conditions (Translation: author): Anyone who uses or recommends general terms and conditions of business containing terms, that are not binding according to ss 307–309 BGB, can be claimed for injunctive relief or withdrawal of the recommendation.

4 Astrid Stadler, 'Beseitigungsklagen durch Verbände im AGB-Recht' in Caroline Meller-Hannich and others (eds), *Festschrift für Eberhard Schilken* (CH Beck 2015) 481; BGH, Judgment of 14 December 2017, I ZR 184/15; Caroline Meller-Hannich, 'BGH, Judgment of 14 December 2017, I ZR 184/15' [2018] JZ 629, 623 (note).

5 Eberhard Schilken, 'Überlegungen zur Umsetzung der Empfehlungen der Europäischen Kommission zum kollektiven Zivilrechtsschutz in Deutschland' in Bettina Limperg and others (eds), *Festschrift 200 Jahre Carl Heymanns Verlag* (Heymanns 2015) 125; Beate Gsell and Johannes Rübbeck, 'Beseitigung als Folgenbeseitigung? – Kollektivklagen der Verbraucherverbände auf Rückzahlung unrechtmäßig erzielter Gewinne' [2018] Zeitschrift für die gesamte Privatrechtswissenschaft 409.

The elimination of consequences can blur the limit to the right to damages and the skimming of profits. Therefore, in view of the higher conditions of the law on damages, an individual compensation may not be granted by way of elimination action. As far as the use of general terms and conditions is concerned, however, according to the case law,[6] a repayment obligation with regard to sums recovered illegally exists. It is still unclear whether this jurisprudence will continue to prevail. This is to be welcomed, at least in the case of low-value damages, in which associations file skimming of actions.[7]

b) The Act against Unfair Competition (Gesetz gegen den unlauteren Wettbewerb, UWG)

A claim for elimination due to unfair competition is provided in section 8 of the UWG. Competitors are entitled to take action as well as consumer and business associations.

Both Case 1 and Case 2 will qualify as an unfair commercial practice within the definition of section 8 of the UWG. However, here, too, affected consumers and investors are not considered direct beneficiaries. In addition, an individual claim for damages as a result of the elimination of consequences cannot be granted in view of the specifically regulated higher requirements of the law on damages.

c) Antitrust Law (Gesetz gegen Wettbewerbsbeschränkungen, GWB)

Also, the claim for elimination according to section 33 of the GWB is to be combined with an injunction claim. In addition, the GWB expressly provides for special claims for damages as well as skimming off entitlements, so that their specialty supplants the claim for damages as a form of elimination. That being said, neither Case 1 nor Case 2 will be a restriction of competition since it requires either an agreement restricting competition or a dominant position within the market.

2. *Compensation of Damages*

a) Case 1

Case 1 concerns claims between car buyers and automakers. Unlike between buyer and seller there is no purchase contract between buyer and manufacturer.

---

6 OLG Dresden, Judgment of 10 August 2018, 14 U 82/16.

7 Caroline Meller-Hannich, *Sammelklagen, Gruppenklagen, Verbandsklagen – Bedarf es neuer Instrumente des kollektiven Rechtsschutzes im Zivilprozess?, Gutachten A zum 72. Deutschen Juristentag* (CH Beck 2018) A 56 (hereafter Meller-Hannich, Gutachten).

In addition, the case law largely and rightly rejects a guarantee contract between the buyer and the manufacturer with regard to the compliance with the emission values.[8] Therefore, no contractual claims, but only non-contractual claims, in particular from tort law, have to be considered.[9]

Tort law claims exist only in case of an infringement of an absolute right, e.g. property, body, health (section 823 paragraph 1 of the BGB[10]), in case of a violation of a statute that is intended to protect another person (section 823 paragraph 2 of the BGB) or in case of intentional damage in a manner contrary to public policy (section 826 of the BGB[11]). Only under section 823 paragraph 2 of the BGB and section 826 of the BGB do claims exist even if a pure financial loss has been suffered.

Since the car buyers, if at all,[12] suffered only a financial loss, but not a damage of an absolute right, a claim under section 823 paragraph 1 of the BGB will drop out. A claim under section 823 paragraph 2 of the BGB requires, as mentioned, the violation of a protection law. There is agreement in both case law and science that the European rules on type approval, which prohibit exhaust gas manipulation, do not constitute protection laws within the definition of this standard.[13] A protection law would indeed be the offence of fraud under section 263 of the Criminal Code (Strafgesetzbuch, StGB) – but it regulates only

---

8 For instance, OLG Braunschweig, Judgment of 19 February 2019, 7 U 134/17 (appeal permitted); OLG Schleswig-Holstein, Judgment of 13 November 2019, 9 U 120/19; different view: Markus Artz and Jan Dirk Harke, 'EU-Übereinstimmungsbescheinigung als Auskunfts- und Garantievertrag' [2017] NJW 3409.

9 For criminal and private law aspects see Christoph Schmid, 'Germany' in Marco Frigessi di Rattalma, *The Dieselgate, A Legal Perspective* (Springer 2017) 27.

10 S 823 of the BGB Liability in damages (Translation: Langenscheidt Translation Service, updated by Neil Mussett via <http://www.gesetze-im-internet.de>): (1) A person who, intentionally or negligently, unlawfully injures the life, body, health, freedom, property or another right of another person is liable to make compensation to the other party for the damage arising from this. (2) The same duty is held by a person who commits a breach of a statute that is intended to protect another person. If, according to the contents of the statute, it may also be breached without fault, then liability to compensation only exists in the case of fault.

11 S 826 of the BGB Intentional damage contrary to public policy (Translation: Langenscheidt Translation Service, updated by Neil Mussett <http://www.gesetze-im-internet.de>): A person who, in a manner contrary to public policy, intentionally inflicts damage on another person is liable to the other person to make compensation for the damage.

12 Since the Kraftfahrtbundesamt has allowed the continued use of the vehicles, damage can ultimately only be seen in the reduced resale value.

13 For instance OLG München, Judgment of 20 January 2020, 21 U 5072/19; OLG Braunschweig, Judgment of 19 February 2019, 7 U 134/17 (appeal permitted); LG Aachen, Judgment of 3 May 2018, 10 O 364/17; LG Marburg, Judgment of 26 June 2018, 7 O 90/16; Christian Armbrüster, 'Herstellerhaftung für abgasmanipulierte Fahrzeuge' [2019] ZIP 837; different view Jan Dirk Harke, 'Herstellerhaftung im Abgasskandal' [2017] VuR 83 (hereafter Harke, 'Herstellerhaftung'); see for a general court decision overview: Alexander Sievers, 'Rechtsprechungsübersicht zur Abgasthematik' [2016] DAR 543; [2017] DAR 538; [2018] DAR 534; [2019] DAR 489 (hereafter Sievers, 'Rechtsprechungsübersicht').

the criminal liability of natural persons, but not of companies; in addition, the fraud is not relevant in its conditions: the negotiations and the property orders did not take place between the manufacturer and the car buyers. At least when viewed directly the manufacturer is not enriched.

Therefore, only claims for intentional immoral damage according to section 826 of the BGB are left to be considered. Here, the conditions are much higher. In addition to an offence against public policy with intent, causality between immorality and damage is required. The burden of proof for all constituent elements, including causality, lies on the injured party.

There are good legal arguments for both affirming the claim and rejecting it.

In many legal proceedings, the plaintiffs have failed to present and prove the necessary facts. Therefore, at least in the years 2015 to 2017 there was a tendency in the case law of renouncing claims of intentional immoral injury.[14] In the meantime, however, case law seems to be proceeding in another direction.[15]

Upper courts have already confirmed first instance judgments against the automaker, such as in January 2019 the Higher Regional Court of Cologne,[16] in March 2019 the Higher Regional Court of Karlsruhe,[17] in June 2019 the Higher Regional Court of Koblenz,[18] in November 2019 the Higher Regional Court (*Kammergericht*) of Berlin[19] and in January 2020 the Higher Regional Court of Munich.[20] The case law nowadays increasingly assumes a so-called secondary burden of presentation of the facts by the automaker or even a reversal of the burden of proof. The courts argue that it is impossible for the car buyer to explain and prove the relevant facts and that the car manufacturer can no longer rely on clarifying the circumstances.

And indeed, time can make a difference here. Justifiably, after a certain period of time, it can be expected that the automaker himself will be in a position to clarify the issues surrounding exhaust gas manipulation within his company. If he fails to do so, this has an impact on the burden of proof, in favour of the plaintiff.

---

14 For instance, LG München II, Judgment of 25 November 2016, 12 O 1482/16; Overview Sievers, 'Rechtsprechungsübersicht' (n 13).

15 LG Hildesheim, Judgment of 17 January 2017, 3 O 139/16; LG Krefeld, Judgment of 13 February 2019, 2 O 313/17; LG Augsburg, Judgment of 14 November 2018, 021 O 4310/16; OLG Karlsruhe, Order of 5 March 2019, 13 U 142/18; OLG Köln, Order of 3 January 2019, 18 U 70/18; OLG Koblenz, Judgment of 12 June 2019, 5 U 1318/18; KG Berlin, Judgment of 18 November 2019, 24 U 129/18; OLG Hamm, Judgment of 10 September 2019, 13 U 149/18; OLG Karlsruhe, Judgment of November 19 2019, 17 U 146/19; OLG Koblenz, Judgment of September 16 2019, 12 U 61/19; OLG Köln, Judgment of 4 October 2019, 19 U 98/19; Pro defendant (=manufacturer): OLG München, Judgment of 6 September 2019, 14 U 416/19; OLG Dresden, Judgment of 20 August 2019, 9 U 2067/18; OLG Celle, Order of 1 July 2019, 7 U 33/19.

16 OLG Köln, Order of 3 January 2019, 18 U 70/18.

17 OLG Karlsruhe, Order of 5 March 2019, 13 U 142/18.

18 OLG Koblenz, Judgment of 12 June 2019, 5 U 1318/18.

19 KG Berlin, Judgment of 18 November 2019, 24 U 129/18.

20 OLG München, Judgment of 15 January 2020, 20 U 3219/18.

However, we also see court decisions which deny a claim under Section 826 of the BGB, if the car was bought after the manufacturer informed the general public about the manipulations in 2015.[21]

Since many of the disputes are also settled or the courts do not allow an appeal, one had to expect a BGH decision until May 2020.[22] The Sixth Civil Senate of the BGH, which is responsible, *inter alia*, for the right of tort, has scheduled the first hearing for 5 May 2020.[23] On 25 May 2020, the BGH ruled in favour of the purchaser of a used car and awarded him damages in the amount of the purchase price. However, the buyer must return the car and pay compensation for its use.[24]

The question of liability arising from an intentional tort under section 826 of the BGB has also been the subject of the model declaratory procedure initiated by the Verbraucherzentrale Bundesverband (VZBV) (see Section I.B.1.d)).[25] Its completion, it must be said, would have taken some time. The parties, however, reached an out-of-court settlement at the end of February 2020.[26] The plaintiff will therefore withdraw the claim and a court decision will not be attained.

The scientific literature is also in disagreement regarding this issue.[27] It has also proposed additional claim bases found in a number of very different approaches, such as liability of the automaker from pre-contractual fault or selection default.[28] Even in the scientific literature, however, the tendency towards the affirmation of a claim for damages also goes against the automakers.

It must be clarified that claims under tort law underlie a longer limitation period than claims under sales law. The limitation period in case of a pecuniary loss is three years (section 195 of the BGB) and commences at the end of the year

21 The courts differ in their opinion of the exact date on which the information by the automaker was sufficient to deny a claim under s 826 of the BGB, for instance OLG München, Judgment of 20 January 2020, 21 U 5972/19 (press release on 2 October 2015 and enabling car buyers to determine whether their car was affected by the manipulations on various websites); OLG Karlsruhe, Judgment of 9 January 2020, 17 U 133/19 (statement on 10 December 2015 to the general public admitting the manipulations and statement on 16 December 2015 waiving claims of time limitation until 31 December 2017).

22 Only a few appeals are pending before the BGH, for instance BGH, VIII ZR 61/19; VI ZR 252/19; VI ZR 292/19; VI ZR 354/19.

23 BGH, 'Erster Verhandlungstermin in den sogenannten VW-Verfahren (VI ZR 252/19) am 5. Mai 2020, 9.30 Uhr' (Press Release no 166/2019, 19 December 2019) <http://juris.bundesgerichtshof.de/cgi-bin/rechtsprechung/document.py?Gericht=bgh&Art=pm&pm_nummer=0166/19>.

24 BGH, Judgment of 25 May 2020, VI ZR 252/19, NJW 2020, 1962.

25 OLG Braunschweig, Order of 26 November 2018, 4 MK 1/18.

26 Verbraucherzentrale 'Vergleich zwischen vzbv und Volkswagen steht: Wie es jetzt weitergeht' <https://www.verbraucherzentrale.de/wissen/vertraege-reklamation/kundenrechte/vergleich-zwischen-vzbv-und-volkswagen-steht-wie-es-jetzt-weitergeht-29738>.

27 For instance, Thomas Riehm, 'Dieselgate und das Deliktsrecht' [2016] DAR 12.

28 Harke, 'Herstellerhaftung' (n 13) 83; different view for instance: OLG München, Judgment of 5 September 2019, 14 U 416/19.

in which the obligee obtains knowledge of the circumstances giving rise to the claim (section 199 paragraph 1 of the BGB).

In summary, it should be noted here that, at least according to the current tendency in case law, claims for damages are affirmed.

b) Case 2

Article 14 of the Market Abuse Regulation[29] (MAR) prohibits insider trading. The prohibited practices described there are also punishable under section 119 paragraph 1 of the Securities Trading Act (Wertpapierhandelsgesetz, WpHG).[30] An insider trading occurs when an individual acquires or sells a financial instrument directly or indirectly using insider information for their own or third-party account, article 8 paragraph 1 sentence 1 of the MAR.

If a member of the Executive Board, while aware of the emissions manipulation, sells his shares before such a notice is disclosed, it will be considered an instance of punishable insider dealing. In practice, however, precisely the elements of time needed for gaining knowledge, especially in temporally extended situations, are very problematic. This can paradigmatically be seen in two capital investment model proceedings recently filed at the Higher Regional Court of Braunschweig and the Higher Regional Court of Stuttgart, in which, among other things, the courts are concerned with the timing of the knowledge of insider information and the knowledge/knowledge pooling within an organisation.[31] The claimant discusses periods from 2007 to 2011, which refer to a warning from the supplying company Bosch, the investigation of the US environmental authorities as well as various internal technician information.

As far as the claim for damages of investors is concerned, the decisive starting point is not the criminal liability, but the late ad hoc announcement of insider information. As a claim for compensation for investors, the duty to publish ad hoc information with insider information, which is standardised in the WpHG and sanctioned with compensation, can be taken into consideration.

Sections 13, 15, 37b paragraph 1 and section 37c of the WpHG in the version valid until 1 July 2016 apply to the older facts. In the meantime, these regulations

---

29 Regulation (EU) No 596/2014 of the European Parliament and of the Council of 16 April 2014 on market abuse (Market Abuse Regulation – MAR) [2014] OJ L173/1.

30 See Thomas MJ Möllers and Pirmin Herz, 'Anmerkung zu einer Entscheidung des BGH, Beschl. v. 10.01.2017, 5 StR 532/16 – Die Neufassung von Strafbestimmungen im Kapitalmarktrecht hat auch unter Berücksichtigung unionsrechtlicher Aspekte keine Generalamnestie in Bezug auf Insiderhandel und Marktmanipulation zur Folge' [2017] WuB 309; Thomas MJ Möllers and Pirmin Herz, 'Generalamnestie von Kursmanipulationen im Kapitalmarktrecht? Sanktionslücken durch das Redaktionsversehen des Gesetzgebers und der untaugliche Rettungsversuch des BGH' [2017] JZ 445.

31 OLG Braunschweig, Order of 12 August 2019, 3 Kap 1/16; OLG Stuttgart, Order of 27 March 2019, 20 Kap 2/17; 20 Kap 3/17; 20 Kap 4/17.

have been replaced by sections 97,[32] 98 of the WpHG. These expressly refer to the already mentioned MAR. According to article 17 of the MAR, there is an obligation to publish insider information without delay. The damage claim of section 97 of the WpHG is linked to their violation.

In addition to the insider information and its omitted ad hoc notification, the claim for compensation presupposes that the investor has acquired or sold the securities in consequence of the omission and thus suffered damage. So, the 'crash of the course' is not enough, unless a purchase or sale act is added.[33]

In addition to the claim under the WpHG, claims under general civil law are not excluded. In particular, a claim according to section 826 of the BGB for intentional immoral injury must be taken into consideration. In addition, a claim under section 823 paragraph 2 of the BGB due to the violation of commercial law, securities law, and stock corporation law protection provisions is conceivable.[34]

For all claims, the causality between the omitted information and the investment, the so-called Abschlusskausalität, plays an important role. The decisive factor is who will bear the burden of proof for this causality. This is highly controversial in science and practice.[35] The same applies to the question of whether transaction damage alone or course difference damage are recorded.[36]

It is difficult to predict when the procedure before the Higher Regional Court of Braunschweig will lead to a binding result.

It is also problematic in this context that there are questions of coordination between the procedure before the Higher Regional Court of Braunschweig and the one before the Higher Regional Court of Stuttgart. The question is whether the case against VW has a blocking effect on the proceedings against Porsche Holding.[37]

---

32 S 97 of the WpHG Liability for damages due to failure to publish inside information without undue delay (Translation via BaFin.de): '(1) If an issuer whose financial instruments have been admitted to trading on a trading venue in Germany or who has applied for the financial instruments to be admitted to trading on a regulated market or multilateral trading facility in Germany fails to publish, without undue delay, inside information that directly relates to that issuer in accordance with Article 17 of Regulation (EU) No. 596/2014, that issuer is liable to compensate a third party for losses arising from the failure to publish if that third party 1. bought the financial instruments after the failure to publish and still owns the financial instruments when the inside information becomes known, or 2. bought the financial instruments before the event triggering the inside information and sells them after failure to publish that information. (2)–(5) (…).'

33 Thomas Meschede, 'Dieselgate: Denkbare Anspruchsgrundlagen für Schadensersatzansprüche von Porsche-Aktionären und Erwerbern von Derivaten auf VW-Aktien gegen die Volkswagen AG' [2017] ZIP 215 (hereafter Meschede, 'Dieselgate').

34 Meschede, 'Dieselgate' (n 33) 215.

35 Details see LG Braunschweig, Order of 5 August 2016, 5 OH 62/16.

36 Further details see LG Braunschweig, Order of 5 August 2016, 5 OH 62/16; Meschede, 'Dieselgate' (n 33) 215.

37 OLG Stuttgart, Order of 27 March 2019, 20 Kap 2/17; 3/17; 4/17: the proceeding in Braunschweig blocks the proceeding in Stuttgart.

It must be remembered that in such cases a legal appeal to the BGH is always permissible, so that a longer procedure will still be expected.

3. *Skimming of Profits*

There are claims for the skimming of profits in the case of infringements of the unfair competition law (section 10 of the UWG) or antitrust law (sections 34, 34a of the GWB).

The skimming of profits in the unfair competition law can be asserted by the authorised associations, which are also authorised to bring injunctions. Competitors are not entitled to profit.

The skimming of profits in the antitrust law can be asserted by the antitrust authority as well as by authorised associations.

A special feature of unfair competition and of antitrust law is that any claims for damages and penalties for profits are deducted from the skimming off. With regard to the quantification of profits, antitrust law provides for the possibility of an estimate.

It is of particular importance in both unfair competition law and antitrust law that a skimming off of profits can only be possible in the event of intentional infringement. Proof of intent is difficult to ascertain. Also in terms of presentation and evidence of profit and its quantification and causality, the standards have high hurdles. Overall, the judicial practice in Germany shows that these complaints have rarely been collected and have little chance of achieving success. They are also particularly risky for the suing associations because they have to pay for any costs incurred in a lost process and are not allowed to retain the profits in the event of winning a lawsuit. Therefore, there is no incentive to file such lawsuits. The results of the last German Jurists Forum (Deutscher Juristentag) have therefore positioned itself in such a way that the prerequisites of unfair competition law and antitrust lawsuits should be lowered and that associations should be able to profit from won processes, for example by the possibility of financing further claims.[38]

B. COLLECTIVE REDRESS/REPRESENTATIVE ACTIONS

1. *Representative Actions*

The German system relies primarily on representative actions, filed by associations. Overall, the injunctions of associations can point to a long tradition.

---

38 Deutscher Juristentag, 'Beschlüsse' (72. Deutscher Juristentag, Leipzig, 26–28 September 2018) nos 12 and 14 <http://www.djt.de/fileadmin/downloads/72/Beschluesse_gesamt_final.pdf> (hereafter DJT, 'Beschlüsse').

However, they also exist as the only collective legal instruments of significant practical importance.[39] Original payment claims of associations are unknown. Associations may only claim for omission, skimming of profits, following an individual assignment and they may file test cases. In detail, the following applies.

a) Injunctions

Basis for injunctions from associations have already been mentioned in section 1 of the UKlaG (injunction for the recommendation or use of unlawful terms and conditions), section 2 of the UKlaG (injunction for anti-consumer law practices), section 8 of the UWG (injunction for unfair commercial practices), section 33 of the GWB (injunctions for antitrust violations). They are of no relevance to Case 1 and Case 2 because these are closed cases. Injunctions have only a preventive effect and are only likely to succeed in the event of imminent injury or recurrence. Only the removal of consequences can be considered under the conditions described above (see Section I.A.1.a)).

b) Collective Representative Action after Individual Assignment

Associations can assert bundled individual claims. However, the relevant standard of section 79 paragraph 2 sentence 2 no 3 of the ZPO[40] always requires an individual assignment or authorisation as well as the organisation of these assignments by an association which collects individual claims and asserts each individual claim in court. According to experience, the effort is time-consuming and the courts are authorised to separate the processes again. The plaintive associations are also the ones to bear the legal costs risk. The possibilities of bundling are therefore rarely used and not very effective.

c) Skimming of Suits

Also, the above explained suits for skimming of profits in unfair competition and antitrust law (see section I.A.3.) are designed as a representative action, filed by an association.

---

39 Caroline Meller-Hannich and Armin Höland, 'Evaluierung der Effektivität kollektiver Rechtsschutzinstrumente' (2011) <http://www.bmel.de/SharedDocs/Downloads/Service/AnWis/Heft523.pdf?__blob=publicationFile> (hereafter Meller-Hannich and Höland, 'Evaluierung').

40 S 79 of the ZPO Proceedings the parties may pursue without being represented by counsel (Translation: Samson-Übersetzungen GmbH, Dr. Carmen von Schöning via <http://www.gesetze-im-internet.de>): '(1) (…) (2) The parties may have themselves represented by counsel as attorneys-in-fact. Above and beyond this, the following are authorised to represent parties as attorneys-in-fact: 1. (…); 2. (…); 3. Consumer centres and other publicly subsidised consumer associations, where they are collecting claims of consumers in the context of their scope of responsibilities; 4. (…). (3)–(4) (…).'

d) Model Declaratory Suit

In November 2018, Germany implemented a model declaratory suit, with which associations are allowed to have facts and legal issues determined in court, which in turn has a binding effect on the individual processes of registered consumers. The individual application for a model declaratory action also has a statute-barred effect. The model declaratory suit is regulated in sections 606ff[41] of the Code of Civil Procedure (Zivilprozessordnung, ZPO). The statute of limitations arises from section 204 paragraph 1 no 1a of the BGB.[42] These standards also give rise to a number of limitations on the admissibility of designation actions, for example with regard to the authorised bodies, the conditions of the applications and the necessary quorum.

So far, eight claims have been filed,[43] two of which are inadmissible because the plaintiff is not an entitled institution within the meaning of section 606 of the ZPO:[44]

- 2 March 2020 Verbraucherzentrale Sachsen e.V. ./. Sparkasse Zwickau
  - Higher Regional Court of Dresden 5 MK 1/20
  - 'Calculation of interest in saving contracts'
- 27 January 2019 vzbv ./. Insolvenzverwalter der BEV Bayerischen Energieversorgungsgesellschaft mbH
  - Higher Regional Court of München – MK 2/19
  - 'Bonus for new customers before minimum contract period ends'
- 8 November 2019 Verbraucherzentrale Sachsen e.V. ./. Erzgebirgssparkasse
  - Higher Regional Court of Dresden – 5 MK 2/19
  - 'Calculation of interest in saving contracts'
- 17 June 2019 Verbraucherzentrale Sachsen e.V. ./. Stadt- und Kreissparkasse Leipzig
  - Higher Regional Court of Dresden – 5 MK 1/19
  - 'Calculation of interest in saving contracts'

---

41 S 606 of the ZPO Model declaratory suit (Translation: author): 'With a model declaratory suit qualified entities can sue to establish the existence or non-existence of factual or legal prerequisites for the existence or non-existence of a claim or a legal relationship (determination goals) between a consumer and an entrepreneur (…). (2)–(3) (…).'

42 S 204 of the BGB Suspension of limitation as a result of prosecution of rights (Translation: author): '(1) The limitation period is suspended by 1. (…) 1a. the filing of a model declaratory action, for a claim, which a creditor has registered effectively to the registry of actions and the case of the registered claim has the same facts as the determination goals of the model declaratory action. 2. (…) (2)–(3).'

43 The litigation register can be accessed via <http://www.bundesjustizamt.de/DE/Themen/Buergerdienste/Klageregister/Bekanntmachungen/Klagen_node.html>.

44 See OLG Stuttgart, Judgment of 20 March 2019, 6 MK 1/18.

- 10 May 2019 DMB Mieterverein München ./. Max-Emanuel Immobilien GmbH
  - Higher Regional Court of Munich – MK 1/19[45]
  - 'Rent increase and modernisation measures'
- 21 February 2019 Schutzgemeinschaft für Bankkunden e.V. ./. Bisnode Deutschland GmbH
  - Higher Regional Court of Frankfurt am Main – 24 MK 1/18
  - 'Top ratings'
- 26 November 2018 vzbv ./. Volkswagen AG
  - Higher Regional Court of Braunschweig – 4 MK 1/18[46]
  - 'Tort law and emission manipulation'
- 20 November 2018 Schutzgemeinschaft für Bankkunden e.V. ./. Mercedes Benz Bank AG
  - Higher Regional Court of Stuttgart – 6 MK 1/18
  - 'Right of withdrawal'

The mentioned action *vzbv v Volkswagen* concerns Case 1: the main goal here is to ascertain whether buyers may have a tort claim against automakers.

The benefit of the model declaratory action is that it allows the court to establish, with binding effect, facts and legal issues which are relevant to a variety of individual procedures. In addition, the statute-barred effect of the application to the procedure is to be evaluated as an advantage, since it spares the individual claim (for the moment). In addition, filing applications in a declaratory claim is easier and involves less risk for associations than the process of bundling claims.

The big disadvantage of the model declaratory action, however, is that it cannot lead to a performance obligation of the defendant. The finding has no further legal consequences, so that neither injured parties are compensated, nor a business practice is prohibited in the future. Only if an injured party becomes active on its own after the determination judgment, can he or she receive compensation. In the individual process the consumer can benefit from the binding effect of the model determination. It will, however, remain to be clarified to what extent the model determination is a prejudice for the dispute over individual damage; likewise, the 'whether' and the amount of individual damage are not yet the subject matter of the model declaratory.

45 See OLG München, Judgment of 15 October 2019, MK 1/19; an appeal has been lodged by the defendant, see BGH, VIII ZR 305/19 (pending).

46 Interlocutory decisions and information given by the court can be accessed via <http://www.bundesjustizamt.de/DE/Themen/Buergerdienste/Klageregister/Klagen/201802/Verfahren/Verfahrensstand.html?nn=11994364>.

2. *No German Class Action*

Group lawsuits or class action lawsuits are unknown in German law. Consumers and investors must individually file their individual claims. Only the general rules, such as the suspension of parallel processes within the framework of section 148 of the ZPO, of model-process agreements or the joint-venture pursuant to sections 59ff of the ZPO, provide for the approaches for joint settlement of similar issues. Therefore, at the last German Jurists Forum (Deutscher Juristentag) an opt-in group action was proposed.[47]

3. *Limited Class Action under the Capital Markets Model Case Act (Kapitalanlegermusterverfahren, KapMuG). Concerns in Particular Case 2*

Of course, especially in the field of capital investment law, the investor model procedure is worth mentioning, which presents itself as a limited class action. It is a process specifically fitting our Case 2.

Indeed, Case 2 is currently underway at the Higher Regional Court of Braunschweig and at the Higher Regional Court of Stuttgart:

- Volkswagen AG
  - Higher Regional Court of Braunschweig – 3 Kap 1/16
  - 'Damages for late ad hoc information?'
- Porsche Automobile Holding SE
  - Higher Regional Court of Stuttgart – 20 Kap 2/17; 3/17; 4/17
  - 'Independent ad hoc duty of the holding company?'

It concerns the above-mentioned question of the ad hoc notification obligation and the liability towards investors (see Section I.A.2.b)). While the procedure before the Higher Regional Court of Braunschweig is directed against VW, the one before the Higher Regional Court of Stuttgart is directed against Porsche Holding. In the latter case, there is the question of the holding company's independent ad hoc obligation for the conduct of the subsidiary. Overall, questions of knowledge aggregation play a decisive role. How must or may inside information be passed on within a group? Can knowledge distributed in the company be aggregated 'like a mosaic'? Do the proceedings against the subsidiary block the proceedings against the holding?[48]

---

47 DJT, 'Beschlüsse' (n 38).

48 OLG Stuttgart, Order of 27 March 2019, 20 Kap 2/17: The proceeding in Braunschweig blocks the proceeding in Stuttgart.

The KapMuG also requires an individual action by each victim in the capital investment model procedure.[49] However, the proceedings are suspended in the case of corresponding applications for the purpose of exemplary decision by the Higher Regional Court. After the model decision, the individual proceedings must be completed. In addition, as soon as the model proceeding has been initiated, a damaged investor will be able to register for it even without bringing an action, according to a 2012 amendment. However, this application has only a statute-barred effect (section 204 paragraph 1 no 6a of the BGB). A binding to the model decision does not arise.[50] If the KapMuG is not renewed, it is going to expire on 1 November 2020 (section 28 of the KapMuG).

By way of illustration, the key difference between the capital investment model procedure and the model declaratory suit is that the investor process is generated from individual actions already filed, one of which is a model claim. In contrast, the model declaratory action is initiated by an association and the persons concerned sue only after completion of the model procedure. In addition, the investor model procedure is limited to capital investment law, whereas the model declaratory action concerns consumer law. The application for the process has a statute-barred effect in both types of proceedings; but only in the case of a model declaratory, the application alone already has binding effect on the model decision. In contrast, a binding effect on the model decision in investment law only exists if it is individually complained of; the registration alone is not enough.

Overall, the investor model process has been proven to be very complicated and cumbersome due to the many interdependent procedural steps.[51] The biggest weakness is that every individual investor must file a lawsuit themselves to be involved in the process and obtain a performance title. However, when it comes to the trial, the individual's claim is inevitably suspended. Thus, investors cannot participate without individual legal action and, at the same time, accept in the collective interest a significant delay in their individual proceedings as a result of the compulsory suspension. In any event, according to the model procedure,

---

49 S 1 of the KapMuG Scope (Translation: Jane Yager for the Federal Ministry of Justice and Consumer Protection via <http://www.gesetze-im-internet.de>): '(1) This Act applies to civil disputes in which: 1. A claim for compensation of damages due to false, misleading or omitted public capital markets information, 2. A claim for compensation of damages for the use of false or misleading public capital markets information or for failure to offer clarification about the false or misleading nature of public capital markets information, or 3. A claim to fulfilment of contract, which is based on an offer under the Securities Acquisition and Takeover Act, including a claim under Section 39 (3) sent. 3 and 4 of the Stock Exchange Act is asserted. (2) (…).'

50 See Thomas MJ Möllers, in Heribert Hirte and Thomas MJ Möllers (eds), *Kölner Kommentar zum WpHG* (2nd edn, Carl Heymanns 2014) §§37b, c WpHG para 534.

51 Case Study Telekom-Process: Christopher Hodges, *The Reform of Class and Representative Actions in European Legal Systems* (Hart Publishing 2008) 76.

the coping with the suspension of the suspended proceedings is due to the judiciary. This does not contribute to an effective discharge. The aforementioned possibility of simple registration does not compensate for this disadvantage, since, although it has limitation-inhibiting effect, it brings about no involvement of the applicant in the process. In order to preserve the statute-barred effect on a permanent basis, moreover, legal action must still be taken, as section 204 paragraph 1 no 6a of the BGB requires this action to be brought about within three months. In addition, a dependency on the model case is a prerequisite for the statute of limitations. If it lacks, the statute-barred effect is eliminated. On the positive side, however, the possibility for settlements exists (sections 17–19 of the KapMuG). This opens the discussion for more complex mass damages. Though, there would be no need for a model procedure, because in a settlement, facts and legal issues, the clarification of which the model procedure precisely is made for, remain open.

4. *Entitled Entities*

Only authorised associations according to the UklaG are entitled to file a representative action. In total, there are three major groups of suitors:

1. The qualified entities within the meaning of sections 3, 4 of the UKlaG. These are the associations that have been entered in the list at the Federal Office of Justice or the European Commission (section 3 paragraph 1 sentence 1 no 1, section 4 of the UKlaG).
2. Associations representing the interests of certain companies (section 3 paragraph 1 sentence 1 no 2 of the UKlaG).
3. The Chambers of Commerce and Industry and Chambers of Crafts (section 3 paragraph 1 sentence 1 no 3 of the UKlaG).

It may be stated that the legislator insists on a mixture of business and consumer associations. Particularly effective in practice are the consumer centres and the Wettbewerbszentrale.[52] They belong to the qualified entities within the definition of sections 3, 4 of the UKlaG. Few complaints are made by the Chambers of Commerce and Industry and Chambers of Crafts. In part, however, they seem to pass on the irregularities to the Wettbewerbszentrale.

Some laws, however, make extensions and others make restrictions on this *locus standi*. This is particularly noticeable in the case of the model declaratory act. Here, there are greater restrictions on the *locus standi* in section 606 paragraph 1 sentence 2 of the ZPO. In contrast, there are additional legal actions for competitors and commercial customers in the UWG and the GWB.

---

52 Meller-Hannich and Höland, 'Evaluierung' (n 39).

The reasons for the limitations and extensions in the legal standing are not always fully comprehensible. In part, they are based on the scope of the specific legislation. Thus, an additional control of general terms and conditions in Germany in the entrepreneurial field exists, so that the involvement of business associations makes sense. Similar reasons exist for the inclusion of companies in the area of cartel damages. On the other hand, the model declaratory action has been specifically developed under consumer law, so that it was restricted to consumer associations. However, some of these restrictions are also politically motivated, for example because of fear of abuse.[53]

5. *Finance*

The entitled entities are financed by the public sector and by private donors. They carry the legal costs risk but are not financially involved in the success of lawsuits.

6. *Collective Settlements*

Both the capital investment model procedure and the model declaratory action provide for the possibility of a court settlement. There is no possibility of judicial approval of out-of-court settlements. Nevertheless, there was an explicit reference to the Dutch WCAM in the reform process of the KapMuG.[54] However, the hopes for a far-reaching out-of-court settlement procedure have not materialised.

C. SUBSTANTIVE ASSIGNMENT MODELS – PROCESS-BASED BUNDLING OF COMPENSATION CLAIMS (MYFLIGHT/MYRIGHT ETC.)

These models have only recently been around and, at least, they have not proven to be very successful thus far. The case law places higher demands on the bundled assertion of consumer claims by means of private assignment models.[55]

---

53 For instance, 'Beschlussempfehlung und Bericht des Ausschusses für Recht und Verbraucherschutz' (2018) BT-Drucks 19/2741, 22ff <https://dip21.bundestag.de/dip21/btd/19/027/1902741.pdf>.

54 Xandra Kramer, 'Enforcing mass settlements in the European Judicial Area: EU policy and the strange case of Dutch collective settlements' in Christopher Hodges and Astrid Stadler (eds), *Resolving Mass Disputes. ADR and Settlement of Mass Claims* (Edward Elgar Publishing 2013) 63, 73.

55 See OLG Düsseldorf, Judgment of 18 February 2015, VI U (Kart) 3/14; Rolf Hempel, 'Ende des kollektiven Rechtsschutzes im deutschen Kartellrecht' [2015] NJW 2077 (hereafter Hempel, 'Ende des kollektiven Rechtsschutzes'); Astrid Stadler, 'Die Bündelung von gleichgerichteten

A common place of jurisdiction for consumer claims does not yet exist. If a law enforcement company that is in the process of asserting claims as a result of assignments is unable to pay the substantial litigation costs to be incurred in the event of litigation, an assignment may be ineffective. Process financing options and contingency fees are only possible under tighter conditions. The question of whether the platform 'myright' of the registered collection service provider Financialright GmbH in the future will bring forth success for car buyers (Case 1), still remains open. Financialright GmbH finances the proceedings and mandates the lawyers. Organisationally, this is a complex procedure. The assignee incurs relatively high costs in the case of the success following the process. The question of whether this model is allowed remains open for every individual case. Conflicts may exist with both the prohibition of the lawyer's success fee and with the legal service law (Rechtsdienstleistungsgesetz, RDG).[56] The corresponding activities show deficits in the regulation of private bundling options by the legislator. After all, in November 2019, the BGH decided in favour of a platform bundling and taking the claims of tenants together to court.[57]

II. PUBLIC LAW

A. DO ELIMINATIONS OF CONSEQUENCES, DAMAGES AND SKIMMING OF PROFITS (BY FINES) EXIST?

In German antitrust law, there is the special feature that the court, which decides on damage claims of victims, is bound by the findings of a cartel offence on the part of the antitrust authority, section 33b of the GWB. As a result, follow-on lawsuits undertaken by private individuals are facilitated by regulatory investigations. In addition, antitrust investigations by antitrust authorities impede upon the statute of limitations for antitrust claims, section 33h paragraph 6 of the GWB. This prevents the damage claims of injured parties from becoming statute-barred. A further relief is experienced by the cartel victims by a claim for the release of evidence and the provision of information against any individual who may possess appropriate evidence, section 33g of the GWB.

Ansprüchen durch Inkassozession – Geschäftsmodelle zur Prozessfinanzierung auf dem Prüfstand, zugleich Besprechung von LG Düsseldorf, Urteil v. 17.12.2013 – 37 O 200/09' [2014] JZ 613; Caroline Meller-Hannich, 'Schrems v Facebook' [2019] ZEuP 202 (note).

56 See Kai von Lewinsky and Tim Kerstges, 'Interessenkonflikte zwischen der Tätigkeit als Prozessfinanzierer und Inkassounternehmen im Lichte des §4 RDG' [2019] ZZP 132, 177; Meller-Hannich, 'Rechtsdurchsetzung im digitalen Binnenmarkt: Legal Tech, Online Dispute Resolution, Plattformklagen – die Zukunft des Zivilprozesses?' in Matthias Weller and Matthias Wendland (eds), *Digital Single Market* (Mohr Siebeck 2019) 143.

57 BGH, Judgment of 27 November 2019, VIII ZR 285/18.

In addition, in antitrust law, the skimming off is not only possible in the above-mentioned cases of an association becoming active, but also directly by the antitrust authority, section 34 of the GWB (see Section I.A.3.). Again, it goes without saying that a profit deduction is only possible in the case of intentional infringements. Claims for damages and fines take precedence over the profit reduction.

Corresponding rules regarding the interaction between regulatory and private enforcement do not exist in unfair competition law and private consumer law. The antitrust law is characterised in a special way by official structures. However, in none of our initial cases would it be considered relevant.

In capital investor law official structures also exist (see Section II.B.), wherein, however, no comparable link with the private claims of injured parties is provided.[58] For our initial Case 2, it is not the antitrust authority that is responsible, but the Federal Financial Supervisory Authority (Bundesanstalt für Finanzdienstleistungsaufsicht – BaFin). However, their activities do not concern damages and profits.

It must be remembered that the mixture of public and private enforcement, which was hitherto only rooted in antitrust law, provides little remedy, at least with regard to compensation for dispersed low-value damages caused. Nevertheless, the proceedings remain complex and claims for damages in the case of antitrust encroachment are very rare, also as a follow-on complaint.[59] It is not expected that this would work better in other areas of law – in any case with regard to dispersed damages. Incidentally, antitrust law sees itself as only conditionally suitable for comparison in view of its other objectives and structures.[60] This is shown by the fact that the specialty of the leniency program and the fine regulation play a major role here.[61] In recent years, however, the Bundeskartellamt has increasingly been given consumer protection tasks; initial studies relate to comparison platforms,[62] for example. Strengthening the

---

58 See Thomas MJ Möllers and Bernhard Pregler, 'Zivilrechtliche Rechtsdurchsetzung und kollektiver Rechtsschutz im Wirtschaftsrecht' (2012) 176 ZHR 144.

59 To the difficulties Franz Böni and Alex Wassmer, 'Sammelklagen als Instrument der Kartellrechtsdurchsetzung' [2015] EWS 130; Philipp Eckel, 'Kollektiver Rechtsschutz gegen kartellrechtliche Streuschäden. Das Vereinigte Königreich als Vorbild?' [2015] WuW 4; Hempel, 'Ende des kollektiven Rechtsschutzes' (n 55) 2077; Markus Langen and Lars Teigelack, 'Amerikanische Verhältnisse im Kartellrecht oder Ende des Abtretungsmodells? Zur gebündelten Durchsetzung von Schadenersatzansprüchen de lege lata' [2014] BB 1795.

60 Christoph Brömmelmeyer, 'Kollektiver Rechtsschutz im Kartellrecht' in Christoph Brömmelmeyer (ed), *Die EU-Sammelklage* (Nomos 2013) 57.

61 Daniela Seeliger, 'Kollektiver Rechtsschutz im Kartell- und Wettbewerbsrecht' in Caroline Meller-Hannich (ed), *Kollektiver Rechtsschutz im Zivilprozess* (Nomos 2008) 73.

62 Bundeskartellamt, 'Sektoruntersuchung Vergleichsportale' (April 2019) <http://www.bundeskartellamt.de/SharedDocs/Publikation/DE/Sektoruntersuchungen/Sektoruntersuchung_Vergleichsportale_Bericht.html>.

antitrust authorities or establishing comparable authorities in consumer law and unfair competition law will in any case only supplement and not replace civil-procedural instruments.

B. COMPARED TO PRIVATE ENFORCEMENT – HOW STRONG IS THE MONITORING AND LAW ENFORCEMENT BY PUBLIC AUTHORITIES OR OTHER PUBLIC BODIES?

In the capital market law (Case 2), the former supervisory authorities for credit and securities trading as well as for the insurance industry were merged more than 15 years ago to form a German Federal Financial Supervisory Authority (BaFin). One of BaFin's tasks involves combating insider trading. The agency routinely observes trading activity on the basis of the reportable transactions. In addition, BaFin reviews ad hoc disclosures by listed companies, including information from investors or other authorities or from the press. It intervenes when a company does not publish ad hoc publicity information that is subject to publicity, late, incorrectly, or incompletely. Also, Boards and Supervisory Boards of listed companies which buy or sell their own shares must report this to BaFin. The corresponding financial market powers of BaFin are regulated in sections 6ff of the WpHG.

The Kraftfahrtbundesamt, on the other hand, is the authority relevant to Case 1. It is responsible for the type-approval process and certifies that a particular type of vehicle complies with the requirements of the EU type-approval Regulation. Regarding the type approval, this depends on the approval for road use according to the Road Traffic Licensing Ordinance (Straßenverkehrszulassungsordnung – StVZO). The Kraftfahrtbundesamt is also responsible for market surveillance and product recalls.

In addition, in accordance with the Federal Immission Control Act (Bundesimmissionsschutzgesetz – BImSchG), air quality plans can be established (section 47 of the BImSchG) and environmental zones with driving restrictions for certain motor vehicles can be set up (section 40 of the BImSchG). Administrative Courts have already issued a series of driving bans on diesel vehicles through a judicial decision.[63]

The key difference between private enforcement and the monitoring and enforcement by public bodies is that the authorities have *ex officio* investigative and enforcement powers and can intervene preventively. Private enforcement always has limits which can only be offset by regulatory activities. This includes, for example, the determination of facts and the prevention and sanctioning of

63 Summarising Kurt Faßbender, 'Der Dieselskandal und der Gesundheitsschutz. Zugleich ein Beitrag zur Zulässigkeit von Fahrverboten für Dieselfahrzeuge' [2017] NJW 1995.

legal violations through licensing and control procedures as well as fines and criminal proceedings. Both private law enforcement and public enforcement can have a deterrent effect. However, private law enforcement only has it if it takes place realistically wise and provides painful sanctions.[64] At present, therefore, the deterrent effect of private law enforcement in Germany is very low. However, on the other hand, authorities have limited ability to provide for compensation, and if the 'precautionary principle' fails and the damage has been done, only private enforcement remains for compensation purposes.

III. GENERAL PROCEDURAL LAW

A. IS A SIMULTANEOUS COEXISTENCE OF SEVERAL LEGAL ACTIONS POSSIBLE?

The simultaneous coexistence of several individual legal actions with the same subject matter is not possible, section 261 paragraph 3 no 1 of the ZPO. Several investor model procedures with the same determination objective are also mutually exclusive, section 7 of the KapMuG.[65] This also applies to several model declaratory actions for the same facts of life and the same determination objective, section 610 paragraph 1 of the ZPO. However, several association injunctions against the same General Terms and Conditions or anti-consumer law practices may be brought about simultaneously.

In the case of individual and collective actions, the KapMuG lays down that the individual claim is suspended as long as the model procedure is in progress and continued after the model decision, section 8 of the KapMuG. Injunctions and individual actions ultimately do not affect each other. In the case of a model declaratory action, a previously filed individual claim is suspended (section 613 paragraph 2 of the ZPO), a later one will be deemed inadmissible (section 610 paragraph 3 of the ZPO).

B. DOES FACILITATION TO GIVE PROOF EXIST: HOW IS THE BURDEN OF PROOF DISTRIBUTED?

As a rule, the plaintiff bears the burden of proof. In the sale of consumer goods, there is a facilitation to give proof in the case of defects occurring within

---

64 Steven VanUytsel, 'Collective actions in a competition law context – reconciling multilayer interests to enhance access to justice?' in Stefan Wrbka and others (eds), *Collective Actions. Enhancing Access to Justice and Reconciling Multilayer Interests?* (Cambridge University Press 2012) 57, 86ff.

65 OLG Stuttgart, Order of 27 March 2019, 20 Kap 2/17; 20 Kap 3/17; 20 Kap 4/17.

six months after delivery, it is assumed that the item was defective at the time of delivery, section 477 of the BGB. In tort law and investment law, there are no specific evidence facilitations. In case law, however, the possibility of a so-called secondary burden of presentation has generally been developed, which the courts are now also applying in cases such as Case 1.[66] The secondary burden of presentation concerns cases in which the evidence-laden party's lecture is not possible or unreasonable, while the adversary is aware of all the essential facts and it is reasonable for him to provide details.

C. ARE THERE ANY DEMANDS FOR INFORMATION AGAINST THE ALLEGED INJURING PARTY?

In addition to the possibility of applying the secondary burden of presentation, there is the possibility of the opposing party to require documents which are in possession of the other party, section 142 of the ZPO.

D. WHAT IS THE BINDING EFFECT OF JUDGMENTS FOR SUBSEQUENT PROCEEDINGS?

In individual proceedings, a judgment binds only to the relatively narrow limits of legal force, sections 322ff of the ZPO. This concerns only the parties and their legal successors and only the subject matter of the dispute and, in terms of time, only to those facts which have arisen up until the end of the oral proceedings.

Between the collective proceedings of the KapMuG and the individual proceedings as well as between the model declaratory suit and the individual proceedings, there are relatively complicated and in detail controversial binding effects.[67] In principle, the binding effect which exists within the KapMuG works in such a way that the model decision binds the trial courts in all suspended proceedings, so that the courts must decide on the basis of the legally binding

---

66 See OLG Hamm, Judgment of 10 September 2019, 13 U 149/18; LG Bonn, Judgment of 7 March 2018, 19 O 327/17; LG Hildesheim, Judgment of 17 January 2017, 3 O 139/16; in this context Thomas Pfeiffer, 'Organwissen und Grenzen der sekundären Darlegungslast' [2017] ZIP 2077; Steffi Lehre and Ellen Stamer, 'Sekundäre Darlegungs- und Beweislast' [2017] DAR 510; Julia Habbe and Konrad Gieseler, 'Beweiserleichterungen bei (angeblich) fehlerhaften Ad-hoc-Mitteilungen?' [2016] Neue Zeitschrift für Gesellschaftsrecht 454.

67 See Caroline Meller-Hannich, 'Das Kapitalanleger-Musterverfahrensgesetz (KapMuG) – Eine Zwischenbilanz' [2011] ZBB 180 (hereafter Meller-Hannich, 'Kapitalanleger-Musterverfahrensgesetz'); Gesa Lutz in Volkert Vorwerk and Christian Wolf (eds), *BeckOK ZPO* (32nd edn, CH Beck 2019) §§606ff ZPO.

determination goals, see section 22 of the KapMuG.[68] In the case of the model declaratory action, the binding effect of the model decision extends to all registered consumers, who do not have to file suit themselves. The binding effect refers to the individual proceedings of registered consumers following the model procedure, insofar as they are affected by the aims of determination and the facts of the case, section 613 of the ZPO.[69]

E. ARE THERE ANY PROCEDURAL SIMPLIFICATIONS IN CONSUMER AND CAPITAL MARKET LAW?

There is no general consumer jurisdiction. However, for the relatively comprehensive area of the off-premises contracts, an exclusive local jurisdiction is stipulated, section 29c of the ZPO. In addition, in relation to consumers' jurisdiction agreements, riotous admittance and jurisdiction-based fulfilment arrangements are possible only to a limited extent, sections 29, 38, 39, 40 of the ZPO.

In capital market law, there is an exclusive place of jurisdiction according to section 32b of the ZPO. This concerns false, misleading or omitted public capital market information, such as ad hoc releases, prospectus liability, and investment advice.[70]

For procedures dealing with a small amount in dispute (up to €600) there are procedural simplifications, such as a waiver of a hearing, section 495a of the ZPO. Overall, in proceedings up to a value of €5,000, the representation by a lawyer is not mandatory, section 78 of the ZPO, section 23 no 1 of the GVG.[71]

However, there are exceptions within certain capital market disputes, section 71 paragraph 2 nos 3 and 4 of the GVG. This is applicable to Case 2. Therefore, it could not be handled before the district court, but would have to be heard before the regional court, where having a lawyer is compulsory.

68 S 22 of the KapMuG Effect of the Model Case Ruling (Translation: Jane Yager for the Federal Ministry of Justice and Consumer Protection via <http://www.gesetze-im-internet.de>): '(1) The model case ruling shall be binding on the courts trying all proceedings that have been suspended pursuant to Section 8 (1). (…) (2)–(5) (…).'

69 S 613 of the ZPO Binding effect of the model declaratory action (Translation: author): 'The declaratory judgment is binding for the court deciding on an action between a registered consumer and the defendant, if the decision affects the declaratory goals and the facts of the model declaratory case. (…) (2) (…).'

70 For details see Robert Bey in Hanns Prütting and Markus Gehrlein (eds), *Zivilprozessordnung* (Luchterhand 2018) §32b, mn 2; Meller-Hannich, 'Kapitalanleger-Musterverfahrensgesetz' (n 67) 180.

71 Details see Caroline Meller-Hannich, 'Begriff und Leitbild des Verbrauchers im Zivilprozess' in Markus Artz and others (eds), *Wer ist der Verbraucher?* (Nomos 2018) 193.

Finally, it should be noted that for minor claims of up to €750, in some federal states there is the obligation to go through a conciliation procedure before filing an action, section 15a of the EGZPO.

F. WHEN IS THE STATUTE OF LIMITATION FOR COLLECTIVE REDRESS SUSPENDED?

Injunction actions have no statute-barred effect, which is an important criticism point directed at them.[72] The statute-barring effect of antitrust investigations has been pointed out (see Section II.A.). The individual registration for a model declaratory action and an investor model procedure has a statute-barring effect, see section 204 paragraph 1 no 1a and 6a of the BGB.[73]

G. WHO BEARS THE LITIGATION RISKS?

This applies to the 'loser pays' rule (section 91 of the ZPO). Therefore, the litigation risk is carried by both sides – the cost risk being realised on the part of the process loser.[74]

H. WHO RECEIVES ANY AWARDED OR SETTLED DAMAGES OR SKIMMED PROFITS?

Skimmed off profits are designated for the treasury (see section 10 of the UWG, sections 34, 34a of the GWB), while damages are paid to the victims.

IV. CRITICAL EVALUATION AND PROPOSALS *DE LEGE FERENDA*

In *substantive law*, it is necessary to clarify which responsibilities within companies and groups apply to the knowledge available only to several employees. The violation of standards for the prevention of exhaust gas manipulation should be

72 Meller-Hannich, Gutachten (n 7) A 56.

73 For details see Caroline Meller-Hannich in Beate Gsell and others (eds), *beck-online. Großkommentar BGB* (CH Beck 2019) §204 BGB.

74 Details see Burkhard Hess and Rudolf Hübner, 'Germany' in Christopher Hodges and others (eds), *The Costs and Funding of Civil Litigation. A Comparative Perspective* (Hart Publishing 2010) 349.

regarded as a violation of a protection law in the sense of section 823 paragraph 2 of the BGB. The conditions for skimming off should be reduced.

In *procedural law*, a class-action claim for performance and the possibility of judicial approval of out-of-court collective agreements should be introduced. Whether the concepts proposed by the EU-"New Deal for Consumers" will suffice remains doubtful.

Rather, the new model declaratory suit (sections 606ff of the ZPO) will lead to disappointment, seeing that cumbersome, long-lasting, and often unsuccessful follow-up proceedings are to be expected. This will disappoint the legitimate expectation for an effective judicial guarantee and will lead to liability risks for the qualified associations.

The KapMuG should be modified and kept in practice; thus far, no current extension is being considered in a specific legislative procedure. If nothing happens, the KapMuG is expected to expire on 1 November 2020.

The long German tradition of representative action has in principle proven itself worthy. Injunctive actions by associations should, however, have a statute-barring effect.

Public and private enforcement should be seen as complementary and conditional enforcement channels rather than as competing alternatives.

Further criticism and suggestions for improvement are to be found in the relevant text.

ENFORCING CONSUMER AND CAPITAL MARKETS LAW IN ENGLAND AND WALES

John Sorabji*

* John Sorabji, Dr., MA (Oxon), MPhil, LLM, Senior Teaching Fellow, University College London, Faculty of Laws.
All UK legislation is freely available at <http://www.legislation.gov.uk>. Relevant court rules concerning civil procedure, the Civil Procedure Rules, are available at <http://www.justice.gov.uk/courts/procedure-rules/civil/rules>.

I. INTRODUCTION

This chapter considers the approach that can be taken to the enforcement of consumer protection and capital markets law in England and Wales (England). It does so through a consideration of two case studies[1] that form the focus of this chapter, which are based on litigation arising from alleged infringements of consumer protection law and capital markets law by Volkswagen, which have been the subject of proceedings in a number of jurisdictions (the diesel scandal).

A. THE DIESEL SCANDAL IN ENGLAND

The diesel scandal has had a more limited impact in England than it has in, for instance, Germany or the US, both in terms of governmental or regulatory action and in terms of criminal and civil proceedings.

1 See Introduction Section IV.A.

In respect of the former, it was initially considered by a UK Parliamentary Committee, the Transport Committee.[2] It took evidence concerning the issue and then raised its concerns with the UK Government[3] and issued a report into the diesel scandal in July 2016.[4] Its primary focus was an apparent lack of action by the UK Government and various investigatory and regulatory authorities. As it noted, no real action was taken by the government:

> The Secretary of State said that in the UK, VW could face action from the Serious Fraud Office (SFO), the Competition and Markets Authority (CMA) and himself under the Road Vehicles (Approval) Regulations 2009. In practice little action has been taken.[5]

Additionally, authorities such as the Serious Fraud Office (SFO) and Competition and Markets Authority (CMA) could have taken action, but they did not take any or any substantive action either. They, the Transport Select Committee concluded, had 'taken a softer approach to investigating VW compared to European counterparts'.[6] The SFO was noted to have reported that it was co-ordinating with counterparts in other European Union Member States. In point of fact, in 2015 the SFO had previously been reported to be considering whether to investigate Volkswagen for 'corporate criminality' arising from the diesel scandal.[7] No further public comment on any potential or actual investigation has been made public, either since then or since the Select Committee's report and its statement concerning the action the SFO was taking in 2016. The CMA had also not commenced any formal investigation but was assessing the situation.[8] More significantly it could not seek damages for individual consumers. The reason

---

2 The House of Commons' Select Committee on Transport, Volkswagen Group emissions violations one-off session and follow-up session (12 October 2015, 25 January 2016 and 20 February 2017). <http://www.parliament.uk/business/committees/committees-a-z/commons-select/transport-committee/inquiries/parliament-2015/volkswagen-group-emissions-violations-15-16/publications/>.

3 Letter from Lillian Greenwood MP, Chair of the Transport Committee, to Jesse Norman MP, Parliamentary Under Secretary of State for Transport (18 December 2017) <http://www.parliament.uk/documents/commons-committees/transport/Response-from-Lilian-Greenwood-MP-to-Jesse-Norman-MP-re-VW-emissions-scandal-18-12-2017.pdf>.

4 The House of Commons' Select Committee on Transport, Volkswagen emissions scandal and vehicle type approval, (16 July 2016) <http://www.publications.parliament.uk/pa/cm201617/cmselect/cmtrans/69/6902.htm> (hereafter Committee, 'Approval').

5 Ibid, ch 2 para 27.

6 Ibid, ch 2 para 28.

7 Laura Hughes, 'Volkswagen faces Serious Fraud Office investigation' *The Daily Telegraph* (London, 27 October 2015) <http://www.telegraph.co.uk/motoring/car-manufacturers/volkswagen/11959009/Volkswagen-faces-Serious-Fraud-Office-investigation.html> (hereafter Hughes, 'Volkswagen').

8 It was also reported in October 2015 that the CMA was considering such an investigation into Volkswagen, ibid.

for the latter point no doubt being that its ability to secure damages was limited to breaches of competition law, which at that time had not been suggested as an aspect of the scandal. Finally, the Transport Select Committee noted that the Secretary of State could, in principle, prosecute Volkswagen for breaches of the Road Vehicles (Approval) Regulations 2009 (see below). No action had been taken, although the Select Committee acknowledged that the Department of Transport had been receiving legal advice 'on the evidence base for a successful prosecution and the procedural steps required for such a prosecution since February 2016'.[9] No further action had then, or since appears to have, been taken.

The UK Government's approach has not, it would appear, to have stemmed from an absence of appreciation of the issue, or from any conclusion that it has no bearing on or relevance to the UK and to UK consumers. It stems from a principled position that any action in the UK by or on behalf of the Government ought properly to await the outcome of action brought in Germany against Volkswagen. As the Under Secretary of State put it,

> Among EU states, it is for the German Government in the first place to take legal action given that the vast majority, if not all, of the potential wrongdoing is likely to have occurred at Volkswagen AG in Germany, where the relevant engines were developed, manufactured and type-approval tested and the Secretary of State has discussed this issue with his German counterpart. The starting point of any investigation will be to establish the wrongdoing which occurred at Volkswagen AG, and it would be inappropriate, and jurisdictionally difficult, to carry out a separate investigation in parallel with the German authorities. The Department hopes to see results from the German investigation soon and, at that point, will be in a position to reassess the prospects of a successful prosecution in the UK, based on the evidence available as a result of any German prosecution.[10]

The position appears to be then that what might seem to be an apparent lack of action on the part of UK authorities does not arise from any perception that the diesel scandal does not raise genuine issues of concern in the UK. On the contrary, it arises out of a deliberate decision to await developments, and the conclusion of investigations, in Germany by relevant German authorities. The UK is not then, in a sense, declining jurisdiction or declining to take action. It is staying its own investigations pending the outcome of those, in what the UK

---

9 Committee, 'Approval' (n 4) ch 2 para 29.

10 Letter from Jesse Norman MP, Parliamentary Under Secretary of State for Transport to Lillian Greenwood MP, Chair of the Transport Committee (11 December 2017) <http://www.parliament.uk/documents/commons-committees/transport/Letter-from-Jesse-Norman-MP-to-Lilian-Greenwwod-MP-re-VW-emissions-issue-11-12-2017.pdf> (hereafter Norman, 'Letter').

Government has concluded is the primary forum where any alleged wrongdoing took place.

The position in respect of criminal and civil proceedings is more nuanced. In contrast to Germany and the US, only the scenario set out in Case 1 has been the subject of civil proceedings in England concerning Volkswagen: the VW NOx Emissions Group Litigation.[11] In so far as that litigation is concerned, as of March 2019, 117,000 claimants had issued claims against Volkswagen and joined the group litigation;[12] this would appear to represent just under 10 per cent of all affected vehicles.[13] In April 2020, the High Court considered two preliminary issues in the proceedings, which affected some 91,000 group claimants. Those issues were:

> '(1) Issue 1: Is the High Court of England and Wales bound (having regard to the terms and operation of the EC Type Approval legislation and pursuant to its duty

---

11 See <http://www.gov.uk/guidance/group-litigation-orders#VW-NOx-emissions-group-litigation>. The Group Litigation Order (GLO) in this litigation was made on 11 May 2018. The issues that have been pleaded in the various claims that form part of the group litigation, i.e. the common issues to be determined are, as noted in the GLO Register, as follows:

'Defining issues:

The matters set out below for the purposes of CPR 19.11 are intended to identify the high level GLO issues to assist in the management of the GLO, and are not intended as a substitute for particularised pleadings. These GLO issues will be likely to require revision and review as the matter progresses, including when pleadings are finalised. Accordingly, no party makes or is deemed to make any admission by reason of the matters set out below.

(1) Whether any of the 1st to 4th Defendants knowingly or recklessly made false representations in relation to vehicles manufactured with EA 189 engines affected by the NOx issue ("affected vehicles"), with the intention of deceiving Claimants, on which those Claimants relied and were caused to suffer loss.
(2) Whether there was any breach of the implied term of satisfactory quality in contracts relating to affected vehicles between Claimants and the 6th Defendant (VWFS), 7th Defendant (Inchcape), or any other Authorised Dealership.
(3) Whether Claimants have any right to redress in relation to affected vehicle under Part 4A of the Consumer Protection from Unfair Trading Regulations 2008.
(4) Whether there was an unfair relationship between Claimants who entered into finance agreements with the 6th Defendant (VWFS) in respect of affected vehicles such that a remedy ought to be ordered.
(5) Whether any of the 1st to 4th Defendants acted in breach of obligations under EC Regulation 715/2007 in relation to affected vehicles so as to give rise to an actionable claim in damages as a breach of statutory duty or a sui generis tort.
(6) Whether Claimants have suffered any recoverable loss in respect of any cause of action above.'

12 *Crossley & Ors v Volkswagen Aktiengesellschaft & Ors* [2019] EWHC 698 (QB) at [1] <http://www.bailii.org/ew/cases/EWHC/QB/2019/698.html>. This was the first case management decision in the group litigation and provides detail concerning the issues. It held that a number of the common issues, those relating to breaches of European Union law, would be dealt with as preliminary issues, see [28] and [112–14].

13 Norman, 'Letter' (n 10) 6.

of sincere cooperation) by the finding of the competent EU type approval authority (the KBA, in this case) that a vehicle contains a defeat device in circumstances where that finding could have been, but has not been, appealed by the manufacturer; and/or is it an abuse of process for the Defendants to seek collaterally to attack the KBA's reasoning or conclusions by denying that the affected vehicles contain defeat devices?

(2) Issue 2: Where a vehicle's engine control unit is capable of identifying the New European Driving Cycle test and operates in a different mode during the test by altering the rate of exhaust gas recirculation to reduce NOx emissions, does the vehicle contain a "defeat device" within the meaning of Article 3(10) of Regulation 715/2007/EC?' The first pre-trial hearings in the proceedings took place in October and December 2019.'[14]

The High Court held, on Issue 1, that it was bound by any findings of a competent EU type approval authority; hence it was bound by findings of the German Federal Motor Transport Authority (KBA).[15] It further held on that Issue, that it was an abuse of process for the defendants to attempt to collaterally attack the KBA's findings through an attempt to argue that the vehicles subject to the claims did not contain a defeat device. On Issue 2, it held that the affected vehicles did contain a defeat device. Having determined those preliminary issues, the proceedings are likely to move to trial, subject to any appeal from the High Court's decision on Issues 1 and/or 2, in 2021.[16]

The scenario in Case 2 has been the subject of litigation arising from alleged market abuse by Tesco, the supermarket.[17] In so far as criminal proceedings are concerned, none have as yet become a matter of public record. No prosecutions have, as yet, been brought before the courts, in respect to either Case 1 or Case 2, which is consistent with the approach of the UK authorities noted by the Transport Select Committee.

In this chapter, three areas are considered: first, public law issues relating to the diesel scandal. This encompasses potential criminal and regulatory action that could be taken; secondly, private law actions that could be taken; and

---

14 *Crossley & Ors v Volkswagen Aktiengesellschaft & Ors* [2020] EWHC 783 (QB) at [9].

15 It also held that it was not, in the circumstances of the case, also bound by the contents of a letter sent by the UK's Vehicle Certification Agency, as it did not amount to a binding decision and neither had Skoda made any formal admission regarding defeat devices in its communications with it; see *Crossley & Ors v Volkswagen Aktiengesellschaft & Ors* [2020] EWHC 783 (QB) at [422]–[436].

16 Jemma Slingo, 'VW prepares for epic emissions scandal trial' (*The Law Gazette*, 11 October 2019) <http://www.lawgazette.co.uk/news/vw-prepares-for-epic-emissions-scandal-trial/5101782.article>.

17 See, Financial Conduct Authority, 'Tesco to pay redress for market abuse' (23 August 2017) <http://www.fca.org.uk/news/press-releases/tesco-pay-redress-market-abuse> (hereafter FCA, 'Press Release'). For details of the criminal proceedings brought in respect of this matter see, *Serious Fraud Office v Tesco Stores Ltd*, The Crown Court at Southwark (Case no U20170287, 10 April 2017, unrep.) <http://www.judiciary.uk/wp-content/uploads/2019/01/sfo-v-tesco-stores-ltd-2017-approved-final.pdf>.

finally, civil procedural mechanisms available for the effective management of civil actions. This chapter does not consider the form of collective action and collective settlement procedures, which are available in the UK Competition Appeal Tribunal. It does not as those procedures are only available for actions for damages arising from alleged competition law breaches, and would primarily stem from action taken by the CMA (noted above).[18] As such they are not available in either of the scenarios outlined in the case studies. It may be the case, however, that if competition law breaches, such as any potential breach of article 101 of the TFEU, then such collective proceedings for competition law damages for consumers, either on an opt-in or opt-out basis, could be pursued against Volkswagen.

II. PUBLIC LAW ISSUES

There are a number of potential public, including criminal and regulatory, actions that could be brought in respect of the two case studies.

A. CRIMINAL OFFENCES

There are a number of possible criminal offences that could be pursued in respect of the two case studies.

1. *Offences under the Fraud Act 2006*

The Fraud Act 2006, section 1, created a general offence of fraud, conviction for which can result in a sentence of ten years' imprisonment or an unlimited fine, or both.[19] A person is guilty of fraud if they commit fraud by false representation

---

18 For details see, Competition Appeals Tribunal, *Guide to Proceedings 2015*, <http://www.catribunal.org.uk/sites/default/files/2017-12/guide_to_proceedings_2015.pdf>; and, s 47B of the Competition Act 1998 (as amended) <http://www.legislation.gov.uk/ukpga/1998/41/section/47B>.

19 Fraud Act 2006, s 1,

> '(1) A person is guilty of fraud if he is in breach of any of the sections listed in subsection (2) (which provide for different ways of committing the offence).
> (2) The sections are—
> (a) section 2 (fraud by false representation),
> (b) section 3 (fraud by failing to disclose information), and
> (c) section 4 (fraud by abuse of position).
> (3) A person who is guilty of fraud is liable—
> (a) on summary conviction, to imprisonment for a term not exceeding 12 months or to a fine not exceeding the statutory maximum (or to both);
> (b) on conviction on indictment, to imprisonment for a term not exceeding 10 years or to a fine (or to both) …' <http://www.legislation.gov.uk/ukpga/2006/35/section/1>.

(Fraud Act 2006, section 2[20]), fraud by failing to disclose information (Fraud Act 2006, section 3[21]), or fraud by abuse of position (Fraud Act 2006, section 4[22]). Additionally, the Fraud Act 2006, section 7, also creates the offence of making or supplying articles for the use in frauds. On conviction this too carries a maximum penalty of ten years' imprisonment or an unlimited fine, or both.[23] Finally, where the foregoing offences are committed by a corporate body, then its senior management (directors, secretary, management etc.) could be liable for prosecution and conviction of those offences if they 'consented to' or 'connived' in the offending.[24] This requires individual members of senior management to take an active part in the criminal conduct.[25] The test for dishonesty as an element of these various offences is that set out in *Ivey v Genting Casinos (UK) Ltd* (2017).[26] It requires that:

> … the fact-finding tribunal must first ascertain (subjectively) the actual state of the individual's knowledge or belief as to the facts. The reasonableness or otherwise of

---

20 See <http://www.legislation.gov.uk/ukpga/2006/35/section/2>.

21 See <http://www.legislation.gov.uk/ukpga/2006/35/section/3>.

22 See <http://www.legislation.gov.uk/ukpga/2006/35/section/4>.

23 Fraud Act 2006, s 7,

> '(1) A person is guilty of an offence if he makes, adapts, supplies or offers to supply any article—
> (a) knowing that it is designed or adapted for use in the course of or in connection with fraud, or
> (b) intending it to be used to commit, or assist in the commission of, fraud.
> (2) A person guilty of an offence under this section is liable—
> (a) on summary conviction, to imprisonment for a term not exceeding 12 months or to a fine not exceeding the statutory maximum (or to both);
> (b) on conviction on indictment, to imprisonment for a term not exceeding 10 years or to a fine (or to both) …' <http://www.legislation.gov.uk/ukpga/2006/35/section/7>.

24 Fraud Act 2006, s 12,

> 'Subsection (2) applies if an offence under this Act is committed by a body corporate.
> (2) If the offence is proved to have been committed with the consent or connivance of—
> (a) a director, manager, secretary or other similar officer of the body corporate, or
> (b) a person who was purporting to act in any such capacity,
> he (as well as the body corporate) is guilty of the offence and liable to be proceeded against and punished accordingly.
> (3) If the affairs of a body corporate are managed by its members, subsection (2) applies in relation to the acts and defaults of a member in connection with his functions of management as if he were a director of the body corporate.' <http://www.legislation.gov.uk/ukpga/2006/35/section/12>.

25 See guidance issued by the Crown Prosecution Service, 'Legal Guidance – Fraud and economic crime', <http://www.cps.gov.uk/legal-guidance/fraud-act-2006> (hereafter CPS, 'Guidance').

26 *Ivey v Genting Casinos (UK) Ltd* [2017] UKSC 67; [2018] AC 391 at [74].

> his belief is a matter of evidence (often in practice determinative) going to whether he held the belief, but it is not an additional requirement that his belief must be reasonable; the question is whether it is genuinely held. When once his actual state of mind as to knowledge or belief as to facts is established, the question whether his conduct was honest or dishonest is to be determined by the fact-finder by applying the (objective) standards of ordinary decent people. There is no requirement that the defendant must appreciate that what he has done is, by those standards, dishonest.

Investigations and prosecutions in respect of offences of fraud can either be brought by the police and Crown Prosecution Service (CPS) or the SFO, as that latter body has a statutory remit to investigate 'any suspected offence which appears to (the SFO's Director) on reasonable grounds to involve serious or complex fraud'.[27] In both the present case studies, and in respect of the diesel scandal, the appropriate body for investigating and prosecuting would be the SFO due to the serious nature of the potential offending.

Turning specifically to the two case studies, and by analogy to the diesel scandal itself, prosecutions could arise in a number of situations. In so far as Case 1 is concerned, the most likely form of prosecution would arise against the corporate body, directors and senior managers for fraud by false representation, concerning the emission value data, fraud by failing to disclosure information, i.e. the true emission values, and, fraud by abuse of position, through using their positions of responsibility to procure false emission data and the development and use of devices to create such false data. Additionally, if emission value data was manipulated through the application of a computer programme installed in the vehicles, a prosecution under Fraud Act 2007, section 7 could be brought.[28] In so far as Case 2 is concerned, prosecutions could, in principle, be pursued for fraud by false representation, fraud by failing to disclose information, and as in the Tesco case, for fraud by abuse of position. Such prosecutions could be brought against directors, senior managers as well as the corporate body. To secure convictions it would, variously, be necessary to demonstrate that the emission value data was false, that the individuals concerned, and the company itself, were responsible for the false data, and that dishonesty was involved to the requisite standard.

2. *Conspiracy to Defraud*

English law contains both criminal offences that arise under statute, such as the Fraud Act 2006, and under common law, i.e. its judge-made law. One such common law offence is that of conspiracy to defraud. A conspiracy arises where

---

27 Criminal Justice Act 1987, s 1 <http://www.legislation.gov.uk/ukpga/1987/38/section/1>.

28 In October 2015 it was reported that the SFO was considering investigating Volkswagen for issues of 'corporate criminality', see Hughes, 'Volkswagen' (n 7).

there is an agreement between at least two people to enter into criminal activity; in this case to commit fraud. The conspiracy need not be put into effect; the offence of conspiracy is complete when agreement is reached.[29] It is irrelevant to the offence whether it is put into effect, or whether the parties to the conspiracy change their minds before putting it into effect: repentance and withdrawal from the conspiracy are only relevant, if that, in respect of sentence.[30] The nature of the common law offence of conspiracy was summarised by Lord Diplock in *Scott v Commissioner of Police of the Metropolis* (1975) as follows:

> … (2) Where the intended victim of a 'conspiracy to defraud' is a private individual the purpose of the conspirators must be to cause the victim economic loss by depriving him of some property or right, corporeal or incorporeal, to which he is or would or might become entitled. The intended means by which the purpose is to be achieved must be dishonest. They need not involve fraudulent misrepresentation such as is needed to constitute the civil tort of deceit. Dishonesty of any kind is enough.
>
> (3) Where the intended victim of a "conspiracy to defraud" is a person performing public duties as distinct from a private individual it is sufficient if the purpose is to cause him to act contrary to his public duty, and the intended means of achieving this purpose are dishonest. The purpose need not involve causing economic loss to anyone.[31]

Again, the test of dishonesty is that set out in *Ivey v Genting Casinos (UK) Ltd* (2017). Additionally, there is a statutory offence of conspiracy, which arises under the Criminal Law Act 1977, section 1.[32] Prosecutions can be brought for both offences.[33] Upon conviction of common law and statutory conspiracy, an individual may be sentenced according to the tariff applicable to the offence of fraud, i.e. a maximum sentence of ten years' imprisonment or an unlimited fine, or both.[34] Assuming the elements of both common law and the statutory offence of conspiracy were made out, prosecutions could in principle succeed against the directors and any senior managers of the company in Case 1 arising

---

29 *R v Tibbits & Windust* [1902] 1 KB 77, 89.

30 *O'Connell v R* [1844] 5 St Tr (NS) 1; *R v Aspinall* [1876] 2 QBD 48; *R v Gortat and Pirog* [1973] Crim L R 648; *R v Bolton* [1992] 94 Cr App R 7.

31 *Scott v Commissioner of Police of the Metropolis* [1975] AC 819, 841 per Lord Diplock.

32 See <http://www.legislation.gov.uk/ukpga/1977/45/section/1>.

33 *R v Rimmington* [2005] UKHL 63; [2006] AC 459 at [30], 'I would not go to the length of holding that conduct may never be lawfully prosecuted as a generally-expressed common law crime where it falls within the terms of a specific statutory provision, but good practice and respect for the primacy of statute do in my judgment require that conduct falling within the terms of a specific statutory provision should be prosecuted under that provision unless there is good reason for doing otherwise.'

34 Criminal Law Act 1977, s 3 and CPS, 'Guidance' (n 25), Inchoate Offences <http://www.cps.gov.uk/legal-guidance/inchoate-offences>.

out of any decision to utilise devices to produce false emission data, with the aim of causing financial loss to the individual purchasers of their vehicles. That financial loss would, it would appear, relate to the value of the car purchased. Equally, the conspiracy to defraud could relate to the provision of false emission data to public officials responsible for vehicle licensing, with the intention of causing them to act contrary to their public duty to licence vehicles properly under the Road Vehicles (Approval) Regulations 2009.

3. *Offences under the Theft Act 1968*

Liability could also arise under the Theft Act 1968, section 17, which creates the offence of fraud by false accounting.[35] As with offences under the Fraud Act 2006, where this offence is committed by a corporate body, its officers, if they consented or connived in the criminality, may too be prosecuted under this offence.[36] Additionally under section 19 of the 1968 Act, a director may be liable of the offence of issuing false statements with the intent to deceive members or creditors of a corporate body.[37] The maximum sentence for these three offences is seven years' imprisonment. In principle this offence could arise in Case 2 in so far as the individual who provided the insider information was also involved in producing any false accounting record that was published to the market.

4. *Offences under the Road Vehicles (Approval) Regulations 2009*

Finally, two possible offences could arise under regulation 33(4)[38] and/or regulation 33A of the 2009 Regulations. The latter provision, however, only applies to conduct that occurred post-5 October 2018, as it was inserted into the 2009 Regulations as a consequence of the diesel scandal in order to render the use of defeat devices, such as those alleged to have been used by Volkswagen, a specific offence.[39] Both offences could, in principle, apply in the first case study.

Regulation 33(4) of the 2009 Regulations, which attracts a maximum sentence of £5,000 if proceedings are brought in the Magistrates' courts, or an unlimited fine if brought in the Crown Court, creates the offence of knowingly or recklessly supplying false information for the purpose of road vehicle approval by the

35 See <http://www.legislation.gov.uk/ukpga/1968/60/section/17>.

36 See <http://www.legislation.gov.uk/ukpga/1968/60/section/18>.

37 See <http://www.legislation.gov.uk/ukpga/1968/60/section/19>.

38 SI 2009/707, <http://www.legislation.gov.uk/uksi/2009/717/contents/made>.

39 SI 2018/737, <http://www.legislation.gov.uk/uksi/2018/673/contents/made>.

Vehicle Certification Authority.[40] Regulation 33A of the 2009 Regulations makes it an offence to market or register in the UK a vehicle that has an unlawful defeat device fitted. An offence is committed for each vehicle placed on the market or registered.[41] Upon conviction a person guilty of manufacturing such a vehicle and marketing or registering it, is liable for imprisonment of up to three months per offence, in an individual rather than a corporate body, and/or a fine. A civil penalty may also be imposed of up to £50,000 payable to the VCA. Should a civil penalty be paid to the VCA no criminal penalty will be imposed. A civil penalty may only be imposed if it appears, on the balance of probabilities to the VCA, that a criminal offence has been committed by the person, and that criminal proceedings have not been initiated against the person and the person has no reasonable excuse for committing the offence.[42]

---

40 Regulation 2009/707, regulation 33

'… (4) A person commits an offence if, in supplying information or producing a document for the purpose of these Regulations, that person—
(a) makes a statement which that person knows to be false in a material particular or recklessly makes a statement which is false in a material particular, or
(b) produces, provides, sends or otherwise makes use of a document which that person knows to be false in a material particular or recklessly produces, provides or sends or otherwise makes use of a document which is false in a material particular.
(5) A person who contravenes regulation 16, 22(1) or 23(1) commits an offence.
(6) A person guilty of an offence under paragraph (4) or (5) is liable—
(a) on summary conviction, to a fine not exceeding the statutory maximum, or
(b) on conviction on indictment, to a fine.'

<http://www.legislation.gov.uk/uksi/2009/717/regulation/33/made>.

41 Regulation 33A,

'(1) A person who is a manufacturer is guilty of an offence if a motor vehicle manufactured by that person—
(a) is placed on the market or registered in the United Kingdom; and
(b) that motor vehicle is fitted with a defeat system which is not permitted.
(2) A separate offence under paragraph (1) is committed in respect of each such motor vehicle placed on the market or registered.
(3) A defeat system is not permitted unless—
(a) in the case of a motor vehicle to which Regulation (EC) 595/2009 applies, the fitting and operation of the defeat system is explained in the extended documentation package submitted by the manufacturer to the approval authority (as defined in Article 3(29) of the Framework Directive) when applying for emissions type approval for that vehicle; or
(b) in the case of a motor vehicle to which Regulation (EC) 715/2007 applies—
(i) its use falls within one of the exceptions listed in Article 5(2)(a) to (c) of that Regulation; and
(ii) in respect of a motor vehicle submitted for emissions type approval after 16th May 2016, the fitting and operation of the defeat system is explained in the documentation package submitted by the manufacturer to the approval authority (as defined in Article 3(29) of the Framework Directive) when applying for emissions type approval for that vehicle …'

<http://www.legislation.gov.uk/uksi/2018/673/regulation/16/made>.

42 See 2009 Regulations, sch 7 paras 2 and 3.

5. *Consumer Protection from Unfair Trading Regulations 2008*

The Consumer Protection from Unfair Trading Regulations 2008,[43] which implemented the Unfair Commercial Practices Directive (UCPD, Directive 2005/29/EC) into UK Law, provides a further basis of criminal liability in respect of the two case studies. Its particular focus would be Case 1. Regulation 3 of the 2008 Regulations prohibits unfair commercial practices,[44] of which the most pertinent to the present case study and the diesel scandal is that prohibited by regulations 5 and 6 of the 2008 Regulations: the prohibition on misleading actions[45] and on

43 SI 2008/1277, <http://www.legislation.gov.uk/uksi/2008/1277/contents/made>.

44 Regulation 3,

'(1) Unfair commercial practices are prohibited.
(2) Paragraphs (3) and (4) set out the circumstances when a commercial practice is unfair.
(3) A commercial practice is unfair if—
  (a) it contravenes the requirements of professional diligence; and
  (b) it materially distorts or is likely to materially distort the economic behaviour of the average consumer with regard to the product.
(4) A commercial practice is unfair if—
  (a) it is a misleading action under the provisions of regulation 5;
  (b) it is a misleading omission under the provisions of regulation 6; …' <http://www.legislation.gov.uk/uksi/2008/1277/regulation/3/made>.

45 Regulation 5,

'(1) A commercial practice is a misleading action if it satisfies the conditions in either paragraph (2) or paragraph (3).
(2) A commercial practice satisfies the conditions of this paragraph—
  (a) if it contains false information and is therefore untruthful in relation to any of the matters in paragraph (4) or if it or its overall presentation in any way deceives or is likely to deceive the average consumer in relation to any of the matters in that paragraph, even if the information is factually correct; and
  (b) it causes or is likely to cause the average consumer to take a transactional decision he would not have taken otherwise.
(3) A commercial practice satisfies the conditions of this paragraph if—
  (a) it concerns any marketing of a product (including comparative advertising) which creates confusion with any products, trade marks, trade names or other distinguishing marks of a competitor; or
  (b) it concerns any failure by a trader to comply with a commitment contained in a code of conduct which the trader has undertaken to comply with, if—
    (i) the trader indicates in a commercial practice that he is bound by that code of conduct, and
    (ii) the commitment is firm and capable of being verified and is not aspirational,
  and it causes or is likely to cause the average consumer to take a transactional decision he would not have taken otherwise, taking account of its factual context and of all its features and circumstances.
(4) …' <http://www.legislation.gov.uk/uksi/2008/1277/regulation/5/made>.

misleading omissions.[46] Action in respect of the Regulations is a matter for the CMA. Again, liability for action taken by a corporate body may also be visited on its managers if they consented or connived in its carrying out.[47] Upon conviction from a prosecution brought in the Magistrates' court, a maximum fine of £5,000

---

46 Regulation 6,

'(1) A commercial practice is a misleading omission if, in its factual context, taking account of the matters in paragraph (2)—
(a) the commercial practice omits material information,
(b) the commercial practice hides material information,
(c) the commercial practice provides material information in a manner which is unclear, unintelligible, ambiguous or untimely, or
(d) the commercial practice fails to identify its commercial intent, unless this is already apparent from the context,
and as a result it causes or is likely to cause the average consumer to take a transactional decision he would not have taken otherwise.
(2) The matters referred to in paragraph (1) are—
(a) all the features and circumstances of the commercial practice;
(b) the limitations of the medium used to communicate the commercial practice (including limitations of space or time); and
(c) where the medium used to communicate the commercial practice imposes limitations of space or time, any measures taken by the trader to make the information available to consumers by other means.
(3) In paragraph (1) "material information" means—
(a) the information which the average consumer needs, according to the context, to take an informed transactional decision; and
(b) any information requirement which applies in relation to a commercial communication as a result of a Community obligation.
(4) ...' <http://www.legislation.gov.uk/uksi/2008/1277/regulation/6/made>.

47 Regulation 15,

'(1) Where an offence under these Regulations committed by a body corporate is proved—
(a) to have been committed with the consent or connivance of an officer of the body, or
(b) to be attributable to any neglect on his part,
the officer as well as the body corporate is guilty of the offence and liable to be proceeded against and punished accordingly.
(2) In paragraph (1) a reference to an officer of a body corporate includes a reference to—
(a) a director, manager, secretary or other similar officer; and
(b) a person purporting to act as a director, manager, secretary or other similar officer.
(3) Where an offence under these Regulations committed by a Scottish partnership is proved—
(a) to have been committed with the consent or connivance of a partner, or
(b) to be attributable to any neglect on his part,
the partner as well as the partnership is guilty of the offence and liable to be proceeded against and punished accordingly.
(4) In paragraph (3) a reference to a partner includes a person purporting to act as a partner.'
<http://www.legislation.gov.uk/uksi/2008/1277/regulation/15/made>.

can be imposed, while if a prosecution is brought in the Crown Court, two years' imprisonment could be ordered and/or an unlimited fine.[48]

B. REGULATORY MEASURES

There is one specific regulatory measure that could be taken in addition to, or in the alternative to, criminal proceedings. The particular focus of this mechanism is the situation outlined in the second case study. It arises under the Financial Services and Markets Act 2000, and concerns market abuse. In principle, as a consequence, the following regulatory measures could be applied in the second case study.[49]

1. *Financial Services and Markets Act 2000 Pre-2016*

Prior to 3 July 2016, when the Financial Services and Markets Act 2000 (FSMA) was amended by the Financial Services and Markets Act 2000 (Market Abuse) Regulations 2016, which in turn reflected Regulation (EU) No 596/2014 of the European Parliament and of the Council of 16 April 2014 on market abuse (the Market Abuse Regulation), regulatory action could have been taken by the Financial Conduct Authority (FCA). Specifically, it could have investigated the individual member of the company's management in the second case study, and by analogy Volkswagen in the diesel scandal, under what was then FSMA, section 118.[50] The specific forms of market abuse in this context would have been insider dealing, contrary to what was section 118(2), or of trading relying on information not generally available to those trading in the market, contrary to section 118(4). The member of the management board selling their shares would fall under the ambit of both sections. Should a positive finding be made under these provisions, the FCA could, in its absolute discretion, impose an unlimited fine under FSMA, section 123 (as it then was).[51] Where it was considering issuing a fine, the FCA had to first issue a warning notice setting out

48 Regulations 9, 10 and 13 of the 2008 Regulations <http://www.legislation.gov.uk/uksi/2008/1277/regulation/13/made>.

49 As they were in the Tesco case, see below (n 62).

50 See <http://www.legislation.gov.uk/ukpga/2000/8/section/118/2014-12-15>.

51 S 123,

> '(1) If the FCA is satisfied that a person ("A")—
> (a) is or has engaged in market abuse, or
> (b) by taking or refraining from taking any action has required or encouraged another person or persons to engage in behaviour which, if engaged in by A, would amount to market abuse,
> it may impose on him a penalty of such amount as it considers appropriate.

that fact to the individual concerned under FSMA, section 126.[52] If it were then to issue a fine, it then had to issue a Decision Notice to that effect, from which the individual could refer the matter to the relevant tribunal.[53]

In addition to action against regulatory fines against individuals the FCA could also have taken action to secure compensation for individuals who had suffered a loss as a consequence of the market abuse. Under FSMA, section 383, at that time, the FCA had power, where there had been a finding of market abuse, to apply to the court for an order requiring such an individual to pay such damages.[54] In assessing the level of damages to be paid, the court had to take account of the nature of the profits made as a result of the market abuse and the loss suffered by the individuals to whom damages are to be paid.

2. *Financial Services and Markets Act 2000 Post-2016*

In July 2016 the FSMA market abuse regime changed as a consequence of the 2016 Regulations and the Market Abuse Regulation. This extended the

---

> (2) But the FCA may not impose a penalty on a person if, having considered any representations made to it in response to a warning notice, there are reasonable grounds for it to be satisfied that—
> (a) he believed, on reasonable grounds, that his behaviour did not fall within paragraph (a) or (b) of subsection (1), or
> (b) he took all reasonable precautions and exercised all due diligence to avoid behaving in a way which fell within paragraph (a) or (b) of that subsection.
> (3) If the FCA is entitled to impose a penalty on a person under this section it may, instead of imposing a penalty on him, publish a statement to the effect that he has engaged in market abuse.'

<http://www.legislation.gov.uk/ukpga/2000/8/section/123/2014-12-15>.

52 S 126,

> '(1) If the FCA proposes to take action against a person under section 123, it must give him a warning notice.
> (2) A warning notice about a proposal to impose a penalty must state the amount of the proposed penalty.
> (3) A warning notice about a proposal to publish a statement must set out the terms of the proposed statement.'

<http://www.legislation.gov.uk/ukpga/2000/8/section/126/2014-12-15>.

53 S 127,

> 'If the FCA decides to take action against a person under section 123, it must give him a decision notice.
> (2) A decision notice about the imposition of a penalty must state the amount of the penalty.
> (3) A decision notice about the publication of a statement must set out the terms of the statement.
> (4) If the FCA decides to take action against a person under section 123, that person may refer the matter to the Tribunal.'

<http://www.legislation.gov.uk/ukpga/2000/8/section/127/2014-12-15>.

54 See <http://www.legislation.gov.uk/ukpga/2000/8/section/383/2013-04-01>.

FCA's regulatory powers through repealing the provisions, referred to above, and inserting sections 122A to 131AE into FSMA.[55] These provisions provide the FCA with a range of investigatory powers, e.g. to require the provision of information from issuers, managers of issuers or those closely connected to such managers, to enter premises, and retain documents; with powers to require market actors to issue corrective statements; with power to suspend trading by market actors; to impose an unlimited fine on individuals or issue a written censure of those individuals who have been found to have engaged in market abuse; and, the power to suspend such individuals from holding or selling financial instruments. Before taking such steps the FCA must issue the individual with a warning notice setting out the proposed action, which the individual concerned may refer to the Upper Tribunal in order to challenge the proposed action. The substantive provisions concerning the prohibition on persons of insider dealing and market manipulation are contained in articles 14 and 15 of the Market Abuse Regulation.[56] That Regulation will continue to form part of UK law, as retained EU law[57] following the UK's withdrawal from the European Union.[58] Regulatory liability, and a penalty, may also arise where the FCA concludes that a person has breached corporate governance rules.[59]

III. PRIVATE LAW ISSUES

Individual consumers who had suffered loss as a consequence of the actions described in the two case studies could potentially bring a number of different claims seeking redress. Such private law claims could proceed at the same time as any criminal or regulatory proceedings were ongoing. There is nothing to prevent such multiple forms of proceeding being brought simultaneously. By way of example, in the Tesco case,[60] which is broadly comparable to Case 2, criminal proceedings were taken forward at the same time as public regulatory action, and at the time that private law actions were taken. The criminal

55 See the Financial Services and Markets Act 2000 (Market Abuse) Regulations 2016, SI 2016/680 <http://www.legislation.gov.uk/uksi/2016/680/contents/made>.

56 The power to impose penalties for breaches of these articles is contained in FSMA, s 123. The power to prohibit individuals from managing or dealing in breach of these articles is contained in FSMA, s 123A.

57 European Union (Withdrawal) Act 2018 (Withdrawal Act), s 3 <http://www.legislation.gov.uk/ukpga/2018/16/section/3/enacted>.

58 Ibid, ss 1 and 20 (2) <http://www.legislation.gov.uk/ukpga/2018/16/contents/enacted>; The European Union (Withdrawal) Act 2018 (Exit Day) (Amendment) (No 2) Regulations 2019, SI 2019/859.

59 See FSMA, s 90 <http://www.legislation.gov.uk/ukpga/2000/8/section/91>.

60 FCA, 'Press Release' (n 17).

prosecution culminated in a deferred prosecution agreement (DPA)[61] for Tesco Stores Plc for false accounting, whilst individual prosecutions continued against specific directors.[62] As part of the DPA, Tesco agreed to pay a financial penalty of nearly £129 million as well as the full costs of the criminal prosecution. It is also reported to have agreed to a regulatory finding of market abuse, contrary to, the then in force, FSMA, section 118(7), with the FCA. The consequence of which was that it agreed to pay approximately £85 million into a statutory compensation scheme under FSMA, section 384, with compensation then being available to approximately 10,000 investors both individual and institutional.[63] One consequence of this for private law actions against Tesco was that should the individual claimants accept compensation under the scheme, they had to release Tesco from any potential civil liability, i.e. accepting compensation acted as an effective settlement or waiver of the claimant's strict private law rights.[64] A similar approach could be taken in respect of the matters outlined in Case 2, should multiple forms of proceedings be taken forward. Where civil proceedings are concerned multiple causes of action can, and should if available, be pursued in a single claim by each individual claimant.[65]

Turning to the two case studies, the following private law actions could potentially be pursued against the corporate bodies and/or their directors or senior managers. They are as follows.

A. BREACH OF IMPLIED TERM UNDER THE SALE OF GOODS ACT 1979

Section 14 of the Sale of Goods Act 1979[66] implies into contracts to which the Consumer Rights Act 2015 does not apply, i.e. those entered into prior

---

61 A DPA is a form of plea-bargaining approach introduced into the English criminal justice via sch 17 of the Crime and Courts Act 2013 <http://www.legislation.gov.uk/ukpga/2013/22/schedule/17/enacted>. It enables a defendant in criminal proceedings to enter into a binding agreement with the CPS, whereby prosecution will be deferred for a set period upon the defendant complying with various conditions under the agreement.

62 The prosecution of the directors ultimately failed. The case was thrown out by the judge without having to be put to a jury, see Max Walters, 'SFO under fire for "fundamental misunderstanding" in Tesco trial' (*The Law Gazette*, 6 December 2018) <http://www.lawgazette.co.uk/law/sfo-under-fire-for-fundamental-misunderstanding-in-tesco-trial/5068603.article>. The failure called into question whether a DPA should have been entered into by Tesco.

63 For an outline see Clyde & Co, 'Tesco: DPA and redress scheme announced … but what of the shareholder action?' <http://www.clydeco.com/blog/insurance-hub/article/tesco-dpa-and-redress-scheme-announcedbut-what-of-the-shareholder-action>. The scheme was put in place and run by KPMG, see <http://www.home.kpmg/uk/en/home/services/advisory/tesco-scheme.html>.

64 Damien Bryne Hill et al, *Class Actions in England and Wales* (Sweet & Maxwell 2018) 442 (hereafter Bryne Hill, 'Class Actions').

65 CPR r 7.3 <http://www.justice.gov.uk/courts/procedure-rules/civil/rules/part07#7.3>.

66 See <http://www.legislation.gov.uk/ukpga/1979/54/section/14>.

to 1 October 2015,[67] an implied term that the goods are of satisfactory quality. This includes fitness for purpose, durability and safety. Such actions would lie between the consumer and the business from whom the purchased the vehicle, i.e. the person with whom the consumer entered the sales contract.

B. ACTIONS UNDER THE CONSUMER PROTECTION ACT 1987

Under sections 2 and 5 of the Consumer Protection Act 1987 a producer of a product can be held liable for any damage arising from a defect in it caused to a consumer. Damage refers to personal injury, death or damage to land. In the present case studies, this would thus only apply if it could be shown that a consumer had suffered personal injury as a consequence of the manufacturer in the first case study manipulating the emission data, and that the means by which it did so was a product defect. It might be thought to be unlikely that such a claim would be capable of being borne out, given the need to demonstrate personal injury as a consequence of excess vehicle emissions.

C. ACTIONS FOR FALSE MISPRESENTATION UNDER THE MISREPRESENTATION ACT 1967 OR FOR THE TORT OF DECEIT

Two possible actions could arise. The first would be for false misrepresentation. This arises under the Misrepresentation Act 1967, section 2.1.[68] It applies where an individual enters a contract following a misrepresentation made by another person and as a consequence has suffered loss.[69] The misrepresentation need only be false and not fraudulent. In Case 1, such false representations could include representations concerning the vehicle's emission data. Where the person making the representation proves that they had reasonable grounds to believe and did believe in the truth of the state at the time the contract was made, damages will not be available. In Case 1 it must be questionable at best if such could be borne out. The nature of damages is tortious and equate to those that would otherwise be available under the tort of deceit.

---

67 Generally, this has been overtaken by comparable provision in the Consumer Rights Act 2015, see s 9 <http://www.legislation.gov.uk/ukpga/2015/15/section/9/enacted>. However, as the case studies are assumed to refer to conduct carried out prior to its entry into force on 1 October 2015, it would not apply and civil claims would thus need to be brought under the 1979 Act, see Consumer Rights Act 2015 (Commencement No 3, Transitional Provisions, Savings and Consequential Amendments) Order 2015/1630, art 3.

68 See <http://www.legislation.gov.uk/ukpga/1967/7>.

69 Damages are not available under the 1967 Act if they are available under Part 4A of the Consumer Protection from Unfair Trading Regulations 2008, see the 1967 Act, s 2(4).

The second form of action would arise under the tort of deceit.[70] This arises where loss has arisen as a consequence of a representation made by an individual to another individual, where that representation is false and the individual making it either knows it to be false or is reckless as to its truth. Where deceit is established all damage flowing directly from the contract is recoverable, even if the damages were not foreseeable.[71] Rescission may also be available as a remedy.[72] In the circumstances set out in the first case study, it is possible that, unusually, the tort of deceit could be made out.

D. ACTION FOR REDRESS UNDER PART 4A OF THE CONSUMER PROTECTION FROM UNFAIR TRADING REGULATIONS 2008

Part 4A of the Consumer Protection from Unfair Trading Regulations 2008 introduced a number of specific remedies to protect consumers from unfair trading practices. Specifically, breach of the 2008 Regulations creates a civil right of action for consumers under regulations 27A to 27J. Claims arise when consumers enter into contracts with businesses,[73] where the business has engaged in a 'prohibited practice' under, as relevant here, regulation 5 of the 2008 Regulations, i.e. they have engaged in a 'misleading practice', i.e. in Case 1, a practice to mask the true emissions data for the manufactured vehicles. Successful actions provide a basis to rescind, i.e. unwind a consumer contract and/or provide an entitlement to damages; damages under the Regulations unlike normal contractual damages are recoverable for 'alarm, distress or physical inconvenience or discomfort which the consumer would not have suffered if the prohibited practice in question had not taken place'.[74]

E. AN ACTION FOR BREACH OF OBLIGATIONS ARISING UNDER EC REGULATION 715/2007 AMOUNTS TO A BREACH OF STATUTORY DUTY OR OTHER TORTIOUS LIABILITY

One of the issues in the VW NOx Emissions Group Litigation[75] is whether an action lies for breach of statutory duty or another form of *sui generis* tortious

---

70 *Derry v Peek* [1889] 14 App Cas 337.

71 *Smith New Court Securities Ltd v Scrimgeour Vickers (Asset Management) Ltd* [1997] AC 254.

72 See generally Hugh Beale, *Chitty on Contracts* (33rd edn, Sweet & Maxwell 2018), chs 7, ss 3 and 4.

73 The term used in the Regulations is 'trader', but this has a wide definition and encompasses anyone engaged in a commercial practice in respect of their business, see *R (Surrey Trading Standards) v Scottish and Southern Energy Plc* [2012] EWCA Crim 539; [2014] LLR 780.

74 Regulation 27J(1)(b) of the 2008 Regulations. Ordinarily such damages are not available for contract claims, see *Jarvis v Swans Tours Ltd* [1973] QB 233.

75 See (n 11).

liability arises for breach of the obligations by a manufacturer for breach of the Type Approval Regulation, i.e. the regulation governing approval of motor vehicles in respect of environmental emissions.[76] Assuming it is established that such tortious liability exists, then the normal measures of tortious damages would apply.

F. AN ACTION UNDER FSMA FOR MARKET ABUSE

At the present time it is unclear whether there is a private cause of action for market abuse. Prior to the Market Abuse Regulation coming into force, it was held that there was no such private cause of action in English law, see *Hall v Cable and Wireless Plc* (2009).[77] Given the Court of Appeal decision in *R (United Road Transport Union) v Secretary of State for Transport* (2013),[78] which rejected the contention that such a private right and cause of action arose under Regulation 561/2006 in circumstances where individuals had other available remedies, it may be the case that given the existence of regulatory action and regulatory compensation for market abuse, the courts may also refuse to affirm the existence of such a private right. Given the possibility of such alternative regulatory or compensatory measures available in relation to breaches of the Type Approval Regulation, as above, the same position may be taken by the English courts in respect of the question whether such a private action arises as a *sui generis* tort.

IV. CIVIL PROCEDURAL MECHANISMS CONCERNING PRIVATE ACTIONS

In this part of the report, a number of discrete questions concerning English civil procedure and its applicability to the prosecution of private law claims is considered. As English civil procedure is generally trans-substantive, i.e. the same procedure applies irrespective of the cause of action, there are no general procedural simplifications for consumer or capital market law claims. Simplification may be applicable, however, depending on the value of specific claims. Assuming, for instance, that the individual claims in Case 1 were below

---

76 European Parliament and Council Regulation (EC) No 715/2007 of 20 June 2007 on type approval of motor vehicles with respect to emissions from light passenger and commercial vehicles (Euro 5 and Euro 6) and on access to vehicle repair and maintenance information [2007] OJ L171/1.

77 *Hall v Cable and Wireless Plc* [2009] EWHC 1793 (Comm); [2011] BCC 543.

78 *R (United Road Transport Union) v Secretary of State for Transport* [2013] EWCA Civ 962; [2014] 1 CMLR 25.

£10,000, they would be allocated to the small claims procedure (CPR Pt 27[79]). That has a simplified form of process, with limited disclosure of evidence, limited expert evidence, short trials of one hour to half a day, relaxation of the rules of evidence, and a more investigative approach by the judge trying the claim than is ordinarily the case in England's adversarial process. Such simplification would be unlikely to be applied to capital market law claims, except where individual shareholder's claims were also within the small claims limit.

In each of the forms of multi-party action to be discussed below, any relevant limitation period (under the Limitation Act 1980[80]) would cease to run from the point in time that the individual claim is issued. Limitation periods are not capable of suspension. This is the case even for the representative action, described below, where limitation continues to run for represented parties.[81] This position was criticised in 2008 by the Civil Justice Council, in its Report on Collective Redress Reform in England, which noted that primary legislation would be needed to rectify this position.[82]

A. WHAT FORMS OF COLLECTIVE ACTIONS ARE AVAILABLE (CLASS ACTION, REPRESENTATIVE ACTION, ETC.)?

There are a number of means by which multi-party litigation can be conducted. They can be divided into two categories: first, case management measures; and secondly, collective redress mechanisms. In respect of the second category, it would not be appropriate to describe the mechanisms as collective proceedings, as only one of them – as will be seen – is a true collective proceeding. The case management mechanisms are: test cases; joinder of proceedings; and consolidation of proceedings. The collective redress mechanisms are: Group Litigations (GLOs) under CPR rr 19.1–19.15 and CPR PD19B;[83] and, representative actions under CPR r 19.6.[84]

---

79 See <http://www.justice.gov.uk/courts/procedure-rules/civil/rules/part27>.

80 See <http://www.legislation.gov.uk/ukpga/1980/58/contents>.

81 *Moon v Atherton* [1972] 2 QB 435 (hereafter *Moon v Atherton*).

82 John Sorabji, Michael Napier and Robert Musgrove (eds), *'Improving Access to Justice through Collective Actions' – Developing a More Efficient and Effective Procedure to Collective Actions: Final Report* (Civil Justice Council of England and Wales, London, November 2008) 125–27, 145ff <http://www.judiciary.uk/wp-content/uploads/JCO/Documents/CJC/Publications/CJC+papers/CJC+Improving+Access+to+Justice+through+Collective+Actions.pdf>; Ministry of Justice, *The Government's Response to the Civil Justice Council's Report: 'Improving Access to Justice through Collective Actions'* (Ministry of Justice, London, July 2009).

83 See <http://www.justice.gov.uk/courts/procedure-rules/civil/rules/part19#III> and <http://www.justice.gov.uk/courts/procedure-rules/civil/rules/part19/pd_part19b>.

84 See<http://www.justice.gov.uk/courts/procedure-rules/civil/rules/part19#II>. The representative action is, in fact, the original form of class action: see, John Sorabji, 'The Hidden Class Action in English Civil Procedure' (2009) 28 CJQ 498.

The different mechanisms are as follows, in respect of each mechanism however it should be noted that the decisions do not bind other future claims except and in so far as the doctrine of precedent operates.

1. *Case Management Mechanisms*

a) Test Cases

Where a large number of individual claims share a common legal or factual issue, it is possible for one or a small number of them to be treated by the civil courts as a 'test case'. Where this occurs one or two claims will be selected by the court to go forward to trial and judgment; although that does not preclude the parties from settling those claims. Selection of the case or cases to go forward is not subject to any specific rules. There is no science to it, although generally the most representative case will be selected to go forward by a procedural judge. Where a test case settles prior to judgment, the court will then select a further case to go forward as a new test case. There is no specific procedural rule dealing with test cases, they are managed under the court's general case management powers in CPR r 3.1[85] or its inherent jurisdiction.

Once a case is selected to go forward, the other claims will be subject to either a formal stay of proceedings or an 'informal stay'; the former occurs by way of a formal court order, the latter, through the courts simply not listing the other claims for hearing until the test cases have been resolved. Unlike the test case procedure in, for instance, Germany,[86] the judgment in the test case does not bind the parties in the other claims. Its effect is to determine the common legal or factual issue only. As a precedent on the legal or factual issue, the test case decision will serve as a basis upon which the other claims can be settled by agreement or discontinued by the claimants. Alternatively, it can serve to narrow the issues in dispute in those other claims, enabling them to proceed to trial on the issues that are unique to those individual claims in a more efficient and cost-effective manner.

A recent example of this approach in the field of consumer protection is the 'bank charges' litigation. Thousands of individual claims were issued by bank customers against their banks. The claims alleged that the customers had been charged unlawful penalty charges for going overdrawn on their accounts. A single claim was selected to go forward to consider the legal issue as to whether the bank charges were unlawful penalties. In this case the claimant that brought

---

85 See <http://www.justice.gov.uk/courts/procedure-rules/civil/rules/part03#3.1>.

86 Michael Stuerner, 'Model case proceedings in the capital markets – tentative steps towards group litigation in Germany' (2007) 26 CJQ 250.

the test case was a regulatory body, the Office of Fair Trading,[87] as in this case it had at the time a statutory basis on which to bring the claim concerning the legal issue,[88] which concerned the correct interpretation of regulation 6(2) of the Unfair Terms in Consumer Contracts Regulations 1999 (SI 1999/2083). In the absence of that any one of the individual claims brought by a bank customer could have been selected to go forward.[89]

Test cases could be used in either of the scenarios set out in the case studies provided that sufficient numbers of claims arising from the scenarios were issued by individual claimants.

b) Consolidation or Joinder of Individual Proceedings

Two more formal case management mechanisms for dealing with multi-party litigation are consolidation of proceedings under CPR r 3.1(2)(g)[90] and joinder of proceedings under CPR r 3.1(2)(h).[91]

Consolidation can be ordered where large numbers of claims raise a common issue of fact or law and the relief claimed arose out of or relates to the same factual matrix. It would thus be a potential means of managing the claims arising in the two case studies. The effect of consolidation is to merge the multiple individual claims into a single claim with multiple claimants (or defendants). In one example of this procedure over 3,000 individual claims were consolidated into a single claim with over 3,000 claimants and one defendant.[92] Once claims are consolidated, as a general rule, the various claimants must be represented by the same legal representative.[93]

Joinder is similar to consolidation except that the multiple individual claims remain individual sets of proceedings. It simply ensures that the various claims are case managed and then tried together. Thus increasing procedural efficiency and cost-effectiveness, while removing the risk of multiple inconsistent decisions taken by different judges on the same or similar issue.

Of the two forms of proceedings it is likely that consolidation would be more appropriate for the first, the consumer, case study, whereas joinder would be more appropriate for the second, the capital markets, case study. While there are no specific rules or guidelines for the court to consider in exercising its case management discretion to order consolidation or joinder, it would do so

---

87 It was dissolved in 2014, and its consumer protection responsibilities transferred to the Trading Standards Service.
88 See Enterprise Act 2002, pt 1 <http://www.legislation.gov.uk/ukpga/2002/40/part/1>.
89 See *The Office of Fair Trading v Abbey National Plc* [2010] 1 AC 696.
90 See <http://www.justice.gov.uk/courts/procedure-rules/civil/rules/part03#3.1>.
91 See <http://www.justice.gov.uk/courts/procedure-rules/civil/rules/part03#3.1>.
92 *Lubbe v Cape Plc* [2000] 1 WLR 1545.
93 Bryne Hill, 'Class Actions' (n 64) 9.

according to the CPR's overriding objective (CPR r 1[94]). That requires the court, amongst other things, to ensure that claims are tried proportionately, which includes at proportionate cost, that they secure equality of arms, and are tried as economically and efficiently as possible.

A court would be likely to hold that where there are large numbers of consumer claims, which in Case 1 are likely to be allocated to the small claims track (as individual claims below the value of £10,000), they ought to be subject to consolidation. In that way, economies of scale for the claimants can be promoted by requiring one legal representative to act for the parties, and by providing for the individual claimants to be jointly and severally liable for the litigation costs, i.e. sharing the litigation risk, and through these points promoting greater equality of arms. Where, as in the capital markets case, there is the possibility that a number or a large number of the claimants would be sophisticated investors, each bringing high or relatively high-value claims, the same issues would not arise and the court would be more likely to join the claims, or permit one or several to go forward as test cases.

2. *Collective Redress Mechanisms*

a) The Representative Action

This form of collective proceeding was devised as an action in Chancery proceedings in the Middle Ages. It is the original form of class action. It is however, in England, almost entirely incapable of use, and as a consequence has been the subject of sustained and detailed academic and other criticism.[95] It would not be available for claimants in either of the two case studies. The representative action has the following features.

First, it enables an individual with a claim against a defendant to seek permission to bring those proceedings not only on their own behalf but also as the representative of all other individuals who have the 'same interest' in the claim against the defendant, i.e. to bring the proceedings in their own and in a representative capacity.[96] If permission is granted by the court for the claim to continue as a representative action, it does so as a form of opt-out representative action.[97]

Secondly, the represented parties are not joined to the action. They are before the court by representation only. This means that while they will be bound by

---

94 See <http://www.justice.gov.uk/courts/procedure-rules/civil/rules/part01>.

95 Rachael Mulheron, 'Emerald Supplies Ltd v British Airways plc: A Century Later, the Ghost of Markt Lives On' (2009) 8 Comp Law 159; Rachael Mulheron, 'A missed gem of an opportunity for the representative rule' (2012) 23 EBLR 1–49.

96 CPR r 19.6.

97 *The Irish Rowan* [1991] 2 QB 206, 227–41.

any judgment in the proceedings,[98] it can only be enforced against them with the court's permission.[99] Two consequences of this are: first, that evidentiary disclosure obligations which apply to parties do not apply to members of the represented class. They only apply to parties; and, secondly, the representative party is solely liable for the costs of the litigation.[100] Should a representative party or winning defendant seek to recover their costs from the representative class,[101] or should a defendant seek disclosure from a member of the represented class, they would therefore need to obtain a court order to that effect.[102]

Thirdly, as a general rule damages cannot be obtained via a representative action. Its primary form of relief is a declaration in respect of the 'same interest'. In limited circumstances, where the global quantum of damage to the representative class is ascertainable, damages may be awarded.[103] In the Bank Charges litigation, if a representative action could have been brought damages would,[104] in principle, have been an available remedy, as the global quantum of loss was readily ascertainable by reference to the charges incurred by each of the claimants. In tortious claims that is not however the case, as each individual claimant's damages will be a matter of separate findings on the medical evidence. There is no basis under the representative action for aggregation of damages or estimation methods to be used to determine tortious losses.

A representative action would not be available to claimants in either of the two case studies. This is the case because the claimants would not satisfy the 'same interest' test. Intuitively this would seem a perverse result where, as in both case studies, the same legal issue or issues will arise and the same factual issues underpin both. The difficulty arises, however, because of the extremely narrow definition of 'same interest' that is applied, and which was recently reaffirmed by the Court of Appeal in *Emerald Supplies Ltd v British Airways Plc*.[105]

To have the 'same interest' requires the class members to: i) have a 'common interest', which would arise for instance if they were all parties to the same contract; ii) have a common grievance; and iii) seek a remedy that benefits all class members in common, i.e. a declaration, an injunction, albeit not damages.[106]

---

98 *Commissioners of Sewers of the City of London v Gellatly* [1876] 3 ChD 610 at [616]; *Moon v Atherton* (n 81).

99 CPR r 19.6(4).

100 *Moon v Atherton* (n 81).

101 *Handforth v Storie* [1825] 2 Sim & St 196 at [198].

102 *Chandra v Mayor* [2016] EWHC 2636 (Ch).

103 *EMI Records Ltd v Riley* [1981] 1 WLR 923.

104 A representative action could not have been brought however as the individual claims would not have satisfied the 'same interest' criterion.

105 *Emerald Supplies Ltd v British Airways Plc* [2011] Ch 345; the test was originally set out in *Markt & Co Ltd v Knight Steamship Co Ltd* [1910] 2 KB 1021.

106 Ibid.

In neither of the case studies would the claimants meet the first, common interest, criterion. In the consumer case study, the class members would not all be party to a common contract. They would have entered into separate contracts to purchase the cars with different car dealers. In the capital markets case, the share purchases would again not be pursuant to a single common share purchase agreement. Moreover, in neither case study do the individual class members, seek a common remedy, i.e. one beneficial to all of them. They seek individual remedies, which depend upon a calculation of their own individual losses.

b) The Group Litigation Order

The Group Litigation Order (GLO) is a recent innovation.[107] It was introduced in 2000. It is a sophisticated form of case management device, where multiple claims give rise to common or related issues of fact or law. There is no need, as in the case of the representative action, for there to be a 'same interest' across the various claims or claimants. A GLO is 'not a form of representative action and representative claimants or defendants are not identified or selected'.[108] The GLO is a very flexible form of multi-party action and such orders have been made where as few as 18 claimants[109] have brought claims and where as many as 40,000 and more claimants have brought claims.[110]

A GLO can be made where a large number of claims with a common issue are issued by individual claimants. On application by one or more of those claimants, the court can consider whether to make a GLO. If it does so, before the GLO is made the order must be approved by a senior member of the civil judiciary (the Master of the Rolls, the President of the Queen's Bench Division, or the Chancellor of the High Court).[111] If a GLO is made, a register of claims subject to the order is created.

To come within the ambit of the order, claims must opt-in by having their details entered on the register.[112] Claims within the scope of the GLO but not entered on the GLO register by the time required for registration will be stayed pending the outcome of the GLO proceedings. Where a GLO is made a single judge will be appointed to manage the GLO proceedings.[113] While each claim within the GLO remains an individual claim, any judgment or order made in

---

107 CPR rr 19.10–19.15.
108 Bryne Hill, 'Class Actions' (n 64) 12.
109 *The Corby Group Litigation* [2009] EWHC 1944 (TCC).
110 *Kimathi v Foreign and Commonwealth Office* [2015] EWHC 3432.
111 CPR PD 19 para 3.3.
112 CPR PD 19 para 6.1.
113 CPR PD 19 para 8.

the GLO proceedings binds those claims within it.[114] This includes orders for documentary disclosure.[115] In managing the claims within a GLO, the court may direct that one or a small number of the claims may proceed as test cases. Claims within a GLO are liable for a share of the costs of the litigation.[116]

As noted above, a GLO has been made in the Volkswagen litigation which is being pursued in England. Given that it is readily apparent that the scenario set out in Case 1 could, and in all likelihood would, be subject to a GLO procedure.

It is not apparent that shareholder claims have been brought in England against Volkswagen. Should claims comparable to those set out in the second case study be issued, it would be likely that – assuming sufficient numbers were brought – that either on the application of one or several individual claimants or on the court's own motion a GLO would be made. As Bryne et al have rightly noted, a GLO is a 'natural' approach for shareholders' actions to take.[117] There are two instances where a GLO has been made in shareholder actions brought in situations analogous to that in Case 2: first, the RBS Rights Issue Litigation;[118] and, secondly, the Lloyds/HBOS Litigation.[119] A GLO was refused in respect of individual shareholder actions brought against Tesco.[120]

B. WHO IS ENTITLED TO BRING ACTION?

Civil proceedings can only be brought by a claimant that has an interest in the litigation, i.e. that they have a cause of action against the defendant. This is the case for all the procedural mechanisms through which multi-party actions can be litigated, including GLOs[121] and the representative action.[122]

---

114 CPR r 19.12(1).

115 CPR r 19.12(4).

116 CPR PD para 16.1.

117 Bryne Hill, 'Class Actions' (n 64) 383.

118 <http://www.gov.uk/guidance/group-litigation-orders#lloyds-HBOS-litigation>.

119 <http://www.gov.uk/guidance/group-litigation-orders#rbs-rights>.

120 *Manning & Napier Fund v Tesco Plc* [2017] EWHC 2203 (Ch). The claims continue, see for instance, *Omers Administration Corp v Tesco Plc* [2019] EWHC 109 (Ch).

121 As noted above a GLO is simply a device to aggregate individual claims to enable their efficient management. It is not a representative or class action. As such each claim within the GLO is a claim brought by an individual who themselves has a cause of action against the defendant.

122 CPR r 19.6(1) makes this limitation explicit for representative actions, as it provides that,

'Where more than one person has the same interest in a claim –

(a) the claim may be begun; or
(b) the court may order that the claim be continued,

by or against one or more of the persons who have the same interest as representatives of any other persons who have that interest.'

As such it is not possible for so-called 'ideological' claimants, i.e. campaigning bodies, consumer rights bodies, regulatory bodies or Ombudsman to bring litigation in a representative capacity. The one exemption to this is, as in the case of the Office of Fair Trading noted above, a regulator body that is authorised by statute to bring a claim, albeit not a representative claim, seeking declaratory relief. In the Bank Charges litigation, the declaration sought was as to the nature of the bank charges, i.e. unlawful penalty charge or not.

Given this, in neither of the case studies could damages actions be brought on behalf of individuals who had suffered a loss as a result of the alleged consumer protection breaches or capital markets law breaches by any individual, body or organisation that did not itself have the same interest in the litigation as those individuals.

C. HOW CAN COLLECTIVE REDRESS ACTIONS POSSIBLY BE FINANCED?

Collective redress actions can be funded in any of the ways that other forms of civil litigation can be financed. As such the available funding mechanisms for the two case studies are:

- Private funding by the individual claimants;
- Before or after-the-event insurance policies, to the extent they are available;
- Third-party litigation funding, including crowd-funding;
- Conditional fee funding (CFAs) or Damages-based Agreements under Courts and Legal Services Act 1990, section 58 and section 58AA.[123] This has historically been a common form of funding for GLOs.[124]

If private funding were not available should a GLO be made in Case 1, it would be expected that either BTE or ATE insurance would be available, but that also third-party funding could be used.[125] In respect of Case 2, given the funding arrangements that appear to have been used in comparable litigation, i.e. the

123 See <http://www.legislation.gov.uk/ukpga/1990/41/section/58>; <http://www.legislation.gov.uk/ukpga/1990/41/section/58AA>.

124 Bryne Hill, 'Class Actions' (n 64) 328–329.

125 It was reported in the Volkswagen GLO that at least some of the claimants were being funded by way of a third-party funding arrangement: see, Neil Rose, 'London firm secured third-party funding to bring first group action against VW – and on a DBA' (*Litigation Futures*, 9 January 2017) <http://www.litigationfutures.com/news/london-firm-secured-third-party-funding-bring-first-group-action-vw-dba>.

RBS Rights Issue Litigation,[126] both third-party funding and ATE insurance funding would be expected to be relied upon.

In each of the forms of action, set out above, the parties bear the litigation risks, i.e. they are at risk of adverse costs. In the GLO situation, the GLO parties will, however, only be liable for common costs, i.e. those attributable to the common issue. In the representative action, as noted above, the representative party bears the costs risk, subject to any contrary order by the court. Where third-party funding is taken out, the funder will however be potentially liable for the litigation costs attributable to the level of their funding, i.e. if they funded 30 per cent of the claimants' costs, they would in principle be liable to pay 30 per cent of any costs recoverable by a successful defendant.[127]

D. ARE THERE ANY SPECIAL MECHANISMS FOR ACHIEVING COLLECTIVE SETTLEMENTS?

There are no specific civil procedural mechanisms or schemes for achieving collective settlements.

E. HAVE SUBSTANTIVE ASSIGNMENT MODELS DEVELOPED FOR THE PROCESS-BASED BUNDLING OF COMPENSATION CLAIMS?

The assignment of a bare cause of action is not generally permitted in English law.[128] Assignment models have not therefore developed to bundle compensation claims. In contrast to assignment models, there has been a growth in claims management, which is subject to statutory regulation by the Financial Conduct Authority.[129] Claims management companies (CMCs) are businesses that seek to promote the bringing of claims, enable them to be bundled together thus facilitating single common representation by specific law firms, and through bundling promote forms of collective settlement.[130] Claims managed by CMCs

---

126 *Re RBS Rights Issue Litigation* [2017] 1 WLR 3539.

127 *Arkin v Borchard Lines Ltd* [2005] 1 WLR 3055; *Chapelgate Credit Opportunity Master Fund Ltd v Money* [2020] EWCA Civ 246.

128 *Trendtex Trading Corp v Credit Suisse* [1982] AC 679.

129 Financial Conduct Authority, 'Using claims management companies' (7 March 2019, updated 30 August 2019) <http://www.fca.org.uk/consumers/using-claims-management-companies>.

130 Financial Guidance and Claims Act 2018, pt 2 <http://www.legislation.gov.uk/ukpga/2018/10/part/2/enacted>.

are not assigned or transferred to them; the cause of action remains at all times that of the individual claimant.

F. ARE REMEDIES SUCH AS ELIMINATIONS OF CONSEQUENCES, DAMAGES AND SKIMMING OF PROFITS AVAILABLE?

In the two case studies, contractual or tortious damages would be available.[131] Damages under FSMA, section 90A, are, it is believed, available as tortious damages. As yet there is no authority on the issue. In the Tesco litigation a number of different bases on which damages are claimed have been put forward; the most likely applicable basis for calculating loss might be thought to be the difference between the price paid for the shares and the price that would have been paid for them but for the alleged misleading information.[132] Should damages be awarded they are payable directly to the parties. There is no basis in any of the actions, particularly the representative action, for damages to be held by lawyers pending identification of represented class members and thereafter possible *cy pres* distributions as is the case in the US.[133] This is the case due to the limited availability of damages awards in representative actions.

Rescission of the share purchase is also an available remedy for misrepresentation. As such it would be available, in principle, in both case studies, i.e. unwinding both transactions.

G. DOES FACILITATION TO GIVE PROOF EXIST: HOW IS THE BURDEN OF PROOF DISTRIBUTED?

The burden of proof in English civil proceedings generally lies on the party 'asserting the affirmative of [an] issue'.[134] That is not altered in any of the mechanisms used to manage multi-party actions.

---

131 The basis on which tortious damages would be calculated in Case 2 has not however been subject to a decision in England, see Bryne Hill, 'Class Actions' (n 64) 438ff. It is suggested that the measure of damages would be the difference between the price paid and the real value of the shares at the time of the shares were purchased. As Bryne Hill et al put it, this would mirror the approach taken in the US.

132 Bryne Hill, 'Class Actions' (n 64) 437.

133 See the discussion and recommendation for reform on this point in the Civil Justice Council's 2008 Report (n 79) 181.

134 Adrian Keane and Paul McKeown, *The Modern Law of Evidence* (12th edn, Oxford University Press 2018) 106–09.

H. ARE THERE ANY DEMANDS FOR INFORMATION AGAINST THE ALLEGED INJURING PARTY?

In any of the multi-party procedures the various mechanisms for the taking of evidence apply. They are not varied or altered by dint of the fact that, for instance, a representative action or GLO is made.

As such a defendant (the alleged injury party) in both case studies would, in principle, be subject to the obligation to disclose documentary information, including that contained in electronic documents, further to the disclosure process. In Case 1, this obligation would be governed by the generally applicable rules governing disclosure set out in CPR Pt 31.[135] In respect of the second case study, as such proceedings would in all likelihood proceed in the High Court's Business and Property Courts, they would be subject to a pilot scheme for disclosure that is currently applicable to all proceedings in those courts, which is contained in CPR PD51U.[136]

In both case studies, the claimants could also seek interim orders for the provision of evidence under CPR Pt 25,[137] i.e. orders: for the detention, custody or preservation of relevant property; for the inspection of relevant property; for the taking of a sample of relevant property; for the carrying out of an experiment on or with relevant property. Such orders may become relevant to test, if necessary, the manufacturer's testing facilities and or machinery, or the vehicles upon which any vehicle testing was carried out in so far as that was relevant to any issue in dispute or defence advanced.

---

135 See <http://www.justice.gov.uk/courts/procedure-rules/civil/rules/part31>.

136 See <http://www.justice.gov.uk/courts/procedure-rules/civil/rules/practice-direction-51u-disclosure-pilot-for-the-business-and-property-courts>.

137 See <http://www.justice.gov.uk/courts/procedure-rules/civil/rules/part25>.

ENFORCING CONSUMER AND CAPITAL MARKETS LAW IN ITALY

Marcello GABOARDI*

* Marcello Gaboardi, PhD, Assistant Professor of Civil Procedure Law and Bankruptcy Law, Bocconi University of Milan, School of Law. Free websites for Jurisprudence and statutes: Italian Supreme Court of Cassation: <http://www.cortedicassazione.it/corte-di-cassazione/>; Official Report of Italian Statutes: <http://www.gazzettaufficiale.it/homePostLogin;jsessionid=qwVVOvUeUAurvBnU7eAfrQ__>; Consumer Code: <http://www.mise.gov.it/index.php/it/mercato-e-consumatori/tutela-del-consumatore/codice-del-consumo>; Civil Code: <http://www.gazzettaufficiale.it/dettaglio/codici/codiceCivile>; Code of Civil Procedure: <http://www.gazzettaufficiale.it/dettaglio/codici/proceduraCivile>.

I. INTRODUCTION

The impact of the Dieselgate case in Italy has been limited to date. While in other countries the case has generally had severe and significant outcomes, in Italy it has not yet yielded remarkable results.

Four years after Volkswagen AG admitted in September 2015 that it cheated American diesel emissions tests, Volkswagen Group Italia (VGI) – that is the Italian subsidiary of Volkswagen AG – is still battling criminal investigations and investors' lawsuits. In 2016, public prosecutors in the Italian city of Verona, where VGI has its headquarters, brought charges against former VGI managers over their roles in the *Dieselgate* scandal. According to the newspaper reports, the Italian public prosecutors have accused the former president of the board of directors, the former chief executive officer and the former general manager of a particularly serious fraud when they failed to stop the malicious practice in Italy, which dates back to 2009. The prosecutors state that VGI managers would have been conscious that Volkswagen AG was selling manipulated vehicles in Italy by installing a software which was designed to hide the real reason for the increased levels of pollutants in normal vehicle usage.[1]

Preliminary investigations are being carried out by public prosecutors. But those investigations have not yet been completed. The technical report ordered by the Verona court in 2016 was recently filed. In light of the newspapers, in March 2019 the experts appointed by the court would have realised the software changes constituted a defeat device prohibited under Italian law.[2] Notwithstanding this conclusion, the appointed experts would also have stated that the decision of Volkswagen AG to offer to the cars' owners involved in the Dieselgate scandal the substitution of the responsible software with a correct one would have significantly reduced the detrimental consequences of defeated devices.[3] It is worth noting that if VGI managers will be found guilty of the crimes they are accused of, that outcome will be also relevant as a potential indicator of their civil liability in the Dieselgate case, because it is highly likely that a civil court would be strongly influenced by the reasons to declare the VGI managers' criminal liability. But this kind of judicial ascertainment lacks in Italy because Italian civil judges have not yet ruled on that case.

---

1 See Coordinamento delle associazioni per la difesa dell'ambiente e dei diritti degli utenti e dei consumatori (Codacons), 'Dieselgate, l'inchiesta chiusa dopo 4 anni. Migliaia le parti civili pronte a battere cassa' (7 August 2019) <http://www.codacons.it/dieselgate-l-inchiesta-chiusa-dopo-4-anni-migliaia-le-parti-civili-pronte-a-battere-cassa/>.

2 Ibid.

3 See Coordinamento delle associazioni per la difesa dell'ambiente e dei diritti degli utenti e dei consumatori (Codacons), 'Dieselgate, riconosciuto in Italia l'inganno di Volkswagen. Ma i risarcimenti restano lontani' (28 March 2019) <http://www.codacons.it/dieselgate-riconosciuto-in-italia-l-inganno-di-volkswagen-ma-i-risarcimenti-restano-lontani/>.

In 2016, an Italian consumer association (*Altroconsumo*) brought a class lawsuit in the appellate court of Venice against Volkswagen. The lawsuit was certified as a class action in 2017. In the class certification order the Italian court declared that

> Volkswagen's advertising and marketing green claims appear to be in contrast with the company's behavior denounced by the consumer association, and involved the installation of an EGR device, capable of reducing car emissions during tests and thus of misleading consumers about the car features.[4]

In particular, 76,000 consumers have joined the class action. The named plaintiff has claimed compensation of 15 per cent of the value of each car were sold in Italy. The first hearing for the assessment of the 76,000consumers' declarations was initially set for February 2019, but the workload forced the court to postpone the hearing to May 2019. Therefore, there is still no decision on the merits. The decision will probably be taken no later than mid of 2020.

Finally, it is also worth noting that in 2015 the Italian Antitrust Authority – that is an administrative branch – investigated whether VGI engaged in improper commercial practices by promoting its vehicles as meeting emissions standards which it failed to reach without a defeat device.[5] The Italian antitrust regulator has actually fined VGI €5 million for its Dieselgate software manipulation. The fine amounts to over €7 for each of the 700,000 affected cars sold in Italy since 2009.[6] VGI has immediately appealed the fine to the competent Italian regional administrative court. In 2019, however, the Italian court has rejected the VGI appeal, so that the fine has been confirmed as 'economically adequate and consistent with the Italian antitrust law.'[7]

4 See Appellate Court of Venice, 25 May 2017, no 12489/2017. These are the original words of the appellate court of Venice: 'i green claims propri della campagna di marketing pubblicitario di commercializzazione dei veicoli a marchio VW appaiono in contrapposizione con la condotta denunciata dalla associazione dei consumatori e consistita nella istallazione del dispositivo EGR, in grado di ridurre in sede di test le emissioni inquinanti dei veicoli, e appaiono tali da indurre in errore il consumatore in ordine alle caratteristiche del veicolo stesso'. The translation in the text is by the author.

5 See Autorita' Garante della Concorrenza e del Mercato (AGCM), 'Istruttoria Antitrust sul caso Volkswagen per pratica commerciale scorretta' (2 October 2015) <http://www.agcm.it/media/comunicati-stampa/2015/10/alias-7881>.

6 See Autorita' Garante della Concorrenza e del Mercato (AGCM), 'Testo del provvedimento PS10211' <http://www.agcm.it/dotcmsDOC/allegati-news/PS10211_Volkswagen_ENG.pdf>.

7 See Regional Administrative Court of Rome, 31 May 2019, no 6920. These are the original words of the Administrative Court: 'l'Autorità ha quantificato la sanzione pecuniaria in modo proporzionato e conforme alle disposizioni legislative di riferimento'. The translation in the text is by the author. See also Giovanni Posio, 'Italy' in Marco Frigessi di Rattalma (ed), *The Dieselgate. A Legal Perspective* (Springer 2017) 47ff.

These results show the weaknesses of the Italian legal system with respect to public and private enforcement of consumer and capital market law. The public enforcement depends entirely on criminal prosecutions, while the Antitrust Authority has a limited role to play because its power to fine the wrongdoer in case of unfair commercial practices is legally determined (the fine cannot be less than €5,000, but it cannot exceed €5,000,000).[8] Besides, it is worth noting that the Antitrust Authority lacks any effective means to reach a settlement of criminal investigations and legal fines in connection with legal violations concerning unfair commercial practices. These factors significantly reduce the impact of public enforcement of consumer and capital market law within the context of the Italian legal system.

On the other side, the private enforcement of consumer and capital market law revolves entirely around civil litigation. Stakeholders are entitled to bring individual or collective lawsuits for money damages against the wrongdoer before national courts. Those civil lawsuits can be brought not only for compensating individual damages, but also for preventing future violations of legal provisions. Nevertheless, the fact that private enforcement depends entirely on civil litigation is seriously problematic because Italian civil litigation traditionally suffers the pain of unreasonable length of civil proceedings.[9] The excessive length of civil court cases inevitably reduces the efficacy of private enforcement in promoting the protection of consumers or investors. If private enforcement of consumer and capital market law must be viewed as severely harmed by the unreasonable length of civil proceedings, the appropriate response can be a civil litigation based on the advantages of representative litigation. Individual consumers or investors are entitled to bring class lawsuits for money damages against the wrongdoer before national courts. Similarly, consumer or investor associations are empowered to bring representative lawsuits for precautionary or preventive orders against the wrongdoer. As one shall see, these legal instruments increase the efficiency of private enforcement of consumer and capital market law. They represent a crucial point that enables consumers and investors to achieve objectives such as damages compensation or the prevention of future violations.

8 See art 27 of the Italian Consumer Code 2005 (Legislative Decree no 206/2005) (hereafter Italian Consumer Code).

9 See the 2018 Report of the Italian Parliament on the unreasonable length of civil proceedings in Italy, Camera dei Deputati Servizio Studi, 'Ragionevole durata del processo' (22 March 2018) <http://www.camera.it/temiap/documentazione/temi/pdf/1104921.pdf>; see also Remo Caponi, 'The Performance of the Italian Civil Justice System: An Empirical Assessment' (2016) 2 The Italian Law Journal 15.

II. THE ITALIAN CONSUMER AND CAPITAL MARKET LAW

While the preceding Section I has sought to provide a comprehensive account of which legal actions the Italian legal system endorsed as remedies for the violation of consumer rights in the Dieselgate scandal, Sections II and III survey the theoretical and historical grounds on which consumer protection is commonly justified in Italy. Finally, Section IV describes extensively the Italian legal system as constructed around the private enforcement of consumer and capital market law rather than its public enforcement.

Since 2005, the Italian legislator crafted the new regulatory regime of consumer law within the context of the European Union law. By contrast, the evolution of capital market law toward the existing legal pattern was longer and more complicated. Notwithstanding this difference, however, it is worth noting that, in both cases, the existing Italian legal framework gradually emerged from the European normative premises that provided a principled basis for the implementation of substantive and procedural safeguards within the universe of consumer and capital market law. By adopting the legal perspective of the European Union institutions, the Italian law changed over time and adapted to the new legal backdrop.[10]

It is also worth noting that the Italian legal system's ability to adapt to the new European legal requirements manifested itself not only in terms of legislative enactment, but also in terms of interpretative adjustment. The Italian legal framework became more robust and nuanced. But that result depended on a web of normative and interpretative efforts that determined – and, in part, continue to determine – the living legal framework for the protection of individual rights within the context of consumer and capital market law. Such a legal framework can be properly defined as living, the author believes, because it cannot be reduced to a set of legal amendments, but it undoubtedly includes the relevant part of the national case law. That is, the new legal framework encompasses judicial interpretation and understanding about the European Union legislation on the one hand and the legal rules adopted by national legislator in accordance

---

10 See ECJ, Joined Cases C-240/98, C-241/98, C-242/98, C-243/98 and C-244/98 *Océano Grupo Editorial SA v Rocío Murciano Quintero* [27 June 2000] ECR 2000 I-4941, para 27 stating that, under the European Union law, Member States were called upon 'to implement adequate and effective means to prevent the continued use of unfair terms, (and to pay careful attention to the fact that) those means (we)re to include allowing authorised consumer associations to take action in order to obtain a decision as to whether contractual terms drawn up for general use are unfair and, if need be, to have them prohibited, even if they have not been used in specific contracts'; ECJ, C-372/99 *Commission of the European Communities v Italian Republic* [24 January 2002] ECR 2002 I-819.

with the European law itself on the other hand. Moreover, the judicial activism often serves as a counterweight against a certain Italian legislative immobilism that impedes – or, at least, delays – the passage of important legal measures according to the European legal principles. And this legislative hesitation easily runs into a problem of legal inadequacy. In fact, if the Italian Parliament hesitates to comply with the European Union regulations or adopt the European Union directives, judicial activism reduces not only the distance between the European and Italian legal rules but also the risk of inconsistent interpretation and application of law.

Even if the European national courts have a crucial, though debatable, role to play in filling the gap, what starts the engine of legal changes remains the legislative action – that is, the Italian Parliament and its amendments of national rules over time in order to adapt to changing European backdrop on matters of consumer and capital market protection. While legislative activism promotes legal uniformity, certainty, and predictability, judicial activism is not sufficiently strong and coherent to outweigh the risks of misinterpretation and misapplication of law.

III. HISTORICAL PREMISES

The process of legal adaptation to the European Union law has had a late start in Italy. The most important and comprehensive effort to enrich the protection of consumers against harmful commercial activities was expended in 1996 to amend the Italian Civil Code.[11] That amendment reshaped several legal provisions concerning the individual protection on matters of contract rights and commercial transactions in light of the consumer's rights. The underlying theory coheres with the protection of the weaker party in the European contract law. According to such a theory, the various factors that naturally inform the relationship between the consumer and the producer – such as asymmetry in the allocation of information, personal and market conditions, and difference in the bargaining power – make it necessary to convert that naturally unbalanced relationship into a legally balanced relationship. In this way, the producer is put in the position of complying with a set of duties that reflects the legislative intent to protect the consumer's rights.

---

11 See arts 1469-bis–1469-sexies of the Italian Civil Code 1942 (Royal Decree no 262/1942) (hereafter Italian Civil Code); see also art 25 of the Italian Law no 52/1996 concerning the adaptation of the Italian legal system to the European Community law on several matters. In 2005, as explained below, arts 1469-bis–1469-sexies were abrogated by the Italian Consumer Code 2005 (Legislative Decree no 206/2005).

When the amendment of 1996 entered into force, there emerged the touchstone for broader reforms of traditional legal measures. The enactment of the Italian Consumer Code in 2005 was undoubtedly the turning point in the protection of consumers.[12] The Code was based in large part on the content of preexisting legal rules. The Italian Parliament simply reframed several legal provisions into a unique, coherent legislative act.[13] Thus, the Code maintains continuity over time by creating a stable framework for consumers. But it also reduces the hazards of interpretative divergence in the adjudication of disputes. The Code promotes the stability and predictability of decision-making that is now driven by a uniform legal framework – just as, it ensures that consumers properly understand the ways in which they can present their case before the courts.

The enforcement of consumer law also depends on the regulatory regime of civil litigation. Civil actions undoubtedly play an essential role in the analysis of consumer protection against unfair practices and harmful behaviours. The fundamental role of civil litigation, as understood traditionally and in part even today, is to allow individuals to bring damages suits in the courts. But it requires the expenditure of significant resources – economic and otherwise – to reach the appropriate result. Moreover, individual lawsuits ensure individual protection, so that individual litigation reveals itself as economically inefficient. Factual and legal similarities are evident in the dynamics of consumer law cases. It is worth noting, with respect of cases involving similar, if not serial, property or contract rights, that fact-finding process revolves around the same factual and legal questions. Much the same is true of the application of tort law to consumer law cases in which, for example, unfair commercial or competitive practices on the one hand and sales of defective goods on the other hand authorise lawsuits for money damages against the wrongdoer.

For several years the solution to those problems, which depends on reshaping individual litigation into representative lawsuits, continued to prove elusive. Such an approach was in large part defined by a common feature of the European legal systems – that is, their remarkable tendency to resist abandoning the traditional ideal of individual litigation. Notwithstanding this resistance, the consumer law has played a relevant role in inciting – or, better yet, reinforcing – this legal change. In fact, Italian law already allowed certain individuals and organisations to bring lawsuits in national courts on behalf of other stakeholders. For example, some four decades before the enactment of the Italian Consumer Code, in cases involving the violation of crucial employees' rights, such as the right to organise

12 See Italian Consumer Code (n 8).

13 For example, arts 33–37 of the Italian Consumer Code (n 8) replaced arts 1469-bis–1469-sexies of the Italian Civil Code (n 11). The text of legal provisions remained substantially unchanged.

and to bargain collectively or the right to strike, the Italian law authorised – and continues to authorise – the labour unions to bring preventive lawsuits against the employer on behalf of the collectivity of employers.[14]

Those measures served as a starting point for transforming some notable exceptions into something more efficient and theoretically coherent. Since that moment, the legislative approach to the legal protection of consumers is radically changed. It is not surprising that the most revolutionary change revolves around the subjects that the Consumer Code authorises to bring lawsuits on behalf of consumers. That change remains revolutionary because it reflects the formal move away from a legal system that was exclusively-individual-litigation oriented toward a legal system that is equally-individual-and-representative oriented. While consumers continue to be individually entitled to bring damages suits against the wrongdoer, the Consumer Code allows consumer organisations to contribute to the protection of the collective interests of consumers against unlawful practices.

Consumer organisations can be described as representative subjects. In other words, the Italian law authorises them to bring lawsuits – or, better yet, only certain types of lawsuits – on behalf of a given category of consumers. As discussed in detail below, while consumer organisations are exclusively entitled to bring provisional or protective suits on behalf of represented consumers, since 2010 an amendment to the Italian Consumer Code also authorises both individual consumers and representative entities to bring damages suits on behalf of a given category of stakeholders – that is, the class members. The difference between these legal rules depends on the different effects of the judicial decisions. Generally, provisional and protective measures prevent the wrongdoer from continuing to do something whenever it threatens to create immediate harms to consumers. In such cases, the judicial order produces the same effect in favour of all consumers – that is, it protects the collective interest of consumers. Instead, when legal rules authorise representative lawsuits for money damages against the wrongdoer, they aim at protecting individual rights of consumers. In such cases, the judicial decision produces different, though similar, effects in favour of each consumer.[15]

Beyond these differences, the legal change occurred in 2005 and in 2010 promoted consumer protection in important ways. New legal rules reinforce

---

14 See art 28.1 of the Italian Workers Statute of 1970 (Law no 300/1970). The Statute was amended in 1977 and 1990.

15 See generally Geoffrey Hazard, 'The Effect of the Class Action Device upon Substantive Law' (1972) 58 FRD 299, 309; Arthur R Miller, 'Of Frankenstein Monsters and Shining Knights: Myth, Reality, and the Class Action Problem' (1979) 92 Harv L Rev 664, 668; David Rosenberg, 'Class Actions for Mass Torts: Doing Individual Justice by Collective Means' (1987) 62 Ind LJ 561. For the Italian debate, see also Andrea Giussani, *Azioni Collettive Risarcitorie nel Processo Civile* (Il Mulino 2008).

consumer protection by increasing the number of subjects who are entitled to bring lawsuits in national courts against the wrongdoer. Moreover, the new legal framework ventures far beyond authorising individual lawsuits for money damages. It encompasses representative actions aimed at preventing new unfair practices coming to pass as well as representative actions aimed at compensating individual damages.

IV. THE ENFORCEMENT OF THE ITALIAN CONSUMER AND CAPITAL MARKET LAW THROUGH THE LENS OF COMPARATIVE ANALYSIS

A. THE REPRESENTATIVE NATURE OF DISPUTES CONCERNING THE ENFORCEMENT OF CONSUMER AND CAPITAL MARKET LAW

The enforcement of Italian consumer and capital market law embraces the essential features of representative litigation. In common law tradition the protection of individual rights revolves primarily around representative litigation when a collective interest or several individual interests are implicated by a given event, such as breaches of contract or unfair commercial or competitive practices. Instead, civil law legal systems can be described as deeply rooted in the ideal of individual litigation. The point is that, notwithstanding some similarities, the dynamics of representative action departs from the traditional mechanism for promoting individual protection in civil litigation.

Allowing representative subjects, such as consumer organisations, to bring suits on behalf of stakeholders is the primary way of departing from the mechanism of individual litigation.[16] It is worth noting that representative disputes emerge within the context of the European legal systems as the result of specific legislative choices about the subjects who are entitled to apply to the courts on behalf of stakeholders. In 2005, the Italian law has authorised certain representative subjects to promote the collective interests of consumers by bringing provisional or protective suits against the wrongdoer.[17] Indeed, according to the Italian Consumer Code, the entities that are exclusively entitled to bring those representative lawsuits are defined as 'consumers and

16 See John C Jr Coffee, 'Understanding the Plaintiff's Attorney: The Implications of Economic Theory for Private Enforcement of Law through Class and Derivative Actions' (1986) 86 Colum L Rev 669, 682.

17 See arts 139 and 140 of the Italian Consumer Code (n 8).

users associations.'[18] They must be able to represent consumers and users at the national level. And they must be enrolled in a public register before petitioning the court. Further, imposing a set of legal requirements on those associations, such as an exclusive purpose concerning the protection of consumers or users, a minimum number of members, and the functioning over a period of three years, reflects significant regard for the importance of durability and adequacy of representation.[19]

In 2010, the Italian legislator has also looked to the 'consumers and users associations' as one potential alternative to individuals in order to bring lawsuits for money damages on behalf of stakeholders.[20] If consumers are individually entitled to bring a lawsuit for money damages on behalf of other consumers, they can also designate a given association as representing them before the court. In such a case the representative nature of disputes does not depend on the fact that the association serves the collective interests of consumers. And that is just what associations tend to do, as noted above, when they petition the court for a provisional or protective measure on behalf of consumers. By contrast, when associations bring a lawsuit for money damages, it serves the individual interests of consumers who designated it as petitioner. In such a case the representative nature of disputes depends on the fact that a single consumer is entitled to take a legal action for money damages on behalf of other consumers. Therefore, the petitioner serves as a named plaintiff by protecting those individual interests that cannot be undermined by a common event without the payment of compensation.

B. THE ENFORCEMENT OF THE ITALIAN CONSUMER LAW THROUGH PRECAUTIONARY AND INJUNCTIVE MEASURES

The collective interests of consumers enjoy legal protection under the Italian law. Along with the protection of collective interests in civil litigation comes enhanced the possibility of settling the case through a compromise.

In cases where collective interests are involved, consumers are not entitled to bring their claims in national courts individually. They must avail themselves of another subject – that is, a given consumer or user organisation – to bring their claims collectively. Because collective interests reflect the common interest of consumers as a qualified group, their protection cannot depend on individual

18 See art 137 of the Italian Consumer Code (n 8).
19 Ibid.
20 See art 140-bis of the Italian Consumer Code (n 8).

initiatives.[21] Such initiatives, indeed, would allow consumers to bring their individual claims instead of their collective claim. For example, when unfair competitive practices threaten to damage those who have signed commercial agreements with the same producer, there emerges the need for protecting not only individual interests but also a collective interest. While individual interests require consumers to bring individually damages lawsuits, the collective interest requires a general approach. In other words, it requires invoking a judicial measure that produces effects in favour of both harmed and not harmed consumers.

Sympathy for these arguments reaches all the way to the European institutions.[22] According to European Union law, the Italian Consumer Code authorises consumer organisations to bring civil actions in courts – more precisely in first instance courts – in order to obtain:

1. *preventive measures* – that is, precautionary measures aimed either at preventing the wrongdoer from doing something whenever it threatens to create immediate harms to consumers or directing the wrongdoer to continue to do something going forward whenever its interruption threatens to harm consumers;[23] or
2. *injunctive measures* – that is, injunction orders aimed at properly correcting or eliminating the harmful effects of the unfair practice or behaviour of the wrongdoer against consumers;[24] or
3. *informative measures* – that is, further injunction orders aimed at publicising orders *sub* (1) or (2) on national and local newspapers when the publication reveals itself as amenable to contribute or facilitate the correction or the elimination of the harmful effects caused by the wrongdoer.[25]

This legal framework bears some resemblance to a large part of the other European legal systems. For instance, the protection of collective interests revolves

---

21 That conclusion is supported by several decisions of the Italian Supreme Court of Cassation. See Cass civ, 28 March 2006, no 7036, FI 2006, I, 717.

22 See Fabrizio Cafaggi and Hans-W Micklitz, 'Collective Enforcement of Consumer Law: A Framework for Comparative Assessment' (2008) 16 ERPL 391; Willem van Boom and Marco Loos, 'Effective Enforcement of consumer Law in Europe: Synchronizing Private, Public, and Collective Mechanisms' (2008) <http://www.researchgate.net/publication/254916563_Collective_enforcement_of_consumer_law_securing_compliance_in_Europe_through_private_group_action_and_public_authority_intervention>. For the Italian debate see also Vincenzo Zeno Zencovich and Maria Cecilia Paglietti, *Diritto processuale dei consumatori* (EGEA 2009) 51 (hereafter Zeno Zencovich and Paglietti, *Diritto processuale*).

23 See art 140.1.a of the Italian Consumer Code (n 8).

24 See art 140.1.b of the Italian Consumer Code (n 8).

25 See art 140.1.c of the Italian Consumer Code (n 8); see Ilaria Pagni, 'Tutela individuale e tutela collettiva nella nuova disciplina dei diritti dei consumatori' in Angelo Barba (ed), *La disciplina dei diritti dei consumatori e degli utenti* (Jovene 2000) 162, 166.

around the role of representative subjects, such as consumer organisations, in German and French legal systems. The scope of representative measures can be generally defined as preventive and remedial. The preventive nature of those measures depends on the need for preserving collective interests and avoiding the violations of collective rights and expectations. Their preventive nature thus emerges in the precautionary measures *sub* (1). By contrast, their remedial nature emerges within the context of injunctive orders *sub* (2). In fact, even if consumer organisations are not empowered to bring representative lawsuits for money damages against the wrongdoer, judicial orders aimed at correcting or eliminating the harmful effects of the wrongdoer's unfair practices or behaviours can be described as remedial measures. They reflect legal reactions to practices or behaviours that are aimed not only at continuing to damage consumers who were already harmed, but also at damaging consumers who were not still harmed.

C. THE ENFORCEMENT OF THE ITALIAN CONSUMER LAW THROUGH SETTLEMENTS

As noted above, a particular way in which the Italian law permits consumer organisations to enforce the consumer law is allowing them to promote an agreement with the wrongdoer.

According to the Italian Consumer Code, consumer organisations can submit a proposal to settle the case – or, better yet, the harmful consequences of the wrongdoer's unfair practices or behaviours – before certain public institutions, such as the Italian Chamber of Commerce, that are expressly designated by existing legal rules.[26] In particular, the Italian Consumer Code authorises representative subjects to settle claims, issues or defences as appropriate in accordance with the specific procedure adopted by the public institution that will be appointed as mediator between the parties. Therefore, the agreement represents the result of collective efforts to mediate in the dispute – the consumer organisation, the wrongdoer, and the public institution are called upon to channel their efforts through the formal process ruled by law.[27] However, the agreement is subject to judicial supervision that has the effect of giving the power to approve or veto settlement to the competent first instance court, which in turn is asked to solicit the views of the wrongdoer before making the decision.[28]

26 See art 140.2 of the Italian Consumer Code (n 8).
27 It is worth noting that the duration of mediation procedure is established by law in 60 days. See art 140.2 of the Italian Consumer Code (n 8).
28 See art 140.3 of the Italian Consumer Code (n 8).

That mediation procedure represents a preliminary matter. The Italian law requires the consumer organisation to submit the proposal to settle the case before it decides to apply to the court in order to obtain a provisional or protective measure. That does not mean that consumer organisations must deem themselves barred from bringing provisional or protective lawsuits against the wrongdoer before they have submitted a proposal to settle the case. It simply means their proposal matters. In other words, the Italian law contemplates the possibility that the resolution of the dispute between consumers and the wrongdoer is best promoted by adopting a voluntary agreement between them. Nevertheless, consumer organisations are not obliged to submit their proposal before petitioning the court. When the dispute between consumers and the wrongdoer comes before a registered consumer organisation,[29] it is simply entitled to submit a proposal to settle the case when it appears right to do so. However, just as consumer organisations can submit their proposals, so, too, can the wrongdoer. In fact, according to the Italian Consumer Code, consumer organisations are asked to send a formal notice to the wrongdoer before petitioning the court. That notice orders the recipient to stop his (or her) unfair and harmful practice or behaviour. If the wrongdoer does not submit a proposal to settle the case before the competent institution within 15 days, the consumer organisation is entitled to bring the lawsuit in court against the wrongdoer.[30] Therefore, the compromise simply remains an alternative to civil litigation – an alternative that both the consumer organisation and the wrongdoer can choose when they prefer to avoid litigation, for reasons ranging from uncertainty about their length and conclusion to a simple desire to avoid the spotlight.

As a practical matter, consumer organisations generally give little, and sometimes even negative, weight to compromise. The distance between the claims of consumers and the wrongdoer, the limited capacity of organisations to completely understand the claims of consumers, and the notable lack of expertise that generally characterises institutions appointed as mediators reduce the appeal and practicality of that option. Notwithstanding these limitations, when the parties are bound by judgment or compromise under the Italian Consumer Code, the court is asked to set a deadline by which the wrongdoer must comply with judicial orders and establish the payment of a sum of money – that is, a penalty – for each day of delay or for any breach of judicial orders.[31] That rule provides a potentially important incentive for consumers

---

[29] As noted above, the consumer organisations that are entitled to bring lawsuits in nation courts in order to obtain provisional or protective measures must be enrolled in a public register. The same is true of those consumer organisations that are called upon to submit proposals to settle the case. See art 137 of the Italian Consumer Code (n 8).

[30] See art 140.5 of the Italian Consumer Code (n 8).

[31] See art 140.7 of the Italian Consumer Code (n 8).

to resolve the dispute with the wrongdoer collectively because it threatens to extend the binding effects of judicial order over time – that is, beyond those unfair practices or behaviours on which the judgment or settlement is based.

D. THE ITALIAN CLASS LITIGATION: A WAY OF CONSUMER PROTECTION

The European Union law has ultimately led the Italian Parliament to amend the Consumer Code providing an additional incentive for consumers to protect their individual rights.[32] Since 2010, the Italian legislator allows individual consumers to bring class lawsuits in national courts on behalf of other consumers when the lawsuit challenges a practice or behaviour that affects all the putative class members.[33] As noted above, they are entitled to bring class lawsuits individually or through a representative subject. However, even when they opt to delegate a representative organisation, consumers bring their suit as representative parties on behalf of all members of the class.

The admissibility of class action depends on whether all requirements listed in article 140-bis of the Italian Consumer Code are satisfied before the court will certify the case as a class action.[34] The named plaintiff has the burden of proving that the requirements for class certification are satisfied. This set of requirements bears relevant similarities to that of other European and Anglo-American legal systems. For example, Rule 23 of the US Federal Rules of Civil Procedure requires the existence of 'questions of law or fact common to the class'[35] before the case will be certified as a class action. Under Rule 19.10 of the English Civil Procedure Rules the group litigation order likewise requires that claims 'give rise to common or related issues of fact or law'.[36]

On these points, the Italian Consumer Code embraces similar rules. The court – that is, the court of first instance – must evaluate whether the individual rights of named plaintiff can be described as homogenous. Phrased in terms of the Italian Consumer Code, the class action can be brought for the protection of 'individual homogenous rights'. This requirement is intended to ensure that the

---

32 See Michele Taruffo, 'La tutela collettiva: interessi in gioco ed esperienze a confronto' in Claudio Belli (ed), *Le azioni collettive in Italia. Profili teorici e applicativi* (Cedam 2017) 14.

33 See generally Claudio Consolo and Beatrice Zuffi, *L'azione di classe ex art. 140-bis cod. cons.* (Cedam 2012) (hereafter Consolo and Zuffi, *L'azione di classe*); Romolo Donzelli, *L'azione di classe a tutela dei consumatori* (Jovene 2011); Remo Caponi, 'Azioni collettive: interessi protetti e modelli processuali di tutela' (2008) 5 RDP 1205 (hereafter Caponi, *Azioni collettive*).

34 See art 140-bis of the Italian Consumer Code (n 8).

35 See rule 23.a.2 of the US Federal Rules of Civil Procedure.

36 See rule 19.10 of the English Civil Procedure Rules.

named plaintiff will represent the best expectations of class members in cases involving:

1. *contractual rights* when breaches of contracts derive from similar situations in which a given entrepreneur breaches contracts with consumers concerning the same type of factual conditions or economic clauses;[37] or
2. *contractual and non-contractual rights* when a given type of flawed product or service harms consumers (for example, when a product presents unreasonably dangerous defects or when a financial service impedes stakeholders from accessing to essential information), allowing for money damages against producers, suppliers, or retailers;[38] or
3. *contractual and non-contractual rights*, when consumers are harmed by given commercial or competitive unfair practices, such as deceptive business practices, abuses of market dominance, or collusive agreements, allowing for money damages or restitutions against the same wrongdoer.[39]

While the scope of class action in Anglo-American models is defined broadly to encompass all situations where the number of parties is sufficiently large so that 'joinder of all members is impracticable',[40] the Italian legislator has narrowly tailored its regulation of class action to serve compelling interests of consumers.[41] This type of limitations has become part of a large number of European legal systems. It reflects the fact that, over the past decades, the European Union institutions have focused more of their attention to the protection of consumers than any other types of stakeholders. The reason for favouring special protection of consumers is that there is an attentive approach to the weaker commercial party in matters of contracting and commercial transactions – that is, a party who is inherently subject to inequality of bargaining powers or contractual imbalance. It also reflects the scepticism of civil lawyers toward representative litigation. Just as organisations or unions can bring representative lawsuits on

---

37 The consumer class protection literally refers to 'the contractual rights of a plurality of consumers who are involved in a homogenous situation against the same business'. It also refers to those situations in which consumers are parties to a contract of adhesion under the Italian Civil Code. See art 140-bis.2.a of the Italian Consumer Code (n 8). See also arts 1341 and 1342 of the Italian Civil Code (n 11).

38 The consumer class protection literally refers to 'the individual homogenous rights of consumers with respect to products or services even when they are not parties to a contract'. See art 140-bis.1.b of the Italian Consumer Code (n 8).

39 The consumer class protection literally refers to 'the homogenous rights to the compensation of damages occurred to consumers or users for unfair commercial or competitive practices'. See art 140-bis.1.c of the Italian Consumer Code (n 8). See also Consolo and Zuffi, *L'azione di classe* (n 33) 66.

40 See rule 23.a.1 of the US Federal Rules of Civil Procedure.

41 See Zeno Zencovich and Paglietti, *Diritto processuale* (n 22) 58.

behalf of certain categories of stakeholders such as consumers or workers,[42] so, too, can the named plaintiff on behalf of the class of consumers. Thus, the Italian representative litigation must be interpreted and applied in a restrictive manner on the understanding that representative lawsuits and class actions are, and will remain, means of protecting only certain types of stakeholders.

According to the Italian Consumer Code, the court are asked to consider a question of homogeneity – meaning substantial commonality – among claims before the case is decided on the merits. This requirement can be depicted as a typicality test because it ensures that there exists strong similarities between the interests of class representative and those of absent class members. If the claim of class representative arises from the same event or course of conduct as the class members' claims, and if it involves the same legal rules or remedies, the case will be certified as a class action. In both situations, differences among the claims can exist, but they do not prevent a class certification if they are compatible with the homogeneity of claims.

The court is also called upon to decide questions regarding the ability of the named plaintiff to adequately represent the class. The Italian law requires the court to be particularly attentive to this requirement. Indeed, crucial issues arise in evaluating whether class representative improperly deviate from the interests of class members. Even if the court can exercise discretion in determining the degree of class-representative adequacy, potential conflicts of interest and deficiencies in economic integrity are sufficient to render class representative inadequate.[43] Crucial to class actions is a need to protect the interests of class members who play a less active role than parties engaged in conventional litigation. The fate of a class action cannot be influenced by unfair behaviours of class representative, such as a personal friendship between the named plaintiff and lawyer or agreements that threaten to harm some class members and benefit others. Thus, the class representative adequacy constitutes a significant obstacle to misusing or abusing the opportunity to bring a class action.

Finally, and most importantly for present purposes, the Italian class litigation proceeds on an opt-in basis. While the traditional model of Anglo-American class litigation provides that class actions, once certified, have binding effect on whomever the court finds to be within the membership of the class, in the Italian class litigation class members are entitled to declare to opt-in to the class membership. In other words, class members are called upon to determine that their claims against the wrongdoer refer to the same type of breach of contract or legal duty. In this way, class actions certified under article 140-bis of the Italian Consumer Code have binding effect on those class members who opted in to the

---

42 See supra Section IV.A.

43 See art 140-bis.6 of the Italian Consumer Code (n 8). See also Consolo and Zuffi, *L'azione di classe* (n 33) 185; Caponi, *Azioni collettive* (n 33) 1210.

class and whom the court defined as members. Though the written declarations of class members can be deemed integral to protecting individual consent to class action, they cannot be described as complaints. Only the named plaintiff can properly assert a claim in which a demand for relief against the respondent is included. By contrast, class members provide the court and their opponent with the grounds upon which their claims rest. By presenting to the court their claims, class members reveal their consent to class action or, in the words of the Italian law, their '*adesione*' – which is to say, acceptance – to class action.[44]

There is little practical difference between the complaint of class representative and the declaration of class member. While the motion of class representative must be served on the respondent no later than 20 days prior to the hearing on the motion, the declaration of class members must be filed with the court – that is, with the clerk of the court – within a reasonable time after class certification.[45] Even if the distinction between complaint and declaration implies that it is the claim of class representative that can be defined as the request to the court that seeks an order on the merits, both the class representative and class members are equally bound by the judgment. The declarations of class members serve no effects other than to accept the judgment on the merits. By accepting the class action, class members implicitly waive any individual lawsuit for money damages or restitution against the respondent.[46] In the end, one might define the role of class members as a joint participation to class litigation, while we have to deny that they can play any proper role as parties to the proceedings. Once class members have accepted the class action, they can only wait for the judgment.

The complaint of class representative must be served not only on the respondent, but also on the attorney general.[47] Even when he is served with a copy of the complaint, he is not obliged to intervene. In these cases, the service is required as a means of informing the attorney general that a party has chosen to seek a class certification. This rule should be amended because the participation of the attorney general to a class litigation is irrelevant to prosecuting the respondent for violations of criminal law. It would be more reasonable to expect the attorney general to be served with a copy of the complaint rather than to grant him the ability to intervene in the civil proceedings.

---

44 See art 140-bis.3 of the Italian Consumer Code (n 8).

45 Whether the time between class certification and filing is reasonable is a question left to the discretion of the court. Nevertheless, the Italian law requires that class members' declarations are to be filed with the clerk of court within, at most, 120 days after the publication of notice of class certification on newspapers or periodicals that are of general circulation in a particular province or city. See art 140-bis.3 and 9.b of the Italian Consumer Code (n 8).

46 See art 140-bis.3 of the Italian Consumer Code (n 8). See also Consolo and Zuffi, *L'azione di classe* (n 33) 132; Caponi, *Azioni collettive* (n 33) 1212.

47 See art 140-bis.5 of the Italian Consumer Code (n 8).

E. THE NEW ITALIAN CLASS ACTION: A GENERAL WAY OF STAKEHOLDER PROTECTION

Finally, it is worth noting that the Italian legislator has recently enacted a new regulatory regime of the Italian class action that will implement the Italian Code of Civil Procedure.[48] It will enter into force only in April 2020 when it will abrogate the class litigation ruled by article 140-bis of the Italian Consumer Code. The most important feature of the new class action is represented by the extent of its subjective and objective relevance. Class litigation will be not only a way of protecting the consumers' interests, but it will become a general way of implementing individual protection by applying to the court.

The new regulatory regime allows individuals and organisations to bring lawsuits for money damages on behalf of the class against a wrongdoer. The scope of the new Italian class action is not limited to those situations that are expressly determined by law, but it can be defined as broad and general. In any situations in which stakeholders can assert a violation of individual rights, they are entitled to bring such collective redress on behalf of the class.[49] The homogeneity among the situation in which the representative plaintiff is involved and situations in which class members are individually involved is the new requirement for the certification of class action. Putting this new requirement aside, the new legal regime maintains the same approach of the consumer class action.

On the procedural ground, the Italian class action continues to proceed on an opt-in basis. However, it is important noting that the possibility of class members to adhere to class litigation is not limited to a preliminary moment during the litigation itself, but it is now ensured even when the collective case has been already decided on the merits.[50] Class members will probably evaluate in a more cautious way their right to participate in class litigation because they will be informed about the judicial order on the merits – that is, how the case has been decided, which type of compensation has been ordered, and so on. Another important element of the new legal framework is the fact that both the court and the class representative are entitled to submit respectively to the parties and the wrongdoer a proposal to settle the case. The new legal provisions expressly grant class members who have decided to adhere to the class action the ability to participate in the agreement.[51]

---

48 See Italian Law no 31/2019 concerning the new Italian class action. The new legal rules will be introduced within the context of the Italian Code of Civil Procedure 1940 (Royal Decree no 1443/1940) (hereafter Italian Code of Civil Procedure).

49 See art 840-bis of the Italian Code of Civil Procedure (n 48).

50 See art 840-sexies.1.e of the Italian Code of Civil Procedure (n 48).

51 See art 840-quaterdecies of the Italian Code of Civil Procedure (n 48).

F. CONCLUSION

The Italian system of enforcing consumer and capital market law is the result of a complex legislative process. Such a process is strongly embedded within the European legal context. As noted above, the Italian system revolves around two peculiar tools. When individual litigation is not able to ensure an effective outcome for consumers, the Italian law allows them to bring a precautionary lawsuit or a class lawsuit in courts. While the precautionary litigation is aimed at protecting the collective interest of consumers, the class litigation is aimed at ensuring protection to individual rights and interests. The possibility to decide the case through a settlement is a real and practical opportunity for consumers and the wrongdoer. It is true not only when the violation of collective interests arises, but also when individual interests are at stake. In fact, even when the named plaintiff brings a class lawsuit on behalf of the class members, proposals to settle the case can be submitted to the entire class for approval. On this point, it is worth noting that the new Italian regulatory regime of class action reinforces the benefits of compromise for the parties.

V. THE APPLICATION OF ITALIAN CONSUMER AND CAPITAL MARKET LAW

The editors have assigned two hypothetical cases concerning two likely scenarios related to several points discussed in the debate over the Dieselgate scandal. As noted above, the consumer and capital market law must be applied flexibly to ever-changing circumstances. The efficacy and soundness of the legal system require that all remedies be infused with adapting force. The legal system's ability to adapt and respond to ever-changing circumstances depends on a web of theoretical and technical factors that determine the proper ends of consumer and capital market law. But examining the Italian legal framework does not end the inquiry into its enforcement. There remains the deeper question of how Italian consumers can react in any given case under existing legal rules. For these purposes, addressing a concrete legal problem is a proper method for assessing the soundness of applicable legal rules.

Bearing in mind the foregoing description of the Italian legal system, one can turn to the analysis of the assigned hypothetical cases.[52]

[52] See Introduction Section IV.A.

A. INTRODUCTION

Case 1 requires answering the question of whether those consumers who purchased defective vehicles are entitled to receive payment for their losses. At the same time, this case requires considering the legal consequences of protecting harmed consumers under existing legal rules. Consumers can individually or collectively bring lawsuits for money damages to the national courts. But they are also empowered to obtain precautionary orders that impede the automobile manufacturer to manipulate the emission values of its vehicles and to sell defective vehicles. Finally, it is worth noting that the behaviour of manufacturer is detrimental not only in terms of its effect on consumers who purchased (or risked purchasing) defective vehicles, but also in terms of fostering unfair commercial or competitive practices. Similarly, Case 2 revolves around the abusive use of confidential information on the capital market (insider trading).[53] According to Italian law, this kind of unlawful behaviour allows public prosecutors to investigate the member of the management board in order to ascertain his or her criminal liability. At the same time, Italian law authorises the Italian National Commission for Companies and the Stock Exchange to impose a fine ranging from €20,000 to €3,000,000 on the wrongdoer when he buys, sells or performs other operations, directly or indirectly, on his own behalf or on behalf of third parties on financial instruments by using confidential or inside information.[54]

Therefore, the analysis of Cases 1 and 2 can be usefully divided into three inquiries: the perspective of public law, the perspectives of private law and civil procedure and the perspective of general procedural law.

B. LEGAL ANALYSIS

1. *The Perspective of Public Law*

As noted above, the public enforcement of consumer and capital market law can be viewed as limited to (i) criminal prosecution when the wrongdoer's behaviour is relevant under criminal law and (ii) certain types of administrative actions when the wrongdoer's behaviour manifests itself in terms of unfair commercial or competitive practices.

The criminal prosecution warrants protection exclusively on public and general grounds. It secures the conviction and punishment of one accused of

---

53 See art 184 of the Italian Law on financial intermediation (Legislative Decree no 58/1998) (hereafter Italian Law on financial intermediation).

54 See art 187-bis of the Italian Law on financial intermediation (n 53).

crime. For example, with respect to Case 1, thus, a criminal prosecution would be substantially aimed at punishing the manufacturer when the manipulation of emission values could be described (and proved) as a conscious behaviour of the wrongdoer. It is plausible that a criminal accusation specifies that the wrongdoing on the part of the accused constitutes a violation of the law in terms of criminal fraud or environmental disaster according to the implications of the wrongdoing. If the wrongdoing imposes economic losses on those who purchased the manipulated vehicles, it will reasonably be relevant as a potential fraud. Instead, if the wrongdoing can be described as a complex behaviour whose impact is too broad to involve only the purchasers, it could be relevant as an environmental disaster. Although the emission values manipulation can create losses for those who purchased defective vehicles, it can also impose significant environmental harm. For example, the manipulation's harmfulness might occasionally be determined by its tendency to generate air pollutant emissions. These emissions could harm individual and environmental health.

In such cases, the Italian criminal law can affect the accused with imprisonment and/or fine. But it also provides a means of eliminating consequences and damages. This is true of Case 1 and Case 2. According to Italian criminal procedure law, those who are harmed by the crime are entitled to bring damages suits against the wrongdoer within the context of criminal proceedings.[55] That possibility allows those who are harmed to obtain the payment of compensation as well as the relinquishment of benefits or the return of money or other property obtained through an improper means.[56]

In cases involving the emission values manipulation, the public enforcement of Italian consumer and capital market law also depends on the possibility of administrative fines. In particular, the Italian Antitrust Authority is empowered to inhibit the continuation of unfair commercial and competitive practices and eliminate their harmful effects.[57] During the investigation, the Authority may request information or documentation from the wrongdoers or other subjects related to the wrongdoers.[58] If the wrongdoers do not comply with the request, the Authority is empowered to apply a fine from €2,000 to €20,000.[59] If the information or documentation provided is not truthful, the Authority can apply

55 See art 185.2 of the Italian Criminal Code 1930 (Royal Decree no 1398/1930) (hereafter Italian Criminal Code).

56 See art 185.1 of the Italian Criminal Code (n 55). It is also worth noting that, according to art 186 of the Italian Criminal Code, the publication of the judgment can be ordered by the judge when it serves as a means to repair the moral damage that was caused by the crime.

57 See art 27.2 of the Italian Consumer Code (n 8).

58 Ibid.

59 See art 27.4 of the Italian Consumer Code (n 8).

a fine from €4,000 to €40,000.[60] If the wrongdoers should be held responsible for the unfair commercial practices they voluntarily take, the Authority is empowered to (i) prohibit unfair practices to be initiated or even continued[61] and (ii) apply a fine from €5,000 to €5,000,000, taking into account the severity and length of the violation.[62] If the wrongdoer does not comply with such orders, the Authority can apply a further fine from €10,000 to €5,000,000.[63] In the most serious cases, the Authority can also order the suspension of the business activity for a period not exceeding 30 days.[64]

As noted above, this legal framework suggests that Italian public authorities have limited powers to control the violation of consumer and capital market law.[65] Similarly, they have limited powers to enforce consumer and capital market law within the context of public law. The complexity of criminal investigations, the length of criminal proceedings, and the limits that public law imposes on authorities in determining fines increase the likelihood that public enforcement of law proves difficult to articulate in a way that satisfies efficiency expectations.

2. *The Perspectives of Private Law and Civil Procedure*

As we have seen, the private enforcement of consumer and capital market law is called upon to play a crucial role within the Italian legal system. This kind of enforcement revolves entirely around representative and collective actions. In cases involving individual expectations, consumers are individually entitled to bring damages suits against the wrongdoer in national courts. But individual lawsuits create costly inefficiencies in the protection of consumers because unfair commercial or competitive practices generally impose little harms and little economic losses. By introducing both (i) a representative action aimed at impeding unfair commercial or competitive practices[66] and (ii) a class action aimed at ensuring payments to compensate consumers from the harms caused by the unfair commercial practices,[67] the Italian Consumer Code of 2005 provides comfort to consumers notwithstanding their limited individual resources.

As noted above, registered consumer associations are exclusively entitled to bring the representative lawsuits *sub* (i) on behalf of those consumers who

60 Ibid.
61 See art 27.8 of the Italian Consumer Code (n 8).
62 See art 27.9 of the Italian Consumer Code (n 8). See also supra Section I.
63 See art 27.12 of the Italian Consumer Code (n 8).
64 Ibid.
65 See supra Section I.
66 See art 140 of the Italian Consumer Code (n 8).
67 See art 140-bis of the Italian Consumer Code (n 8).

are harmed by unfair commercial or competitive practices.[68] By contrast, both registered consumer associations and individual consumers are entitled to bring the class lawsuits *sub* (ii) on behalf of those class members who decide to expressly adhere to the class action.[69]

The Italian legal system provides no financial relief for those who decide to bring a representative or collective action under the Italian Consumer Code. The Italian legal system is still rather unfamiliar with litigation funding. There are neither national rules nor standards in this respect. However, even though collective redress actions are not financed by third parties, consumers are generally spared from expending the resources needed to bring representative or collective actions in national courts. Both the representative lawsuits *sub* (i) and the class lawsuits *sub* (ii) are generally brought by the consumer associations that incur the costs of litigation.

As noted above, the parties may normally settle both their representative disputes *sub* (i) and their class disputes *sub* (ii) with the approval of the court. In particular, Italian law authorises consumer associations to settle representative disputes *sub* (i) before they are brought in national courts,[70] but it requires that proposals to settle the case be submitted to both the wrongdoer and the court for approval.[71] Italian law also authorises class representatives to settle class actions *sub* (ii). However, the proposals to settle the case can exert their binding force only if they are approved by the wrongdoer and class members, so that only those class members who expressly approve the proposal are bound to follow the compromise.[72]

Nevertheless, even though there are not special mechanisms for achieving collective agreements under existing legal rules, the new Italian legal regime on class action – a regime that will enter into force in April 2020[73] – provides that, during the class litigation, the court is empowered to articulate a proposal for settling the case.[74] The proposal must be submitted to the class representative and the wrongdoer for approval. If the parties approve the proposal, their settlement must be served on class members.[75] Because Italian class action proceeds on an

---

68 See art 139 of the Italian Consumer Code (n 8).

69 See art 140-bis.1 of the Italian Consumer Code (n 8).

70 See art 140.2 of the Italian Consumer Code (n 57). It is worth noting that the Italian law also authorises the wrongdoer to submit proposals to settle the case to the counterparty – that is, the consumer association – when the representative lawsuit has been *already* brought in national courts (though not decided). See art 140.6 of the Italian Consumer Code (n 8).

71 See art 140.3 of the Italian Consumer Code (n 8).

72 See art 140-bis.15 of the Italian Consumer Code (n 8).

73 See supra Section IV.E.

74 See art 840-quaterdecies.1 of the Italian Code of Civil Procedure (n 48) as introduced by the Italian Law no 31/2019 concerning the new Italian class action (hereafter Italian Law no 31/2019).

75 Ibid.

opt-in basis,[76] only those class members who have expressly decided to adhere to the class litigation are also asked to join the settlement. The new Italian law also authorises the wrongdoer and the class members representative who is specially appointed by the court in the judgment in which it declares that the case is closed[77] – that is, the ruling that adjudicates the class representative's claim – to articulate a proposal for settling the case.[78] The proposal must be served on those class members who have decided to adhere to class litigation for their approval.[79] The settlement can exert its binding force only with the approval of the court.[80]

According to Italian legal system, substantive assignment models have not developed for the process-based bundling of compensation claims. Many claims of class members are simply gathered by consumer associations when they decide to bring class lawsuits on behalf of other stakeholders. Nevertheless, such models would be consistent with the Italian rules of civil procedure because they simply allow putative class members to collectively enhance their claims.

As has been seen, the private enforcement of Italian consumer and capital market law revolves around remedies such as eliminations of consequences, damages, and skimming of profits. While representative actions *sub* (i) are aimed at impeding future infringements of individual rights such as unfair commercial or competitive practices, class actions *sub* (i) are aimed at ensuring the payment of compensation. In particular, when consumer associations choose to bring representative actions *sub* (i) in national courts, they are entitled to seek not only judicial orders for stopping or prohibiting unfair practices but also judicial orders for eliminating the harmful consequences of unfair practices.[81] By contrast, when consumer associations or individual consumers choose to bring class-wide lawsuits in national courts, they are entitled to claim their rights to compensation or restitution.[82]

The burden of proof is ordinarily distributed both in representative actions *sub* (i) and class actions *sub* (ii). This ordinary distribution entails that the plaintiffs – that is, consumer associations in actions *sub* (i) and consumer associations or individual consumers in actions *sub* (ii) – are generally asked to prove the material facts that are relevant to the claim, while the wrongdoer

---

76 See supra Section IV.D.

77 See art 840-sexies.1.g of the Italian Code of Civil Procedure (n 48) as introduced by the Italian Law no 31/2019 (n 74).

78 See art 840-quaterdecies.2 of the Italian Code of Civil Procedure (n 48) as introduced by the Italian Law no 31/2019 (n 74).

79 See art 840-quaterdecies.3 of the Italian Code of Civil Procedure (n 48) as introduced by the Italian Law no 31/2019 (n 74).

80 See art 840-quaterdecies.5 of the Italian Code of Civil Procedure (n 48) as introduced by the Italian Law no 31/2019 (n 74).

81 See art 140.1 of the Italian Consumer Code (n 8).

82 See art 140-bis.1 of the Italian Consumer Code (n 8).

is generally asked to prove the material facts that are relevant to the defence. However, Italian law facilitates the plaintiff in proving the material facts. When consumer associations bring representative lawsuits *sub* (i) in national courts, the fact-finding process is much simpler than the ordinary discovery procedure because the court is empowered to acquire the proofs in the way that it deems more appropriate.[83] To facilitate the fact-finding process, national courts can avail themselves of statistical data and presumptions even within the context of the new legal regime of Italian class actions *sub* (ii).[84] With respect to class actions, however, there is also a new legal rule that dictates the extent to which the judicial power to acquire proofs can be exercised to enhance the efficiency of discovery procedure by, among other things, performing time-saving strategies. According to this new legal regime, the court is empowered to proceed in the way it deems more appropriate to accomplish the evidentiary acts which are relevant with respect to the class dispute.[85] Even if the judicial power to accomplish the evidentiary acts is discretionary, the new Italian law requires judicial respect for the parties' equal opportunity to defence in accordance with the due process rule under article 111 of the Italian Constitution.[86]

Finally, it is worth noting that the inquiry into the new Italian class action highlights the potential importance of factors like the role played by the alleged injuring party – that is, the respondent – within the context of discovery procedure. In particular, the Italian law provides that, upon motion of the class representative, national courts may order the wrongdoer to exhibit in the proceeding those proofs, such as documents or other things, that are necessary to decide the case.[87] The Italian law considers the authority of national courts to order the exhibition of documents in the proceeding based on factors including their evidentiary weight, the costs of their exhibition, and the relevance of confidential information.[88] If the respondent disregards the judicial order, a pecuniary fine may be applied (from €10,000 to €100,000).[89]

---

83 See art 140.8 of the Italian Consumer Code (n 8). See also art 669-sexies.1 of the Italian Code of Civil Procedure (n 48).

84 See art 840-quinquies.4 of the Italian Code of Civil Procedure (n 48) as introduced by the Italian Law no 31/2019 (n 74).

85 See art 840-quinquies.2 of the Italian Code of Civil Procedure (n 48) as introduced by the Italian Law no 31/2019 (n 74).

86 See art 111 of the Italian Constitution of 1948.

87 See art 840-quinquies.5 of the Italian Code of Civil Procedure (n 48) as introduced by the Italian Law no 31/2019 (n 74).

88 See art 840-quinquies.6 of the Italian Code of Civil Procedure (n 48) as introduced by the Italian Law no 31/2019 (n 74).

89 See art 840-quinquies.11 of the Italian Code of Civil Procedure (n 48) as introduced by the Italian Law no 31/2019 (n 74).

3. *The Perspective of General Procedural Law*

The Italian legal system can raise concerns by permitting several legal actions to coexist in the course of a single dispute involving consumer or capital market law. The coexistence of representative actions *sub* (i) and class actions *sub* (ii) as well as the coexistence of two or more representative actions *sub* (i) or two or more class actions *sub* (ii) is considered under existing legal rules. While the coexistence of two or more representative actions *sub* (i) allows national court to consolidate litigations upon application of a party when they are related – that is, when the claims give rise to common issues in fact or law.[90] Similarly, the coexistence of two or more class actions *sub* (ii) allows national courts to consolidate litigations. But those consumers who are similarly situated than class members are entitled to bring other class actions in national courts only if the claims of class representatives are filed with the court within the time frame the court has provided for the adhesion of class members.[91] According to the Italian Consumer Code, class members are called upon to adhere to class action within the time frame the court expressly provides when it certifies the case as a class action.[92] However, it is established that the court cannot serve this rule discretionary, because the Italian law authorises class members to adhere to class litigation within 120 days after the class certification will be published (on newspapers or online) under existing legal rules.[93]

It is worth noting that the new regulatory regime of class actions allows those stakeholders who are similarly situated than class members to bring other class lawsuits in national courts within 60 days after the claim of class representative is filed with the court – or, more precisely, after it is published online.[94] Therefore, the new Italian law does not permit additional motions to

---

90 See art 140.9 of the Italian Consumer Code (n 8); see also arts 40 and 274 of the Italian Code of Civil Procedure (n 48).

91 See art 140-bis.14 of the Italian Consumer Code (n 8). As noted above, according to the Italian Consumer Code, class members are called upon to adhere to class action within the time frame the court expressly provides when it certifies the case as a class action. However, it is established that the court must serve this rule at least 120 days after the class certification will be published (on newspapers or online), see art 140-bis.9 of the Italian Consumer Code (n 8).

92 Ibid.

93 See art 140.9.b of the Italian Consumer Code (n 8). According to the new legal regime of class action, instead, this time frame can range *from 60 days to 150 days* after the court certifies the case as a class action or adjudicates the class representative's claim. See arts 840-quinquies.1 and 840-sexies.1.e of the Italian Code of Civil Procedure (n 48) as introduced by the Italian Law no 31/2019 (n 74).

94 See art 840-quater.1 of the Italian Code of Civil Procedure (n 48) as introduced by the Italian Law no 31/2019 (n 74). It is also worth noting that, according to the new regulatory regime, the complaint of class representative must be published online within ten days after it has been filed with the court. See art 840-ter.2 of the Italian Code of Civil Procedure (n 48) as introduced by the Italian Law no 31/2019 (n 74).

be filed with the court after that timeframe even though the additional motions concern the same kind of infringement of the law and the same respondent.[95] If additional motions are brought in national courts after that timeframe, the new motions cannot be filed with the court, and thus no additional sanctions will be imposed on the wrongdoer. By contrast, additional motions can be filed with the court until 60 days after the claim of class representative is filed with the court. In this case, national courts are expressly permitted to consolidate litigations upon application of a party.[96]

As has been seen, the legal regime of class actions provides procedural simplifications. They are particularly relevant to the extent they increase the efficacy of the fact-finding process and discovery procedure following the class certification.[97]

While the parties to a representative lawsuit *sub* (i) are directly bound by the judgment, those consumers who are represented by the consumer association that brought the lawsuit in court and, generally, those consumers who endured unfair commercial or competitive practices can avail themselves of the injunction order whereby the court stopped or prohibited those practices. By contrast, class actions certified under existing legal rules have binding effect on the class representative, the respondent, and whomever the court finds to be within the membership of the class because of their adhesion to the class action. The Italian law does not contemplate a binding effect of decisions *sub* (i) or *sub* (ii) on subsequent proceedings. This preclusion depends on the fact that, as has been seen, the Italian law provides the court with the power to refuse, under certain conditions, to certify the case as a class action. In particular, the class certification must be rejected when the claim of class representative is filed with the court after the timeframe established by law or provided by the court. With respect to representative actions *sub* (i), the crucial point is that consumer associations are empowered to seek an injunctive order that is able to protect all consumers, even if they brought the lawsuits in court only on behalf of a part of consumers affected by unfair practices.

The timeframe where consumers need to take action to seek collective redress after injury or damage depends on whether the cause of action involves a contract, personal injury, fraud, or other claims. Italian law classifies the statutes of limitations based on the distinction between contractual and extra-contractual liability. Generally, the statute of limitations for filing a lawsuit based upon personal injuries caused by the negligence of another person might be five years from the date of the accident under Italian legal rules. By contrast, in

95 See art 840-quater.1 of the Italian Code of Civil Procedure (n 48) as introduced by the Italian Law no. 31/2019 (n 74).

96 Ibid.

97 See supra Section V.B.2.

cases involving a breach of contract, the statute of limitations is generally longer than the time limits on personal injury cases. For example, breach of contract can be as long as ten years according to Italian law. The statute of limitations is suspended when the plaintiff brings the lawsuit – that is, both the representative lawsuit *sub* (i) and the class action *sub* (ii) – in the court. More precisely, the statute of limitations is suspended when the lawsuit is filed with the court in accordance with the Italian Code of Civil Procedure.[98]

According to Italian legal system, the respondent – that is, the wrongdoer – is called upon to bear the litigation risk. This risk can be understood as the possibility that legal action will be taken because of unfair commercial or competitive practices. The general rule governing the costs of litigation is that the loser in legal proceedings is required to incur the legal costs of the successful party. It is also worth noting that the Italian class action, as has been seen, proceeds on an opt-in basis. The opt-in mechanism occasionally imposes additional costs on the respondent because issues such as the legitimacy of class members or their membership to the class can arise from the respondent's right to provide the court with information about the evidence that will be used to defend against those class members who decided to adhere to the class litigation. However, the disclosure of class membership can impose significant costs on the respondent.

Finally, Italian law provides that both class representative and class members receive awarded and settled damages. Within the context of class action *sub* (ii), the existing legal regime requires the wrongdoer to make the payment of compensation to the class representative only when it is not a consumer association but an individual consumer.[99] Instead, the wrongdoer is always obliged to make the payment of compensation to class members after they have chosen to adhere to the class litigation.[100] Within the context of representative action *sub* (i), instead, the existing legal rules allow the court to order to the wrongdoer the payment of a fine on the application of consumer association. That fine can range from €516 to €1,032 for each infringement of the injunctive order that prohibits or impedes unfair commercial or competitive practices.[101] The same is true of the delay in performing the injunctive order. However, according to Italian law, the fine is received by the State in order to promote the protection of consumers' rights.[102]

98 See arts 2943.1 and 2945.2 of the Italian Civil Code (n 11).

99 See art 140-bis.2 of the Italian Consumer Code (n 8). Therefore, when the class representative is a consumer association, the claimant seeks relief to determine exclusively the respondent's liability.

100 See art 140-bis.12 of the Italian Consumer Code (n 8).

101 See art 140.7 of the Italian Consumer Code (n 8).

102 Ibid.

C. CONCLUSIONS

It is possible to conclude, following Case 1, that the purchasers are certainly entitled to bring class lawsuits for money damages against the manufacturer. The Italian Consumer Code authorises both individual purchasers both their representative associations to bring the class action on behalf of those other purchasers who have bought the same kind of vehicle whose emission values are manipulated. In Case 2, instead, it is highly likely that public prosecutors and the Italian National Commission for Companies and the Stock Exchange investigates the member of the management board who employs confidence information for achieving unjustified enrichment.

ENFORCING CONSUMER AND CAPITAL MARKETS LAW IN LITHUANIA

Egidija TAMOŠIŪNIENĖ* and Remigijus JOKUBAUSKAS**

* Egidija Tamošiūnienė, Dr., Judge at the Court of Appeal of Lithuania, Professor of practice at Vilnius University.

** Remigijus Jokubauskas, Adviser of the Division of Court Practice at the Court of Appeal of Lithuania. A freely accessible website for all Lithuanian legal acts: <http://www.e-tar.lt>. In this chapter, the versions of national laws which existed until 1 January 2020 are used.

This chapter describes public and private enforcement of consumer and capital market law in Lithuania. It is based on the analysis of two cases involving the diesel emissions scandal: Case 1 and Case 2. This chapter focuses on the public monitoring by governmental authorities of economic operators (traders) and liability for unfair competition. Also, it explains individual and collective mechanisms for private enforcement of consumer law in civil proceedings. In cases of large-scale infringements, the modern legal system shall ensure the same level of judicial defence which is guaranteed in individual cases. However, the model of individualistic civil proceedings which is based on individual and active involvement and participation of all parties is unable to deal with the challenges deriving from large-scale infringements.[1] A novelty in this area in Lithuania is the right to file a class action. A class action is particularly relevant for enforcement of individual and collective legal remedies. Furthermore, this report covers private enforcement of capital market law in case of bad faith actions in the sale and purchase contract of corporate's shares.

The chapter consists of four parts: Public Law (Section I), Private Enforcement of Consumer Law (Section II), General Procedural Law (Section III), Protection of Rights in the Capital Market (Section IV) and conclusions (Section V).

I. PUBLIC LAW

This section of the chapter explains which public authorities protect consumer rights and what sanctions they can impose for violation of consumer law, according to the Case 1 example and discuses other relevant questions.

A. DO ELIMINATIONS OF CONSEQUENCES, DAMAGES AND SKIMMING OF PROFITS (BY FINES) EXIST?

Consumer law is enforced by various public authorities in Lithuania. Some public authorities focus on specific market areas (energetics, financial services)

1 Vytautas Nekrošius and others, 'Class claim as means to speed up civil process' (2016) 98 Teisė 18 (hereafter Nekrošius and others, 'Class claim').

and some of them deal with the general enforcement of consumer law. The State Consumer Rights Protection Authority (lt. *Valstybinė vartotojų teisių apsaugos tarnyba*) (thereafter – *Authority*) and the Competition Council of the Republic of Lithuania (lt. *Lietuvos Respublikos konkurencijos taryba*) (thereafter – *Council*) are the main governmental institutions which deal with protection of consumer rights. The primary tool for public enforcement of consumer law is imposition of sanctions (fines) to economic operators (traders) which have infringed consumer rights and fair competition.

Article 46(5) of the Constitution[2] establishes that the State defends the interests of consumers. Defence of consumer public interest is defined as submission of an action (claim) for protection of consumer public interest to recognise or amend legal relations, prohibit (break off) actions (inaction) of the vendor or provider of services, which violate the general lawful consumer interests and are unfair to consumer and incompatible with the fair business practice or violate the Civil Code,[3] the Law on Protection of Consumer Rights of the Republic of Lithuania[4] or other legal acts.[5] Consumers' associations also can protect consumer public interest under certain conditions.[6] Consumer public interest is principally coupled with the basic values in the society which are established, protected and defended by the Constitution.[7] In administrative proceedings, when consumer interests are defended, three conditions shall be established: existence of public interest, special status (only persons recognised by the law can file a claim) and legal basis (such right shall be established by the law).[8]

The Authority implements state policy in protection of consumer rights and ensures protection of them.[9] It also monitors compliance of products with the legal requirements for safety, quality, marking,[10] imposes measures established by law[11] and protects consumer public interest.[12] Thus, the Authority has the power to investigate and protect consumer interests in case of a purchased faulty product.

---

2 Constitution of the Republic of Lithuania (hereafter Constitution).

3 Civil Code of the Republic of Lithuania (hereafter Civil Code).

4 Law on Protection of Consumer Rights of the Republic of Lithuania (hereafter Law on Protection of Consumer Rights).

5 Ibid, art 30(2).

6 Ibid, art 31.

7 Supreme Administrative Court of Lithuania, Ruling of 19 September 2013, A-502-586-13 Public search for all judgments of Lithuanian courts <http://liteko.teismai.lt/viesasprendimupaieska/detalipaieska.aspx?detali=2>.

8 Supreme Administrative Court of Lithuania, Ruling of 15 October 2013, A-146-585-13.

9 Law on Protection of Consumer Rights of the Republic of Lithuania, art 11(1).

10 Ibid, art 12(1)(1).

11 Ibid, art 12(1)(7).

12 Ibid, art 12(1)(8).

The Law on Prohibition of Unfair Commercial Practices[13] which implements the Unfair Commercial Practices Directive,[14] establishes prohibition of unfair commercial practices, types and cases of unfair commercial practices, authorities responsible for monitoring compliance with the provisions of this law, and liability for infringement of this law.[15] This law is applicable for commercial activities before, during and after a commercial transaction.[16] It also explicitly prohibits unfair competition.[17]

Misleading commercial practices which may infringe consumer rights is defined as misleading actions or omissions.[18] Misleading actions are defined as provision of fraudulent information or information, which is actually accurate but deceptive or likely to deceive an average consumer and he or she may be encouraged to make such decision which he would not have made in other circumstances.[19] The Authority controls how economic operators comply with the Law on Prohibition of Unfair Commercial Practices.[20] The Authority has the right to obtain information and documents from state and municipal institutions and bodies, and other persons necessary for investigating the violation;[21] obtain information and documents from economic traders;[22] require economic operators and other persons responsible for commercial practices to present oral or written explanations;[23] impose fines or warnings[24] and impose a provisional measure (to cease unfair commercial activities).[25] According to the relevant case law, actions which are contrary to the requirements of professional diligence do not necessarily have to cause consequences, meaning that they do not have to distort consumer economic actions, since influence on consumer activities can be established when there is a possibility of such influence.

The Law on Prohibition of Unfair Commercial Practices establishes the procedure of investigation of unfair commercial practices. Consumers, governmental and municipal institutions, consumers' associations have the right

---

13 Law on Prohibition of Unfair Commercial Practices for Consumer of the Republic of Lithuania (hereafter Law on Prohibition of Unfair Commercial Practices).
14 European Parliament and Council Directive 2005/29/EC of 11 May 2005 concerning unfair business-to-consumer commercial practices in the internal market [2005] OJ L149.
15 Law on Prohibition of Unfair Commercial Practices for Consumer of the Republic of Lithuania, art 1.
16 Ibid, art 1(2).
17 Ibid, art 3(1).
18 Ibid, art 4.
19 Ibid, art 5(1).
20 Ibid, art 9(1).
21 Ibid, art 10(1)(1).
22 Ibid, art 10(1)(1).
23 Ibid, art 10(1)(3).
24 Ibid, art 10(1)(4).
25 Ibid, art 10(1)(5).

to appeal to the Authority for the infringement of this law.[26] The Authority may, within its competence, impose a fine from €289 to €8,688, if this fine does not exceed 3 per cent of the annual income of the economic operator in the previous financial year of the economic operator for unfair commercial practices.[27] In cases where the infringement is of minor importance, it does not cause substantial harm to the interests of consumer protected by this law, the Authority may impose a penalty (warning) on economic operators in accordance with the criteria of fairness and reasonableness.[28] It shall consider aggravating and mitigating circumstances, nature, scope and duration of the violation.[29] The investigation procedure of unfair commercial practices is regulated in detail in the Rules on Investigation of the Infringements of the Law on Prohibition of Unfair Commercial Practices for Consumer.[30]

The Council deals with unfair competition and protection of consumer as well. The Law on Competition[31] prohibits economic operators to conduct any actions which violate fair practice of business and good customs, when such actions can impede possibilities of another economic operator to compete.[32] One of the examples of unfair competition established by this law is to mislead or provide false information of economic operators about itself or another economic operator's quantity, quality, composition, peculiarities of consumption, place of production, method, prices of goods or reticence about risks, linked with the consumption of such goods, recycling or other usage.[33]

The Council has the right to oblige economic operators to cease illegal activities, restore the previous situation or eliminate consequences of the infringement[34] and impose fines.[35] Sanctions may be imposed for the infringements of the Law on Competition no later than five years from the date of the infringement and, if there is a continuous or persistent infringement, from the date of the last action or termination.[36]

The Council imposes fines considering such criteria: danger, duration of the infringement, mitigating and aggravating circumstances, impact of each economic operator if the infringement was committed by few economic operators, the value of sold goods directly or indirectly related to the infringement.[37]

26 Ibid, art 15(1).
27 Ibid, art 13(1).
28 Ibid, art 13(1).
29 Ibid, art 13(3–5).
30 Rules on Investigation of the infringement of the Law on Prohibition of Unfair Commercial Practices for Consumer adopted by the Order of the Minister of Justice, no 1R-68.
31 Law on Competition of the Republic of Lithuania (hereafter Law on Competition).
32 Ibid, art 15(1).
33 Ibid, art 15(2).
34 Ibid, art 35(1)(1).
35 Ibid, art 35(1)(4).
36 Ibid, art 35(3).
37 Ibid, art 37(1).

If the infringer disputes the fine, the court has to analyse whether the Council acted in accordance with these rules.[38]

Nevertheless, not each infringement of unfair competition is investigated. The Council investigates acts of unfair competition only if such actions infringe interests of the majority of economic operators or consumers.[39] Therefore, the authority of the Council to impose pecuniary penalties is not coupled with the infringement of individual (single) interests. Fines for the actions of unfair competition are up to 3 percent of gross annual income of the economic operator in the previous financial year.[40] Thus, even though the Council enjoys significant discretion for imposition of fines, it is restricted by the general principles (proportionality and equal assessment) and special rules which regulate the imposition of fines.[41]

To sum up, consumer law is enforced primarily by defence of consumer public interests and imposition of fines on economic operators (traders). The Authority has a right to file an action to the court for protection of consumer public interest. However, such practice is not popular. Thus, currently private enforcement of consumer law is a more efficient and practical solution in such situations.

B. COMPARED TO PRIVATE ENFORCEMENT: HOW STRONG IS THE MONITORING AND LAW ENFORCEMENT BY PUBLIC AUTHORITIES OR OTHER PUBLIC BODIES?

Monitoring and enforcement of consumer rights are performed by several public institutions in Lithuania. The Authority and the Council are the main public bodies in this area.

According to the Statute,[42] the Council performs certain functions related to the monitoring of competition. The Council monitors how economic operators and entities of public administration comply with the requirements established by the Law on Competition,[43] investigates and examines infringements of the Law on Competition and other laws and impose sanctions for infringers according to the laws;[44] recourses to the court to protect public interests established by the Law on Competition,[45] monitors competition and provides conclusions and

38 Supreme Administrative Court of Lithuania, Ruling of 4 March 2015, A-1672-822/2015.
39 Law on the Competition of the Republic of Lithuania, art 16(4).
40 Ibid, art 36(2).
41 Administrative Court of Lithuania, Ruling of 4 March 2015, A-1672-822/2015.
42 Statute of the Competition Council of the Republic of Lithuania (hereafter Statute).
43 Ibid, art 8(1).
44 Ibid, art 8(5).
45 Ibid, art 8(6).

suggestions to the Parliament or the Government regarding the appropriate measures to ensure effective competition.[46]

The Authority performs specific market monitoring functions related to the protection of consumer interests and fair competition. Since the Authority is a subject of public administration, it acts in the framework of administrative law. The general legal basis of monitoring of economic operators derives from article 36^1 of the Law on Public Administration of the Republic of Lithuania. Monitoring should be compatible with these principles: minimal and proportional burden of monitoring, non-discrimination, planning, publicity, provisions of methodical assistance, separation of functions, assessment of risk.[47]

The Rules[48] regulate the order of annual monitoring. The purpose of this monitoring is to provide methodical assistance to economic operators for assessment of information of economic operators, communicate with them and consult questions which fall under the competence of the Authority and implement other means of preventive character, which help economic operators to follow the legal requirements. Measures are imposed on economic operators only when the goals of monitoring cannot be achieved by other lawful means and also in order to prevent damage to the society and interests of other persons.[49] Monitoring shall be proportional[50] and without discrimination to economic operators.[51] Monitoring can encompass the whole economic operator or part of it. At the same time no more than two monitoring procedures of the economic operator can be carried out.[52] When planning monitoring activities of economic operators, the Authority considers consumer requests, information provided by the consumer associations, information received from the governmental and municipal institutions, publicly announced information, other relevant circumstances.[53]

A few types of monitoring are established. One of the types of the monitoring is monitoring in the area of commercial practices for consumers. In such cases the Authority demands the economic operator to provide certain necessary information. If the Authority identifies a possible infringement of the Law on Prohibition of Unfair Commercial Practices, it can set up a term of at least one month to eliminate economic activities which may be contrary to the said law.[54] If the economic operator does not implement the decision or fails to provide a

---

46 Ibid, art 8(9) (n 42).

47 Law on Public Administration of the Republic of Lithuania, art $36^2(1)$.

48 Rules of the Monitoring Conducted by the Authority adopted by the Order of the Chairperson of the State Consumer Rights Protection Authority no 1-57 (hereafter Rules).

49 Ibid, art 4.

50 Ibid, art 5.

51 Ibid, art 6.

52 Ibid, art 7.

53 Ibid, art 8.

54 Ibid, art 12.1–12.3.

motivated explanation, the Authority has a right to commence the investigation procedure.[55] The results of the monitoring could be also used in the private enforcement of consumer law in the civil proceedings.

II. PRIVATE ENFORCEMENT OF CONSUMER LAW

This section of the chapter explains what mechanisms of private enforcement of consumer law are available in Lithuania in large-scale infringements, according to the Case 1 example and discusses other relevant questions.

A. TYPES OF INDIVIDUAL ACTION AND COLLECTIVE REDRESS

At the highest level the guarantees of protection of consumer rights are enshrined in article 46(5) of the Constitution, which establishes that the state defends the interest of consumers; this constitutional provision is one of the fundamental principles of Lithuanian economy and it is implemented through the system of lower power legal norms.

In Lithuanian legal system consumers can enforce their rights by addressing to the economic operator (trader) or commencing proceedings in pre-trial dispute settlement institutions and (or) courts.[56] Nevertheless, in situation of a large-scale infringement of consumer rights, it is likely that proceedings in the court would be commenced right away. In the situation of a large-scale infringement of consumer rights three options for civil proceedings are available for consumers:

- an individual action;
- optional procedural joinder;
- a class action.

Thus, a consumer can either file an individual action to the court or protect his or her rights together with a group of consumers (optional procedural joinder or a class action). Each of these options are explained.

1. *An Individual Action*

According to article 5(1) of the Code of Civil Procedure,[57] every person who considers that his or her civil rights have been violated, has a right to

55 Ibid, art 12.4.
56 Law on Protection of Consumer Rights of the Republic of Lithuania, art 20(1).
57 Code of Civil Procedure of the Republic of Lithuania (hereafter Code of Civil Procedure).

file an action to the court.[58] Also, in consumer disputes a consumer can be represented by the association of consumers in the court if certain requirements are met.[59]

The case law has established that consumers should be protected in the adjudication. The Supreme Court of Lithuania has repeatedly stated that protection of consumer rights is a constitutional principle of the administration of the state economy (article 46(5) of the Constitution, article 6.188 of the Civil Code), disputes related to protection of consumer rights often exceed the limits of private relations, protection of consumer rights shall be regarded as the public interest, not only for the consumer but also for a large part of society; the current legislation and case law confirm that the specificity of the dispute arising from a consumer contract determines that courts shall be active in the proceedings.[60] However, what does this active court's role actually mean in practice? First, it means that the court has to take care of a faire, good faith, fast and appropriate settlement of the case. Second, the court may apply additional legal remedies which are not demanded by the claim.[61] Also, the court should offer to take care or representation if the consumer fails effectively defend and explain negative consequences of inappropriate representation.[62]

Nevertheless, the fact that the case is related to a consumer contract, does not eliminate the duty of a claimant (a consumer) to collect and submit relevant evidence. A claimant shall prove the circumstances on which he or she relies.[63] The active role of the court shall not infringe the principle of adversary proceedings which means that each party shall prove the circumstances upon which the party relies unless the law establishes that certain circumstances shall not be proved.[64]

2. *Optional Procedural Joinder*

Another option in situations, involving a number of related persons is optional procedural joinder (lt. *neprivalomas procesinis bendrininkavimas*).[65] It is likely that in a large-scale infringement of consumer rights individual disputes between the economic trader and consumers may be sufficiently interlinked, including similar factual circumstances and legal questions. In such case centralisation of claims may be particularly effective.

58 Ibid, art 5(1).
59 Ibid, art 56(1)(6).
60 Supreme Court of Lithuania, Ruling of 17 November 2017, e3K-3-414-421/2017.
61 Supreme Court of Lithuania, Ruling of 21 February 2014, 3K-3-42/2014.
62 Supreme Court of Lithuania, Ruling of 7 November 2018, e3K-3-409-1075/2018.
63 Code of Civil Procedure, art 178 (n 57).
64 Supreme Court of Lithuania, Ruling of 15 July 2015, e3K-3-420-969/2015.
65 Code of Civil Procedure, art 43(1)(2) (n 57).

An action may be brought by several claimants together or against several defendants if the subject of the claim is of the same nature, based on the same matter of factual and legal issues, when each separate claim could be a subject of an independent action (optional procedural joinder).[66] In every case optional procedural joinder is an option, but not an obligation, meaning that claimants have a right, but not a duty to submit an action together since individual actions could be submitted as well. One of the major incentives for option procedural joinder would be procedural efficiency and reduced litigation costs.[67]

In optional procedural joinder each participant (a claimant) acts on his/her own behalf.[68] However, participants may agree to have the case conducted by one of them.[69] Each participant shall have the right to act independently. All participants, for whom the case is not closed, shall be summoned to the court hearing.[70] Also, each participant has a right to submit an individual action to the court, but their connection is based on identity of reliefs, nature of obligations, facts and the legal questions.[71] If an action is submitted by several claimants, the court has also to decide whether there is a sufficient connection between the claims of each claimant. When several claimants submit joined claims or they are submitted against several defendants the court has a right to separate one or more claims into a separate case, if it is more appropriate to deal with them separately.[72] The court after establishing that several cases of a single type in which the same parties are participating or that several cases are based on claims of a single claimant against different defendants or actions of different claimants against the same defendant have been filed in the court(s), can join these cases into a single case in order to hear them together if in such case the disputes would be heard more expeditiously and lawfully as well as in cases when claims are intertwined and due to this it is impossible to examine them separately.[73] In general, the institution of joining of cases is applicable when a part of circumstances which should be determined overlap and it causes the need to assess the same arguments of the parties and evidence. Joining of cases in such instance complies with the principles of process efficiency and economy and allows to settle the dispute between the parties faster and more efficiently, prevents the adoption of different rulings on the matter and suspension of one of the cases.

66 Ibid, art 41(1)(2).
67 Supreme Court of Lithuania, Ruling of 22 December 2010, 3K-7-521/2010.
68 Code of Civil Procedure, art 44(1) (n 57).
69 Ibid, art 44(2).
70 Ibid, art 44(4).
71 Supreme Court of Lithuania, Ruling of 5 December 2018, e3K-3-478-687/2018.
72 Code of Civil Procedure, art 137(2) (n 57).
73 Ibid, art 136(4).

Noteworthy, each claimant acts independently from each other and actions of one claimant do not have impact on the rights and duties of the others.[74] For instance, if one claimant files an appeal, it will have no impact on other claimants and each of them should defend his or her rights against the judgment of the first instance court only by filling an appeal.[75] Similarly, if one claimant files a cassation claim, the court of cassation will analyse only the part of the judgment of the court of appeal which is related to the claimant who filed the claim.[76] Agreement of all participants is mandatory to conclude a peace agreement, except for cases when this action is performed within the scope of claims.[77]

In case of a large-scale infringement of consumer rights an optional procedural joinder may be a reasonable choice. However, claimants would have to prove that their claims sufficiently intertwine and are based on the same factual circumstances and legal questions. In such disputes optional procedural joinder may be advantageous for both parties. For claimants it would help to harmonise legal defence and possibly reduce litigation costs. For the defendant it allows to avoid litigation in multiple cases which would inevitably increase litigation costs and may harm procedural efficiency. Also, centralisation of claims may be useful for harmonisation of the case law. Multiple litigation proceedings which basically relate to the same subject matter may hamper unanimous interpretation and application of law. Possibility to deal with such large-scale civil disputes in one case would allow to look for a common solution.

3. *A Class Action*

Class actions are particular in a way that they aim to combine a big class of persons' identical or similar claims which arise from the same mass violation of law.[78] It manifests either through certain legislative initiatives on the EU level, or when instances of mass damage are revealed.[79] The European civil proceedings doctrine has stated for many years that a class action should ensure the recovery of small damages (which are smaller than the cost of litigation), the pursuit of which on a case-by-case basis would be too expensive;[80] it should also ensure potentially better protection of consumer rights and environmental interests.

74 Supreme Court of Lithuania, Ruling of 5 December 2018, e3K-3-478-687/2018.
75 Supreme Court of Lithuania, Ruling of 22 December 2010, 3K-7-521/2010.
76 Supreme Court of Lithuania, Ruling of 4 July 2018, 3K-3-213-687/2018.
77 Code of Civil Procedure, art 44(3) (n 57).
78 Nekrošius and others, 'Class claim' (n 1) 18.
79 Caroline Meller-Hannich, *Sammelklagen, Gruppenklagen, Verbandsklagen – bedarf es neuer Instrumente des kollektiven Rechtsschutzes Im Zivilprozess?* (CH Beck 2018) 9.
80 Monika Rejdak and Pawel Pietkiewicz, *Ustawa o dochodzeniu roszczen w postępowaniu grupowym. Komentarz* (Lexis Nexis 2011) 16.

A class action is established in Chapter XXIV^{1} (articles 441^{1}–41^{17}) of the Code of Civil Procedure. The general rules of civil proceedings are applicable for a class action unless the special rules established in this chapter regulate otherwise.[81] This option is available only if certain requirements set out in the Code of Civil Procedure are met. If these requirements are not met, ordinary civil proceedings should be commenced instead (an individual action or an optional procedural joinder). A class action is explained as mechanism of defence of collective interests.[82]

The right to file a class action is a novelty in Lithuanian civil proceedings. Nevertheless, a class action has not been popular since the new regulation entered into force. One of the reasons is that there are no and should not be many appropriate mass disputes, compared to the situations of individual disputes. During the period of 2015–18 claimants filed a class action in ten cases. As regards the admissibility of a class action, the courts in Lithuania have found in some cases that the action is based on different factual circumstances and non-identical material legal norms, also the claimants failed to use the pre-trial dispute resolution system. In other cases the courts have refused to accept a class action because of the following grounds: the claims of the group did not meet the criterion of common facts, so the class action was not a more expedient, effective and appropriate way of resolving the particular dispute than an individual action; failure to follow the pre-trial dispute settlement procedure, as well as failure to comply with the rules of jurisdiction and eliminate deficiencies of the claim. These examples show that persons have sought to use a class action only in few cases and only two of these cases were successful. Currently, in one class action case the representative of the group of investors (the Investors' Association) argues that non-redemption of the third-party BAB bank Snoras bonds acquired by the claimants is an insured event and insurance payments shall be awarded. A class action is submitted in another case in which the subject matter of the claim is the right to purchase land without auction.

The *travaux préparatoires* of the adoption of the class action regulation suggest that the goal of this procedure is to facilitate litigation in cases involving a large group of persons who are linked with factually and legally homogenous claims deriving from identical factual circumstances and the same legal basis.[83] Thus, two aspects are particularly important for a class action: a quantitative criterion (a number of persons) and a sign of commonality (the members of the group are related with similar material relation and the common interests for the

---

81 Supreme Court of Lithuania, Ruling of 14 February 2019, 3K-3-40-313/2019.

82 Ibid.

83 Resolution of the Government of the Republic of Lithuania concerning the adoption of approval of a class action, Lietuvos Respublikos Vyriausybė, 'Nutarimas dėl Grupės ieškinio koncepcijos patvirtinimo' (13 July 2011 no 885).

outcome of the case). A class action should allow defendants to save financial, human, and time resources to defend against multiple claims, and distribute them more rationally and to avoid divergent court judgments and ensure legal certainty. Namely, one of the reasons for the adoption of the regulation of a class action was protection of consumers.[84]

One of the most important issues related to the institution of a class action is its scope, i.e. the relationship from which the claims derive. Article $441^1(2)$ of the Code of Civil Procedure establishes that a class action can be filed when the claim is based on identical or similar factual circumstances and it aims at using the same remedies for a class of natural or legal persons who brought an action to defend their identical or similar substantive rights or interests safeguarded by law. This feature is particularly stressed in the case law by indicating that a class action is dedicated to such cases where homogeneous legal and factual claims of applicants are resolved; and the aim of a class action is to use the same remedies for a class of natural or legal persons to defend their identical or similar substantive rights or interests safeguarded by law in a more effective and appropriate manner.[85] However, soon after the introduction of 'wide application' class action, concerns were raised that such a system may give rise to the abuse of this institution, when claims would be brought and based on false circumstances for purely economic reasons.[86] Therefore, Lithuania is among the few EU Member States which established the system of a wide-application class action, which can be restricted solely by the sameness and similarity of claims, and minimal requirements for the size of a class. The aim of such regulation is to develop as favourable conditions as possible for the application of this institution in practice and to improve the prospects of recovering collective small damages. However, the case law in the last three years shows that this institution has not become a part of society's legal culture yet, since it is used rather seldom and, unfortunately, not effectively.

A class action could be filed when a certain similar link between all persons in the group is established. If all persons in the group are not connected by identical or similar legal relations, a class action should not be accepted.[87] There is no specific requirement for a subject matter of a class action, meaning that is possible in all civil proceedings. Participation of an attorney is mandatory in a class action.[88]

A pre-trial dispute settlement procedure is set up before a class action is filed to the court. The representative of the group shall notify the defendant

---

84 Ibid.

85 Court of Appeal of Lithuania, Ruling of 19 July 2018, e2-860-302/2018.

86 Rimantas Daujotas, 'Class action in Lithuania – practical implementation issues' (2016) 101 Teisė 29–48.

87 Court of Appeal of Lithuania, Ruling of 10 July 2015, e2-816-157/2015.

88 Code of Civil Procedure, art 4411 (3) (n 57).

about intention to file a class action by sending a written claim. Such claim should include a description of the group, demands and warning that the group will recourse to the court unless demands are not fulfilled in time. Such period should not be less than 30 days. If the defendant does not respond in time, it is deemed that demands were not fulfilled.[89] This procedure is not applicable if other laws establish certain mandatory pre-trial dispute settlement procedure.[90]

A class action can be filed to the court if all these requirements are met:

1. it is filed for the dispute according to the circumstances laid down in article 441^1(2) of the Code of Civil Procedure;
2. a class action is more expedient, effective and appropriate to settle a concrete dispute than individual actions;
3. the pre-trial dispute settlement procedure set out in article 441^2 of the Code of Civil Procedure has been followed;
4. the group has an appropriate representative.[91]

Also, a couple more special requirements for a class action shall be satisfied:

1. at least 20 natural or legal persons submit a claim which expresses their will in writing to be participants of the group and file an action to the court;
2. the group has a groups' attorney.[92]

The Supreme Court of Lithuania has summarised these requirements and concluded that basically a class action is based on two assumptions: first, willingness of the group of persons to defend their rights by a class action, second, the court's assessment that the dispute, pursuant to its nature, complies with certain legal requirements.[93]

One of the major requirements which shall be established is that a class action would be more expedient, effective and appropriate to settle a concrete dispute instead of filling individual actions. In other words, the court should analyse whether a class action would be a better solution for a specific legal dispute than individual actions. There are no guidelines in the Code of Civil Procedure as to which criteria are applicable for such assessment and the court should analyse all relevant circumstance of each individual case. Also, if pecuniary claims (lt. *turtiniai ginčai*) are submitted by the class action, they must be individualised. This requirement is coupled with the need to examine each claim appropriately.

---

89 Ibid, art 441^2 (1).
90 Ibid, art 441^2 (2).
91 Ibid, art 441^3 (1). The second requirement (a class action is more expedient, effective and appropriate to settle a concrete dispute than individual actions) was abolished in January 2020.
92 Ibid, art 441^3 (2)(1–2).
93 Supreme Court of Lithuania, Ruling of 14 February 2019, 3K-3-40-313/2019.

Nevertheless, the court shall analyse relevant facts in each case pursuant to the subject matter of the dispute, the nature of the claim and avoid disproportional burden to the claimant to provide all relevant circumstances.[94] Formal procedural shortcomings should not hinder the implementation of the right to file a class action.[95]

The Code of Civil Procedure establishes the requirements for a class action and its annexes.[96] One of the main requirements is to substantiate why the claims should be more expediently, effectively and appropriately tried in a class action procedure. The group which files a class action shall be represented by the representative who signs a class action on behalf of the group and represents the interests of the group together with the group's attorney.[97]

The position of the member of the group should be briefly explained. All members of the group are regarded as claimants. In general, all members of the group are presented by the representative of the group. If the member of the group submits a pecuniary claim, he or she shall also submit all relevant evidence. The member has a right to leave the group and file an individual claim.[98]

The court is also active if the case in which a class action is filed. In such cases the court can: summon other members of the group;[99] suggest to the representative of the court to change the attorney if the attorney does not properly represent the interests of the group in court proceedings;[100] suggest to the group to change the representative of the group if the representative does not properly represent the interests of the group;[101] decide on the expediency, effectiveness and appropriateness of further examination of the case in accordance with the rules of a class action if the number of the members of the group decreases.[102] These actions relate to the effective case management.

For a class action for a non-pecuniary claim the stamp duty is €500. This stamp duty is shared equally between the members of the group.[103] If pecuniary claims of individual nature are submitted, the claims shall be aggregated and the amount of stamp duty shall be calculated according to the general rules of the Code of Civil Procedure. Each member of the group has to the share stamp duty proportionally to the amount of the individual claim.[104] The same rules are applicable to an appeal or cassation claim in a class action case.

---

94 Ibid.

95 Ibid.

96 Code of Civil Procedure, art 441^{3} (3–4) (n 57).

97 Ibid, art 441^{3} (3)(8).

98 Ibid, art 441^{5}.

99 Ibid, art 441^{11} (1).

100 Ibid, art 441^{11} (2).

101 Ibid, art 441^{11} (3).

102 Ibid, art 441^{11} (4).

103 Ibid, art 441^{16} (1).

104 Ibid, art 441^{16} (2).

Certain types of court judgments are established in cases in which a class action is filed: a common judgment (lt. *bendras sprendimas*) is rendered by the court after hearing the claims of the class action in the oral procedure, which is common to all members of the group;[105] an intermediate judgment (lt. *tarpinis sprendimas*) is made after an oral assessment of the group's collective claims on the facts uniting the group that is common to all members of the group and rendered in cases in which individual pecuniary claims are submitted;[106] an individual judgment (lt. *individualus sprendimas*) is rendered in a written procedure (or, after the oral procedure) according to the valid intermediate decision which examined individual pecuniary claims of each member of the group.[107]

To sum up, a class action model in Lithuania is an appropriate mechanism for the disputes involving multiple consumers' claims which derive from similar factual circumstances and legal issues. Even though a class action shall meet several criteria, its application in consumer disputes, such as described in the Case 1 example is particularly possible. It should be particularly attractive since individual claims can be submitted by the class action, meaning that each member of the group can seek individual redress. Such individualisation of claims allows each member to demand specific remedies (for instance, a specific amount of damages to be paid) which derive from the same factual circumstances and legal matter.

B. SUBSTANTIVE ASSIGNMENT MODELS – PROCESS-BASED BUNDLING OF COMPENSATION CLAIMS

In general, a creditor may without consent of a debtor assign to another person all or a part of the claim provided that the transfer does not contradict with laws or the contract, or the claim is not related with the person of a creditor.[108] No specific rules of assignment of compensation claims are established for the claims which derive from consumer law.

C. ARE REMEDIES SUCH AS ELIMINATIONS OF CONSEQUENCES, DAMAGES AND SKIMMING OF PROFITS AVAILABLE?

Irrespective of which option of civil defence in consumer disputes is used, the general rules of legal remedies are applicable. A claimant has to choose the

105 Ibid, art 441^{9} (1).
106 Ibid, art 441^{9} (2).
107 Ibid, art 441^{9} (3).
108 Civil Code, art 6.101(1) (n 3).

most appropriate individual remedies in each case. Regarding possible legal remedies, elimination of negative consequences[109] and (or) compensation of damages[110] are both available in civil proceedings. A claimant can demand a full compensation of suffered damages (*restitutio in integrum*). The purpose of *restitutio in integrum* is to return the person to the situation in which they were before the infringement.[111] However, specific legal remedies which may be found in other states like skimming of profits are not established as a legal remedy in Lithuanian civil law.

D. DOES FACILITATION TO GIVE PROOF EXIST? HOW IS THE BURDEN OF PROOF DISTRIBUTED? ARE THERE ANY DEMANDS FOR INFORMATION AGAINST THE ALLEGED INJURING PARTY?

The parties must prove the circumstances used as a basis to substantiate their claims except for circumstances which are considered indemonstrable in accordance with the procedure defined by the Code of Civil Procedure.[112] Nevertheless, the court is more active in cases which involve protection of consumer rights. It can recover evidence from persons that may not be obtained by other participants in the proceedings,[113] collect evidence *ex officio* in cases defined by the Code of Civil Procedure and other laws.[114]

III. GENERAL PROCEDURAL LAW

This section of the chapter discusses the relevant issues of general procedural law which relate to enforcement of consumer law.

A. IS A COEXISTENCE OF SEVERAL LEGAL ACTIONS POSSIBLE?

A person has to choose a certain way how to defend rights in civil proceedings. It means that a claimant has to choose either to defend rights individually

109 Ibid, art 1.138(1).
110 Ibid, art 1.138(6).
111 Supreme Court of Lithuania, Ruling of 7 January 2017, 3K-3-44/2015.
112 Code of Civil Procedure, art 178 (n 57).
113 Ibid, art 160(1)(2).
114 Ibid, art 160(1)(6).

(an individual action) or collectively (optional procedural joinder or a class action). Also, when separate similar actions are filed, the court can join cases into a single case under certain circumstances. Noteworthy, if a class action is filed and a person files an individual action which is based on analogous or similar factual circumstances and analogous or similar demands to the same respondent seeking for the same legal redress, such claimant can withdraw the action and become the member of the group which filed the class action.[115]

B. ARE THERE ANY PROCEDURAL SIMPLIFICATIONS IN CONSUMER AND CAPITAL MARKET LAW?

There are no procedural simplifications in consumer and capital market law. However, the court is more active in cases which involve protection of consumer rights. In such cases the court can recover evidence from persons that may not be obtained by the participants in the proceedings,[116] collect evidence *ex officio*.

C. WHAT IS THE BINDING EFFECT OF DECISIONS FOR SUBSEQUENT PROCEEDINGS?

In the Lithuanian legal system, the rule of precedent exists. Courts shall be bound by the rules of interpretation of law formed in analogous or essentially similar cases.[117] Judicial practice shall be amended and the new rules for the interpretation of law in analogous or similar cases may be created only in cases when it is inevitable or objectively necessary.[118] The Supreme Court of Lithuania shall develop a uniform court practice in the interpretation and application of statutes and other legal acts.[119] These rules of formation of judicial practice are applicable in consumer disputes as well.

D. WHEN IS THE STATUTE OF LIMITATION FOR COLLECTIVE REDRESS SUSPENDED?

No specific statute of limitation is established for collective redress. The general limitation period is ten years.[120] However, a three-year limitation

---

115 Ibid, art 441[10].
116 Ibid, art 160(1)(2).
117 Law on Courts of the Republic of Lithuania, art 33(4).
118 Ibid, art 33(4).
119 Ibid, art 23(2).
120 Civil Code, art 1.125(1) (n 3).

period is established for compensation of damage, including claims for the compensation of damage caused by defective production.[121] The limitation period begins when the person became aware or should have become aware of the violation of his or her rights.[122] Suspension of the statute of limitation is possible in exceptional cases.[123]

E. WHO BEARS THE LITIGATION RISKS?

In civil proceedings the rule 'loser-pays' is applicable.[124] Thus, if the action is dismissed, the claimant has to pay litigation costs.

The model of limited allocation of procedural costs in cases of a class action is applicable. According to article 98(1) of the Code of Civil Procedure, the party in whose favour the ruling was made shall be awarded by the court from the second party the litigation costs for the assistance of attorney or attorney's assistant who participated in the hearing of the case as well as for the help in preparing documents and consultation. The maximum amounts of such costs are established in the recommendations "On the maximum amount of fees of aid granted by an attorney or attorney's assistant in civil cases" adopted by Order of the Minister of Justice of the Republic of Lithuania of 2 April 2004. These recommendations set the maximum amount of fees payable to an attorney or attorney's assistant for the legal aid.

The recommendations separately recommend the amount of maximum fees for separate legal service (for instance, filing of a claim, drafting of an appeal or cassation claim). It does not establish any rules on reimbursement of litigation costs in cases in which a class action is filed, but according to the general rules, the court, when deciding with the issue of such costs, may take into account such significant criteria as complexity of the case, complexity of legal service, necessity of special knowledge, novelty of the legal issues and behaviour of the litigants during the proceedings, attorney's work time and other important circumstances. The Supreme Court of Lithuania has found that litigation costs related to the hearing of the case shall be real. Thus, in all cases, the award of such costs for the help of the attorney or attorney's assistant is subject to the criterion of reality. It requires that these persons have been paid for the legal service, the winning party has suffered litigation costs of representation in the civil proceedings and provided evidence to the court in the manner prescribed by the law. In such cases litigation costs are understood as "spent costs".[125]

121 Ibid, art 1.125(8).
122 Ibid, art 1.127(1).
123 Ibid, art 1.129(1).
124 Code of Civil Procedure, art 93(1) (n 57).
125 Supreme Court of Lithuania, Ruling of 23 January 2017, 3K-3-7-687/2017.

Litigation costs incurred by the winning party shall be awarded by the court from the other party.[126] When the court awards litigation costs for the group which is the winning party, it is deemed that costs are awarded to each member of the group in equal parts according to article 93 of the Code of Civil Procedure. If an intermediate ruling is made, this rule is applicable only to litigation costs related to this ruling. Litigation costs related to the individual pecuniary claim of members of the group after the ruling is rendered are distributed to each member of the group who submitted a pecuniary claim. A member of the group who leaves the group shall cover only litigations costs which are related to his or her procedural actions before the withdrawal.[127]

F. WHO RECEIVES ANY AWARDED OR SETTLED DAMAGES OR SKIMMED PROFITS?

Damages in civil proceedings are awarded to the person who suffered them.

IV. PROTECTION OF RIGHTS IN THE CAPITAL MARKET

This section of the chapter explains protection of rights in the capital market in cases, according to the Case 2 example.

Basically, no specific civil judicial proceedings or legal remedies exist for the situation described in the Case 2 (when the value of shares of the company is manipulated and the buyer of the shares suffers damages). The general rules for civil liability and civil proceedings would be applicable in such a case. Nevertheless, such a dispute could raise complex legal questions. For instance, how should the grounds for civil liability (unlawful actions, causation, fault, damages) be established, how should the value of the sold shares be assessed and calculated? How does the link of causation between the allegedly unlawful seller's actions and the damages suffered by the buyer exist? Could it be regarded as a common business practice in the market of shares?

Failure to reveal important information about the object of the purchase-sale contract before the conclusion of the contract, could be regarded as bad faith actions of the seller. A creditor and a debtor shall act in good faith, reasonably and justifiably when the obligation is created and performed.[128] The obligation to

126 Code of Civil Procedure, art 93(1–2) (n 57).
127 Ibid, art 441[17].
128 Civil Code, art 6.4 (n 3).

act in accordance with good faith in contractual relationships is also established specifically in the law of contracts.[129] The principle of good faith is applicable throughout of period of the contract, including pre-contractual relations and negotiations.[130] This obligation creates a requirement to act *bona fides* and in accordance with the fair commercial practice.

One of the aspects of the principle of good faith in the law of contracts is disclosure of relevant information. The parties are bound to disclose to each other information they have and which is of essential importance for the conclusion of the contract.[131] This information depends on the type, nature and goals of the contract, the legal status of the parties and other relevant circumstances.[132] It seems that information related to the value of shares in the sale and purchase contract of shares may be regarded as essential information for the conclusion of such contract. If the value of shares decreases immediately after the conclusion of the contract and the seller was aware of such decrease in value, it may be regarded as bad-faith actions of the seller. Consequently, the breach of the principle of good faith may give rise to civil liability.

Another relevant question is determination of the value of the shares and amount of damage. In such case the need for an expert's examination would be very likely since specific knowledge and experience is required.[133] The court should find what the value was of the shares before the conclusion of the contract and how it changed later.

V. CONCLUSIONS

In Lithuania public enforcement of consumer law is coupled with the public interest. The primary tool for enforcement of consumer law is imposition of fines to economic operators which infringe fair competition rules. Skimming of profits as a public enforcement tool is not established. Monitoring of economic operators is carried out by the public authorities and regulated in detail.

It is doubtful whether for the illegal actions described in the Case 1 criminal liability could be imposed. There is no specific provision for the violation of consumer rights in the Criminal Code of the Republic of Lithuania. Thus, legal remedies established by administrative and civil law shall be used.

Three options for private enforcement of consumer law exist in civil proceedings. Since there are no requirements for which legal mechanism should

129 Ibid, art 6.158(1).
130 Supreme Court of Lithuania, Ruling of 15 January 2019, e3K-3-89-915/2019.
131 Civil Code, art 6.163(4) (n 3).
132 Supreme Court of Lithuania, Ruling of 5 July 2017, e3K-3-309-378/2017.
133 Code of Civil Procedure, art 212(1) (n 57).

be used, consumers are free to choose to enforce their rights individually or collectively in each case. In such cases as described in the Case 1 example an optional procedural joinder or a class action would be an appropriate tool to defend consumer rights and interests in large-scale infringements. In such cases one of the major requirements are consumers' willingness to enforce their rights collectively and similar factual circumstances and legal remedies. Additionally, a class action would be possible if such a procedure was more efficient and expedient than submission of numerous individual claims to the court. Noteworthy, the court shall engage in active case management in consumer disputes, meaning that the court can recover necessary evidence *ex officio* and help the weaker party (a consumer) in the proceedings to defend rights.

No special mechanism for protection of rights in the capital market is established for cases such as described in the Case 2 example. If an action is filed for damages caused by the seller's failure to reveal essential information to the buyer before the conclusion of the contract, it shall be qualified as bad faith actions in pre-contractual relationships. In such case the general rules of civil liability are applicable.

There is no specific case law of statutory regulation concerning the diesel emissions scandal. There could a couple of reasons for this. First, the car market in Lithuania is significantly smaller than the markets of other countries in which the diesel scandal has attracted a lot of attention. Second, the use of collective consumer right enforcement mechanisms is still rare in consumer disputes. Thus, the general public may not be aware of the existing legal mechanisms for collective defence and (or) this scandal simply has not caused significant negative consequences. Finally, it is known that car owners in Lithuania have chosen alternative technical solutions offered by the manufacturer and helped to solve pollution problems.

ENFORCING CONSUMER AND CAPITAL MARKETS LAW IN THE NETHERLANDS

Willem H. van Boom* and Charlotte M.D.S. Pavillon**

* Willem H. van Boom, Dr., Professor of Civil Law, University of Leiden, School of Law.

** Charlotte M.D.S. Pavillon, Dr., Professor of Private Law, in particular of Consumer Law, University of Groningen, School of Law.

A freely accessible website where the cited cases can be found is <http://www.rechtspraak.nl>. A freely accessible website where most of the cited statutes can be found is <http://www.dutchcivillaw.com>.

I. PUBLIC LAW

A. CONSUMER LAW (CASE 1)[1]

1. Do Eliminations of Consequences, Damages and Skimming of Profits (by Fines) Exist?

The 2006 Wet handhaving consumentenbescherming (Act on Consumer Protection Enforcement) brought the Dutch consumer authority into existence. This authority merged with the Competition Authority in 2013 and now goes by the name of the Netherlands Authority for Consumers and Markets (ACM).[2]

Under public law, the abovementioned sanctions do not exist. However, the ACM may impose fines for violations committed by traders. When setting the amount of the fine, it has to take into account 'the infringing trader's turnover, net profit as well as any fines imposed for the same infringement in other

[1] See Introduction Section IV.A.

[2] Sjoerd Ammerlaan and Dirk Janssen, 'The Dutch Consumer Authority: an introduction' in Willem H van Boom and Marco BM Loos (eds), *Collective enforcement of consumer law in Europe. Securing compliance in Europe through private group action and public authority intervention* (Europa Law Publishing 2007) 107–21.

Member States'.[3] The exact amount of the fine depends on the seriousness and the duration of the violation, and on the specific circumstances of the case. If there have been repeat offences or if the investigation has been obstructed, the fine may be set higher. On the other hand, fines may also be lowered, for example if the aggrieved parties were compensated by the infringers. The fine must be proportional to the violation of the law but it must also have a sufficiently deterrent effect, not just on the infringer himself, but also on other companies. Fines are therefore published on the website of the ACM.[4] The maximum fines were raised in 2014 – fines can now be as high as €900,000 or 10 per cent of the relevant turnover – but temporally speaking these new rules were held not to apply to the fact pattern of Dieselgate.

The ACM established in 2017 that between 2009 and 2015 Volkswagen AG had acted in breach of section 8.8 of the Act on Consumer Protection Enforcement in conjunction with the rules on unfair commercial practices implementing the Unfair Commercial Practices Directive (UCPD), more specifically section 6:193b, paragraphs 1 and 2, opening lines and under (a) of the Dutch Civil Code (acting contrary to the requirements of professional diligence); section 6:193c, under (b) of the DCC (provision of misleading information); and section 6:193g, opening lines and under (d) of the DCC (black list of misleading commercial practices).[5]

The ACM has established that Volkswagen AG misled consumers in the sale of its diesel cars with type EA 189 engines. Volkswagen advertised these cars as environmentally friendly, while the results of emission tests had been manipulated by illegal software. In 2017, the Dutch Consumers' Association (Consumentenbond) asked ACM to launch an investigation into Volkswagen. The ACM subsequently investigated whether the company had misled consumers and established that, in the period between 2009 and 2015, Volkswagen misled consumers about the most important features of its cars. As a result, consumers may have made a different decision than if they had received the correct information. Diesel cars with type EA 189 engines of the brands Volkswagen, Audi, ŠKODA and Seat were presented as sustainable and environment-friendly, while the test results were not reliable due to the installed software. By using this 'defeat device' software, Volkswagen's actions have been in breach of the requirements of professional diligence. Moreover, Volkswagen had wrongly claimed that the cars complied with the approval requirements for admission to the European market.

---

3 'ACM Fining Policy Rule' (1 July 2016) <http://www.acm.nl/sites/default/files/documents/2017-10/2014-acm-fining-policy-rule-amended-on-july-1-2016.pdf>.

4 'ACM Mission and strategy' <http://www.acm.nl/en/about-acm/mission-vision-strategy/our-powers>.

5 The cited statutes can be found at: <http://www.dutchcivillaw.com/civilcodebook066.htm>.

After establishing the violation of the UCPD rules, the ACM has imposed a fine of €450,000 on Volkswagen AG.[6] This is the maximum fine that the ACM was able to impose for a breach of the UCPD in the period before the legal amendment. What is more, the ACM held that it could only impose one fine of €450,000 because the different infringements could be attributed to only one single offence, i.e. the application of the 'defeat device' software. The ACM has upheld the fine on administrative appeal. Volkswagen has used a further opportunity for administrative appeal with the District Court of Rotterdam. The public hearing took place on 16 December 2019.

2. *Compared to Private Enforcement: How Strong is the Monitoring and Law Enforcement by Public Authorities or Other Public Bodies?*

Private enforcement in the Netherlands is founded both on civil law procedures and on self-regulation (the so-called 'private foundation', the Dutch Consumer Complaint Boards are exemplary[7]). Private enforcement entirely depends on the initiative of private parties and the ACM only takes action when private parties fail to effectively tackle breaches of consumer law. The ACM came into being because the power of consumers to discipline the market was insufficient but 'it is statutorily obliged to organize a national forum[8] in order to ensure that its actions are aligned with private initiatives to protect the consumer'.[9]

The ACM has limited resources and is not able to address every violation of consumer law. Therefore, it has to prioritise its actions. The ACM selects the cases it deals with by answering three questions: What is the magnitude of the harm to consumers? What public interest is at stake? And is the ACM able to take action effectively?[10] The ACM may choose from a wide range of enforcement instruments: from awareness campaigns to hard sanctions such as fines. In most cases, the ACM uses a mix of instruments in order to address the underlying causes of violations, and to prevent repeat offences. It may apply a gradual, responsive approach, starting with warnings and ending with sanctions. This tailor-made approach has however been criticised for not paying enough attention to its actual deterrent effect.[11] The enforcement style of the ACM is

---

6 'ACM fines Volkswagen for misleading practices in diesel scandal' (28 November 2017) <http://www.acm.nl/en/publications/acm-fines-volkswagen-misleading-practices-diesel-scandal>.

7 <http://www.degeschillencommissie.nl/english/>.

8 The so-called 'Maatschappelijk Overleg'.

9 Anita Vegter, 'Toezicht op consumentenrechten en het Private Fundament' (*15th International Association of Consumer Law conference*, Amsterdam, 29 June 2015) <http://www.acm.nl/nl/publicaties/publicatie/14528/Speech-Anita-Vegter-Toezicht-op-consumentenrechten-en-het-Private-Fundament>.

10 See <http://www.acm.nl/en/about-acm/mission-vision-strategy/our-mission>.

11 ACM, 'Eindrapport evaluatie Autoriteit Consument en Markt' (7 December 2015) <http://www.kwinkgroep.nl/publicatie/eindrapport-evaluatie-autoriteit-consument-en-markt-acm/>.

perceived as entailing a rather soft approach, giving violators a 'second chance' before facing hard sanctions. This may lead to calculating behaviour and there are concerns among stakeholders and business managers about the extent to which violators are treated equally in similar circumstances and about the market knowledge of the ACM.[12] In the case of Dieselgate, the fine was immediately imposed, without a previous warning.

In the Volkswagen case, the ACM has played a coordinating and initiating role in the collaboration between European regulators. The joint regulators have required Volkswagen to resolve the problems of consumers with diesel cars and to treat consumers with diesel cars with modified software in an 'expedient and accommodating manner'.[13] In July 2018, 80 per cent of diesel cars in Europe (75 per cent in the Netherlands) had been repaired without any additional costs. Volkswagen has however not complied with the requirement to provide a full guarantee on the diesel cars after repair.[14] It has merely promised to take complaints connected to these repairs seriously. If necessary, individual Member States may take follow-up actions to compel Volkswagen to take further steps on specific issues. The authors are not aware of any follow-up actions.

B. CAPITAL MARKET LAW (CASE 2)[15]

1. Do Eliminations of Consequences, Damages and Skimming of Profits (by Fines) Exist?

Under public financial law, such sanctions do not exist. The Autoriteit Financiële Markten (Netherlands Authority for the Financial Markets; AFM) is the competent authority. The supervision of Dutch stock markets is regulated by the Wet op het financieel toezicht (Financial Supervision Act). The AFM is committed to promoting fair and transparent financial markets. In this respect, it enforces the EU's Market Abuse Regulation (MAR).[16]

---

12 ACM, 'Resultaten Reputatieonderzoek' (23 August 2018) <http://www.acm.nl/sites/default/files/documents/2018-08/resultaten-reputatieonderzoek.pdf>.

13 'Volkswagen is taking steps to solve consumer issues with diesel cards in the EU' (17 July 2018) <http://www.acm.nl/en/publications/volkswagen-taking-steps-solve-consumer-issues-diesel-cars-eu>.

14 'The European Commission and EU consumer authorities publish final assessment of dialogue with Volkswagen' (Brussels, 17 July 2018) <http://europa.eu/rapid/press-release_IP-18-4549_en.htm>.

15 See Introduction Section IV.A.

16 Mario Hössl-Neumann and Andreas Baumgartner, 'Dealing with Corporate Scandal under European Market Abuse Law: The Case of VW' (2018) 37 EU Law Working Papers <http://www-cdn.law.stanford.edu/wp-content/uploads/2018/11/hoessl_baumgartner_eulawwp37.pdf>; Loes Lennarts and Joti Roest, 'Netherlands: Protection of Investors and the Compensation of their Losses' in Pierre-Henri Conac and Martin Gelter (eds),

The AFM may impose administrative fines upon companies for disseminating incorrect or misleading information and for violating disclosure requirements. The degree of seriousness and duration of the offence, and the degree of culpability of the offender with regard to the offence are taken into consideration when setting the amount of the fine. Consideration is also given to whether the offence has previously been committed and to the proceeds that have been realised. Finally, the offender's ability to pay is taken into account.[17] With the implementation of the MAR the maximum fines to be imposed have significantly increased. These million fines have not yet been imposed.

The AFM may also fine individuals who are aware of actions constituting the offence by the company (knowledge of the forbidden character of such actions is not required), and have the power and obligation to take necessary measures to prevent such actions.[18] The AFM is not entitled to settle compensation claims with offenders, nor does it have the competence to allocate (a portion of) pecuniary sanctions to an investors indemnification fund.[19]

2. *Compared to Private Enforcement: How Strong is the Monitoring and Law Enforcement by Public Authorities or Other Public Bodies?*

Private enforcement aims at compensating investors who have sustained losses. The practice of class actions and collective settlement of investor claims is well developed in the Netherlands.[20] The Association of Stockholders (*Vereniging van Effectenbezitters*, VEB) is powerful and the number of investor claims has raised significantly in the past 15 years (thanks to the WCAM, see below). The VEB has issued a claim against car manufacturer Volkswagen for the losses incurred by investors pursuant to the infringement of US environmental legislation.

Public enforcement complements private enforcement by serving a different goal, i.e. promoting fair and transparent financial markets. However, public bodies often face criticism mainly for being too mild in their approach and for adopting a wait-and-see strategy. Public authorities supervising the financial markets (this also includes the Dutch central bank) have been criticised after

Global Securities Litigation and Enforcement (Cambridge University Press 2019) 469–516 (hereafter Lennarts and Roest, 'Netherlands').

17 <http://www.afm.nl/en/over-afm/werkzaamheden/maatregelen/boetehoogte>.

18 College van Beroep voor het bedrijfsleven, 14 August 2018, ECLI:NL:CBB:2018:400 – Imtech; College van Beroep voor het bedrijfsleven, 14 August 2018, ECLI:NL:CBB:2018:401 – Imtech.

19 Lennarts and Roest, 'Netherlands' (n 16) 469–516.

20 Tomas Arons and Willem H van Boom, 'Beyond Tulips and Cheese: Exporting Mass Security Claim Settlements from the Netherlands' (2016) 6 EBLR 857–83.

failing to adequately address the problems and eventual collapse of the DSB Bank.[21] Recent criticism pertains to the AFM's oversight arrangements.[22]

In disclosing inside information, the main rule is that inside information which directly concerns the issuer involved must be disclosed as soon as possible by the issuer.[23] For its supervision of compliance with this disclosure obligation, the AFM disposes of a variety of enforcement mechanisms. Among them is the imposition of an order for incremental penalty payments or an administrative fine, including publication of this. The AFM can also report the matter to the Public Prosecution Service.[24] It may also take a trade measure, i.e. suspend trading if damaging and unlawful information inequality or misleading/ incorrect information is present in the market.

Insider dealing or any attempt to engage in insider dealing is prohibited. The AFM proactively monitors behaviours, orders and transactions of investors in the market. If necessary, the AFM conducts an investigation into the compliance with the prohibition of insider dealing. The proactive supervision by the AFM of compliance by issuers with their obligations, such as publishing inside information as soon as possible, functions as an important means of detecting possible violations. The framework for supervising compliance with the MAR enables the AFM to obtain information from anyone that might reasonably be expected to possess information relevant for this supervision. If transactions or activities violate the insider dealing regulation, an administrative or criminal sanction can be imposed. In other words, the AFM has the authority to fine the infringer itself or to refer the matter to the Public Prosecution Service.

The AFM budget is paid by the parties under supervision. The government does not contribute to the budget but is entitled to income generated by the AFM through administrative fines and orders for incremental penalty payments, to the extent this amount on a yearly basis exceeds €2.5 million.

In order to fine Volkswagen, the AFM must first look for evidence determining whether Volkswagen failed to disclose information about cars that did not comply with EU emission standards when it issued certain securities to investors (and whether insider trading has taken place as suggested by Case 2). The authors are not aware of any ongoing enforcement action by the Dutch AFM in this respect.

---

21 A liability claim against the AFM was however rejected in 2014: Hoge Raad, 21 November 2014, ECLI:NL:HR:2014:3349 – AFM-DSB.

22 Stephanie Wix, 'Netherlands' regulator faces criticism after courts overrule sanctions' (*The Accountant*, 8 January 2018) <http://www.theaccountant-online.com/News/netherlands-regulator-faces-criticism-after-courts-overrule-sanctions-6022014>.

23 <http://www.afm.nl/en/professionals/onderwerpen/marktmisbruik/openbaarmaking-voorwetenschap>.

24 <http://www.afm.nl/en/professionals/onderwerpen/marktmisbruik/voorwetenschap-mm-be>.

II. PRIVATE LAW/CIVIL PROCEDURE: CONSUMER AND CAPITAL MARKET LAW (CASE 1 AND CASE 2)

A. TYPES OF COLLECTIVE ACTIONS

There are four instruments available in civil proceedings.

First, Dutch law allows voluntary aggregation of individual claims based on voluntary joinder or consolidation of claims. Such aggregation can be troublesome if the individual claims pertain to damages because the principle of Dutch law of damages is that as far as quantum is concerned, each claim must be assessed individually. However, the aggregation can be efficient because Dutch courts will try to answer questions of wrongfulness, protective scope of the rule, fault and causality (to the extent possible) in the abstract so that the questions common to the entire group of claimants are answered consistently and efficiently as much as possible.[25]

Second, there is a general rule on representative action, which authorises representative organisations to initiate a collective representative action in the civil courts.[26] Such organisations need to be an association or foundation and their articles of association/foundation and byelaws need to state that their aim is to represent a specified group of persons or specific and commonly shared interests. In the representative action procedure, the representative foundation/association may (1) seek a declaratory judgment to the benefit of interested parties that are alleging the defendant has acted wrongfully against these parties, and is thus legally obliged to do something or to abstain from doing something towards them; (2) seek injunctive relief in the form of either a positive mandatory injunction or a prohibitory injunction; (3) seek performance of a contractual duty of the defendant owed to various interested parties; or (4) seek the termination or rescission of a contract between the defendant and various interested parties. The crucial limitation to the representative action is that the claim cannot be for individual damages for the interested parties.[27]

Third, in response to the aforementioned limitation to the representative action, the 2005 Collective Settlement of Mass Damage Act (Wet collectieve

---

25 See, e.g. Hoge Raad, 27 November 2009, ECLI:NL:HR:2009:BH2162 – World Online; Hoge Raad, 5 June 2009 ECLI:NL:HR:2009:BH2815 – De Treek/Dexia.

26 Arts 3:305a-c of the DCC. See also Franziska Weber and Willem H van Boom, 'Dutch Treat: the Dutch Collective Settlement of Mass Damage Act (WCAM 2005)' (2011) 1 Contratto e impresa/Europa 71ff.

27 Art 3:305a (3) of the DCC: 'A legal claim as meant in paragraph 1 may be brought to court in order to force the defendant to disclose the judicial decision to the public, in a way as set by court and at the costs of the persons as pointed out by the court. It cannot be filed in order to obtain compensatory damages.'

afwikkeling massaschade (WCAM)) was introduced. Briefly explained, the WCAM operates as follows. First, an amicable settlement agreement concerning payment of compensation is concluded between the allegedly liable party or parties on the one hand, and a foundation or association acting in the aligned common interest of individuals involved (and injured) on the other; the parties to the agreement then jointly petition the Amsterdam Court of Appeals to declare the settlement binding on all persons to whom damage was caused; these interested persons are not summoned in this procedure but are notified by post or by newspaper announcement. The Amsterdam Court hears the arguments of all interested parties and considers several points concerning the substantive and procedural fairness and efficiency of the settlement (e.g. amount of compensation, adequate representation of interested parties). If the Court rules in favour of the settlement, it declares the settlement binding upon all persons to whom damage was caused and who are accommodated by the settlement, leaving non-willing parties with the opportunity to opt out within a certain period, after which the opt-out option lapses. The WCAM 2005 has been used frequently since its enactment and can be called a successful tool to efficiently settle and put claims to rest. The WCAM settlements mostly concern capital markets litigation.

Fourth, in 2019, the Collective Mass Damages Action Act (Wet afwikkeling massaschade in collectieve actie; WAMCA) was enacted. It came into force on 1 January 2020.[28] The Act applies to collective actions if the underlying event(s) date from 15 November 2016 or later (that latter date being the date of introduction of the Bill to Parliament). The WAMCA 2019 builds on the three previous instruments. It opens up the possibility of class action proceedings initiated by a representative association or foundation provided it represents these interests under the terms of its articles of association and these interests are sufficiently safeguarded by the governance structure of the association/foundation. Moreover, the association/foundation does not have standing if its directors have a commercial motive to directly or indirectly profit from the action. The collective claim needs to be registered in a central register; this allows consolidation of several claims. The claim needs to have a sufficiently close relationship with the Netherlands. Then, an exclusive group representative (the EGR, or 'lead claimant') is appointed to represent all claimants and interested parties. After the appointment, such claimants and interested parties have the opportunity to opt out from the proceedings. Then, the defendant(s) and EGR are under a duty of best efforts to negotiate a settlement before the case goes to trial. If a settlement is reached, it will be reviewed and declared binding by the court, after which a second opt-out period starts to run. If no settlement is reached, the proceedings continue and the court may award damages to the

[28] Staatsblad 2019, 130 and Staatsblad 2019, 446.

interested parties behind the EGR. It may also dismiss the claim. The court decision has *res judicata* effect for all those who did not opt out.

Note that it is doubtful that a Dieselgate fact pattern can be adjudicated under the WAMCA regime, assuming that most of the wrongful acts have occurred before 15 November 2016.[29] Also, it should be borne in mind that the WAMCA regime is different as regards foreign claimants.[30] A claim vehicle will only have standing in court concerning foreign claims if there is a sufficiently close connection with the Dutch jurisdiction. If the underlying claims represented by the claim vehicle meet this requirement, the case can be heard. However, if the case is one for a collective compensation, persons belonging to the precisely specified group who are not domiciled or resident in the Netherlands are only bound by the court-imposed scheme if they have opted into the proceedings. To do so, they must inform the court registry in writing that they agree to have their interests represented in this collective action within a time limit to be determined by the court (at least one month). This means that if a Dutch foundation starts a representative group action for collective compensation in the interest of consumers affected by a company that has wrongfully caused damage to consumers in Germany and the Netherlands, the court will first test whether there is a sufficiently close connection with the Dutch jurisdiction. If there is, the proceedings will affect Dutch consumers who are part of the 'precisely specified group' unless they opt out. It will affect the German consumers only if they opt in (unless the court sees good grounds to bind foreign consumers on an opt-out basis).[31] Note that this is not the case with a 'lone standing' WCAM settlement procedure; there, German consumers can derive benefits from the settlement declared binding unless they opt out.

B. SUBSTANTIVE ASSIGNMENT MODELS – PROCESS-BASED BUNDLING OF COMPENSATION CLAIMS

Assignment of claims falls under the first instrument mentioned above. It is relatively straightforward under Dutch law: unless the claim is unassignable,

[29] The WAMCA has not yet entered into force but has, to some extent, a 'retroactive' effect, thanks to which the new procedure may prove useful in Dieselgate. The WAMCA is applicable provided that the underlying event(s) date from 15 November 2016 or later. This requirement could perhaps be met if the action does not focus on the misleading practices prior to that date but on the fact that by failing to offer appropriate solutions in the past four years, the harm inflicted on car owners has been perpetuated.

[30] Willem H van Boom and Charlotte MDS Pavillon, 'The Netherlands takes collective redress to a next level. An introduction to the Collective Redress of Mass Damages Act 2019' (2019) 4 Zeitschrift für Verbraucherrecht 133.

[31] See art 1018f (5) of the DCCP (after entry into force of the WAMCA).

it can be assigned by means of a written and signed document by the assignor. Notification of the debtor can be substituted by a simple procedure involving official date stamping of the document by the Dutch tax office. Thus, individual claims can be assigned to a genuine buyer or to a claims agency for the purpose of debt collection.[32] There are no rules against using assignment by claims agencies in a 'no cure no pay' construction. In this sense, anyone can open up shop as a claims broker. Attorneys, however, are not allowed to charge contingency fees of this sort.

C. ARE REMEDIES SUCH AS ELIMINATIONS OF CONSEQUENCES, DAMAGES AND SKIMMING OF PROFITS AVAILABLE?

Generally speaking, in claims for damages (based on tort or contract), the damaged party has a right to be brought in the position – financially speaking – he would have been in but for the tort or non-performance of the contractual duty. In other words, he has a right to compensation either in money or otherwise.[33] The court has the authority (but not the duty) to assess the damage by reference to the amount of profit the liable party gained by his behaviour[34] (article 6:104 of the DCC[35]). Although this instrument is not a proper instrument for skimming off profits, it can be used for that purpose in deserving cases. If, however, the damage of the claimants is calculable, it seems unlikely that the profit can serve as a gauge for damages.[36]

D. DOES FACILITATION TO GIVE PROOF EXIST – HOW IS THE BURDEN OF PROOF DISTRIBUTED?

An investor or a consumer who has been misled by Volkswagen, has to state and prove to establish causation in order to claim compensation for his/her

32 Hoge Raad, 27 November 2009, ECLI:NL:HR:2009:BH2162 – World Online. Attorneys are not allowed to act as assignee of claims which are subject of ongoing litigation in their district; see art 3:43 of the DCC.

33 Art 6:95ff of the DCC.

34 Art 6:104 of the DCC.

35 'If someone, who is liable towards another person on the basis of tort or a default of complying with an obligation, has gained a profit because of this tort or non-performance, then the court may, upon the request of the injured person, estimate that damage in line with the amount of this profit or a part of it.'

36 Cf Hoge Raad, 24 December 1993, ECLI:NL:HR:1993:ZC1202 – Wayen-Scheers/Naus; Hoge Raad, 18 June 2010, ECLI:NL:HR:2010:BM0893 – illegal subletting.

financial loss. The general rule with respect to the burden of proof applies: the party invoking a certain legal consequence must prove the necessary facts and circumstances. Pursuant to a special rule or based on the requirements of reasonableness and fairness the burden of proof may be allocated differently between the parties (article 150 of the Dutch Code of Civil Procedure). Those requirements allow for a shift of the burden of proof. A court may for example choose to adopt a rebuttable presumption of causation.

In this area, the 2009 *World Online* ruling by the Hoge Raad may be relevant.[37] There, it was decided that a misleading prospectus could be presumed to have influenced the buying behaviour of stock owners. The Hoge Raad alleviated the burden of proof for claimants in view of the European law background of the prospectus liability and the European law mandate of effective and dissuasive enforcement. As a result, in prospectus liability cases, the court may presume that the misleading prospectus influenced the investor's decision unless the specific circumstances of the case point in a different direction. Whether this EU principle of effectiveness plays a role elsewhere is not certain.[38]

E. ARE THERE ANY DEMANDS FOR INFORMATION AGAINST THE ALLEGED INJURING PARTY?

Pursuant to articles 87 and 88 of the DCCP, the court may hold an oral hearing at any stage of the proceedings, either to investigate whether a settlement is possible or to obtain additional information from the parties.[39] The court may do so either at its own initiative or at the request of one or more of the parties. There is no general discovery or disclosure under Dutch procedural law. Depending on the circumstances, a party may be obliged by the court to submit information and documents that are relevant to the case. If parties fail to do this, the court can draw adverse inferences if it deems appropriate. However, privileged data or documents are protected against disclosure, unless privilege has been waived.

---

37 Hoge Raad, 27 November 2009, ECLI:NL:HR:2009:BH2162 – World Online.

38 Cf Hoge Raad, 30 January 2015, ECLI:NL:HR:2015:178 – Staatsloterij/Loterijverlies. The Hoge Raad upheld in that ruling the declaratory judgment that the Dutch State Lottery had breached the misleading advertising directive: 'Dutch Supreme Court: State Lottery misled players over winning odds' (30 January 2015) <http://www.barentskrans.nl/en/news/lottery-misled-players/>. The burden of proof for claimants was however not alleviated.

39 Tom Claassens, 'Litigation in the Netherlands – A Practitioner's Guide' (2013) <http://loyensloeffwebsite.blob.core.windows.net/media/2116/litigation-in-the-netherlands-x.pdf>.

III. GENERAL PROCEDURAL LAW

A. CONSUMER AND CAPITAL MARKET LAW (CASE 1 AND CASE 2)

1. *Is a Simultaneous Coexistence of Several Legal Actions Possible?*

Collective actions can co-exist with a joinder, a test case or the bundling of claims by an entrepreneurial party.[40] Such collective actions do not deprive the aggrieved parties of their individual right to litigate. Under the WCAM, individuals would need to opt out from the court-approved settlement to secure their individual rights.[41]

To date, several actions – collective actions and bundled claims – have simultaneously been initiated both by consumers and investors (VEB, stichting Investor Settlement Foundation, Consumentenclaim, Diesel Emissions Justice Foundation[42]).[43] Some of these organisations/foundations under Dutch law are still trying to settle. The only pending representative consumer action is the action brought before the Amsterdam District Court. The only pending representative investors' action is the one initiated by the VEB in February 2016.

2. *Are there Any Procedural Simplifications in Consumer and Capital Market Law?*

No, there are no specific procedural simplifications in consumer and capital market law. The rules governing collective procedure are the same, irrespective of the legal provisions underlying the claim.

3. *What is the Binding Effect of Decisions for Subsequent Proceedings?*

Court decisions, even decisions by the Hoge Raad, are not binding on courts in deciding future cases. There is no rule of precedent in Dutch law. Even the

---

40 Ilja Tillema, *Entrepreneurial Mass Litigation; Balancing the Building Blocks* (Erasmus University Rotterdam 2019) 268–69.

41 Under the WAMCA, individual proceedings can be suspended upon request of the most appropriate party (art 1018m of the DCCP).

42 'Dieselgate: lawyers back legal action for Europeans affected by the scandal' <http://www.euronews.com/2019/11/28/dieselgate-lawyers-back-legal-action-for-europeans-affected-by-the-scandal>.

43 'Overzicht: Claims tegen Volkswagen vanwege dieselschandaal' (13 June 2017) <http://www.nu.nl/volkswagen-schandaal/4211413/overzicht-claims-volkswagen-vanwege-dieselschandaal.html>.

Supreme Court itself is not bound by its own decisions and from time to time amends its earlier opinions and judgments. The binding effect of collective action judgment is restricted to the representative organisation and the defendant.

Decisions of the Hoge Raad, however, are often followed by the lower courts. A lower court will generally take a test case judgment as a starting point. The same goes for a collective action judgment. Both can constitute the basis of a settlement. Individual circumstances define the possibility to challenge this judgment and to deviate from it.

This also holds particularly true for preliminary rulings issued by the Supreme Court upon the request of lower courts. In 2013, a procedure of referencing for preliminary rulings to the Dutch Supreme Court in civil cases came into existence. In cases in which the need for a landmark ruling is felt – often cases of mass damages – the Act on Requests for a Preliminary Ruling to the Hoge Raad enables civil courts to obtain in an early stage the answer to a pressing legal question. The new procedure has proven to be successful. The Act has furthered the development of civil law: development of the law, legal uniformity and legal certainty have all been stimulated by it.[44]

4. *When is the Statute of Limitations for Collective Redress Suspended?*

There are two limitation periods in damages actions. First, there is a limitation period of five years for a claim for compensation of damage. The limitation period begins on the day following the one on which the claimant was aware of both the damage and the identity of the person responsible for the damage. There is also a long-stop period of 20 years following the event that caused the damage.

The limitation period can be interrupted by sending a letter to the allegedly liable party (stating in unequivocal wording that the party is deemed liable and the rights to claim compensation are reserved) or by initiating legal proceedings. This starts a new period of five years. In 2014, the Hoge Raad held that a representative association or foundation could, for the benefit of all potential claimants it represents, interrupt the statute of limitations by sending such a (pre-litigation) letter to potential defendants.[45]

5. *Who Bears the Litigation Risks?*

In a summons procedure where a collective claim is submitted, the principle is that 'the loser pays'. So, if the claim fails the claimant organisation will be ordered

---

44 <http://www.wodc.nl/binaries/2631-summary_tcm28-124548.pdf>.

45 Hoge Raad, 28 March 2014, ECLI:NL:HR:2014:766 – VEB NCVB/Deloitte Accountants.

to pay court fees and the defendant's attorney fees. However, as a rule, the 'loser pays' rule means that the cost awards consist of fixed and therefore predictable amounts in court fees; the opposing party's attorney's fees are calculated on the basis of a crude tarification model, which means that the amounts are predictable and very low. The actual attorney costs almost always go beyond these tariffs, which means that even a winner loses somewhat. This prospect is thought to both deter overly litigation-happy parties and ensure access to justice for less pecunious parties.[46]

6. *Who Receives Any Awarded or Settled Damages or Skimmed Profits?*

Any awarded damages or profits accrue to the claimants in case of a voluntary joinder of individual claims. Under the WAMCA 2019, the court will award damages to groups of interested parties in accordance with their group characteristics ('damage scheduling').[47]

In Case 2, the damage suffered does not concern consumers as such but investors who see the value of their stock plummet. The main line of defence of the manufacturer will likely be that there is no causation between the late notification of the damage: the stock value would have decreased just as well if the exchange would have been informed earlier. This defence will not help if, due to the tortious manipulation, there is damage in the difference between the hypothetical situation (i.e. the hypothetical current market value of the shares without the manipulation) and the actual situation (i.e. the market value of the shares after the manipulation came to light).

Whether the illicit gains obtained by the board member can be skimmed off to the benefit of the aggrieved shareholders remains to be seen. The first hurdle is whether the act by the board member was wrongful vis-à-vis all shareholders (or only in relation to the actual shareholders he sold his shares to). If the tort lies in the trading as such and not so much in the fact that he was complicit in keeping information from the market, then it is debatable whether the board member actually acted wrongfully vis-à-vis any and all shareholders. The second hurdle is causation: what damage did he cause to the shareholders by selling his shares? In such cases, where damage is difficult to assess, the court may label the profits as the damage suffered by the shareholders. That would mean that the board

46 Note that under the WAMCA 2019, in a collective claims action the court has the authority to award the respondent(s) the attorney tariff multiplied by five if the claim is apparently frivolous. Conversely, if the respondent is ordered to pay damages to the interested parties, the court may also award 'reasonable and proportionate court costs and other costs that the successful party has incurred'. See art 1018l of the DCCP (after coming into force of the WAMCA 2019).

47 Art 1018i of the DCCP (after coming into force of the WAMCA 2019).

member can be held to account for the profits and that the shareholders have a right to skim off these profits.

B. RECENT DEVELOPMENTS

1. *Consumer Law (Case 1)*

The foundation Stichting Volkswagen Car Claim has hoped (and still hopes?) for an appropriate settlement, of which a financial compensation may be a part. The foundation is privately funded, and private investors will probably get up to 15–18 per cent of the damages/compensation awarded. Car owners may join the collective action for free. Thousands of owners have done so; the foundation, however, is acting in the interest of all 180,000 involved car owners in the Netherlands (the number of applicants is not a prerequisite for standing).

After the negotiations hit a dead-end street – discussions have not even been entered – the foundation filed collective (representation) action proceedings under article 3:305a of the DCC at the Amsterdam District Court against *inter alia* Volkswagen, Audi, Škoda, SEAT, Dutch importer PON, software supplier Bosch and the official Dutch Volkswagen dealers on 2 May 2018. The foundation has requested the court to declare that the sales contracts can be terminated, that Dutch car owners are authorised to return the affected vehicles to the Dutch dealers (authorised Volkswagen dealers) and to receive a full refund of the purchase price. For consumers and business drivers who have purchased the affected cars second-hand, the foundation is demanding a declaration that Volkswagen c.s. have acted unlawfully.[48] The claim is, among other legal grounds, based on national laws transposing the Consumer Sales Directive[49] and the UCPD. In order to establish the breach of the UCPD, the administrative decision of the ACM might be helpful, though not decisive. If the court honours the foundation's claims, car owners may use this judgment in a subsequent (individual) procedure.[50] Another possibility is that Volkswagen offers an appropriate solution such as a hardware-repair; the software-fix already offered by Volkswagen does not suffice according to the foundation. It has indeed led to new problems and many complaints.

48 <http://www.stichtingvolkswagencarclaim.com/progress-process>.

49 A potential problem is the notice of default: a consumer should inform the seller that a lack of conformity exists to benefit from his rights. This may jeopardise the availability of the remedies under the consumer sales directive.

50 In individual procedures car owners will face the potentially difficult task of proving that the damages they suffered were caused by Volkswagen's misleading practices.

During the first stage of the proceedings, only the former board members of Volkswagen objected to the jurisdiction of the District Court of Amsterdam. Volkswagen and the other defendants accepted the jurisdiction of the District Court of Amsterdam. Since the proceedings against the defendants will be dealt with simultaneously, the proceedings against the former board members would delay the progress of the proceedings against Volkswagen and the other defendants. To prevent this delay the foundation decided to remove the indictment against the former directors from the summons proceedings. The former directors can be sued in a separate procedure if need be.

The second stage, in which the Amsterdam District Court had to address all kinds of other formal questions such as to the admissibility of the claim, was completed on 20 November 2019.[51] The Court gave all parties – after exchanging written documents – the opportunity to explain their views orally during a plea that was held in October 2019. Most collective claims of the foundation were declared admissible. The interests the action aims to protect were considered to be 'sufficiently similar'. The Court considered it plausible that Dutch car owners have suffered damage from Dieselgate. Two claims, however, were not admissible: a declaratory judgment that car owners are not obliged compensate the seller after dissolving the sales contract for the use of the vehicle and a declaratory judgment that dealers are responsible for unfair commercial practices. Both claims require that (diverging) individual circumstances are taken into account and thus pertain to interests that are not sufficiently similar.

The Court will now examine the merits of the admissible claims in the third, final stage of the proceedings. The hearing will take place at the beginning of June 2020.

2. *Capital Market Law (Case 2)*

Volkswagen is currently defending a representative shareholder case based on a liability claim. The representative action proceedings under article 3:305a of the DCC were initiated in February 2016 by the VEB with a writ of summons. The VEB acts for those Volkswagen shareholders who (1) held Volkswagen shares on Friday evening 18 September 2015 after trading hours, (2) bought these Volkswagen shares through an investment account in the Netherlands or through a Dutch bank or broker, and (3) have incurred a loss.[52]

The Netherlands have in recent years become a preferred forum for investor actions from around the world. The aforementioned Dutch initiative, organised

---

51 Rechtbank Amsterdam, 20 November 2019, ECLI:NL:RBAMS:2019:8741.

52 'VEB holds Volkswagen liable for investor losses' (25 September 2015) <http://www.veb.net/artikel/05790/veb-holds-volkswagen-liable-for-investor-losses>.

on behalf of Volkswagen securities holders whose investment interests were harmed as a result of the emissions-related scandal may represent the most significant effort since the *Converium* case to try to use the Dutch WCAM procedure on behalf of an aggrieved class of investors. This initiative raises a number of potentially complicated questions about jurisdiction, priority, potential preemption, and international comity.[53] It is rather uncertain whether the Dutch mechanisms can be used where the alleged wrongdoing took place outside the Netherlands and there are no other factors connecting the case to Netherlands.[54] For instance, at this very moment a preliminary ruling from the CJEU is pending on request of the Hoge Raad in another mass damage case. The question is on the international jurisdiction of the Dutch court (article 7, introductory sentence and paragraph 2 of the Regulation Brussels I-bis (Brussels I Recast, no 1215/2012)).[55] The Supreme Court has asked the CJEU whether article 7(2) of the Brussels I-bis regulation should be interpreted as meaning that the direct occurrence of purely financial damage to an investment account held in the Netherlands as a result of investment decisions made under the influence of widely distributed but incorrect, incomplete or misleading information from an international listed company, provides a sufficient starting point for assuming international jurisdiction of Dutch courts.[56] In the meantime the collective proceedings against Volkswagen were stayed. It is expected that the outcome of this preliminary ruling procedure has implications for the Volkswagen case.

---

53 Kevin M LaCroix, 'Dutch Shareholder Foundation Seeks to Represent Global Class of VW Investors' (*The D&O Diary*, 17 February 2016) <http://www.dandodiary.com/2016/02/articles/international-d-o/dutch-shareholder-foundation-seeks-to-represent-global-class-of-vw-investors/>.

54 Kevin M LaCroix, 'Dutch Court Dismisses Collective Investor Action Against BP on Jurisdictional Grounds' (*The D&O Diary*, 13 October 2016) <http://www.dandodiary.com/2016/10/articles/international-d-o/dutch-court-dismisses-collective-investor-action-bp-jurisdictional-grounds/>; <http://www.issgovernance.com/file/publications/764v4s5.pdf>.

55 Hoge Raad, 14 June 2019, ECLI:NL:HR:2019:925; Marcus Wagemakers, 'Supreme Court seeks answers from the european Court of Justice in BP case' (16 June 2019) <http://www.mwagemakers.nl/supreme-court-seeks-answers-from-the-european-court-of-justice-in-bp-case/>.

56 Sjoerd Yntema, 'Deepwater Horizon' (*Leiden Law Blog*, 27 June 2019) <https://leidenlawblog.nl/articles/deepwater-horizon>.

ENFORCING CONSUMER AND CAPITAL MARKETS LAW IN PORTUGAL

Henrique Sousa ANTUNES*

* Henrique Sousa Antunes, Dr., Associate Professor, Catholic University of Portugal, School of Law.
Statutes can be found at <http://www.pgdlisboa.pt>; judgments can be found at <http://www.dgsi.pt>.

I. PUBLIC LAW

A. DO ELIMINATION OF CONSEQUENCES, DAMAGES AND SKIMMING OF PROFITS (BY FINES) EXIST?

1. *Administrative Offences*

a) Case 1[1]

The Advertising Code (approved by Decree-Law 330/90, 23 October) is relevant on this issue. Given that advertising must respect the truth and not distort

[1] See Introduction Section IV.A.

the facts (article 10(1)), statements on the characteristics of the good being advertised must be accurate and capable of being proven, at any time, before the competent authorities (article 10(2)). Thus, the authority with competence to initiate the administrative offence proceedings where there is misleading advertising in terms of Decree-Law 57/2008, 26 March (transposing Directive 2005/29/EC, of the European Parliament and of the Council, of 11 May 2005, concerning unfair business-to-consumer commercial practices in the internal market), may require the advertiser to present proof of the material accuracy of the information actually contained in the advertising (article 11(1) and (2) of the Advertising Code). If the proof demanded is not presented or is insufficient, the information is presumed to be inaccurate (article 11(3)). The unfair commercial practice mentioned constitutes an administrative offence punishable with a fine of between €3,000 and €44,891.81, these amounts being applicable to legal persons (article 21 of Decree-Law 57/2008, cited above).

Furthermore, in line with article 114(4) of the Highway Code (approved by Decree-Law 114/94, 3 May), a manufacturer or seller that places on the market vehicles, systems, components or accessories in breach of the rules governing their manufacture and trading is punished with a fine of between €600 and €3,000 in the case of a natural person or between €1,200 and €6,000 in the case of a legal person and with loss of the objects, which must be apprehended when the infringement is confirmed.

In certain circumstances, the amount of these sanctions may be higher due to the profit obtained from the practice of the unlawful act: article 18(2) of the Administrative Offences Act (approved by Decree-Law 433/82, 27 October) lays down that:

> if the agent gains from the infringement an economic benefit which can be calculated as being higher than the upper limit of the fine, and there are no other means to eliminate it, the fine may be raised up to the amount of the benefit, although this increase may not be more than one third of the upper limit established by law.

The fine may, therefore, not actually disgorge the gain. Given that the determination of the sanction also depends on the seriousness of the administrative offence, the fault and the economic situation of the agent (article 18(1)) it is possible, at least in theory, to calculate an amount which, inclusively, is below the established upper limit.

In this case, if, as shall be seen, compensation includes restitution of unlawful profit, awarding the injured parties the economic gains obtained with the practice of the unlawful act would harm the application of the aforementioned rule.

b) Case 2[2]

Providing information on the issuing entity that is not complete, truthful, current, clear, objective and lawful constitutes a very serious administrative offence punishable with a fine of between €25,000 and €5,000,000 (articles 7(1), 388(1) and 389(1) a) of the Securities Code, approved by Decree-Law 486/99, 13 November).

The use or transfer of privileged information also constitutes a very serious administrative offence, unless it also constitutes a crime, as does breach of the prohibition on market manipulation, again unless it also constitutes a crime. Both are punishable with a fine between the amounts indicated above (article 399-A(1) a) and b) of the Securities Code).

Both natural persons and legal persons may be guilty of administrative offences (article 401(1) of the Securities Code). Legal persons are responsible for acts performed by members of their governing bodies, their authorised agents, representatives or employees, acting in the performance of their duties or in their name or on their behalf (article 401(2) of the Securities Code). The legal persons' liability does not exclude individual liability of their agents (article 401(4) and (5) of the Securities Code).

According to article 388(2) of the Securities Code, the upper limit of the fine is the highest of the following amounts: (i) three times the economic benefit obtained, even if totally or partially in the form of losses potentially avoided (sub-paragraph a)); (ii) for administrative offences for use or transfer of privileged information and market manipulation, 15 per cent of the turnover (sub-paragraph c)).

Article 404(1) a) of the Securities Code adds: in addition to the fine, an additional sanction may be applied of apprehension and loss of the benefit obtained by the infringer through the practice of an administrative offence. Meanwhile, pursuant to article 406(2) of the Securities Code, the proceeds from the fines and the apprehended economic benefit revert in their entirety to the Investors Compensation System.

2. *Criminal Law*

a) The Grounds of Liability

i) Case 1

The behaviour described in Case 1 is relevant in the criminal sphere. Besides potentially constituting some types of environmental crimes (articles 272(1) c),

[2] See Introduction Section IV.A.

279 and 279-A of the Criminal Code – release of toxic gases, pollution, activities that are harmful to the environment), the manufacturer's conduct is also equivalent to the crime of deception and, possibly, qualified deception if the patrimonial loss caused is of a high amount (article 217(1) of the Criminal Code defines deception as follows:

> Whoever, with the intention to obtain for himself or for a third party unlawful enrichment, by means of an error or mistake regarding facts that he deceptively induces, leads another to practice acts that cause him, or that cause another person, patrimonial damage is punished with a prison sentence of up to three years or with a fine).

ii) Case 2

In line with article 378 of the Securities Code, insider trading is a crime. According to the first paragraph of this article, whoever has privileged information due to his position as a member of an administrative body and, on the basis of that information, sells securities is punished with a prison sentence of up to five years or with a fine. Privileged information is unpublished information that, being accurate and relating, namely, to an issuer of securities, would be capable, if publicised, of significantly influencing the respective price in the market (paragraph 4). The member of the management board will, therefore, be liable.

Providing false information on the polluting values of automobiles manufactured by the issuer appears to be a crime of market manipulation. Article 379(1) of the Securities Code punishes with a prison sentence of up to five years or a fine whoever disseminates false, incomplete, exaggerated, biased or misleading information if this is capable of artificially changing the regular functioning of the securities market. The sanctions are increased to eight years' imprisonment or a fine of up to 600 days if the conduct described caused or contributed to an artificial change in the regular functioning of the market (article 379(2) of the Securities Code). Pursuant to paragraph 3 of this article, acts capable of artificially changing the regular functioning of the market are acts which, namely, can modify the conditions for setting the prices or the normal conditions of supply or demand of securities. Both the legal person and whoever acts as a member of one of its bodies are responsible (articles 11 and 12 of the Criminal Code).

b) Skimming of Profits

i) Case 1

Article 110 of the Criminal Code (loss of proceeds and gains) lays down that advantages gained from a typical unlawful act are declared lost in favour of the State. Such gains are deemed to be all things, rights or advantages that constitute an economic benefit, directly or indirectly resulting from that act, for the agent or for another person (paragraph 1, sub-paragraph b)). Paragraph 3 of the article adds that loss of the gains mentioned occurs even if these were subsequently reinvested, also covering any quantifiable gains that have resulted therefrom. Pursuant to paragraph 6, the provisions of the article do not harm the rights of the injured party.

Protection of the rights of the injured party was considered in the light of a traditional understanding of the effects of civil liability, hence excluding restitution of the unlawful profit obtained by the agent (in fact, the rules on unjust enrichment or improper *negotiorum gestio* are rarely applied with this purpose). And yet, as one sees it, restitution of the profit is, as it shall be seen, a natural effect of civil liability.

Consequently, if compensation includes restitution of unlawful profit, allocation of the economic gains obtained by the agent to the State is not a legitimate solution. Indeed, it will be recalled that, according to article 110(6) of the Criminal Code, application of the rule does not harm the rights of the injured party.

ii) Case 2

The provisions of article 380-A of the Securities Code, on the apprehension and loss of criminal gains, appear to go against the interpretation of the Criminal Code argued. If the unlawful act gives rise to patrimonial gains, the amounts are declared lost in the final court decision (paragraph 1). Patrimonial gains are actual gains obtained and costs and losses avoided with the practice of the act, regardless of the final use that the agent (defendant) has given these and even if they are subsequently lost (paragraph 2). The amount apprehended is allocated to reparation of any injured parties who presented their claim in the criminal proceedings, and 60 per cent of the remaining amount is declared lost in favour of the State and 40 per cent in favour of the Investors Compensation System (paragraph 3). This distribution denies allocation of the profit to the injured parties, wrongly, in the authors' opinion.

It should be mentioned, however, that in the case of insider trading, article 449(1) of the Companies Code, approved by Decree-Law 262/86, 2 September, establishes that the perpetrator of the unlawful act must indemnify those who have been harmed, paying them an amount equivalent to the amount of the patrimonial advantage achieved.

B. COMPARED TO PRIVATE ENFORCEMENT: HOW STRONG IS THE MONITORING AND LAW ENFORCEMENT BY PUBLIC AUTHORITIES OR OTHER PUBLIC BODIES?

No relevant data is available, although public enforcement prevails.

II. PRIVATE LAW/CIVIL PROCEDURE

A. COLLECTIVE ACTIONS

1. *What Forms of Collective Actions are Available (Class Action, Representative Action, etc.)? Who is Entitled to Bring Action?*

Joinder is a classic instrument of collective legal protection (article 267 of the Code of Civil Procedure): it allows for the joining of actions when, having been proposed separately, these may be brought together in a single suit where the presuppositions of the admissibility of litis consortium, coalition, opposition or counterclaim are confirmed.

With regard to representative group litigation, Portuguese law has implemented a general set of rules in this area (Law 83/95, of 31 August, on the right to take part in administrative proceedings and the right of popular action). The legislator gave effect to article 52(3) of the Constitution of the Portuguese Republic, of 1976, in the version which resulted from the constitution amendment of 1989.[3] Up until then, the law only entertained the possibility of a popular action of a corrective nature, for the jurisdictional control of certain acts of the Administration, and a popular action of a suppletory nature, which aimed at overcoming the omissions of local public entities in the defence of property and rights of the Administration. The law in force extended popular action to prevention, to the prosecution of offences and to claims for damages. Besides this, it has changed from simply being a means of controlling the activity of the

[3] The law currently in force states that: 'Everyone shall be granted the right of popular action, either personally or via associations that purport to defend the interests in question, including the right of an aggrieved party or parties to apply for the corresponding compensation, in such cases and under such terms as the law may determine, in particular to: a) promote the prevention, cessation or judicial prosecution of offences against public health, consumer rights, the quality of life or the preservation of the environment and the cultural heritage; b) safeguard the property of the State, the Autonomous Regions and local authorities'.

Administration to also being a means by which individuals can bring actions against the acts or omissions of other individuals.[4]

a) Case 1

According to article 1(2) of Law 83/95, popular action includes, amongst other interests protected by the law, public health, the environment, quality of life, consumers' rights, cultural heritage and the public domain. Standing is granted to any citizen who enjoys civil and political rights, and to associations and foundations who defend the interests provided for in article 1, regardless of whether they have a direct interest in the claim or not. This is set out in article 2(1).

It should be added that paragraph 2 of the same article grants standing to local authorities concerning the interests of all those who are officially resident in their district. The question being dealt with is the supra-individual protection of diffuse interests and collective interests, and also homogeneous individual (fragmented) interests or rights with the *res judicata* binding all members of the class who have not exercised their right to opt out.

It is worth distinguishing the standing of natural persons from that of legal persons, given the decision of the legislator to provide additional provision regarding the latter (article 3). It is a subject of debate whether the reference to any citizen includes foreigners and stateless persons. In the positive sense, one can argue that the constitutional right to access to the courts is not tied up with the nationality of the interested party being Portuguese.[5]

With regard to legal persons, article 3 sets out that the requirements for associations or foundations to have active standing are that they have legal personality, that there is a connection between the aims expressly set out in their statutes and the interests they are pursuing with the popular action, and that they do not exercise any kind of professional activity in competition with the activity of companies or independent professionals.

It may be questioned whether these requirements are sufficient. In particular, there is no mention of the personal or material base of the legal person (for example, the number of members or the endowment to the foundation) or its organisation. The participation of other interested parties in the action, controlling the conduct of the claimant, association or foundation does, however, mean that it is possible to overcome any inconveniences resulting from

---

4 See José Robin de Andrade, *A Acção Popular no Direito Administrativo Português* (Coimbra Editora 1967) 6ff; Paulo Otero, 'A Acção Popular: configuração e valor no actual direito português' (1999) 59 Revista da Ordem dos Advogados 871ff.

5 Miguel Teixeira de Sousa, *A Legitimidade Popular na Tutela dos Interesses Difusos* (Lex 2003) 178 (hereafter Teixeira de Sousa, *A Legitimidade Popular*).

a more liberal option from the legislator in the granting of active standing in proceedings.[6]

The claimant in the popular action is granted standing as a representative, acting in the defence of all those interested parties who do not reject such representation. Article 14 clarifies that popular action corresponds to a form of representative litigation. The law establishes a special regime of representation: the claimant represents on his own initiative, and without the need for a mandate or express authorisation, all the other holders of the rights or interests in question who have not exercised the right to exclude themselves as set out in article 15 (opt-out regime), with the consequences of the law under appreciation.

Naturally, the combination of representative standing with the opt-out system presupposes recognition of guarantees to the holders of the affected rights or interests. Article 13 of the law of popular action (Law 83/95) establishes a special regime of dismissal of the complaint: the complaint should be dismissed if the judge considers that it is highly improbable that it will proceed, having heard the Public Prosecutor and made the preliminary inquiries that he considers justified or that the claimant or the Public Prosecutor request. Also, herein lies the role of the Public Prosecutor. In particular, it may replace the claimant in the case of withdrawal from the suit, or a transaction or behaviour which is harmful to the interests in question (article 16(1)).[7]

The Consumer Protection Act (Law 24/96, 31 July) establishes a special rule regarding standing to bring a popular action. Consumers and consumers' associations, despite not being directly harmed, have active standing, in the terms of Law 83/95 (article 13, sub-paragraph b)). In 2014, the legislator also gave standing to the Public Prosecutor and the General-Directorate for Consumers (Law 47/2014, 28 July).

Under the Consumer Protection Act, article 17 sets out the notion and requirements demanded of consumers' associations for standing to be recognised to bring a popular action: according to the provisions of that law, consumers' associations are non-profit-making associations with legal personality and the main aim of protecting the rights and interests of consumers in general or of their members as consumers (article 17(1)). With regard to the scope of action, the law provides for three types of associations: consumers' associations may

6 Ibid, 181.

7 Limitation of the *res judicata* to the parties in the action, a sanction which, as shall be seen, the law provides to the judge, allows the latter to accompany the Public Prosecutor in confirming adequacy of representation. It should, however, be noted that, because of the distinct nature of the two judicial entities, although either of them may react to a conflict of interests between the claimant in the popular action and the holders of interests represented, only the Public Prosecutor may sanction the procedural choices of the claimant or the lack of diligence employed in the action (for comments on this, see Teixeira de Sousa, *A Legitimidade Popular* (n 5) 241).

be national, regional or local, according to the extent of their intervention and if they respectively bring together 3,000, 500 or 100 members (article 17(2)). Concerning their scope, the law divides the entities in question into general interest consumers' associations and specific interest consumers' associations. In either case, there is a need for the organs of the association to be freely elected by a universal and secret ballot of all of the members. General interest associations are those whose aim, as stated in their statutes, is the protection of consumers' rights in general. Specific interest associations are any other associations of consumers of particular goods or services (article 17(3)). Lastly, for the purposes of the provisions of the law for consumer protection, article 17(4) regards consumers' cooperatives as being equivalent to consumers' associations.

b) Case 2

The Securities Code provides, in articles 31 and 32, for the possibility of recourse to popular action for the protection of homogeneous individual interests or collective interests of investors in securities, giving standing to non-institutional investors, to associations for the protection of investors and to foundations whose aim is the protection of investors in securities. Article 32 establishes the requirements for standing to be conferred on associations. Besides having the protection of the interests of investors in securities as the principal aim of their establishment, they must have at least 100 members, natural persons, who are not institutional investors, and must have been in operation for more than a year.[8]

2. *How can Collective Redress Actions Possibly be Financed?*

Regarding funding, according to article 4(1) b) of the Regulations on Legal Costs (approved by Decree-Law 34/2008, 26 February), any person, foundation or association is exempt from costs when they exercise the right of popular action provided for in the terms of the Constitution and the ordinary law. Paragraph 5 of the article provides the caveat that exempt persons are liable to pay costs, in general terms, when it is concluded that the claim is clearly without merit. Furthermore, pursuant to paragraph 6, the exempt party is liable, after all, for the costs it gave rise to in the case, when its claim is totally defeated.

---

8 On this subject, see Sofia Nascimento Rodrigues, *A Protecção dos Investidores em Valores Mobiliários* (Almedina 2001) 57ff.

Lastly, except for cases of lack of funds, governed by the law on access to the law and to the courts, the exemption from costs does not cover reimbursements to the successful party for party costs, which, in such cases, the exempt party will bear (paragraph 7).

This general rule must be combined with Law 83/95. According to article 20, prepayment of costs is not required (paragraph 1), the plaintiff, in the event of the claim only partially proceeding, is exempt from the payment of costs (paragraph 2), and in the case of total failure of the claim, he is only responsible for an amount to be determined by the judge, somewhere between 10 per cent and 50 per cent of the costs that would normally be due, depending on his financial situation and the substantive or procedural reason for the dismissal of the action (paragraph 3). The Consumer Protection Act refers to Law 83/95 (article 18(1) n)).

It should be added that: (i) There is a public support system for those who are not in a position financially to bear the ordinary costs of an action, called judicial support. Briefly, this can take the form of payment of the fees of a lawyer selected by the party (with limits), appointment of a lawyer, or waiving or deferment of the payment of costs. However, these benefits should be 'paid back' if the beneficiary comes to acquire sufficient means; (ii) The funding of potential plaintiffs by third-party payers seems possible; (iii) Lawyers are prohibited from entering into *quota litis* agreements.

3. *Are there Any Special Mechanisms for Achieving Collective Settlements?*

Article 33 of the Securities Code provides for the creation of a service aimed at voluntary mediation of conflicts between non-professional investors and, among others, issuers. The Securities Commission organises this service (Conflicts Mediation Service). According to article 34 of the Code, the mediation procedures must obey principles of impartiality and expediency and must be free of charge (paragraph 1). If the conflict relates to homogeneous individual interests or collective interests of investors, associations for the protection of investors may take the initiative regarding mediation and participate in it, as the principal or accessory (paragraph 2). The procedure is confidential, the mediator is bound by secrecy in relation to all the information he obtains during the mediation, and the Securities Commission is prohibited from using, in any proceedings, information that has come to its knowledge, exclusively, in the mediation procedure (paragraph 3). The mediator may attempt conciliation or propose to the parties a solution that he considers most appropriate (paragraph 4). A written agreement resulting from the mediation has the nature of an out-of-court settlement (paragraph 5).

4. *Substantive Assignment Models – Process-Based Bundling of Compensation Claims*

Due to the Portuguese legal framework, which favours compensatory collective redress, these models have not appeared. Such models would be admissible on the basis of express representation of the claimants and the admissibility of multiple parties in proceedings.

Without prejudice to that written above, it may be noted that the Bar Association Statute (approved by Law 145/2015, of 9 September) prohibits client recruitment. According to article 90(2) h), lawyers have the duty in relation to the community not to solicit for clients, themselves or via an intermediary. Meanwhile, regarding fees, it is important to consider the Portuguese rules. According to article 105 of the Bar Association Statute, the following are criteria for calculating fees: the importance of the services provided, the difficulty and urgency of the matter, the amount of intellectual creativity involved in the service provided by the lawyer, the result obtained, the time spent, the responsibilities taken on by the lawyer and any other professional uses (3). The fees should be adequate reward for the services provided and should be paid in cash, with the possibility of the parties agreeing on a fixed sum (1). Payment of an hourly rate, periodic payments or payments per service are therefore accepted. The lawyer should present the client with the fees total divided into a list of the services provided (2).

In his relationship with the client, it is the lawyer's duty to inform him, if he so requests, of the criteria used for calculating his fees, indicating, whenever possible, the approximate total amount (article 100(1) a) of the Bar Association Statute). Considering the applicable competition rules, a tariff for fees is excluded.

Quota litis (a share of the amount awarded) is prohibited but success fees are given legitimacy. This is set out in article 106 of the Bar Association Statute:

> 1. Lawyers are prohibited from entering into *quota litis* agreements; 2. A *quota litis* agreement is an agreement made by a lawyer and his client, before the final conclusion of the case in which the latter is a party, such that the right to fees is exclusively dependent on the result obtained in the case and as a result of which the client agrees to pay the lawyer a portion of the result that he obtains, whether this consists of a quantity of money or of any good or value; 3. An agreement which consists of the prior calculation of the amount of fees, even if this is a percentage, according to the value of the case entrusted to the lawyer, or through which, in addition to the fees calculated according to other criteria, it is agreed that there shall be a bonus depending on the result obtained, shall not be considered a *quota litis* agreement.

B. ARE REMEDIES SUCH AS ELIMINATIONS OF CONSEQUENCES, DAMAGES AND SKIMMING OF PROFITS AVAILABLE?

1. *Remedies (Elimination of Consequences, Damages)*

a) Case 1

The purchasers suffer harm (firstly, the defect in the purchased item; secondly, the loss of the value of the automobiles purchased). The situation will be analysed in terms of B2C relationships.[9]

The Consumer Protection Act establishes a set of rights that provide the basis for the liability of the manufacturer and of the seller.

Article 3 a) and d) grant the consumer the right to receive goods and services of quality and the right to information. According to article 4:

> goods and services intended for consumption must be capable of meeting the purposes for which they are intended and of producing the effects attributed to them, according to legally established standards, or, in the absence of these, in a manner appropriate to the consumer's legitimate expectations.

Article 8 rules on the right to information. Pursuant to 1 a) of this article, the supplier must inform the consumer, in a clear, objective and appropriate manner, both during the negotiations stage and when a contract is being entered into, of the main characteristics of the goods being supplied. Paragraph 2 provides that the duty to inform also extends to the manufacturer. Additionally, according to article 10 of the Advertising Code, the information must respect the truth, not distorting the facts (paragraph 1), and statements on the origin, nature, composition, properties and conditions of purchase of the goods being advertised must be accurate and capable of being proven, at any time, before the competent authorities.

This framework, as shall be seen, enables the application of the sanctions set out in the sale of consumer goods regime (see note 9). Article 2(1) establishes

---

9 Art 913ff of the Civil Code, on the legal rules governing the sale of defective products, is applicable to relations between a private individual and a non-professional seller (C2C) or between two professionals (B2B). It may be noted, however, that according to art 4(6) of the rules on the sale of consumer goods (Decree-Law 67/2003, 8 April, resulting from the transposition of Directive 1999/44/EC of the European Parliament and of the Council of 25 May 1999 on certain aspects of the sale of consumer goods and associated guarantees [1999] OJ L171/12), the rights granted to the consumer by the said rule are transferred to the third-party purchaser of the good.

the requirement that the goods must be in conformity with the sale and purchase contract. A lack of conformity is presumed in the situations contained in paragraph 2 of the same article. Sub-paragraphs a), c) and d) seem applicable in the case under analysis: (i) the good is not in conformity with the description of it given by the seller or does not possess the qualities of the good that the seller presented to the consumer as a sample or model (sub-paragraph a)); (ii) the good is not suitable for the use normally given to goods of the same type (sub-paragraph c)); (iii) the good does not display the normal qualities and performance of goods of the same type and which the consumer may reasonably expect, given the nature of the good and, possibly, public statements regarding its specific characteristics made by the seller, the producer or its representative, namely in advertising or on the label.[10] According to article 3(1) of the rules on the sale of consumer goods, the seller is responsible to the consumer for the lack of conformity that existed when the good was delivered.

Article 4 lists consumers' rights: repair of the good, its replacement, an appropriate reduction in the price and termination of the contract (paragraph 1). The consumer may exercise, as an alternative, any of the aforesaid rights, provided that choice does not prove impossible or constitute an abuse of rights, in general terms (paragraph 5).

Meanwhile, and without prejudice to the said rights against the seller, article 6 provides for direct liability of the producer, with the consumer being able to demand from the former repair or replacement of the defective item. This choice is only restricted if the option proves impossible or disproportionate, taking into account the value that the good would have in the absence of that non-conformity, the importance of the latter and the possibility of the alternative solution being given effect without serious inconvenience to the consumer (paragraph 1).

The rights afforded to the consumer are affected by the limits on the guarantee periods and on the exercise of rights:[11] in the case of a movable good, rights may be exercised when the lack of conformity is revealed within two years of the good's delivery (article 5(1)). During that time, the lack of conformity must be reported within two months of the consumer first detecting it, or

---

[10] Pursuant to art 1-B, d) of the rules on the sale of consumer goods, the producer is the manufacturer of a consumer good, the importer of the consumer good in European Community territory or any other person who presents himself as a producer by indication of its name, brand or other identifying mark of the product.
In line with art 7(5) of the Consumer Protection Act, 'specific and objective information contained in advertising messages of a given good, service or right are deemed to be part of the content of contracts that are entered into after they have been broadcast, and any contract clauses to the contrary are deemed not to have been written'.

[11] Favourable to the application of the expiration periods set out in art 5 to the producer's direct liability (art 6), see João Calvão da Silva, *Venda de Bens de Consumo. Comentário. Decreto-Lei n.º 67/2003, de 8 de Abril. Directiva n.º 1999/44/CE* (4th edn, Almedina 2010) 137 (hereafter Calvão da Silva, *Venda de Bens de Consumo*).

otherwise those rights will expire (article 5-A(2)). If the lack of conformity is reported, the consumer's rights expire two years after the date this occurs (article 5-A(3)).

One may note, however, that, in the terms of article 8(1) Directive 1999/44/EC, the rules on the sale of consumer goods do not harm the national rules governing contractual or non-contractual liability. Accordingly, the Civil Code provides that, where there is wilful intent (Case 1 refers to manipulation by the manufacturer), the purchaser may bring an action to rescind the contract within one year of his becoming aware of the defect (article 905, applicable to the sale of defective goods by remission from article 913(1) and article 287(1)) and regardless of whether it is reported (article 916(1)) or he may exercise the right to have the item repaired or replaced (article 914), subject only to the general rules on limitation periods (article 298(1)).[12]

It is considered, however, that, besides the rights set out in article 4 of the rules on the sale of consumer goods, consumers also benefit from the application of rules that establish duties to indemnify. Let one see.

According to article 8(5) of the Consumer Protection Act, a supplier of goods that breaches the duty of information is liable for the damage it causes to the consumer. The other parties involved in the production-to-distribution chain that have also breached the duty of information are jointly liable.

Likewise, article 12 of the Consumer Protection Act provides:

> 1. The consumer has the right to be compensated for damage to property and personal injuries resulting from the supply of defective goods or services; 2. The producer is liable, regardless of fault, for damage caused by defective products it places on the market, in the terms of the law.

It should be stressed that paragraph 1 above appears to include the manufacturer within its scope.

Given the practical importance of this latter rule, a brief look at its application appears to be justified. In the understanding of some, the right to compensation lapses in line with the forfeiture established for the exercise of the rights set out in the rules on the sale of consumer goods.[13] The authors would disagree. The legislator refers to the right to be indemnified as compensation for any harm suffered by the consumer, covering, simultaneously, consequential damages and the devaluing derived from the defect. This is the meaning of the general affirmation of the right to compensation in the Consumer Protection Act and

---

12 Thus, Pires de Lima and Antunes Varela, *Código Civil Anotado, vol II* (4th edn, Coimbra Editora 1997) 211.

13 In this sense, João Calvão da Silva, *Compra e Venda de Coisas Defeituosas. Conformidade e Segurança* (5th edn, Almedina 2008) 135ff; and João Calvão da Silva, *Venda de Bens de Consumo* (n 11) 122.

of the silence, on this matter, in the rules on the sale of consumer goods. The consumer's property is therefore protected from harm involving fault which, corresponding to defects at the time the good is delivered, only appears at a time after the forfeiture has passed.[14] A natural effect of this option is the competence of the general rules on limitation periods (article 498 of the Civil Code – according to paragraph 1, the right expires when the first of two time limits is reached: 20 years from the harmful fact or three years from the date that the injured party became aware of the right afforded to him, although without knowing the person responsible for the harm and the full extent of the damage).

If one returns to the original version of the Consumer Protection Act, it will be seen that article 12 reads:

> 3. The rights granted to the consumer pursuant to paragraph 1 lapse at the end of any of the periods referred to in the previous paragraph without the consumer having reported the fact, or once six months have passed since it was reported, not counting for the purpose the time spent on repair operations; 4. Without prejudice to the provision in the previous paragraph, the consumer has the right to be compensated for damage to property and personal injuries resulting from the supply of defective goods or services.

The wording of the article appears to clarify that the right to compensation is not affected by the forfeiture laid down for the other rights of the consumer, being covered only by the rules of limitation periods established by the civil law.

It may also be recalled that the rules on the sale of consumer goods do not harm the national rules governing contractual or non-contractual liability. Therefore, if the Civil Code is applied to the case under analysis, the purchaser would have one year from becoming aware of the defect to react, by bringing an action to rescind the contract, and the seller who had acted with wilful intent would be required to compensate the buyer for the harm the latter would not have suffered if the sale and purchase had not been entered into (article 908, applicable to the sale of defective goods by remission from article 913(1)). This is a situation of pre-contractual civil liability, to which the general rules on limitation periods are applied (article 227(2), with remission to article 498, both of the Civil Code).

Besides the provisions already considered, the case in question warrants recourse to the rules applicable to unfair commercial practices of companies in their relations with consumers (Decree-Law 57/2008, cited above). Article 5(1)

---

14 These only make sense when the compensation accompanies the other rights in situations of no-fault civil liability.

of this decree-law states: 'A commercial practice is unfair if it is contrary to professional diligence, and materially distorts or may materially distort the economic behaviour of the consumer to whom it is addressed or that it affects regarding a certain good or service'. Moreover, according to articles 6 b) and 7(1) of that regime, unfair practices are, in particular, misleading actions that consist of providing false information about the main characteristics of a good, the results that can be expected from its use, or the results and material features of tests or checks carried out on the good (article 7(1) b)). It is, however, necessary for the false information to lead the consumer to take a transactional decision that he would not have taken otherwise (article 7(1)).

Article 14 of Decree-Law 57/2008 lays down that contracts entered into under the influence of an unfair commercial practice are voidable at the consumer's request (paragraph 1). This, as an alternative to rescission, may require modification of the contract according to fairness considerations (paragraph 2).

Article 15 of the same decree-law establishes civil liability of the agent: 'A consumer injured due to the effect of any unfair commercial practice prohibited in the terms of this decree-law is compensated in general terms'.

Portuguese law provides, therefore, an appropriate response to the injured party's compensation claim, covering, at the same time, the contractual liability of the seller and the non-contractual liability of the manufacturer. It thus falls outside the following considerations of the European Commission on the Proposal for a Directive of the European Parliament and of the Council amending Council Directive 93/13/EEC of 5 April 1993, Directive 98/6/EC of the European Parliament and of the Council, Directive 2005/29/EC of the European Parliament and of the Council and Directive 2011/83/EU of the European Parliament and of the Council as regards better enforcement and modernisation of EU consumer protection rules [COM (2018) 185 – adopted as Directive (EU) 2019/2161 of the European Parliament and of the Council of 27 November 2019]:

> On individual remedies, the proposal requires Member States to ensure that consumers harmed by unfair commercial practices have access to at least the contractual remedy of contract termination and the non-contractual remedy of compensation for damages. In particular, the 'Dieselgate' controversy (where car manufacturers installed technology in cars to cheat emissions tests) has shown that non-contractual remedies, such as the extra-contractual right to compensation for damages, can sometimes be more important for consumers than contractual ones. In the Dieselgate case, many consumers have not been able to claim remedies even in Member States that already provide remedies for victims of unfair commercial practices. This is because the available remedies are only contractual. The remedies can therefore only be applied against the consumers' contractual counterparts, who in this case are usually the car sellers and not the car manufacturers.

In the light of this framework, the main consumer rights protection association in Portugal, Deco, proposed, recently, a popular action against manufacturers and importers of automobiles with manipulated emission figures. It claimed, in short: (i) rescission of the contract and, therefore, that the vehicles be returned to the defendants, with payment of an amount equivalent to the amount given to American consumers; (ii) repair of the vehicles at no cost, if this proves appropriate and the consumers choose to continue with the contract; (iii) in the case of vehicles acquired through rental or leasing contracts, the possibility of the consumers putting an end to those contracts (without paying any commissions or the remaining instalments); (iv) in the case mentioned in (iii), the alternative of repairing the vehicles, if this is possible; (v) compensation for the harm suffered due to the false information and the depreciation of the affected vehicle, namely at the time of any resale, in an amount equivalent to the amount that one of the manufacturers agreed to pay to American consumers or, alternatively, 15 per cent of the vehicle's purchase value (estimated devaluation).

b) Case 2

In this case, the injured parties are investors in shares of the automobile vehicle manufacturers. With regard to civil liability, there is a situation of harm resulting from breach of a protective provision (*Schutzgesetz*). In the terms of article 483(1) of the Portuguese Civil Code, unlawfulness may take two main forms: breach of the right of another or breach of 'any legal provision intended to protect the interests of others'. The second type of unlawfulness occurs when the law directly protects private interests by imposing duties on subjects bound to comply with the provision. Only in this situation is pure economic loss protected.

Article 7 of the Securities Code has the characteristics of a protective provision. It lays down that information on issuers must be complete, truthful, current, clear, objective and lawful, regardless of the means of dissemination and even if the information is included in advice, a recommendation, an advertising message or a credit rating report (paragraphs 1 and 2). The general rules on advertising apply to advertising related to financial instruments and activities regulated in the Securities Code (paragraph 4).

These rules seek to directly protect investors and entitle them to compensation in the event of false information about an entity issuing securities. While it is true that, in the terms noted, grounds would exist for the duty to indemnify under the general principle of article 483 of the Civil Code, article 485 of the Civil Code sets out, specifically, civil liability for information, imposing the obligation to compensate if, having the duty to provide information, the agent has acted negligently or with the intention to harm (paragraph 2). Additionally, in the terms of article 30 of the Advertising Code, the advertiser, the entity benefiting from the advertising, is liable for harm caused to third parties due to the dissemination of unlawful advertising messages (paragraph 1).

Regarding insider trading, article 449(1) of the Companies Code establishes that a member of a management body who, having knowledge of facts related to the company that have not been publicised and that may influence the securities issued by it, sells shares in that company, thereby attaining a profit or avoiding a loss, must compensate the injured parties, paying them an amount equivalent to the amount of the patrimonial gain achieved. If it is not possible to identify the injured parties, the infringer must pay the said compensation to the company.

2. *Remedies (Skimming of Profits)*

In Portuguese private law, as happens in other legal systems in continental Europe, the removal of the benefits obtained by the injuring party as a result of his committing the unlawful act falls, in theory, to unjust enrichment. However, there appears to be a predominant opinion which is inclined towards restricting the obligation to disgorge to the impoverishment, if this is less, or, according to those who do not agree with this limit, to the amount which corresponds to the market value of the good that the debtor has unlawfully appropriated.[15]

The disgorgement of profits resulting from the interference in the proper order of things is, therefore, governed by recourse to other sources, namely to the law on *negotiorum gestio*.[16] The alternative appears to be clearly unsatisfactory. The duties of the principal to waive his right to compensation, to reimburse the intervener for the expenses incurred and to compensate him for the loss he has suffered (article 469 of the Civil Code) are somewhat of a paradigm.

In several instruments, in particular of European Law, the duty to indemnify is designed as a remedy that transfers the profit to the injured party. There has been the opportunity to argue that compensation is, indeed, the natural place for restoring unlawful gains, but, in any case, the emergence of new legislative solutions makes such a response clear.

In the authors' view, handing over of the profit is due as an effect of civil liability. This duty lies in the relational dimension of the general principle established by the legislator with regard to the obligation to indemnify.[17]

---

15 See, for all, Luís Menezes Leitão, *O Enriquecimento Sem Causa no Direito Civil* (Centro de Estudos Fiscais 1996) 910ff.

16 See, for all, Júlio Gomes, *O Conceito de Enriquecimento, o Enriquecimento Forçado e os Vários Paradigmas do Enriquecimento sem Causa* (Universidade Católica Portuguesa 1998) 801.

17 This theory was initially presented in: Henrique Sousa Antunes, 'Das Funções Reconstitutiva e Punitiva da Responsabilidade Civil Extracontratual' in Agostinho Cardoso Guedes and Nuno Manuel Pinto Oliveira (eds), *Colóquio de Direito Civil de Santo Tirso – O Código Civil 50 Anos Depois: Balanço e Perspetivas* (Almedina 2017) 491ff.

In the terms of article 562 of the Civil Code, 'whoever is obliged to repair harm must restore the situation that would exist if the event that obliged the repair had not occurred'. The rule has been interpreted with reference to restoring the property of the debtor, forgetting, it must be stressed, the relational extent that the principle implies.

The law imposes a duty on the injuring party to recreate the hypothetical situation that his intervention made impossible. That alternative reality must, necessarily, include the position of the agent. If the injuring party obtained a patrimonial benefit from his behaviour, it is fiction to state that restitution is different from reconstituting the situation that would exist.

In the authors' opinion, it should be acknowledged, however, that taking back the gain obtained by the agent follows even the most traditional understanding of compensation, considering that illegally obtained profit constitutes separate non-patrimonial damage suffered by the injured party.[18] The extent to which the Portuguese legal system allows compensation for non-patrimonial damage may be recalled. According to article 496(1) of the Civil Code, any non-patrimonial damage which, due to its severity, warrants legal protection is indemnifiable.

In the authors' view, relevant non-patrimonial damage occurs whenever an economic benefit for a third party is the result of the culpable sacrificing of rights of the injured party. It is damage which is born out of a rupture in the fair patrimonial relationship between individuals. Compensation for this damage may only, naturally, be achieved by passing into the sphere of the injured party the advantages that the third party obtained unlawfully.

The insufficiencies of unjust enrichment, with regard to its object and in relation to its consequences, the artificial nature of recourse to improper *negotiorum gestio*, and, possibly, its perverse effects, the limitation on the analogous application of the rules of possession, the extent to which compensation for non-patrimonial damage has been accepted in Portuguese law, capable of being adapted to the evolution of social circumstances, the aim of satisfying the injured party in relation to whom the damage is recognised, the sense of justice, should entitle the judge, in this area, to order restitution from the injuring party of the net profits resulting from his behaviour.

---

18 Henrique Sousa Antunes, *Da Inclusão do Lucro Ilícito e de Efeitos Punitivos entre as Consequências da Responsabilidade Civil Extracontratual* (Coimbra Editora 2011) 205ff. The authors' theory has already been well received by other authors. See, for example, Maria da Graça Trigo, 'Responsabilidade civil por violação de direito intelectual' (2011) LII – 3 and 4 Revista de Direito e de Estudos Sociais 161–71; José Carlos Brandão Proença, 'A responsabilidade civil extracontratual nos 50 anos de vigência do Código Civil: um olhar à luz do direito contemporâneo' in José Carlos Brandão Proença (ed), *Estudos de Direito das Obrigações* (Universidade Católica Editora 2018) 101ff.

C. DOES FACILITATION TO GIVE PROOF EXIST? HOW IS THE BURDEN OF PROOF DISTRIBUTED?

In the terms of article 342(1) of the Civil Code, 'the one who invokes a right must prove the facts that constitute the alleged right'. It is a known fact, however, that the burden of proof is reversed when there is a legal presumption (article 344(1) of the Civil Code).

From a general perspective, it should also be stated that in the area of non-contractual liability, the injured party must prove the fault of the originator of the harm, unless there is a legal presumption of fault (article 487(1) of the Civil Code), and that, in the area of contractual liability, the debtor must prove that the lack of compliance or defective compliance with the obligation is not a result of his own fault (article 799(1) of the Civil Code). In other words, in the contract arena, the injured party benefits from a presumption of fault.

1. *Case 1*

Article 2 of the rules on the sale of consumer goods establishes presumptions of non-conformity with the contract. When transposing Directive 1999/44/EC, the Portuguese legislator chose to use a presumption of non-conformity, rather than accept the presumption of conformity provided for in the Directive.

According to article 3 of Decree-Law 67/2003, the seller is liable for non-conformity at the time when the good is delivered to the consumer (paragraph 1). The injured party, besides not having to prove the non-conformity of the good due to the presumption of article 2(2), is also relieved from proving that such non-conformity existed on the date the good was delivered. In fact, according to article 3(2) of this decree-law, non-conformities that come to light within two years of the delivery date for tangible movable goods or five years for immovable goods are presumed to have existed on that date, unless this is incompatible with the nature of the good or with the characteristics of the non-conformity.

In the exercise of a direct action of the consumer against the producer, article 6(2) a) and c) of the rules on the sale of consumer goods presumes that the non-conformity is attributable to the producer, insofar as it is up to the latter to prove that the defect resulted, exclusively, from statements of the seller on the good and its use, or from misuse, or that, considering the circumstances, the defect did not exist when it placed the good in circulation.

Although the rule seems, in this case, to be difficult to apply for the benefit of consumers, article 23 of the Law on Popular Action lays down no-fault civil liability whenever acts or omissions of the agent result in an affront to rights or interests protected by the law in question and within the scope of and following on from an objectively dangerous activity.

In the terms of article 30(2) of the Advertising Code, advertisers are presumed to be civilly liable for damage caused by the dissemination of unlawful advertising messages, unless they prove that they had no prior knowledge of the advertising message conveyed.

D. ARE THERE ANY DEMANDS FOR INFORMATION AGAINST THE ALLEGED INJURING PARTY?

Parties determine the subject matter of the proceeding, which indirectly limits the scope of evidence. Within those limits, the judge is also recognised as having initiative in the collection of evidence in order to reach the real truth (article 411 of the Code of Civil Procedure). A request is provided that the court may compel the other party to present documents which it has in its power (articles 429ff of the Code of Civil Procedure) or to make a statement on facts that are prejudicial to it (articles 452ff of the Code of Civil Procedure).

Under article 17 of the Law on Popular Action, it is understood that within the scope of the fundamental issues defined by the parties, the judge is responsible on his own initiative for collecting evidence, not being bound by the will of the parties.

III. GENERAL PROCEDURAL LAW

A. IS A COEXISTENCE OF SEVERAL LEGAL ACTIONS POSSIBLE?

According to article 71 of the Code of Criminal Procedure, 'a claim for civil compensation based on the practice of a crime is presented in the respective criminal proceedings, and can only be presented separately, before the civil court, in the cases provided for in the law' (principle of adhesion). Article 72 of the Code sets out the situations in which the claim for compensation may be presented separately.

In the criminal proceedings, the claim for civil compensation is presented by the injured party, who is deemed to be a person who has suffered harm caused by the crime (article 74(1) of the Code of Criminal Procedure). Although Portuguese criminal law lays down that the injured party may become a party assisting the Public Prosecutor – *assistente* (article 68(1) of the Code of Criminal Procedure) and, accordingly, cooperate with the Public Prosecutor, it allows the injured party to present the claim for compensation separately without becoming an *assistente* (article 74(1) of the Code of Criminal Procedure).[19] The injured party's intervention in the proceedings is then limited to arguing and proving the claim for civil compensation, and he is given the rights that the law bestows on parties assisting the Public Prosecutor for that purpose (article 74(2) of the Code of Criminal Procedure).

The claim for civil compensation may be presented in the criminal proceedings against persons with merely civil liability and such persons may intervene voluntarily in those proceedings (article 73(1) of the Code of Criminal Procedure). According to article 74(3) of the Code, 'the civil defendants and the interveners have the same position in the proceedings as the defendant regarding arguing and proving the civil matters judged in the proceedings, and each of the defences is independent'.

In Case 1 that is under appreciation, it seems that the claim for compensation may be presented separately from the criminal proceedings, since criminal proceedings regarding the crime of deception are dependent on a complaint (article 217(3) of the Criminal Code and article 72(1) c) of the Code of Criminal Procedure). It can also be seen that presenting a claim for compensation separately is an option. If this possibility is used, the criminal *res judicata* does not have *erga omnes* effect, thereby safeguarding the discussion of the facts in civil proceedings.

The law recognises the possibility of intervention in an action of a criminal nature. Article 25 of Law 83/95 grants standing to holders of the right of popular action to make a denunciation, complaint or notification to the Public Prosecutor (*Ministério Público*) or to join proceedings. This fact does not, however, influence the system of criminal procedure, excluding, accordingly, the possibility of a popular criminal action or proceedings.[20]

Meanwhile, if the same fact constitutes, simultaneously, a crime and an administrative offence, the perpetrator will be punished for the crime, without

---

19 It should be stressed, however, that, in line with art 69(2) of the Code of Criminal Procedure, 'it is especially incumbent on the parties assisting the Public Prosecutor to: a) Intervene in the inquiry and in the preliminary stage by providing evidence and by requesting that steps deemed necessary be taken and to be given information on any court decisions related to such activities; b) Bring charges independent from those of the Public Prosecutor and, in case of proceedings depending upon private accusation, even when the Public Prosecutor decides not to prosecute; c) Lodge appeals against any decisions affecting them, even if the Public Prosecutor has not done so. To this end, the party assisting the Public Prosecutor shall have access to any indispensable procedural data, without to prejudice to the regime applicable to secrecy during the inquiry stage'. The law gives entities with standing to exercise popular action the right to become complainants in the respective criminal proceedings (art 25 of Law 83/95).

20 See Teixeira de Sousa, *A Legitimidade Popular* (n 5) 132ff.

prejudice to the application of the additional sanctions imposed for the administrative offence (article 20 of Decree-Law 433/82). Article 420(1) of the Securities Code provides otherwise, however, allowing accumulation of the penalty for the practice of the crime and the fine for the practice of the administrative offence. This rule does not exclude a double penalty where infringements are apparently concurrent, as such violating the constitutional principle of *ne bis in idem* and therefore being unconstitutional.[21]

Article 420(2) excludes, however, the possibility of being found guilty of both the crime and the administrative offence of use or transfer of privileged information and breach of the prohibition on market manipulation (article 399 – A(1) a) and b) of the Securities Code). In such cases, if the act is attributable to the same perpetrator on the basis of the same judgement of guilt, there is only the possibility of criminal proceedings.

B. ARE THERE ANY PROCEDURAL SIMPLIFICATIONS IN CONSUMER AND CAPITAL MARKET LAW?

One procedural simplification is the creation of 'Justices of the Peace', who also have competence for consumer disputes (Law 78/2001, 13 July). Justices of the peace can only decide on cases involving amounts up to €15,000. Once the case is received in the Justice of the Peace Courts, pre-mediation takes place, if the parties have not rejected that possibility. The objective of this phase is to explain to the parties what mediation consists of and to check how receptive they are to a possible settlement. In the absence of a settlement, the trial is held, with rules that enable greater expediency in the proceedings. Decisions delivered by the justices of the peace have the same value as decisions delivered by a court of first instance.

Also, when transposing Directive 2013/11/EU, of the European Parliament and of the Council, on alternative dispute resolution for consumer disputes, Law 144/2015, 8 September, established the legal framework for extra-judicial resolution mechanisms for consumer disputes. The specific arbitration centre for the automobile sector is CASA (*Centro de Arbitragem do Sector Automóvel* – Automobile Sector Arbitration Centre).

---

21 In this sense, Augusto Silva Dias, *Direito das Contra-Ordenações* (Almedina 2018 – reprint) 152ff.

C. WHAT IS THE BINDING EFFECT OF JUDGMENTS FOR SUBSEQUENT PROCEEDINGS?

It is necessary to distinguish between situations that are only judged in the civil arena and those in which there are decisions of a criminal or administrative offence nature. Thus:

1. In the civil arena, once a decision becomes *res judicata*, the decision on the contested material relationship has binding force within the proceedings and outside of them within the limits established by articles 580 and 581 of the Code of Civil Procedure (article 619(1) of the Code of Civil Procedure). Given that the *lis pendens* and *res judicata* to which the said articles refer require repetition of a case, measured by the identity of the subjects, the effects and the legal facts, the decision in an individual action does not constitute *res judicata* in relation to another action based on similar facts, but with different subjects;
2. Regarding popular action, article 19 of Law 83/95 provides, in relation to the effects of *res judicata*, that decisions pronounced which have become *res judicata*, except where these result from insufficient evidence, or when the judge should decide alternatively, considering the actual motivations of the concrete case,[22] have *erga omnes* (towards all) effect, but excluding the holders of rights or interests who exercise the right to exclude themselves from the representation (1).[23] Portuguese Law has adopted an opt-out regime: once the writ for popular action has been received, the judge summons the holders of the interest in question, the purpose being for them to state whether they intend to intervene in the case in their own name or whether they accept representation by the claimant, with no express declaration being understood as acceptance of the representation (article 15(1) of Law 83/95). In that case, any decisions pronounced are applicable to them. Holders may refuse the representation up until the end of the production of evidence or an equivalent phase, by express declaration in the case records (article 15(4)).
3. If the claim for compensation is presented in criminal proceedings, the criminal decision, whether a conviction or acquittal, that considers the civil claim constitutes *res judicata* in the terms in which the law affords

22 This occurs when the judge considers there has been inadequate representation of absent interests, see Teixeira de Sousa, *A Legitimidade Popular* (n 5) 241.

23 For comments on this, see José Lebre de Freitas, 'A acção popular do direito português' (2003) 24 sub judice 19ff.

res judicata effect to civil rulings (article 84 of the Code of Criminal Procedure);

4. If the claim for compensation is presented separately from the criminal proceedings, the criminal ruling has effects on civil actions where legal relations dependent on the practice of the infringement are being discussed: (i) a definitive conviction constitutes a rebuttable presumption of the existence of the facts on which the conviction is based (article 623 of the Code of Civil Procedure); (ii) a definitive acquittal constitutes a rebuttable presumption of the inexistence of the facts with which the defendant was charged (article 624(1) of the Code of Civil Procedure). It should be stressed that the said presumption prevails over any presumptions of fault established in the civil law (article 624(2) of the Code of Civil Procedure);
5. The final decision of administrative proceedings and the *res judicata* of a court decision that assess the act as an administrative offence or as a crime rule out re-appreciation of that act as an administrative offence (article 79(1) of Decree-Law 433/82, cited – general rules on administrative offences). Once a court decision that assesses the act as an administrative offence becomes *res judicata*, the possibility of it being re-assessed as a crime is also ruled out. (Article 79(2) of Decree-Law 433/82, cited – general rules on administrative offences);
6. A decision of an administrative authority that applies a fine or an additional sanction lapses if the defendant is found guilty in criminal proceedings for the same act (article 82(1) of Decree-Law 433/82, cited above). The same is true in relation to the final decision of criminal proceedings which, when it is not a conviction, proves incompatible with the application of the fine or additional sanction (article 82(2) of Decree-Law 433/82, cited above). The same happens with an acquittal for the same act, if the decision is based on the confirmation that the agent did not practice the act charged or practiced it justifiably or without fault;[24]
7. Articles 30(1) and 77(1) of the Criminal Code and 19 of the general rules on administrative offences equate the real concurrence and ideal concurrence of crimes and administrative offences and restrict sentencing or the administrative decision, respectively, to one single penalty or one single fine.

---

[24] Paulo Pinto de Albuquerque, *Comentário do Regime Geral das Contra-Ordenações (à luz da Constituição da República e da Convenção Europeia dos Direitos do Homem)* (Universidade Católica Editora 2011) 329.

D. WHEN IS THE STATUTE OF LIMITATION FOR COLLECTIVE REDRESS SUSPENDED?

According to article 11 of the Proposal for a Directive of the European Parliament and of the Council of 11 April 2018 on representative actions for the protection of the collective interests of consumers, and repealing Directive 2009/22/EC [COM(2018) 184 final]:

> Member States shall ensure that the submission of a representative action as referred to in Articles 5 and 6 shall have the effect of suspending or interrupting limitation periods applicable to any redress actions for the consumers concerned, if the relevant rights are subject to a limitation period under Union or national law.

Without prejudice to the absence of a rule that refers specifically to popular action, article 323(1) of the Civil Code allows for the limitation period to be interrupted. According to this rule, a summons or judicial notification of any act that expresses, directly or indirectly, the intention to exercise a right, regardless of which case the act belongs to and even if the court is not competent, interrupts the limitation period. Given that civil popular action can take any of the forms set out in the Code of Civil Procedure, but that article 14 of Law 83/95 establishes special rules of procedural representation, the intention to exercise the right is, in the authors' opinion, simultaneous with the summons for intervention of the holders of the interests in question in the action (article 15 of the aforementioned Law 83/95) if that occurs before the summons of the defendant. Here there is also sufficient publicising and, pursuant to article 323(4) of the Civil Code, any other judicial means by which the person against whom the right may be exercised is made aware of the act is equivalent to the summons or notification.

It is important to make a few observations regarding the participation of interested parties in the action: (i) article 14 clarifies that popular action corresponds to a form of representative litigation. The law establishes a special regime of representation: the claimant represents on his own initiative, and without the need for a mandate or express authorisation, all the other holders of the rights or interests in question who have not exercised the right to exclude themselves as set out in article 15 (opt-out regime), with the consequences of the law under appreciation; (ii) Once the writ for popular action has been received, the judge summons the holders of the interest in question.

The summons is by means of an advertisement publicised in any form of the media or press, depending on whether general or geographically specific interests are at issue (article 15(2)). The law does not require personal identification of those at whom the advertisement is directed, it being sufficient for the summons to refer to them as holders of the interests at stake, mentioning, also, the action in question, the identity of the claimant, or at least of the first claimant where there are several, the identity of the defendant or defendants, and sufficient reference to the claim and the reason for it.

Where it is not possible to specify the individual holders, the summons uses the circumstance or characteristic that is common to all of them, such as the geographical area in which they reside or the group or community that they make up (article 15(3)).

E. WHO BEARS THE LITIGATION RISKS?

Civil litigation is the reference here. In Portuguese legislation the principle of *victus victori* (the loser pays principle) applies. One may read, in article 527(1) and (2) of the Code of Civil Procedure:

> 1 – The decision which judges the action or any of its incidents or appeals shall order costs to be borne by the party which has given rise to them or, where there is no successful party in the action, whoever gains advantage; 2 – It is understood that the defeated party gives rise to the costs, in the proportion in which he is so defeated.

The rule is not absolute, however, excluding mere failure from constituting the grounds for allocating costs. This fact allows some legal theory to recognise subjective reasons in the responsibility for costs, without the law making that requirement explicit.[25] Fault in the proceedings therefore very often constitutes a justification for the assumption of charging costs, even when the party wins the action.[26] What is at issue, fundamentally, is the lack of procedural interest. Article 534 (Acts and measures which are not included in the general rule on costs) and article 535 (Responsibility of the claimant for the costs) of the Code of Civil Procedure outline situations of fault in the use of proceedings.

One may read in paragraphs 1 and 2 of the first rule:

> 1. The responsibility of the defeated party regarding costs does not cover superfluous acts and incidents (...); 2. Acts and incidents which are unnecessary for the declaration or defence of the right shall be considered superfluous. The costs of these acts shall be borne by whosoever requested them (...).

Article 535(1) provides: 'When the defendant has not given rise to the action and does not contest it, the costs are paid by the claimant'. Among the facts

---

[25] In a different sense is the rule for the sharing of costs where the action subsequently becomes impossible or useless not through any fault of the parties, under the terms of art 536 of the Portuguese Code of Civil Procedure.

[26] In this sense, Paula Costa e Silva, *A Litigância de Má Fé* (Coimbra Editora 2008) 640ff.

described in paragraph 2 of this article are situations in which the obligation of the defendant is only due at the time of the summons or after the action has been proposed, or where the claimant, although benefiting from a right which is clearly enforceable, uses declarative proceedings.

Regarding the first situation mentioned, one may also refer to article 610 (Judgment in the case of unenforceable obligation), which establishes that if the obligation is unenforceable when the action is brought and the defendant contests the enforceability of the provision, without litigating with regard to the existence of the duty (2), the claimant shall bear the costs and pay the fees of the defendant's lawyer (3). Thus, both in the provisions of article 535 and underlying that which is laid down in article 610,

> the use of the court proved to be totally unnecessary since the attitude of the defendant suggested that he would have complied with the obligation by which he was bound. The claimant won the action, but since it was unnecessary, he gave rise to the legal costs, and consequently should bear them.[27]

If the successful party used legal proceedings, where, however, it was possible to choose alternative dispute structures, he shall bear his costs, except when the counterparty has made the use of that alternative means of dispute resolution unfeasible (article 533(4)).

Article 537(2) of the Code of Civil Procedure rules on costs in the situation of settlement in the following terms:

> In the case of settlement, the costs are shared in half, unless there is an agreement to the contrary, but when the settlement is made between a party who is exempt or dispensed from paying costs and another who is not exempt or dispensed, the judge, after consultation with the Public Prosecutor's Office, shall determine the proportion in which the costs must be paid.

The procedural costs include the justice fee, the charges and the party costs. The justice fee is understood to be the amount due for each party's impulse in the proceedings, and is fixed according to the amount and the complexity of the case. The charges in the case are the expenses that are a result of the development of the case, based on the acts requested by the parties or ordered by the judge in the case. The party costs correspond to the sums spent by the party on the case and which the law states shall be compensated by the other party. In these are included, namely, the justice fees paid, the charges actually borne by the party, the remuneration of the enforcement agent and any expenses paid by him, and the fees of the legal representative and any expenses paid by him.

---

27 Ibid, 463.

Regarding the latter category, there is a legal limit of a sum equivalent to half of the value of the justice fees paid by both parties. This is set out in articles 529 and 533(2) of the Code of Civil Procedure and article 26(3) of the Regulations on Legal Costs.

It should be remembered that, according to the law on popular action (article 20), prepayment of costs is not required (paragraph 1), the plaintiff, in the event of the claim only partially proceeding, is exempt from the payment of costs (paragraph 2), and in the case of total failure of the claim, he is only responsible for an amount to be determined by the judge, somewhere between 10 per cent and 50 per cent of the costs that would normally be due, depending on his financial situation and the substantive or procedural reason for the dismissal of the action (paragraph 3). Also, the judge in the case will decide on the compensation of the legal expenses the successful party is entitled to receive from the unsuccessful party, depending on the complexity of the case and the amount in discussion (article 21).

F. WHO RECEIVES ANY AWARDED OR SETTLED DAMAGES OR SKIMMED PROFITS?

Repair of mass injury received particular attention from the legislator in articles 22ff of Law 83/95. Article 22, which sets down the subjective liability of the agent, distinguishes between compensation for injury to identified holders of interests, calculated under the general terms of civil liability (3) and the global fixing of compensation for violation of the interests of unidentified holders (2). Interpretation of the rules appears to give rise to different readings. Summarising the trends in question, what is at issue is the greater or lesser extent of collective protection of homogeneous individual interests. There are those who restrict the global compensation to violation of collective or diffuse interests[28] or, at least, to situations where the amount due to each of the injured parties is of a small amount, not justifying the costs inherent in calculating the individual harm.[29] That is the reason why, together with the need to prevent repetition of the unlawful behaviour regarding repair of the individual injury, it is legitimate

28 One can read in the Judgment of the Supreme Court of Justice, 7 October 2003, 03A1243: 'Although the interpretation of this legal rule [art 22 (3) of Law 83/95] gives rise to many doubts, it seems clear to us that the compensation in question only takes place when the interests violated are actual diffuse interests and not, as in the present case, homogeneous individual interests (interests of entitled persons who, if unidentified, may perfectly be identified: the subscribers to a fixed telephone service who, during the period considered, had paid the activation charge)' (at <http://www.dgsi.pt>).

29 Teixeira de Sousa, *A Legitimidade Popular* (n 5) 170ff.

to index the compensation to the profits of the agent. In the authors' opinion, as, indeed, has already been written on another occasion, the mention that the law makes of identified holders of rights is understood as a reference to those who, in fact, intervene in the action or reject representation by the claimant.[30] This, therefore, distances the fear of harm to injured parties based on an '(...) arbitrary demarcation of the object of the popular action brought by the popular claimant'.[31] Between the conditioning of collective appreciation of civil liability for violation of homogeneous individual rights or interests by the prevalence of common issues over individual issues, which is considered appropriate, and its restriction to harm of low value, wide scope should be recognised for standing for global compensation. In support of this conclusion, article 31(2) of the Securities Code provides that a decision in favour of the plaintiffs in a popular action must indicate the entity charged with receiving and managing the damages due to persons not individually identified. The following may be nominated: a guarantee fund, an association for the protection of investors or one or several holders of rights to damages who have been identified in the action. The rule is linked, inextricably, to homogeneous individual interests.[32]

In the law of popular action, the legislator did not establish any system for sharing the global compensation between injured parties. Regarding this issue, the following has been written:

> (...) it seems to us that *de iure condendo* (in law as it should be) the payment should be made by resorting exclusively to arbitration, setting up a highly specialized court or arbitration committee alongside the court in question which processes the payment of all the indemnities. This process would thus be relatively simple, non-litigious, informal, and with low costs and would increase the number of injured parties that would come to court to receive compensation.[33]

Once the compensation had been paid, there would be significant advantage in the collective execution of the patrimony of the debtor.[34]

30 Henrique Sousa Antunes, 'Apontamento sobre a Responsabilidade Civil do Fabricante de Tabaco' (2003) XVII Direito e Justiça 202ff.

31 Teixeira de Sousa, *A Legitimidade Popular* (n 5) 174.

32 See J Oliveira Ascensão, 'A Acção Popular e a Protecção do Investidor' (2001) 11 Cadernos do Mercado de Valores Mobiliários 65: 'The holders of rights who are not individually identified are the parties who are individually harmed that did not take part in the action. This is confirmed by Paragraph 3: damages which are not paid as a result of the statute of limitations or the impossibility of identifying the respective holders revert to the guarantee fund. Only individual parties may be unable to be identified'.

33 António Payan Martins, *Class Actions em Portugal* (Edições Cosmos 1999) 122.

34 Ibid, 123.

It is relevant to mention the Draft Bill for a Consumers Code, a proposal presented in 2006 that was not passed. According to the Draft Bill, popular action would be exercised under the terms of Law 83/95, with the specifics of the articles subsequent to it.

The provisions of articles 554 and 555 were especially relevant, since they filled a gap in the law of popular action. Article 554 established, with regard to reparative protection, that, once the substance of the request for compensation had been confirmed, the decision would designate the General-Directorate for Consumers (then, the Institute for the Consumer) as the competent body to receive and manage the amount of the order and fix the criteria to be observed in its distribution to the holders who were not identified by name in the proceedings. The court would be able to apply a compulsory pecuniary sanction which would be sufficient to encourage voluntary compliance with the obligations placed on the defendant, under the terms of article 829-A of the Civil Code.

It should be highlighted that, according to article 555, the procedure for sharing the amount fixed as global compensation would be conducted officiously by the General-Directorate for Consumers, and should be begun within 30 days of the decision becoming *res judicata* and concluded within 180 days (1 and 2).

Considering that, in the terms described above, criminal or administrative offence sanctions may include restitution of unlawful profit, recipients of this can be identified in the following terms:

1. According to article 110(6) of the Criminal Code, loss of gains in favour of the State does not harm the rights of the injured party. Thus, assessing, namely, the consequences of the crime of deception, the profit will be, totally or partially, intended for the holder of the violated right, due to the application of the rules on unjust enrichment, of the law on *negotiorum gestio* or of the rules on the obligation to indemnify, as we have argued;
2. Regarding the fine applicable to an unfair commercial practice, article 18(2) of the Administrative Offences Act lays down that:

   > if the agent gains from the infringement an economic benefit which can be calculated as being higher than the upper limit of the fine, and there are no other means to eliminate it, the latter may be raised up to the amount of the benefit, although this increase may not be more than one third of the upper limit established by law.

   Here also, the solution is subsidiary in relation to the applicable civil law rules;
3. On the crimes of insider trading and market manipulation, article 380-A of the Securities Code provides with regard to the apprehension and loss of criminal gains: if the unlawful act gives rise to patrimonial gains, the amounts are declared lost in the final conviction (paragraph 1). Patrimonial gains are actual gains obtained and costs and losses avoided with the

practice of the act, regardless of the final use that the agent (defendant) has given these and even if they are subsequently lost (paragraph 2). The amount apprehended is allocated to reparation of any injured parties who presented their claim in the criminal proceedings, and 60 per cent of the remaining amount is declared lost in favour of the State and 40 per cent in favour of the Investors Compensation System (paragraph 3). This distribution denies allocation of the profit to the injured parties, wrongly, in the authors' opinion.

4. In the situation where information is provided that is not complete, truthful, current, clear, objective and lawful, article 388(2) of the Securities Code lays down that the upper limit of the fine is the highest of the following amounts: (i) three times the economic benefit obtained, even if totally or partially in the form of losses potentially avoided (sub-paragraph 1.); (ii) for administrative offences for use or transfer of privileged information and market manipulation, 15 per cent of the turnover (sub-paragraph 3.). Meanwhile, in the terms of article 406(2) of the Securities Code, the proceeds from the fines and the apprehended economic benefit revert in their entirety to the Investors Compensation System.

The Investors Compensation System is a legal person in public law, created by Decree-Law 222/99, 22 June, and intended to protect small investors, if a participating entity does not have the financial capacity to reimburse or return the money or financial instruments belonging to them.

PART II

BEYOND EUROPE

ENFORCING CONSUMER AND CAPITAL MARKETS LAW IN AUSTRALIA

Peter CASHMAN*

---

* Peter Cashman, *LLB, Dip Crim (Melb), LLM, PhD (Lond)*; Barrister; Adjunct Professor, University of New South Wales, Faculty of Law; formerly Professor, University of Sydney, School of Law, Kim Santow Chair in Law and Social Justice.
Information on class actions in the Federal Court of Australia is available at: <http://www.fedcourt.gov.au/law-and-practice/class-actions/class-actions>.
Reported and unreported Australian cases, from all state and federal jurisdictions, together with legislation, can be found on the database of the Australasian Legal Information Institute (AustLII) at: <http://www.austlii.edu.au>. Another legal database with Australian cases and legislation can be found at: <http://jade.io>.

Volkswagen was ranked ninth of the Fortune 500 companies in 2018 with revenue in 2018 of US$278 billion. Revenue growth since 2004 has been 152 per cent.[1] Around the time of the announcement of the emissions scandal in late 2015 it had just achieved prominence as the largest manufacturer of vehicles in the world.

In Australia, purchasers of the affected vehicles which are the subject of the present proceedings referred to in this chapter paid around A$5 billion for the vehicles.[2]

This chapter examines the enforcement of consumer and capital market law in Australia with particular reference to recent litigation in the Federal Court of Australia arising out of the diesel emissions scandal. This encompasses an assessment of public sanctions, private claims and procedural law in general and class action mechanisms in particular.

In keeping with the focus of this publication there is an evaluation of the domestic legal procedures and remedies available in the event of:

- an automobile manufacturer producing motor vehicles with emission values that are manipulated resulting in a material defect in the vehicle whereby consumers who purchase such vehicles suffer a loss of the vehicle's value as a result of such defect (Case 1);[3] and
- a material decrease in the share price following disclosure to the Stock Exchange of information concerning the manipulation of the emission values (Case 2).

The 'hypothetical' scenario in Case 1 is of course based on the present VW diesel emissions scandal. This scandal has given rise to protracted legal proceedings in the Federal Court of Australia against various Volkswagen, Audi and Skoda entities. This litigation is examined in some detail below.

---

1 As reported in *The Australian* (Surry Hills, 22 August 2019) 25.
2 Based on an estimated average of A$50,000 per vehicle for 100,000 vehicles.
3 See Introduction Section IV.A.

The Case 2 scenario is presently the subject of extensive litigation in Europe and elsewhere on behalf of shareholders who claim to have suffered loss and damage as a result of the decline in the value of relevant shares. At present there is no equivalent litigation against VW entities in Australia although Australian litigation funders are involved in financing shareholder litigation against VW entities in other jurisdictions. The substantive and procedural law relevant to shareholder litigation in Australia is examined below.

I. PRIVATE LAW AND CIVIL PROCEDURE

Statutory class actions were first introduced in Australia on 4 March 1992 in the Federal Court as a result of Part IVA of the Federal Court of Australia Act 1976 (Cth) coming into operation. Statutory class action procedures are now available in the Federal Court of Australia and in the Supreme Courts of five states: Victoria; New South Wales, Queensland, Western Australia and Tasmania.[4]

The statutory regime in each Australian jurisdiction is similar. The key features may be summarised as follows:

- The threshold criteria for the commencement of a class action are minimalist (seven or more persons, with claims against the same person, arising out of the same similar or related facts giving rise to a substantial common question of law or fact).
- There is no certification. A class action can be commenced if the abovementioned criteria are satisfied, without judicial approval being required.
- It is an 'opt-out' regime. Persons falling within the definition of the defined class are included whether or not they are aware or consent. They may be excluded by taking formal steps to 'opt out'.
- In the dieselgate context: the class action regime is, in theory, available to both consumers and shareholders. It was utilised by consumers (discussed below) but not by shareholders, at least in Australia (see below).
- Commercial litigation funders may be able to take a percentage of the amount recovered by class members if the claim is successful. Historically this was achieved by individual class members entering into litigation funding agreements with the commercial litigation funder. Recently, Australian courts have often made 'common fund' orders whereby the litigation funder may be entitled to recovery of a percentage from the

4 The Western Australian and Tasmanian reforms to introduce class actions in the Supreme Courts in those jurisdictions have only recently been introduced.

class as a whole, if the case is successful, without individual contractual arrangements being entered into.[5] The court determines the reasonableness of the amount payable to the litigation funder at the conclusion of the proceedings. Although both the Federal Court and the NSW Court of Appeal have held recently that Australian (federal and state) courts have power to make common fund orders in class action litigation, the High Court of Australia has recently determined that there is no power to make such an order (pursuant to section 33ZF of the Federal Court of Australia Act 1976 (Cth)) at the outset or during the course of the litigation.[6] At the time of writing it remains a vexed question as to whether such an order can be made at the conclusion of the proceedings following a settlement (pursuant to section 33V(2)) or judgment.

- Lawyers are not allowed to charge fees calculated as a percentage of the amount recovered. Normally legal fees are calculated based on hourly rates with a further 'uplift' (of up to 25 per cent of the hourly rate) payable if the fees are only payable in the event of success in the litigation. However, the Australian Law Reform Commission has recently recommended that the law should be changed to permit percentage-based fees, subject to a number of specified conditions.[7]
- Although the courts have a general discretion in relation to the making of orders for costs, at the conclusion of the proceedings the successful party will usually obtain an order from the court that the losing party pay (most of) the legal costs incurred in conducting the litigation.
- The lead applicant is personally liable for any adverse costs order[8] whereas the class members are not liable for adverse costs.[9]

---

5 *Money Max Int Pty Ltd (Trustee) v QBE Insurance Group Ltd* [2016] FCAFC 148 (Murphy, Gleeson and Beach JJ). All federal common fund orders made up to the end of 2018 are summarised in the empirical report available at <http://ssrn.com/abstract=3326303>.

6 The New South Wales Court of Appeal decision is: *Brewster v BMW Australia Ltd* [2019] NSWCA 35 and the Full Federal Court of Australia decision is: *Lenthall v Westpac Life Insurance Services Ltd* [2019] FCAFC 34. The High Court decisions are: *BMW Australia Ltd v Brewster* and *Westpac Banking Corporation v Lenthall* [2019] HCA 45 (4 December 2019).

7 On 24 January 2019, the Attorney-General for Australia tabled in Parliament: Australian Law Reform Commission (ALRC), *Integrity, Fairness and Efficiency – An Inquiry into Class Action Proceedings and Third-Party Litigation Funders, Final Report 134* (Commonwealth of Australia 2018) <http://www.alrc.gov.au/inquiry-categories/class-action-proceedings-and-third-party-litigation-funders> (hereafter Australian Law Reform Commission (ALRC), *Integrity, Fairness and Efficiency*).

8 Usually in a funded case the commercial litigation funder will indemnify the lead applicant in respect of any order for costs or security for costs. Often there will also be an after the event insurance (ATE) policy taken out with a commercial insurer whereby the insurer assumes liability to pay any such costs in consideration for the payment of a (substantial) premium. Often the premium is as high as one-third of the limit of indemnity required. Usually the majority of the premium amount is only payable upon a successful outcome.

9 In some limited circumstances a class member may become liable for certain costs: e.g. if they become appointed as a sub-group representative or if they take steps in the litigation

- The limitation periods in respect of the causes of action relied upon by the class members are suspended upon the filing of the action.

The advantage of the Australian 'opt-out' class action regime compared with jurisdictions which have an 'opt-in' requirement is starkly apparent from the experience to date in the dieselgate litigation. The class actions in the Australian litigation were commenced on behalf of the purchasers of *all* affected vehicles in Australia and thus comprise around 100,000 consumers. By way of contrast, the English Group Litigation scheme requires each claimant to commence an individual proceeding in the High Court. Proceedings have been commenced to date by approximately 95,000 UK consumers. Thus, the number of claimants in the Australian and UK proceedings are roughly similar. However, in the UK there are approximately 1.2 million affected vehicles. Thus, the UK claimants comprise less than 8 per cent of affected consumers in the UK. Similarly, in other European jurisdictions where those affected are required to take individual steps to commence proceedings, or to have proceedings commenced on their behalf, the total number of those making claims is substantially less than the total population of persons with similar claims.

The following part of this chapter focuses on three main recent developments concerning class actions in Australia:

- recent doctrinal and procedural developments;
- some findings from empirical research; and
- policy developments with particular reference to the recent reports of the Victorian and Australian Law Reform Commissions concerning commercial litigation funding and class actions.[10]

A. DOCTRINAL AND PROCEDURAL DEVELOPMENTS

In relatively recent decisions Australian courts have resolved hitherto perplexing questions about:

1. whether class actions can be commenced on behalf of only some of those who may fall within the group affected by the conduct giving rise to class action proceedings;
2. whether in cases involving multiple respondents all class members have to have an individual claim against each of the respondents; and

---

in connection with the resolution of individual issues in respect of their particular claim.

10 This part of the chapter is based in part on an unpublished paper by the author: Peter Cashman, 'Class Action Developments: the Good, the Bad and the Ugly' (Civil Justice Research Conference, Sydney, February 2019).

3. in the case of commercially funded proceedings, whether the funder may obtain an entitlement to a commission from all of the class members, not just those who may have entered into contractual litigation funding agreements.

To date these questions have been answered (1) yes; (2) no and (3) no, respectively. However:

- the judicial determination of the first question is under attack on policy grounds and the subject of proposals for legislative reform, discussed below;
- the judicial determination of the second question may not have finally determined the issue;
- the judicial resolution of the third question is limited to interlocutory orders made at the outset or during the course of the proceeding and, as noted below, the Court may have power to make such an order at the conclusion of the proceedings in connection with settlement approval or following judgment.

Each of these matters is considered in more detail below.

1. Limited or Open Classes?

In *Multiplex*[11] the Full Federal Court determined that limited or 'closed' classes were permissible under the class action regime provided for in Part IVA of the Federal Court of Australia Act 1976 (Cth) given that the legislation expressly provides that a class action may be commenced by or on behalf of 'some or all' who have 'claims'[12] as 'representing some or all of them'.[13] This issue was previously the subject of divided judicial views of members of both the Federal Court and the Victorian Supreme Court.

The Full Court resolution of this relatively straightforward matter of statutory interpretation has precipitated a policy debate about the relative merits of 'open' compared with 'closed' classes. This has been driven in part by the fact that in many instances, particularly before the decision of the Full Court in *Money-Max* (discussed below), many commercially funded class actions were commenced on behalf of classes limited to those who had entered into litigation funding arrangements which in some cases comprised

11 *Multiplex Funds Management Ltd v P Dawson Nominees Pty Ltd* (2007) 164 FCR 275.
12 S 33C requires that such 'claims': be 'against the same person'; are in respect of or arise out of the same, similar or related circumstances and give rise to a substantial common issue of law or fact.
13 Federal Court of Australia Act 1976 (Cth), s 33C.

only those potential class members with the largest claims (e.g. institutional shareholders in shareholder class actions).

The adverse policy consequence of this development is obvious. What was intended as an 'open' class action regime had been, in the view of some, subverted by the introduction of commercial litigation funding arrangements which were, historically at least, constrained by the commercial necessity to sign up persons with claims in order to obtain a legal entitlement (under contract law) to a share of the money recovered by funded class members.

Accordingly, there has been a policy move to amend the class action legislation to require that all class actions be commenced as open classes. According to the ALRC, this recommendation 'is primarily directed at ensuring that the class action regime does not require potential group members to sign up with a lawyer or funder in order to participate'.[14] According to the ALRC, the Federal Court has the necessary discretion to distinguish between a proceeding where the class is defined 'reasonably' and one where the 'description of the class is crafted to require the signing up with a lawyer or funder to participate.'[15]

Although historically there appeared to be a notable transition from open to limited classes with the introduction and expansion of commercial litigation funding, this appears to have been reversed, particularly following the decision of the Full Federal Court in *Money Max* to allow funders to obtain a (judicially approved) commission from class members as a whole, not just those who had entered into litigation funding arrangements (and without the onerous and expensive requirement to engage in 'book-building').

The policy arguments considered by the ALRC in its recent report focus primarily on the contrast between open classes and classes limited to class members who have signed litigation funding or legal representation agreements.

However, the circumstances where it may be desirable or necessary to limit the ambit of the class are much more complex. Such situations include (a) those where an open class may encompass an unwieldly and enormous number of people (such as in the Vitamins price fixing cartel class action); (b) cases where there may be different and difficult causation issues amongst different subsets of potential class members (such as in the Vioxx and silicone breast implant litigation); (c) situations where many of those with eligible claims may only be entitled to a very modest amount, and where problems of proof and transaction costs may make the pursuit of claims on behalf of many such persons impractical or unduly expensive[16] (such as in the Nurofen litigation).

---

14 Australian Law Reform Commission (ALRC), *Integrity, Fairness and Efficiency* (n 7) 3.18.

15 Ibid.

16 The legislation presently provides a mechanism for the dismissal or stay of cases actions where the costs to the respondent of identifying class members and distributing money to

In the context of investor or shareholder litigation it is difficult to contend that all class actions should be commenced on behalf of all those who suffered loss, regardless of the quantum of individual claims.

Leaving aside policy considerations, the legislative solution recommended by the ALRC is problematic. The ALRC in its suggested legislative amendments has proposed that section 33 (1) of the Federal Court of Australia Act 1976 (Cth) should be amended to read: 'a proceeding may be commenced by one or more of those persons as representing all of them' (i.e. by deleting the words 'some or' after the word 'representing' in the present provision).

If the requirement is to commence the proceeding on behalf of 'all' persons who have claims and who meet the requirements of section 33(1)(a) (numerosity), (b) (similarity) and (c)(commonality) it is not clear how the concept of 'all' is to be operationalised or interpreted in practice. In a personal injury or product liability claims for personal injuries, would this require the class to be defined to include all persons who have suffered any form of personal injury or financial loss, regardless of the type or quantum of the claim and without regard to whether there may be causation complications associated with some types of claims? In a price-fixing case would this require all persons who may have suffered loss to be included, including first-tier commercial purchasers and all ultimate consumers who may have purchased a product or service at an inflated cost, regardless of the quantum of such increased cost and the invidious difficulties in dealing with the so-called pass-on defence?

Even if the ambit of the class is to be left to judicial discretion, this may not be an appropriate role for the court and may involve difficult questions in which uncertainty and value judgments may loom large.

2. *Common Fund Orders*

In *Money Max*[17] the Full Federal Court held that the Federal Court had power to make an interlocutory order allowing a commercial funder of the litigation to obtain a commission or percentage of the successful recovery from all class members (i.e. not just those who had entered into contractual litigation funding arrangements).

The judicial power to make such an order has been held to be derived from section 33ZF and section 23 of the federal legislation. The former provides that the Federal Court may make 'any order the Court thinks appropriate or necessary to ensure justice is done in a proceeding'.[18]

---

them would be excessive having regard to the likely total amounts in issue: see, e.g. Federal Court of Australia Act 1976 (Cth), s 33M.

17 *Money Max Int Pty Ltd (Trustee) v QBE Insurance Group Ltd* (2016) 245 FCR 191.

18 See generally, in addition to the decision in *Money Max: Pearson v State of Queensland* [2017] FCA 1096 (Murphy J); *Caason Investments Pty Ltd v Cao (No 2)* [2018] FCA 527; *Lentall v Westpac Life Insurance Services Ltd* [2018] FCA 1422.

The power to make such orders was the subject of appeals in two cases, one in the Federal Court (*Lenthall v Westpac Banking Corporation*) and one in the NSW Supreme Court (*Brewster v BMW Australia*). In both cases the appeals/applications for leave to appeal were instigated by the respondent/defendants, notwithstanding the fact that the exercise of the power in question does not (directly) affect them. A common fund order would only take money out of the pockets of successful class members after the respondents had been ordered, or agreed, to part with it other than pursuant to the judicial power(s) relied upon in making common fund orders. In neither case has any issue of standing been raised. In the NSW Supreme Court the question of power was remitted directly to the Court of Appeal by the docket judge (Sackar J) without having made any order in the proceeding before him (one of the many Takata air bag cases).[19]

Both appeals were recently heard before a joint sitting of the Full Federal Court and the NSW Court of Appeal. The appellants contended, *inter alia*, that neither the Federal Court nor the Supreme Court is empowered by their respective federal and state class action legislation to make an interlocutory order of the type in question.

In the *Lenthall* proceedings in the Federal Court the application for leave to appeal contended, *inter alia*, that section 33ZF of the Federal Court of Australia Act 1976 (Cth) did not empower Justice Lee in that case to make the common fund orders that were made[20] on the grounds that the making of such an order is an exercise of power which is neither a judicial power nor incidental to the exercise of judicial power. If such a power exists it is contended by the defendant/respondents that such a common fund order is derived from a law which is invalid because it provides for the acquisition of property (of group members) in favour of the funder otherwise than on just terms, contrary to section 51 (xxxi) of the Australian Constitution. This is not the first time that class action provisions have been subject to challenge on constitutional grounds.

In *Bright v Femcare* Finkelstein J sitting as a member of the Full Federal Court noted that:

> There is a disturbing trend that is emerging in representative proceedings which is best brought to an end. I refer to the numerous interlocutory applications, including interlocutory appeals, that occur in such proceedings. ... it is not unknown for respondents in class actions to do whatever is necessary to avoid a trial, usually by causing the applicants to incur prohibitive costs. The court should be astute to ensure that such tactics are not successful.[21]

---

19 *Owen Brewster v BMW Australia Ltd* [2018] NSWSC 1602.
20 *Lenthall v Westpac Life Insurance Services Ltd* [2018] FCA 1422.
21 *Bright v Femcare* [2002] FCAFC 243 at [160].

That admonition has not been adopted. Class actions remain the subject of enduring interlocutory disputation and appeals.[22] As Lee J has more recently observed:

> Part IVA ... has reached its silver anniversary. Born in controversy, in its turbulent infancy procedural disputation was its almost constant companion. As it matured, and the more the adjectival law and the lore of Part IVA developed, the disputation lessened. Despite this, procedural arguments still recur; indeed, they are often the same arguments in different guises ....[23]

At the hearing of the appeals in respect of common fund orders some of the debate and argument focused on whether the court(s) might be empowered to make a common fund order, as a final order at the conclusion of the proceedings, pursuant to other sections of the federal and state legislation governing judgments and settlements, rather than on an interlocutory basis said to be empowered by section 33ZF.

In separate judgments, both the Full Court and the NSW Court of Appeal accepted that the respective courts were empowered to make common fund orders. Thus, it was accepted (subject to the decision of the High Court on appeal, discussed below) that even if an order could be made early on an interlocutory basis there is no certainty that at the conclusion of the case the order will not be varied in light of the ultimate outcome. Moreover, although Lee J specified a percentage amount (provisionally) payable to the funder in *Lenthall*, in *Money Max* the Full Federal Court made it clear that court approval of a reasonable funding commission rate is to be left to a later stage when more probative and more complete information would be available to the court, which was likely to be at the stage of settlement approval or the distribution of damages.[24]

Although the defendant/respondents do not have a direct interest in a common fund order in challenging the power to make such orders they presumably are motivated by a desire to circumvent or frustrate the commercial

---

22 Some of the reasons for this are discussed by Bernard Murphy, 'Class Actions and the National Court Framework' (*Legal Leaders Briefing, Law Council of Australia*, 7 December 2015) <http://www.fedcourt.gov.au/digital-law-library/judges-speeches/justice-murphy/murphy-j-20151207>.

23 *Dillon v RBS Group (Australia) Pty Ltd* [2017] FCA 896. A paper in which there is reference to the case: Michael Lee, 'Certification of Class Actions: A "Solution" in Search of a Problem' (Commercial Law Association Seminar 'Class Actions-Different Perspectives', 20 October 2017) <http://www.fedcourt.gov.au/digital-law-library/judges-speeches/justice-lee/lee-j-20171020> goes on to note that many of the issues that have been the subject of interlocutory disputation, including 'the power of the Court to make common fund orders' 'have all been resolved'. However, many new avenues for interlocutory disputation have opened up and old ones are being revisited.

24 *Money Max Int Pty Ltd (Trustee) v QBE Insurance Group Ltd* (2016) 245 FCR 191 at [11].

funding of class actions against them. The recent legal challenge joins a long list of challenges to commercial litigation funding arrangements by parties sued in class actions.

The acceptance, prior to the High Court decision on appeal, that a common fund order can be made early in the proceedings appears to have led to the desirable policy result that open class actions have become more commercially attractive to litigation funders, with a consequential decrease in 'closed' class actions. However, this has led to one undesirable consequence. The attractiveness of common fund orders appears to have spurred an increase in duplicative and competing class actions instituted with financial support from a multiplicity of Australian and international funders. Thus, the Full Federal Court's prediction in *Money Max* that this would have the reverse effect[25] does not appear to have been borne out.

In any event, in its recent decision in the appeals from the decisions of the Full Federal Court and the NSW Court of Appeal, the High Court held (by majority[26]) that the courts below had no power to make common fund orders on an interlocutory basis. As noted above, it remains unclear whether common fund orders are not permissible *in any circumstances* or whether such an order may still be made *at the conclusion of the proceeding* at the settlement or judgment stage (pursuant to section 33V(2) or section 33Z). This issue is presently under consideration in a number of cases, including in the VW dieselgate class action litigation. In what appears to be the most recent decision dealing with this issue, Justice Beach of the Federal Court of Australia made the following observation:

> … the issue before the High Court in *BMW Australia Ltd v Brewster* (2019) 94 ALJR 51 did not concern a settlement approval process. Relatedly, it did not discuss the ambit of the power under s 33V(2). Moreover, and I say this with some hesitation although after careful reflection, there is no considered majority dicta which clearly precludes s 33V(2) from being used for that purpose.[27]

3. *Claims against Multiple Defendants*

In 2000 the Full Federal Court (Sackville J, with whom Spender and Hill JJ agreed) decided that it was a requirement in class action proceedings commenced in the Federal Court under the federal legislation that where there are multiple respondents each class member is required to have an individual

---

25 *Money Max Int Pty Ltd (Trustee) v QBE Insurance Group Ltd* (2016) 245 FCR 191 at [14].

26 The majority judgments comprised the joint decision of Kiefel CJ, Bell and Keane JJ and the separate individual judgments of Nettle J and Gordon J. Gageler J and Edelman J each delivered separate dissenting judgments.

27 McKay Super Solutions Pty Ltd v Bellamy's Australia Ltd (No 3) [2020] FCA 461 at [31].

claim against each respondent.[28] As that requirement was not satisfied in that case the proceedings were terminated. The decision is obiter as the issue was not argued. The lawyers for the claimants conceded the point.

Things have moved on. In *Bray v Hoffman-La Roche*[29] the majority in a differently constituted Full Court disagreed with the decision in *Nixon*. A later Full Federal Court subsequently held that there is no requirement in multi-respondent class actions for each class member to have a claim against every respondent. In *Cash Converters International Limited v Gray*[30] the Full Federal Court determined that a proper construction of section 33C (1) does *not* require that every group member have a claim against all respondents. Provided that the threshold requirements for commencing a class action are satisfied in respect of the claim of the applicant, the applicant may join as respondents persons or entities against who only some class members have claims.

This issue has been resolved (for the time being at least) after 15 years of disputation and differing judicial views. Thus, it is not necessary for all group members to have a claim against every respondent, provided that at least seven group members have claims against each respondent; the applicant has a claim against each respondent and the proceedings satisfy the other threshold requirements of section 33C of the Federal Court of Australia Act 1976 (Cth). However, the issue of whether or not seven or more group members are required to have claims against each of the respondents did not arise for judicial resolution on the facts of *Cash Converters* because it was accepted that this 'requirement' was satisfied. Thus, as one law firm has noted, the reasoning of the Court on this issue is not binding and may give rise to further legal challenge.[31]

At the state level, in NSW the class action legislation was drafted so as to get around this impediment. Section 158(2) of the Civil Procedure Act provides that a 'person may commence representative proceedings on behalf of other persons against more than one defendant irrespective of whether or not the person and each of those persons have a claim against every defendant in the proceedings.' As noted by Garling J in two decisions, this does not require the plaintiff or the group members to have a claim against every defendant joined.[32]

---

28 *Philip Morris (Australia) Ltd v Nixon* (2000) 170 ALR 487. See generally Vince Morabito, 'Class Actions against Multiple Respondents' [2002] FLR 11.

29 *Bray v Hoffman-La Roche* (2003) 130 FCR 317 (Carr and Finkelstein JJ; Branson J dissenting).

30 *Cash Converters International Ltd v Gray* (2014) 223 FCR 139 (Jacobson, Middleton and Gordon JJ).

31 Peter O'Donahoo and Jenny Campbell, 'Client Update: Court takes an expansive view of the threshold requirements for class actions against multiple respondents' (*Allens Linklaters*, 8 September 2014) <http://www.allens.com.au/pubs/ldr/culdr8sep14.htm>.

32 *Giles v Commonwealth of Australia* [2014] NSWSC 83 at [68]; *Rickhuss v The Cosmetic Institute Pty Ltd* [2018] NSWSC 1848 at [34]. See also the decision of Beech-Jones J in

Although the NSW provisions provide that it is not necessary for all group members to have claims against all defendants, the legislation is silent as to what the minimum requirements are. This may give rise to further controversy.

B. FINDINGS FROM RECENT EMPIRICAL RESEARCH

Leaving aside doctrinal developments, there are some interesting implications from recent empirical research. The recent ALRC and VLRC reports on funding and class actions (discussed below) contain valuable information, although neither commission embarked upon major empirical research.

A significant amount of empirical data is available in respect of the operation of the Australian class action regime(s). This has been compiled and analysed principally by Professor Vince Morabito of Monash University in Melbourne.[33]

The 25th anniversary of the federal regime was in 2017. From 4 March 1992 to date over 600 class actions have been commenced. Approximately three-quarters were in the Federal Court. There is an increasing proportion of claims in respect of financial products and securities (about 50 per cent). This reflects the increasing proportion of funded cases. Around 70 per cent of class actions commenced in recent years are funded by a commercial funder. Most cases were commenced in NSW. There has also been a marked increase in competing class actions filed by different law firms (some of which are funded by different commercial funders) in respect of the same events.

According to Morabito[34] the class actions commenced in Australia to date comprise primarily: shareholder class actions (115); investor class actions (11); product liability class actions (78); mass tort class actions (66) and employment class actions (65).

As part of his ongoing monumental research Professor Morabito has shed some useful light on class action practice in a recent report.[35]

The report seeks, *inter alia*, to 'rectify an incorrect perception regarding the overall sums that class action defendants have agreed to pay in order to settle

---

Rodriguez & Sons Pty Ltd v Queensland Bulk Water Supply Authority t/as Seqwater (No 5) [2015] NSWSC 1771 a class action arising out of the Brisbane floods.

33 See, e.g. the report by Vince Morabito, 'An Evidence-Based Approach to Class Action Reform in Australia: Competing Class Actions and Comparative Perspectives on the Volume of Class Action Litigation in Australia' (2018) <http://papers.ssrn.com/sol3/papers.cfm?abstract_id=3212527>.

34 Vince Morabito, 'Empirical Perspectives on 27 Years of Class Actions in Australia' (University of Melbourne Master's program on Class Actions, Melbourne, July 2019).

35 Vince Morabito, 'An Evidence Based Approach to Class Action Reform in Australia: Common Fund Orders, Funding Fees and Reimbursement Payments' (2019).

class action proceedings in this country'.[36] According to Morabito there have been (only) 16 class action settlements for amounts in excess of A$100 million over a period of 27 years.

The report also presents a preliminary analysis of the proportion of successful class action outcomes that have been consumed by legal fees and funding commissions.

Analysis of the relevant data shows that about 27 per cent of all settlement proceeds (arising out of settlements approved by the court) have been applied towards the funding fees of the commercial funder financing the litigation.[37] The median figure is 25 per cent.

This does not include reimbursement of the costs outlaid by funders in financing the litigation. When such cost recovery is factored in, according to Morabito, in about two-thirds of all funded cases settled in the study period, more than 50 per cent of the settlement proceeds were left for distribution to class members.

To these data may be added cases which settled without the commencement of a class action or cases which settled after a class action was commenced but where the case was no longer proceeding as a class action. Combing these categories of cases with the former results in an outcome whereby 27.1 per cent of the settlements went to the funders by way of commission.

In his report Professor Morabito also examines common fund orders in class actions in the aftermath of the decision in *Money Max* (referred to above). What is interesting is that what appears to have become something of a feeding frenzy among funders, resulting in a multiplicity of competing class actions, has had at least one positive outcome. Increased competition has placed downward pressure on funding fees. Funders competing with each other have been prepared to reduce their commissions in the hope of obtaining a judicial imprimatur to allow their funded case to continue, in preference to other competitors. In the competition for cases law firms have also proposed constraints on fees generated.

One important policy development, discussed further below, is the proposal by the ALRC that solicitors be allowed to conduct class actions on the basis of a (judicially approved) percentage fee payable upon success and the recommendation that this not be permitted in combination, in any individual case, with a funder seeking payment of a percentage commission. If these proposals are implemented,[38] competition between solicitors and funders, and

---

36 Ibid, 7.

37 Ibid, 11.

38 At the time of writing the Victorian Government has recently introduced legislation to permit lawyers to act on a percentage contingent fee basis in class actions in the Supreme Court of Victoria.

between law firms, is likely to place further downward pressure on funding commissions.

In his report Morabito also examines reimbursement payments to class representatives who have incurred time and expense in connection with the conduct of the proceedings. Such payments have become relatively routine.[39]

C. POLICY DEVELOPMENTS

As noted above, both the VLRC and the ALRC have recently made various recommendations in relation to litigation funding and class actions. The VLRC report was tabled in the Victorian Parliament on 19 June 2018.[40] The report makes 31 recommendations for reform. The ALRC Report was published on 24 January 2019.[41] The report makes 24 recommendations for reform. A detailed consideration of these reform proposals is outside the scope of the present chapter. The following section of this chapter focuses on the consumer class actions (and regulatory proceedings) against VW, Audi and Skoda in Australia.[42]

II. THE CURRENT CONSUMER AND REGULATORY PROCEEDINGS IN AUSTRALIA ARISING OUT OF THE DIESEL EMISSIONS SCANDAL[43]

Five class actions seeking damages seeking civil penalties were conducted before Justice Foster in the Federal Court of Australia.[44] Two regulatory proceedings seeking civil penalties were also before Justice Foster. All proceedings have recently been resolved on terms discussed below.

---

39 See, e.g. *Caason Investments Pty Ltd v International Litigation Partners No 3 Ltd* [2018] FCAFC 176 (Allsop CJ, Middleton and Perram JJ).

40 Victorian Law Reform Commission (VLRC), 'Access to Justice – Litigation Funding and Group Proceedings' (Victorian Government Printer 2018) <http://lawreform.vic.gov.au/sites/default/files/VLRC_Litigation_Funding_and_Group_Proceedings_Report_forweb.pdf>.

41 Australian Law Reform Commission (ALRC), *Integrity, Fairness and Efficiency* (n 7).

42 The position summarised is as at 2 August 2019. In the interests of brevity, some aspects of the proceedings have been simplified.

43 This section of the chapter is based in part upon the paper presented by the author at the seminar in Augsburg, Germany in May 2019 which focused on consumer and capital market law in various jurisdictions, with particular reference to the diesel emissions scandal.

44 The writer is one of the counsel acting for the applicant and class members in the *Cantor* and *Tolentino* class actions.

Pre-trial stages of all proceedings were dealt with concurrently. As noted above, the class actions encompass approximately 100,000 class members. A settlement of all of these actions has recently been agreed to by the parties. The settlement reached in the five class actions required court approval before it can be implemented. The hearing at which court approval was sought was held using video conference facilities on 26 March 2020. On 1 April 2020 Justice Foster made orders approving of the settlements. Reasons have recently been delivered (see the update below).

The recent settlement agreement was reached on the eve of the 'second stage' trial which was due to commence in the Federal Court on 23 September 2019. Under the terms of the proposed settlement, the respondents to the five class actions agreed to pay an amount of between A$87 million and A$127.1 million, depending on the number of class members who participate. Average payments to participating class members were originally estimated to be between a maximum of A$2,900 and A$1,400. The respondents have also agreed to pay the legal costs incurred by the applicants and class members on top of the compensation amounts.

The process for registering claims was completed recently. Approximately 40,000 class members registered valid claims within the required time. Thus, as Justice Foster noted in his orders approving the settlement: Volkswagen AG will pay approximately A$120 million; the estimated average settlement payment for each participating vehicle is A$2,800; different payments will be made for different types of vehicles and depending on their age, with the range of payments to be approximately A$1,589 to A$6,554.

Justice Foster also approved of the payment of legal costs to the two law firms conducting the five class action proceedings, which are to be paid by Volkswagen AG on top of the abovementioned settlement amount. The amounts approved had been assessed as reasonable by a costs expert. Thus, in the case of Maurice Blackburn an amount of A$43,296,810 was approved. In the case of Bannister Law an amount of A$7,589,396 was approved. Thus, on the assumption that the respondents' legal costs are no less than those of the applicants, the total legal costs of the Australian class action proceedings exceeded A$100 million.

The regulatory proceedings were the subject of a penalty hearing in the Federal Court in late 2019. At around the same time that agreement was reached to settle the five Australian class actions in late September 2019 agreement was also reached between the ACCC and the respondents to the two proceedings brought by the regulator. It was agreed between the parties that VW AG would pay a penalty of A$75 million and an amount of A$4 million in legal costs, subject to approval of the Federal Court. However, the presiding judge, Justice Foster, had other ideas. He indicated in court that in his view a higher penalty was warranted.

On 20 December 2019 he handed down a detailed 111-page judgment in which he concluded that the pecuniary penalty should be increased to A$125 million, plus an amount of A$4 million for legal costs.[45]

Justice Foster found that in the period from 1 January 2011 to 3 October 2015 in respect of 57,082 Volkswagen branded vehicles, the first respondent (VWAG) had submitted documents to the relevant regulatory body seeking approval for the import of the vehicles into Australia for use as road vehicles.

In such approval applications VWAG had impliedly represented that each of the vehicles would, when imported into Australia and supplied for on-road use, comply with Australian Design Rule 79 (ADR 79) (which relates to emission control for light vehicles and prescribes the maximum emissions of NOx that vehicles could emit whilst undergoing a standardised testing procedure).

The implied representations were found to be false because (a) each of the vehicles was fitted with software that operated in two modes (during testing and on-road use) and (b) if the vehicles had been subject to testing whilst operating on the 'on-road' mode determined by the software (Mode 2) the vehicles would have exceeded the NOx emission limits prescribed by ADR 79. Such false representations were found to contravene section 29(10)(a) of the Australian Consumer Law.

Justice Foster also found that VWAG had made further false representations that the vehicles in question complied with ADR 79 for the purpose of obtaining (low) air pollution ratings on the Green Vehicle Guide website administered by the Australian Department of Infrastructure and Regional Development (DIRD).

The history of the Australian regulatory proceedings and class actions proceedings is outlined in detail in Justice Foster's judgment. His findings and conclusions will no doubt be of interest to those involved in the ongoing conduct of regulatory, consumer and shareholder proceedings in other jurisdictions, including in Europe. According to Justice Foster '[t]he conduct of VWAG encompassed by the admitted contraventions is corporate conduct of the worst possible kind'.[46]

In March 2018 a hearing in respect of a number of separate questions, including whether the affected vehicles in Australia are fitted with illegal 'defeat devices', was heard over several weeks before Foster J (the Stage 1 Trial). The judgment on the separate questions was yet to be handed down when the recent settlement agreements were reached. This judgment would have

45 *Australian Competition and Consumer Commission v Volkswagen Aktiengesellschaft* [2019] FCA 2166.

46 Ibid at [234].

been of some international significance given that the grounds upon which the respondents have denied that the Australian cars were fitted with illegal defeat devices are also being relied upon in proceedings in a number of other jurisdictions.

For example, in the UK Group Litigation similar grounds have been relied on. However, in a recent judgment Mr Justice Waksman of the High Court (Queens Bench Division) of England and Wales rejected the contentions of the defendants and held that the affected UK vehicles did contain a prohibited defeat device.[47] He also found that the High Court was bound by the finding of the competent EU Type Approval authority that the affected vehicles contained a defeat device and that it was an abuse of process for the defendants to seek collaterally to attack this by denying that the affected vehicles contained a defeat device.

As noted above, a six-week joint trial of all the Australian proceedings was scheduled to commence in Sydney in late September 2019 (the Stage 2 Trial) before Justice Foster, four years after the initial class actions were commenced.

Thereafter a Stage 3 trial would have been held to determine, *inter alia*, civil penalties and exemplary damages.

The five class actions comprise two conducted by the Bannister Law (BL) firm (the *Cantor* and *Tolentino* proceedings) and three conducted by Maurice Blackburn (MB) (the *Dalton, Richardson* and *Roe* proceedings).

The BL class actions were commenced in September 2015, not long after the defeat device scandal became known, and were funded by a commercial litigation funder.

The BL proceedings were strategically confined to the Australian corporations and to strict liability causes of action in order to expedite resolution of the cases and to reduce costs and forensic complication. This did not occur given that all of the class actions and regulatory proceedings were proceeding concurrently.

An application for a *common fund* order was made in the BL proceedings but not pressed prior to the settlement given an application by the respondents seeking to stay or dismiss the BL proceedings. That application was renewed by the funder when the recent settlement was reached but recently rejected by Justice Foster in making orders approving of the settlement.

The MB class actions were commenced not long after the BL proceedings. MB was acting on a no-win no-fee arrangement having signed up a large number of class members to a fee and retainer agreement whereby they have agreed to pay a share of the costs of conducting the litigation, out of any damages recovered if they were successful.

---

47 *Crossley & Ors v Volkswagen Aktiengesellschaft & Ors* [2020] EWHC 783 (QB) (6 April 2020).

A. THE PARTIES SUED IN THE AUSTRALIAN PROCEEDINGS

In the BL proceedings:

- The respondent to the *Cantor* proceedings is the Australian company, Audi Australia Pty Ltd.
- The respondent to the *Tolentino* proceedings is the Australian company Volkswagen Group Australia Pty Ltd.

In the MB proceedings:

- The respondents to the *Dalton* proceedings are Volkswagen AG and Volkswagen Group Australia Pty Ltd.
- The respondents to the *Richardson* proceeding are Audi AG and Audi Australia Pty Ltd.
- The respondents to the *Roe* proceeding are Skoda Auto AS, Volkswagen Australia Group Pty Ltd and Volkswagen AG.

B. THE CLASSES IN THE AUSTRALIAN PROCEEDINGS

The five class actions comprise classes which substantially overlap although clients of the respective law firms are excluded from the ambit of the classes represented by the other law firm.

Approximately 2,700 of the 100,000 Australian class members have opted out. The opt-out process was the subject of some controversy between the parties.[48] As noted above, around 40,000 class members filed valid timely claims to participate in the settlement.

Leaving aside the differences in the ambit of the classes, the primary difference between the class actions is that:

- The BL class actions are confined to the Australian corporate entities and plead only cause so faction for which liability is strict.
- The MB class actions encompass the same (strict liability) causes of action as the BL proceedings but also include additional causes of action which require proof of intention or knowledge.
- Also, in addition to compensation, the MB class actions seek an award of exemplary damages and an account of profits.
- The MB class actions are against both the Australian and the European corporate entities.

48 See the decision in *Cantor v Audi Australia Pty Ltd (No 2)* [2017] FCA 1042 (Foster J).

C. THE CLAIMS FOR COMPENSATORY DAMAGES

The applicants were required to provide further particulars of the claims for damages. The BL applicants provided the following particulars of their claims for compensatory damages.

Each applicant's claim for loss and damage is for the reduction in value (the Loss) between (a) the actual price paid for the vehicle (the Purchase Price) and (b) the actual value of the vehicle with a defeat device as at the date of purchase, being the value of the vehicle which is non-compliant with applicable Australian regulations for registration and on-road use (the Actual Value).

In the alternative to 1: The claim for loss and damage is the amount of the Purchase Price, less an allowance for usage upon return of the car. The calculation for the value of usage is:

$$\frac{\textit{kilometers driven at the date of judgment}}{\textit{expected kilometers}} \times \textit{purchase price}$$

In the alternative to 1 and 2: The loss or damage is the difference between the current market value of the vehicle and the amount which would have been the current market value but for the presence of the defeat device and the VW emissions scandal, calculated in accordance with the methodology employed by the applicants' expert.

The compensatory damages sought by the applicants in the MB proceedings comprises (a) the purchase price paid for the vehicles less an amount representing the value of the vehicles as scrap metal or the value of the components sold as parts, or (b) the additionally depreciated value of the vehicles in the aftermath of the dieselgate scandal. The applicants in the MB proceedings also sought an account of profits and exemplary (or punitive) damages.

In preparation for the second stage trial each of the parties had also adduced expert evidence concerning the questions of whether the 'fix' of the vehicles gave rise to additional problems in terms of increased wear and tear on the engines and components parts, additional costs of servicing and parts replacement and increased fuel consumption.

D. THE REGULATORY PROCEEDINGS

The regulatory proceedings seeking civil penalties were commenced by the Australian Competition and Consumer Commission (ACCC) in 2016 and 2017.

- The respondents to proceedings NSD 1462 of 2016 (the *VW Penalty Proceedings*) are the German parent, Volkswagen AG, and the Australian company, Volkswagen Group Australia Pty Ltd.

- The respondents to proceeding NSD 322 of 2017 (the *Audi Penalty Proceedings*) are Audi AG and Audi Australia Pty Ltd.

In the regulatory proceedings the ACCC relied on causes of action in respect of, *inter alia*, conduct alleged to be misleading or deceptive or likely to mislead or deceive and false representations. The relief sought encompassed pecuniary penalties and corrective advertising. The question of public enforcement is discussed further below.

E. THE TECHNICAL ISSUES IN DISPUTE

Prior to the Stage 1 Trial a conferral between experts took place. Subsequently various documents were exchanged between the parties with a view to reaching agreement on the technical issues in dispute. Although agreement was reached on a number of technical issues in relation to the operation of the exhaust gas recirculation system (EGR), the SCR system, oxides of nitrogen and remedial measures (as set out in an Agreed Technical Document) critical issues remained in dispute at the Stage 1 Trial.

F. THE DENIAL THAT THE VEHICLES HAVE PROHIBITED DEFEAT DEVICES

Although the respondents admitted that the cars were programmed to operate in two modes, one during laboratory testing (Mode 1) and another whilst driven on the road (Mode 2), they have continued to deny that this comes within the definition of a prohibited 'defeat device'.

In summary, the respondents' forensic position was that the admitted software manipulation did not fall foul of the prohibition on 'defeat' devices for three main reasons:

First, it was contended that the relevant comparisons (to determine whether any element of design any part of the emission control system so as to lead to the *reduced* effectiveness of the emission control system) requires a comparison or consideration of the vehicles operating in both Modes 1 and 2 in normal road conditions, i.e. *on the road*, rather than a comparison between the vehicles *undergoing testing* and driven *on the road.*

Second, because the (admitted) manipulation affected the operation of the EGR system the respondents contended that the EGR system does not form part of the 'emission control system' within the meaning of the regulatory prohibition on 'defeat' devices.

Third, in considering the meaning of *reduced* effectiveness of the emission control system it was said to be necessary for the applicants to establish that the *overall* effectiveness of the emission control system has been reduced, not merely the effect on *NOx* emissions.[49]

The applicants in the three groups of proceedings contended that the respondents' construction of the defeat device prohibition should be rejected. The forensic position adopted by the respondents in the Australian proceedings appears to be inconsistent with or contradicted by, *inter alia*:

- the determination by the EPA in the US;
- the defendants' admissions in the US proceedings;
- the determinations by the KBA in Germany;
- the findings of numerous German courts to date;
- the regulatory determinations by other regulators in Europe, including in the Netherland and in Italy;
- the multitude of unqualified admissions in internal documents and business records of a number of the respondents; and
- the corporate conduct of the respondents in seeking to remove the software in question and replace it, at considerable expense, with software that does not give rise to differential emissions during laboratory testing and on road use of the vehicles.

The applicants contended that there is a perverse logic in the respondents' contention that in order to determine whether a vehicle contains a prohibited defeat device it is necessary to compare their operation in *both* modes *on the road*, when the first mode (Mode 1) was designed to operate following recognition that the vehicle was being tested in the laboratory and for the purpose of lowering NOx emissions below the prescribed limits, *during testing*, in order to obtain regulatory approval.

In any event, even if the first abovementioned contention of the respondents is accepted, the applicants contended that it is clear from (a) the documentary evidence adduced in the Australian proceedings, (b) the expert evidence relied upon by the applicants in those proceedings and (c) the Technical Documents agreed between the parties in the Australian litigation, that the vehicles will start operating on the road in Mode 1 (at least where there is a cold start) and then, upon recognition that the vehicle is not being tested on a laboratory dynamometer (in accordance with the NEDC time-distance parameters) it will switch from Mode 1 to Mode 2.

[49] There are additional arguments in relation to the Audi Q5 vehicles and the SCR which are not dealt with here.

G. THE ALLEGED COMPLIANCE WITH REGULATORY REQUIREMENTS

At the Stage 1 Trial, the respondents contended, *inter alia*, that the original certification by European testing authorities was sufficient to establish compliance with applicable Australian regulatory requirements.

In their submission to the Federal Court of Australia, they argued that when the Australian statutory scheme is construed as a whole it operates in a manner whereby once an Emission Type Approval is granted in respect of a particular vehicle and that approval is provided to Australian authorities as *proof* of compliance with the European standard, the vehicle is deemed to comply with the Australian regulatory requirements and the technical requirements thereof. This is said to be so without any proof of compliance with the underlying requirements. Thus, so it was contended by the respondents, in the absence of any further evaluation on the part of Australian authorities to assess compliance, the European approval is proof of compliance with Australian regulatory requirements.

H. THE APPLICANTS' POSITION IN RELATION TO REGULATORY COMPLIANCE

Each of the applicants in the Australian class actions and regulatory proceedings rejected this approach to the construction of the Australian regulatory provisions. The applicants argued, *inter alia*, that where there is not in fact *actual* compliance with critical provisions of the applicable standards (in this instance in relation to maximum permissible NOx emission levels) a construction of regulations that requires that the submission of a European Type Approval conclusively establishes compliance with such standards is perverse.

Moreover, the applicants contended that the European Type Approvals and Australian regulatory approvals were obtained by fraudulent or deceptive means.

The respondents' construction of both the Type Approval process and the defeat device definition, if accepted, would amount to a forensic defeat device that would both: (a) render the entire regulatory regime for controlling emissions harmful to human health and the environment ineffectual and (b) deprive the specific prohibition of defeat devices of any force.

At the Stage 1 Trial the applicants contended, and called expert evidence from numerous experts to establish, *inter alia*, that the EGR system is part of the emission control system, the cars are in fact fitted with prohibited defeat devices and the initial certification by European authorities does not suffice to establish compliance with Australian regulatory standards. The applicants also agreed with and adopted the technical explanation of the relevant automotive engineering issues as stated by the German Federal Motor Transport Authority (the KBA) and communicated to VW AG, in October 2015, as to why the EGR *is* part of the mission control system and why the affected vehicles *do* contain a prohibited defeat device. That determination was not the subject of an appeal by any of the European entities.[50]

Alternatively, the class action applicants contended that the admitted manipulation of the operation of the vehicles (through the use of Mode 1 during laboratory testing and Mode 2 during on-road use) amounts to a 'prohibited *defeat device equivalent*' if it does not come within the technical ambit of the regulatory prohibition on 'defeat' devices.

At the Stage 1 Trial expert evidence on behalf of the applicants was adduced by experts from a number of countries.

I. THE RESPONDENTS' FAILURE TO CALL ANY EXPERT EVIDENCE

Not long before the start of the Stage 1 trial, the respondents informed the parties and the Court that they did not intend to call any of the experts who had prepared and submitted expert evidence. Thus the 1st Stage Trial proceeded without the respondents calling any witnesses. As noted above, Foster J had not delivered judgment following the Stage 1 Trial prior to the recent announcement of a settlement of both the class actions and the regulatory proceedings. However, many of the same arguments relied upon by the respondents in the Australian proceedings were also relied upon by the defendants in the UK Group Litigation but rejected by Mr Justice Waxman in a recent determination of preliminary issues which were ordered to be tried.[51]

J. PROCEDURAL DISPUTATION

During the course of the Australian proceedings, there were numerous interlocutory applications, including in relation to, *inter alia*, disputed claims of privilege, the overlapping proceedings, notices to admit facts, interrogatories, pleading issues and discovery.

---

50 The question of whether the German KBA determinations could be appealed, under German law, was the subject of controversy, and expert evidence, in the UK Group Litigation.

51 *Crossley & Ors v Volkswagen Aktiengesellschaft & Ors* [2020] EWHC 783 (QB) (6 April 2020).

The respondents provided redacted copies of regulatory determinations by the German KBA claiming privilege over the redacted portions. This proceeded to a separate hearing before another Federal Court Judge who upheld the respondents' contentions.[52]

Until recently there had been no court-ordered mediation although the issue has been raised in court.[53] A recent mediation was held by agreement between the parties and this resulted in the abovementioned settlement.

Prior to the recent settlement, there continued to be considerable procedural disputation in relation to, *inter alia*:

- confidentiality orders sought by the respondents to prevent public disclosure of certain information and documents and
- whether further interrogatories should be permitted to obtain additional answers to three categories of questions from 79 current and former employees in respect of their roles, responsibilities and knowledge of various matters over almost a ten-year period.

The respondents pleaded and continued to contend that if the affected vehicles did contain a defeat device or a defeat device equivalent (which was denied), they did not have the requisite knowledge of such matters as is required by section 139B of the Competition and Consumer Act 2010 (Cth), nor did any person who was the directing mind and will of the companies have the requisite state of mind in respect of the common law causes of action brought against them in the MB proceedings.

As such, the applicants in the BL (and ACCC) proceedings had the onus of identifying the individuals they say had the requisite knowledge, and how those individuals' state of mind is to be attributed to each of the respondents. The respondents' position was that the impugned conduct was not done with the authority of the respondents.

The applicants in the MB proceedings contended that it is apparent from the respondents' previous answers to interrogatories, as well as discovered documents, that numerous employees, at various levels within the organisations, had knowledge of the 'cheating software' which is at the heart of the litigation.

In addition to the vexed issue of 'who knew what and when', there was continuing controversy over whether the European-based respondents (sued in the MB and ACCC proceedings but not in the BL proceedings) carried on business, *in Australia*, at relevant times so as to subject them to Australian laws that do not have extra-territorial effect.

52 *Cantor v Audi Australia Pty Ltd* [2016] FCA 1391 (Bromwich J).

53 In late 2018 the BL applicants wrote to the respondents proposing mediation and the appointment of US lawyer Ken Feinberg as a mediator. The proposal was not accepted by the respondents.

K. DISCOVERY OF DOCUMENTS

In relation to discovery: the respondents identified over 100 million potentially relevant documents, including some 11 million recently discovered. Most are in German and the respondents contended that any English translations of such documents are privileged. With a view to expediting and reducing the cost of the initial review, a process for technical-assisted review (TAR) of such documents using predictive coding was implemented.

L. EVIDENCE FOR THE SECOND-STAGE TRIAL

Prior to the recent settlement agreement, the applicants had served and filed with the Federal Court their evidence, including expert evidence, to be relied upon at the 2nd Stage Trial. In addition to evidence by the applicants, that evidence encompassed expert evidence from expert witnesses from a number of countries. Much of the respondents' evidence had also been recently filed and served on the parties and the applicants had prepared and served evidence in reply.

M. COMMON AND INDIVIDUAL ISSUES

There was discussion between the parties as to what 'common issues' would be resolved at the second stage trial and what 'residual issues' (in addition to penalties in the regulatory proceedings and exemplary damages in the MB proceedings) would still need to be determined following judgment after the second stage trial.

N. THE TECHNICAL SOLUTION OR FIX

The respondents continued to contend that the *technical solution* which is being implemented in Australia and elsewhere in the world, whereby the cars are being re-programmed to only operate in one 'mode' during both testing and on-road use (the Fix), will not have any adverse impact on vehicle performance or fuel economy.

As noted above, expert evidence to the contrary was filed by the applicants in the Australian proceedings. This issue would have been dealt with in the Second Stage trial but for the recent settlements. The respondents had served their evidence in respect of this issue and the applicants had served evidence in reply.

The applicants in the class action proceedings filed written submission with the Court in respect of the common questions to be determined at the second stage trial. The BL submissions may be summarised as follows.

The BL applicants contended that the parties and the Court should seek to resolve the *common questions* to be determined at the second stage trial rather than, at this stage, seek to determine what additional issues will require resolution once such questions are determined. This is in part because such *residual issues* will largely depend on how the common questions were resolved. Accordingly, the BL submissions were directed to the common questions to be determined at the second stage trial.

As noted above, the causes of action relied upon by the Bannister Law (BL) applicants (in both the *Cantor* and *Tolentino* proceedings) are limited to:

- Misleading and deceptive conduct or conduct likely to mislead or deceive;
- Non-compliance with the pleaded consumer guarantees (under the ACL[54]);
- Breach of the implied term as to merchantable quality (with the meaning of section 74D of the TPA); and
- Failure to comply with Australian safety standards.

Liability in respect of each such cause of action is strict and is to be determined on the basis of *objective*, as distinct from *subjective*, considerations.

Assuming that the judgment in respect of the separate questions was to the effect that the affected vehicles were fitted with a prohibited defeat device (or defeat device equivalent) and assuming that liability was established in favour of the applicants at the second stage trial, the Court would then have been required to determine, in respect of the lead applicants, what the appropriate measure of their loss and damage is.

At the second stage trial the Court would also have been required to determine competing legal and factual contentions concerning the impact of the implementation of the technical measures ('the Fix') on the performance of affected vehicles. Until these competing factual and legal contentions have been determined it is difficult, if not impossible, to determine what residual issues in respect of loss and damage would need to be determined, at a later stage, in respect of the claims of owners of affected vehicles who have agreed to 'the Fix'. In view of recent Court approval of the settlement, these issues will now not be determined.

O. THE CONTINUING SAGA

Until the recent settlement, there was no end in sight to the Australian litigation and the costs incurred to date are enormous.

---

54 Competition and Consumer Act 2010 (Cth), sch 2.

Moreover, the Australian cars remain on the road and the NOx emissions continue to exceed the permissible regulatory limits. The question of whether cars that have had 'the Fix' implemented now comply with regulatory emission limits remains a vexed issue.

III. PUBLIC ENFORCEMENT

As noted above, the Australian consumer class action proceedings were being dealt with concurrently in the Federal Court with the *regulatory* proceedings, seeking civil *penalties*, commenced by the Australian Competition and Consumer Commission.

The parties to the regulatory proceedings reached a settlement agreement not long after the settlement agreement was reached in the class action proceedings. Under the proposed agreement to resolve the regulatory proceedings it was agreed that Volkswagen AG would pay a civil penalty of A$75 million. However, the presiding judge, Justice Foster increased this and imposed a penalty of A$125 million.[55] This is now on appeal to the Full Federal Court.

In Australia, at a federal level, there are three main statutory bodies concerned with public enforcement. They are: the Australian Competition and Consumer Commission (ACCC),[56] the Australian Securities and Investment Commission (ASIC)[57] and the Australian Prudential Authority (APRA).[58]

The ACCC is an independent Commonwealth statutory authority whose role is to enforce the Competition and Consumer Act 2010 (Cth) and a range of additional legislation, promoting competition, fair trading and regulating national infrastructure. This may include proceedings against those involved in various forms of conduct in breach or contravention of Australian law, including participants in cartels.

Although the ACCC may seek individual remedies by way of a class action on behalf of consumers who have suffered loss or damage, each individual consumer must agree to the pursuit of such a claim and thus this 'opt-in' procedure is limited in its effectiveness.

ASIC is an independent Australian government body that acts as Australia's corporate regulator. ASIC's role is to enforce and regulate company and financial services laws to protect Australian consumers, investors and creditors.

---

55 *Australian Competition and Consumer Commission v Volkswagen Aktiengesellschaft* [2019] FCA 2166 (20 December 2019).

56 Australian Competition and Consumer Commission (ACCC) <http://www.accc.gov.au>.

57 Australian Securities and Investment Commission (ASIC) <http://www.asic.gov.au>.

58 Australian Prudential Authority (APRA) <http://www.apra.gov.au>.

ASIC has powers to begin a civil action to recover damages or property for persons (including companies) who have suffered loss:[59] ASIC's discretion about whether or not to commence section 50 proceedings is wide.[60]

For the purpose of recovery of *damages*, both the ACCC and ASIC can only bring proceedings on behalf of persons who *consent*.

Notwithstanding this limitation, both the ACCC and ASIC have important powers to *compulsorily* obtain information in connection with matters under investigation by them. In some instances information obtained pursuant to such investigations may be made available to litigants who are pursuing separate legal proceedings, including by way of a class action. A detailed consideration of these important avenues for enforcement and information gathering is outside the scope of the present chapter.

The third federal regulatory body, APRA, is an independent statutory authority that supervises institutions across banking, insurance and superannuation and promotes financial system stability in Australia.

In addition to the federal regulatory regimes there are, at state and territory level, additional regulatory bodies involved in consumer protection.

IV. THE LAW AND PROCEDURE IN RESPECT OF CLAIMS BY INVESTORS AND SHAREHOLDERS

Given that the existing statutory class action regimes in Australia may be utilised for the purpose of recovering damages on behalf of investors who have suffered loss as a result of unlawful conduct, it is of interest to examine the substantive statutory provisions that may be relied on in securities class action litigation in Australia.

In most investor class actions in Australia shareholders have claimed that the defendant company and/or its directors and officers had engaged in activities that constituted a breach of the *misleading or deceptive conduct* provisions under the Corporations Act 2001 (Cth). It is frequently pleaded that directors and officers of the company had provided inaccurate or incomplete financial statements. Of particular significance in Australia are the

---

59 See ASIC Act 2001, s 50; and National Credit Act 2009, s 275 (s 50 proceedings).

60 The power to commence such proceedings includes four elements: there must be an investigation or compulsory examination under the ASIC Act 2001 or National Credit Act 2009; it must appear to ASIC to be in the public interest to begin and carry on the proceedings; recovery of damages or property are sought (e.g. where there is a damages claim for fraud, negligence, default, breach of duty or other misconduct committed in connection with a matter to which ASIC's investigation or examination related); if the proceedings are to be commenced on behalf of a person that person must give their written consent.

somewhat onerous *continuous disclosure* obligations. A detailed consideration of these statutory provisions is outside the scope of the present chapter.

The legal bases of liability in investor or shareholder cases have been considered in a number of Australian cases.[61] Detailed empirical information on shareholder class actions in Australia is provided in a recent report by Professor Vice Morabito.[62]

Although there have been many securities class actions in Australia only a small number have gone to trial and to date only one has resulted in a judgment[63] with another recently decided case dealing with relevant issues.[64]

As Justice Lee of the Federal Court has recently observed:

> The post-Aristocrat securities class action not only has a common form, but often has a familiar genesis and development. A significant drop in the value of securities is scrutinized to determine whether it is likely that the relevant drop had been occasioned by the late revelation of material information. Premised on assumptions that: (a) the value of the relevant security reflects the expected discounted value of future cash flows to the security holders; and (b) that the security operates in an efficient market, the information released prior to the price-drop is reviewed to ascertain whether it was likely to have caused the market to alter its expectation of future cash flows (hence causing a repricing of the security to reflect these

61 These include: *Australian Securities and Investments Commission v Westpac Banking Corporation (No 2)* (24 May 2018) [2018] FCA 751 (Beach J); *Perera v GetSwift Ltd* (23 May 2018) [2018] FCA 732 (Lee J) (in the context of competing class actions); *Caason Investments Pty Ltd v Cao (No 2)* (16 April 2018) [2018] FCA 527 (Murphy J); *Smith v Leveraged Equities Ltd [No 3]* (29 March 2018) [2018] WASC 84 (Allanson J); *Australian Securities and Investments Commission v Cassimatis (No 9)* (22 March 2018) [2018] FCA 385 (Dowsett J); *In the matter of DSHE Holdings Ltd* (recs and mgrs apptd) (In Liq) (9 February 2018) [2018] NSWSC 82 (Black J); various judgments involving *Equititrust Ltd (In Liq) (Receiver Appointed) (No 1)* (2 February 2018) [2018] FCA 39 (Foster J) (in the context of an application to amend the pleadings); (No 5) (17 January 2018) [2018] FCA 11; 124 ACSR 115 (Foster J); *Rushleigh Services Pty Ltd v Forge Group Ltd (In Liquidation) (Receivers and Managers Appointed)* (31 January 2018) [2018] FCA 26 (Markovic J); *Sadie Ville Pty Ltd v Deloitte Touche Tohmatsu (A Firm) (No 2)* (19 December 2017) [2017] FCA 1574 (Moshinsky J); *Sadie Ville Pty Ltd v Deloitte Touche Tohmatsu (A Firm)* (9 October 2017) [2017] FCA 1202; 123 ACSR 223 (Moshinsky J); *Australian Competition and Consumer Commission v The Construction, Forestry, Mining and Energy Union (No 2)* (5 October 2017) [2017] FCA 1191 (Middleton J); *Whittenbury v Vocation Ltd* (4 October 2017) [2017] FCA 1185 (Middleton J); *Gloucester Shire Council v Fitch Ratings, Inc (No 2)* (16 March 2017) [2017] FCA 248 (Wigney J); and *Money Max Int Pty Ltd (Trustee) v QBE Insurance Group Ltd* (26 October 2016) [2016] FCAFC 148; 245 FCR 191; 338 ALR 188 (Murphy, Gleeson and Beach JJ).

62 Vince Morabito, 'Shareholder class actions in Australia – myths v facts' (2019) <http://papers.ssrn.com/sol3/papers.cfm?abstract_id=3484660>.

63 *TPT Patrol Pty Ltd as trustee for Amies Superannuation Fund v Myer Holdings Ltd* [2019] FCA 1747(Beach J).

64 *Masters v Lombe (Liquidator); In the matter of Babcock & Brown Ltd (in Liq)* [2019] FCA 1720 (Foster J).

altered expectations). Analysis takes place as to whether there is a sufficient basis for assuming the existence of contravening conduct during a period anterior to the revelation (this will usually involve close consideration of any relevant disclosures and available analyst reports). Further analysis is undertaken as to the size of the potential loss that may be related to the suspected contravening conduct over an identified period (the duration of which is identified by the preceding analysis).

(…) One matter left out of this historical survey is a characteristic of this type of litigation, which is both striking and singular. That is, that since the *Aristocrat* class action, there have been over 60 funded securities class actions commenced but not one of these actions has proceeded to the delivery of judgment following a fully contested hearing (albeit two have settled after an initial trial, but before judgment and at least one has settled during the course of the initial trial).[65]

There are some as yet unresolved issues including the extent to which some variation of the well-known US concept of 'fraud on the market' will ultimately find favour in Australian jurisprudence.

In explaining why no Australian securities class action had proceeded to judgment (until recently) Justice Lee observed as follows:

There are a number of reasons why this might be the case. First, such litigation is expensive. Secondly, it involves risk as at least one issue, commonly described as 'market based causation', is yet to receive express acceptance by the High Court (notwithstanding its acceptance by Perram J, in obiter, in Grant-Taylor v Babcock and Brown Ltd (in liq) [2015] FCA 149; (2015) 322 ALR 723 at 765–66 [219]–[20]; in the decision of the Full Court (on a pleading dispute) in Caason Investments Pty Ltd v Cao [2015] FCAFC 94; (2015) 236 FCR 322 at 333 [68] per Gilmour and Foster JJ; the decision of Brereton J in Re HIH Insurance Ltd (in liq) [2016] NSWSC 482; (2016) 335 ALR 320; and the relatively recent observations of two Full Courts as to indirect causation in ABN AMRO Bank NV v Bathurst Regional Council [2014] FCAFC 65; (2014) 224 FCR 1 at 272 [1375]–[76] per Jacobson, Gilmour and Gordon JJ and Chowder Bay Pty Ltd v Paganin [2018] FCAFC 25 at [61] per Besanko, Markovic and Lee JJ). Thirdly, speaking generally, many cases have involved a real risk for the respondent of proof of contravening conduct, as such costly litigation is likely to be commenced only when the subjective view of those commencing the litigation is that it is likely that contravening conduct will be able to be established; this is because it is only in such circumstances that there is an efficient allocation of the resources of the funder (although, it must be said, these subjective views may well be wrong and a more competitive funding market and the entry of different players may lead to some cases being commenced which would not otherwise have been prosecuted at a more embryonic and 'risk averse' stage of the development of securities class actions). Fourthly, connected to the previous point, respondents and insurers have generally been likely to seek to minimize risk by being

65 *Perera v GetSwift Ltd* (2018) [2018] FCA 732 at [11] and [30].

open to settlement, provided an acceptable sum can be agreed (including in cases of real risk for the respondent where the amount paid cannot be characterized as payment of a 'nuisance sum').[66]

To this list Lee J added what he described as a further and potentially worrisome reason for cases not proceeding to judgment following an initial trial which was said to arise out of the desire of commercial funders to obtain a quick financial return.[67]

The lack of judgments in securities class actions and the unresolved issue of '*market-based causation*' were also referred to in a discussion paper by the Australian Law Reform Commission in connection with its inquiry into class actions and litigation funding.[68]

In terms of remedies in shareholder or investor litigation, the conventional measure of damages under Australian law is the difference between the price actually paid and the actual or 'market' value of the shares in light of (a) the disclosure of hitherto undisclosed facts and/or (b) the correction of misleading or deceptive statements.[69] The need to establish a causal relationship between the conduct and losses in question is highlighted by the recent Federal Court judgments of Beach J[70] and Foster J.[71]

V. SOME CONCLUSIONS

The Australian experience to date in the VW diesel emissions litigation is illustrative of the ongoing problem of costs and delay in class action litigation. The stonewall defence(s) relied upon by the respondents to the Australian litigation, which appears to be part of a coordinated worldwide forensic position, appears to raise some concerns about access to justice and ethical standards governing the conduct of class actions and civil litigation generally.

It would appear to be clear that the statutory class action regime in Australia, and the substantive law able to be relied upon by both consumers and

---

66 *Perera v GetSwift Ltd* (2018) [2018] FCA 732 at [31].

67 *Perera v GetSwift Ltd* (2018) [2018] FCA 732 at [32].

68 Australian Law Reform Commission (ALRC), 'Inquiry Into Class Action Proceedings and Third-Party Litigation Funders; discussion paper 85' (Commonwealth of Australia 2018) 29 and notes 71 and 72.

69 Based on the decision of the High Court in *Potts v Miller* [1940] HCA 43; 64 CLR 282 and subsequent jurisprudence.

70 TPT Patrol Pty Ltd as trustee for Amies Superannuation Fund v Myer Holdings Ltd [2019] FCA 1747.

71 *Masters v Lombe (Liquidator); In the matter of Babcock & Brown Ltd (in Liq)* [2019] FCA 1720. See also: Michael Duffy, 'Causation in Australian Securities Class Actions: Searching for an Efficient but Balanced Approach' (2019) 93 ALJ 833.

investors who have suffered loss as a result of unlawful conduct, are both more advantageous than the procedural redress mechanisms and substantive law applicable in many other jurisdictions, including most if not all of those in Europe.

Whilst the recent settlements in the Australian litigation are to be welcomed, had the matters proceeded to trial the judgments in the Australian diesel emissions litigation would no doubt have been of particular interest to those seeking to pursue claims in other jurisdictions.

Addendum and Update

At the time of going to press there were a number of significant further developments in relation to class actions and litigation funding in Australia. These are summarised below.

1. *Judgment of Federal Court approving settlement of VW class actions*

Having made orders approving of the settlement of the Australian VW class actions on 1 April 2010 (referred to in this chapter) a judgment by Justice Foster was handed down on 13 May 2020.[72] This sets out his reasons for approving the settlement and rejecting the funding application made by the funder in the two BL proceedings. Importantly, his Honour determined that the relevant Australian vehicles were fitted with 'defeat devices' which were prohibited under Australian regulations which mirrored European regulations.[73]

2. *Federal Parliamentary Inquiry into class actions & litigation funding*

Recently the Australian Government announced a further inquiry into litigation funding and the regulation of the class actions industry. The Inquiry is to be conducted by the Parliamentary Joint Committee on Corporations and Financial Services. The Committee is to report by 7 December 2020.

3. *Modification of corporate continuous disclosure laws*

The Australian Government has introduced a 'temporary' six-month modification of corporate continuous disclosure laws during the Covid 19 crisis. Under the changes the relatively broad continuous disclosure obligations have been modified so that liability of companies and their officers under the *Corporations Act 2001* (Cth) will only arise (in respect of continuous disclosure requirements) where there was relevant 'knowledge, recklessness or negligence' in respect of the disclosure or non-disclosure of price sensitive information.

---

72 *Cantor v Audi Australia Pty Limited (No 5)* [2020] FCA 637.

73 United Nations Economic Commission for Europe Regulation 83, Uniform Provisions Concerning the Approval of Vehicles with Regard to the Emission of Pollutants According to Engine Fuel Requirements (UNECE Reg 83), which is an international instrument given legal effect in Australia through ADR 79. See [195].

4. *Regulatory requirements imposed on litigation funders*

On 22 May 2020 the Commonwealth Treasurer announced that the Australian Government would introduce regulations that would require third party litigation funders to obtain an Australian Financial Services License and treat funded class actions as managed investment schemes.

5. *Decision of NSW Court of Appeal in relation to class closure*

On 22 April 2020 the NSW Court of Appeal held that a 'class closure' order made by the presiding judge in the Taka air bag class action litigation was not within the power of the Court conferred by s 183 of the *Civil Procedure Act 2005* (NSW).[74] This has important implications in all Australian jurisdictions where class actions are conducted.

6. Legislation has recently been passed by Parliament in the State of Victoria to permit a representative party in a class action in the Supreme Court to apply to the Court for an order that the legal costs payable to the plaintiff's legal representative be in the form of a contingency fee calculated as a *percentage* of the amount recovered and for those costs to be shared between the plaintiff and all group members. The Court may make such an order if it is satisfied that it is appropriate or necessary to ensure that justice is done in the proceeding. If such an order is made by the Court and the class action is unsuccessful, the plaintiff's law firm is liable to pay any costs of the proceeding awarded to the defendant. The Court may also order that the plaintiff's law firm give security for the defendant's costs (*Justice Legislation Miscellaneous Amendments Act 2020* (Vic) passed on 18 June 2020).

A detailed consideration of each of these matters is beyond the scope of the present chapter.

---

[74] *Haselhurst v Toyota Motor Corporation Australia Ltd t/as Toyota Australia* [and other proceedings] [2020] NSWCA 66.

ENFORCING CONSUMER AND CAPITAL MARKETS LAW IN BRAZIL

Claudia Lima MARQUES*

* Claudia Lima Marques, full professor in Private International Law (Federal University of Rio Grande do Sul, UFRGS, Porto Alegre, Brazil). Chair of the Committee of International Protection of Consumers of the International Law Association (London). Director of International Association of Consumer Law – IACL and the Center for European and Germany Studies, CDEA-DAAD, Porto Alegre. *Doctor iuris utriusque* (Ruprecht-Karls Universität Heidelberg), *Legum Magister* (Eberhard-Karls-Universität Tübingen), diploma in European Integration (Universität des Saarlandes), SDJ (UFRGS). Former President of *Asociación Americana de Derecho Internacional Privado* (ASADIP, Asunción) and BRASILCON (Brazilian Institut for Consumer Law and Policy, Brasilia).
The author thanks PhD candidate Guilherme Mucelin (UFRGS) and Dr. Laís Bergstein for suggestions and contributions to the text.

I. INTRODUCTION

As a non-expert in Capital Market Law,[1] this chapter will focus in particular on the Brazilian approach to enforce consumer law, explaining the dialogue between collective consumer law and the general civil procedural law and how Brazilian Consumer Law has responded to the 'Dieselgate' scandal[2] and similar schemes to deceive consumers.

The so-called 'Dieselgate'[3] case shows how differently the national consumer law responses to global schemes to deceive consumer are. Brazil, a country that has had a Consumer Code since 1990, an adapted 'Brazilian-class action'[4] or collective action and also a very active National Administrative

---

1 The author's only contribution in this regard was helping coordinate the translation from German into Portuguese of the book: Siegfried Kümpel, *Direito do Mercado de Capitais* (Renovar 2007).

2 The VW Dieselgate scandal is primarily an environmental scandal, see Guillaume P Chossière and others, 'Public health impacts of excess NOx emissions from Volkswagen diesel passenger vehicles in Germany' (2017) 12(3) Environmental Research Letters <http://www.iopscience.iop.org/article/10.1088/1748-9326/aa5987/pdf> (hereafter Chossière and others, 'Public health impacts'), saying that road 'transportation emissions account for approximately 50% of the total health impacts from ambient air pollution in Europe (OECD 2014)'.

3 Dieselgate is so described: 'In September 2015, the Volkswagen Group (VW) admitted the use of "defeat devices" designed to lower emissions measured during VW vehicle testing for regulatory purposes. Globally, 11 million cars sold between 2008 and 2015 are affected, including about 2.6 million in Germany.' (Chossière and others, 'Public health impacts' (n 2) 1.) 'In January 2016, and following orders by the KBA (2015), VW started to recall affected vehicles with the aim of reducing their NOx emissions to an as-yet unspecified level. The modification costs per car have been reported to amount to 60 EUR, excluding the value added tax. We assume that the vehicle modification can be completed within 1 hour, including time required to travel to and from the modification site. Applying an average value-of-time of 40 EUR per hour, modification of one vehicle incurs a total cost of approximately 100 EUR. The overall cost of the recall would then be 240 million EUR. This estimate does not include other costs such as increased fuel expenses or social costs of additional carbon emissions (…).' (Chossière and others, 'Public health impacts' (n 2) 11 (citations omitted)).

4 About the adaptation of the North-American class action to the current model of a Brazilian 'class-action', see Antonio Gidi, 'Class Actions In Brazil – A Model for Civil Law Countries' (2003) 51 Am J Comp L 311, 323 (hereafter Gidi, 'Class actions in Brazil'): 'The Brazilian class action traces its origins to academic papers delivered in Italy in the 1970s, when a group of Italian scholars began studying American class actions and publishing articles and books on the subject. The most influential of the Italian works in Brazil were written by Mauro Cappelletti, Michele Taruffo, and Vincenzo Vigoriti. The Italian academic movement was warmly received in Brazil by important legal scholars. Shortly thereafter, José Carlos Barbosa Moreira, Ada Pellegrini Grinover, and Waldemar Mariz Oliveira Júnior, three of the most distinguished Brazilian jurists, published important articles on class action suits. The reputation of these jurists and their continuous research and lobbying efforts, as well as the undeniable importance of the provision, contributed to the introduction of the class action in the Brazilian system. The intellectual support of reputable scholars unlocked the doors of the Brazilian system to class actions.'

System to Consumer Protection,[5] with more than 600 consumer authorities (PROCON)[6] in the country, can be an interesting example of how an emergent country fights against global schemes.

In the 21st century, the international protection of consumers should be a 'global' policy,[7] a minimum standard of the international society and a universal cross-regional 'demand'.[8] Since the beginning, consumer law and policy had an international calling (in French: *vocation international*),[9] because problems and models of consumer protection are normally very similar in national, regional, supranational and global markets.[10] Consumers are also important actors in the globalisation process.[11] However, the truth is that, besides the UN Guidelines on Consumer Protection (UNGCP) from 1985, revised in 1999 and 2015, there is no other universal – or 'global'– legal instrument (either soft or hard law) on consumer protection.[12] People all agree that consumer law on its current scale has an international dimension,[13] but until today – unlike environmental law –, there is no single global convention or binding international legal instrument on consumer protection issues.[14]

---

5 See more information in Marcelo Gomes Sodré, *Formação do Sistema Nacional de Defesa do Consumidor* (Revista Dos Tribunais 2007) 148 (hereafter Sodré, *Formação do Sistema*).

6 See the association of 200 of these state and city consumer enforcement agencies in ProconsBrasil (Associação Brasileira dos Procons). The most important (and old) PROCON is from São Paulo State <http://www.procon.sp.gov.br/> (hereafter Procon São Paulo).

7 See about the definition of consumer in Global North and South, Beate Gsell and others (eds), *Wer ist der Verbraucher? Verbraucherbegriffe, Verbraucherleitbilder und situative Differenzierungen im Verbraucherschutz* (Nomos 2018) (hereafter Gsell and others, *Wer ist der Verbraucher?*).

8 Antônio Herman Benjamin, 'Consumer Protection in Less-Developed Countries: The Latin American Experience' in Iain Ramsay (ed), *Consumer Law in the Global Economy* (Ashgate 1996) 49.

9 Thierry Bourgoignie, *Éléments pour une théorie du droit de la consummation* (Story 1988) 215ff.

10 Claudia Lima Marques, 'A proteção do consumidor: aspectos de direito privado regional e geral' in *XXVII Curso de Derecho Internacional-OEA/CIJ* (Secretaría General-Subsecretaria de Asuntos Jurídicos 2001) 657 (hereafter Marques, 'A proteção do consumidor').

11 Erik Jayme, 'Le Droit International Privé du Nouveau Millénaire: la Protection de la Personne Humaine Face à la Globalisation' (2000) 282 Collected Courses of the Hague Academy of International Law 147 (hereafter Jayme, 'Le Droit International Privé').

12 See Claudia Lima Marques, 'Towards a global approach to protect foreign tourists: building governance through a new cooperation net in consumer and tourist issues' in Anibal Sierraltra and Claudia Lima Marques (eds), *Derecho internacional, mundialización y gobernanza* (CEDEP/ASADIP 2012) 425 (hereafter Marques, 'Towards a global approach').

13 So open their book Geraint Howells, Iain Ramsay and Thomas Wilhelmsson, 'Consumer law in its international dimension' in Geraint Howells, Iain Ramsay and Thomas Wilhelmsson (eds), *Handbook of Research on International Consumer Law* (2nd edn, Edward Elgar 2010) 1 (hereafter Howells, Ramsay and Wilhelmsson, 'Consumer law').

14 Claudia Lima Marques, '25 Years to Celebrate: Horizons of the 1990's Brazilian Protection Code and new Horizons, Especially on the Protection of Consumers' in Claudia Lima Marques and Wei Dan (eds), *The future of international protection of consumers* (PPGD/UFRGS 2016) 111 (hereafter Marques, '25 Years'). Also in Claudia Lima Marques and

When Case 1[15] is examined, one sees how little coherence there is among the legal responses issued by different jurisdictions. Perhaps an international joint response would be better.

In Brazil, the particular 'Dieselgate' case was considered 'not so severe', because only 17,057 Volkswagen diesel cars (Amarok-2011 and partially 2012) were equipped with the problematic software, that identified an inspection and corrected the pollution emissions only then.[16] On the other hand, the Brazilian Consumer Code has very strict rules on the veracity of information given to consumers (as well as environmental information)[17] and considers advertising a contractual offer, so the legal responses in Brazil were based on information deficit (a R$7,2 million – circa €1.8 million – fine from the Secretary of Consumer Defense-SENACON)[18] on breach of environmental regulation (R$50 million – circa €12.5 million – fine from the Environmental Agency-IBAMA).[19]

So in order to respond to the questions raised by the reference case, this chapter will be divided into two sections: The first will explain the Brazilian Consumer Law system, its enforcement authorities and the Brazilian General Procedural Law; and the second will examine the Brazilian private enforcement and the law enforcement by public institutions in this particular case.

Wei Dan (eds), *Consumer Law and Socioeconomic Development: National and International Dimensions* (Springer 2017) 103 (hereafter Marques and Dan, *Consumer law*).

15 See Introduction Section IV.A.

16 Information from the Brazilian Ministry of Justice (Ministério da Justiça e Segurança Pública, Secretaria Nacional do Consumidor (SENACON), Departamento de Proteção e Defesa do Consumidor (DPDC), 'Nota Técnica n.º 54/2019/CSA-SENACON/CGCTSA/DPDC/SENACON/MJ' (File nº 08012.000153/2016-03) 2 <http://www.defesadoconsumidor.gov.br/images/Notas_Técnicas/Nota_Técnica_54.pdf> (hereafter SENACON, 'Nota Técnica').

17 See also Cláudio José Franzolin and Luciane Klein Vieira, 'Emissões de poluentes em veículos e empresas transnacionais: a tutela ambiental na sociedade de consumo e os desafios no cenário internacional' (2019) 121 Revista de Direito do Consumidor 459 (hereafter Franzolin and Vieira, 'Emissões de poluentes'). The authors explain: 'Considering that transnational automobile manufacturers are trademark owners of internationally respected brands, this paper highlights the need that such companies compulsorily incorporate ecological values, regardless in which country their vehicles are sold, in this way, to enhance both sustainable production and consumerism, and to stimulate social development mainly in economically and politically under-developed countries, if such countries are in a position of dependence of these vehicle manufacturers.' See about the 11 million Volkswagen cars with problems at the software in the world and the US$4.3 billion fine in the USA: G1, 'Volkswagen diz que vai pagar multa de US$4,3 bi por fraude nos EUA' (10 January 2017) <http://www.g1.globo.com/carros/noticia/2017/01/volkswagen-diz-que-vai-pagar-multa-de-us-43-bi-por-fraude-nos-eua.html>.

18 The Title of the Technical note is: 'Processo Administrativo. Ofensa ao dever de informação e violação de normas do órgão regulador. Software que otimizava as emissões de óxidos de nitrogênio durante os testes laboratoriais alterando os resultados sobre as emissões de poluentes. Aplicação de sanção de multa no valor de R$7.200.000,00 (Sete milhões e duzentos mil reais).'

19 *Auto de Infração* 9082389-E from IBAMA, Process no 02001.007032/2015-46, Decision 191/2017, not yet paid.

II. NOTIONS OF THE BRAZILIAN CONSUMER LAW SYSTEM, ENFORCEMENT AUTHORITIES AND THEIR DIALOGUE WITH THE BRAZILIAN GENERAL CONSUMER AND PROCEDURAL LAW

The Brazilian Federal Constitution of 1988 has consolidated the ideal of a collective redress in Brazil, including several references to the defence of collective interests (title II, chapter 1, article 5, X, XIV, XXI, XXXV), the right to compensations, including for moral damages (article 5, V), in consumer (articles 5, XXXII and 170, V) and environmental protection (articles 235 and 170, VI), granted procedural rights (article 5, LIV, LV, LVI, LX, LXXVIII), a collective *mandamus* and *habeas data* (article 5, LXIX, LXIXI, LXXII, LXXVII) and raised the human dignity to its fundamental principle.

Article 5, XXXII of the Federal Constitution mentions consumer protection as a fundamental right.[20] Article 170, V mentions consumer protection as a principle of the public order and as a limit to party autonomy and economic freedom:

> Article 170
>
> The economic order, founded on the appreciation of the value of human work and on free enterprise, is intended to ensure everyone a life with dignity, in accordance with the dictates of social justice, with due regard for the following principles: ... IV – free competition; V – consumer protection; VI – environment protection, which may include differentiated treatment in accordance with the environmental impact of goods and services and of their respective production and delivery processes; (...).

In article 48 of the dispositive part of the Federal Constitution, we can find a mandate addressed to the Parliament to elaborate a Consumer Code in 120 days:

> Article 48
>
> The National Congress, within one hundred and twenty days of the promulgation of this Constitution, shall draw up a consumer defense code.[21]

---

20 Patricia Galindo Fonseca, *Droit de la protection du consommateur au Québec et au Brésil – Une analyse comparée* (IEIM 2016) 15 (hereafter Fonseca, *Droit de la protection*).

21 See Gustavo Tepedino, 'Les contrats de consommation au Brésil' in Arnold Wald and Camille Jauffret-Spinosi (eds), *Le droit Brésilien: hier, aujourd'hui et demain* (Société de Législation Comparée 2005) 433 (hereafter Tepedino, 'Les contrats'). See also Jan Peter Schmidt, *Zivilrechtskodifikation in Brasilien* (Mohr 2009) 230 (hereafter Schmidt,

Professor Ada Pellegrini Grinover wrote:

> The Brazilian Constitution of 1988 establishes the public civil action as a procedural tool for group litigations in order to protect any diffuse and collective interests, irrespective of the matter. The Law of the Public Action, 1985, extended, in 1990, the subject-matter of the action in accordance with the Constitution and the Consumer Defense Code (1990), whose procedural rules apply to the protection of any diffuse and collective interests (of indivisible nature), also irrespective of the matter, and recognized the category of the homogeneous individual interests, which correspond to the class actions for damages in the North American Law.[22]

In 1998, the Brazilian Federal Constitution also included a chapter about Public Prosecution (Attorney's General Office, *Ministério Público*, article 129) and created the pro-bono legal defence office (*Defensoria Pública*), both with *locus standi* in consumer issues (article 82 of the Brazilian Consumer Code (CDC)).

A. OVERVIEW OF THE BRAZILIAN CONSUMER LAW AND ENFORCEMENT SYSTEM

Since 1965 Brazil has known a 'public' collective suit (*ação popular*, Act 4.717/1965) used for rather political and environmental issues.[23] In 1985, at the end of the Brazilian Military Dictatorship, the Act no 7347 was published, which established the Collective Action in order to protect 'diffuses and collective interests' and created a federal fund to compensate collective damages (*Fundo de Reconstituição dos Bens Lesados*).[24] Act 7347, 2015 was 'an important milestone in the transformation of the "classic" civil procedure, conceived under individual and formalistic bases.'[25] The Brazilian Consumer Code has completed the so-called 'system' of collective redress in Brazil, allowing

Zivilrechtskodifikation): 'Ganz konkret ordnet schließlich Art. 48 der verfassungsrechtlichen Übergangsbestimmungen die Ausarbeitung eines Verbraucherschutzgesetzbuches (Código de Defesa do Consumidor, transl. by the author) innerhalb 120 Tagen nach der Verkündigung der Verfassung an. Die Entscheidung darüber, in welcher gesetzlicher Form das Thema Verbraucherschutz geregelt werden sollte, wurde also bereits von der verfassungsgebenden Versammlung getroffen.'

22 Ada Pellegrini Grinover, 'Cultural Dimensions of Group Litigation (Brazilian National Report)' (2012) 214 Revista de Processo 361 (hereafter Grinover, 'Cultural dimensions').

23 Ana Luisa Tarter Nunes, *Execução do direito individual homogêneo pelo autor coletivo* (Gazeta Jurídica 2018) 19 (hereafter Nunes, *Execução do direito*).

24 João Batista de Almeida, *Aspectos controvertidos da ação civil pública* (3rd edn, Revista dos Tribunais 2011) 37 (hereafter Almeida, *Aspectos controvertidos*).

25 Heloisa Carpena, 'SOS Collective Action' (2019) 3 Macau Journal of Brazilian Studies, not yet published, 5 of the original text (hereafter Carpena, 'SOS'). Thanks to the author for allowing its use in this chapter.

injunction and compensation in a procedure of this nature.[26] As the President of the Drafting Committee for the Consumer Defense Code, Ada Pellegrini Grinover states:

> In Brazil, all types of provisions may be requested in the public civil action: judgments of declaratory, constitutive and condemnatory nature both as to compensation for damage and by means of injunctions.

The Consumer Defense Code-CDC (Law 8.078 of 11 September 1990) has created a new classification of collective interests (article 81 of the CDC), which allows individual and collective action to exist at the same time. The Consumer Defense Code's legal classification of collective interest involved is the following:

> Article 81
>
> The defense of victims' best interests and rights can be exercised in court individually or collectively.
>
> Sole paragraph. Collective defense will be used when the case includes:
>
> I - interests or diffuse rights, in other words, in the scope of this Code, trans-individual rights of an indivisible nature in which the parties involved are indeterminate persons connected by circumstances of fate;
>
> II - collective interests or rights, in other words, in the scope of this Code, transindividual rights of an indivisible nature, in which the involved party is a group, category or class of people connected amongst each other or with the defending party through a judicial relationship;
>
> III - homogeneous individual interests or rights, so understood those resulting from a common origin.[27]

The Public Civil Action Act 7.347, 1985 and the Brazilian Consumer Code Act 8.078, 1990 entitle the Public Prosecutor (*Ministério Público*); the Public Defender (*Defensoria Pública*); Union, States, the Federal District and

26 Claudia Lima Marques and Patrícia Galindo da Fonseca, 'Consumer Protection in Brazil' in Hans-W Micklitz and Geneviève Saumier (eds), *Enforcement and Effectiveness of Consumer Law* (Springer 2018) 99, 113 (hereafter Marques and Fonseca, 'Consumer Protection').

27 In 2012, Grinover, 'Cultural dimensions' (n 22) 363, affirms that the objective of both Brazilian class action and the North American damages class action are the same: 'The group litigation in Brazil has changed the face of justice, from an individual model to a social model. The protection of the rights in both the North American and the Brazilian systems may have differences in terminology but, substantially, there are no differences: the so-called diffuse or collective interests in Brazil are similar to those protected by Rules 23 (b) 1 and 23 (b) 2 and the homogeneous individual interests are correspondent with Rule 23 (b) 3.'

Municipalities; other public entities and associations (that must have at least one year of existence) to bring action (*Locus Standi*), but not to the individual.

The CDC also regulated the collective *Res Judicata, a res judicata ergu omnes,*[28] *ultra-parts,*[29] *secundum eventum litis* (article 103 of the CDC), in a way that individual claims would remain unaffected in case the collective suit was lost (article 104 of the CDC). The system can be summarised as a collective enforcement in two degrees or stages: recognition of redress and individual or collective redress for a fund.[30] The damages can be deposited in a federal (or state) fund. The consumer associations may obtain financial aid from the State, but normally they are exempt from litigation costs.[31]

The CDC made several simplifications to consumer law procedure, such as the shifting of burden of proof declared by the judge (article 6, VIII) and the distribution of the burden of proof established by law, in case of defective products (article 12, paragraph 2).[32] It has also assured to the Public

---

28 See controversy with the Act 1570, 1997 trying to limit the effects to the 'limits of territorial jurisdiction of the judge', in Ada Pelegrini Grinover, 'A ação civil pública refém do autoritarismo' (1999) 96 Revista de Processo 28 (hereafter Grinover, 'A ação civil'). See also Carpena, 'SOS' (n 25), mentions that only by the Decision of the Superior Court of Justice – Brazil. STJ, *Recurso Especial* 1243887/PR, Supreme Justice Luis Felipe Salomão, 19 October 2011, published in DJe 12 December 2011, the problem was resolved.

29 See also Grinover, 'A ação civil' (n 28) 28ff.

30 As addresses Sérgio Cruz Arenhart, 'The Brazilian Collective Redress System' in Alan Uzelac and Cornelis Hendrik (Remco) van Rhee (eds), *Transformation of Civil Justice: Unity and Diversity* (Springer 2018) 240 (hereafter Arenhart, 'The Brazilian'): '(…) to balance the purpose of a class action and individual rights, the statute created a two-stage procedure. The first part consists of collective proceedings, leading to the judgement of the dispute. Upon having determined the defendant's liability, the second stage begins, authorizing the victims (individuals) to initiate – to their own benefit – the enforcement of the decision. Therefore, the system operates within a collective-individual rationale, allowing the victim to choose to benefit or not from the judgement. In any case, if no individual shows up for enforcement, any potential collective plaintiff may request the enforcement of the decision. In this case, the money collected goes to the public funds (…)'.

31 Grinover, 'Cultural dimensions' (n 22) 365, affirms: 'Counsel fees are not a problem in Brazil, since the standing to sue in a public civil action is not granted to the individual and the lawsuits are filed by public entities or associations that go to court with the assistance of their own attorneys. The associations are, by law, exempt from the payment of court costs and attorney fees to the opposing party, except in the case of bad faith.'

32 Carpena, 'SOS' (n 25) 7 at the original, states: 'The standard of proof in collective actions has been poorly discussed so far, although it is one of the main aspects regarding the effectiveness of the collective custody. Particularly when the trial is referred to individual homogeneous rights, the victims must prove the amount of damages only when the enforcement suit is presented, according to arts 95 and 97 of the Code, rules that are often poorly interpreted. The scope of the collective actions for individual damages is limited to declaring a defendant's liability. In case the action is successful, each individual class member must bring his or her own case to court, to establish that the claimant is a member of the group (causation) and to prove the amount and extent of the individual damages suffered (…). The ideological plaintiff, as the representative of the group, frequently faces difficulties to satisfy his burden of proof, therefore, it would not be reasonable for him to face the same burden

Prosecutor and Public Defender the possibility to sue with no litigation costs and risks of condemnation and legal aid to the consumer if he or she proves to be financially incapable. Here the Civil Procedure Code brings a favourable rule to consumers that may be used *ex vi* article 7 of the CDC: The §°1 of article 373 of the Civil Procedure Code/2015 gives the judge the power to shift the burden of proof 'due to peculiarities of causes related to the impossibility or extreme difficulties to the party to meet the burden pursuant to the caput or when it is easier to the other party to obtain the evidence'.

Brazil knows a very strong role of the public prosecutor (*Ministério Público*) or the Attorney General's Office, due to their investigative prerogative (called 'public civil inquest'/*inquérito civil público*). They can impose 'recommendations', make 'agreements' imposing changes to eliminate consequences or damages,[33] as well as agreements and standards to practical collective redress and finally they can impose fines (directed to a collective fund). Or else, they can also – at end of the inquiry – choose to file a class actions against the enterprises to protect all classes of collective interests.[34]

The civil inquiry means that the Public Prosecutor (and nowadays the agencies, like SENACON and IBAMA) can demand information from professionals and also from the alleged injured party, if there are any. It is to note that the inquiry can be initiated *ex officio*. The *custos legis* the Attorney General's Office is always notified and there is a new National Register of collective redress.[35] There have

the individual plaintiff does. According to the procedural rules for collective protection of rights, the individual situations will be presented before the judge only in the settlement and enforcement suit. If the claim is granted the collective judgment will benefit the members of the group, who may then file an action for calculation of damages and enforcement according to articles 96 to 99 [of CDC]'.

33 Arenhart, 'The Brazilian' (n 30) 233.

34 The leading judgment was summarised as follows: '*Extraordinary appeal. Constitutional. Legitimacy of the Public Prosecutor's Office to promote public civil action in defense of diffuse interests, collective and homogeneous. School fees: Federal prosecution office's standing to sue.* 1. The Federal Constitution gives prominence to the Attorney General's Office (…) 5. The so-called school fees, when abusive or illegal, can be challenged by way of public civil action, at the request of the Attorney General's Office, because although they are homogeneous rights of common origin, they are subspecies of collective interests, protected by the State by this procedural mean as stated in art 129, III, of the Brazilian Federal Constitution. 5.1. Minding a theme linked to education, constitutionally protected as administration's duty and obligation of all (FC, art 205), the Prosecutor's Office is invested of the standing to sue, patent the legitimacy *ad causam*, when the right being sought to protect is inserted in the orbit of collective interests, in segment extremely sensitive and socially relevant that, above all, it is recommended the administration protection. Extraordinary appeal known and provided for, drift away the alleged illegitimacy of the Prosecutor's Office, aiming the defense of the interests of a collective, determine the referral of the case back to the Court of origin, to proceed in the trial of the action.' (Brazil. Supreme Court of Justice (STF), Tribunal Pleno, RE 163,231, Supreme Justice Maurício Corrêa, julg. 26 February 1997, DJ 29 June 2001 PP-00055 Ement Vol-02037-04 PP-00737) (translation by Carpena, 'SOS' (n 25) 4 at the original).

35 See <http://www.cnmp.mp.br/direitoscoletivos/>.

been more than 2,000 victories in consumer collective actions/agreements brought by the Public Prosecutors in Brazil.[36]

B. SPECIAL CHARACTERISTICS OF THE NATIONAL CONSUMER PROTECTION SYSTEM AND THE COLLECTIVE REDRESS SYSTEM OF THE BRAZILIAN CONSUMER CODE

The Brazilian Consumer Code contains 119 articles, not only in substantive (civil and administrative) matters, but also in procedural issues as well as five articles of a criminal nature.[37] The CDC is the most important legal basis for consumers' collective redress and its characteristics, like its basis on the administrative and public enforcement, should be noted.

As this author and Fonseca have written:[38]

> Articles 105 and 106 of the CDC aim to set up a national consumer protection system.[39] The objectives of the system are established in Articles 4 and 5 of the CDC, grouped under the title 'the national policy of consumer relations.'[40] The Article 4 describes the goals of the system and lists its principles. The Article 5 lists the institutions that play an important role in the implementation of this policy and those that may cooperate with the authorities in this regard. The combined efforts of all State agencies, both federal and local, municipalities and the civil society for the

---

36 See the victories on class actions and agreements by Public Prosecutors, available at <http://rj.consumidorvencedor.mp.br/>. See more in Heloisa Carpena, 'Consumidor Vencedor. Um projeto do Ministério Público do Rio de Janeiro em busca da efetividade na defesa dos interesses individuais homogêneos dos consumidores' (2013) 86 Revista de Direito do Consumidor 75 (hereafter Carpena, 'Consumidor Vencedor').

37 The CDC is composed of six Parts: I. Consumer Rights; II. Penal Infractions; III. Consumer Defense in Court; IV. National Consumer Defense System; V. Collective Consumer Convention; VI. Final Provisions. As this author has written with Fonseca, 'Consumer Protection' (n 26) 101: 'The first Part contains all the basic concepts of the CDC: the notions; principles and goals, as well as all CDC's substantive provisions. The first three chapters of the CDC are the most important and compose the general section. The first defines the scope of the CDC (Articles 1, 2 and 3); the second deals with its objectives and its fundamental principles (Articles 4 and 5); the third lists the consumer's basic rights but not all of them (Articles 6 and 7). Section 6 is a summary of the substantive and procedural rights addressed in the CDC. Chapter IV of first part regulates the quality of products and services as well as compensation for damages, including the regime of liability of the product or service. Chapter V deals with commercial practices (supply, advertising, abusive practices, debt collection, database and consumers' database) and Chapter VI establishes contractual protection (standards on the interpretation of contracts, the obligation to inform unfair terms and guarantees). Administrative sanctions are the subject of Chapter VII.'

38 Marques and Fonseca, 'Consumer Protection' (n 26) 100–01.

39 See more information in Sodré, *Formação do Sistema* (n 5) 148ff.

40 Antônio Herman Benjamin, Claudia Lima Marques and Bruno Miragem, *Comentários ao Código de Defesa do Consumidor* (4th edn, Revista dos Tribunais 2013) 226ff (hereafter Benjamin, Marques and Miragem, *Comentários*).

implementation of consumer rights are essential to the national consumer protection system.

The joint action brought by the institutions responsible for the implementation of the national consumer protection policy is crucial to ensure the effectiveness of the Brazilian consumer defense system. Such action involves: mutual and continuous exchange regarding the institutions' activities; coordination among agencies to ensure the consistent implementation of policies; mutual cooperation; communication and joint action regarding the initiatives carried out, the information gathered and results. (…)

The CDC addresses the procedural aspects of consumer protection in Part III. Part IV establishes the elements of the national consumer protection system that aim to bring together state and municipal consumer protection institutions, as well as public and private ones, and to coordinate initiatives regarding the Department of Protection and Consumer Protection (DPDC), designated as the body primarily responsible for policy in this area in Brazil. Part V introduces the collective consumption agreement, enabling ad hoc civil institutions along with organizations representing enterprises to establish the terms of certain consumer relations, including price, quality, quantity, warranty and product features and services.

The CDC is, as a legal microsystem, designed to ensure that custody, through four different types of legal protection: (a) civil protection especially in provisions on trade practices and unfair terms, but not exclusively; (b) criminal protection through the establishment of a wide range of criminal consumption offenses; (c) judicial protection resulting in procedural standards; (d) administrative protection by the establishment of an institutional system on the field of consumer law.

Furthermore:[41]

The Brazilian courts are the most prominent actors in charge of the enforcement of consumer law, but the public prosecutor and the public defender play also an important role.[42] The two main administrative institutions for consumer protection in the Brazilian institutional framework of consumer protection are the Department of Consumer Protection (located in Brasilia, the capital) and the PROCONs. PROCONs are public consumer protection agencies that may belong to the states or municipalities. PROCON's main task is providing consumers with information about their rights. In addition, PROCONs publish books on various topics and organize regular courses and lectures on various aspects of the protection and defense of consumers.

The legal basis for that authority is in the Brazilian Consumer Code (CDC), Act 7.347 of 24 July 1985 and the Decree 2.181/97.

---

41 Marques and Fonseca, 'Consumer Protection' (n 26) 104.

42 See for all discussion in regard to the role played by Brazilian actors in charge of consumer laws enforcement, Fonseca, *Droit de la protection* (n 20) 368–99, 414–28.

In Brazil, one must pass a public selection, examinations and titles to become a judge. This is the way to access a judicial career. The Order of Brazilian Lawyers participates in all phases of this selection. It is necessary to have three years of experience to be a candidate. A successful public selection is followed by an appointment as substitute judge, always in the lower courts. The Federal Constitution provides a career development system in Article 93 I. Promotion to higher courts is based on seniority and merit.

Public selection is also the way to access a career as a prosecutor or as a member of the legal assistance (Public Defender). PROCONs are very well known as well as the small claims courts (*Juizado Especial Cível – JEC*), however they are only available in the states' capitals and in average-sized or big cities across the country. In that case, the consumidor.gov (federal internet mediation platform) and the State Attorneys (*Ministério Público*) fulfill that role. The service provided by PROCON is available in 26 states, the Federal District and 400 municipalities. The system covers 683 units spread over 531 cities. These PROCONs meet a monthly average of 220,000 consumers.

About collective redress, this author and Fonseca also affirm that:[43]

In Brazil, the system of representation of the collective consumer rights in court is wide open because of the diversity of possible claims in one procedure – injunction and compensation.[44] There is the possibility of obtaining compensation for damage caused both to homogeneous individual interests of consumers and to their collective interest, as independent from the general interest. (…) Since 1965, the Brazilian civil procedural system recognizes the collective redress. The *Lei de Ação Popular* (Act 4.717 of 29 June 1965) allowed the citizen to file an injunction against the public government in order to nullify a potentially harmful act to a public property related to art, landscape, history and tourism or a public act that could harm the environment. In 1985, the *Lei de Ação Civil Pública* has institutionalized the injunction collective redress and has added the consumer's protection to the environment, artistic, historical, landscape and touristic public property as the public interests to be protected. Five years later, the Brazilian Consumers Code establishes a new instrument of collective redress in the Brazilian civil procedural: the class action format. The interest protected in this kind of collective redress is called *direito individual homogêneo* by the Brazilian law. Brazilian judges and the doctrine unanimously declare the absolute compatibility of those different means of collective redress in the Brazilian procedural system. The Brazilian consumer law recognizes three different types of consumers interests protected in the collective redress (1) protection of diffuse interests, (2) protection of collective interests and (3) protection of homogeneous individual interests. This is the designation adopted by the Brazilian law to the consumer interests protected

---

43 Available at <http://rs.consumidorvencedor.mp.br/>.

44 See Patrícia Galindo Fonseca, 'Le dynamisme du droit brésilien de la consommation' (2011) 23.1 Revue québécoise de droit international 115.

in a class action: homogeneous individual interests. Besides, the protection of these three categories in a single lawsuit is possible.[45] The CDC recognizes the right for various entities to file an injunction or a class action: the consumer civil associations, the public prosecutor, the Union, the States and the municipalities, the public bodies responsible for consumer protection (PROCON) and public defenders. Therefore, in the Brazilian system, there is no criteria to distinguish the collective redress as an injunction or a class action because both kinds of collective redress are accepted. Besides that, all the organizations mentioned above have the power to initiate the two kinds of lawsuits. One can join the lawsuit initialized by another plaintiff. Rather than contradictory, these forms of collective representation are seen as complementary.[46] Prevention lawsuits (injunctions) stand alongside with compensation ones (class actions). The total amount of cases of collective redress that have been recorded in 2015 is not quantified. Only some organizations keep a public record of collective redress cases. Public prosecutors of the State of Minas Gerais, for example, won more than two hundred class actions in many fields, such as feeding, trade, education, finances, housing, information, internet, recreation, defective products and services and transport. There is no national statistics data available about how many cases of collective redress occurred in the last three years, but the *Ministério Público* from Rio de Janeiro has a site with all victories of the *Ministério Público* in the country,[47] so in the last years there are 129 victories, with redress to consumers, in *ações coletivas* and 209 victories in *ações civis coletivas* registered in this site. The site has the claims state by 25 Brazilian States, so the number of all consumer collective actions is difficult to achieve.

About the specialised agencies on consumer enforcement:[48]

A restructure of the national consumer protection policy, which intended to strengthen the public structures, followed this institutional reform. Reforms at the institutional level were introduced, concerning the coordination of the national consumer protection a mandate recognized to Department of Consumer Protection and Defense (DPDC). A decree issued in May 2012 provided the creation of a new

45 'Il est donc possible d'introduire dans une même action collective une demande de protections des intérêts collectifs (la demande d'annulation d'une clause abusive) et une demande de protection des intérêts individuels homogènes. Tel serait le cas, par exemple, d'une clause abusive insérée dans un contrat d'adhésion. Si le parquet entame une action collective et demande la nullité de cette clause, les droits collectifs de tous ceux ayant signé le même contrat d'adhésion se trouveront protégés. S'il y a eu des dommages causés par cette clause, le parquet peut encore demander l'indemnisation. Certains systèmes mixtes reconnaissent encore la juxtaposition de la protection des intérêts diffus, comme le système brésilien. Par exemple, lorsqu'on ajoute une exigence du fournisseur, l'enjoignant de ne pas insérer une pareille clause dans les futurs contrats', Fonseca, *Droit de la protection* (n 20) 475.

46 That is why Fonseca nominates the Brazilian collective redress system of 'mixed system', regarding the objective and the subjective criteria. The first classification calls for an injunction (prevention lawsuit) or a class action (compensation) whereas the subjective classification concerns the plaintiff. The author considers it a strong point in the Brazilian consumer system. (Fonseca, *Droit de la protection* (n 20) 171–83, 255–90).

47 See <http://rs.consumidorvencedor.mp.br/>.

48 Marques and Fonseca, 'Consumer Protection' (n 26) 118–19, 109.

institution with the exclusive mandate to coordinate the national consumer system: the Consumer's National Bureau (*Secretaria Nacional do Consumidor*, its official abbreviation is SENACON). The Decree 7.738/2012 modified Article 106 of the Consumer code and Article 3 of Decree 2.181/1997, establishing the Consumer's National Bureau as the coordinator of the national consumer defense system. More specifically, it states that this bureau has the role of the planning, developing, coordinating and implementing national policy regarding consumer relations. The first tasks of consumer's National Office are the management of the national information system for consumer protection, the organization of the National School of Consumer Protection, the activities related to health protection and consumers security, the repression of illegal practices and the development of regulations. By this institutional change within the Ministry, the Government seeks to give more visibility, importance and autonomy to its division responsible for consumer protection. Indeed, the way federal departments are established in Brazil, the divisions named *Secretaria* have a higher hierarchical importance than *Departments*.

The Department of Protection and Consumer Protection (DPDC) is the agency responsible for coordinating the National Consumer Defense System. It aims to ensure the effectiveness of interventions in favor of consumers. The DPDC is the only department of the Consumer's National Bureau (*Secretaria Nacional do Consumidor*), a division of the Ministry of Justice. Even though the primary responsibility of the Consumer's National Bureau and the Department is the coordination of the National Consumer Defense System (SNDC), it is important to emphasize that those organisms do not have a coercive power vis-à-vis other institutions members of the National Consumer Defense System, particularly the PROCONs, whose autonomy is conserved. Furthermore, the Department regularly organizes seminars and conferences on the daily work of the national consumer protection system and their actors, about their needs and interests, as well as current issues. The Department managed to create discussions on various consumer topics towards consensual and harmonious solutions by bringing together players from across the country. The Department consists of four sections: one in charge of technical consultations and administrative proceedings (*Coordenação-Geral de Consultaria Técnica e Processos Administrativos);* a section responsible for articulation and supervision of institutional relations (*Coordenação-Geral de Articulação e Relações Institucionais*); a section responsible for research and monitoring of market players (*Coordenação-Geral de Estudos e Monitoramento de Mercado*) and a section in charge of the National Information System on consumer protection (*Coordenação-Geral do Sistema Nacional de Informações de Defesa do Consumidor).*

The DPDC is responsible for storing all data on all complaints made by consumers through the more than 600 PROCONs in Brazil in a platform called SINDEC[49] and also for organising a public mediation platform, called

49 See <http://dados.mj.gov.br/dataset/cadastro-nacional-de-reclamacoes-fundamentadas-procons-sindec>.

'consumidor.gov'.[50] SENACON and DPDC department offices are located in the federal capital Brasília and its attributions are enumerated in article 106 of the CDC and Decree 2.181/ 97.[51]

Finally, it should be noted that articles 55 to 60 of the CDC provide the list of possible administrative sanctions and fines. If mediation fails and the administrative procedure concludes that the enterprise committed a violation, PROCON can issue an administrative penalty, and so can SENACON-DPDC. In this system, there is no *bis in idem*.[52] The notification must include the following information: the CDC rule that was violated and the description of facts that led to the offence report; identification of who committed the acts; criteria that led to the establishment liability, the penalty chosen and the justification regarding the proportionality of the imposed penalty. As shall be seen in the Dieselgate these were the most efficient responses to settle this global scandal.

III. BRAZILIAN PRIVATE ENFORCEMENT AND THE LAW ENFORCEMENT BY PUBLIC INSTITUTIONS IN THE DIESELGATE SCANDAL

Unlike the US, public law enforcement in Brazil is more efficient than private by skimming of profits and imposing fines to eliminate the consumer

---

50 See <http://www.consumidor.gov.br/pages/principal/?1556997942608>.

51 See Benjamin, Marques and Miragem, *Comentários* (n 40) 2235ff.

52 So the leading case at the Superior Court of Justice, STJ: '*Administrativo e consumidor – Publicidade Enganosa – Multa Aplicada por PROCON à Seguradora Privada – Alegação de bis in idem, pois a pena somente poderia ser aplicada pela SUSEP – Não-Ocorrência – Sistema Nacional de Defesa do Consumidor – SNDC – Possibilidade de aplicação de multa em concorrência por qualquer órgão de defesa do consumidor, público ou privado, federal, estadual, municipal ou distrital.* 1. A tese da recorrente é a de que o Procon não teria atribuição para a aplicação de sanções administrativas às seguradoras privadas, pois, com base no Decreto n. 73/66, somente à Susep caberia a normatização e fiscalização das operações de capitalização. Assim, a multa discutida no caso dos autos implicaria verdadeiro bis in idem e enriquecimento sem causa dos Estados, uma vez que a Susep é autarquia vinculada ao Ministério da Fazenda; enquanto que o Procon, às Secretarias de Justiça Estaduais. 2. Não se há falar em bis in idem ou enriquecimento sem causa do Estado porque à Susep cabe apenas a fiscalização e normatização das operações de capitalização pura e simples, nos termos do Decreto n. 73/66. Quando qualquer prestação de serviço ou colocação de produto no mercado envolver relação de consumo, exsurge, em prol da Política Nacional das Relações de Consumo estatuída nos arts. 4º e 5º do Código de Defesa do Consumidor (Lei n. 8.078/90), o Sistema Nacional de Defesa do Consumidor – SNDC que, nos termos do art. 105 do Código de Defesa do Consumidor é integrado por órgãos federais, estaduais, municipais e do Distrito Federal, além das entidades privadas que têm por objeto a defesa do consumidor. Recurso ordinário improvido.' (STJ, RMS 26.397/BA, Rap. Humberto Martins, 4 January 2008, published in DJe 11 April 2008).

damages. 'Public civil Inquiry' by the Public Prosecutor (*Ministério Público*) and Brazilian class actions (normally proposed by the Public Prosecutors)[53] can be better than private enforcement at determining what the compensation of individual and collective damages concern. The key element is the strong system of 'monitoring' and law enforcement by public authorities and some agencies, like the Environmental agencies (IBAMA) and consumer agencies (federal one, SENACON and state and municipal consumer agencies, the PROCONs).

A. *DE LEGE LATA*: BRAZILIAN LAW ENFORCEMENT IN THE DIESELGATE SCANDAL

In Brazil, the problem affected only 17,057 Volkswagen diesel cars (Amarok-2011 and partially 2012), which were equipped with the problematic software.[54] As explained before, the national system allows each agency to impose penalties. On breach of environmental regulation, 'Volkswagen do Brazil' received a fine of R$50 million – circa €12.5 million – from the environmental agency IBAMA in 2015, maintained by the Ministry of Environment in 2017, but has not yet paid.[55] In 2015, one week after IBAMAS's fine, due to the violation of consumer regulation Volkswagen received a fine (16 November 2015) of R$8.3 million for 'fraud' against consumers from the PROCON from the State São Paulo, where 'Volkswagen do Brasil' has its head office. The fine has not yet been paid either.

On 29 September 2015, SENACON, the Consumer Secretary of the Ministry of Justice opened an investigation against Volkswagen.[56] After communication, Volkswagen answered to SENACON that at the time they could not identify the number of cars affected in Brazil, asking for more time to answer it, because they needed to 'consult the mother company in Germany'.[57] But on 21 October 2015, 'Volkswagen do Brasil' informed the Ministry of Justice.[58] After that, SENACON demanded the data from the environmental agency IBAMA and its proceedings,[59] but the fine proceeding were only officially established by

53 Carpena, 'SOS' (n 25) 1 at the original, affirms that 70 per cent of the class actions are proposed by the Public Prosecutors and other public authorities (Public Defenders, Agencies, etc.).
54 SENACON, 'Nota Técnica' (n 16) 2.
55 Auto de Infração 9082389-E from IBAMA, Processo 02001.007032/2015-46, Decision 191/2017, not yet paid.
56 SENACON, 'Nota Técnica' (n 16) 1, n 2.
57 SENACON, 'Nota Técnica' (n 16) 1, n 3.
58 SENACON, 'Nota Técnica' (n 16) 2, n 4–6.
59 SENACON, 'Nota Técnica' (n 16) 2, n 7.

the SENACON on 11 March 2016.[60] 'Volkswagen do Brasil' has alleged that the emissions of the Amarok cars were allowed in Brazil in 2011 and 2012 (n 11 of the Technical Note)[61] and that there was no need to recall the vehicles.

On 4 July 2016, IBAMA determined the recall of the Amarok cars for 'environmental fraud' on the emissions and 'Volkswagen do Brasil' has promised the Ministry of Justice to proceed to recall and take all measures needed to 'stop' and 'compensate' for the damages.[62] On 30 March 2017, the Ministry of Environment maintained the R$50 million fine.[63] 'Volkswagen do Brasil' alleged then that the software was not active in the Brazilian vehicles and that the recall was 'voluntary'.[64] SENACON focused on the violation of Brazilian Consumer Code information duties,[65] abusive commercial practice in Brazil affecting the freedom of choice of the Brazilian consumers[66] and imposed a R$7.2 million – circa €1.8 million – fine,[67] not yet paid. It is interesting to note that the SENACON fine was calculated to be R$14 million but the 'good behaviour' of the company and the 'voluntary' recall reduced the fine to almost half, to R$7.2 million on 6 February 2019, circa R$1 million less than the Procon-SP's fine of 2015!

Individual lawsuits could not be found at the Superior courts, but Brazil has not developed a substantive assignment model for the process-based compilation of compensation claims, like 'my right', which is initially allowed. Normally, the consumers and lawyers form a new consumer association with the victims from the event. The CDC created a kind of 'master agreement' or mass mediation tool, very rarely used:

> TITLE V – Collective Convention about Consumption – Article 107
>
> Civil consumer entities and associations of suppliers and unions of economic scope may regulate, through a written convention, consumer relations aimed that establishing conditions relative to price, quality, quantity, warranty, and the

---

60 SENACON, 'Nota Técnica' (n 16) 3, n 9.

61 In the original: '11. No tocante às possíveis violações ao CDC, a Representada alegou que não houve prática abusiva por não se utilizar funcionalidade de software capaz de otimizar o índice de emissões. Alegou que "no Brasil, durante a Fase PL4 do PROCONVE, quando se deu a homologação do modelo, o limite de emissão de NOx era de 1,0g/km, conforme Resolução CONAMA n. 315/2002. Ou seja, em ambos os cenários testados, as emissões estavam abaixo do limite, o que comprova que o item não estava ativo e não provocou alterações nos limites e exigências previstos à época da legislação". Segundo a Representada, apesar da existência do dispositivo, ele não teria estado ativo e provocado alterações nos limites legais de emissões.' SENACON, 'Nota Técnica' (n 16) 3.

62 SENACON, 'Nota Técnica' (n 16) 3–4, n 12.

63 SENACON, 'Nota Técnica' (n 16) 4, n 13.

64 SENACON, 'Nota Técnica' (n 16) 4, n 14.

65 SENACON, 'Nota Técnica' (n 16) 4–5, n 15–22.

66 SENACON, 'Nota Técnica' (n 16) 6–7, n 23–27.

67 SENACON, 'Nota Técnica' (n 16) 7–8, 30–33.

characteristics of products and services, as well as complaints and consumer conflict composition.

§1. The convention will be mandatory as of the moment the document is registered by an official notary's office.

§2. The convention will only be binding for those who are members of the signing entities.

§3. Any suppliers who disassociate themselves from the entity in update after the document has been registered will still be bound by the convention.

So, this kind of 'compiled actions' system is possible in the Brazilian procedural landscape. This may be a solution because, according to the current jurisprudence, the statute of limitation for collective redress is five years after the event and it differs from the statute of limitation for individual redress (from one year, three years to ten years, depending on the applicable legislation, Civil Code or Consumer Code, 60 days to five years). However, the statute of limitation for individual and collective redress is suspended by the 'public civil inquiry' (article 26 paragraph 2) and when 'the defect is not visible, the period for complaints begins at the moment when the defect is noticed' (article 26 paragraph 3),[68] which indicates that the recall can be used as a starting point. Since the software 'defect' is also an environmental 'defect', the five-year period of article 27 of the CDC will probably be applied by the court. That means that 'right to claim compensation' for such a defect is probably open in Brazil. A consumer mass mediation is also possible (normally with the Public Prosecutor involved as *custos legis*).

It is interesting to note that a similar problem happened with an imported product in 2011 in Brazil. The product was a 'natural catalyser' made by the

---

68 Also in environmental cases, see leading case of the Superior Court of justice-STJ, Recurso Especial 1.641.167-RS: '*Recurso especial. Direito civil e ambiental. Contaminação ambiental por produtos químicos utilizados em tratamento de madeira destinada à fabricação de postes. Omissão, contradição e obscuridade. Ausência. Princípio da adstrição ou congruência. Interpretação ampla da inicial. Possibilidade. Dano ambiental individual. Prescrição. Termo inicial. Ciência inequívoca. Precedentes. Ação coletiva. Interrupção da prescrição de ações individuais. Possibilidade.* 1[...] 4. O dano ambiental pode ocorrer na de forma difusa, coletiva e individual homogêneo este, na verdade, trata-se do dano ambiental particular ou dano por intermédio do meio ambiente ou dano em ricochete. 5. Prescrição: perda da pretensão de exigibilidade atribuída a um direito, em consequência de sua não utilização por um determinado período. 6. O termo inicial do prazo prescricional para o ajuizamento de ação de indenização por dano ambiental suportado por particular conta-se da ciência inequívoca dos efeitos decorrentes do ato lesivo. Precedentes. 7. O ajuizamento de ação versando interesse difuso tem o condão de interromper o prazo prescricional para a apresentação de demanda judicial que verse interesse individual homogêneo. 8. Necessidade, na hipótese dos autos, da completa instrução processual. 9. Recurso especial conhecido e não provido.' (STJ, Recurso Especial 1641167/RS, Rap. Nancy Andrighi, j. 13 March 2018, published in DJe 20 March 2018).

Euro Fuel saver SRL that claimed to help cars save 12 per cent of gasoline and 80 per cent in the emission. In reality, it was only a 'magnet'. The Public Prosecutor from the State of Rio Grande do Sul opened a public inquiry to investigate the fact and proposed a collective action based on misleading advertising in 2012.[69] The final decision was given by the Court of Rio Grande do Sul in 27 September 2018. The importer was condemned to pay R$300,000 for 'collective social damages', which were deposited at the federal fund (*Fundo de Reconstituição dos Bens Lesados*), and to compensate individual damages that will be defined in a second individual or collective proceeding.[70]

B. *DE LEGE FERENDA* SUGGESTIONS: THE CURRENT REFORM ON CONSUMER LAW

The current goal of consumer policy in Brazil is adapting the 1990 Consumer Code to the new digital challenges and also dealing with the consumer credit and the over-indebtedness issue.[71] The two reform bills for the Consumer Code are PL 3515, 2015 and PL 3514, 2015. The first one concerns prevention and resolution of consumer over-indebtedness.[72] The second one,

---

69 A similar case of an imported software alleged to 'reduce' emissions and the use of gasoline was decided in a collective action as misleading advertising, see Case APC 70077905719, Supreme Court of Rio Grande do Sul (TJRS), decided on the 27 September 2018 assuring redress of individual damages plus collective 'moral' damage. In the original: '*Apelação cível. Direito privado não especificado. Ação coletiva de consumo. Economizador de combustível. Redução da emissão de poluentes. Publicidade enganosa. Conduta abusiva da ré. Dano moral coletivo configurado.* – No caso, o produto divulgado pela empresa ré não apresenta as qualidades e não produz efeitos anunciados, caracterizando-se como propaganda enganosa. – Assim, cabia à demandada o ônus da prova da qualidade do produto, da veracidade e correção da informação, nos termos do art. 38 do CDC, prova da qual não se desincumbiu. – Ainda que não individualmente quantificados os consumidores neste momento processual, restou consagrado no artigo 95 do CDC, a possibilidade de condenação genérica sem fixação do quantum, cabendo a cada consumidor, em sede de liquidação de sentença, comprovar os eventuais prejuízos para ressarcimento, motivo pelo qual deve ser mantida a condenação a danos materiais individualmente considerados. – Para configurar o dano moral coletivo é preciso que o fato transgressor seja de razoável significância e desborde os limites da tolerância, devendo ser grave e suficiente para produzir verdadeiros sofrimentos, intranquilidade social e alterações relevantes na ordem extrapatrimonial coletiva, o que se configurou no caso dos autos. Portanto, vai mantido o quantum indenizatório, assim como o valor fixado a título de multa por descumprimento. Apelo Desprovido. Unânime.' (Brazil. Rio Grande do Sul Court of Justice. *Apelação Cível* no 70077905719, Décima Sétima Câmara Cível, Tribunal de Justiça do RS, Relator: Gelson Rolim Stocker, Julgado em 27 September 2018). Available at <http://www.tjrs.jus.br/>.

70 Nunes, *Execução do direito* (n 23) 129.

71 Claudia Lima Marques, 'Der Schutz der Verbraucher in einer globalisierten Welt' in Karlheinz Sonntag (ed), *Heidelberger Profile – Studium Generale* (Universitätsverlag Winter 2012) 153 (hereafter Marques, 'Der Schutz').

72 See Fonseca, *Droit de la protection* (n 20) 291ff.

PL 3514, 2015 concerns e-commerce and uses the EU law for national and international e-commerce and distance sales as a model. Those bills are based on the French legislation model on prevention and resolution of consumer over-indebtedness (PL 3515, 2015) and on the Brazilian Proposal[73] to the CIDIP VII (later 2017 Mercosur Treaty) on applicable law to consumer contracts (PL 3514, 2015).[74]

The third Bill, concerning procedural issues (PL 282,2012) was not accepted by the Senate.[75] Instead, the Brazilian Parliament approved a new Civil Procedure Code (CPC) in 2015, which has been in force since 18 March 2016.[76] The new code has developed a new collective action instrument similar to a 'Musterverfahren', the so-called 'Incident for the resolution of repetitive cases' ('Incidente de Resolução de Demandas Repetitivas', arts 976 to 987

---

73 See Claudia Lima Marques, 'Consumer Protection in Private International Law Rules: the need for an interamerican Convention on the law applicable to some consumer contracts and consumer transactions (CIDIP)' in Thierry Bourgoignie (ed), *Regards croisés sur les enjeux contemporains du droit de la consommation* (Éditions Yvon Blais 2006) 145 (hereafter Marques, 'Consumer Protection').

74 See Marques, '25 Years' (n 14).

75 See the 12 objectives of the Bill 282 explained by Prof. Ada Grinover, Head of the Committee in this part: 'Por determinação do então Presidente do Senado, José Sarney, foi constituída comissão, presidida pelo Ministro do STJ Herman Benjamin, com a incumbência de apresentar projetos de lei setoriais de atualização do CDC, com expressa proibição de qualquer retrocesso. Em setembro de 1990, foram encaminhados ao Senado três Projetos de Lei nesse sentido: … 3. Projeto de Lei que altera o Código de Defesa do Consumidor, para aperfeiçoar a disciplina das ações coletivas.É deste último que vamos nos ocupar. O objetivo geral da proposta era reforçar a efetividade das ações coletivas e incentivar a desjudicialização das demandas. Em especial, a proposta pretendia, em síntese: 1. Complementar e esclarecer a definição dos direitos individuais homogêneos. 2. Reforçar a presunção legal da relevância social e jurídica da tutela coletiva. 3. Dar prioridade de processamento e julgamento às ações coletivas, com possibilidade de suspensão das individuais. 4. Explicitar a possibilidade de controle difuso de constitucionalidade nas ações coletivas. 5. Retocar as regras de competência, para evitar a proliferação de ações decorrentes da competência concorrente. 6. Reforçar o incentivo à atuação das associações de defesa do consumidor. 7. Incluir capítulos regulando o procedimento da ação coletiva e os cadastros nacionais de processos coletivos e compromissos de ajustamento de conduta. 8. Reforçar a adaptabilidade do procedimento e a conciliação nas ações coletivas e cuidar do procedimento. 9. Reforçar a regulamentação das indenizações individuais. 10. Incluir a Defensoria Pública no rol dos legitimados, bem como a Advocacia Pública e as Agências reguladoras na proteção dos consumidores. 11. Reforçar a coisa julgada erga omnes e os efeitos da sentença. 12. Preservar o CDC como fonte principal do microssistema de processos coletivos e regular a prescrição das pretensões coletivas e sua execução. Todavia, esse projeto, que trazia alguns avanços, também caiu no limbo e a última informação que se tem é a de que foi arquivado no final da legislatura passada.' (Ada Pelegrini Grinover, 'Requiem para a reforma dos processos coletivos' (2017) 265 Revista de Processo 213, 217–18 (hereafter Grinover, 'Requiem').

76 Maria Angélica Feijó and Ronaldo Kochen, 'What to expect from the new Brazilian Civil Procedure Code of 2015' (2015) 20 ZZPInt 363 (hereafter Feijó and Kochen, 'What to expect').

of the CPC/2015).[77] However, the President vetoed the article about transformation of an individual lawsuit into a collective redress (article 333)[78] in order to preserve the current collective action system proposed by the CDC. It is not certain how the two collective tools 'Incident proceedings for the resolution of repetitive cases' and the Brazilian class action will be used by the judge.[79]

---

77 The Brazilian authors mention that the model was the Kapitalanleger-Musterverfahrensgesetz in Germany, see Feijó and Kochen, 'What to expect' (n 76) 371.

78 See Claudia Lima Marques, 'Nota sobre a proteção do consumidor no novo Código de Processo civil (Lei 13.105/2015)' (2016) 104 Revista de Direito do Consumidor 555, 56 (hereafter Marques, 'Nota'): 'Dentre as normas processuais interessantes no que se refere às ações coletivas, está também foi o veto presidencial ao art. 333 e inciso XII do art. 1015, com a seguinte mensagem (Mensagem nº 56, de 16 de março de 2015): art. 333. Atendidos os pressupostos da relevância social e da dificuldade de formação do litisconsórcio, o juiz, a requerimento do Ministério Público ou da Defensoria Pública, ouvido o autor, poderá converter em coletiva a ação individual que veicule pedido que: I – tenha alcance coletivo, em razão da tutela de bem jurídico difuso ou coletivo, assim entendidos aqueles definidos pelo art. 81, parágrafo único, incisos I e II, da Lei nº 8.078, de 11 de setembro de 1990 (Código de Defesa do Consumidor), e cuja ofensa afete, a um só tempo, as esferas jurídicas do indivíduo e da coletividade; II – tenha por objetivo a solução de conflito de interesse relativo a uma mesma relação jurídica plurilateral, cuja solução, por sua natureza ou por disposição de lei, deva ser necessariamente uniforme, assegurando-se tratamento isonômico para todos os membros do grupo. §1º Além do Ministério Público e da Defensoria Pública, podem requerer a conversão os legitimados referidos no art. 5º da Lei nº 7.347, de 24 de julho de 1985, e no art. 82 da Lei nº 8.078, de 11 de setembro de 1990 (Código de Defesa do Consumidor). §2º A conversão não pode implicar a formação de processo coletivo para a tutela de direitos individuais homogêneos. §3º Não se admite a conversão, ainda, se: I – já iniciada, no processo individual, a audiência de instrução e julgamento; ou II – houver processo coletivo pendente com o mesmo objeto; ou III – o juízo não tiver competência para o processo coletivo que seria formado. §4º Determinada a conversão, o juiz intimará o autor do requerimento para que, no prazo fixado, adite ou emende a petição inicial, para adaptá-la à tutela coletiva. §5º Havendo aditamento ou emenda da petição inicial, o juiz determinará a intimação do réu para, querendo, manifestar-se no prazo de 15 (quinze) dias. §6º O autor originário da ação individual atuará na condição de litisconsorte unitário do legitimado para condução do processo coletivo. §7º O autor originário não é responsável por nenhuma despesa processual decorrente da conversão do processo individual em coletivo. §8º Após a conversão, observar-se-ão as regras do processo coletivo. §9º A conversão poderá ocorrer mesmo que o autor tenha cumulado pedido de natureza estritamente individual, hipótese em que o processamento desse pedido dar-se-á em autos apartados. §10. O Ministério Público deverá ser ouvido sobre o requerimento previsto no caput, salvo quando ele próprio o houver formulado.'
Inciso XII do art 1.015. 'XII – conversão da ação individual em ação coletiva;' Razões dos vetos 'Da forma como foi redigido, o dispositivo poderia levar à conversão de ação individual em ação coletiva de maneira pouco criteriosa, inclusive em detrimento do interesse das partes. O tema exige disciplina própria para garantir a plena eficácia do instituto. Além disso, o novo Código já contempla mecanismos para tratar demandas repetitivas. No sentido do veto manifestou-se também a Ordem dos Advogados do Brasil – OAB.'

79 New art 139 of the Civil Procedure Code gives power to the judge to act *ex officio*, but states a dialogue between these sources: 'X – When encountering various repetitive individual demands, the judge may provoke the Attorney General's Office, the Public Defender's Office and, to the extent possible, other plaintiffs to which refer Arts. 5 of Act n. 7347, of 24th of July

The Bill 282, 2012 should respond to some still unanswered questions on the reference case, Dieselgate. For example, the Bill 282, 2012 had a specific article about the collective action's priority vis-à-vis the individual one (new paragraph 3 to article 81 of the CDC). In Brazil a coexistence of several legal actions and the coexistence of collective and individual based on the same facts are possible,[80] but the 'respective cases' are quicker than the 'Brazilian class actions' and they can be decided first.[81] Another issue regulated by the Bill 282, 2012 and without solution until nowadays is the different statute of limitation for individual and collective redress in Brazil (new paragraph 5 to article 81 of the CDC).

Finally, allow a decision by Supreme Justice Antônio Herman Benjamin (STJ) to be quote about the importance of the Brazilian collective redress system and the collective suits:[82]

> (...) 5. Access to Justice is no rhetoric guarantee, because its concrete effectiveness depends on the enforcement of all other fundamental rights. Within his significance attributed by the Welfare State, the expression goes beyond the access to the courts, to include the access to Law itself, meaning, to a fair legal order (= enemy of imbalances and averse to presumption of equality), known (= socially and individually recognized) and enforceable (= effective). 6. If the norm of the Ancien Régime was the judicial enforcement provided individually, drop-by-drop, in the post-industrial society, even for pragmatic reasons of efficiency and survival of the judiciary framework, the collective suits are the only possible response to the mass litigation issues, which are organized around rights and diffuse interests, collective stricto sensu and individual homogeneous (art 81 CDC). 7. In addition to benefiting the victims, who see their demands being resolved uniformly and with institutional support, the ad causa legitimacy of the Attorney General's Office and of the NGOs for the proposal of Collective Actions honors and favors the Judiciary itself, which, through this way, while continuing to fulfill its high constitutional mission, prevents the drain of hundreds, thousands and even millions of individual disputes. (...)

If this Bill 282, 2012 that aims to reform the procedural chapter of the Consumer Code is not approved by the Parliament, one should be looking for other solutions for the mass conflicts in Brazil – a country with more than 29 million

---

of 1985, and n. 82 of Act N. 8078, of 11th of September of 1990, to, if appropriate, promote the filing of the respective class-action suit'. (Translation by Carpena, 'SOS' (n 25) 6 in original 6.)

80 See art 83 of the CDC: 'In order to defend the rights and interests protected by this Code, all sorts of actions capable and enforcing the Code are permissible.'

81 Nunes, *Execução do direito* (n 23) 92ff.

82 Brazil. Superior Court of Justice (STJ), Recurso Especial 347.752/SP, Min. Herman Benjamin, j. 8 May 2007, publ. DJe 11 April 2009.

new claims each year[83] – and this solution is, in the authors' opinion, effective public enforcement and private collective suits to consumer redress.

IV. FINAL OBSERVATIONS

This brief text has showed that in emergent economies the role of the State remains necessary to enforce consumer law (and environmental standards!). Global challenges such as the 'Dieselgate' case (or the 'resistance' of the Tobacco Industry to compensate damages to other countries that are not the USA and its 'master agreement') shows us that the national legislation is no longer enough to assure fair consumer standards in all markets. In the authors' opinion, cooperation between States is needed. Perhaps the IGE – Intergovernmental Group of Experts – at UNCTAD can help the emergent economies and underdevelopment world respond to such challenges.

83 Exactly 29.1 million new actions in 2017 (latest data available), see *Conselho Nacional de Justiça*, Available at <http://www.cnj.jus.br/pesquisas-judiciarias/justica-em-numeros/>. From then 12.1 per cent settled by conciliation and an average of 1.819 cases/year per judge. Arenhart, 'The Brazilian' (n 30) 241 quotes a study from 2010 that shows that in São Paulo, 51 per cent of the cases are consumer cases, while public litigation represented 43 per cent.

ENFORCING CONSUMER LAW IN CHINA

Tong ZHANG*

In the 2015 VW scandal, the consumer's interest was damaged by VW's manipulation of results in laboratory emission tests. The Volkswagen Group has paid a great price for the relevant litigations, recalls and compensations. Based on the VW case and the reference Case 1,[1] from the perspective of Chinese law,

* Tong Zhang, Dr., LL.M. (Frankfurt am Main), Professor, China University of Political Science and Law, Jean Monnet Chair, Director of the Centre for European Studies. This work was supported by the China National Social Science Funding Program (Contract No 1717BFX195).

1 See Introduction Section IV.A.

this chapter will analyse the types of possible remedies for Chinese consumers when facing similar situations. Consumers could seek remedy through either private or public enforcement of law. This chapter focuses on the possible ways to achieve such remedies.

I. THE VOLKSWAGEN EMISSIONS SCANDAL'S INFLUENCE ON THE CHINESE MARKET

The Volkswagen emissions scandal, in which the automobile manufacturer manipulated the laboratory test result of its automobiles' emissions, was exposed on 18 September 2015. This scandal has also dragged VW into a series of criminal investigations and civil lawsuits in many countries. Germany, Italy, the US and Australia have initiated investigations against the Volkswagen Group and its products.[2]

This incident has drawn intense attention from many countries. However, China, as VW's largest market around the globe, has not shown great concern over this scandal.

According to the manufacture record and sales record of both SAIC Volkswagen and FAW-Volkswagen, none of the VW products manufactured or sold under joint venture between VW and the Chinese local company has been involved in the VW emissions sandal. The only type of product that may face impact from such scandal is the Tiguan with four-cylinder diesel engine. A total of 1.946 of this type of automobile was imported by Volkswagen China.[3] Thus, the manager of public relations and sales department (SAIC Volkswagen) claimed that the automobiles related to the VW scandal were not manufactured and would not be manufactured in China. More precisely, China has banned the manufacture of such types of automobile. Because of that, even if VW is deeply tangled in the scandal, it would not influence VW products' manufacture or sales in China.[4] Some scholars considered a common view among Chinese public to be the major reason that obstructs the sales of diesel engine car in China: old-styled diesel engine cars had existed in China for a relatively long period in the past and had created an impression among general public that diesel cars are too noisy and produce too much pollution.[5]

---

2 Shen Zhenyi, 'The Volkswagen Emissions Scandal Continues' (2016) 7 Prosecutorial View 57.

3 'Volkswagen China has made Official Announcement Regarding to the Volkswagen Emissions Scandal' <http://auto.ifeng.com/pinglun/20150926/1047581.shtml>.

4 'The Manufacture and Sales of Volkswagen's Automobile Products were not influenced by the Volkswagen Emissions Scandal' <http://sputniknews.cn/china/201511111016963698/>.

5 'From the Volkswagen Emissions Scandal: Eight Types of Conclusions in China on Diesel Engine Auto' <https://club.autohome.com.cn/bbs/thread/65fc2ee0bad1e4a1/45765485-1.html>.

What would the Chinese Government's official attitude towards the Volkswagen emissions scandal be? When searching relevant governmental subdivisions' official website, there are quite a number of recall announcements regarding VW's products, but most of them concern other types of defect, such as the safety airbag's flaw. One could not find any result mentioning the attitude or opinion of a corresponding department against the VW scandal.[6] Therefore, it can be said that although Chinese media has provided relatively thorough news coverage regarding the Volkswagen emissions scandal,[7] the VW case has not yet raised great concern in China, which is mainly caused by the fact that the sales of diesel engine cars in China are relatively low to the extent that they could be ignored.[8]

Observing the law, VW's wrongful manipulation harms multiple legal interests greatly – it hurts the rightful interest of the consumers, society's public environmental interest, as well as the interest of the company's shareholders,[9] it violates laws of different fields such as environmental protection, consumer protection, market competition, finance, tax, etc., which may lead to corresponding legal consequence(s) that VW must bear.[10]

For consumers, VW has provided them with diesel engine automotive products which did not satisfy statutory delivery standard. These automobiles have a serious defect related to emissions technology applied on them which, on the one hand, may not directly threaten consumers' health or safety; on the other hand, however, VW has obviously harmed the lawful right of the consumers by purposefully concealing its products' defect and using software to create false results in order to deceive the consumers. Under situations such as this, based on purchase contract, consumers of these automobiles may require VW to provide remedies which include the recall and replacement of defected automobiles. Other than that, consumers may also file a lawsuit against VW's fraudulent act and request compensation for relevant loss.

Based on the VW case and reference case 1, from the perspective of Chinese law, this chapter will analyse the types of possible remedies for Chinese consumers when facing similar situations. This discussion will consider both the public and private enforcement of Chinese consumer protection law.

---

6 For examples, the ones of Ministry of Commerce, State Administration for Market Regulation, and Ministry of Ecology and Environment using 'Volkswagen', 'emission(s)' and(or) 'diesel' as keyword(s), have not displayed any official announcement regarding Volkswagen's emissions incident.

7 For example, China's famous internet media such as people.com.cn, qq.com, and news.sohu.com, etc. have many reports and commentary articles on the incident.

8 Wei Jinqiao, 'Why doesn't anyone in China Care about the Volkswagen Emissions Scandal?' <http://www.sohu.com/a/37104667_122189>.

9 Xia Xiaoxiong, 'The Three Types of Interest harmed by the Volkswagen Emissions Scandal' *Economic Information Daily* (Beijing, 25 May 2016) 6.

10 Yang Xiande, 'Litigation Process Relating to the Volkswagen Emissions Scandal in the US' *Procuratorate Daily* (Beijing, 1 August 2017) 3.

The enforcement of legislation on the protection of consumers has experienced a transformation: Once it could only be enforced through private interest litigation, now public interest litigation has also become a way to enforce such legislation. It is also worth noting that there is a trend to diversify the form of public interest litigation. These changes would also lead to a structural change in the ways of enforcing such legislation: Once private enforcement was the major type of enforcement which was mostly done through civil litigation providing remedies to specific consumers who suffered loss. And now, public enforcement aiming at protecting trading order will gradually take the leading role.[11]

In China, the development of legislation on consumers' protection related strongly with the change in government's policy. The creation of such legislation has not resulted from the development of traditional civil legislation. Indeed, it was influenced by the change in civil legislation that took place around the same time period. However, Chinese legislation on consumers' protection really originated from the domain of public law and has been gradually improved to what it is today.[12] One may observe these transformations in the 2013 revision of the Law of the People's Republic of China on the Protection of Consumer Rights and Interest (hereinafter referred to as the Law on the Protection of Consumer)[13] – Chapter IV and Chapter V of the act has strengthened state and social organisations' duties to protect consumers' right and interest.[14]

II. PRIVATE ENFORCEMENT OF CHINESE CONSUMER LAW

A. REMEDIES FOR CONSUMERS: INITIATING LEGAL ACTION AS AN INDIVIDUAL

Private enforcement of law is the major way to protect private interest. It is carried out by private parties, mostly by the consumers who suffered loss.

---

11 Liu Shuilin and Lu Bo, 'The Change of Forms in the Legislation on the Protection of Consumer's Right and Interest – An Analysis Based on Economics' (2016) 6 Journal of Shanghai University of Finance and Economics 101, 102.

12 Yang Qin, 'The Development of Chinese Legislations for Protection of Consumer in Sixty Years' (2009) 6 Journal of Guizhou University (Social Sciences) 38.

13 In 1993, China adopted its first official version of the Law of the People's Republic of China on the Protection of Consumer Rights and Interests. 19 years later, on 25 October 2013, China adopted the latest revision of that statute. This amended version came into effect on 15 March 2014.

14 Fang Ying, 'On the Organization System of Consumers' Rights and Interests Protection: A Perspective of "State-Society" Cooperation Governance' (2018) 2 Journal of Guangzhou University (Social Science Edition) 62.

These consumers could file civil lawsuits to seek remedies. These actions serve majorly and directly to protect the consumer's personal interest and provide relevant remedies.

As to the Chinese cases of individuals enforcing law on consumers' protection, the number of such cases are quite limited. Reasons behind this phenomenon include Chinese traditional reluctance of litigation, the high expense of litigation, as well as other problems which made relevant legislations seemed incomplete. Under the system nowadays, consumers should be encouraged to apply legislation which protect consumers' rights by initiating legal action as an individual.

In the reference case, after purchasing an automobile, the consumer found out that its actual emission exceeded its prescribed amount. Thus, the automobile could be seen as a defective product. There are several different legislations in the Chinese legal system, according to which consumers can initiate legal action as individuals and request relevant remedies.

1. *Remedies in Non-Conformity*

a) Special Legislation

The current legislation mainly includes two special legislations on consumer protection: The Law on the Protection of Consumer and the Product Quality Law.[15] The former includes the systematic regulation of consumer protection issues, while the latter focuses on tort law issues in relation to product liabilities.

In the reference case, consumers may demand the business operator to bear civil liability in accordance with the Law on the Protection of Consumer. Article 24 has described the situations where the commodities or services provided by business operators fail to meet the quality requirements. When facing such situations, consumers may 'return them in accordance with the provisions of the state or as agreed upon by the parties or require business operators to fulfil their obligations of replacement or repair, among others'. Article 52 described that, under certain circumstances, business operators shall 'assume civil liability in accordance with the law or as agreed by the parties, including but not limited to repair, remanufacture, replacement, return

15 The Product Quality Law came into force in 1993, which was amended in 2000 and 2009. The current law is the 2009 amendment version, including 74 articles and six chapters which are general principles, supervision and control of product quality, product quality responsibilities and obligations of producers and sellers, damages, penalty provisions and supplementary provisions.

of goods, making up shortage of commodities, refunding payments for goods or services, or compensation for losses'.[16]

b) General Private Law

The General Provisions of the Civil Law,[17] the Contract Law and the Tort Law constitute the general legal framework involving consumer protection issues such as remedy for breach of contract and tort liability. Article 128 of the General Provisions of the Civil Law has included the Law on the Protection of Consumer into China's civil law system by clarifying that the latter are banded by basic provisions provided by the former.[18]

Besides the Law on the Protection of Consumer, the consumer found out that the automobile's actual emission exceeded its prescribed amount. Thus, the automobile could be seen as a defected product. According to article 101 of the Contract Law, for defected products, consumers may demand that the business operator bear the liability for the breach of contract, including: repairing or substituting the goods; reducing the price; allowing the consumer to return the goods; etc. This depends on the content of the contract, as well as the actual performance of his/her obligations, the business operator will bear one or more of such liabilities accordingly.

c) Specific Regulations or Administrative Measures

Besides the legislations listed above, there are other protective legislations for consumers of specific types of merchandise. For example, the General Administration of Quality Supervision, Inspection and Quarantine, one of China's administrative departments, has deliberated and adopted the Provisions on the Liability for the Repair, Replacement and Return of Household Automotive Products (Hereinafter referred to as the Provisions on Household Automotive Products).[19] This act is aimed at implementing the Law on the

---

16 Article 52 of the Law on the Protection of Consumer: 'Where the commodities or services provided by business operators have caused property damage to consumers, business operators shall assume civil liability in accordance with the law or as agreed by the parties, including but not limited to repair, remanufacture, replacement, return of goods, making up shortage of commodities, refunding payments for goods or services, or compensation for losses.'

17 The General Provisions of the Civil Law of the People's Republic of China adopted and came into force in 2017.

18 Art 128 of the General Provisions of the Civil Law: 'Where any laws have special provisions on the protection of civil rights of the minors, the elderly, the disabled, women, and consumers, among others, such special provisions shall apply.'

19 The Provisions on Household Automotive Products is issued on 29 December 2012 by the General Administration of Quality Supervision, Inspection and Quarantine and come into force on 1 October 2013. It contains nine chapters (General Provisions, Obligations of

Protection of Consumer in the industry of household automotive products by specifying certain obligations of business operator – the 'three guarantees'.[20] It is a set of special concepts which originated and develops in China. The three guarantees are the liabilities for the repair, replacement and return of household automotive products with a 'product quality problem' – meaning that 'the normal use of a household automotive product is affected or impossible or the quality of a household automotive product does not comply with the quality status prescribed by regulations or standards or explicitly stated by the enterprise'. According to article 4 of the Provisions on Household Automotive Products, the three guarantees shall be assumed by the sellers.[21] After assuming the three guarantees according to the relevant provisions, a seller is entitled to reimbursement by the producer or any other business operator if the producer or other business operator is actual liable. Chapter V of the act provides the content of three guarantees with more details.[22]

To sum up, with the Law on the Protection of Consumer, the Contract Law and the Provisions on Household Automotive Products, China has provided detailed and practical legislations which describe the obligations borne by business operators of household automotive products. Under situations in accordance with those described in these acts, consumers of household automotive products shall be entitled to request business operators to bear

---

Producers, Obligations of Sellers, Obligations of Repairers, Three Guarantees, Exemption from Three Guarantees, Resolution of Disputes, Penalty Provisions, Penalty Provisions) and 48 articles.

20 'Three Guarantees' describe three types of guarantees made by business operators to consumers for protection of the latter's rights and interests. In 2001, Chinese legislation had established 'three guarantees for mobile phone' and 'three guarantees for telephone'. This event triggered a massive debate on whether 'three guarantees' were already outdated. Some scholars considered 'three guarantees' as a remnant of the past planned economy and thus, it is unnecessary to keep them in today's legislation. These scholars advocate the abolishment of 'three guarantees'. But the government department that had been in charge of designing the 'three guarantees', disagreed. According to the government's opinion: 'Three guarantees' had been proved by practice to be effective in protecting consumer's rights and interests. Based on this opinion, after establishing 'three guarantees for mobile phone' and 'three guarantees for telephone', 'three guarantees for computer' and 'three guarantees for audiovisual products' were later added into Chinese legislation.

21 Art 4 of the Provisions on Household Automotive Product: 'The three guarantees as mentioned in these Provisions shall be assumed by the sellers in accordance with law. After assuming the three guarantees according to the relevant provisions, a seller shall be entitled to reimbursement by the producer or any other business operator if the producer or other business operator is liable. Business operators of household automotive products may enter into contracts among them to agree on the assumption of three guarantees, which, however, shall not infringe upon the lawful rights and interests of consumers and shall not exempt themselves from the three guarantees and quality obligations as prescribed in these Provisions.'

22 Arts 17 to 28, Chapter V. Provisions on Household Automotive Product.

the liability for the breach of contract and request the fulfilment of the 'Three Guarantees'. As to the famous Xi'an case[23] at the beginning of April 2019, the dealer clearly violated both the Provisions on Household Automotive Product and the Law on the Protection of Consumer. Both acts provide that it is for the consumer, not the dealer, to decide whether the car shall be replaced, repaired or returned. The auto dealer and consumer eventually settled their dispute through conciliation: The dealer agreed to replace the car with a new one and provided other compensations to the consumer.[24]

However, some scholars are sceptical about whether the three guarantees have strengthened the protection of consumer, or in fact have them inappropriately limited (decreased) consumer's right and interest.[25] Their arguments are based on article 101 of the Contract Law and article 52 of the Law on the Protection of Consumer. These two provisions provide that consumers could request

---

23 On 9 April 2019, a young woman in Xi'an (a Chinese city) spent CN¥ 660,000 to purchase a Mercedes-Benz. However, five minutes after she concluded the sales contract with the dealer (an auto sales and service shop named 'Lizhixing'), when the car was still inside Lizhixing, its engine started to leak. The consumer had negotiated with the dealer three times within 15 days. However, the dealer refused to take responsibility and denied the consumer's request for a replacement or return of the automobile. Later, the dealer came to terms but only agreed to replace a new engine for the original vehicle. Unable to find other available methods, the woman eventually paid a visit to the shop, tried to defend herself by sitting on the hood of the car in question and explained her story to the crowd while crying. This incident was filmed and went viral – it was viewed 350 million times in two days. The dealer in this incident insisted that, since the automobile had been sold, the dealer only needed to bear responsibility in accordance with the three guarantees. According to the dealer's understanding, the three guarantees only require the replacement of the engine; as to other losses mentioned by the consumer, they shall be borne by the consumer no matter whether the car had left the shop or not. However, the dealer's opinion is really a mistaken understanding of law. It is clearly provided in the Provisions on Household Automotive Product that: Where there is a leakage of fuel of a household automotive product within 60 days from the date of issuance of the purchase invoice by the seller or within the mileage of 3,000 km (whichever is earlier), if the consumer chooses to replace or return the household automotive product, the seller shall be responsible for the replacement or return free of charge. According to this provision, the consumer has the right to request a replacement or returning the car. See: 'Female Graduate Tried to Protect her Lawful Right by "Making A Scene", Xi'an Administration for Market Regulation Has Opened Investigation on the Car's Dealer' *Sanqin Daily* (Xian, 13 April 2019) 1.

24 The agreement reached between the consumer and the dealer provides that: (1) the dealer will replace the car in question with a new one of the same type, the consumer could still make payment through a bank loan; (2) the dealer will make a full refund of the so-called 'financial service fee' (which is about CN¥ 10,000); (3) that Mercedes-Benz will invite the consumer to visit its factory and assembly line in Germany and explain the relevant process to the consumer; (4) as a present, the consumer will be given a ten-year period of 'one-on-one' VIP service; (5) that Mercedes-Benz will organise a birthday celebration for the consumer and pay all related expense. See: 'The Conciliation of Xi'an Mercedes-Benz Case' *Shanxi Dushi Kuai Bao* (Xian, 18 April 2019) 1.

25 Zhong Ruihua, 'A Comprehensive Critique on "Three Guarantees"' (2005) 2 Tsinghua University Law Journal 93.

the repair, remanufacture, replacement, return of goods, make up shortage of commodities, refund of payments for goods or services, or compensation for losses. In other words, these two provisions have provided a much larger range of rights and interests for consumers in comparison with the three guarantees which only list three of them. Because of that, the implementation of three guarantees could easily lead to an actual nullification of other remedies provided by the Contract Law and the Law on the Protection of Consumer.

2. *Punitive Compensation*

The situation described by the reference case may constitute 'consumer deception and fraud' (also named as 'deceptive and fraudulent practices'). Such practices refer to that, while providing commodities or services, a business operator mislead his/her consumer with false or other illicit means which infringe upon the consumer's lawful rights and interests. When business operators engaged in deceptive and fraudulent practices, according to article 54 (second paragraph) of the Contract Law, the injured party shall have the right to modify or revoke such contract.[26] Besides that, according to the second paragraph of article 113 of the Contract Law, the business operator who commits deceptive and fraudulent activities while providing commodities or services to the consumer shall be liable for paying compensation for damages in accordance with the Law on the Protection of Consumer.[27]

The 2013 revision of the Law on the Protection of Consumer includes a system of punitive compensation.[28] This represents China's progress and

---

26 Second paragraph, art 54 of the Contract Law: '(...) If a contract is concluded by one party against the other party's true intentions through the use of fraud, coercion, or exploitation of the other party's unfavorable position, the injured party shall have the right to request the people's court or an arbitration institution to modify or revoke it. (...)'.

27 Art 113 of the Contract Law: 'Where a party fails to perform its obligations under the contract or its performance fails to conform to the agreement and cause losses to the other party, the amount of compensation for losses shall be equal to the losses caused by the breach of contract, including the interests receivable after the performance of the contract, provided not exceeding the probable losses caused by the breach of contract which has been foreseen or ought to be foreseen when the party in breach concludes the contract.'
The business operator who participates in deceptive and fraudulent activities in providing to the consumer any goods or services shall be liable for paying compensation for damages in accordance with the Law of the People's Republic of China on Protection of Consumer Rights and Interests.

28 The punitive compensation first appeared in art 49 of Law on the Protection of Consumer (came into effect on 1 January 1994). In the subsequent ten years, using art 49 as their model, regulations on punitive compensation were added into the Contract Law (came into effect on 1 October 1999), the Interpretation of the Supreme People's Court on the Relevant Issues concerning the Application of Law for Trying Cases on Dispute over Contract for the Sale of Commodity Houses (Interpretation 7 [2003] of the Supreme People's Court), the Food Safety Law (2009 revision, its latest revision is a 2018 Amendment) and the Tort Law (came into effect on 1 July 2010).

research on such systems in the past 20 years or so.[29] According to the first paragraph of Act.55 of the Law on the Protection of Consumer, business operators that fraudulently provide commodities or services shall, as required by consumers, increase the compensation for consumers' losses, and the increase in compensation shall be three times the payment made by a consumer for the commodity purchased or the service received or be 500 yuan if the increase as calculated before is less than 500 yuan, except as otherwise provided for by the law. The second paragraph of article 55 provides that: where business operators knowingly provide consumers with defective commodities or services, causing death or serious damage to the heath of consumers or other victims, the victims shall have the right to require business operators to compensate them for losses in accordance with articles 49 and 51 of this Law and other provisions of laws, and have the right to claim punitive compensation of not more than two times the amount of losses incurred. These regulations on punitive compensation are entirely new to Chinese law.

The sentence 'increase the compensation for consumers' losses' (in the first paragraph of article 55) has shown that punitive compensation is an 'extra compensation' to consumers' loss. In other words, it is only given to the consumer who suffers actual losses caused by the business operator's engagement in deceptive and fraudulent practices.

The Law on the Protection of Consumer has also clarified the meaning of 'losses' – it refers to the losses generated by the death or severe health issues of the consumer or other victims, which is caused by defected commodities or services. Articles 49 and 55 have listed five types of possible losses (relevant compensation included): (1) Medical expenses, care expenses, travel expenses, and other reasonable expenses incurred for treatment and rehabilitation; (2) lost wages; (3) expenses on assisting devices for disability and disability compensation; (4) funeral expenses and death compensation; (5) compensation for the infliction of mental distress.[30]

---

29 Zhu Guangxin, 'The Development and Application of Punitive Compensation' (2014) 3 Soc Sci China 110.

30 Art 49 of the Law on the Protection of Consumer: 'Where the commodities or services provided by business operators have caused personal injuries to consumers or other victims, business operators shall compensate them for medical expenses, care expenses, travel expenses, and other reasonable expenses incurred for treatment and rehabilitation, as well as lost wages. If disabilities are caused to them, business operators shall also compensate them for expenses on assisting devices for disability and pay disability compensation. If death is caused to them, business operators shall also pay funeral expenses and death compensation.' Art 51 of the Law on the Protection of Consumer: 'Where business operators insult or defame, search the persons of, violate the personal freedom of, or otherwise infringe upon the personal rights of consumers or other victims, inflicting serious mental distress on the victims, the victims may claim damages for the infliction of mental distress.'

There have been more and more cases in which Chinese courts find for consumers' demand of punitive compensation from business operators who engaged in deceptive and fraudulent practices. For example, there was a case in 2018[31] where the court decided that the dealer had engaged in deceptive and fraudulent practices and thus granted the consumer's requests which made the total amount of compensation around CN¥ 2,700,000.[32]

B. REMEDIES FOR A GROUP OF CONSUMERS: REPRESENTATIVE ACTION

Defective products or business operators' misbehaviour may affect many consumers. However, when singled out, the injury suffered by one consumer may seem to be quite slight. Thus, to avoid further trouble, individual consumers tend not to seek remedy actively. To deal with this phenomenon, many countries in the world (China included) have designed a suitable system for litigation that arises from disputes shared by a group of consumers. Class action is a typical type of litigation filed by injured consumers. In China, class action is also called as representative action.

Articles 52 and 54 of the Civil Procedure Law of the People's Republic of China (hereinafter referred to as the Civil Procedure Law) provide two forms of representative litigation – representative litigation with a certain number of parties, and representative litigation with an uncertain number of parties. The differences between these two forms are as follows. As to the former, when the action is filed, the number of parties on each side are certain; the subject matter of action for each party is either the same, or is of the same kind. As to the latter, when the action is filed, it is sure that the number of parties on one side is more than one, but the exact number remains uncertain; the subject matter of action for each party must be of the same kind; the people's court may publish

31 Ms Wang Yajun from Hangzhou Zhongsheng Star Automobile Company had purchased an imported Mercedes-Benz CLS which cost her CN¥ 700,000. However, she was later told that she could not get a license plate for the car as the dealer (an auto sales and service shop) had changed some parts of the car without proper permission, and the tyres were no longer considered as 'new'. Ms Wang Yajun demanded that the dealer should change all the parts back into the car's original version and compensate her CN¥ 50,000. After being refused, Ms Wang Yajun filed a lawsuit against the dealer, requested a full refund, plus a punitive compensation three times the original payment. The first trial court decided that the dealer had engaged in deceptive and fraudulent practices and thus granted the consumer's requests which made the total amount of compensation around CN¥ 2,700,000. The dealer appealed. Recently, the appellate court made its decision on this case which was to sustain the judgment of the first trial.

32 *Wang Yajun v Hangzhou Zhongsheng Star Automobile Sales and Service Co, Ltd Sales Contract Dispute* (Judgment) [2017] No 4434 <http://wenshu.court.gov.cn/list/list/>.

a notice to describe the case and claims and notify right holders to register with the people's court within a certain period of time.

Representative litigation with any uncertain number of parties is the so-called 'class action'. The Civil Procedure Law clearly stated that class action in the Chinese legal system applies a 'joining system'. Article 54 of the Civil Procedure Law regulates the procedures of joining representative litigation and the procedure of recommending a representative or representatives. That clause also provides the effectiveness of the court's decision in representative litigation. Articles 77, 79 and 80 of the new Judicial Interpretation of the Civil Procedure Law provide more detailed explanation of article 54 of the Civil Procedure Law.

As to Chinese application of representative action, it constantly runs into difficulties in civil court. For example: in 2001, Yang Jianchu, along with 36 other consumers, filed a case against Ericsson (China) company. The Court of Chaoyang District in Beijing estimated that there might be more than 500 right holders relevant to this case. Later, this court dismissed this case based on the fact that many consumers had provided an invoice with differences in the product's price. Eventually Yang Jianchu filed his personal claim instead of a class action.[33]

C. RECEIVING REMEDIES: PUBLIC INTEREST ACTION

In some scenarios, private interest litigation could not provide sufficient protection for consumers. At the same time, it would also be impractical for consumers to expect full protection from public enforcement of the law. These two facts provide the justification to strengthen other forms of private enforcement of the law, such as civil public interest litigation.

Public interest litigation was introduced into the Chinese civil system in 2012. Article 55 of the Civil Procedure Law (2012 revision) clearly established public interest litigation, though its content is 'generalised and directive'. Details of public interest litigation for certain type of cases was 'left to be separately provided by other legislation'.[34] Thus, in other words, detailed regulations on public interest litigation could not be found in the Civil Procedure Law, such as: the qualification of the subject, the types of litigation, as well as the procedure rules applied in such litigations, etc.

---

33 'Case concerning Yang Jianyu against Ericsson (China) Company Mobile Phone Quality Dispute' <http://www.pkulaw.cn/case/>.

34 Du Leqi, 'The Limitation of Public Interest Litigation for Protection of Consumer and its Countermeasure – A Critique on Art. 47 of the Law of the People's Republic of China on the Protection of Consumer Rights and Interests' (2014) 10 Theory Monthly 99.

Article 47 of the Law on the Protection of Consumer[35] could be seen as providing details for article 55 of the Civil Procedure Law. The former, together with representative action, was considered extremely helpful for consumers. As they effectively solved the two typical problems many consumers would encounter in litigation – high expense and low benefit. This clause formally established public interest litigation in the domain of the protection of consumers which is very meaningful. Because, in many cases when the losses suffered by a single consumer are observed, the amount of the loss could be considered as too small to claim. Article 47 provides an effective means to deal with such a problem. However, article 47 has its flaws: This provision limits the plaintiff of consumption-related public interest litigation to 'the China Consumers' Association (CCA)[36] and the consumer associations formed in provinces, autonomous regions, and municipalities directly under the Central Government'. This limitation greatly narrows the subjects to file public interest litigation and definitely weakens public interest litigation's function as private enforcement of the law.[37]

Public interest civil litigation is regulated under article 55[38] of Civil Procedure Law. The 'authority or relevant organisation' in the first paragraph of article 55 refers to administrative departments in charge of environmental resources, CCA,[39] other public interest social groups, etc. The most interesting provision in article 55 is that it allows a 'relevant organisation', which is not of direct interest to the case, to file a lawsuit over 'conduct (...) damages the public interest'. This provision marks China's historical breakthrough in its procedural law regarding to the plaintiff's qualification.[40] The scope of 'an authority

35 Art 47 of the Law on the Protection of Consumer: 'For infringement upon the lawful rights and interests of vast consumers, the China Consumers' Association and the consumer associations formed in provinces, autonomous regions, and municipalities directly under the Central Government may file lawsuits in the people's courts.'

36 CCA was founded on 26 December 1984, via the approval of the State Council of the People's Republic of China.

37 Xiao Jianguo and Huang Zhongshun, 'Research on the Qualification of Parties in Consumption Related Public Interest Litigation – with Commentary on the draft of Art. 19 of the Law on the Protection of Consumer' (2013) 6 Journal of Shandong Police College 5.

38 The first paragraph of art 55 of Civil Procedure Law: 'For conduct that pollutes environment, infringes upon the lawful rights and interests of vast consumers or otherwise damages the public interest, an authority or relevant organization as prescribed by law may institute an action in a people's court.'

39 Art 36 of the Law on the Protection of Consumer: 'Consumer associations and other consumer organizations are social organizations legally formed to exercise social supervision over commodities and services and protect the lawful rights and interests of consumers.' Also see art 37 (Law on the Protection of Consumer) which describes one of the CCA's public duties as 'for infringement upon the lawful rights and interests of consumers, supporting the victims in filing lawsuits or, in accordance with this Law, filing lawsuits'.

40 Huang Jinrong, 'Progress and Flaw in Legislation on Public Interest Litigation – A Commentary on Art. 55 of Civil Procedure Law' (2014) 2 Research on Rule of Law 102.

or relevant organisation' is extremely broad. In a way, one could say that article 55 has included every type of organisation as a qualified plaintiff to file a public interest litigation. Does that mean that article 55 does not provide any limitation at all? The answer is no, and the reality may be quite contrary to 'no limitation'. Article 55 provides limitations on the plaintiff's qualification by adding 'as prescribed by law' after 'an authority or relevant organisation'. This means that an authority or organisation is not qualified to file public interest litigation, unless other legislations provide that this authority or organisation is qualified to be a plaintiff of a public interest litigation.

In the latest revision of Civil Procedure Law (2017 revision), an additional regulation on public interest litigation was added into article 55.[41] If there is a conduct that undermines the protection of the ecological environment and resources, interests in the field of food and drug safety, or any other conduct that damages social interest, the procuratorate may file a lawsuit in the people's court if other departments or organisations with the relevant authority neglects its duty to file litigation or refuses to file such litigation. This newly added regulation clearly extends the types of qualified party to file public interest litigation.

Allowing a prosecutorial department to file public interest administrative litigation is meaningful to the rule of law: it is based on the necessity to supervise administrative power. When administrative departments neglect their duty or abuse their power, under certain circumstances, the procuratorate will file charges against the misbehaving departments – this represents the judicial power's supervision over administrative power. Under such practice, the exercise of administrative power will gradually follow the rule of law. This is very important for China to achieve governance in accordance with the law and create a system in which power serves right.[42] According to the second paragraph of article 55, public interest administrative litigation filed by the procuratorate is a safety net kind of regulation: no matter whether other authorities or organisations file public interest litigation or not, the procuratorate always has ways to

---

41 The second paragraph of art 55 of Civil Procedure Law: 'Where the people's procuratorate finds in the performance of functions any conduct that undermines the protection of the ecological environment and resources, infringes upon consumers' lawful rights and interests in the field of food and drug safety or any other conduct that damages social interest, the procuratorate may file lawsuit. Besides this, another prerequisite for procuratorate to undertake public interest administrative litigation is that other authority or organization must have not yet filed a similar public interest litigation. If an authority or organization has already filed a lawsuit, the procuratorate may take part in by providing its support to such lawsuit.'

42 Jiang Tao, 'Filing Public Interest Administrative Litigation by Procuratorate: Research over A Chinese Problem' (2015) 6 Tribune of Political Science and Law 17.

participate in such litigation – either by filing a lawsuit or providing support to lawsuits filed by others.[43]

Therefore, to protect the lawful interests and rights of consumers, in China the CCA and the consumer associations formed in provinces, autonomous regions and municipalities could directly file public interest litigation in court. Also, based on the will to protect their own personal interest and interests of other similar consumers, there is a possibility for individuals to file public interest litigation. Besides that, procuratorates may provide support to public interest litigation. Procuratorates may even bring up administrative public interest litigation if no other association files charges against business operators based on public interest.

III. PUBLIC ENFORCEMENT OF CHINESE CONSUMER LAW

China has already established a relatively complete system for the protection of consumers. Yet for consumers who seek to protect their lawful right and interest, they still face many challenges or even difficulties. The ineffectiveness in law enforcement is the basic reason behind these phenomena. In other words, there are duties that could only be borne by the state. However, in reality, some of these duties are left untaken care of.

China does not have a tradition to set private law apart from public law. Thus, even in the domain of private law, administrative regulation may apply.

---

43 There are many cases of public interest administrative litigation, either filed by the procuratorate or administrative departments. Here are some examples: *People's Procuratorate of Laoling City, Dezhou City, Shandong Province v Jinxin Chemistry Factory* (environmental pollution case); *People's Procuratorate of Pinghu City, Zhejiang Province v Jiaxing Lvyi Environmental Protection Service Ltd etc.* (environmental pollution case); case filed by People's Procuratorate of Chengjiang Town, Yunnan Province on arsenic pollution in Yangzonghai lake; *Guiyang City Administration on Red Maple Lake, Baihua Lake and Aha Dam v Tianfeng Chemistry Ltd* (pollution case); *Kunming City Administration on Environmental Protection v Kunming Sannong Agricultural and Livestock Ltd* (water pollution case); *Jiangyin City Administration on Environmental Protection v Wang and Ma* (water pollution case). The above cases are sourced from: <http://www.pkulaw.cn/case/>. Regional government and judicial departments also established many relevant regulations, in order to allow public interest administrative litigation to be either filed by the procuratorate or administrative departments. For example, Kunming Intermediate People's Court along with People's Procuratorate of Kunming has established Opinions on Several Issues Concerning the Processing of Public Interest Civil Litigation (for Trial Implementation); Wuxi Intermediate People's Court along with People's Procuratorate of Wuxi has recently established Trial Implementation on Processing Public Interest Civil Litigation Concerning Environmental Problem. See: 'Plan for the Pilot Project of Reform of Instituting Public Interest Litigations by the Procuratorial Organs' Procuratorate Daily (Beijing, 3 July 2015) 1.

Nowadays, there is a trend to protect consumers through private law and a trend to decrease administrative regulation regarding protection of consumers. However, such trends are mostly among countries in which the market economy has fully developed. As for China, the protection of consumers is still based on an idea in which administrative regulation plays a major role.[44] In comparison with the remedies provided by private law, remedies in public law mostly take the form of administrative departments' direct supervision on business operators. 'Strong state and weak society' had once been a trait of China and still has some influence over China nowadays. This trait has brought a series of challenges for social organisations, such as consumer associations, to fully realise their function. In the future, to better enforce protection of consumers, China should still try to establish a 'state – society' co-regulation system so that legislation would be more practical and consumer associations would function better.[45]

Public enforcement of law is a very important aspect in the protection of consumer. Public enforcement of law is provided in, for example, Chapter IV ('Protection of Lawful Rights and Interests of Consumers by the State') of the Law on the Protection of Consumer. This chapter clearly provides that the people's governments at all levels shall strengthen their leadership, organise, coordinate and supervise the relevant administrative departments in satisfactorily protecting the lawful rights and interests of consumers, and fulfil their duties in protecting the lawful rights and interests of consumers. The relevant state organs shall, in accordance with the provisions of laws and regulations, punish the illegal or criminal acts of business operators infringing upon the lawful rights and interests of consumers in providing commodities or services.[46]

---

44 Cui Jizi, *Comparative Studies on Consumer Contracts Law of East Asia* (Peking University Press 2013) 149.

45 Fang Ying, 'Consumer Association System for Protection of Consumer – under the Perspective of "State – Society" co-regulation' (2018) 2 Journal of Guangzhou University (Social Science Edition) 67.

46 Content relating to public enforcement of law could also be found in Chapter VII ('Legal Liability') of the Law on the Protection of Consumer. It bans business operators from engaging in certain types of activities, such as: providing commodities or services not in compliance with the requirements for the protection of personal and property safety; adulterating commodities, passing fake commodities off as genuine ones, or passing inferior commodities off as superior ones, or passing non-compliance commodities off as compliance ones; deliberately delaying or unreasonably refusing consumers' requests for repair, remanufacture, replacement, return of goods, making up shortage of commodities, refunding payments for goods or services, or compensation for losses. For the business operators who commit such activities, art 56 of the Law on the Protection of Consumer: '(...) in addition to corresponding civil liabilities, (those business operator shall) be governed by other applicable laws and regulations which provide for the punishing authorities and forms of punishment; or in the absence of such provisions in laws or regulations, the administrative departments for industry and commerce or other relevant administrative departments shall order them to make correction, and may, according to the circumstances, warn the business operators, confiscate their illegal income, impose a fine of not less than the illegal income but

In the reference case, the manufacturer manipulated the test result of its vehicles' emission. The actual emission of the automobile exceeds its prescribed value. The right and interest of the consumers of such automobiles were thus injured. Remedies could be sought through public enforcement of law. According to the Law on the Protection of Consumer and the Criminal Law of the People's Republic of China (hereinafter referred to as the Criminal Law), relevant administrative departments of quality supervision and supervision may impose administrative punishment to related business operators and supervise the manufacture of that line of automobiles; under certain circumstances, there is the possibility that manufacturers may be subject to criminal liability in accordance with the law.

A. ADMINISTRATIVE SUPERVISION

The Law on the Protection of Consumer has provided administrative departments' duties on supervising business operators which are in the form of: the right to conduct spot check and inspection of the commodities and services provided by business operators;[47] the right to accept and process consumers' complaints;[48] the right to impose administrative sanctions[49] etc. These are very important means to protect consumers' rights and interests.

In the reference case, manufacturer manipulated the test result of its vehicles' emissions. The actual emission of the automobile exceeds its prescribed

not more than ten times the illegal income or, if there is no illegal income, a fine of not more than CN¥ 500,000, or impose a combination of the above penalties on them; and if the circumstances are serious, order them to suspend business for rectification or revoke their business licenses.'

47 Art 33 of the Law on the Protection of Consumer: 'The relevant administrative departments shall, within their respective functions, conduct spot check and inspection of the commodities and services provided by business operators on a regular or unscheduled basis, and publish the results thereof in a timely manner. Where the relevant administrative departments discover and determine that the commodities or services provided by business operators are defective and may endanger the personal or property safety, they shall immediately order the business operators to take measures such as cessation of sale, issuance of a warning, recall, harmless treatment, destruction, and cessation of production or service.'

48 Art 32 of the Law on the Protection of Consumer: 'The administrative departments for industry and commerce of the people's governments at all levels and other relevant administrative departments shall take measures to protect the lawful rights and interests of consumers within their respective functions in accordance with the provisions of laws and regulations. The relevant administrative departments shall hear the opinions of consumers, consumer associations, and other organizations on issues concerning the transactions of business operators and the quality of commodities and services, and investigate and address such issues in a timely manner.'

49 Art 34 of the Law on the Protection of Consumer: 'The relevant state organs shall, in accordance with the provisions of laws and regulations, punish the illegal or criminal acts of business operators infringing upon the lawful rights and interests of consumers in providing commodities or services.'

value – since this can be seen as a defect, the legislation on 'recall of defective products' may be applied. Article 33 of the Law on the Protection of Consumer provides regulation on recall of defective products and cessation of relevant production. However, article 33 does not include a detailed definition of 'defective'. Expenses (such as transportation fee or expenses for substitute) may be caused by recall – article 33 does not provide how these expenses shall be borne either.

There are two other legislations on the recall of defective automotive products, though both are on the lower level in the hierarchy of law. These two legislations are: Regulation on the Administration of Recall of Defective Auto Products, and Measures for the Implementation of the Regulation on the Administration of the Recall of Defective Auto Products. These two legislations provide much detailed information on different aspects relating to the recall of defective automotive products, such as: information management, defect investigation, recall implementation and administration, legal liability, etc. They are aiming at enforcing article 19[50] and Chapter IV ('Protection of Lawful Rights and Interests of Consumers by the State') of the Law on the Protection of Consumer.

B. ADMINISTRATIVE MEDIATION

Both the role of consumer and business operator are gradually becoming more vital in a country's economy and social life. Together with that, the role of administrative law enforcement in punishing misbehaviour of business operators, in protecting consumers, as well as in maintaining market order are also becoming more significant. Because of that, Chinese legislators have gradually focused on establishing a proper administrative mediation system as one of the means to protect consumers. Mediation is an important way to settle disputes, which always existed in Chinese legal tradition. It is widely accepted by members of society and deeply rooted in Chinese culture. Article 39 of the Law on the Protection of Consumer[51] provides regulation on mediation.

---

50 Art 19 of the Law on the Protection of Consumer: 'After discovering any defects which may endanger personal or property safety in their provided commodities or services, business operators shall immediately report to the relevant administrative departments and inform consumers; and take measures such as cessation of sale, issuance of a warning, recall, harmless treatment, destruction, and cessation of production or service. If the measure of recall is taken, business operators shall reimburse consumers for necessary expenses incurred for the recall of commodities.'

51 Art 39 of the Law on the Protection of Consumer: 'Where any dispute over consumer rights and interests arises between business operators and consumers, consumers may settle the dispute by the following means: (...) (2) Requesting mediation by a consumer association or any other mediation organization legally formed.'

CCA is a consumer association specialised in processing consumer's complaint and mediation. CCA contains different levels of consumer associations which were approved respectively by people's governments of similar level.[52] Although it is provided in article 12 of the Law on the Protection of Consumer that 'consumers shall have the right to form social organizations in accordance with the law to protect their lawful rights and interests', up until today, there are not many Chinese non-governmental consumer organisations, the CCA is the only national consumer organisation of China. To a certain degree, this phenomenon limits the rise of consumers' power which makes it harder to promote a 'consumer movement' in China. This is also one of the reasons why China has not been able to provide a high-level protection for consumers.[53]

Article 36 of the Law of the Protection of Consumer describes the overall function of CCA as follows: 'Consumer associations and other consumer organizations are social organizations legally formed to exercise social supervision over commodities and services and protect the lawful rights and interests of consumers.' The actual meaning of such a function could be reflected through article 37, which provides eight types of public duties that the CCA should perform, such as: guiding the consumers; providing information and a consultation service to consumers; accepting complaints of consumers, investigating the complaints, mediating between the concerned parties; bringing claims to courts on behalf of consumers; etc.[54]

---

52 These associations registered in civil affairs departments as 'non-governmental organization'. However, comparing with other non-governmental organisations, the CCA has some unique characters: it was founded by the government in accordance with law; most of its funding comes from governmental funding. Thus, the CCA is a social organisation with characters similar to governmental organisation.

53 Sun Ying, 'The reconstruction of Chinese consumer organization under the latest Amendment of the Law of the Protection of Consumer' (2013) 4 China Legal Science 98.

54 Art 37 of the Law on the Protection of Consumer: Consumer associations shall perform the following public duties: '(1) Providing consumption information and consultation services to consumers, increasing consumers' ability to protect their lawful rights and interests, and guiding consumption in a civilized, healthy, resource conservation, and environmental protection manner; (2) participating in the development of laws, regulations, rules, and mandatory standards related to consumer rights and interests; (3) participating in the supervision and inspection of commodities and services conducted by the relevant administrative departments; (4) reporting or inquiring about issues concerning the lawful rights and interests of consumers to the relevant authorities and providing recommendations; (5) accepting complaints of consumers, investigating the complaints, mediating between the concerned parties; (6) when necessary, authorizing an appraisal by a qualified appraiser, which shall issue an appraisal opinion, if a complaint involves any quality problems of commodities or services; (7) for infringement upon the lawful rights and interests of consumers, supporting the victims in filing lawsuits or, in accordance with this Law, filing lawsuits; (8) exposing and criticizing through mass media the acts infringing upon the lawful rights and interests of consumers.'

C. ADMINISTRATIVE PENALTY

In China, Industry and Commerce Administrative departments comprehensively regulate market participants and their operation in market. These departments are the most important administrative departments to enforce protection of consumer.

The State Administration for Industry and Commerce of the People's Republic of China (SAIC) had established the Temporary Measures for the Processing of Consumer's Complaints by Industry and Commerce Administrative Departments and Measures for Penalties against Deception and Fraud on Consumer. These two regulations represented SAIC's effort in enforcing protection of consumer within its authority.

Article 56 of the Law on the Protection of Consumer[55] also provides contents on administrative penalty. In addition to punishment in accordance with laws and regulations, the punishing authorities shall enter the violations into their credit files and disclose them to the public.

The most commonly used administrative penalties imposed on the business operators who engaged in illegal operation or other misbehaviour banned by

---

[55] Art 56 of the Law on the Protection of Consumer: 'Under any of the following circumstances, business operators shall, in addition to corresponding civil liabilities, be governed by other applicable laws and regulations which provide for the punishing authorities and forms of punishment; or in the absence of such provisions in laws or regulations, the administrative departments for industry and commerce or other relevant administrative departments shall order them to make correction, and may, according to the circumstances, warn the business operators, confiscate their illegal income, impose a fine of not less than the illegal income but not more than ten times the illegal income or, if there is no illegal income, a fine of not more than 500,000 yuan, or impose a combination of the above penalties on them; and if the circumstances are serious, order them to suspend business for rectification or revoke their business licenses: (1) Providing commodities or services not in compliance with the requirements for the protection of personal and property safety. (2) Adulterating commodities, passing fake commodities off as genuine ones, or passing inferior commodities off as superior ones, or passing non-compliance commodities off as compliance ones. (3) Producing commodities expressly eliminated by the state, or selling expired or deteriorated commodities. (4) Forging the origins of commodities, forging or falsely using the factory names and addresses of others, tampering with the date of production, or forging or falsely using certification marks and other quality marks. (5) Selling commodities not inspected or quarantined as required, or forging the inspection or quarantine results. (6) Promoting commodities or services in a false or misleading manner. (7) Refusing or delaying the measures ordered by the relevant administrative departments, such as cessation of sale, issuance of warnings, recall, harmless treatment, destruction, and cessation of production or service, for their defective commodities or services. (8) Deliberately delaying or unreasonably refusing consumers' requests for repair, remanufacture, replacement, return of goods, making up shortage of commodities, refunding payments for goods or services, or compensation for losses. (9) Infringing upon the human dignity or personal freedom of consumers or infringing upon the right of consumers to legal protection of personal information. (10) Otherwise infringing upon consumer rights and interests, punishable according to laws or regulations.'

law which result in consumers receiving defective product(s), in reality, are confiscation of their illegal income and (or) fine.

D. CRIMINAL PUNISHMENTS

In recent years, more and more countries have turned to criminal legislation to seek better protection of consumer.[56] In the Chinese market, incidents in which business operators infringed upon consumers' rights and interests have continually happened. Some of these incidents showed sufficient ill will or malice that criminal legislation has inevitably become the last but necessary resort to enforce protection of consumer. Article 57 of the Law of the Protection of Consumer has clearly stated that: Business operators which are suspected of any crime for infringing upon the lawful rights and interests of consumers in providing commodities or services in violation of this Law shall be subject to criminal liability in accordance with the law. Such legislations mostly appear in Section 1, Chapter III of the Criminal Law. Article 140 of the Criminal Law provides crimes of manufacturing and selling fake and shoddy products.[57]

In Chinese legislation, the *actus reus* for the crime of manufacturing and selling fake and shoddy products not only requires the perpetrator to perform an illegal act, but also requires that the act has produced a severe consequence. That is to say, if a person has manufactured and sold fake or shoddy products, but such misbehaviour has not created a consequence severe enough to satisfy the requirements of article 140, this person would not be considered as having committed a crime. One of the Chinese Criminal Law's important traits is these combined requirements that an act of crime must be 'both illegal and reaching

56 Qiao Xinsheng, *Pandect of Law on the Protection of Consumer* (China Procurational Press 2018) 60.

57 Art 140 of the Criminal Law: 'Any producer or seller who mixes up or adulterates products, passes fake imitations for genuine, sells seconds at best quality price, or passes unqualified products as qualified ones, with a sale amount of not less than 50,000 yuan and not more than 200,000 yuan, is to be sentenced to not more than two years of fixed-term imprisonment or criminal detention and may in addition or exclusively be sentenced to a fine of not less than 50 percent and not more than 200 percent of the sale amount; when the sale amount is not less than 200,000 yuan and not more than 500,000 yuan, is to be sentenced to not less than two years and not more than seven years of fixed-term imprisonment and may in addition be sentenced to a fine of not less than 50 percent and not more than 200 percent of the sale amount; when the sale amount is not less than 500,000 yuan and not more than 2 million yuan, is to be sentenced to not less than seven years and may in addition be sentenced to a fine of not less than 50 percent and not more than 200 percent of the sale amount; when the sale amount is not less than two million yuan, is to be sentenced to 15 years of fixed-term imprisonment or life imprisonment and may in addition be sentenced to a fine of not less than 50 percent and not more than 200 percent of the sale amount or confiscation of property.'

certain degree of severity'.[58] As to crimes of manufacturing and selling fake and shoddy products, the degree of severity was described as 'a sale amount of not less than CN¥ 50,000'.[59] The legislation does not concern other circumstances which might increase the social harm brought by the manufacture or sale of fake and shoddy products, such as the scale or ways of manufacture, the actual function of the products, etc. However, as a matter of fact, the severity of manufacturing and selling fake and shoddy products is not only affected by the sale amount, but also by other circumstances. When evaluating the social harm brought by an illegal act, the legislation should take those circumstances into consideration as well.

IV. CONCLUSION

China has already established a relatively complete system for the protection of consumers. However, China is experiencing a transformation in its society, it is now a so-called 'risk society'. Under these circumstances, many consumers in the Chinese market have experienced incidents in which their rights and interests were injured. To seek an effective counter-measurement, China must improve both its private and public enforcement of law.

The improvement of the private enforcement of law must start with providing a better system for consumers to seek remedy of their private rights. The most typical way is to establish a proper system for consumers' class action. This system can effectively solve problems encountered by many injured consumers – there may be a lot of consumers facing similar defective products, however, the degree or amount of loss suffered by each one of them may be too small. Today in many countries around the world, the system within the legislation for the protection of consumers have changed greatly – earlier it only provided regulations for private interest litigation, now it consists of regulations for both private and public interest litigation. In many foreign countries, there has also been a trend to diversify public interest litigation. China has followed this trend. Its 2013 and 2017 revisions of the Law on the Protection of Consumer provide the public interest litigation. Private interest litigation under the legislation for the protection of consumer may sometimes benefit the protection of public interest.

The legislation on protection of the consumer is experiencing a transformation from individual-protection-oriented to public-interest-protection-oriented. This means state intervention is a need and a must. Thus, one may observe public

---

58 Li Jie, 'A Critique on the Features of Criminal Legislation on the Protection of Consumer' (2004) 5 Journal of Henan Administrative Institute of Politics and Law 78.

59 See art 140 of the Criminal Law.

enforcement of such legislation through administrative enforcement and judicial activities. These activities are led by state departments and social organisations with the goal of preventing the misbehaviour that injures order in transaction for consumption. Such activities are referred to as public enforcement of law. Some of the remedies depend fully on government intervention, for example, the inspection and evaluation of defect products, the recall of defective products, the administrative penalty. One may observe these transformations in the 2013 revision of the Law on the Protection of Consumer – Chapter IV and Chapter V of the act has strengthened state and social organisations' duties to protect consumers' rights and interests.

ENFORCING CONSUMER AND CAPITAL MARKETS LAW IN THE UNITED STATES

Amy J. SCHMITZ*

Consumers with similar claims in the United States (US) often join forces to pursue remedies using class actions. This allows them to obtain remedies with little cost and effort and serves a 'private attorney general' function by bringing light to purchase problems and deceptive practices that may otherwise

* Amy J. Schmitz, Elwood L Thomas Missouri Endowed Professor of Law, University of Missouri, School of Law, Center for the Study of Dispute Resolution.
I thank Kelli Reichert, Rachel Mitchell, Sam Obscherning and Andrew Johnson for their research assistance. I also thank Professors Gsell and Möllers, and all the participants in the Enforcing Consumer and Capital Market Law in Europe Conference in Augsburg, Germany.
List of websites with related information: <http://www.epa.gov/vw>; <http://www.cand.uscourts.gov/crb/vwmdl>; <http://www.ftc.gov/enforcement/cases-proceedings/162-3006/volkswagen-group-america-inc>.
Note that no one open database has all the cases and documents, as many are accessible through subscription-based databases as is customary for many publications in the US.

be ignored. This is especially true in small dollar claims, where the cost to individually litigate is disproportionate to the eventual judgment. However, some have criticised class actions in the US for forcing settlements and padding the pockets of lawyers, while leaving consumers with minimal pay-outs. This chapter will provide an overview of how enforcement and class actions operate in the US, using the Volkswagen (VW) case as an example. This chapter will also initiate ideas for using online dispute resolution (ODR) for consumer claims as means for expanding access to remedies and opening an alternative to class actions. The hope is that this chapter will engage renewed interest in global access to remedies, especially in cases like Dieselgate where consumers throughout the world suffer similar harms.

I. INTRODUCTION

Borders lose meaning as consumers purchase goods from all over the world and manufacturers set up shop overseas. However, borders matter when disputes develop due to jurisdictional differences in laws and procedures for obtaining remedies. This is especially true when it comes to deceptive trade practices, like when Volkswagen (VW) used software in its diesel engines to manipulate emission levels.[1] This manipulation gave rise to 'Dieselgate' and an eruption of lawsuits in the US that have helped many consumers obtain compensation. Meanwhile, some have complained that many consumers in Europe have yet to receive remedies due to arguably limited procedures for obtaining redress on such mass claims.[2]

Consumers all over the world may suffer the same harms but have very different remedies depending on where they live. For example, many consumers in the US obtained remedies related to Dieselgate before their European counterparts. It is therefore critical to consider legal redress mechanisms on a global scale. Businesses and policymakers must address differences in consumer redress systems and collaborate to create mechanisms that operate efficiently and fairly for consumers regardless of residence.

Accordingly, this chapter uses the VW example to provide a snapshot of consumer redress processes in the US, with special focus on the tandem power

1 Maria Juul, 'Lawsuit Triggered by the Volkswagen Emissions Case' (*European Parliamentary Research Service Briefing*, May 2016) 1 <http://www.europarl.europa.eu/RegData/etudes/BRIE/2016/583793/EPRS_BRI(2016)583793_EN.pdf>.

2 Kevin Tarsa, 'Won't Get Fooled Again: Why VW's Emissions Deception is Illegal in Europe and How to Improve the EU's Auto Regulatory System' (2017) 40 B C Int'l & Comp L Rev 315, 317–42 (hereafter Tarsa, 'EU's Auto Regulatory System').

of government enforcement actions alongside class actions. In the case of VW, for example, consumers' recovery resulted from government action as well as simultaneous class actions. Class actions are important in the US because they allow consumers to act as 'private attorneys general' in bringing lawsuits as a group of harmed individuals and shedding light on improprieties that the government would likely pursue, given the resources. Indeed, class relief has been the primary means for consumers to pursue remedies in business-to-consumer (B2C) transactions.

However, these traditional American remedial processes have diminished due to the strict enforcement of pre-dispute arbitration under the Federal Arbitration Act (FAA).[3] This jurisprudence has arguably threatened public awareness and enforcement of substantive consumer protection law.[4] Businesses may use arbitration and class waiver provisions to privatise consumers' access to remedies, and potentially escape legal reforms.[5] In contrast, the European Union (EU) has been more proactive in its refusal or reluctance to enforce pre-dispute arbitration clauses in B2C contracts.[6]

Meanwhile, policymakers around the world are developing online dispute resolution (ODR) systems for expanding access to remedies in B2C purchases. For example, the EU has adopted a Directive on Alternative Dispute Resolution for Consumer Disputes (the 'ADR Directive')[7] and a Regulation on Online Dispute Resolution for Consumer Disputes (the 'ODR Regulation'),[8] which work in tandem to require Member States to implement ODR systems for consumer claims. Furthermore, the United Nations Commission on International Trade Law (UNCITRAL) spent many years advancing ODR for cross-border

---

3 Federal Arbitration Act (FAA), 9 U.S.C. §§201–08, 301–07 (1970) (implementing the NY Convention under §§201–08 and the Panama Convention under §§301–07); Christopher R Drahozal, 'New Experiences of International Arbitration in the United States' (2006) 54 Am J Comp L 233, 233–55 (noting how the US's strict enforcement of arbitration is distinct).

4 J Maria Glover, 'Disappearing Claims and the Erosion of Disappearing Claims and the Erosion of Substantive Law' (2015) 124 Yale LJ 3052, 3070–84 (hereafter Glover, 'Disappearing Claims and Erosion').

5 Ibid, 3080–82; see also Jean R Sternlight, 'Mandatory Binding Arbitration Clauses Prevent Consumers from Presenting Procedurally Difficult Claims' (2012) 42 Sw U L Rev 87, 94–98.

6 James R Bucilla II, 'The Online Crossroads of Website Terms of Service Agreements and Consumer Protection: An Empirical Study of Arbitration Clauses in the Terms of Service Agreements for the Top 100 Websites Viewed in the United States' (2014) 15 Wake Forest L Rev 102, 133–49.

7 European Parliament and Council Directive 2013/11/EU of 21 May 2013 on Alternative Dispute Resolution for Consumer Disputes and amending Regulation (EC) 2006/2004 and Directive 2009/22/EC (Directive on consumer ADR) [2013] OJ L165/63.

8 European Parliament and Council Regulation (EU) 524/2013 of 21 May 2013 on Online Dispute Resolution for Consumer Disputes and amending Regulation (EC) 2006/2004 and Directive 2009/22/EC (Regulation on consumer ODR) [2013] OJ L165/1.

ecommerce through its Working Group III on Online Dispute Resolution.[9] Furthermore, ODR projects in the courts are flourishing throughout the world.[10]

Nonetheless, class actions are not dead in the US, and they are important in the consumer redress ecosystem. They continue to serve an important role in providing remedies for small dollar claims, and bringing light to issues that impact the public. Indeed, class actions serve a private attorney general function. However, they also generate criticism for padding pockets of lawyers and arguably extorting settlements from deep pocket companies. Of course, consumers who have obtained remedies through class actions and government enforcement mechanisms in cases like Dieselgate are not complaining.

Accordingly, Section II of this chapter will provide background on the lawsuits launched in the US related to the VW diesel emissions cases, and the laws and procedural mechanisms that empowered these claims. Section III will then dive deeper into consumer remedy procedures in the US, and explain some of the debates regarding class actions and arbitration clauses. Section IV will then initiate ideas for using ODR to resolve class action debates, and allow for an alternative mechanism for promoting fairness, transparency, and efficiency while expanding consumers' access to remedies with respect to deception and product claims. Section V will conclude.

II. THE DIESELGATE SCANDAL IN THE US

A. CONCERT OF GOVERNMENT AND CONSUMER CLAIMS

The facts of VW's manipulation of emissions serve as a background for studying consumer remedies in mass claims, especially with respect to deceptive practices. The US part in the saga that has come to be known as 'Dieselgate' began in the autumn of 2015, when the US Environmental Protection Agency (EPA) issued a notice of violation of the Clean Air Act to German automaker VW.[11] The agency found that since 2009, VW intentionally programmed turbocharged direct injection (TDI) diesel engines to activate their emissions controls only during laboratory emissions testing.[12] This manipulation deceptively caused

9 UN Commission on International Trade Law Working Group III, 33rd Session, 'Draft outcome document reflecting elements and principles of an ODR process' (New York, 29 February–4 March 2016, UN Doc. A/CN.9/WG.III/WP.140) <https://undocs.org/en/a/cn.9/wg.iii/wp.140>.

10 Amy J Schmitz, 'Expanding Access to Remedies through E-Court Initiatives' (2019) 67 Buff L Rev 101–73 (hereafter Schmitz, 'Expanding Access').

11 Tarsa, 'EU's Auto Regulatory System' (n 2) 315–25.

12 Environmental Protection Agency, 'Learn About Volkswagen Violations' (*EPA*, 11 August 2017) <http://www.epa.gov/vw/learn-about-volkswagen-violations>.

the vehicles' nitrogen oxides (NOx) readings to meet US standards during regulatory testing, but emit up to 40 times more NOx in real-world driving.[13] VW deployed this programming software in about 11 million cars worldwide, including 500,000 in the US, in model years 2009 through 2015.[14]

This manipulation caused financial, as well as emotional and psychological, injuries to consumers who felt betrayed.[15] VW purposefully targeted environmentally conscious, or 'green', consumers through advertisements stating that its diesel engines ran on clean energy.[16] Consumers were therefore aghast when they learned that they had purchased vehicles that were not only dirtier than advertised, but so dirty that it was illegal to drive them in the US.[17] This news destroyed the value of the cars, and inflicted identity harm on consumers when they realised they had been lured into harming the environment which they had actively sought to protect through their purchase of the vehicle.[18] Nonetheless, the VW case was particularly appalling because of the nature of the promises that they made and their active manipulation to hide the truth.[19]

In most circumstances, this type of case can be difficult for consumers to pursue. Consumers usually face obstacles in detecting, proving, and measuring damages with respect to deception – especially when the main harm is damage to one's psyche.[20] However, in the case of VW, multiple government agencies and the US Justice Department acted swiftly to pave the way for consumer compensation. Moreover, the VW case involved more than simply psychic, or identity, harm. It was coupled with financial loss.[21]

Specifically, the US Department of Justice filed a civil suit against VW on behalf of the EPA on 4 January 2016.[22] This complaint centred on the fact that VW's emissions exceeded the levels deemed acceptable by the EPA. Additionally, it stated that the company violated the Clean Air Act by introducing vehicles into commerce that have a design that differs from that relayed to the EPA and the

13 Jack Ewing, 'Ex-Volkswagen C.E.O. Charged With Fraud Over Diesel Emissions', *The New York Times* (New York, 3 May 2018).

14 Ibid.

15 Sarah Dadush, 'Identity Harm' (2018) 89 U Colo L Rev 863, 863–75 (hereafter Dadush, 'Identity Harm').

16 Ibid, 889ff.

17 Ibid, 891.

18 Ibid, 892–92.

19 Ibid, 902.

20 Ibid.

21 John C Cruden, 'Dieselgate: How the Investigation, Prosecution, and Settlement of Volkswagen's Emissions Cheating Scandal Illustrates the Need for Robust Environmental Enforcement' (2018) 36 Va Envtl LJ 118, 120 (hereafter Cruden, 'Dieselgate').

22 United States Department of Justice, 'United States Files Complaint Against Volkswagen, Audi, and Porsche for Alleged Clean Air Act Violations' (4 January 2016) <http://www.justice.gov/opa/pr/united-states-files-complaint-against-volkswagen-audi-and-porsche-alleged-clean-air-act>.

California Air Resources Board (CARB).[23] The Clean Air Act section (a)(3)(b) 'prohibits the manufacture, selling, or installation of any device that intentionally circumvents EPA emission standards by bypassing, defeating, or rendering inoperative a required element of the vehicle's emissions control system'.[24] The Act also prohibits selling vehicles that are not covered by certificates of conformity under section 203(a)(1).[25] Accordingly, it is no surprise that defeat devices are prohibited, and VW's actions clearly violated federal and state environmental laws.[26]

In addition to these actions, the US Department of Justice's Criminal Division, Fraud Section, worked with the US Federal Bureau of Investigation (FBI) and EPA Criminal Investigation Division in pursuing VW for criminal actions. This led to VW pleading guilty to three felony counts on 10 March 2017.[27] Additionally, on 3 May 2018, the former VW CEO was indicted for conspiracy and wire fraud related to the emissions violations.[28]

At the same time, the US Customs and Border Protection (CBP) investigated a claim concerning customs violations.[29] The CBP is responsible for regulating customs laws and working with other agencies on matters involving health, safety and border security.[30] VW's misrepresentations regarding thousands of vehicles entering the US violated US customs laws.[31] Accordingly, VW's guilty pleas included felony importation of vehicles while making false statements about their compliance with emissions standards.[32] VW paid a $2.8 billion criminal penalty, as well as a $1.45 billion civil penalty to settle its claims with the CBP and EPA. This was the largest civil penalty for customs violations in US history.[33]

---

23 Ibid.

24 Environmental Protection Agency, 'Laws and Regulations Related to Volkswagen Violations' <http://www.epa.gov/vw/laws-and-regulations-related-volkswagen-violations>.

25 Ibid.

26 Ibid. When the EPA finds that a significant number of vehicles are nonconforming with the articulated standards, it can order a recall of vehicles by the manufacturer.

27 United States Department of Justice, 'Volkswagen AG Pleads Guilty in Connection with Conspiracy to Cheat U.S. Emissions Tests' (10 March 2017) <http://www.justice.gov/opa/pr/volkswagen-ag-pleads-guilty-connection-conspiracy-cheat-us-emissions-tests>.

28 United States Department of Justice, 'Former CEO of Volkswagen AG Charged with Conspiracy and Wire Fraud in Diesel Emissions Scandal' (3 May 2018) <http://www.justice.gov/opa/pr/former-ceo-volkswagen-ag-charged-conspiracy-and-wire-fraud-diesel-emissions-scandal>.

29 Cruden, 'Dieselgate' (n 21) 134.

30 Customs and Border Protection, 'CBP Joins DOJ, FBI, and EPA in Announcing a Settlement Against Volkswagen as a Result of Their Scheme to Cheat U.S. Emissions Test' (12 January 2017) <http://www.cbp.gov/newsroom/spotlights/cbp-joins-doj-fbi-and-epa-announcing-settlement-against-volkswagen-result-their>.

31 Ibid.

32 Ibid.

33 Ibid.

The US Federal Trade Commission (FTC) also pursued a claim alleging unlawful deception under the FTC Act.[34] This act outlaws '[u]nfair methods of competition in or affecting commerce, and unfair or deceptive acts or practices in or affecting commerce.'[35] The FTC alleged that VW was engaged in unlawful deception of its customers by relaying to customers that the sold vehicles were environmentally friendly and conformed to emissions standards.[36] The complaint details how the company misrepresented the vehicles with respect to clean energy, as well as value.[37]

The FTC focused its claims under section 5(a) of the FTC Act because these were clearly 'deceptive acts or practices affecting commerce.'[38] Additionally, the FTC noted that VW's 'misrepresentations' included its failure to disclose material facts.[39] These claims ended with a stipulated order for a permanent injunction and monetary judgment on 28 June 2016.[40] The injunction included a ban on the advertisement, sale, or distribution of vehicles with a defeat device, and also placed a ban on VW's misrepresentations.[41] The order also hit VW financially with a $10.03 billion settlement.[42] This money was placed in a funding pool to pay consumers wronged by the company's policies.[43] The FTC settlement further required that VW allow consumers to force VW to buy back their affected vehicles or obtain free Approved Emissions Modifications if consumers wished to keep their cars.[44] The settlement also allocated compensation for individuals who had leases terminated after 28 September 2015, as well as sellers who lost money due to the dip in value after the scandal broke.[45]

34 Cruden, 'Dieselgate' (n 21) 133.

35 15 U.S.C.S. §45.

36 Cruden, 'Dieselgate' (n 21) 133.

37 *Federal Trade Commission v Volkswagen Group of America, Inc*, Case 3:16-cv-01534 at 1–13 (N.D. Cal) (29 March 2016) <http://www.ftc.gov/system/files/documents/cases/160329volkswagen_cmpt.pdf>.

38 Ibid, 13.

39 Ibid.

40 *In Re: Volkswagen 'Clean Diesel' Marketing, Sales Practices, and Products Liability Litigation*, Case 3:15-md-2672 at 1 (N.D. Cal) (28 June 2016) <http://www.ftc.gov/system/files/documents/cases/proposed_partial_stipulated_order_filed_copy_0.pdf>.

41 Ibid, 11–12.

42 Ibid, 13.

43 Ibid. Section IV of the FTC settlement order describes the monetary terms of the agreement between VW and the FTC. Section V goes on to describe an escrow account for whatever funds are needed in the case of a suit. The terms stated, in part: 'the Court enters Judgment in the amount of ten billion and thirty-three million dollars ($10,033,000,000.00) against Defendant and in favor of the FTC. Defendant shall satisfy the Judgment fully by establishing a Funding Pool in this amount, and making the payments to consumers required by Sections VII, VIII, IX, X, and XI of this Order. Defendant may use satisfaction of this Order to meet its obligations under the DOJ Consent Decree and/or the Class Action Settlement Agreement to the extent provided for in those settlements'.

44 Ibid.

45 Ibid, 25.

On the state level, every state has some form of an 'Unfair, Deceptive, or Abusive Acts or Practices' statute.[46] States may also have their own environmental laws. For example, the State of California filed a lawsuit against VW on 27 June 2016, based upon the regulatory authority of the CARB.[47] Similarly, the State of Oklahoma brought an action against VW, and entered into a settlement on 6 June 2018, for $8.5 million.[48] Oklahoma claimed that VW violated the Oklahoma Consumer Protection Act by installing software in diesel vehicles to manipulate emissions, thus engaging in false and deceptive advertising.[49] Oklahoma planned to use all settlement proceeds to help enforce Oklahoma consumer protection laws through education and mediation programs designed to protect individuals from deceptive or fraudulent practices.[50]

Beyond these government-led actions, consumers launched their own private actions.[51] These actions mainly included statutory claims focused on misrepresentation, concealment, unfair business practices, and breach of consumer protection laws such as the FTC Act.[52] For example, in a class action settlement applicable to purchases of 3-L vehicles, the court looked to the FTC settlement regarding the 2-L vehicles.[53] The court thus approved the same general remedies as that under the FTC settlement and the 2-L claims. These settlements generally allowed eligible and former lessees, and eligible and former owners of the 2-L and 3-L vehicles to force a buyback, a trade-in, or an emission modification subject to the approval of the EPA or CARB.[54] Additionally, the settlements required VW to create an Escrow Account for submitted claims.[55]

46 NCLC, 'State-by-State Summaries of State UDAP Statutes' (10 January 2009) <http://www.nclc.org/images/pdf/udap/analysis-state-summaries.pdf>.

47 Cruden, 'Dieselgate' (n 21) 133–34.

48 Alexa St John, 'Volkswagen, Oklahoma Reach $8.5M Settlement over Diesel Emissions Suit' (*Automotive News*, 8 June 2018) <http://www.autonews.com/article/20180608/OEM/180609776/volkswagen-oklahoma-reach-8-5m-settlement-over-diesel-emissions-suit> (hereafter Alexa St John, 'Volkswagen').

49 *Oklahoma v Volkswagen*, CJ-2016-3047 at 1 (6 June 2018); Alexa St John, 'Volkswagen' (n 48).

50 Jack Money 'Oklahoma, Volkswagen Settle Suit Related to Deceptive Advertising, Attorney General Announces' *The Oklahoman* (Oklahoma City, 7 June 2018) <https://newsok.com/article/5597217/oklahoma-volkswagen-settle-suit-related-to-deceptive-advertising-attorney-general-announces>.

51 Cruden, 'Dieselgate' (n 21) 129–34.

52 *In Re: Volkswagen 'Clean Diesel' Marketing, Sales Practices, and Products Liability Litigation*, WL 2212783 at 2 (N.D. Cal. 2017).

53 Ibid, 2.

54 Ibid, 5.

55 Ibid, 8. An initial funding amount will be maintained by VW, with the company being required to deposit more money each time it falls below a certain point. Unused funds at the end of the Settlement Benefit Period will revert back to VW.

These were in addition to the buy-/lease-backs or emission modifications, and millions of dollars were set aside for emissions mitigation efforts.[56]

Notably, these settlements did not clog courts throughout the nation. Instead, the Judicial Panel on Multidistrict Litigation (JPML) combined filed cases to the Northern District of California.[57] The situation clearly called for consolidation of the ever-growing universe of lawsuits in order to allow for orderly discovery and greater efficiencies.

However, this consolidation in California came with some controversy. The court noted that no party opposed centralisation, but that 28 separate transferee districts had been nominated by the various litigants. The court ultimately chose to transfer the then-pending 63 actions before the JPML (as well as the 451 potentially related actions that by this time had been filed in over 60 districts across the country) to Breyer J in part due to his experience with complex litigation.[58]

In sum, these various class and government actions generally required VW to either buy back the cars, or to fix the cars so that their emissions were within the legal limits.[59] Accordingly, these government and class actions worked in concert to provide consumers with some form of recovery.[60] In most cases, the compensation ranged from $12,500 to $44,000.[61] Nonetheless, consumers could not 'double-dip' and receive compensation for the same injury from both a class action and another lawsuit. At the same time, VW was ordered to contribute billions of dollars to advance climate mitigation efforts and zero emission cars.[62]

Although this appears to have been a victory for US consumers, it should not be overstated. VW was the world's largest automaker at the time, the fraud had been on-going for seven years, over 500,000 Americans were affected, and VW's conduct broke both consumer and environmental law. This set it up for a perfect storm of litigation.[63] Some have also questioned whether VW truly

---

56 Charles R Breyer, 'Executive Summary of Final Class Settlement Program for 3.0 Liter Engines' <http://www.cand.uscourts.gov/judges/breyer-charles-r-crb/in-re-volkswagen-clean-diesel-mdl/final-3-0-l-settlement/>.

57 *In Re: Volkswagen 'Clean Diesel' Marketing, Sales Practices, and Products Liability Litigation Transfer Order*, Case MDL 267 (4 October 2017) United States Judicial Panel on Multidistrict Litigation; see also Joseph Allen MacDougald, 'United States of America' in Marco Frigessi di Rattalma (ed), *The Dieselgate: A Legal Perspective* (Springer 2017) 88–120.

58 Cruden, 'Dieselgate' (n 21) 131.

59 Dadush, 'Identity Harm' (n 15) 863–916.

60 Edith Ramirez, 'Road Cleared for VW to Compensate Consumers' (*Federal Trade Commission*, 25 October 2016) <http://www.ftc.gov/news-events/blogs/business-blog/2016/10/road-cleared-vw-compensate-consumers>.

61 Ibid. The American consumers who were not compensated were those who had purchased cars but had resold them before the scandal broke. See Dadush, 'Identity Harm' (n 15) 900–18.

62 See Dadush, 'Identity Harm' (n 15) 900–18.

63 Dadush, 'Identity Harm' (n 15) 918–22.

learned its lesson. The first audit of VW's efforts to comply with its agreement with the US Justice Department and the State of California indicated VW's continuing lack of transparency.[64] VW was slow to change, and German prosecutors have asserted that some VW officials meddled with their investigation. Furthermore, VW-owned Audi AG also used illegal software that manipulates emissions in about 60,000 of its best-selling diesel-powered vehicles, leading to the arrest of its CEO, Rupert Stadler.[65] The former VW CEO, Martin Winterkorn, was also indicted, leading many to question VW's claims that this scandal was merely the product of a few lower-level engineers.[66]

B. SHAREHOLDER AND INVESTOR CLAIMS

When Dieselgate broke, investors began to panic as they watched VW's value plummet. Stock and bond values dropped quickly, leading to investor lawsuits.[67] The claims alleged fraud on the part of VW, and based such claims upon the US Securities Exchange Act.[68] In one action, for example, the claimants stated that VW engaged in material misrepresentations and omissions in the company's compliance with emission standards and financial management, which in turn led to declining values for their American Depository Receipts (ADRs).[69]

Related issues also led to bondholder suits in the Northern District of California.[70] One suit, which was first filed on 20 June 2016, was a class action brought by a Puerto Rican employee pension fund (Puerto Rico Government Employees and Judiciary Retirement Systems Administration) and BRS (Boston Retirement System).[71] It was part of the multi-district litigation noted above, *In re: Volkswagen 'Clean Diesel' Marketing, Sales Practices and Products Liability Litigation*.[72] Investors claimed that they purchased expensive VW bonds after reading documents that lacked information about the emissions tampering that eventually led to the Volkswagen emissions scandal.[73] The Volkswagen attorneys

---

64 William Boston, 'Report on Volkswagen's Changes Since Emissions Scandal Cites Lack of Transparency' *Wall Street Journal* (New York City, 27 August 2018) <http://www.wsj.com/articles/report-on-volkswagens-changes-since-emissions-scandal-cites-lack-of-transparency-1535374982?mod=searchresults&page=11&pos=12>.

65 Ibid.

66 Ibid.

67 *In re Volkswagen 'Clean Diesel' Mktg., Sales Practices, & Prods. Liab. Litig.*, 2672 CRB (JSC) U.S. Dist. 1109, 798–99 (N.D. Cal. 4 January 2017).

68 Ibid, 803–04.

69 Ibid, 799.

70 Dorothy Atkins, 'VW, Bondholders Spar Over Axing the Emissions Fraud Suit' (*LAW 360*, 3 August 2018) <http://www.law360.com/articles/1069951> (hereafter Atkins, 'Bondholders Spar').

71 *BRS v Volkswagen AG et al.*, 3:15-MD-02672WESTLAW (7 August 2018).

72 Atkins, 'Bondholders Spar' (n 70).

73 Ibid.

argued that the bondholders have not sufficiently shown that they relied upon bond-offering documents in making the investments, and that since bondholders are not owed a fiduciary duty, they have no legal basis for the suit.[74] In response, the plaintiffs have argued that an investment firm purchased the bond for the fund and was required to read the offering.[75] The court has stayed the discovery process, and there has been no final determination on this action as of the time this chapter was written.[76]

C. CONSEQUENCES AND COMPLIANCE

It is difficult to gather all the statistics and data regarding the overall impact and consequences of the various actions that took place in the US with respect to Dieselgate. According to the independent claims supervisor who administered claims with the consolidated cases in California, 482,632 consumers had submitted claims for VW 2-Liter vehicles alone.[77] Of those, 373,623 owners and lessees resolved their disputes in the consolidated cases.[78] This resulted in a total of $7.8 billion that VW paid to consumers, while VW either removed from commerce or properly modified approximately 93.4 per cent of these subject 2-Liter vehicles by the end of 2018.[79]

Additional reports were filed regarding the 3-Liter VW vehicles. As of 13 March 2019, 70,839 3-Liter VW consumers had submitted claims in the consolidated litigation and 64,885 had accepted settlement offers, totalling $1.03 billion.[80] Of the 17,123 completed claims for 3-Liter Generation One vehicles, 16,002 consumers elected a buyback or trade-in remedy.[81] In addition, 45,045 consumers with 3-Liter Generation Two vehicles had successfully completed their vehicle modifications, which was their limited remedy under the settlement.[82] Moreover, as of the March 2019 report, VW either removed

74 Ibid.

75 Ibid.

76 Ibid; see also Nicholas Iovino, 'Volkswagen Can't Dodge Securities Class Action' (*Courthouse News Service*, 7 September 2018) <http://www.courthousenews.com/volkswagen-cant-dodge-securities-class-action/>.

77 Ankura Consulting Group, 'Report of independent claims supervisor on Volkswagen's progress and compliance related to 2.0 liter resolution agreements entered October 25, 2016' (26 November 2018) 5 <http://www.cand.uscourts.gov/crb/vwmdl/claims-reports>.

78 Ibid.

79 Ibid, 6. The terms of the settlement called for 85 per cent to have been removed or modified by 1 May 2018.

80 Ankura Consulting Group, 'Report of independent claims supervisor on Volkswagen's progress and compliance related to 2.0 liter resolution agreements entered May 17, 2017' (13 March 2019) 4 <http://www.cand.uscourts.gov/crb/vwmdl/claims-reports>.

81 Ibid.

82 Ibid.

from commerce or properly modified approximately 90 percent of all subject 3.0-Litre Vehicles (Generation One and Two).[83] In totality, this gives a sense of compliance in that the court administrator has been following up and publishing these reports.

Indeed, the concert of claims was all part of a coordinated effort in the US.[84] Furthermore, the EPA settlement established serious financial penalties for failure to comply.[85] If VW failed to meet set deadlines for compliance, it would have to pay millions of dollars in fines per each deadline missed.[86] At the same time, 'the total $2.7 billion funding for the mitigation trust fund is intended to fully mitigate the total, lifetime excess NOx emissions from the 2.0 liter vehicles.'[87] Furthermore, as noted above, $225 million was allocated to the mitigation trust through the 3.0-Litre VW settlement, and VW was required to invest $2 billion 'toward improving infrastructure, access and education to support and advance zero emission vehicles'.[88]

The EPA is monitoring VW's compliance.[89] For example, the personnel who test VW vehicles for emissions compliance must be independent from those who design their vehicles.[90] VW has also introduced a steering committee to monitor compliance with the Clean Air Act.[91] Strict procedures have now been implemented to ensure VW's honesty in emissions testing and a whistleblower system has been established to prevent future violations.[92]

Meanwhile, the FTC settlement also aims to ensure compliance.[93] It specifically provides for additional money damages to compensate consumers for the harm caused by VW's deceptive advertising.[94] The FTC also secured injunctive relief to forbid devices that could be used to falsify emissions testing and to prohibit VW from making deceptive misrepresentations about their vehicles' environmental benefits.[95] The settlements outline a number of

---

83 Ibid, 5. These numbers are similarly in excess of the settlement's 85 percent minimum.

84 Nick Conger and Julia Valentine, 'Reference News Release: Volkswagen to Spend Up to $14.7 Billion to Settle Allegations of Cheating Emissions Tests and Deceiving Customers on 2.0 Liter Diesel Vehicles' (*EPA*, 2017) <http://www.epa.gov/enforcement/reference-news-release-volkswagen-spend-147-billion-settle-allegations-cheating> (hereafter Conger, 'News Release').

85 Ibid.

86 Ibid.

87 Environmental Protection Agency, 'Volkswagen Clean Air Act Civil Settlement' <http://www.epa.gov/enforcement/volkswagen-clean-air-act-civil-settlement> (hereafter EPA, 'Clean Air Act').

88 Conger, 'News Release' (n 84).

89 EPA, 'Clean Air Act' (n 87).

90 Ibid.

91 Ibid.

92 Ibid.

93 Ibid.

94 Ibid.

95 Ibid.

requirements related to claims processing, including the implementation and maintenance of a website for consumers to learn about and submit claims for relief.[96]

Some also question the large awards and ask whether they are punitive in nature. For example, in one of the VW cases, the attorney fees equalled nearly US$1 million while the compensatory recovery was less than US$50,000, leading VW to challenge the award as violating the Due Process Clauses of the United States and Oklahoma Constitutions.[97] The court rejected this argument, explaining that while it is true that punitive damages will be limited where they are found to be so exorbitant that they deprive a person of 'life, liberty, or property without due process of law', mere attorney fee awards that are compensatory in nature are not subject to these constraints.[98] The attorney fees in this case were considered compensatory rather than punitive in nature.[99]

In contrast to attorney fee awards, punitive damages are meant to be punitive. Nonetheless, they are also subject to limits, as articulated in *BMW of North America, Inc v Gore.*[100] In that case, the US Supreme Court set out guideposts for determining when punitive damages awards violate Constitutional due process. A court will consider: (1) the degree of reprehensibility of the defendant's conduct, (2) the disparity between the harm or potential harm suffered by the plaintiff and the punitive damages award, and (3) the difference between the punitive damages award and the civil penalties authorised or imposed in comparable cases.[101]

Accordingly, punitive damages assessed in VW cases would be scrutinised from this vantage point. In one of the VW cases, for example, the court noted how punitive damages would be appropriate, within reason. Plaintiffs alleged that VW represented that its TDI diesel-engine cars were environmentally friendly, when in fact VW knew that the cars utilised software to evade emissions testing and emitted nitrogen oxides at levels far exceeding the legal limits. Accordingly, the court found that punitive damages would be proper in VW cases.[102] Nonetheless, under the consolidated litigation, most damages were assessed for specific components of the redress: buy-backs, modifications, damage mitigation, compliance, etc.

---

96 United States District Court Northern District of California San Francisco Division, 'Order Entering the Federal Trade Commission's Amended Second Partial Stipulated Order for Permanent Injunction and Monetary Judgment' (17 May 2017) 45 <http://www.cand.uscourts.gov/crb/vwmdl>.

97 *Hess v Volkswagen Group of America, Inc*, 398 P.3d 27, 27–31 (Ok. App. 2017).

98 Ibid, 30–34.

99 *Action Marine, Inc v Cont'l Carbon Inc*, 481 F.3d 1302, 1321 (11th Cir. 2007).

100 *BMW of North America, Inc v Gore.*, 517 U.S. 559, 560–70 (1996).

101 Ibid, 574–76.

102 *In re Volkswagen 'Clean Diesel' Marketing, Sales Practices, and Products Liability Litigation*, WL 957578 (N.D. Cal. 27 February 2019) (slip copy).

III. PRIMARY PROCESSES FOR PURSUING CONSUMER MASS CLAIMS

A. GOVERNMENT ACTIONS BASED ON STATUTORY CLAIMS

As the VW case illustrates, there are several laws in the US that may apply in deceptive practices cases. First, there are the various criminal actions that the government may launch against a company violating laws such as the Clean Air Act and criminal fraud statutes.[103] However, when it comes to seeking redress for consumers, civil actions launched by federal agencies like the FTC are paramount. For example, the FTC Act protects consumers from 'unfair methods of competition in or affecting commerce, and unfair or deceptive acts or practices in or affecting commerce'.[104] A deceptive act includes 'a representation, omission, or practice that [is] likely to mislead a consumer acting reasonably in the circumstances, to the consumer's detriment'.[105] This description fits perfectly in the VW case.

Other laws address illegal profits skimming, which occurs when companies do not disclose their full income on tax returns.[106] Additionally, US consumers may use the Magnuson-Moss Act for breach of warranty claims.[107] Under that Act, there is an implied warranty of merchantability, and companies must follow clear rules to disclaim or limit the warranty.[108] In the case of VW, consumers argued that VW did not adequately label its vehicles, and the vehicles did not 'pass without objection in the trade as designed, manufactured, and marketed'.[109] At the state level, consumers may also rely on their state 'Unfair, Deceptive, or Abusive Acts or Practices' statutes, as noted above.[110]

---

103 Environmental Protection Agency, 'Laws and Regulations Related to Volkswagen Violations' <http://www.epa.gov/vw/learn-about-volkswagen-violations> and <http://www.epa.gov/vw/laws-and-regulations-related-volkswagen-violations>.

104 15 U.S.C.S. §45 (PL 115–230, approved 2 August 2018).

105 *Sw. Sunsites v FTC*, 785 F.2d 1431, 1435 (9th Cir. 1986).

106 Department of Justice, 'Georgia Couple Sentenced to Prison for Tax Fraud' (7 October 2015) <http://www.justice.gov/opa/pr/georgia-couple-sentenced-prison-tax-fraud>. A federal bill was introduced, but not enacted, that would have focused upon skimming profits, the Equity Skimming Prevention Act. Equity Skimming Prevention Act, 1994 Bill Tracking s 2462, 103 Bill Tracking s 2462, 1994 Bill Tracking s 2462.

107 *David Doebler v Volkswagen Group of America, Inc*, 1:15-cv-23753-PCH (7 October 2015) <http://www.truthinadvertising.org/wp-content/uploads/2015/10/Doebler-v-Volkswagen-complaint.pdf>.

108 Ibid, 15.

109 Ibid.

110 NCLC, 'State-by-State Summaries of State UDAP Statutes' (10 January 2009) <http://www.nclc.org/images/pdf/udap/analysis-state-summaries.pdf>.

In some situations, state Attorneys General also may bring suits on behalf of the residents of their states.[111] These actions, referred to as *parens patriae* suits, are akin to private class actions in that they allow for injunctions, civil penalties, and public compensation.[112] At the same time, state Attorneys General may join together for these lawsuits.[113] This can be problematic in some cases.[114] For example, there may be a battle among Attorneys General to capture the spotlight and appear as the 'champion' in the action, which can thwart progress toward remedies.[115] In addition, harmed consumers may end up with lesser remedies, especially those from less populous or less wealthy states that lack bargaining power in comparison with large, prosperous states.[116]

Nonetheless, it is important to note that government actions do not usually take the place of private class actions in the US. Instead, government enforcement actions may simply provide for settlements that set the stage for consumers to obtain redress. This is demonstrated above with respect to the EPA and FTC actions paving the way for consumer redress. Moreover, as the VW case exemplifies, multiple actions may coexist in the US. This is true for consumer and governmental actions, allowing companies like VW to get hit from many angles.

For example, in *United States v Kordel*, the court held that a governmental agency does not have to choose one course of proceedings. In other words, an agency is free to bring both civil and criminal proceedings at a single point in time.[117] Accordingly, it was appropriate for the EPA to seek both criminal and civil penalties against VW concurrently. The Ninth Circuit similarly held that simultaneous criminal and civil investigations did not violate a defendant's Fifth Amendment protections against double jeopardy.[118] Moreover, government and citizen lawsuits may occur in concert, again as seen in the VW case.

---

111 Elysa Dishman, 'Class Action Squared: Multistate Actions and Agency Dilemmas' (19 September 2018) BYU Law Research Paper 18–21 <https://papers.ssrn.com/sol3/papers.cfm?abstract_id=3252149>.

112 Ibid, 8–12.

113 Ibid, 15.

114 Ibid, 22.

115 Ibid, 24.

116 Ibid, 53. These actions may also raise separation of powers issues when a state essentially 'borrows' law of another state by joining forces. For example, one state with weak data protection laws may nonetheless join with other states that have stronger data protection laws, and effectively borrow their enforcement authority by fully sharing in the final settlement.

117 *United States v Kordel*, 397 U.S. 1, 11–13 (1970).

118 *United States v Stringer*, 535 F.3d 929, 942 (9th Cir. 2008). The US Supreme Court denied certiorari, leaving the Ninth Circuit Court's decision standing. See also, *Stringer v United States*, 555 U.S. 1049 (2008).

B. SHAREHOLDER DERIVATIVE ACTIONS

Shareholder derivative actions allow a shareholder to step into the shoes of the corporation and sue company officers/directors over losses due to breach of fiduciary duty.[119] In order to step into the shoes of the corporation, however, a shareholder is first required to request that the officers take an action, or else plead facts that show why such a demand would be futile.[120] Derivative lawsuits are often unhelpful in that the business judgment rule protects most decisions by corporate officers[121] and monetary relief belongs to the corporation.[122] Accordingly, most harmed shareholders in the VW case chose to proceed in a class action where they could recover their losses.

For example, Arkansas State Highway Employees' Retirement System (ASHERS) and the Miami Police Relief and Pension Fund (Miami Police) led a class action shareholder lawsuit against VW. The shareholders alleged extensive fraud and securities violations against VW, several subsidiaries, and, Winterkorn and Diess (individually), connected to the sale and purchase of ADRs like those noted above.[123] To support their claims, the plaintiffs relied on the Securities Exchange Act[124] and rule 10b-5.[125] Section 10(b) states that it is unlawful:

> To use or employ, in connection with the purchase or sale of any security registered on a national securities exchange or any security not so registered, or any securities-based swap agreement any manipulative or deceptive device or contrivance in contravention of such rules and regulations as the Commission may prescribe as necessary or appropriate in the public interest or for the protection of investors.[126]

Similarly, rule 10b-5 prohibits a wide range of deceitful acts or fraud in a securities sale.[127]

The plaintiffs also alleged that VW, Winterkorn and Diess caused the subsidiaries to violate section 10(b) and rule 10b-5 by asserting power and

---

119 See, e.g. *Meyer v Fleming*, 327 U.S. 161, 167 (1946) (describing derivative suits as remedies when management uses 'fraud, neglect of duty, or other cause' to ignore corporate duties); *Ross v Bernhard*, 396 U.S. 531, 534 (1970) (stating that derivative suits are remedies for possible abuse by corporate directors and officers).

120 See Fed. R. Civ. P. 23.1(b)(3).

121 Ann M Scarlett, 'Imitation or Improvement? The Evolution of Shareholder Derivative Litigation in the United States, United Kingdom, Canada, and Australia' (2011) 28 Ariz J Int'l & Comp L 569, 578–79.

122 Ibid, 576.

123 *In re: Volkswagen 'Clean Diesel' Marketing, Sales Practices, and Products Liability Litigation*, 2672 CRB (JSC)WL 2956503 (N.D. Cal. 2016) (hereafter Consolidated Securities Class Action Complaint).

124 15 U.S.C. §78j(b).

125 17 C.F.R. §240.10b-5.

126 15 U.S.C. §78j(b).

127 17 C.F.R. §240.10b-5.

control over them through misleading statements and omissions, and other deceitful conduct.[128] To support this count, the plaintiffs relied on section 20(a) of the Securities Exchange Act.[129]

Section 20(a) states that,

> Every person who, directly or indirectly, controls any person liable under any provision of this chapter or of any rule or regulation thereunder shall also be liable jointly and severally with and to the same extent as such controlled person to any person to whom such controlled person is liable (including to the Commission in any action brought under paragraph (1) or (3) of section 78u(d) of this title), unless the controlling person acted in good faith and did not directly or indirectly induce the act or acts constituting the violation or cause of action.[130]

In August 2018, the parties in this particular case agreed to a US$48 million settlement, which was approved by the court in October.[131]

C. CLASS ACTIONS

Although some view class actions as a recent phenomenon, class actions in the form of 'bills of peace' originated in old common law.[132] In essence, they allowed a representative to bring or defend a suit on behalf of an entire group of individuals.[133] In modern US law, class actions have been incorporated in the larger procedural scheme under the Federal Rules of Civil Procedure (FRCP). Specifically, FRCP 23 formalises the procedure for the formation of class actions.[134] Furthermore, the FRCP was amended in 1966 to shift the procedure from 'opt-out' to an 'opt-in' default, meaning that individuals now must opt out of a class action to avoid being a member.[135] At the same time, FRCP rule 23(c)(2) places the burden on the petitioner to bear the cost of the notice for the class action.[136]

The class action rules also provide for a 'common funding mechanism.'[137] This requires all beneficiaries of a class action to contribute to a common fund

128 See Consolidated Securities Class Action Complaint (n 123) 466–78.
129 15 U.S.C. §78t(a).
130 15 U.S.C. §78t(a).
131 Nicholas Iovino, 'Volkswagen Settles US Investor Suit for $48 Million' *Courthouse News* (Pasadena, 28 August 2018).
132 Thomas D Rowe Jr, 'A Distant Mirror: The Bill of Peace in Early American Mass Torts and Its Implications for Modern Class Actions' (1997) 39 ACJ 712.
133 Ibid.
134 Fed. R. Civ. P 23.
135 Nyal D Deems, 'The Cy Pres Solution to the Damage Distribution Problems of Mass Class Actions' (1974–75) 9 Ga L Rev 893.
136 Fed R Civ P 23 (c)(2).
137 Fed R Civ P 23 (h) (2003 amend Comm N).

for maintaining a class action.[138] Nonetheless, class action rules also allow for a shift in the usual US rule requiring parties to pay their own legal fees.[139] This means that state or federal laws may permit plaintiffs in class actions to recover attorney fees from the defendant if their suit is successful.[140] However, defendants have no analogous right if their defence is successful, and these rules differ depending on the basis of the underlying claims.[141] Furthermore, law firms often take class actions on a contingency basis, meaning that attorneys only get paid from the amount that they recover on behalf of the class members.

Class actions in the US also benefit from rules requiring courts to give full faith and credit to the judgments of other states under the US Constitution.[142] Additionally, federal courts also must give state judgments full faith and credit.[143] Nonetheless, courts in different states may not always have to abide by evidentiary rulings that conflict with their laws.[144] There may also be different nuances among states, and different judges may view class actions differently.

D. CAUTION ON CONTRACTUALLY REQUIRED ARBITRATION IN THE US

Any discussion of class actions in the US must include a caution on the power of arbitration clauses. Class actions are arguably disappearing in the U.S. due to the proliferation of arbitration clauses with class relief waivers.[145] Many businesses insist upon class action waivers in all of their consumer contracts to save litigation costs and hide claims from the public eye.[146] Indeed, VW sought to preclude consumers' claims based on arbitration clauses in their purchase agreements with the dealerships.[147] The problem for VW, however, was that it was not a party to the dealership agreements containing the arbitration clauses.

138 Ibid.

139 Janet Cooper Alexander, 'An Introduction to Class Action Procedure in the United States' (Debates over Group Litigation in Comparative Perspective Conference, Geneva, 21–22 July 2000) <https://law.duke.edu/grouplit/papers/classactionalexander.pdf>.

140 Ibid.

141 Ibid.

142 *V.L. v E.L.*, 136 S. Ct. 1017, 194 L.Ed.2d 92 (2016).

143 *Kremer v Chem. Constr. Corp*, 456 U.S. 461 (1982).

144 *Baker v GMC*, 522 U.S. 222, 241 (1998). In *Baker v GMC*, the Supreme Court rejected the claim that 'full faith and credit' must be granted to another state's evidentiary ruling that conflicts with a given state's laws.

145 Brian T Fitzpatrick, 'The End of Class Actions?' (2015) 57 ACJ 161.

146 Ibid, 164–97.

147 *Robinson v New Jersey Transit Rail Operations, Inc*, Civil Action 2:14 Civ. 2679 (D.N.J. 2017) (denying enforcement of an arbitration clause to preclude a lawsuit against VW).

Nonetheless, VW would have been able to preclude class actions launched by consumers who were parties to contracts with arbitration clauses.[148]

The presence of arbitration clauses is important because unlike the EU, the US insists on strict enforcement of pre-dispute arbitration clauses under the Federal Arbitration Act (FAA).[149] The US has been exceptional in its enforcement of consumer arbitration, even when statutory claims are at stake.[150] Courts in the US have uniformly held that arbitration is not subject to constitutional due process requirements, and construe arbitration clauses broadly to cover tort and statutory claims regardless of whether a clause gives express notice of such coverage.[151] Additionally, arbitrators in the US rarely order class arbitration in the wake of the US Supreme Court's ruling in *Stolt-Nielsen S.A. v Animalfeeds Int'l Corp.*[152] Furthermore, many companies use arbitration clauses that expressly preclude any class relief.[153] This has gained popularity in light of Supreme Court jurisprudence.[154]

In contrast to the FAA, Annex 1[q] of the E.U. Directive 13/93 makes pre-dispute arbitration clauses 'prima facie' invalid.[155] Furthermore, the EU ADR Directive states that nationally certified ADR/ODR entities cannot use pre-dispute arbitration clauses and allows Member States to deny certification of arbitration schemes altogether, as seen in Germany.[156] Additionally, the European Court of Justice has ruled in *Mostaza Claro v Centro Movil Milenium* that courts should examine arbitration clauses in consumer contracts to ensure fairness.[157] This contrasting law on arbitration is problematic, especially with

148 Beasley Allen, 'Judge Denies VW Arbitration Bid in Engine Defect Suit' (*Jere Beasly Report*, 9 June 2017) <http://www.jerebeasleyreport.com/2017/06/judge-denies-vw-arbitration-bid-engine-defect-suit/>.

149 *AT&T Mobility, L.L.C. v Concepcion*, 131 S. Ct. 1740, 1743–56 (2011); *Stolt-Nielsen S.A. v AnimalFeeds Int'l Corp*, 130 S. Ct. 1758 (2010); *Rent-A-Ctr, W., Inc v Jackson*, 130 S. Ct. 2772, 2777–80 (2010).

150 See, *Rodriguez de Quijas v Shearson/Am. Express, Inc*, 490 U.S. 477, 485–86 (1989) (overruling prior opinion to hold securities claims arbitrable); *Green Tree Fin. Corp v Randolph*, 531 U.S. 79, 89–92 (2000) (finding TILA claims may be subject to binding arbitration under the FAA).

151 See, *Gilmer v Interstate/Johnson Lane Corp*, 500 U.S. 20, 624–26 (1991) (finding statutory age discrimination statute could be subject to arbitration).

152 *Stolt-Nielsen S.A. v AnimalFeeds Int'l Corp*, 130 S. Ct. 1758 (2010).

153 Peter B Rutledge and Christopher R Drahozal, 'Contract and Choice' [2013] B Y U L Rev 1, 38 ('Of the arbitration clauses in the sample [of credit card agreements], forty-four of forty-seven clauses (or 93.6%) (covering 99.9% of the credit card loans outstanding) waived any right to class arbitration.').

154 *AT&T Mobility, L.L.C. v Concepcion*, 131 S. Ct. 1740, 1743–56 (2011).

155 Council Directive 93/13/EEC of 5 April 1993 on unfair terms in consumer contracts [1993] OJ L95/34.

156 Directive 2013/11/EU of the European Parliament and of the Council of 21 May 2013 on alternative dispute resolution for consumer disputes and amending Regulation (EC) 2006/2004 and Directive 2009/22/EC Directive on consumer ADR [2013] OJ L165/63.

157 ECJ, C-168/05 *Elisa María Mostaza Claro v Centro Móvil Milenium SL* [26 October 2006] ECR 2006 I-10421.

respect to international consumer contracts.[158] Moreover, consumers often forego claims rather than file individual arbitration claims.[159]

Legal economists may argue that the curtailment of legal action is beneficial to the extent that it generates cost savings that companies may pass on to consumers through lower prices and better products and services.[160] However, public action is often necessary to uncover product defects, initiate recalls, and inform other consumers about systemic or firm-specific problems. Accordingly, class actions play an important role in providing information about consumer issues. They also allow individuals to assert small dollar claims in an economical manner, thereby making vindication of their rights feasible in such consumer cases.[161]

That is not to say that class actions are ideal.[162] Some have criticised class actions for failing to provide just compensation. Additionally, complex class certification rules have hindered the efficiency and deterrence goals of class actions.[163] At the same time, some have noted that attorney's fees and litigation costs may deplete class awards and settlements, leaving the injured consumers with very little redress.[164] Accordingly, the following section invites consideration of Online Dispute Resolution (ODR) coupled with a 'trip wire' for mass claims to assist consumers in quickly obtaining remedies for deceptive practices such as those seen in the VW case.

IV. USING TECHNOLOGY TO ADDRESS CONSUMER DECEPTION

Technology provides new means for advancing consumer protection by assisting with resolution of consumer deception claims in an efficient and fair manner. Specifically, ODR could expand access to remedies for consumer

---

158 Glover, 'Disappearing Claims and Erosion' (n 4). With the growth of mandatory arbitration clauses, businesses have gained quasi-lawmaking powers that significantly decrease the compensatory and public deterrent objectives of consumer protection laws.

159 Aaron Blumenthall, 'Circumventing Concepcion: Conceptualizing Innovative Strategies to Ensure the Enforcement of Consumer Protection Laws in the Age of the Inviolable Class Action Waiver' (2015) 103 CLR 699, 700–14.

160 See Stephen J Ware, 'The Case for Enforcing Adhesive Arbitration Agreements – with Particular Consideration of Class Actions and Arbitration Fees' (2006) 5 Journal of American Arbitration 251, 254–64, 292.

161 See Amy J Schmitz, 'Curing Consumers' Warranty Woes through Regulated Arbitration' (2008) 23 Ohio St J on Disp Resol 627, 635–45 (discussing functions of class actions).

162 Linda S Mullenix, 'Ending Class Actions as We Know Them: Rethinking the American Class Action' (2014) 64 Emory L J 399.

163 Ibid, 419–430.

164 George Rutherglen, 'Wal-Mart, AT&T Mobility, and the Decline of the Deterrent Class Action' (2012) 98 Va L Rev In Brief 24, 25–27.

deception claims. This section merely aims to spark conversation, as greater detail regarding such ODR is provided in other publications.[165]

ODR includes use of technology and computer-mediated communication (CMC) to facilitate negotiation, mediation, arbitration and other means of dispute resolution. The prime example of private ODR in the US is eBay's Resolution Center, which processes consumer claims related to website purchases free of charge.[166] For example, when a buyer does not receive an item or the item is not as promised on eBay, the buyer has the right to file an online complaint within 30 days after the latest estimated delivery date. The seller then has three business days to respond in the Resolution Center.[167] If the seller does not respond or provide an adequate remedy, the buyer may ask eBay to assign an ODR neutral to arbitrate.[168] If necessary, eBay may enforce ODR determinations via PayPal, eBay's payment system provider, by setting aside a seller's funds.[169]

At the same time, the EU has incentivised development of ODR through its Regulation, aiming to create an ODR platform, or single point of entry, for consumers and traders seeking to resolve disputes regarding online transactions through ADR/ODR.[170] Although the ADR Directive suggests that consumers' access to ADR/ODR should be free or low cost, it does not specify who will fund developing and maintaining the platform or related services.[171] Instead, it encourages private funding and leaves utilisation of public funds to Member States' discretion.[172]

With this backdrop in the EU and growing ODR in the US and elsewhere, it seems that international efforts could lead to development of a unified ODR system for mass consumer complaints. Government agencies could work together to set up a portal that allows consumers to file claims for free or for a

---

165 See Amy J Schmitz and Colin Rule, *The New Handshake: Online Dispute Resolution and the Future of Consumer Protection* (American Bar Association Section on Dispute Resolution 2017).

166 Colin Rule, 'Making Peace on eBay: Resolving Disputes in the World's Largest Marketplace' [Fall 2008] ACResolution: The Quarterly Magazine of the Association for Conflict Resolution 1–10 (hereafter Rule, 'Making Peace').

167 EBAY, 'Ebay Money Back Guarantee' <http://pages.ebay.com/help/policies/money-back-guarantee.html>.

168 Ibid.

169 Ibid (also giving both parties 30 days to appeal any determinations).

170 European Parliament and Council Regulation (EU) 524/2013 of 21 May 2013 on Online Dispute Resolution for Consumer Disputes [2013] OJ L165/2, recital 18.

171 Directive 2013/11/EU of the European Parliament and of the Council of 21 May 2013 on alternative dispute resolution for consumer disputes and amending Regulation (EC) 2006/2004 and Directive 2009/22/EC (Directive on consumer ADR) [2013] OJ L165/67, recital 41.

172 European Parliament and Council Directive 2013/11/EU of 21 May 2013 on alternative dispute resolution for consumer disputes and amending Regulation (EC) 2006/2004 and Directive 2009/22/EC (Directive on consumer ADR) [2013] OJ L165/68, recital 46.

very low fee.[173] Government regulators such as the Consumer Financial Protection Bureau (CFPB) in the US could also work with their international counterparts to educate the public about this ODR platform, and establish a government-approved trustmark which companies could post if they abide by, and perhaps contribute a small fee toward the maintenance of, this ODR platform.[174]

Of course, adopting ODR requires time and money in creating and maintaining these systems. Implementing ODR is an investment, and it may take time before companies see positive returns for abiding by ODR. For example, it took some time before eBay saw the financial benefits of its investment in ODR.[175] Nonetheless, contextually tailored systems that 'fit the forum to the fuss' pay off, especially when they employ simple and streamlined procedures. Furthermore, companies would benefit from an internationally accepted trustmark system for ODR because it would help consumers feel comfortable purchasing from companies who provide ethical and fair ODR.[176]

In order to gain the right to post the trustmark, companies would have to abide by a system that is accessible and fair. This means that the system would allow consumers to use standard forms, as well as real-time and asynchronous communications for maximum convenience and efficiency. Translation programs also allow for multilingual processes involving parties from varied countries and cultures. ODR also may help empower marginalised groups who fear stereotypes or biases based on appearance, voice or accent.[177]

That does not mean that ODR is the answer for everyone and all disputes. In-person remedy systems must remain accessible, and reforms should address the 'digital divide' in terms of consumers' differential access to and comfort with the internet.[178] Policymakers and businesses must consider ways to expand

---

173 Consumer Financial Protection Bureau, 'Arbitration Study: Report to Congress, pursuant to Dodd-Frank Wall Street Reform and Consumer Protection Act §1028(a)' (March 2015) <http://files.consumerfinance.gov/f/201503_cfpb_arbitration-study-report-to-congress-2015.pdf>.

174 This could mimic the BBB's trustmark program.

175 Rule, 'Making Peace' (n 166) 1–10; Louis F Del Duca, Colin Rule and Kathryn Rimpfel, 'eBay's De Facto Low Value High Volume Resolution Process: Lessons and Best Practices for ODR Systems Designers' (2014) 6 YB on Arbitration and Mediation 204.

176 Amy J Schmitz, 'There's an "App" for That: Developing Online Dispute Resolution to Empower Economic Development' (2018) 32 Notre Dame J L Ethics & Pub Pol'y 1–45 (hereafter Schmitz, 'There's an "App" for That'); republished in Russian with permission at Эми Дж. Шмитц «Для этого есть приложение!» // Посредничество и примирение. Медиация и право. 2018. №1-2 (45). С. 6–51.

177 See ibid, 125–26.

178 US Census Bureau, 'Computer and Internet Use in the United States; Current Population Survey Reports' (Thom File P20-568, 2012) 1.

free or low-cost internet access for vulnerable groups.[179] They also should adopt educational access programs to assist older adults and those with lower education in adopting and using the internet for dispute resolution.

Privacy and security are also essential for ethical ODR.[180] The EU has recognised the importance of such ethical baselines in its ADR Directive and ODR Regulation in that it requires the Commission to publish a list of 'competent [ADR] authorities' in the Member States, and the states shall ensure that ADR entities make publicly available clear and easily understandable information on their compliance with Directive standards – which include attention to privacy and security.[181] Furthermore, this was a central issue addressed in the United Nations Commission on International Trade Law (UNCITRAL) Working Group III, which showed momentum for creating an international ODR portal for cross-border e-commerce, although it ultimately failed to provide consensus.[182]

Accordingly, it seems that an ODR platform dedicated to consumer deception claims may gain traction because it is narrowly focused on one key issue – consumer deception. Furthermore, it is an area that transcends boundaries and requires international cooperation to protect similarly situated individuals throughout the world. Imagine if there were such an ODR portal in the VW case. Consumers throughout the world would have been able to obtain redress more quickly, and on equal playing fields. And regulators near and far would have been able to coordinate their efforts in detecting and shutting down deceptive behaviour.

Again, however, these are merely initial ideas, and this is not a full distillation of ideas for such a process.[183] This is meant to simply plant the seed for international consideration. Further exploration will be developed elsewhere.[184]

---

179 See, e.g. Rebecca R Ruiz, 'F.C.C. Chief Seeks Broadband Plan to Aid the Poor' *The N.Y. Times* (New York City, 28 May 2015) <http://www.nytimes.com/2015/05/28/business/fcc-chief-seeks-broadband-plan-to-aid-the-poor.html> (discussing plan to expand access to the internet for the poor).

180 Ibid.

181 European Parliament and Council Directive 2013/11/EU of 21 May 2013 on alternative dispute resolution for consumer disputes and amending Regulation (EC) 2006/2004 and Directive 2009/22/EC (Directive on consumer ADR) [2013] OJ L165/73 art 7, 1(b).

182 UN Commission on International Trade Law Working Group III, 'Online Dispute Resolution for Cross-Border Electronic Commerce Transactions: Draft Outcome' (2015, U.N. Doc. A/CN.9/WG.III/WP.140).

183 Given space limitations, these ideas will be distilled in other publications.

184 Of course, these are simply initial thoughts and there are many details for later determination. See, e.g. Amy J Schmitz and Colin Rule, *The New Handshake: Online Dispute Resolution and the Future of Consumer Protection* (American Bar Association Section on Dispute Resolution 2017) (proposing an online remedy system to expand consumers' access to remedies and to revive corporate responsibility in consumer contracting) (hereafter Schmitz and Rule, *The New Handshake*). See also, Amy J Schmitz, *Addressing the Class Claim Conundrum with Online Dispute Resolution (ODR)*, [forthcoming 2020] J. of Dispute Resolution.

V. CONCLUSION

The VW case provides a nice case study for exploration of consumer rights with respect to deceptive practices. In the US alone, there were a myriad of government, class, and private claims against VW to obtain redress and punish VW for its manipulations of emissions on its vehicles. Indeed, VW was hit from every angle in the US, and some may see that as effective redress. Certainly, class actions and allowance for consolidated litigation assisted with the effectiveness of these processes because it is rarely worth the cost and stress to assert claims individually.

Nonetheless, class actions have their own drawbacks, and are not ideal in all cases. Pre-dispute arbitration clauses often cut off access to class relief in the US, and consumers sometimes complain that class attorneys are the real winners due to high fees. Moreover, deception claims often cross borders and it seems there should be coordinated efforts to stop deception and provide even redress for consumers. To that end, this chapter concludes by inviting consideration of an international ODR portal for deception claims. Of course, these are ideas that need further development, but ultimately, this would benefit regulators, consumers and companies who abide by consumer protections.[185]

[185] This portal could be developed along the lines discussed by UNCITRAL Working Group III and this author's prior work in Schmitz and Rule, *The New Handshake* (n 184). See also Schmitz, 'Expanding Access' (n 10); Amy J Schmitz, 'A Blueprint for Online Dispute Resolution System Design' (2018) 21 No 7 J Internet L 3–11; Schmitz, 'There's an "App" for That' (n 176).

PART III

THE SUPRANATIONAL PERSPECTIVE

ENFORCING CONSUMER LAW IN EUROPE AND BEYOND

Similarities and Differences

Tanja DOMEJ* and Patrick HONEGGER-MÜNTENER**

I. INTRODUCTION

The diesel emissions scandal presents many facets, even if one looks at it only from the perspective of consumer law and its enforcement. Obviously, the perspective of consumers, particularly those who purchased the manipulated cars, is not the only relevant one. There is a complex relationship between the

* Tanja Domej, Dr., Professor, University of Zurich, Faculty of Law, Chair in Civil Procedure, Private Law, Private International Law, and Comparative Law.
** Patrick Honegger-Müntener, MLaw, Academic Assistant, University of Zurich, Faculty of Law, Chair in Civil Procedure, Private Law, Private International Law, and Comparative Law.

interests of car buyers on the one hand and the interests of public health and the environment on the other. Measures taken by environmental law authorities are not necessarily beneficial for car buyers; and while some car buyers may be outraged that their car is not as environmentally friendly as they thought it would be, others may be more concerned about resale chances or about potential driving bans. The perspective of a sufferer from asthma or an eco-activist might be completely different again.

As regards false representations about car emissions, such behaviour can potentially be addressed from different angles. Besides consumer law and unfair competition law, rules of environmental law that were not designed for the purpose of consumer protection can also come into play. As regards public law sanctions, this chapter will mainly deal with those specifically addressed at behaviour to the detriment of consumers. Thus, it will concentrate on public law sanctions that are meant to sit alongside private law remedies and to reinforce the deterrent effect of such remedies.

There is a significant degree of legal uncertainty and controversy as to whether and in which circumstances a product is defective if it does not meet certain environmental standards.[1] Environmental law largely is not aimed at the protection of individual consumers but at the protection of the environment in general. If the use of a product for the purpose it was intended for is prohibited because it does not meet environmental standards, nobody will doubt that there is a pecuniary damage to the consumer.[2] Even then one might still argue about whether and to what extent the manufacturer or the seller is responsible for the product's compliance with (perhaps future) regulatory standards. In the emissions scandal, it has been frequently argued by manufacturers or sellers that the cars are indeed perfectly fit for service and that no damage was done to the consumers at all, at least as long as they remain free to drive those cars. Reselling value is yet another issue.[3]

1 Sebastian Heselhaus, 'Dieselfahrverbote in deutschen Städten – Grundlagen und Erkenntnisse für das Schweizer Umweltrecht' [2019] Umweltrecht in der Praxis 165, 172ff, 184 (hereafter Heselhaus, 'Dieselfahrverbote'). VW is even trying to prevent the legal uncertainties from being resolved by the national Supreme Courts. However, despite a settlement in the matter, the German Federal Court (*Bundesgerichtshof* – BGH) has not allowed itself to be deterred from a preliminary assessment to the effect that the software manipulations probably constitute a material defect, see BGH, Order of 8 January 2019, VIII ZR 225/17. Furthermore, the German Federal Court affirmed an individual claim for rescission of the purchase contract. However, a compensation for use must be deducted from the purchase price (see BGH, Judgment of 25 May 2020, VI ZR 252/19).

2 Heselhaus, 'Dieselfahrverbote' (n 1) 184.

3 On possible claims arising out of the Dieselgate scandal, see, e.g. the country reports published in [2017] Journal of European Consumer and Market Law 35ff, 85ff; from a German Perspective, Kolja van Lück, 'Kaufrechtliche Ansprüche des Käufers im Diesel-Abgasskandal' [2019] VuR 8; Thomas Riehm, '"Dieselgate" und das Deliktsrecht' [2016] DAR 12; from a Swiss perspective, Arnold F Rusch and Angelo Schwizer, 'Gewährleistung und Haftung bei abgasmanipulierten Fahrzeugen' [2016] AJP 1299.

Only in a limited number of jurisdictions have tools been developed that enable individuals to act against violations of environmental law.[4] Collective instruments are more common. Article 9(2) of the Aarhus Convention[5] and article 11(3) of the Environmental Impact Assessment Directive[6] provide for the possibility of legal action by environmental associations in the event of violations of their participation rights. In addition, article 9(3) of the Aarhus Convention requires that actions of members of the public concerning other environmental law violations must also be admissible. The provision is generally seen as not directly applicable and has not been implemented in many contracting states. However, the ECJ has determined that EU law in conjunction with the Aarhus Convention provides for a right of action when it comes to compliance with EU environmental regulations in the Member States.[7] Against this background, many legal systems have come to acknowledge that NGOs should have standing in certain types of proceedings involving issues of environmental law.[8]

II. PUBLIC ENFORCEMENT

A. ADMINISTRATIVE PROCEEDINGS

Member States of the European Union are obliged by primary law to enforce EU law effectively (article 19(1) TEU[9]). In EU secondary legislation, there is a trend to include provisions explicitly obliging Member States to provide for 'effective, proportionate and dissuasive' penalties for violations of certain provisions of EU law. The Consumer Rights Directive (article 24(1))[10] and the Unfair Commercial Practices Directive (article 13)[11] both include such provisions. There is, however,

4 See, however, from the perspective of EU law, Heselhaus, 'Dieselfahrverbote' (n 1) 174.

5 Convention on access to information, public participation in decision-making and access to justice in environmental matters, done at Aarhus, Denmark, on 25 June 1998.

6 Directive 2011/92/EU of the European Parliament and of the Council of 13 December 2011 on the assessment of the effects of certain public and private projects on the environment [2011] OJ L26/1.

7 See ECJ, C-240/09 *Lesoochranárske zoskupenie VLK v Ministerstvo životného prostredia Slovenskej republiky* [8 March 2011] ECR I-01255, para 44ff; Heselhaus, 'Dieselfahrverbote' (n 1) 175.

8 In Germany, legal standing of environmental associations is subject to the Environmental Remedies Act (*Umwelt-Rechtsbehelfsgesetz*), BGBl. 2017 I 3290. Art 55 of the Swiss Federal Act on the Protection of the Environment (*Umweltschutzgesetz*), SR 814.01, is slightly more restrictive, see Heselhaus, 'Dieselfahrverbote' (n 1) 175 and 182.

9 Consolidated Version of the Treaty on European Union [2012] OJ C326/01.

10 Directive 2011/83/EU of the European Parliament and of the Council of 25 October 2011 on consumer rights, amending Council Directive 93/13/EEC and Directive 1999/44/EC of the European Parliament and of the Council and repealing Council Directive 85/577/EEC and Directive 97/7/EC of the European Parliament and of the Council [2011] OJ L304/64.

11 Directive 2005/29/EC of the European Parliament and of the Council of 11 May 2005 concerning unfair business-to-consumer commercial practices in the internal market and amending Council Directive 84/450/EEC, Directives 97/7/EC, 98/27/EC and 2002/65/EC of

no uniform approach within the EU to the enforcement of consumer law or of the rules on unfair commercial practices, not even where the substantive provisions originate from EU law. The primary responsibility for the enforcement of substantive EU consumer law lies with the Member States. The EU itself only acts reactively.[12] Outside the EU, there is even greater diversity.

In a number of jurisdictions, such as Brazil,[13] China,[14] Denmark,[15] France,[16] Italy,[17] Lithuania,[18] the Netherlands[19] and Portugal,[20] specific administrative

---

the European Parliament and of the Council and Regulation (EC) 2006/2004 of the European Parliament and of the Council [2005] OJ L149/22.

12 On the influence of the EU on the enforcement of consumer law, see Peter Rott, 'The EU Legal Framework for the Enforcement of Consumer Law' in Hans-Wolfgang Micklitz and Geneviève Saumier (eds), *Enforcement and Effectiveness of Consumer Law* (Springer 2018) 249, 262ff, 283 (hereafter Rott, 'The EU Legal Framework').

13 Claudia Lima Marques, 'Enforcing Consumer and Capital Markets Law in Brazil' in this book Section II.A. (hereafter Marques, 'Brazil'); see also Claudia Lima Marques and Patricia Galindo da Fonseca, 'Consumer Protection in Brazil: The 2016 Report for the International Academy of Consumer Law' in Hans-Wolfgang Micklitz and Geneviève Saumier (eds), *Enforcement and Effectiveness of Consumer Law* (Springer 2018) 99, 109ff (hereafter Marques and Galindo da Fonseca, 'Consumer Protection').

14 Tong Zhang, 'Enforcing Consumer Law in China' in this book Section III.A. (hereafter Zhang, 'China'); Dan Wei, 'Enforcement and Effectiveness of Consumer Law in the People's Republic of China' in Hans-Wolfgang Micklitz and Geneviève Saumier (eds), *Enforcement and Effectiveness of Consumer Law* (Springer 2018) 173, 180ff (hereafter Wei, 'Enforcement and Effectiveness').

15 Anders Schäfer, 'Enforcing Consumer and Capital Markets Law in Denmark' in this book Section I.B.1. (hereafter Schäfer, 'Denmark'). However, the fine can only be imposed by the administrative authority itself if it is accepted by the infringer.

16 Emmanuel Jeuland, 'Enforcing Consumer and Capital Markets Law in France' in this book Section I.A. (hereafter Jeuland, 'France'); Sabine Bernheim-Desvaux and Patricia Foucher, 'L'effectivité du droit français de la consommation' in Hans-Wolfgang Micklitz and Geneviève Saumier (eds), *Enforcement and Effectiveness of Consumer Law* (Springer 2018) 287, 289ff (hereafter Bernheim-Desvaux and Foucher, 'L'effectivité').

17 Marcello Gaboardi, 'Enforcing Consumer and Capital Markets Law in Italy' in this book Section I. (hereafter Gaboardi, 'Italy'); Giacomo Pailli and Cristina Poncibò, 'In Search of an Effective Enforcement of Consumer Rights: The Italian Case' in Hans-Wolfgang Micklitz and Geneviève Saumier (eds), *Enforcement and Effectiveness of Consumer Law* (Springer 2018) 349, 350ff (hereafter Pailli and Poncibò, 'Effective Enforcement').

18 Egidija Tamošiūnienė, 'Enforcing Consumer and Capital Markets Law in Lithuania' in this book Section I.A. (hereafter Tamošiūnienė, 'Lithuania').

19 Willem H van Boom and Charlotte MDS Pavillon, 'Enforcing Consumer and Capital Markets Law in The Netherlands' in this book Section I.A.1. (hereafter van Boom and Pavillon, 'Netherlands'); Charles Dybus and Jeroen Lemmen, '"Dieselgate" and Consumer Law: Repercussions of the Volkswagen scandal in the Netherlands' [2017] Journal of European Consumer and Market Law 91, 93ff (hereafter Dybus and Lemmen, 'Dieselgate'); Vanessa Mak, 'Enforcement and Effectiveness of Consumer Law: The Netherlands' in Hans-Wolfgang Micklitz and Geneviève Saumier (eds), *Enforcement and Effectiveness of Consumer Law* (Springer 2018) 391, 394 (hereafter Mak, 'Enforcement and Effectiveness').

20 Henrique Sousa Antunes, 'Enforcing Consumer and Capital Markets Law in Portugal' in this book Section I.A. (hereafter Sousa Antunes, 'Portugal'); António Pinto Monteiro, Sandra Passinhas and Maria Raquel Guimarães, 'Enforcement and Effectiveness of Consumer Law in Portugal: Filling the Gap Between the Law on the Books and the Law in Action' in

authorities are responsible for taking action against infringements of consumer law. These public authorities usually have the power to impose fines, which may vary considerably. In China, for example, a fine corresponding to ten times the illegal income may be imposed.[21] In contrast, in Portugal the maximum fine for misleading advertising is, as a general rule, €44,891.81.[22] In most jurisdictions, fines for breaches of consumer protection law do not seem to be very effective, as far as can be judged on the basis of the national reports. To some extent, this might be due to the fact that the maximum fines are too low where the unlawful practices are very profitable.[23] In the course of the so-called New Deal for Consumers, the EU is trying to address this by introducing 'minimum maximum thresholds' (4 per cent of the trader's annual turnover or €2 million).[24] However, it remains to be seen whether this will increase the effectiveness of public enforcement.

Other jurisdictions, such as Austria,[25] Germany[26] and Switzerland,[27] do not focus on enforcement of consumer law by public agencies but instead largely leave it to private organisations to bring legal action against non-compliant traders.

The case is sometimes made that the enforcement of consumer law might be more effective if administrative authorities or other non-judicial bodies were not

---

Hans-Wolfgang Micklitz and Geneviève Saumier (eds), *Enforcement and Effectiveness of Consumer Law* (Springer 2018) 457, 467ff (hereafter Pinto Monteiro, Passinhas, and Guimarães, 'Enforcement and Effectiveness').

21 Zhang, 'China' (n 14) Section III.C. n 55.

22 Sousa Antunes, 'Portugal' (n 20) Section I.A.1.a). If the profits from the unlawful act exceed the upper limit, the fine may be raised beyond the upper limit, but not by more than a third.

23 In this respect, see Sousa Antunes, 'Portugal' (n 20) Section I.A.1.a); Gaboardi, 'Italy' (n 17) Section I.; Marques and Galindo da Fonseca, 'Consumer Protection' (n 13) 115.

24 Directive (EU) 2019/2161 of the European Parliament and of the Council amending Council Directive 93/13/EEC and Directives 98/6/EC, 2005/29/EC and 2011/83/EU of the European Parliament and of the Council as regards the better enforcement and modernisation of Union consumer protection rules.

25 Petra Leupold, 'Enforcing of Consumer Law in Austria' in this book Section II.A. (hereafter Leupold, 'Austria'); Petra Leupold, 'Enforcing Consumer Rights: Collective Redress in Austria and the European Union' [2019] Journal of European Consumer and Market Law 121, 122 (hereafter Leupold, 'Enforcing Consumer Rights').

26 See Rupprecht Podszun, Christoph Busch and Frauke Henning-Bodewig, 'Consumer Law in Germany: A Shift to Public Enforcement' [2019] Journal of European Consumer and Market Law 75. See, however, n 68 below.

27 In Switzerland, however, private enforcement of consumer law, particularly in the form of collective actions by organisations, has turned out to be largely ineffective. In reaction to this, the Swiss Confederation's right to bring legal action under the Unfair Competition Act in the interest of consumers has recently been extended; however, this is conceptualised as private, not as public enforcement. See Tanja Domej, 'Vor Art. 9–13a' in Reto Heizmann and Leander D Loacker (eds), *UWG Kommentar: Bundesgesetz gegen den unlauteren Wettbewerb* (Dike 2018) paras 4ff; for a sceptical assessment of the chances of success of the federal lawsuit in practice, see Pascal Pichonnaz, 'L'intervention de l'Etat en matière de lutte contre les conditions générales abusives: Trop ou trop peu?' in Eva Maria Belser and Bernhard Waldmann (eds), *Mehr oder weniger Staat?: Festschrift für Peter Hänni zum 65. Geburtstag* (Stämpfli 2015) 373, 384.

only empowered to impose fines, but also to order redress payments to private individuals harmed by unlawful behaviour.[28] This is presented alongside the idea that the civil courts are not fit to deal with these matters appropriately. An example for such an approach is the power of the UK Financial Ombudsman Service to make compensation orders for the benefit of consumers.[29] The Italian Central Bank also has the power to issue orders for redress for violations of customer protection law.[30] In the areas of consumer law affected by the diesel emissions scandal, such models do not seem to exist, as far as can be seen on the basis of the national reports.

In addition to or instead of traditional public enforcement by public authorities using public law sanctions, a model that may be characterised as 'hybrid enforcement'[31] exists in many jurisdictions, such as Australia,[32] Brazil,[33] China,[34] Denmark,[35] Lithuania,[36] Portugal[37] and the US.[38] In other jurisdictions, such as England and Wales, this type of enforcement exists in principle but is not available in the field of consumer law affected by the diesel emissions scandal.[39] Albeit 'hybrid enforcers' are public authorities, they make their claims on behalf of consumers before civil courts and on the basis of private law. Systematically such instruments therefore belong to private enforcement.

28 See Christopher Hodges and Stefaan Voet, *Delivering Collective Redress: New Technologies* (Hart 2018) 7ff (hereafter Hodges and Voet, *Delivering Collective Redress*).

29 See s 229 of the UK Financial Services and Markets Act 2000. In detail, Hodges and Voet, *Delivering Collective Redress* (n 28) 248.

30 See, in more detail, Hodges and Voet, *Delivering Collective Redress* (n 28) 175.

31 See Folkert Wilman, *Private Enforcement of EU Law before National Courts* (Edward Elgar 2015) para 11.30.

32 Peter Cashman, 'Enforcing Consumer and Capital Markets Law in Australia' in this book Section III. (hereafter Cashman, 'Australia').

33 Marques, 'Brazil' (n 13) Section II.A.; further Márcio Flavio Mafra Leal, 'Die Popularklage im brasilianischen Recht' in Alexander Bruns and others, *Festschrift für Rolf Stürner zum 70. Geburtstag* (Mohr Siebeck 2013) 1657, 1666 (hereafter Mafra Leal, 'Popularklage'); Marques and Galindo da Fonseca, 'Consumer Protection' (n 13) 114.

34 Zhang, 'China' (n 14) Section II.C.

35 Schäfer, 'Denmark' (n 15) Section I.C.1.; Erik Werlauff, 'Class Actions in Denmark' (2009) 622 The Annals of the American Academy of Political and Social Sciences 202, 204 (hereafter Werlauff, 'Class Actions'); Lars Lindencrone Petersen and Erik Werlauff, 'Denmark' in Piet Taelman (ed), *International Encyclopaedia for Civil Procedure* (Wolters Kluwer 2019) 1, 66 (hereafter Lindencrone Petersen and Werlauff, 'Denmark'); Hodges and Voet, *Delivering Collective Redress* (n 28) 160.

36 Tamošiūnienė, 'Lithuania' (n 18) Section I.A.

37 Sousa Antunes, 'Portugal' (n 20) Section II.A.1.a); further Pinto Monteiro, Passinhas, and Guimarães, 'Enforcement and Effectiveness' (n 20) 471; Sandra Passinhas, '"Dieselgate" and Consumer Law: Repercussions of the Volkswagen scandal in Portugal' [2017] Journal of European Consumer and Market Law 42, 44 (hereafter Passinhas, 'Dieselgate').

38 Amy J Schmitz, 'Enforcing Consumer and Capital Markets Law in the United States' in this book Section II.A. (hereafter Schmitz, 'US').

39 See John Sorabji, 'Enforcing Consumer and Capital Markets Law in England and Wales' in this book Section IV.B. (hereafter Sorabji, 'England and Wales').

There seems to be significant divergence as to the effectiveness of 'hybrid enforcement' in different jurisdictions. In Denmark, for example, the Consumer Ombudsman (COM) is entitled to bring civil actions on behalf of consumers (including actions for damages and injunctions).[40] However, the COM has not exercised this power in a single case for more than ten years.[41] In contrast, in Brazil 'hybrid enforcement' seems to be of greater practical importance.[42] In the US, claims filed by 'hybrid enforcers' have led to settlements and to substantial compensation payments.[43] Furthermore, proponents of this model argue that the mere possibility of 'hybrid enforcement' creates strong incentives to settle or to compensate consumers if appropriate.[44]

A crucial problem of public and 'hybrid' enforcement is that the responsible authorities often lack sufficient resources for enforcing effectively and consistently.[45] For cross-border contexts, the new Consumer Protection Cooperation (CPC) Regulation[46] aims at enabling national authorities to act more effectively, which might help to make the most of limited resources, at least in cross-border cases.[47] But certainly, that cannot solve the whole problem. One might contemplate creating further obligations for Member States to provide for better funding of consumer protection authorities. But public funds are limited. Consumer protection authorities compete for them with schools, universities, hospitals, social security etc. Some Member States have been hit hard by austerity politics. At least in such Member States, when it comes to the allocation of public funds, it is comprehensible if other issues are prioritised over the protection of consumers, particularly such consumers as can afford buying rather expensive cars.[48]

In addition, it could be problematic if the enforcement of certain types of private law claims were to be largely shifted away from the courts to

---

40 Schäfer, 'Denmark' (n 15) Sections I.C.1. and I.C.3.a)i); Werlauff, 'Class Actions' (n 35) 204; Lindencrone Petersen and Werlauff, 'Denmark' (n 35) 66; Hodges and Voet, *Delivering Collective Redress* (n 28) 161.

41 Schäfer, 'Denmark' (n 15) Section I.C.3.a)i).

42 Marques, 'Brazil' (n 13) Section II.A.; Marques and Galindo da Fonseca, 'Consumer Protection' (n 13) 113ff.

43 Schmitz, 'US' (n 38) Section II.A.

44 See Schäfer, 'Denmark' (n 15) Section I.C.3.a)i); Hodges and Voet, *Delivering Collective Redress* (n 28) 161; Marques, 'Brazil' (n 13) Section II.A.

45 See van Boom and Pavillon, 'Netherlands' (n 19) Section I.A.2.; Schäfer, 'Denmark' (n 15) Section IV.

46 Regulation (EU) 2017/2394 of the European Parliament and of the Council of 12 December 2017 on cooperation between national authorities responsible for the enforcement of consumer protection laws and repealing Regulation (EC) 2006/2004 [2017] OJ L345/1 (hereafter CPC Regulation).

47 See European Commission, 'Consumer Protection Cooperation Network' <https://ec.europa.eu/info/live-work-travel-eu/consumers/enforcement-consumer-protection/consumer-protection-cooperation-framework_en>.

48 See Tanja Domej, 'Die geplante EU-Verbandsklagenrichtlinie – Sisyphos vor dem Gipfelsieg?' [2019] ZEuP 447, 468 (hereafter Domej, 'Verbandsklagenrichtlinie').

administrative agencies, as suggested by some participants to the collective redress debate.[49] In principle, this is compatible with the right of access to court under article 6 of the European Convention on Human Rights, provided that it is possible to bring the case before a court that has full powers to assess the facts and the legal situation if a party is dissatisfied with the administrative authority's decision.[50] Nevertheless, giving administrative authorities the power to make orders for compensation payments to consumers and thus making them assume an important part of the functions that were traditionally exercised by civil courts may create a risk of undermining the rule of law. The way in which the courts establish the facts of the case and the legal situation undoubtedly comes at a price, but so does sacrificing the interest in a solid factual and legal basis for legally binding decisions in favour of speed and 'efficiency'.

B. CRIMINAL PROCEEDINGS

Albeit there has been some harmonisation of substantive criminal law on the EU level, such harmonisation does not yet exist in the fields of unfair competition, consumer law or those issues of environmental law that are implicated by the diesel emissions scandal.[51] Therefore, it is still largely a matter of national law whether the practices uncovered in the diesel emissions scandal are criminal offences and how they are sanctioned. However, in severe cases, the obligation of Member States to provide for effective sanctions for violations of EU law might include an obligation arising under EU law to make certain unlawful conduct criminally punishable, as the ECJ held in the Unilever case.[52]

In some jurisdictions, such as Brazil[53] and China,[54] the violation of consumer law may directly trigger criminal liability. In contrast, in others, such as Austria,[55]

49 Hodges and Voet, *Delivering Collective Redress* (n 28) 303ff.

50 See *Ortenberg v Austria*, App no 12884/87, 25 November 1994, para 31; Jens Meyer-Ladewig, Stefan Harrendorf, and Stefan König, 'Commentary on Article 6 ECHR' in Jens Meyer-Ladewig, Martin Nettesheim and Stefan von Raumer (eds), *EMRK Europäische Menschenrechtskonvention: Handkommentar* (4th edn, Nomos 2017) para 35.

51 See Rott, 'The EU Legal Framework' (n 12) 280ff; on the harmonisation of criminal law on the EU level in general, see Bernd Hecker, *Europäisches Strafrecht* (5th edn, Springer 2015) 147ff, 269ff, 371ff.

52 ECJ, C-77/79 *Österreichische Unilever GmbH and Smithkline Beecham Markenartikel GmbH* [29 January 1999] ECR I-00431, para 36.

53 See Marques, 'Brazil' (n 13) Section II.B.; Marques and Galindo da Fonseca, 'Consumer Protection' (n 13) 115.

54 See Zhang, 'China' (n 14) Section III.D.; Wei, 'Enforcement and Effectiveness' (n 14) 197ff.

55 Leupold, 'Austria' (n 25) Section IV.A.

France (as of recently),[56] Lithuania[57] and Portugal,[58] there are no specific criminal law provisions concerning the violation of consumer rights. The mere violation of consumer law provisions is therefore not sufficient for criminal liability in the latter jurisdictions. Additional requirements would need to be met, for example those of the criminal offence of fraud, deception or environmental crimes.

Apart from the concrete criminal offences, it can be decisive in practice whether only a natural person directly responsible for the violation is criminally liable or whether criminal sanctions are also possible against a corporation as such. Many jurisdictions, such as Austria,[59] Denmark,[60] England and Wales,[61] France,[62] Italy,[63] Netherlands,[64] Lithuania,[65] Portugal[66] and the US[67] have introduced corporate criminal liability to a certain extent. However, there are still jurisdictions that have largely withstood this trend so far, most notably Germany, where only administrative fines (which may, however, be quite hefty)[68] can

---

56 French consumer protection law has traditionally been characterised by criminal sanctions. However, since these were not often applied, the criminal sanctions were mainly replaced by administrative sanctions. See Jeuland, 'France' (n 16) Sections I.A. and I.B.; Bernheim-Desvaux and Foucher, 'L'effectivité' (n 16) 297.

57 Tamošiūnienė, 'Lithuania' (n 18) Section V.

58 Sousa Antunes, 'Portugal' (n 20) Section I.A.2.a)i); Pinto Monteiro, Passinhas and Guimarães, 'Enforcement and Effectiveness' (n 20) 472.

59 Leupold, 'Austria' (n 25) Section IV.A.; see also, for example, Otto Dietrich, 'Modelle eines Unternehmensstrafrechts und ihre Effektivität Österreich – Verbandsverantwortlichkeit' [2016] Neue Zeitschrift für Wirtschafts-, Steuer- und Unternehmensrecht 186.

60 See Deutscher Bundestag, 'Eine Übersicht zum Unternehmensstrafrecht in einzelnen Mitgliedstaaten der Europäischen Union' (2017) <http://www.bundestag.de/resource/blob/539400/9f7fe461015429dc5f71c4c3d2816704/wd-7-070-17-pdf-data.pdf> (hereafter Deutscher Bundestag, 'Übersicht zum Unternehmensstrafrecht').

61 Sorabji, 'England and Wales' (n 39) Section II.A.; Deutscher Bundestag, 'Übersicht zum Unternehmensstrafrecht' (n 60) 18ff.; Patrick Späth, 'Vom Zweck der Bestrafung von Unternehmen: Die neue Sentencing Guideline for Fraud, Bribery and Money Laundering Offences in England und Wales' [2016] Corporate Compliance Zeitschrift 35.

62 See Deutscher Bundestag, 'Übersicht zum Unternehmensstrafrecht' (n 60) 7; Jeuland, 'France' (n 16) Section I.B.

63 See Deutscher Bundestag, 'Übersicht zum Unternehmensstrafrecht' (n 60) 8.

64 See Deutscher Bundestag, 'Übersicht zum Unternehmensstrafrecht' (n 60) 11.

65 See Deutscher Bundestag, 'Übersicht zum Unternehmensstrafrecht' (n 60) 10.

66 See Deutscher Bundestag, 'Übersicht zum Unternehmensstrafrecht' (n 60) 14.

67 Schmitz, 'US' (n 38) Section II.A.; see also Christoph Partsch, 'Hundert Jahre Erfahrung mit einem Unternehmensstrafrecht in den USA' in Eberhard Kempf, Klaus Lüderssen and Klaus Volk (eds), *Unternehmensstrafrecht* (De Gruyter 2012) 55.

68 Staatsanwaltschaft Braunschweig, 'VW muss Bußgeld zahlen' (Press Release, 13 June 2018) <https://staatsanwaltschaft-braunschweig.niedersachsen.de/startseite/aktuelles/presseinformationen/vw-muss-bugeld-zahlen-174880.html>.

currently be imposed on corporations.[69] As far as the diesel emissions scandal is concerned, the national reports have shown differences in the enforcement of criminal law. In the US criminal proceedings were initiated against VW and later against its former CEO (the latter is still pending).[70] Similarly, there are ongoing criminal investigations/proceedings against VW and/or its employees/managers in Austria,[71] France,[72] Germany,[73] Italy[74] and Switzerland.[75] Meanwhile, in China,[76] England and Wales[77] and Denmark[78] no criminal proceedings have yet become a matter of public record. In addition to criminal penalties, in some jurisdictions the profit resulting from illegal behaviour can also be skimmed off.[79]

The effectiveness of public enforcement might increase if not only a corporation itself but also its directors face sanctions in cases of serious infringements even in cases where the directors themselves did not commit a criminal offence. This has been highlighted in discussions in the UK about the reform of the Competition and Markets Authority (CMA).[80] However, in many jurisdictions one may expect grave reluctance towards significant penalties for company directors. Moreover, there will be those who will argue that sooner or later insurance products will develop to cover the risk of such penalties, and that in the long run the whole exercise will mainly result in increased prices for consumers.

---

69 Caroline Meller-Hannich, 'Enforcing Consumer and Capital Markets Law in Germany' in this book Section II.A. (hereafter Meller-Hannich, 'Germany'). The introduction of corporate criminal liability is currently being discussed, see Nicolas Ott and Cäcilie Lüneborg, 'Das neue Verbandssanktionengesetz – Fragen und Auswirkungen für die Compliance-Praxis' [2019] Neue Zeitschrift für Gesellschaftsrecht 1361.

70 Schmitz, 'US' (n 38) Section II.A.; in the VW proceedings, the criminal fine was US$2.8 billion.

71 Leupold, 'Austria' (n 25) Section IV.A.

72 Jeuland, 'France' (n 16) Section I.B.

73 Staatsanwaltschaft Braunschweig, 'Anklage im Diesel-Skandal' (Press Release, 15 April 2019) <https://staatsanwaltschaft-braunschweig.niedersachsen.de/startseite/aktuelles/presseinformationen/anklage-im-diesel-skandal-176101.html> and Staatsanwaltschaft Braunschweig, 'Weitere Anklage im Diesel-Komplex' (Press Release, 1 January 2020) <https://staatsanwaltschaft-braunschweig.niedersachsen.de/startseite/aktuelles/presseinformationen/weitere-anklage-im-diesel-komplex-184131.html>.

74 Gaboardi, 'Italy' (n 17) Section I.

75 Bundesanwaltschaft, 'VW emissions: Online questionnaire for aggrieved parties' (2 September 2019) <http://www.bundesanwaltschaft.ch/mpc/en/home/medien/archiv-medienmitteilungen/news-seite.msg-id-76267.html>.

76 Zhang, 'China' (n 14) Section I.

77 Sorabji, 'England and Wales' (n 39) Section I.A. The reason for this seems to be that the English authorities intend to wait for the results of the German inquiry.

78 Schäfer, 'Denmark' (n 15) Section I.A.

79 See for example Sousa Antunes, 'Portugal' (n 20) Section I.A.2.b)ii).

80 Andrew Tyre, 'Letter to the Secretary of State for Business, Energy and Industrial Strategy' 24 <https://assets.publishing.service.gov.uk/government/uploads/system/uploads/attachment_data/file/781151/Letter_from_Andrew_Tyrie_to_the_Secretary_of_State_BEIS.pdf>.

In some jurisdictions, such as Austria,[81] Denmark,[82] France,[83] Germany,[84] Italy[85] and Portugal,[86] it is possible for injured consumers to assert their civil claims within the framework of criminal proceedings (so-called 'adhesion procedure'). In Switzerland, the Federal Prosecution Office (*Bundesanwaltschaft*), in September 2019, even published a website inviting affected consumers to join the criminal proceedings against Volkswagen and AMAG (the importer of affected cars).[87] It was estimated that 175,000 consumers would be entitled to join.[88]

The adhesion procedure can be an effective instrument for the enforcement of consumer law, as it allows consumers to benefit from the evidence gathered by the prosecution. Furthermore, the financial risk is often lower than in separate civil proceedings, as the plaintiff is normally only liable for costs that were predominantly caused by the civil (adhesion) action. However, there is considerable divergence as to how this model is implemented. In Portugal, for example, a claim for civil compensation based on a crime can only be presented separately before the civil court under specific conditions.[89] In Denmark, if the offence is punishable by imprisonment, the public prosecutor may claim damages on behalf of and for the benefit of the victims.[90] In France, consumer associations may intervene in criminal proceedings along with consumers, but this rarely happens.[91] While in some jurisdictions, such as France[92] and Belgium,[93] the criminal court must rule on the civil claims, in others it may refer the civil (adhesion) action to the civil courts.[94] This power is often used if entertaining the civil (adhesion) action

81 Georg E Kodek, 'Enforcing Capital Markets Law in Austria' in this book Section IV.D. (hereafter Kodek, 'Austria'); see also Hermann Neidhart, 'Adhäsionsverfahren – ein kurzer Ländervergleich' [2006] DAR 415, 416ff (hereafter Neidhart, 'Adhäsionsverfahren'); Harald Koch, *Verbraucherprozessrecht: Verfahrensrechtliche Gewährleistung des Verbraucherschutzes in Europa* (2nd edn, Nomos 2019) 61 (hereafter Koch, *Verbraucherprozessrecht*).

82 Schäfer, 'Denmark' (n 15) Section I.B.2.; Koch, *Verbraucherprozessrecht* (n 81) 61.

83 Jeuland, 'France' (n 16) Section I.B.; Koch, *Verbraucherprozessrecht* (n 81) 61.

84 §403 German Criminal Procedure Code (*Strafprozessordnung* – StPO), BGBl. 1987 I 1074, 1319; see also Neidhart, 'Adhäsionsverfahren' (n 81) 415; Koch, *Verbraucherprozessrecht* (n 81) 61.

85 Gaboardi, 'Italy' (n 17) Section V.B.1.; Pailli and Poncibò, 'Effective Enforcement' (n 17) 355; Neidhart, 'Adhäsionsverfahren' (n 81) 416; Koch, *Verbraucherprozessrecht* (n 81) 61.

86 Sousa Antunes, Portugal (n 20) General Procedural Law I; Neidhart, 'Adhäsionsverfahren' (n 81) 417.

87 Bundesanwaltschaft, 'VW-Abgasmanipulationen – STRAFUNTERSUCHUNG (SV.16.1943-KAU) – UMFRAGE' <http://www.apps.ba.admin.ch/survey/index.php/811366/>.

88 Matthias Pflume, 'Wer will, kann mitklagen' (*Beobachter*, 1 October 2019) <http://www.beobachter.ch/konsum/konsumentenschutz/vw-abgasskandal-wer-will-kann-mitklagen>.

89 Sousa Antunes, 'Portugal' (n 20) Section III.A.

90 Schäfer, 'Denmark' (n 15) Section I.B.2.

91 Jeuland, 'France' (n 16) Section I.B.

92 See Kerstin Spiess, *Das Adhäsionsverfahren in der Rechtswirklichkeit* (LIT 2008) 246ff (hereafter Spiess, *Adhäsionsverfahren*).

93 See Stefaan Voet, 'Cultural Dimensions of Group Litigation: The Belgian Case' (2013) 41 Ga J Int'l & Comp L 433, 446ff.

94 For example, in Germany, see Spiess, *Adhäsionsverfahren* (n 92) 247.

would prolong or complicate the criminal proceedings. Therefore, the adhesion procedure is rarely used in connection with mass consumer disputes in Denmark.[95] In Austria, on the other hand, criminal courts now seem more willing to deal with civil (adhesion) actions than they used to be.[96] Where the civil claim is referred to the civil courts, consumers often still benefit from the evidence collected in the criminal proceedings, even if the outcome may not be legally binding for the civil court.

III. PRIVATE ENFORCEMENT

A. COLLECTIVE ACTIONS

There is a widely shared perception that judicial systems in Europe perform poorly in the resolution of mass disputes and in the adjudication of mass claims. Intense legislative and doctrinal debates about collective actions have been ongoing both at the EU level and at the national level of many Member States (as well as non-Member States) for several years.

EU Member States are currently obliged to enable actions for injunctive relief in the collective interest of consumers under the Injunctions Directive.[97] Collective actions for injunctive relief have made an important contribution to the enforcement of consumer law but they alone cannot ensure the effective private enforcement of consumer law and remove the barriers for access to justice that exist in this area.

As regards collective actions for damages, there are considerable differences between the jurisdictions covered in this book. Specific rules on such actions have not yet been enacted in Austria,[98] China[99] and Germany,[100] whereas they exist, at least in the area of consumer protection law, in Australia,[101] Brazil,[102]

---

95 Schäfer, 'Denmark' (n 15) Section I.B.2.

96 Kodek, 'Austria' (n 81) Section IV.D.

97 Directive 2009/22/EC of the European Parliament and of the Council of 23 April 2009 on injunctions for the protection of consumers' interests [2009] OJ L110/30 (hereafter Injunctions Directive).

98 Petra Leupold, 'Kollektiver Rechtsschutz: Österreich und Deutschland im Vergleich' [2019] ecolex 564, 565 (hereafter Leupold, 'Kollektiver Rechtsschutz'). However, the assignment model (see Section III.A.9.) may be used for the enforcement of damages in mass claim situations.

99 It seems that damages cannot be claimed in public interest actions, see Zou Weining, Wang Lihua and Chen Mingqing, 'China' in Richard Swallow (ed), *The Class Actions Law Review* (Law Business Research 2017) 40, 45.

100 Meller-Hannich, 'Germany' (n 69) Section I.B.2.; further Leupold, 'Kollektiver Rechtsschutz' (n 98) 565.

101 Cashman, 'Australia' (n 32) Sections II., II.B., II.C.

102 Marques, 'Brazil' (n 13) Section II.A.; further Marques and Galindo da Fonseca, 'Consumer Protection' (n 13) 113.

Denmark,[103] France,[104] Italy,[105] Lithuania,[106] Portugal[107] and the US.[108] In the Netherlands a collective action for damages has recently been introduced.[109] Collective actions for damages represent a crucial element of the attractiveness and ultimately of the effectiveness of the enforcement of consumer law in general, even though the practical success of such instruments varies considerably across jurisdictions.

The Commission's proposal for a Representative Actions Directive is intended to oblige Member States to introduce representative actions for damages. However, the scope of the proposed directive is intended to be limited to certain areas of EU law. In the context of the diesel emissions scandal, only misleading advertising might be a possible basis for a collective action based on the implementation of the proposed directive.[110]

Draft rules on collective redress have also been put forward by the Working Group on Parties in the framework of the ELI/UNIDROIT project aiming at the

---

103 Schäfer, 'Denmark' (n 15) Section I.C.2. However, no damages have been approved in the only class action case on damages decided by the Supreme Court, see Christian Alsøe, Søren Henriksen and Morten Melchior Gudmandsen, 'Denmark' in Camilla Sanger (ed), *The Class Actions Law Review* (3rd edn, Law Business Research 2019) 33, 39.

104 Jeuland, 'France' (n 16) Section I.C.; Florian Bien, 'Die neue französische Action de groupe der Verbraucherschutzverbände' [2014] Neue Zeitschrift für Kartellrecht 507, 508 (hereafter Bien, 'Action de groupe'); Koch, *Verbraucherprozessrecht* (n 81) 89.

105 Gaboardi, 'Italy' (n 17) Section V.A.; Giorgio Afferni, '"Opt-In" Class Actions in Italy: Why are they Failing?' [2016] JETL 82 (hereafter Afferni, 'Italy'); Karin Linhart and Eleonora Finazzi Agrò, 'Kollektiver Rechtsschutz in Italien: Die italienische „azione di classe"' [2013] RIW 443, 445 (hereafter Linhart and Finazzi Agrò, 'Italien'); Pailli and Poncibò, 'Effective Enforcement' (n 17) 360.

106 Tamošiūnienė, 'Lithuania' (n 18) Section II.A.3.; Anna Piszcz, 'Compensatory Collective Redress: Will It Be Part of Private Enforcement of Competition Law in CEE Countries?' (2017) 10(15) Yearbook of Antitrust and Regulatory Studies 223, 231; Danguolė Bublienė, 'Recent Collective Redress Developments in Lithuania – Key Issues in Light of the Implementation of the Commission Recommendation' in Eva Lein and others (eds), *Collective Redress in Europe – Why and How?* (British Institute of International and Comparative Law 2015) 153, 156 (hereafter Bublienė, 'Collective Redress').

107 Sousa Antunes, 'Portugal' (n 20) Section II.A.1.; Passinhas, 'Dieselgate' (n 37) 44; Pinto Monteiro, Passinhas, and Guimarães, 'Enforcement and Effectiveness' (n 20) 471.

108 Schmitz, 'US' (n 38) Section II.A.; Peter L Murray, 'The American Class Action – Private Law Enforcement at Work?' in Peter Jung (ed), *Die private Durchsetzung von öffentlichem Wirtschaftsrecht* (Mohr Siebeck 2018) 79, 81ff (hereafter Murray, 'American Class Action').

109 van Boom and Pavillon, 'Netherlands' (n 19) Section II.A.

110 See on the Commission's proposal for example Susanne Augenhofer, 'Die Reform des Verbraucherrechts durch den «New Deal» – ein Schritt zu einer effektiven Rechtsdurchsetzung?' [2019] EuZW 5, 10 (hereafter Augenhofer, 'Reform'); Domej, 'Verbandsklagenrichtlinie' (n 48); Caroline Meller-Hannich, 'Aktuelle Entwicklungen im kollektiven Rechtsschutz' [2019] ecolex 568, 569 (hereafter Meller-Hannich, 'Entwicklungen'); Waltraud Hakenberg and Eva-Maria Kowollik, 'New Deal for Consumers: Europäische Kollektivklage und andere Wege modernerer Durchsetzung von Verbraucherrechten' [2019] EWS 61, 65 (hereafter Hakenberg and Kowollik, 'New Deal'). The European Parliament adopted its legislative resolution at first reading on 26 March 2019 (T8-0222/2019), and the Council laid down its General Approach on 28 November 2019 (ST- 14600/19). The interinstitutional negotiations (trilogue) have been successfully finished on 30 June 2020 (ST-9223/2020).

development of European Rules on Civil Procedure.[111] These draft rules also envisage the possibility to bring collective actions for damages (draft rule X4(1)(e). One should be aware that the ELI/UNIDROIT Rules project is not a legislative initiative but a scientific exercise, at least at this stage. Hopefully, however, the ELI/UNIDROIT draft rules on collective redress might influence future legislative projects at the EU level and in Member States, as they seem to be a better fit for purpose in several respects than the draft Representative Actions Directive.

1. *Standing*

It can be crucial for the success of collective redress instruments who has standing to bring a collective or representative action. Restricting standing to certain 'trustworthy' claimants is sometimes perceived as an important measure to prevent abusive collective actions, particularly in Europe.[112] It should be kept in mind, however, that such restrictions can have a negative impact on the effectiveness of representative actions or give certain organisations an unjustified competitive advantage over others.

The rules on standing vary significantly across the jurisdictions covered in this book. In some, such as Brazil,[113] France,[114] Germany[115] and the Netherlands,[116] only certain organisations can bring representative actions. In others, such as Australia,[117] China,[118] Denmark,[119] Italy,[120] Portugal[121]

---

111 European Law Institute (ELI) and Institute for the Unification of Private Law (UNIDROIT), 'From Transnational Principles to European Rules of Civil Procedure: Presentation and discussion of the draft rules of the Working Group on 'Parties' (Collective Redress) of 26/27 November 2018' (2018) <https://europeanlawinstitute.eu/fileadmin/user_upload/p_eli/Projects/Unidroit_Materials/Trier_2018/WG_Parties_-_Draft_on_Collective_Redress.pdf>. On these proposals, see Vincent Smith, 'Redress through collective actions in Europe: ELI/Unidroit and European Commission proposals' (2019) 24 Uniform Law Review 1.

112 See, for example, Meller-Hannich, 'Germany' (n 69) Section I.B.4.

113 Marques, 'Brazil' (n 13) Section II.A.; Mafra Leal, 'Popularklage' (n 33) 1666; Marques and Galindo da Fonseca, 'Consumer Protection' (n 13) 114.

114 Jeuland, 'France' (n 16) Section I.C.; further Koch, *Verbraucherprozessrecht* (n 81) 84 and 89; Rafael Amaro and others, 'Collective Redress in the Member States of the European Union' PE 608.829 (October 2018) 27 <http://www.europarl.europa.eu/RegData/etudes/STUD/2018/608829/IPOL_STU(2018)608829_EN.pdf> (hereafter Amaro and others, 'EP Study').

115 Meller-Hannich, 'Germany' (n 69) Section I.B.4.; Amaro and others, 'EP Study' (n 114) 27; Leupold, 'Kollektiver Rechtsschutz' (n 98) 564 and 567.

116 van Boom and Pavillon, 'Netherlands' (n 19) Section II.A.; Dybus and Lemmen, 'Dieselgate' (n 19) 93; Amaro and others, 'EP Study' (n 114) 27; Mak, 'Enforcement and Effectiveness' (n 19) 396ff.

117 Cashman, 'Australia' (n 32) Sections I., III.

118 Zhang, 'China' (n 14) Section II.C.

119 Schäfer, 'Denmark' (n 15) Section I.C.3.a)i); Werlauff, 'Class Actions' (n 35) 204; Lindencrone Petersen and Werlauff, 'Denmark' (n 35) 66.

120 Gaboardi, 'Italy' (n 17) Section IV.E. However, associations have to be authorised by consumers, see Afferni, 'Italy' (n 105) 84ff; Amaro and others, 'EP Study' (n 114) 28; Linhart and Finazzi Agrò, 'Italien' (n 105) 445; Pailli and Poncibò, 'Effective Enforcement' (n 17) 360.

121 Sousa Antunes, 'Portugal' (n 20) Section II.A.1.a); further Passinhas, 'Dieselgate' (n 37) 44; Pinto Monteiro, Passinhas, and Guimarães, 'Enforcement and Effectiveness' (n 20) 471.

and the US,[122] both organisations and affected individuals can bring representative actions that can result in compensation orders for the benefit of a group of consumers. In England and Wales, only group members can initiate proceedings that can become part of a group litigation order (GLO).[123]

The criteria and the methods for establishing an organisation's power to bring collective actions vary considerably across jurisdictions. There may be a requirement for such entities to be registered beforehand or a system of ad hoc certification. Typical criteria are the non-profit character of the organisation, the relationship between the organisation's purpose and the collective interests pursued with the action and the representativeness of the organisation, for which the duration of its existence, the number of its members or the range of its activities may serve as indicators.[124]

The legislative project for the enactment of a Representative Actions Directive aims at establishing an obligation for EU Member States to ensure that 'qualified entities', i.e. organisations or public bodies complying with certain criteria, can bring representative actions for injunctive relief and for redress measures. However, no agreement has yet been reached as to the exact criteria for qualification and on the cases in which they should apply.

Individual group members would not be able to bring representative actions under the proposed directive.[125] However, Member States would remain at liberty to allow representative actions brought by group members under their national law. The ELI/UNIDROIT draft rules, in contrast, explicitly provide for the power of ad hoc entities and individuals to bring collective actions, provided that they meet certain criteria (draft rules X2 and X3).

2. *Group Membership*

It can also be crucial for the success of collective redress instruments how membership in the group that may benefit from the outcome of the proceedings is established. In this respect, it is important to distinguish between actions aiming at injunctive or declaratory relief and those aiming at the payment of damages or other redress measures. Representative actions for injunctive or declaratory relief usually do not require any form of consent (either explicit or tacit)

---

122 See Schmitz, 'US' (n 38) Section II.A.

123 Sorabji, 'England and Wales' (n 39) Section IV.B.; further Amaro and others, 'EP Study' (n 114) 27ff. In a group litigation order affecting 91,000 potentially aggrieved customers, the High Court recently ruled, *inter alia*, that the affected vehicles did contain defeat devices (see *Crossley & Ors v Volkswagen Aktiengesellschaft & Ors* [2020] EWHC 783 (QB)).

124 See, for example, Sousa Antunes, 'Portugal' (n 20) Section II.A.1.a); Jeuland, 'France' (n 16) Section I.C.; Gaboardi, 'Italy' (n 17) Section IV.A.; Meller-Hannich, 'Germany' (n 69) Section I.B.4.

125 See Augenhofer, 'Reform' (n 110) 11; from a critical perspective, Hakenberg and Kowollik, 'New Deal' (n 110) 65.

from members of the affected group. Nevertheless, in some jurisdictions, group members may be able to rely formally on the judgment,[126] and in some, such as the US,[127] even an adverse outcome becomes binding against them. Article 10 of the Commission's proposal for a Representative Actions Directive envisages a binding effect of decisions establishing an infringement harming collective interests of consumers in favour of consumers. The European Parliament, at first reading, even introduced a rule providing for the possibility of adverse effects of decisions delivered in proceedings to which the affected consumer was not a party.[128] The Council's General Approach, however, proposes that decisions establishing an infringement should (only) count as evidence of that infringement in proceedings aiming at redress measures. Even where judgments ordering injunctive or declaratory relief are not directly binding in favour or against group members, their *de facto* effects will normally be considerable, not only in favour of affected consumers if an infringement is established but also as regards the deterrence of further actions in the case of an adverse outcome. In view of the problems associated with a *res judicata* effect against persons who were not parties to the proceedings, it seems to be a wiser and more practical approach, therefore, to refrain from giving such judgments a formal *res judicata* effect.[129]

For actions for redress measures, group membership is normally established either on an opt-in or on an opt-out basis, or on the basis of a combination of both. It is theoretically also possible to establish group membership automatically, i.e. without giving group members a choice of opting in or out (as in the US rules on class actions for injunctive and declaratory relief). It seems, however, that such a system currently is not in place in any jurisdiction for representative actions aiming at redress measures.

As regards the jurisdictions covered in this book, France[130] and Italy[131] provide for collective actions for damages that operate on an opt-in basis. In Portugal[132] and the US,[133] an opt-out system is in place. The newly introduced

---

126 See also Section III.A.5.

127 Megan E Barriger, 'Due Process Limitations on Rule 23(b)(2) Monetary Remedies: Examining the Source of the Limitation in Wal-Mart Stores, Inc. v. Dukes' (2012) 15 Journal of Constitutional Law 619, 626.

128 Domej, 'Verbandsklagenrichtlinie' (n 48) 458ff.

129 Domej, 'Verbandsklagenrichtlinie' (n 48) 458ff; on the *de facto* effect, see Tanja Domej, 'Einheitlicher kollektiver Rechtsschutz in Europa?' [2012] ZZP 421, 432 (hereafter Domej, 'Kollektiver Rechtsschutz').

130 Jeuland, 'France' (n 16) Section I.C.; Bien, 'Action de groupe' (n 104) 507; Amaro and others, 'EP Study' (n 114) 23ff.

131 Gaboardi, 'Italy' (n 17) Section IV.D.; Afferni, 'Italy' (n 105) 88; Amaro and others, 'EP Study' (n 114) 23; Linhart and Finazzi Agrò, 'Italien' (n 105) 443 and 446; Pailli and Poncibò, 'Effective Enforcement' (n 17) 361.

132 Sousa Antunes, 'Portugal' (n 20) Section II.A.1.a); Passinhas, 'Dieselgate' (n 37) 44; Pinto Monteiro, Passinhas and Guimarães, 'Enforcement and Effectiveness' (n 20) 471.

133 Schmitz, 'US' (n 38) Section III.C.; Murray, 'American Class action' (n 108) 84.

Dutch collective action for damages will, in principle, also operate on an opt-out basis, but an opt-in system will normally apply to non-resident group members.[134] A combination of both systems can be found in Australia (opt-in system in case of class action by public authority),[135] Denmark (opt-out system can be ordered in case of collective action brought by public authority).[136] In England and Wales, Group Litigation Orders operate on an opt-in basis in the sense that the affected group members must bring individual claims that are then entered on the Group Register (CPR Practice Direction 19B paragraph 6.1A). However, participation is compulsory in the sense that a Group Litigation Order may direct that claims covered by it be transferred to the management court, stayed until further order, and entered on the group register, and that from a specified date claims falling within the scope of the Group Litigation Order should be started in the management court and entered on the group register (CPR rule 19.11(3)(a) and (b)).[137] In this respect, the German Investor Model Procedure (*Kapitalanleger-Musterverfahren*)[138] has some similarities to the Group Litigation Order.[139]

The ELI/UNIDROIT draft rules propose a combined system. In principle, the collective actions should be based on an opt-in system, which cannot be restricted to residents of the jurisdiction (draft rule X30(3)). The court should, however, declare the opt-out system applicable if the individual claims are too small for individual actions and it is to be expected that a significant number of group members would not opt in to the collective action (draft rule X8). The ELI/UNIDROIT draft rules do not provide for an exact delimitation, so the attitude of the courts would be essential in this respect.

The Commission's proposal for a Representative Actions Directive envisages the possibility of redress actions without the need of any 'mandate' from consumers.[140] The European Parliament, at first reading, has retained this possibility, even if only for group members resident within the jurisdiction (see article 16(2a) of the European Parliament's legislative resolution[141]).

134 van Boom and Pavillon, 'Netherlands' (n 19) Section II.A.; see also Amaro and others, 'EP Study' (n 114) 25; Dybus and Lemmen, 'Dieselgate' (n 19) 93.

135 Cashman, 'Australia' (n 32) Sections I., III. Even under the opt-out system, it is permissible to commence a class action on behalf of only some of those who may fall within the group, see Cashman, 'Australia' (n 32) Sections I.A., I.A.1.

136 Schäfer, 'Denmark' (n 15) Section I.C.3.a)ii); Werlauff, 'Class Actions' (n 35) 204; Lindencrone Petersen and Werlauff, 'Denmark' (n 35) 67.

137 See also Sorabji, 'England and Wales' (n 39) Sections I.A. and IV.A.2.a)b); Amaro and others, 'EP Study' (n 114) 25.

138 See the Investor Model Procedure Act (*Kapitalanleger-Musterverfahrensgesetz* – KapMuG), BGBl. 2012 I 2182.

139 The German legislator was indeed inspired by the English GLO procedure, see Caroline Geiger, *Kollektiver Rechtsschutz im Zivilprozessrecht* (Mohr Siebeck 2015) 62.

140 See Domej, 'Verbandsklagenrichtlinie' (n 48) 452.

141 European Parliament legislative resolution of 26 March 2019 on the proposal for a directive of the European Parliament and of the Council on representative actions for the

Meanwhile, the Council's General Approach is based on the idea that group members must at least be able to opt out, and that consumers who are not habitually resident in the Member State where the representative action is brought must explicitly express their will to participate in order to be bound by the outcome of a representative action for redress measures (article 5b(2) and (3) of the Council's General Approach). From the perspective of the Brussels I*bis* Regulation,[142] it would indeed seem problematic to bind consumers to an adverse outcome of a representative action brought outside the Member State of their domicile without their explicit consent.[143] Furthermore, the European Parliament, at first reading, has made an amendment to the Commission's proposal to make clear that participation in a representative action cannot be limited to residents of the jurisdiction (article 6(1a) of the European Parliament's legislative resolution).[144]

The envisaged broad discretion of Member States concerning establishment of group membership for the purposes of representative actions seems almost unavoidable, as it is very difficult to reconcile the divergent views existing across Member States on this hotly debated issue. There is strong evidence that an opt-out system normally generates much higher participation rates than an opt-in system,[145] particularly where the individual claims are small.[146] Considering the default bias and human inertia, this is hardly surprising.[147] However, in the German model declaratory action (*Musterfeststellungsklage*) against *Volkswagen*, registered 262,000 consumers are considered to be eligible for participation in the settlement agreed between the parties.[148] This demonstrates that even in opt-in proceedings, participation can be very significant if the amounts in dispute are non-trivial, confidence in the representative claimant is high and the procedural environment (particularly concerning the risks associated with participating in the group litigation) is attractive.

---

protection of the collective interests of consumers, and repealing Directive 2009/22/EC (COM(2018)0184 – C8-0149/2018 – 2018/0089(COD)) TA/2019/0222 (hereafter European Parliament legislative resolution).

142 Regulation (EU) 1215/2012 of the European Parliament and of the Council of 12 December 2012 on jurisdiction and the recognition and enforcement of judgments in civil and commercial matters [2012] OJ L351/1.

143 Domej, 'Verbandsklagenrichtlinie' (n 48) 452ff.

144 Domej, 'Verbandsklagenrichtlinie' (n 48) 453; Meller-Hannich, 'Entwicklungen' (n 110) 570.

145 Alma M Mozetic, 'Collective redress: a case for opt-out class actions in England and Wales' (2016) 35 C J Q 29, 32f; Rachael Mulheron, 'The Case for an Opt-out Class Action for European Member States: A Legal and Empirical Analysis' (2009) 15 Colum J Eur L 409, 431f.; Schäfer, 'Denmark' (n 15) Section IV.

146 van Boom and Pavillon, 'Netherlands' (n 19) Section II.A.; Cashman, 'Australia' (n 32) Section I.

147 Domej, 'Kollektiver Rechtsschutz' (n 129) 445.

148 <https://www.adac.de/verkehr/musterfeststellungsklage-vw/>. The large number of consumers interested in participating was a significant administrative challenge; see <https://www.zpoblog.de/anmeldung-forderungen-klageregister-musterfeststellungsklage-probleme-johannes-deiss/>.

In some jurisdictions, particularly in Europe, there is strong resistance against an opt-out regime.[149] To some extent, the resistance may be based on the idea that such a regime would encourage undesirable free riding.[150] From a more legal perspective, concerns are raised that the group members' right to be heard would be violated if they were bound by the outcome of proceedings in which they had no say.[151] However, this is not, strictly speaking, a matter of whether a group member needs to become active to introduce proceedings over their claim but of how their procedural position is designed.[152] Furthermore, particularly in Germany, the idea is promoted that an opt-out regime is incompatible with the principle of party disposition, which is – rather questionably – presented as enshrined in constitutional law.[153]

Other concerns relate to the potential for abuse associated with an opt-out regime. There might be abusive practices to the detriment of group members, who, as 'principals' of the action, are in a weak position in relation to the agent that is supposed to further their cause.[154] However, in Europe, the discussion of the abuse potential of collective actions tends to revolve more around the danger of abusive litigation to the defendant's detriment.[155] Yet there is no clear

---

149 Domej, 'Kollektiver Rechtsschutz' (n 129) 445.

150 See, from the point of view of litigation funding, Rachael Mulheron, 'Opting in, opting out, and closing the class: Some Dilemmas for England's Class Action Lawmakers' (2011) 50 Canadian Business Law Journal 376, 400, 402 with reference to Michael Legg and others, 'Litigation Funding in Australia' [2010] University of New South Wales Faculty of Law Research Series 12; on the free rider problem in general, see Ákos Szalai, 'Beyond Opt-in and Opt-out: The Law and Economics of Group Litigation' in Viktoria Harsagi and C H van Rhee (eds), *Multi-Party Redress Mechanisms in Europe: Squeaking Mice?* (Intersentia 2014) 75, 76ff (hereafter Szalai, 'Economics').

151 See Frank Ebbing, 'Die Gruppenklage: Ein Vorbild für das deutsche Recht?' (2004) 103 ZvglRWiss 31, 46ff (hereafter Ebbing, 'Gruppenklage'); Walter H Rechberger, 'Importware Class Action?: Über die Grenzen der Vereinbarkeit eines amerikanischen Rechtsinstituts mit dem österreichischen Zivilprozess-System' in Erwin Bernat, Elisabeth Böhler, and Arthur Weilinger (eds), *Festschrift Heinz Krejci zum 60. Geburtstag: Zum Recht der Wirtschaft* (Österreich 2001) 1831, 1846ff; see also Domej, 'Kollektiver Rechtsschutz' (n 129) 438ff; Axel Halfmeier and Philip Wimalasena, 'Rechtsstaatliche Anforderungen an Opt-out-Sammelverfahren: Anerkennung ausländischer Titel und rechtspolitischer Gestaltungsspielraum' (2012) 67 JZ 649, 652.

152 See Domej, 'Kollektiver Rechtsschutz' (n 129) 438ff.

153 See Ebbing, 'Gruppenklage' (n 151) 46; Burkhard Hess, 'Verbesserung des Rechtsschutzes durch kollektive Rechtsbehelfe?' in Heinz-Peter Mansel, Barbara Dauner-Lieb, and Martin Henssler (eds), *Zugang zum Recht: Europäische und US-amerikanische Wege der privaten Rechtsdurchsetzung* (Nomos 2008) 61, 80; see also Domej, 'Kollektiver Rechtsschutz' (n 129) 438ff.

154 See Ebbing, 'Gruppenklage' (n 151) 39, 42; Szalai, 'Economics' (n 150) 81; Stephan Madaus, 'Keine Effektivität einer Europäischen class action ohne „amerikanische Verhältnisse" bei deren Finanzierung' [2012] ZEuP 99, 110ff (hereafter Madaus, 'Effektivität'); Bernd Scholl, 'Die Musterfeststellungsklage nach §§606ff ZPO: Eine kritische Würdigung mit Bezügen zum französischen, niederländischen und US-amerikanischen Recht' [2019] ZfPW 317, 330 (hereafter Scholl, 'Musterfeststellungsklage').

155 See Ebbing, 'Gruppenklage' (n 151) 39; Scholl, 'Musterfeststellungsklage' (n 154) 329ff.

evidence that an opt-out regime *per se* carries a greater potential for abuse than an opt-in regime. Such potential may at least as much depend on other features of procedural law. In particular, there are those who argue that the ill fame of the US class action is not primarily to be blamed on the opt-out regime applying to it but rather on other features of what is sometimes referred to as the 'toxic cocktail' of US litigation (such as contingency fees, lack of a loser pays system, punitive damages, onerous discovery obligations and low pleading standards).[156] In any case, the discussion on abusive practices in the field of collective litigation, and on safeguards against them, is largely based on rhetoric and anecdotal evidence, but the arguments brought forward do not necessarily stand up to scrutiny where a closer look is taken at actual cases.[157]

3. *Specific Admissibility Criteria and Certification*

The criteria that need to be met for a collective action to be admissible can have a significant impact on the effectiveness of such actions. There is considerable divergence across jurisdictions in this respect. However, usually, jurisdictions that allow collective actions for damages require at least some sort of similarity or commonality of the claims that are subject to the collective action.[158] Furthermore, admissibility of a collective action often depends on its superiority to individual lawsuits.[159] In some jurisdictions, there is a separate certification stage at the outset of the proceedings to determine whether these requirements are met.[160] Where the criteria for admissibility are vague and leave a broad scope of appreciation to the court, this can introduce a significant degree of legal uncertainty and create the risk that disputes about admissibility criteria are used to prolong or obstruct the proceedings.[161] The purported aim of specific admissibility criteria and/or a separate certification stage is that they are needed to prevent abusive collective litigation. However, considering the additional procedural burdens they create, their operation and fitness for purpose should be critically assessed.

---

156 See Domej, 'Kollektiver Rechtsschutz' (n 129) 449ff; Ebbing, 'Gruppenklage' (n 151) 44ff; Astrid Stadler, 'Wider die Mär von der europäischen class action' [2011] VuR 79, 79; Jochen Clausnitzer, 'Experiment EU-Sammelklagen: Brüsseler Podiumsdiskussion mit Wettbewerbskommissarin Neelie Kroes' [2009] EuZW 169, 171.

157 See, in this respect, the very nuanced picture painted in Deborah R Hensler and others, *Class Action Dilemmas* (RAND Institute 2000) 137ff.

158 See, for example, Schäfer, 'Denmark' (n 15) Section I.C.3.a)iii); Tamošiūnienė, 'Lithuania' (n 18) Section II.A.3.

159 See, for example, Tamošiūnienė, 'Lithuania' (n 18) Section II.A.3.

160 See Schäfer, 'Denmark' (n 15) Section I.C.3.a)iii).; Gaboardi, 'Italy' (n 17) Section IV.D.; Tamošiūnienė, 'Lithuania' (n 18) Section II.A.3.; Schmitz, 'US' (n 38) Section III.D.; Linda S Mullenix, 'Ending Class Actions as We Know Them: Rethinking the American Class Action' (2014) 64 Emory L J 399, 419f (hereafter Mullenix, 'Class Actions').

161 From the US perspective Mullenix, 'Class Actions' (n 160) 419ff.

In several jurisdictions covered in this book, such as Denmark,[162] Italy[163] and the US,[164] there seems to be a tendency for the admissibility and certification process to be lengthy or complex, thus reducing the effectiveness of collective actions. In Australia, there seem to be fewer problems with respect to admissibility criteria. It is required for an Australian class action that at least seven persons have a claim against the same person on the same or similar grounds giving rise to a common legal or factual question, but there is no certification stage.[165]

The ELI/UNIDROIT draft rules also provide for specific admissibility criteria. The collective claim must be more efficient for resolving the dispute than a joinder of individual claims, a mass harm of the group members must originate from the same or a series of related events, similar legal and factual questions must arise and (except in cases of urgency) a pre-trial settlement procedure lasting at least three months must have been completed (draft rule X5(1)). These rules also provide for a separate decision on certification ('collective action order', draft rule X6).

Meanwhile, the proposed Representative Actions Directive does not envisage a separate certification stage. Presumably, there would be a degree of autonomy for the Member States as regards the procedural framework for such actions including a potential certification stage. However, Member States would not be at liberty to introduce prerequisites going beyond those contained in the directive for the admissibility of a representative action. In particular, the proposed directive does not establish a superiority requirement. It remains to be seen how a potential numerosity criterion will be handled with respect to the requirement that the representative action must pertain to the collective interest of consumers.

4. *Limitation Periods*

The national reports have revealed significant differences across jurisdictions with regard to limitation periods and their suspension or interruption in the context of collective actions. According to Dutch case law, the limitation period can be interrupted by a pre-litigation letter from a representative association or foundation with effect for all potential claimants.[166] Similarly, a suspension or interruption of the limitation period applies in Australia (filing),[167] Denmark (filing),[168]

162 Schäfer, 'Denmark' (n 15) Section I.C.3.a)iii).

163 Pailli and Poncibò, 'Effective Enforcement' (n 17) 368.

164 See Schmitz, 'US' (n 38) Section III.D. As a result of the case-law the certification stage is typically hotly contested by defendants, see Mullenix, 'Class Actions' (n 160) 419ff.

165 Cashman, 'Australia' (n 32) Section I.

166 See van Boom and Pavillon, 'Netherlands' (n 19) Section III.A.4.

167 Cashman, 'Australia' (n 32) Section I.

168 Schäfer, 'Denmark' (n 15) Section I.C.3.a)iv).

Italy (filing),[169] France[170] and Portugal (clear intention to exercise a right).[171] Meanwhile, in England and Wales, the limitation period only ceases to run once an individual claim is issued.[172] In Brazil, there are different limitation periods for the individual action (from one to ten years) and for the collective action (five years since the event). For the duration of the 'public civil inquiry', both limitation periods are suspended.[173] In Germany, the limitation period for individual claims ceases to run when the individual registration of participation in a model declaratory action is served, subject to the condition that the individual action is brought within three months after the termination of the model declaratory proceedings.[174] This rule, contained in §204(6a) of the German Civil Code (*Bürgerliches Gesetzbuch* – BGB), indicates that the commencement of the model declaratory action as such does not stop the running of the limitation period for individual claims.[175]

Another issue is whether an action for injunctive or declaratory relief brought in the collective interest of consumers stops the limitation period for damages claims that are based on an infringement the action pertains to. Where such actions are conceptualised as individual actions, such as in Austria[176] or Germany,[177] the default position would be that they have no effect on the running of the limitation period for individual claims. Particularly if proceedings in such actions tend to be lengthy and/or if limitation periods are short, this may detract from the effectiveness of injunctive or declaratory relief. To deal with this problem, the proposed Representative Actions Directive contains a provision according to which limitation periods must be suspended or interrupted if a representative action is submitted (article 11 of the Commission's proposal).[178] According to the Council's General Approach, however, an action for redress measures will only suspend or interrupt limitation periods with respect to consumers concerned by it, i.e. those who have opted in or failed to opt out, depending on the applicable system for establishing group membership. Such a restriction seems justified in principle, as otherwise free riding might be

---

169 Gaboardi, 'Italy' (n 17) Section V.B.3.

170 Jeuland, 'France' (n 16) Section I.D.; Bien, 'Action de groupe' (n 104) 508.

171 Sousa Antunes, 'Portugal' (n 20) Section III.D.

172 Sorabji, 'England and Wales' (n 39) Section IV.

173 Marques, 'Brazil' (n 13) Section III.A.

174 Meller-Hannich, 'Germany' (n 69) Section III.F.; Leupold, 'Kollektiver Rechtsschutz' (n 98) 565.

175 Similarly, Johannes Deiss and Johanna Graf, 'Verjährungshemmung durch die Musterfeststellungsklage – diffuse Rechtslage infolge unklarer Neuregelung' (2018) 73 BB 2883, 2883ff; see, however, 'Entwurf eines Gesetzes zur Einführung einer zivilprozessualen Musterfeststellungsklage' BT-Drucks 19/2439, 25 <https://dip21.bundestag.de/dip21/btd/19/024/1902439.pdf>.

176 Leupold, 'Austria' (n 25) Section II.A.; Leupold, 'Enforcing Consumer Rights' (n 25) 122; Leupold, 'Kollektiver Rechtsschutz' (n 98) 565.

177 Meller-Hannich, 'Germany' (n 69) Section III.F.

178 See Augenhofer, 'Reform' (n 110) 12; Meller-Hannich, 'Entwicklungen' (n 110) 570.

encouraged. However, a rule ensuring that late opt out (where possible) does not result in statute-barring of the claim should be considered.

A provision on the suspension of the limitation period is also contained in the ELI/UNIDROIT draft rules. According to draft rule X10(3), the limitation period for individual claims is suspended upon commencement of a collective action. The suspension ends when the collective actions is withdrawn or dismissed, or the group member opts out. However, the remaining limitation period for individual claims only starts six months after the suspension has ended (draft rule X10(A)).

5. *Binding Effect*

The binding effect of judgments on collective actions is usually closely linked to group membership. Where the opt-in system applies, the judgment will generally become binding on all group members who have opted in, whether it is favourable or adverse. This is the case, for example, in Italy[179] and France.[180] In Germany, a judgment given in model declaratory proceedings becomes binding on consumers who have had their claim entered on the register.[181]

In the case of an opt-out regime or of actions that do not require any mandate, the rules may be more nuanced. In Portugal, for example, a judgment on a popular action is in principle binding on all right-holders who do not opt out.[182] However, no binding effect occurs if the decision is based on lack of evidence or if the judge makes a different order.[183] In Brazil, a judgment on a public civil action only has a binding effect if the action is successful.[184]

Normally, judgments from opt-in proceedings will not become binding against third parties. However, article 10 of the Commission's proposal for a Representative Actions Directive contains a provision suggesting that a consumer could rely on a judgment establishing an infringement harming collective interests of consumers even if it was given on the basis of an opt-in representative action in which they did not participate, a rule that would undermine the success of opt-in collective actions and encourage free riding.[185] The proposal is inspired by article 9(1) and (2) of the Damages Directive.[186] These provisions, however, only refer to final decisions of

179 Gaboardi, 'Italy' (n 17) Sections IV.D. and V.B.3.; see further Afferni, 'Italy' (n 105) 88.
180 Jeuland, 'France' (n 16) Section I.D.; Bien, 'Action de groupe' (n 104) 508.
181 Meller-Hannich, 'Germany' (n 69) Section III.D.; Leupold, 'Kollektiver Rechtsschutz' (n 98) 567.
182 Sousa Antunes, 'Portugal' (n 20) Section III.C.; Pinto Monteiro, Passinhas, and Guimarães, 'Enforcement and Effectiveness' (n 20) 471.
183 Sousa Antunes, 'Portugal' (n 20) Section III.C.
184 Marques, 'Brazil' (n 13) Section II.A.
185 For a critical assessment, see Domej, 'Verbandsklagenrichtlinie' (n 48) 456ff.
186 Directive 2014/104/EU of the European Parliament and of the Council of 26 November 2014 on certain rules governing actions for damages under national law for infringements of the competition law provisions of the Member States and of the European Union OJ L 349/1 (hereafter Damages Directive).

national competition authorities or review courts in cases where a follow-up action for damages is brought. The proposal for a Representative Actions Directive seems to be much broader in scope and to refer to all sorts of judgments 'establishing' an infringement, possibly even only as a preliminary issue.[187] The European Parliament made this problematic provision even worse by adding the possibility of an adverse effect towards non-participating consumers, while changing the effect from an irrefutable establishment of the infringement to evidence of its existence or non-existence.[188] The Council, in its General Approach, proposes to return to a one-way effect only for the benefit of affected consumers but to retain the rule that the judgment could only be used as evidence and would not operate as an irrefutable establishment of the infringement. This approach seems preferable to the proposals put forward by the Commission and the Parliament. Nevertheless, it is problematic that there is no distinction between actions requiring a 'mandate' from consumers and those not requiring such a 'mandate'.[189]

As regards the binding effect of collective actions based on an opt-in or an opt-out system, the ELI/UNIDROIT draft rules contain a provision that is much more appropriate than article 10 of the draft Representative Actions Directive in any of the proposed forms. According to draft rule X21(1), final judgments in collective actions are binding on all parties and group members who have opted in or, in the case of the opt-out system, on group members residing in the forum state who have not opted out.

The rule contained in article 10 of the proposed Representative Actions Directive seems better suited for cases where an action for damages (whether individual or collective) is brought as a follow-up to an action for injunctive or declaratory relief, and indeed it is probably mainly targeted at such situations. Today, the approaches of European jurisdictions to this issue vary, as do those of the other jurisdictions covered in this book. In Austria, for example, actions by organisations for injunctive relief are conceived as purely individual actions, and judgments on such actions have no *res judicata* effect for the individuals whose interests the litigation is about.[190] In Germany, meanwhile, §11 of the *Unterlassungsklagengesetz* (Injunctions Act) gives consumers the right to rely on a judgment ordering a trader to refrain from using unfair contract terms.[191] A similar system seems to be in place in Italy.[192]

---

187 Domej, 'Verbandsklagenrichtlinie' (n 48) 456.

188 For a critical assessment, see Augenhofer, 'Reform' (n 110) 12; Domej, 'Verbandsklagenrichtlinie' (n 48) 458ff.

189 Domej, 'Verbandsklagenrichtlinie' (n 48) 456ff.

190 Walter H Rechberger and Daphne-Ariane Simotta, *Zivilprozessrecht* (9th edn, Manz 2017) para 354.

191 Concerning the controversial legal nature of this effect, see Hans-Wolfgang Micklitz and Peter Rott, 'Commentary on §5 *Unterlassungsklagengesetz*' in Wolfgang Krüger and Thomas Rauscher (eds), *Münchener Kommentar zur Zivilprozessordnung* (5th edn, Beck 2017) para 4 with further references.

192 Gaboardi, 'Italy' (n 17) Section V.B.3.

It may suggest itself that the apparent unattractiveness of representative actions for injunctive relief in many jurisdictions is due to the lack of a legally binding effect of judgments in favour of consumers. However, one would need to look carefully at whether such actions are really more attractive if judgments on them become binding on (or at least in favour of) affected consumers. Depending on whether such an effect operates only in favour of consumers or both ways, difficult issues concerning the procedural equality of arms or of the consumers' right to be heard arise.[193]

6. *Litigation Risk and Funding*

Issues of costs and funding have long been among the most controversial in the collective litigation debate. It can be crucial for the success of collective actions how they can be funded, how the litigation risk is distributed and how the collective claimant is remunerated. The answers to these questions vary greatly across jurisdictions.

In the US, the combination of very modest filing fees, the permissibility of contingency fees, the possibility for class counsel to be remunerated out of the proceeds of the action or settlement and the 'American rule' according to which the losing party does not have to bear the opponent's costs creates an environment that incentivises entrepreneurial collective litigation. It is highly disputed whether, on the whole, this is beneficial as it facilitates the enforcement of mass consumer claims[194] or whether adverse effects predominate,[195] considering the potential for abuse that such a model undoubtedly carries.

European jurisdictions traditionally adhere to the loser pays rule.[196] The losing party bears the court fees and must reimburse the winning party for its legal expenses. The litigation risk is usually mitigated by applying tariffs for reimbursable lawyers' fees, meaning that the losing party does not necessarily have to cover the actual expenses incurred by its opponent.[197] Nevertheless, a loser pays system significantly increases the claimant's litigation risk.

---

193 Domej, 'Verbandsklagenrichtlinie' (n 48) 458ff.

194 See, for example, Madaus, 'Effektivität' (n 154).

195 On the purported 'enormous potential for abuse' in the event of a deviation from the loser pays rule, see 'Beschlussempfehlung und Bericht des Rechtsausschusses (6. Ausschuss) zu dem Arbeitsdokument der Kommissionsdienststellen, Öffentliche Konsultation: Kollektiver Rechtsschutz: Hin zu einem kohärenten euuropäischen Ansatz' BT-Drucks 17/5956, 8 para 22 <http://dip21.bundestag.de/dip21/btd/17/059/1705956.pdf>. For a contrasting view, see Andre Fiebig, 'The Reality of U.S. Class Actions' [2016] GRUR Int 313, 315ff with further references.

196 See Amaro and others, 'EP Study' (n 114) 34ff; Kodek, 'Austria' (n 81) Section V.F.; Schäfer, 'Denmark' (n 15) Section III.A.1.; Meller-Hannich, 'Germany' (n 69) Section III.G.; Gaboardi, 'Italy' (n 17) Section V.B.3.; Tamošiūnienė, 'Lithuania' (n 18) Section III.E.; van Boom and Pavillon, 'Netherlands' (n 19) Section III.A.5.; Sousa Antunes, 'Portugal' (n 20) Section III.E.

197 See for example Denmark (Schäfer, 'Denmark' (n 15) Section III.A.1.), the Netherlands (van Boom and Pavillon, 'Netherlands' (n 19) Section III.A.5.) and Portugal (Sousa Antunes, 'Portugal' (n 20) Section III.E.).

Some jurisdictions exempt collective action claimants from paying court fees or from reimbursing the opponent's legal costs. This approach is followed, for example, in Brazil for public civil actions as long as the associations do not act in bad faith.[198] Similarly, in Portugal, any person, foundation or association is to a certain extent exempt from payment of litigation costs for a popular action.[199] Other approaches aim at limiting the litigation risk for the collective action claimant. In England and Wales, for example, the GLO parties are only responsible for the common costs.[200]

Where the collective action claimant does not have the necessary funds, the question of public funding arises. In some jurisdictions, such as Denmark, it seems possible to finance actions that are brought in the public interest on a legal aid basis, even irrespective of the claimant's financial situation.[201] In others, public funding is provided for such litigation outside the legal aid system, either directly by the state or through dedicated public funds, such as the Ontario Class Proceedings Fund or the Québec *Fonds d'aide aux actions collectives*.[202]

Article 15(1) of the Commission's proposal for a Representative Actions Directive calls upon Member States to support qualified entities in order to ensure effective access to collective redress, for example by limiting court fees, by granting qualified entities legal aid or by providing public funding for collective actions. The European Parliament proposes to complement this with a rule obliging Member States to provide 'structural support' to qualified entities (article 15(1a) of the European Parliament's legislative resolution). In addition, the European Parliament's legislative resolution provides for the possibility for Member States to allocate revenues from fines (article 14(3) of the European Parliament's legislative resolution) or unclaimed compensation payments (article 6(4a) of the European Parliament's legislative resolution) to funds established for the financing of collective actions. The Council, in its General Approach, proposes to remove all rules obliging or encouraging Member States to provide financial support for collective actions from the operative part of the directive and to address these issues in the non-binding recitals. Only rules concerning financial stability and independence of qualified entities (article 4a(3)(cb) and (cc) and article 4b(3) of the General Approach), on the possibility to lay down rules for the allocation of unclaimed proceeds (article 5b(6) of the General Approach) and a very vague rule on 'aiming' to

---

198 Marques, 'Brazil' (n 13) Section II.A. fn 31.

199 See Sousa Antunes, 'Portugal' (n 20) Section II.A.2.

200 Sorabji, 'England and Wales' (n 39) Section IV.C.

201 Schäfer, 'Denmark' (n 15) Section III.A.2.a).

202 On possible benefits and problems, see Sonja Keske, Andrea Renda and Roger Van den Bergh, 'Financing and Group Litigation' in Mark Tuil and Louis Visscher (eds), *New Trends in Financing Civil Litigation in Europe* (Edward Elgar 2010) 57, 84ff; Domej, 'Verbandsklagenrichtlinie' (n 48) 468 with further references.

prevent 'insurmountable obstacles' for effectively exercising the right to claim redress measures (article 15 of the General Approach) would remain in the text of the directive. Regardless of which of these proposals, if any, is adopted, the financial viability and attractiveness of collective actions under the proposed directive would be uncertain at best.[203]

The European Parliament has also proposed to include rules in the Representative Actions Directive that would oblige Member States to adhere to the loser pays system for collective actions (article 7a of the European Parliament's legislative resolution) and to ban contingency fees (article 15a of the European Parliament's legislative resolution). Furthermore, all proposals include rules aiming at preventing an influence of third-party funders on the procedural decisions of the qualified entity. While the Commission and the European Parliament have proposed to address this in the context of the rules on collective actions (article 7 of the respective proposals), the Council proposes to deal with this issue in the rules on the designation of qualified entities (article 4a(3)(cb) and (cc) of the General Approach) and on cross-border collective actions (article 4b(3) of the General Approach). While it is curious enough to address this issue in such a way, the effect would be that the restrictions on third-party funding would not apply to domestic collective actions. In this context, one should be aware that it is reasonable to expect that cross-border collective actions (i.e. collective actions brought outside the Member State where the qualified entity is designated) will be a rare phenomenon and domestic collective actions will continue to make up the bulk of collective litigation. If the Council's General Approach were adopted, this would therefore remove much of the sting of the funding rules, however questionable the proposal may seem from a systematic perspective.

The ELI/UNIDROIT draft rules explicitly allow third-party funding but stipulate that the collective claimant must disclose the source of funding and, if requested, the terms of the agreement to the court (draft rule X32).

The rules on third-party funding of collective actions have been and will presumably remain a central battleground in the European collective redress debate. This is not surprising, as the availability of third-party funding is crucial for the financial viability of collective actions in jurisdictions that do not provide either for contingency fee models or for generous public funding to support such actions. Several jurisdictions that do not allow contingency fees permit third-party funding arrangements where the litigation risk is carried by the funder alone, in exchange for the promise of a share of the proceeds in the case of success. However, there remains great divergence across jurisdictions as concerns the practical use of third-party litigation funding. In Denmark,[204]

---

203 Domej, 'Verbandsklagenrichtlinie' (n 48) 468ff; see also Augenhofer, 'Reform' (n 110) 12.

204 Schäfer, 'Denmark' (n 15) Section III.A.2.b).

Italy[205] and Portugal,[206] for example, it seems to be rarely used. Meanwhile, in other jurisdictions, such as Austria,[207] Australia,[208] England and Wales,[209] Germany[210] and the Netherlands,[211] it is an important element of the collective litigation landscape. As regards Germany, however, it should be noted that the German Federal Court (*Bundesgerichtshof* – BGH) has recently given a very problematic judgment that curbs the use of third-party funding for public interest actions for skimming off profits arising from competition law violations.[212] It remains to be seen whether the approach developed in that judgment will also have repercussions on third-party funding in other fields.

7. *Information and Evidence*

As a general rule, in all jurisdictions covered in this book, the burden of proof for all constitutive elements of a claim lies with the claimant.[213] In certain cases, statutory law or case law depart from this principle.[214] At least in some jurisdictions, such as Brazil,[215] Germany[216] and the Netherlands,[217] the burden of proof can be shifted if it is impossible, extremely difficult or unreasonable to obtain evidence for one party and the other party is easily able to access the relevant evidence. Under Portuguese law, there is a presumption that consumer

---

205 Gaboardi, 'Italy' (n 17) Section V.B.3.; on the reasons, see Afferni, 'Italy' (n 105) 98ff.

206 Sousa Antunes, 'Portugal' (n 20) Section II.A.2.

207 Kodek, 'Austria' (n 81) Section V.F.; Leupold, 'Austria' (n 25) Section II.C.; Leupold, 'Enforcing Consumer Rights' (n 25) 123.

208 Cashman, 'Australia' (n 32) Sections I. and I.B.

209 Sorabji, 'England and Wales' (n 39) Section IV.C.

210 Henning Zander, 'Mit hohem Einsatz: Prozessfinanzierung: Aus David gegen Goliath wird immer häufiger Goliath gegen Goliath' [2019] AnwBl 74.

211 See Matthis Peter, *Zivilprozessuale Gruppenvergleichsverfahren: Einvernehmliche Streitbeilegung im kollektiven Rechtsschutz* (Mohr Siebeck 2018) 106ff (hereafter Peter, *Gruppenvergleichsverfahren*); Ianika Tzankova, 'Funding of Mass Disputes: Lessons From the Netherlands' (2012) 8 Journal of Law, Economics & Policy 549, 589.

212 BGH, Judgment of 13 September 2018, I ZR 26/17, [2018] NJW 3581.

213 At least if the claim is brought by the creditor or somebody on their behalf, as opposed to an action for negative declaration by the alleged debtor where there might be divergences with respect to the burden of proof.

214 See for example Sousa Antunes, 'Portugal' (n 20) Section II.C.; van Boom and Pavillon, 'Netherlands' (n 19) Section II.D.; Meller-Hannich, 'Germany' (n 69) Section III.B.; Schäfer, 'Denmark' (n 15) Section III.B.

215 Marques, 'Brazil' (n 13) Section II.A.; see further Marques and Galindo da Fonseca, 'Consumer Protection' (n 13) 108.

216 Meller-Hannich, 'Germany' (n 69) Section III.B., so-called secondary burden of presentation. In the context of the diesel emissions scandal, see LG Kleve, Judgment of 31 March 2017, 3 O 252/16, BeckRS 2017, 106026; OLG München, Judgment of 22 March 2019, 21 U 533/19, BeckRS 2019, 26061.

217 van Boom and Pavillon, 'Netherlands' (n 19) Section II.D.

goods are not in conformity with the contract which, to a certain extent, also operates against producers.[218]

There are considerable differences among jurisdictions regarding the possibility of obtaining information from the opponent or from third parties. In the US, a very far-reaching discovery obligation exists, an element of US civil procedure that is often perceived as a crucial ingredient of what is referred to, particularly by potential defendants, as the 'toxic cocktail' of US litigation. In Brazil[219] and Denmark,[220] where public authorities have the power to bring collective actions, these authorities can benefit from their administrative power and require information from the defendant. Italian[221] and Portuguese[222] law empowers the court to obtain evidence in the way that it deems appropriate, without having to comply with the parties' will. In Lithuania, there appears to be a possibility for the court to obtain evidence *ex officio* in consumer law cases.[223] In England and Wales, there is a disclosure procedure.[224] In Denmark, a private plaintiff can obtain information and documents from the other side if they are sufficiently specified.[225] There is a similar rule in Switzerland,[226] where the opponent's failure to provide such documents will be taken into account in the evaluation of evidence.[227] In Switzerland, it is also possible to order third parties to produce relevant documents,[228] and compulsive measures can be taken against them in the case of unjustified refusal.[229] However, in Switzerland, courts tend to exercise great restraint in the practical application of these rules. In Germany, the traditionally prevailing view is that disclosure obligations require a basis in substantive law. However, there have long been calls to recognise a procedural obligation to cooperate and to produce relevant evidence at the opponent's request.[230]

Article 13 of the Commission's proposal for a Representative Actions Directive also contains a rule on access to evidence for qualified entities. However, it largely refers to national law and appears very vague and weak. Furthermore, it contains an unclear prerequisite that the evidence already presented by the

---

218 Sousa Antunes, 'Portugal' (n 20) Section II.C.

219 Marques, 'Brazil' (n 13) Section II.A.

220 Schäfer, 'Denmark' (n 15) Section III.B.

221 Gaboardi, 'Italy' (n 17) Section V.B.2.

222 Sousa Antunes, 'Portugal' (n 20) Section II.D.

223 Tamošiūnienė, 'Lithuania' (n 18) Section III.B. Generally, the court might be quite active during the group action proceedings, see Bublienė, 'Collective Redress' (n 106) 161.

224 Sorabji, 'England and Wales' (n 39) Section IV.H.

225 Schäfer, 'Denmark' (n 15) Section III.B.

226 See art 160(1)(b) of the Swiss Code of Civil Procedure (*Schweizerische Zivilprozessordnung*).

227 Art 164 of the Swiss Code of Civil Procedure (n 225).

228 Art 160(1)(b) of the Swiss Code of Civil Procedure (n 225).

229 Art 167(1) of the Swiss Code of Civil Procedure (n 225).

230 On the German debate, see Leo Rosenberg, Karl Heinz Schwab and Peter Gottwald, *Zivilprozessrecht* (18th edn, CH Beck 2018) §110 paras 9ff.

qualified entity is 'sufficient to support the representative action'. The European Parliament, at first reading, has proposed to further narrow down the disclosure rule by introducing a requirement of a 'specific and clear[ly] defined' indication of the relevant evidence in the opponent's control and a requirement that the relevant evidence be defined 'as narrowly as possible'. This is topped up with an adequacy and proportionality clause. One may wonder whether such a rule would bring about an enhancement of access to evidence in any European jurisdiction. In some, its transposition might lead to a restriction of such access instead. The Council's proposal is more balanced, and it broadens the scope of the disclosure rule to evidence in the control of third parties. Furthermore, the Parliament's and Council's amendments would make the rule operate both ways, i.e. against the claimant as well as the defendant, which seems reasonable from the perspective of procedural equality of arms.

Information asymmetry is likely to be a regular feature of consumer disputes. Therefore, effective information procurement tools combined with an appropriate distribution of the burden of proof can be crucial for effective access to justice. However, the legitimate interests of the other party need to be considered as well. Unreasonably burdensome disclosure obligations might create false incentives and unnecessarily increase the complexity and costs of litigation. Furthermore, any disclosure rule needs to ensure that legitimate confidentiality interests, including those pertaining to personal data of third persons or trade secrets, are adequately protected. However, this does not necessarily mean that disclosure of sensitive information is excluded, if protection orders (which may, for example, limit or prohibit further use of the information obtained or stipulate that disclosed material be inspected *in camera*) are sufficient to protect legitimate confidentiality interests.[231]

It should also be noted that the problem of access to information does not only arise in collective litigation. Therefore, one may ask how appropriate it is to address it in legislation specifically dealing with such litigation, as in the proposals for a Representative Actions Directive. Creating special disclosure rules, particularly where these are more generous than those applying to individual actions, could only be justified if parties in collective proceedings face difficulties in this regard that do not arise in individual litigation, or, perhaps, if the legislator considers collective actions as preferable to individual ones and therefore wishes to incentivise them. There is no clear indication that any of these rationales is behind the proposed article 13 of the draft Representative Actions Directive. Therefore, there may be a case for rethinking whether a provision on disclosure should be placed in the directive at all.

---

[231] See Tanja Domej, 'Zivilrechtliche Rechtsdurchsetzungsinstrumente' in *Unternehmensverantwortung und internationales Recht, Berichte der Deutschen Gesellschaft für internationales Recht vol. 50* (CF Müller 2020) 229, 259.

8. *Parallel Proceedings*

The coexistence between multiple proceedings may concern either the relationship between several collective actions or the relationship between collective and individual actions. The default approach in civil litigation is that there cannot be multiple proceedings on the same claim between the same parties. Meanwhile, where the claims or the parties are not identical, multiple litigation is possible in principle. One should note that in this context, if A and B each bought a car affected by the diesel emissions scandal, their claims against the manufacturer (or seller, as the case may be) are not identical, but they are independent claims that can be subject to independent court cases.

It can be a difficult policy question how the rules on parallel proceedings should be applied or modified for the purposes of collective litigation. First, it must be determined whether individual actions should be allowed to exist alongside collective actions or whether a pending collective litigation should bar parallel individual proceedings. This is an issue that arises with respect to both opt-in and opt-out regimes, as is demonstrated by the English GLO and the German Investor Model Procedure Act (*Kapitalanleger-Musterverfahrensgesetz* – KapMuG) regimes, which both operate on an opt-in basis but where individual litigation in cases falling within the scope of the collective action cannot be pursued further while the collective litigation is pending. Meanwhile, there are other regimes, including the German *Musterfeststellungsklage* (model declaratory action), that do not preclude potential group members from pursuing their claims individually instead of joining the collective action.[232] Under the *Musterfeststellungsklage* regime, only individual actions by consumers who subsequently register their claims for the purposes of the model declaratory action are suspended (§613 of the German Code of Civil Procedure (*Zivilprozessordnung* – ZPO)[233]), or, if the individual action is brought after registration, inadmissible (§610(3) of the German Code of Civil Procedure). This demonstrates that different regimes for parallel proceedings can even apply within the same jurisdiction. Brazil also allows the coexistence of collective and individual proceedings, and individual actions are often decided more quickly.[234] Lithuania[235] and France[236] let individuals choose between an

---

232 On 25 May 2020, for example, the German Federal Supreme Court (*Bundesgerichtshof* – BGH) upheld an individual action against Volkswagen (see BGH, Judgment of 25 May 2020, VI ZR 252/19, NJW 2020, 1962), while the *Verbraucherzentrale* and Volkswagen have reached a settlement on the *Musterfeststellungsklage* on 28 February 2020 (see Section III.B).

233 German Code of Civil Procedure (*Zivilprozessordnung* – ZPO), BGBl. 2005 I 3202; 2006 I 431; 2007 I 1781.

234 Marques, 'Brazil' (n 13) Section III.B.

235 Tamošiūnienė, 'Lithuania' (n 18) Section III.A.

236 Jeuland, 'France' (n 16) Section I.D.

individual and a collective action as well. The same approach is followed by ELI/UNIDROIT draft rule X10(1). Furthermore, draft rule X10(2) stipulates that in the case of an opt-out collective action, an individual action that is brought during the opt-out period is considered as an opt-out. Meanwhile, after the opt-out period individual actions by group members who have not opted out are no longer admissible (draft rule X10(1)).

Approaches also vary across jurisdictions with regard to the coexistence of multiple collective actions. There are jurisdictions that design such actions as exclusive. The coexistence of several collective actions for the same facts and the same statement at the same time is therefore not permissible. This approach is followed, for example, by the German KapMuG and the German *Musterfeststellungsklage*.[237]

Under the ELI/UNIDROIT Draft Rules, a collective action after its registration is exclusive to the extent that any other court must dismiss any collective action against the same defendant concerning the same mass harm event and in the interest of the same group (draft rule X4bis). This shall apply at least within the same EU Member State. With regard to collective actions in different Member States, the courts shall be obliged to coordinate in order to avoid irreconcilable judgments or settlement approvals (draft rule X29(2)).

On the other hand, in some jurisdictions the coexistence of several collective actions concerning the same harmful event is perfectly admissible. This applies, for example, to Australia,[238] Italy,[239] the US[240] and, for actions aiming at injunctive relief, Germany.[241] However, where that is the case, there may be a possibility or mechanism for consolidating several parallel collective actions. Italian law, for example, empowers the court to consolidate several class actions. Furthermore, it limits the possibility to bring parallel class actions to the time frame the court has provided for the opt-in.[242]

The coexistence of collective proceedings may increase the effectiveness of law enforcement by hitting the infringer from several angles.[243] However, allowing multiple simultaneous collective proceedings concerning the same harmful event might undermine the efficiency gain that is one of the purposes

237 Meller-Hannich, 'Germany' (n 69) Section III.A.

238 Cashman, 'Australia' (n 32) Section II.B.; Michael Legg, 'Australian Law Reform Commission class action and litigation funding report: empowering courts, monitoring funders, supporting contingency fees for class action lawyers and proposing reviews of shareholder class actions and collective redress' (2019) 38 CJQ 478, 486ff.

239 Gaboardi, 'Italy' (n 17) Section V.B.3.

240 Schmitz, 'US' (n 38) Section II.A.

241 Meller-Hannich, 'Germany' (n 69) Section III.A.

242 Gaboardi, 'Italy' (n 17) Section V.B.3.

243 Schmitz, 'US' (n 38) Section III.A.

collective litigation is intended to serve. In addition, the defendant might be subjected to excessive procedural burdens, and if the same individuals were included in several collective actions, this could also be considered as contrary to the principle of procedural equality of arms. In any case, it would be problematic if group members could 'double-dip' because of the coexistence of multiple collective actions.[244]

If multiple parallel collective actions are not allowed, a rule is required as to which action has priority. The first-in-time rule that generally applies in individual litigation (save for cases where a *forum non conveniens* approach is followed) is not necessarily suitable for collective litigation. Where it is followed, there should at least be some investigation into whether the representative that brought the first action is best suited to pursue the action. This issue, however, might also be addressed by holding a 'beauty contest' in the course of the certification procedure, as envisaged in ELI/UNIDROIT draft rule X6(2) and (3).

9. *Assignment Models*

In many jurisdictions, such as Austria,[245] Brazil,[246] Italy,[247] Germany,[248] the Netherlands,[249] Portugal[250] and Switzerland,[251] it is possible to assert claims collectively by means of assignment and bundling of claims. Another possibility, which exists under German law, but not under Swiss[252] or Austrian law,[253] is the assertion of a claim in one's own name on another's behalf (*Prozessstandschaft*).[254] The representative bringing such a claim must be explicitly authorised by the purported creditor, and they must themselves have a legitimate interest to bring the claim.[255] §8(1)(4) of the Legal Services Act (*Rechtsdienstleistungsgesetz*)[256] and §79(2)(3) of the German Code of Civil Procedure authorise certain consumer associations to bring claims on behalf of their members either on such a basis or on the basis of an assignment, or to represent consumers in court.

---

244 Schmitz, 'US' (n 38) Section II.A.
245 Leupold, 'Austria' (n 25) Section II.C.; Leupold, 'Enforcing Consumer Rights' (n 25) 123; Domej, 'Kollektiver Rechtsschutz' (n 129) 429.
246 Marques, 'Brazil' (n 13) Section III.A.
247 Gaboardi, 'Italy' (n 17) Section V.B.2.
248 Meller-Hannich, 'Germany' (n 69) Section I.C.; Leupold, 'Kollektiver Rechtsschutz' (n 98) 565.
249 van Boom and Pavillon, 'Netherlands' (n 19) Section II.B.
250 Sousa Antunes, 'Portugal' (n 20) Section II.A.4.
251 Domej, 'Kollektiver Rechtsschutz' (n 129) 430.
252 See BGer, Judgment of 1 June 2011, BGE 137 III 293, 298.
253 See OGH, Judgment of 26 May 1998, 8 Ob 364/97f.
254 See Domej, 'Kollektiver Rechtsschutz' (n 129) 434 n 80.
255 See BGH, Judgment of 10 June 2016, V ZR 125/15 para 5.
256 Legal Services Act (*Rechtsdienstleistungsgesetz*), BGBl. 2007 I 2840.

Most national reports seem rather sceptical with respect to the bundling of assigned claims as a tool of collective litigation.[257] In Austria, however, it seems to be functioning quite well as a workaround for the lack of specific instruments for the enforcement of mass claims, in spite of the inevitable limitations of this model.[258] However, the success of such workarounds obviously depends on the attitude of the judiciary, particularly the supreme courts, towards this sort of creative use of traditional procedural instruments that were not designed for the purpose they are used for. In Switzerland, a mass claim based on an assignment was brought by a consumer foundation before the *Handelsgericht* (Commercial Court) of Zurich in late 2017 to claim damages for car buyers affected by the diesel emissions scandal.[259] In an order issued in late 2019, the court dismissed the claim as inadmissible, arguing that the purpose of a consumer foundation does not include the enforcement of individual consumers' claims and that therefore the foundation lacks capacity (*Prozessfähigkeit*) for bringing such claims.[260] It remains to be seen whether this questionable view will be confirmed by the Swiss Federal Supreme Court (*Bundesgericht* – BGer).

A different type of assignment model that does not necessarily depend on bundling has been used in several jurisdictions for the enforcement of straightforward mass claims, such as those under the Flight Compensation Regulation. Several platforms have emerged that offer standardised assessment and enforcement of such claims, either on the basis of an assignment or in the customer's name, against a success fee of 20 to 30 per cent of the compensation sum. In Germany, in the aftermath of the diesel emissions scandal, a website has also been established by a German company operating under the name of 'European Consumer Rights ECR GmbH', advertising services around the enforcement of claims on behalf of car buyers. The information presented on the website[261] about the company and its services seems quite opaque. To some degree, this demonstrates that the services offered by public institutions and established consumer organisations are not fully fit for purpose, as it seems that commercial players with an unclear background are able to make relatively easy money by taking sizeable success fees for low-risk litigation.

---

257 See for example Sousa Antunes, 'Portugal' (n 20) Section II.A.4.; Gaboardi, 'Italy' (n 17) Section V.B.2.; Meller-Hannich, 'Germany' (n 69) Section I.C.

258 Leupold, 'Austria' (n 25) Section II.C.; see also Domej, 'Kollektiver Rechtsschutz' (n 129) 430; Leupold, 'Enforcing Consumer Rights' (n 25) 123.

259 Schweizerischer Konsumentenschutz, 'VW-Klage eingereicht: Meilenstein bei der Rechtsdurchsetzung von Massenschäden' <http://www.konsumentenschutz.ch/medienmitteilungen/2017/12/vw-klage-eingereicht-meilenstein-bei-der-rechtsdurchsetzung-von-massenschaeden/>.

260 HGer, Order of 6 December 2019, HG170257-O.

261 <http://www.verbraucherritter.de/>.

B. COLLECTIVE SETTLEMENTS

Collective actions are often settled instead of being fully litigated.[262] This was also the case with the US[263] and Australian[264] litigations in the aftermath of the diesel emissions scandal. In Germany, the *Verbraucherzentrale* and Volkswagen also reached a settlement concerning the model declaratory action (*Musterfeststellungsklage*) brought by the *Verbraucherzentrale.*[265] In several jurisdictions, specific rules for collective settlements have been established, with the principles contained in FRCP rule 23(e) and the corresponding US practice[266] serving as an important inspiration. In particular, the content of such settlements is often subject to more far-reaching scrutiny than that of settlements reached in individual lawsuits among the parties whose rights are being disposed of. The main reason behind such scrutiny is the principal-agent problem occurring in representative litigation. As the represented individuals normally are not in a position to monitor their representative properly, the representative may be tempted to enter into a self-serving settlement, perhaps even in collusion with the opponent ('sweetheart deal'). Scrutiny by the court might also help to protect the defendant from being blackmailed into settling a meritless case. However, making sure that unfounded claims can be effectively defended is probably more important for tackling the latter problem than settlement scrutiny.

In the US, class actions are often certified for settlement purposes only, after a settlement has already been negotiated.[267] While this practice has developed without a specific legislative basis in the US, several jurisdictions have introduced explicit rules on the approval of settlements reached out of court without the necessity of prior litigation. In Brazil, for example, civil consumer entities and economic associations may regulate through a written convention, *inter alia*, consumer complaints and consumer conflict composition. The settlement becomes legally binding upon the members of the organisations signing up to it after registration with a notary. However, this procedure is rarely used.[268]

---

262 From the US perspective, see Murray, 'American Class action' (n 108) 86.

263 See Schmitz, 'US' (n 38) Sections II.A., II.C., and III.A.

264 See Cashman, 'Australia' (n 32) Sections I.B. and II.

265 According to Vebraucherzentrale, 'Vergleich zwischen vzbv und Volkswagen steht: Bis 20. April entscheiden!' <https://www.verbraucherzentrale.de/wissen/vertraege-reklamation/kundenrechte/vergleich-zwischen-vzbv-und-volkswagen-steht-bis-20-april-entscheiden-29738>, the settlement is expected to bring compensation of around €830 million to affected customers. On 20 April 2020, *Volkswagen* issued a press statement according to which at least €620 million would be paid out in total, see <https://www.volkswagen-newsroom.com/de/pressemitteilungen/vw-vergleich-volkswagen-schliesst-200000-vergleiche-auszahlungen-in-hoehe-von-620-millionen-euro-sicher-5968>.

266 See, for example, Peter, *Gruppenvergleichsverfahren* (n 211) 43ff.

267 For a critical perspective on this phenomenon, see Howard M Erichson, 'The Problem of Settlement Class Actions' (2014) 82 Geo Wash L Rev 951ff.

268 Marques, 'Brazil' (n 13) Section III.A.

The Danish system provides for a collective settlement out of court or in court. The former is regularly negotiated by the administrative authority and consumers may join, whereas the latter is subject to the class action regime. This means, *inter alia*, that it requires judicial approval.[269] Similar models exist in France and Italy, either based on an opt-in mechanism and/or subject to court approval.[270] The best-known European settlement-only mechanism, however, is probably the Dutch collective settlement procedure under the WCAM.[271] It allows court approval of a collective settlement agreed between a foundation or association acting on behalf of affected individuals and the infringer. If approved, the settlement becomes legally binding for all members of the represented group who did not opt out.[272] This mechanism was originally introduced without the accompanying possibility of a collective action. This was justified with the argument that such a procedure was well suited for a jurisdiction with a strong settlement culture such as the Netherlands.[273] Obviously, an opt-out based settlement-only regime is particularly attractive for potential defendants, as they can achieve an overall resolution of large-scale disputes without the risk of collective litigation. However, from the perspective of affected individuals, this system can be rather problematic. In the end, the lack of a possibility to bring a collective action for compensatory relief was indeed perceived as a shortcoming by the Dutch legislature as well – which was the reason behind the latest reform.[274]

From the perspective of the protection of affected group members, scrutiny of the settlement by a court is less crucial where such a settlement only becomes effective against them if they explicitly accept it. Therefore, in jurisdictions where an opt-in regime is in place, there is no obvious necessity of introducing a procedure for approval of out-of-court settlements. However, the case could be made that a 'fairness stamp' by a court might encourage affected individuals to accept the settlement, which in turn might reduce the number of cases that become litigious. Nevertheless, court scrutiny is most important if an opt-out regime applies or if the case was originally started on an opt-in basis, but the settlement becomes binding on group members without their explicit consent or maybe even without the possibility of opting out. However, even in such situations, the need for court scrutiny, particularly regarding the fairness (as opposed to the lawfulness) of the settlement, is not universally acknowledged.

---

269 Schäfer, 'Denmark' (n 15) Section I.C.3.e); further Werlauff, 'Class Actions' (n 35) 207; Lindencrone Petersen and Werlauff, 'Denmark' (n 35) 69.

270 See Gaboardi, 'Italy' (n 17) Section V.B.2.; Jeuland, 'France' (n 16) Section I.C.4.

271 Collective Settlement of Mass Damage Act (*Wet Collectieve Afwikkeling Massaschade* – WCAM).

272 van Boom and Pavillon, 'Netherlands' (n 19) Section II.A.

273 See Andreas Mom, *Kollektiver Rechtsschutz in den Niederlanden* (Mohr Siebeck 2011) 330ff.

274 van Boom and Pavillon, 'Netherlands' (n 19) Section II.A.

The Commission's proposal for a Representative Action Directive stipulates an obligation of Member States to provide for the possibility of the court or an authority to invite the parties to a collective action to enter into settlement negotiations (article 8(2) and (3) of the Commission's proposal). Any settlement reached shall be subject to the scrutiny of the court or an authority (article 8(4) of the Commission's proposal). In the case of an approval, there must be an opt-in or an opt-out possibility for individual consumers. Under the Commission's proposal, therefore, national law could not simply bind consumers to a settlement negotiated by the qualified entity on their behalf, even if they previously opted in to the collective action. The Council wants to make the possibility for consumers to opt in to or out of the settlement optional for Member States, regardless of whether the collective action has been brought on an opt-in or on an opt-out basis. The European Parliament even proposes to remove entirely the possibility for consumers to avoid being bound by a collective settlement. According to the Commission's proposal and the European Parliament's position at first reading, the court scrutinising the settlement would have to assess both the legality and the fairness of the settlement (article 8(4) of the respective texts). Meanwhile, the Council's General Approach provides that approval must only be refused if the settlement 'is contrary to mandatory national law or includes conditions which cannot be enforced'. However, it would be optional for Member States to provide that unfairness of the settlement can be a basis for refusing approval.

The Commission's proposal also contains a provision on the approval of collective settlements reached outside a pending collective action. Such settlements would be subject to the same rules on scrutiny as settlements reached within collective action proceedings. Furthermore, they would only be eligible for approval if no other collective action were pending in respect of the same trader and the same practice in the same Member State (article 8(1) of the Commission's proposal), presumably to prevent 'sweetheart deals'.[275] The European Parliament, at first reading, removed this restriction. The Council proposes to drop the entire rule on the approval of settlements reached outside pending litigation, which would presumably mean that it would be entirely up to Member States how to deal with such settlements, perhaps with the exception that an out-of-court settlement may not interfere with the rights of consumers on whose behalf a pending collective action is being litigated by a qualified entity not involved in the settlement.

The ELI/UNIDROIT draft rules contain detailed provisions on both out-of-court and in-court collective settlements. In general, according to draft rule X14, the court should facilitate a collective settlement by appropriate means. An in-court settlement requires the approval of the court (draft rule X18). For this purpose, the court may demand all the information it needs to assess the

---

275 Domej, 'Verbandsklagenrichtlinie' (n 48) 450.

fairness of the proposed settlement and appoint an appropriate expert (draft rule X17(1)). The court must advertise the proposed settlement and consider any comments made by the parties and the group members, and it may consider any other comments as well (draft rule X17(2) and (3)). An approved settlement binds all group members who have already opted in at the time of approval (draft rule X19) or all those who have not opted out (draft rule X20). An out-of-court collective settlement also requires the approval of the court, for which the same standards apply in principle. However, the ELI/UNIDROIT Draft Rules allow the parties to propose either an opt-in or an opt-out system (draft rule X25) and to demand a certain number of group members for the settlement to be effective (draft rule X25 (3)).

The Dutch experience has shown that a well-designed collective settlement procedure may be a successful tool to deal with mass cases effectively but that rules on collective actions may not be relevant only for enabling actual litigation. Indeed, they may be at least as important for incentivising settlement negotiations and for providing an appropriate negotiating balance in such negotiations. However, it would be problematic to conceptualise the enabling of settlements as the primary function of (potential) collective litigation.[276] A state governed by the rule of law must be able to ensure effective enforcement of claims if a settlement is impossible, or a party is unwilling to settle for whatever reason. Furthermore, the courts' role in developing the law might be put in jeopardy if litigating cases through to a final judgment is not a viable option.

IV. CONCLUSION

The jurisdictions covered in this book take very different approaches to the enforcement of consumer law. In some, the focus is on administrative or criminal sanctions, and enforcement of rules aiming at the protection of consumers is mainly seen as a task of public bodies or agencies. In others, private law instruments predominate. However, the boundaries between public and private enforcement are sometimes difficult to draw. Some jurisdictions entrust the enforcement of private law sanctions to public bodies or to publicly

---

[276] See, in this context, Samuel Baumgartner, 'Rechtsdurchsetzung als Aufgabe des Zivilprozesses' (2017) 43 Schweizerische Zeitschrift für Zivilprozess- und Zwangsvollstreckungsrecht 243, 244ff, 250ff; Rolf Stürner, 'Richterliche Vergleichsverhandlung und richterlicher Vergleich aus juristischer Sicht' in Isaak Meier, Hans Michael Riemer and Peter Weimar (eds), *Recht und Rechtsdurchsetzung: Festschrift für Hans Ulrich Walder zum 65. Geburtstag* (Schulthess 1994) 273, 279; Walter Fellmann, 'Der Gerichtliche Vergleich' in Alfred Koller (ed), *Haftpflicht- und Versicherungsrechtstagung 2001: Tagungsbeiträge* (Institut für Versicherungswirtschaft der Universität St. Gallen 2001) 65, 89; Dieter Leipold, 'Der Zivilprozess zwischen Rechtsschutz und gütlicher Konfliktbeilegung' in National and Kapodistrian University of Athens (ed), *Festschrift für Professor Nikolaos K. Klamaris* (Sakkoulas Publications 2016) 443, 449ff.

funded associations, usually by giving them standing to sue in civil courts for this purpose, which may be characterised as 'hybrid enforcement'. In some jurisdictions, public authorities or ombudsmen even have the power in some cases themselves to order redress payments to consumers, but this model of administering collective redress for consumers does not seem to have been relevant so far in the context of the diesel emissions scandal. Redress payments or other methods of repairing the damage to consumers may also be the subject of agreements between traders and public authorities.

In some situations, public enforcement might be preferable to private enforcement. In cases where there is widespread small-scale damage, a fine or disgorgement of profits as a public law sanction could be more acceptable and easier to enforce in many states than creating a private law claim or a specific collective redress mechanism for that purpose, which in the end might not even function because of built-in safeguards or limitations. Nevertheless, as far as private law claims of individual consumers are concerned, there ought to be a functioning judicial mechanism allowing consumers to bring their claims before the court and enabling traders to defend themselves successfully against unfounded claims. Whether a mechanism 'delivers' adequate redress is not just a matter of how much money is paid out to consumers. It is also a matter of the fairness of the underlying procedure, which should always be a primary concern in a jurisdiction based on the rule of law.[277] That is the case even where the amount of individual damages is low. It is all the more so in cases like the diesel emissions scandal where it would be difficult to accept against the background of most European legal traditions to put the enforcement of substantial private law claims into the hands of non-judicial public bodies instead of providing for fair and effective judicial procedures.

There are significant differences between the jurisdictions studied in this book as regards the severity of sanctions faced by car manufacturers and the sums recovered by consumers in the aftermath of the diesel emissions scandal. In the US substantial payments were made, while in Europe those wishing to pursue redress claims faced significant difficulties, both at the substantive and at the procedural level. However, it is difficult to put up one system of consumer law enforcement as a model to be generally followed. Even if substantial payments are ordered or agreed to, this does not necessarily mean that the affected consumers receive full compensation for the harm they incurred. It has been a long-standing criticism against the US system of class actions that counsel tend to profit more from the outcomes of such litigation than the class members whose interests they purportedly represent. Furthermore, the defendant's perspective also needs to be properly taken into account.

277 See Klaus F Röhl, 'Verfahrensgerechtigkeit (Procedural Justice): Einführung in den Themenbereich und Überblick' (1993) 14 Zeitschrift für Rechtssoziologie 1, 1ff.

In Europe, the difficulties encountered by consumers in the aftermath of the diesel emissions scandal have drawn broad attention to the shortcomings and limitations of traditional procedural instruments when dealing with mass harm situations. This has injected new momentum into the debates and controversies around collective redress. It has also provided those making the case for strengthening collective redress instruments with fresh arguments. However, the ongoing legislative process aiming at creating an EU Representative Actions Directive demonstrates that EU-wide consensus on a coherent concept of collective litigation is still lacking and will probably be difficult to achieve in the foreseeable future, at least beyond rather weak minimum standards. This process has also shown that there is still much need for debate and research as regards the effectiveness of different models of mass litigation and collective redress, as well as with respect to the purported potential for abuse that is often used as an argument for curbing the effectiveness of such instruments.

It is a common, and probably justified, critique that the European legislature does not have a coherent vision of collective redress. However, the reason probably is not that the individual actors have no such vision. They just have very different, and often irreconcilable, visions of what the collective redress landscape should look like and, indeed, whether there should be such a landscape at all. It will therefore remain inevitable for some time to forge compromises, and it will also remain inevitable to leave a lot of policy decisions to the Member States. Perhaps that is not all bad. Collective litigation may be an area of law where productive systems competition is possible and different solutions can be tested in different Member States – both based on specific legislation for collective legislation and based on 'workarounds' such as the assignment models. However, in the current political environment it would probably be naïve to expect that the decisive impulses for an effective system of collective litigation will come from the EU level.

PRIVATE ENFORCEMENT IN EUROPEAN CAPITAL MARKETS LAW

Perspectives for a Reform at the Example of the Obligation to Disclose Inside Information

Rüdiger VEIL*

I. INTRODUCTION

The investor lawsuits against VW for failure to disclose inside information[1] cast a spotlight on private enforcement of European capital markets law.

* Rüdiger Veil, Dr., Professor, Ludwig-Maximilians-University of Munich, Law Faculty, Chair of Civil Law and Company Law, Executive Director of Munich Center for Capital Markets Law.

1 The claims for damages against Volkswagen AG are pending at the Braunschweig Higher Regional Court (Oberlandesgericht Braunschweig (OLG Braunschweig)) and the claims for damages against its majority shareholder Porsche Automobil Holding SE are pending at the Stuttgart Higher Regional Court (Oberlandesgericht Stuttgart (OLG Stuttgart)). See Frank Matthias Drost, 'Anlegerklagen im VW-Dieselskandal werden getrennt verhandelt' *Handelsblatt* (Düsseldorf, 12 August 2019) <http://www.handelsblatt.com/finanzen/steuern-recht/recht/urteil-des-olg-braunschweig-anlegerklagen-im-vw-dieselskandal-werden-getrennt-verhandelt/24894846.html?ticket=ST-32819419-dudHHvuAfO32AfP2Nhej-ap1>.

European legislation to date has been limited to harmonising and standardising supervisory law.[2] The European legislature introduced only very few provisions that grant investors claims for damages.[3] Private enforcement is still a matter of national laws. Therefore, this chapter will first outline how private enforcement of capital markets law has developed in selected Member States (Section II.). The research question is whether a legal basis for claims for damages exists in the Member States, granting investors the right to sue the issuer if they are not informed as soon as possible and correctly about inside information, such as compliance-relevant matters of an issuer.

Subsequently, perspectives of private enforcement will be discussed. First, it is debatable whether the ECJ could oblige Member States to ensure effective private enforcement (Section III.). After all, the ECJ has already ruled in competition law that the full effectiveness of European law requires that individual actions for damages must be possible. A second perspective could be to harmonise private enforcement throughout the Union. This has already happened in European competition law by a directive requiring Member States to ensure that any third party may seek compensation for its damages. It will therefore be discussed whether harmonisation in European capital markets law makes sense and which concepts of harmonisation should be considered (Section IV.).

The European market abuse law consists of prohibitions on insider dealing and market manipulation. Furthermore, it provides obligations for the disclosure of directors' dealings and inside information of the issuer to the public. The claims for damages against VW are primarily based on the allegation that VW did not inform capital markets in a timely manner of inside information. This might have violated the ad hoc disclosure obligation (today regulated in article 17 of the MAR). The scope of this chapter is therefore limited to the private enforcement of this obligation. It will not deal with the private enforcement of insider bans and prohibition of market manipulation.

II. PRIVATE ENFORCEMENT OF THE OBLIGATION TO DISCLOSE INSIDE INFORMATION IN EU MEMBER STATES

Private enforcement has two dimensions. On the one hand, it presupposes that investors have the right to demand compensation from another person. Such right can be granted by a special legal basis for claims, which provides

---

2 Cf on the history of European capital markets legislation Rüdiger Veil, '§1 History' in Rüdiger Veil (ed), *European Capital Markets Law* (2nd edn, Hart Publishing 2017) para 1.

3 The most important example is art 35a of the CRA on the liability of credit rating agencies.

detailed prerequisites for compensation. It is also possible that investors refer to general rules of private law, in particular of tort law. On the other hand, private enforcement depends on the possibility for investors to claim damages before courts. In the event of breaches of disclosure obligations under capital markets law, the damage suffered by investors is generally small. However, a large number of investors are typically affected by false information. In the case of so-called scattered damages, it is rational for investors to not file claims for damages because of high-cost risks. Special mechanisms of collective redress are therefore needed to counter the rational apathy of investors.[4]

The following analysis of private enforcement in the EU Member States is limited to the first issue (substantive law). It is based on the country reports on the legal situation in Austria,[5] Denmark,[6] France,[7] Germany,[8] Italy,[9] Lithuania,[10] the Netherlands,[11] Portugal[12] and the UK,[13] but also makes use of the findings obtained in international legal literature.[14]

Before evaluating the national regimes, it should be briefly highlighted that assessing the *effectiveness* of private enforcement is a complex task.[15] First, one has to analyse the prerequisites for all possible civil remedies in depth. The focus is certainly on the rules and regulations, which give investors the right to claim

---

4 Cf Thomas MJ Möllers and Bernhard Pregler, 'Zivilrechtliche Rechtsdurchsetzung und kollektiver Rechtsschutz im Wirtschaftsrecht' (2012) 176 ZHR 144, 151–83.

5 Georg E Kodek, 'Enforcing Capital Market Law in Austria' in this book Section II. (hereafter Kodek, 'Austria').

6 Anders Schäfer, 'Enforcing Consumer and Capital Markets Law in Denmark' in this book Section II.C. (hereafter Schäfer, 'Denmark').

7 Emannuel Jeuland, 'Enforcing Consumer and Capital Markets Law in France' in this book Sections II.B. and II.C. (hereafter Jeuland, 'France').

8 Caroline Meller-Hannich, 'Enforcing Consumer and Capital Markets Law in Germany' in this book Section I. (hereafter Meller-Hannich, 'Germany').

9 Marcello Gaboardi, 'Enforcing Consumer and Capital Markets Law in Italy' in this book Section IV. (hereafter Gaboardi, 'Italy').

10 Egidija Tamošiūnienė and Remigijus Jokubauskas, 'Enforcing Consumer and Capital Markets Law in Lithuania' in this book Section IV. (hereafter Tamošiūnienė and Jokubauskas, 'Lithuania').

11 Willem H van Boom and Charlotte MDS Pavillon, 'Enforcing Consumer and Capital Markets Law in The Netherlands' in this book Sections II. and III.A. (hereafter van Boom and Pavillon, 'The Netherlands').

12 Henrique Sousa Antunes, 'Enforcing Consumer and Capital Markets Law in Portugal' in this book Section II. (hereafter Sousa Antunes, 'Portugal').

13 John Sorabji, 'Enforcing Consumer and Capital Markets Law in England and Wales' in this book Sections III. and IV. (hereafter Sorabji, 'England and Wales').

14 Cf Pierre-Henri Conac and Martin Gelter (eds), *Global Securities Litigation and Enforcement* (Cambridge University Press 2019); Philipp Koch, '§19 Disclosure of Inside Information' in Rüdiger Veil (ed), *European Capital Markets Law* (2nd edn, Hart Publishing 2017) paras 105–24.

15 The contrary positions developed by Rafael La Porta and others, 'What works in Securities Laws?' (2006) 61 JFin 1–32 on the one hand and Howell Jackson and Mark J Roe, 'Public and Private Enforcement in Securities laws: Resource-based evidence' (2009) 93 Journal of Financial Economics 207–38 on the other are legendary.

damages due to incorrect capital market information. However, other legal remedies may also be considered, in particular skimming off profits, as well as contractual rescission and other compensation rights.

With regard to claims for damages under capital markets law, it is of particular interest how the legal systems of the Member States deal with the difficult questions of causation[16] and damage[17] as well as the fault requirements.[18] The investor lawsuits against Porsche and VW have also revealed that general civil law issues play an important role: according to which rules is knowledge (obtained by employees and executive managers) attributed to the issuer?[19] Finally, it is necessary to consider who in a legal procedure bears the burden of proving that the inside information made public was incorrect, that the decision of the investor to acquire or sell shares was based on the inside information and that the issuer acted wilfully or with gross negligence: the investor or the issuer?

The country reports address these aspects, but also show that courts in the Member States have not yet had the opportunity to decide the legal issues. Against this background, it is not possible to give a conclusive answer if private enforcement in these Member States is effective. However, the country reports and other comparative legal literature give an idea as to whether and how legislature in the Member States has dealt with the key problems of investor protection under capital markets law. These findings make it possible to approach the question of the effectiveness of private enforcement in the Member States.

---

16 Causality issues can become relevant at two levels. A civil liability can presuppose, firstly, a causality between the breach of a duty and the transaction (purchase of a security) and, secondly, a causality between the transaction and the loss.

17 The damage can be the difference between the actual and the hypothetical acquisition price (so-called out-of-pocket damage). In addition, the investor may claim payment or the reimbursement of the acquisition price against the return of the shares (in case the shares have meanwhile been sold, the difference between the acquisition price and the disposal price).

18 Liability for damages may be based on intent, gross negligence or simple negligence. US law requires that the perpetrator has acted with scienter (rule 10b-5). The US Supreme Court initially interpreted this element strictly. In *Ernst & Ernst v Hochfelder* 425 US 185 (1976), the court stated: 'In this opinion, the term "scienter" refers to a mental state embracing intent to deceive, manipulate, or defraud.' After several Court of Appeals had recognised a recklessness standard, the US Supreme Court in *Matrixx Initiatives Inc v Siracusano* 563 US 27 (2011) stated: 'We assume without deciding, that the recklessness standard applied by the Court of Appeals is sufficient to establish scienter.'

19 The question of the attribution of knowledge can already become relevant with regard to the obligation to disclose inside information. It is argued in literature that the disclosure obligation pursuant to art 17 of the MAR presupposes that the issuer was aware of inside information. Cf Hans-Christoph Ihrig, 'Wissenszurechnung im Kapitalmarktrecht – untersucht anhand der Pflicht zur Ad-hoc-Publizität gemäß Art. 17 MAR' (2017) 181 ZHR 381. However, it also brought forward that art 17 of the MAR provides the duty to disclose inside information irrespective of whether the issuer had knowledge or not. Cf Michael Nietsch, 'Emittentenwissen, Wissenszurechnung und Ad-hoc-Publizitätspflicht' [2018] ZIP 142.

First of all, it is of interest to know whether special legal bases for claims exist in the Member States. In this case, legislature may have addressed the most relevant complex issues, such as the question of compensation for investors who bought or sold securities on secondary markets. This does not necessarily imply that rulemakers have given an investor-friendly answer to all legal questions. It is also possible that they rely upon courts to put the requirements into more concrete terms and to develop facilitations of evidence for investors.[20] However, it can at least be inferred from regimes providing a special legal basis what importance national legislature attaches to private liability for damages, in particular whether it provides for liability for damages solely for reasons of compensation or (also) for reasons of prevention.

This research project examined the legal situation in nine EU Member States. Only two of them have special legal bases for claims, namely Germany[21] and the UK.[22] The regulatory approach differs in both Member States. In Germany, liability for damages requires that the issuer intentionally or grossly negligently breaches its obligations under article 17 of the MAR. The requirement for fault is presumed, so that the issuer has to exonerate itself. A causal link between an investor's transaction and its loss is generally not necessary. This liability provision not only pursues the purpose of compensating the investor, but also has a certain preventive function, since its requirements are already fulfilled if an issuer violates the disclosure obligation with gross negligence. This is not the case for liability for damages in the UK.[23] The hurdles for civil liability are high. If the publication of inside information was omitted, the issuer is only held liable for intent.[24] If the issuer disclosed inside information to the public incorrectly, investors are entitled to claim damages, if the issuer acted intentionally or recklessly. However, the burden of proof is not facilitated for investors.

There is still no practical experience with the liability regime in the UK. This is different in Germany. In addition to the special statutory liability under the German Securities Trading Act, the Federal Court of Justice (BGH) has recognised in numerous decisions that the issuer and members of the

20 German law provides in s 97 and s 98 of the WpHG for a special statutory liability of the issuer. However, the two provisions do not regulate the nature and extent of damages. These relevant aspects had to be clarified by the Federal Court of Justice (BGH, Judgment of 13 December 2011, XI ZR 51/10).

21 See ss 97, 98 of the WpHG.

22 See s 90A of the FSMA.

23 The high demands on liability for damages can probably also be explained by the fact that the focus in the UK has always been on public enforcement. Private enforcement, on the other hand, plays no relevant role. Liability for damages is criticised by academia above all because it would only lead to pocket-shifting. See Ian MacNeil, 'Enforcement and Sanctioning' in Niamh Moloney, Eilis Ferran and Jennifer Payne (eds), *The Oxford Handbook of Financial Regulation* (Oxford University Press 2015) 280, 293–94 (hereafter MacNeil, 'Enforcement').

24 Cf s 90A sch 10A(3) of the FSMA.

management board are liable to pay damages under tort law.[25] One may complain that the BGH has refused to adopt the fraud-on-the-market theory developed by the US Supreme Court in *Basic v Levison*.[26] The BGH is however quite aware of the evidence problems of investors and recognises under certain conditions evidence facilitations.[27] In addition, the court does not impose excessively strict requirements on the proof of intent.[28]

In the other EU Member States, investors can solely base their claims for damages on the general rules of private law, in particular tort law. There are therefore theoretically legal bases for liability of issuers. However, most of the regimes still have their test ahead of them. Only in Austria[29] and the Netherlands,[30] have courts dealt with the liability of issuers due to failure to disclose inside information. It is noteworthy that the highest Austrian court has developed principles that provide a far-reaching investor protection. In Austria, the issuer may already be liable for damages if the obligation to publish inside information is negligently violated.[31] In the Netherlands, causality and compensation problems typical of investor lawsuits do not yet appear to have been solved by the highest courts.[32]

The conclusion on investor protection through tort law in Europe is ambivalent. Only in a few Member States – Germany, Austria and the UK – private enforcement of the obligation to disclose inside information has been acknowledged by legislature or the Supreme Courts.[33] This is not true for other Member States

---

25 BGH, Judgment of 19 July 2004, II ZR 218/03, BGHZ 160, 134 and BGH, Judgment of 19 July 2004, II ZR 402/02, BGHZ 160, 149; BGH, Judgment of 16 December 2004, 1 Str 420/03, AG 2005, 162; BGH, Judgment of 28 November 2005, II ZR 80/04, AG 2007, 322; BGH, Order of 28 November 2005, II ZR 246/04, AG 2007, 324; BGH, Judgment of 4 June 2007, II ZR 147/05, AG 2007, 620; BGH, Judgment of 4 June 2007, II ZR 173/05, AG 2007, 623; BGH, Judgment of 7 January 2008, II ZR 229/05, AG 2008, 252; BGH, Judgment of 7 January 2008, II ZR 68/06, AG 2008, 254; BGH, Judgment of 3 March 2008, II ZR 310/06, AG 2008, 377.

26 BGH, Judgment of 19 July 2004, II ZR 218/03, BGHZ 160, 134, 144.

27 BGH, Judgment of 19 July 2004, II ZR 218/03, BGHZ 160, 134, 146.

28 BGH, Judgment of 19 July 2004, II ZR 402/02, BGHZ 160, 149, 155.

29 Kodek, 'Austria' (n 5) Section II.B.

30 van Boom and Pavillon, 'The Netherlands' (n 11) Section I.B.2.

31 The Austrian Supreme Court has decided that the regulations on an obligation to publish insider information are to be qualified as so-called protective laws. Consequently, a liability for damages may already exist in the case of simple negligence. Cf Susanne Kalss, Martin Oppitz and Johannes Zollner, *Kapitalmarktrecht – Volume I System* (2nd edn, Linde 2015) 16 para 99.

32 Cf van Boom and Pavillon, 'The Netherlands' (n 11) Section II.D.: 'An investor (…) who has been misled by VW, has to state and prove to establish causation in order to claim compensation for his/her financial loss. The general rule with respect to the burden of proof applies.'

33 In Finland a special legal bases exists as well, cf Ville Pönkä, 'Finland: Protecting Minority Investors and compensating their losses' in Pierre-Henri Conac and Martin Gelter (eds), *Global Securities Litigation and Enforcement* (Cambridge University Press 2019) 303, 315. Spain provides for a special legal bases re: financial information, cf Mónica Fuentes Naharro, 'Spain: Minority Investors' Protection in Spain: Civil Liability Remedies under Securities law' in Pierre-Henri Conac and Martin Gelter (eds), *Global Securities Litigation and Enforcement* (Cambridge University Press 2019) 595, 609.

analysed in this research project.[34] It cannot be ruled out that the courts of these countries (Denmark, France, Italy, Lithuania and Portugal) and those of other EU Member States may find that issuers are liable for damages under tort law.[35] It is open to question, however, whether courts will then recognise the facilitation of evidence in favour of investors re: causality between the transaction and the loss. It is also uncertain whether courts will only accept compensation for so-called out-of-pocket damages or whether they will also grant in rem restitution. The fault requirements (intent or negligence) result from the respective tort law systems and are probably regulated differently in the Member States.

Overall, it cannot be argued that private enforcement of capital market disclosure under MAR has preventive effects in the EU. It has also not yet become apparent that Member States feel exposed to a regulatory competition that will lead to a certain minimum level of investor protection in the medium or long term. The reform in the UK in 2010[36] might be the result of a competition between legal systems or at least between regulatory ideas.[37] Other Member States, on the other hand, have not yet considered it useful to develop an effective regime of private enforcement to attract institutional investors. This is probably due to the fact that a high level of investor protection through civil liability has not yet been a relevant decision-making parameter for institutional investors.

III. THE (POSSIBLE) ROLE OF THE EUROPEAN COURT OF JUSTICE

European law does not explicitly require Member States to introduce private liability of issuers and/or the management board. Nevertheless, one could interpret it this way. In literature, some academics have argued that private enforcement should be recognised under European law for reasons of the *effet utile* of Union law.[38] These scholars refer to decisions of the ECJ in the *Courage* and

34 In Poland, only the general rules of the Civil Code apply. Cf Mariola Lemonnier, 'Poland: Investor Protection in the Polish Capital Market – Selected Issues' in Pierre-Henri Conac and Martin Gelter (eds), *Global Securities Litigation and Enforcement* (Cambridge University Press 2019) 517, 529.

35 Cf Emmanuel P Mastromanolis, 'Greece: Public Enforcement and Civil Litigation in the Greek Paradigm of Minority Investor Protection' in Pierre-Henri Conac and Martin Gelter (eds), *Global Securities Litigation and Enforcement* (Cambridge University Press 2019) 412, 427.

36 The amendments were implemented by the Financial Services and Markets Act 2000 (Liability of Issuers) Regulations 2010; see Louise Gulliver and Jennifer Payne, *Corporate Finance Law* (2nd edn, Hart 2015) 406–504.

37 Cf Malte Wundenberg, 'Perspektiven der privaten Rechtsdurchsetzung im europäischen Kapitalmarktrecht' [2015] ZGR 124, 144–47 (hereafter Wundenberg, 'Perspektiven').

38 Affirmative Alexander Hellgardt, 'Europarechtliche Vorgaben für die Kapitalmarktinformationshaftung' [2012] AG 154, 163ff (hereafter Hellgardt,

Muñoz cases and argue the principles developed by the ECJ would also apply in European market abuse law.

A. CASE LAW

The *Courage* decision concerned the European prohibition of abuse of dominant market positions (at the time governed by article 85 of the EC Treaty). For the ECJ, this is a fundamental provision, which is indispensable for the performance of Community tasks and, in particular, the functioning of the internal market. Regarding individual rights of action, the court stated:

> The full effectiveness of Article 85 of the Treaty and, in particular, the practical effect of the prohibition laid down in Article 85(1) would be put at risk if it were not open to any individual to claim damages for loss caused to him by (...) conduct liable to restrict or distort competition.[39]

It is noteworthy that the ECJ also focused on the preventive effect of the right to claim damages:[40]

> Indeed, the existence of such a right strengthens the working of the Community competition rules and discourages agreements or practices, which are frequently covert, which are liable to restrict or distort competition. From that point of view, actions for damages before the national courts can make a significant contribution to the maintenance of effective competition in the Community.[41]

'Europarechtliche Vorgaben'); Christoph Seibt and Bernward Wollenschläger, 'Revision des Marktmissbrauchsrechts durch Marktmissbrauchsverordnung und Richtlinie über strafrechtliche Sanktionen für Marktmanipulation' [2014] AG 593, 607; Dörte Poelzig, 'Enforcement im deutschen und europäischen Kapitalmarktrecht' [2015] ZGR 801, 815ff (hereafter Poelzig, 'Enforcement'); Jan-Sebastian Schütt, *Europäische Marktmissbrauchsverordnung und Individualschutz* (Dunker & Humblot 2019) (hereafter Schütt, *Europäische Marktmissbrauchsverordnung*); Vassilis Tountopoulos, 'Market Abuse and Private Enforcement' [2014] ECFR 297, 324ff (hereafter Tountopoulos, 'Market Abuse'); according to Thomas MJ Möllers, '§84 Organhaftung' in Peter Derleder, Kai-Oliver Knops and Heinz Bamberger (eds), *Deutsches und europäisches Bank- und Kapitalmarktrecht, Volume 2* (3rd edn, Springer 2017) §84 para 37, 39, the legal situation is open. Other academics reject the idea that the *effet utile* of Union law would require private liability of issuers. Cf Wundenberg, 'Perspektiven' (n 37) 124, 134–35; David Markworth, 'Marktmissbrauchsverordnung und effet utile' (2019) 183 ZHR 46, 64ff (hereafter Markworth, 'Marktmissbrauchsverordnung').

39 ECJ, C-453/99 *Courage Ltd v Bernard Crehan and Bernard Crehan v Courage Ltd and Others* [20 September 2001] ECR 2001 I-06297 para 26.

40 Dörte Poelzig, *Normdurchsetzung durch Privatrecht* (Mohr Siebeck 2012) 143; Schütt, *Europäische Marktmissbrauchsverordnung* (n 38) 155.

41 ECJ, C-453/99 *Courage Ltd v Bernard Crehan and Bernard Crehan v Courage Ltd and Others* [20 September 2001] ECR 2001 I-06297 para 27.

The ECJ was well aware that European law does not provide for specific rules allowing claim of damages. In the court's view, Member States are responsible for ensuring that the law is effectively enforced:

> However, in the absence of Community rules governing the matter, it is for the domestic legal system of each Member State to designate the courts and tribunals having jurisdiction and to lay down the detailed procedural rules governing actions for safeguarding rights which individuals derive directly from Community law, provided that such rules are not less favourable than those governing similar domestic actions (principle of equivalence) and that they do not render practically impossible or excessively difficult the exercise of rights conferred by Community law (principle of effectiveness).[42]

The *Courage* decision seems to be limited to the procedural dimension of private enforcement.[43] In *Muñoz*,[44] the ECJ confirmed these principles of interpretation, but also went a step further and addressed the necessity of legal bases for claims. *Muñoz* concerned a European regulation on quality standards for fruit and vegetables. It did not contain any liability rules. The ECJ considered the question of whether it should be possible for a market participant to enforce compliance with the provisions of the European regulation on quality standards for fruit and vegetables against a competitor in civil proceedings. The Court answered in the affirmative, albeit in very general terms:

> Pursuant to the second subparagraph of Article 189 of the EC Treaty [...] regulations have general application and are directly applicable in all Member States. Accordingly, owing to their very nature and their place in the system of sources of Community law, regulations operate to confer rights on individuals which the national courts have a duty to protect (...).[45]

The ECJ then stated with regard to the purposes of the EU regulation that it must be possible to enforce the rights in civil proceedings:

> Accordingly, the full effectiveness of the rules on quality standards and, in particular, the practical effect of the obligation [...] imply that it must be possible to enforce that obligation by means of civil proceedings instituted by a trader against a competitor.

42 Ibid, para 29.

43 Dissenting opinion: Assimakis P Kominos, 'New Prospects for Private Enforcement of EC Competition Law: Courage v. Crehand and the Community Right to Damages' (2002) 39 CMLR 446, 466: 'In Courage the Court gave appropriate answers to most of these concerns by recognizing a right to damages as a matter of Community rather than of national law (...)'.

44 ECJ, C-253/00 *Antonio Muñoz y Cia SA and Superior Fruiticola SA v Frumar Ltd and Redbridge Produce Marketing Ltd* [17 September 2002] ECR 2002 I-07289.

45 ECJ, C-253/00 *Antonio Muñoz y Cia SA and Superior Fruiticola SA v Frumar Ltd and Redbridge Produce Marketing Ltd* [17 September 2002] ECR 2002 I-07289 para 27.

> The possibility of bringing such proceedings strengthens the practical working of the Community rules on quality standards. As a supplement to the action of the authorities […] it helps to discourage practices, often difficult to detect, which distort competition. In that context actions brought before the national courts by competing operators are particularly suited to contributing substantially to ensuring fair trading and transparency of markets in the Community.[46]

It should first be noted that in neither of the two judgments did the ECJ expressly develop its position on the type of civil remedy that might be required under Union law, i.e. which must be provided for by Member States in their national legal systems. In particular, the ECJ did not elaborate on whether 'civil proceedings' as defined in *Muñoz* implies a (civil) right for third parties to assert claims for damages.[47]

The need for private enforcement is justified in both judgments by the principle of effectiveness. Interestingly, the ECJ did not deal with the public enforcement of Union law (and its effectiveness). Private enforcement seems to have an important complementary function to public enforcement, probably against the background of a lack of access to information by supervisory authorities.[48] The background may have been that public supervision and enforcement of antitrust relevant transactions was low at that time.[49] In order to prevent a loss of protection of competition, the ECJ required a private enforcement.

B. CONCLUSIONS

Enforcement deficits differ in antitrust and capital markets law.[50] Nevertheless, one cannot deny that prohibitions of MAR on insider dealing and market manipulation and the disclosure obligation for issuers provided for in the interests of investors would be strengthened if investors had the right to

---

46 Ibid, paras 30–31.

47 Cf Schütt, *Europäische Marktmissbrauchsverordnung* (n 38) 157.

48 Cf Andrea Biondi, 'Case C-253/00, Antonio Muñoz y Cia, Superior Fruiticola SA v Frumar Ltd, Redbridge Produce Marketing Ltd, Judgement of the Full Court of 17 September 2002' (2003) 40 CMLR 1241, 1246 (note) (hereafter Biondi, 'Case C-253/00'); Micha Cless, *Unionsrechtliche Vorgaben für eine zivilrechtliche Haftung bei Marktmissbrauch* (Dunker & Humblot 2018) 70 (hereafter Cless, *Unionsrechtliche Vorgaben*); Schütt, *Europäische Marktmissbrauchsverordnung* (n 38) 154.

49 Schütt, *Europäische Marktmissbrauchsverordnung* (n 38) 154.

50 Thomas Ackermann, 'Public und private enforcement im Wirtschaftsrecht: Eine fragwürdige Dichotomie' in Matthias Casper and others (eds), *Festschrift für Johannes Köndgen* (RWS Verlag 2016) 1, 15 (hereafter Ackermann, 'Public and private enforcement'). However, one may conclude that only those who have a direct economic interest in the operation of the market would be able to rely on it to sue a competitor, cf Biondi, 'Case C-253/00' (n 48) 1241, 1249 (note)

assert claims under private law.[51] However, it is not possible to predict whether the ECJ would acknowledge a right to claim for damages with regard to the disclosure obligation under article 17 of the MAR. This is even impossible to assess because the principles developed by the ECJ in *Courage* and *Muñoz* on private rights of third parties are very general. In particular, the ECJ did not deal with the prerequisites of a private liability. It is difficult to imagine that the ECJ would require Member States to introduce liability for simple negligence, thus establishing a high level of deterrence through private enforcement.[52]

It would also not be convincing if the ECJ were to derive private rights in the form of claims for damages from the principle of effectiveness of Union law.[53] The European legislature has decided to enforce the prohibitions and disclosure obligations of MAR through a dense net of administrative and criminal sanctions. Regarding the obligation to publish inside information, which is under discussion here, supervisory authorities can take numerous measures and impose sanctions. The authorities have the power to require information from the issuer,[54] may impose a fine on the issuer[55] and have the right and the obligation to publish all measures and sanctions they have taken with regard to the infringement of prohibitions and obligations under the MAR (naming and shaming).[56] The administrative measures and sanctions were considerably tightened by the 2014/2016 reform,[57] so that the expected costs of a breach of the disclosure obligation significantly increased.[58] The public enforcement regime

---

51 The academic discussion about private enforcement in the light of *Courage* and *Muñoz* has so far mainly focused on insider trading (art 14 of the MAR) and market manipulation prohibitions (art 15 of the MAR). The disclosure obligation (art 17 of the MAR) has not been the focus of attention. See Hellgardt, 'Europarechtliche Vorgaben' (n 38) 154; Tountopoulos, 'Market Abuse' (n 38) 297; Poelzig, 'Enforcement' (n 38) 801.

52 Reluctant also Schütt, *Europäische Marktmissbrauchsverordnung* (n 38) 434 (re: liability for simple negligence) and 447 (re: liability of board members).

53 This is also justified in literature with the argument that the European legislature has deliberately chosen to ensure the enforcement of market abuse law through instruments of public enforcement. Cf Markworth, 'Marktmissbrauchsverordnung' (n 38) 66. However, legislative materials do not refer to such a decision by the European co legislators against private enforcement.

54 Cf art 23(2)b of the MAR.

55 Cf art 30(1)a of the MAR.

56 Cf art 34 of the MAR.

57 Supervisory authorities may impose fines of up to 2 per cent of consolidated turnover of the issuer in the event of a breach of the obligation to disclose inside information. Cf art 30(2)(j)(ii) of the MAR.

58 Rüdiger Veil and Alexander Brüggemeier, 'Kapitalmarktrecht zwischen öffentlich-rechtlicher und privatrechtlicher Normdurchsetzung' in Holger Fleischer, Susanne Kalss and Hans-Ueli Vogt (eds), *Enforcement im Gesellschafts- und Kapitalmarktrecht 2015* (Mohr Siebeck 2015) 277, 293 (hereafter Veil and Brüggemeier, 'Kapitalmarktrecht').

(administrative measures and sanctions, criminal sanctions) therefore has a considerable deterrent effect.[59]

It is difficult to assess how effective this enforcement-regime is.[60] On the one hand, administrative sanctions against issuers due to incorrect information of capital markets are rarely imposed across the EU.[61] In addition, the financial and personnel resources of national supervisory authorities in Europe vary widely. On the other hand, it cannot yet be concluded from publicly known data that enforcement mechanisms are deficient in all areas of market abuse law. This applies in particular to the obligation of issuers to publish inside information in accordance with article 17 of the MAR. It is certainly true that globalisation of markets and increasing digitalisation make it difficult to detect market abuse.[62] With regard to the ad hoc disclosure obligation pursuant to article 17 of the MAR, however, no serious enforcement problems due to a lack of access to information by supervisory authorities have become known to date.[63]

From a dogmatic point of view, one may justify liability for damages under private law by referring to the regulatory objectives of MAR.[64] Indeed, the MAR aims at ensuring the integrity of financial markets in the Union and enhancing investor protection and confidence in those markets to protect the interests of investors.[65] Furthermore, recitals of the

59 Reluctant also Schütt, *Europäische Marktmissbrauchsverordnung* (n 38) 215ff; Markworth, 'Marktmissbrauchsverordnung' (n 38) 66. Dissenting opinion: Tountopoulos, 'Market Abuse' (n 38) 297, 325. Cf on the weaknesses of the previous sanctioning system of EU capital markets law by Julia von Buttlar, 'Die Stärkung der Aufsichts- und Sanktionsbefugnisse im EU-Kapitalmarktrecht: ein neues "field of dreams" für Regulierer?' [2014] BB 451, 452–54.

60 The assessment of the effectiveness of a sanctions system is complex, as numerous parameters need to be considered and evaluated, such as the prerequisites of the respective regime, enforcement practices and problems of coordination and cooperation between public authorities. Cf International Organisation of Securities Commissions (IOSCO), *Credible Deterrence in the Enforcement of Securities Regulation* (June 2015) <http://www.iosco.org/library/pubdocs/pdf/IOSCOPD490.pdf>; Veil and Brüggemeier, 'Kapitalmarktrecht' (n 58) 277, 284–89; cf also Philipp Maume, 'Staatliche Rechtsdurchsetzung im deutschen Kapitalmarktrecht: eine kritische Bestandsaufnahme' (2016) 180 ZHR 358, 372ff (hereafter Maume, 'Staatliche Rechtsdurchsetzung') on responsive regulation as an alternative way of state law enforcement; MacNeil, 'Enforcement' (n 23) 280, 283 (the role of discretion).

61 This is a main argument put forward in literature to justify that public enforcement does not work. Cf Schütt, *Europäische Marktmissbrauchsverordnung* (n 38) 293ff.

62 Tountopoulos, 'Market Abuse' (n 38) 297, 325.

63 Of course, supervisory authorities do not have access to internal company information, such as personal, changes in an annual result or compliance-relevant issues. It is therefore by no means certain that they will always be able to take action against incorrect ad hoc disclosure. However, if information about such circumstances 'leaks' and affects the price of a security, the competent supervisory authority may investigate and request information from the issuer. In particular, supervisory authorities also have the power to enter the issuer's business premises and to interview employees.

64 Cf Poelzig, 'Enforcement' (n 38) 801, 815ff.

65 Cf art 1 of the MAR.

MAR acknowledge that manipulation can lead to losses for investors[66] and investors are harmed by manipulation.[67] However, this does not mean that the obligation to disclose inside information must also be enforced by the issuer's liability for damages. The European legislature did not pursue the goal of protecting investors' interests also through mechanisms of private enforcement.[68] Moreover, the recitals only describe the disadvantages of market manipulation and do not allow any conclusions to be drawn as to private liability of issuers.[69]

IV. HARMONISATION OF PRIVATE ENFORCEMENT

A. DEVELOPMENTS IN EUROPEAN COMPETITION LAW

Competition law is characterised by a dualism of law enforcement; private enforcement complements public enforcement. The system of sanctions is characterised by two aims: compensation and deterrence. The aim of deterrence plays a key role. This is particularly evident in public enforcement, which is based on the idea that the expected amount of fines must exceed the expected profit from an infringement.[70]

Against this background, it is of particular interest for enforcement of EU capital markets law that the European legislature harmonised private enforcement of competition law in 2014.[71] Directive 2014/104/EU is described as one of the most significant developments in antitrust law.[72] It requires Member States to lay down in their national law rules ensuring that anyone who has suffered harm caused by an infringement of competition law can effectively exercise the right to claim full compensation for that harm.[73]

The European legislature has put forward a number of arguments for a harmonisation of private liability. Two arguments should be highlighted here. First, Directive 2014/104/EU is based on differences between the rules in the Member States governing actions for damages for infringements of competition

---

66 Recital 44 of the MAR.

67 Recital 47 of the MAR.

68 Cless, *Unionsrechtliche Vorgaben* (n 48) 88.

69 Cless, *Unionsrechtliche Vorgaben* (n 48) 88ff.

70 Cf Thomas Ackermann, 'Prävention als Paradigma: Zur Verteidigung eines effektiven kartellrechtlichen Sanktionssystems' [2010] ZWeR 329, 331.

71 Directive 2014/104/EU of the European Parliament and of the Council of 26 November 2014 on certain rules governing actions for damages under national law for infringements of the competition law provisions of the Member States and of the European Union [2014] OJ L349/1 (hereafter Directive 2014/104/EU).

72 Cf Rupprecht Podszun, 'Streitpunkte der 9. GWB-Novelle' [2017] WuW 114, 115.

73 Cf art 1(1) of Directive 2014/104/EU (n 71).

law. Differences would lead to uncertainty concerning the conditions under which injured parties can exercise the right to compensation. In addition, injured parties would often choose their Member State as the forum in which to claim damages. Thus, discrepancies would lead to an uneven playing field as regards actions for damages and would affect competition on the markets on which those injured parties, as well as the infringing undertakings, operate.[74]

As a second argument for harmonisation, the European legislator highlighted that large-scale infringements of competition law would often have a cross-border element. Thus, a more level playing field for undertakings operating in the internal market should be ensured. It would be appropriate to increase legal certainty and to reduce the differences between the Member States as to the national rules governing actions for dames for infringements of both Union competition law and national competition law.[75]

B. LESSONS FOR A REFORM OF THE EUROPEAN MARKET ABUSE REGIME

1. *Need for a Harmonisation*

The discussion on harmonisation of private enforcement in European capital market law is at the very beginning. So far, attention has focused on public enforcement, which initially was not subject to European harmonisation. In 2009, the High-Level Expert Group on Financial Supervision, chaired by Jacque de Larosière, provided two key recommendations for the further development of EU financial markets law.

Firstly, the Group criticised a divergent implementation of EU directives and a divergent interpretation of transposed law. European legislative acts should in future be adopted as often as possible in the form of regulations (as they are directly applicable). When directives are used, European legislature should make every effort to achieve maximum harmonisation on key points.[76] Second, the Group drew attention to the fact that sanction regimes of Member States were weak and would allow harmful regulatory arbitrage. As a result, the European legislature fundamentally reformed financial markets law by introducing a level playing field (consisting of numerous so-called single rulebooks) and harmonising sanctions. However, the focus has been on supervisory law and public enforcement mechanisms.

---

74 Cf recital 7 of Directive 2014/104/EU (n 71); Heike Schweitzer, 'Die neue Richtlinie für wettbewerbsrechtliche Schadensersatzklagen' [2014] NZKart 335.

75 Cf recital 9 of Directive 2014/104/EU (n 71).

76 Cf Jaques de Larosière, 'The High-Level Group on Financial Supervision in the EU' (Report 2009) 33.

Would harmonisation of private enforcement now make sense? Indeed, there are strong arguments for this. Generally, harmonisation of a legal framework across the Union reduces the transaction costs of cross-border activities[77] and prevents regulatory fragmentation that hampers competition.[78] This research project has revealed significant differences between the rules in the Member States governing actions for damages for infringements of capital markets law, in particular of the duty to disclose inside information. In contrast to competition law, however, there is no serious concern that these discrepancies affect competition on capital markets. Nevertheless, the different legal situation justifies action by European legislature. The issuance and trade of securities generally have a cross-border element. The level of investor protection should not depend on whether a national legal system ensures compensation of damages and strengthens the effectiveness of disclosure obligation through private enforcement. If one sees a central purpose of private enforcement mechanisms in deterrence, harmonisation of private liability is inevitable! Thus, a more level playing field for investors should be ensured.

Finally, a harmonisation of private liability offers the opportunity to coordinate public and private enforcement in order to prevent both over- and under-enforcement.[79] This has been a further argument for the European legislature harmonising private enforcement in competition law. Directive 2014/104/EU is also justified by the idea that the coordination of public and private enforcement should be regulated.[80]

The positive effects of harmonising private liability are well recognised. In the academic discussion, however, scholars have put forward the idea that harmonising private liability would require that supervisory law and public enforcement are largely harmonised.[81] Otherwise, it would not be possible to develop a common understanding of private and public law enforcement.[82] Instead, it would be preferable to leave the development of private enforcement to competing national legal systems.[83]

This argument is no longer convincing. The legal situation and supervisory practices in Europe have changed fundamentally in the last years. Capital markets law (subject to supervision) is largely unified. This applies in particular to the

77 Wundenberg, 'Perspektiven' (n 37) 124, 150; Alexander Brüggemeier, *Harmonisierungskonzepte im europäischen Kapitalmarktrecht* (Mohr Siebeck 2018) 85.

78 Wundenberg, 'Perspektiven' (n 37) 124, 150.

79 The goal should be an optimal enforcement of the standard. See Veil and Brüggemeier, 'Kapitalmarktrecht' (n 58) 277, 279–82; Ackermann, 'Public and private enforcement' (n 50) 1, 10–16.

80 Cf recital 6 of Directive 2014/104/EU (n 71).

81 Wundenberg, 'Perspektiven' (n 37) 124, 154.

82 Wundenberg, 'Perspektiven' (n 37) 124, 155.

83 Wundenberg, 'Perspektiven' (n 37) 124, 159.

market abuse regimes and its disclosure obligations.[84] In addition, enforcement by national authorities is harmonised.[85] There are still differences in the national legal systems, as the MAR is limited to a minimum harmonisation of administrative measures and sanctions. Furthermore, supervisory practices are likely to continue to be inconsistent, as national authorities have traditionally had different philosophies about market supervision.[86] On the other hand, ESMA has the task of coordinating supervisory practices in order to prevent regulatory arbitrage. For this purpose, ESMA conducts peer reviews and discusses live cases with the staff of national supervisory authorities. ESMA also issues Q&A documents to ensure that national authorities act as consistently as possible (article 29(2) of the ESMA Regulation). Against this background, it does not appear likely that NCAs will adopt diametrically opposed supervisory practices. Significant coordination problems and regulatory conflicts between private and public enforcement should no longer be brought forward against a harmonisation of private enforcement.

2. *Concepts*

There are a number of possible ways for the European legislature to harmonise private enforcement. Firstly, lawmakers could adopt a 'small solution' based on the model of the Prospectus Regulation (PR)[87] and the Transparency Directive (TD).[88] Both Level 1 acts provide for rules requiring Member States to introduce private liability.[89] It could be envisaged in the next reform of the MAR that Member States would have to provide for private liability if an issuer infringes its obligation to disclose inside information. Member States would then be free to rely upon general rules (especially tort law) or to introduce a specific legal basis for claims.

---

84 Regulation (EU) No 596/2014 of 16 April 2014 aims at providing a unified legal situation in Europe. The prohibitions and obligations are directly applicable in the Member States. Only the rules on the tasks and powers of competent authorities and on administrative sanctions need to be transposed by the Member States.

85 Regulation (EU) No 596/2014 (n 84) aims at a minimum harmonisation of the legal systems in this respect.

86 See for example Maume, 'Staatliche Rechtsdurchsetzung' (n 60) 358, 375 on different approaches to flexibility of enforcement.

87 Regulation (EU) 2017/1129 of the European Parliament and of the Council of 14 June 2017 on the prospectus to be published when securities are offered to the public or admitted to trading on a regulated market, and repealing Directive 2003/71/EC [2017] OJ L168/30 recital 12.

88 Directive 2004/109/EC of 15 December 2004 of the European Parliament and of the Council on the harmonisation of transparency requirements in relation to information about issuers whose securities are admitted to trading on a regulated market and amending Directive 2001/34/EC [2004] OJ L390/38.

89 Art 11 of the PR; art 7 of the TD.

However, Member States' discretion in implementation already indicates a disadvantage of the approach. The PR and TD give Member States a very broad discretion as to how they transpose the requirements for a private liability. For example, TD limits itself to require that laws, regulations and administrative provisions of the Member States on liability apply to the issuers, the management bodies or the persons responsible within the issuers. The provision does not provide concrete requirements for a liability standard. The existing fragmentation of the national laws would therefore not be adequately addressed. In addition, a sectoral approach would mean that not all parts of corporate disclosure would be considered. It would undermine investor confidence if investors would not be entitled to claim damages in any case of infringements of disclosure obligations.[90]

It is therefore preferable to adopt a directive along the lines of competition law, which obliges the Member States to introduce liability for damages under private law for all disclosure obligations provided for by European law (the so-called 'big solution'). The European legislature should set forth a minimum harmonisation of core issues, such as respondents, requirements of fault (negligence, gross negligence or intent).

Regulatory models already exist in Union law. Firstly, article 35a of the Regulation on Rating Agencies[91] provides for a separate legal basis for a claim in Union law,[92] but refers to national law with regard to central prerequisites for a claim.[93] Discretion of national legislature/jurisprudence is narrowed down by requiring competent national courts to take into consideration the fact that the investor or issuer may not have access to information, which is purely within the sphere of the credit rating agency.[94]

A similar principles-based approach is adopted by Directive 2014/104/EU, which also takes into account that key concepts of private law are not harmonised by EU law but specifies the way of implementation by Member States.

90 Cf Thomas MJ Möllers, 'Anlegerschutz im System des Kapitalmarktrechts' in Stefan Grundmann and others (eds), *Festschrift für Klaus J. Hopt zum 70 Geburtstag* (De Gruyter 2010) 2247, 2260 on the fragmented legal situation in Germany.

91 Regulation (EC) 1060/2009 of the European Parliament and of the Council of 16 September 2009 on credit rating agencies [2004] OJ L302/1 (CRA). The Regulation was amended in 2011 (Regulation (EU) No 513/2011 of the European Parliament and of the Council of 11 May 2011 amending Regulation (EC) No 1060/2009 on credit rating agencies Text with EEA relevance [2011] OJ L145/30) and in 2013 (Regulation (EU) No 462/2013 of the European Parliament and of the Council of 21 May 2013 amending Regulation (EC) No 1060/2009 on credit rating agencies Text with EEA relevance [2013] OJ L146/1).

92 Cf Thomas MJ Möllers and Charis Niedorf, 'Regulation and liability of credit rating agencies – a more efficient European law?' [2014] ECFR 333–63.

93 Terms such as 'damage', 'intention', 'gross negligence', 'reasonable relied', 'due care', 'impact', 'reasonable' and 'proportionate' should be interpreted and applied in accordance with the applicable national law as determined by the relevant rules of private international law. Cf art 35a(5) of the CRA.

94 Cf art 35(4) of the CRA.

Directive 2014/104/EU thus requires Member States to ensure that neither the burden nor the standard of proof required for the quantification of harm renders the exercise of the right of damages practically impossible or excessively difficult.[95] In addition, the directive provides for solutions to the information asymmetries of victims of a cartel infringement.[96]

Finally, the European lawmaker should make clear whether private liability exclusively ensures compensation or whether it (also) has a deterrent purpose. Directive 2014/104/EU does not explicitly address this issue for private enforcement in competition law. The recitals only reflect general ideas of the legislator on the importance of private enforcement.[97] Furthermore, the Directive explicitly acknowledges that 'compensation for the damage suffered'[98] should be ensured and that it does not seek overcompensation through punitive damages or multiple compensation.[99] Member States have to observe the principles of effectiveness and equivalence when determining liability.[100] However, it cannot be concluded from these principles that a liability under private law should also have a deterrent effect. It would be wise to set out more clearly the central purposes of liability for damages in European capital markets law.

V. RESULTS

The liability of issuers under private law for failures to disclose inside information pursuant to article 17 of the MAR is regulated very differently in Europe. Most Member States do not provide for any special legal bases, so that investors can only claim damages from an issuer in these countries under tort law. The courts, however, have so far gained little experience with claims for damages, so that central problems of investor claims under capital markets law have not yet been solved. This is unsatisfactory from a political point of view. An effective system of private enforcement would strengthen the prohibitions of MAR on insider dealing and market manipulation and the disclosure obligations for issuers provided for in the interests of investors. However, it is not to be expected that the ECJ will oblige Member States to provide for a strict liability for damages.

---

95 Cf art 17(1) of Directive 2014/104/EU (n 71).

96 Cf Harald Kahlenberg and Lena Heim, 'Das deutsche Kartellrecht in der Reform: Überblick über die 9. GWB-Novelle' [2017] BB 1155, 1159.

97 According to recital 5 of Directive 2014/104/EU (n 71), actions for damages for breaches of competition law are only one element of an effective system of private enforcement. Recital 6 explains that to ensure effective private civil enforcement and effective public enforcement by competition authorities, both instruments must work together.

98 Recital 12 of Directive 2014/104/EU (n 71).

99 Recital 13 of Directive 2014/104/EU (n 71).

100 Art 4 of Directive 2014/104/EU (n 71).

Thus, the European legislator should take action. It makes sense to harmonise private liability now, as disclosure obligations are largely uniformly regulated in European capital markets law.

Following the example of competition law, European legislature should harmonise private liability by a directive. The directive should not be limited to the disclosure obligations of MAR but should cover all other disclosure obligations for issuers in European capital markets law. It would not make sense to lay down specific and detailed requirements for a private liability in Union law due to the current state of private law harmonisation. However, the European legislature should stipulate a minimum set of principles for private liability, which take into account information asymmetries of investors. The Member States would then have sufficient discretion as to how they implement the principles within their own legal systems.

The European legislator should also determine the purposes of private liability for failures of corporate disclosure. Should liability for damages (only) aim at compensating the damage suffered, or should it also have a deterrent effect? It should also require Member States to deal with the most urgent questions of private liability. In particular, European lawmakers should ensure that Member States address problems of causation and facilitate evidence for investors.

PART IV

LEGAL PRACTICE PERSPECTIVE

PRACTITIONER COMMENT ON CONSUMER LAW ENFORCEMENT IN EUROPE

Lene KOHL*

The VW emission scandal has demonstrated deficits in the enforcement of European consumer rights in practice. While VW customers in other parts of the world, in particular the US,[1] have been compensated within a relatively short time after it became public that Volkswagen AG (VW) had installed illegal defeat devices in 11 million vehicles worldwide, including 8 million vehicles in Europe, many of the affected European consumers are still waiting for redress.

The initial setup in the VW emission scandal is exemplary for big mass tort cases worldwide: On the one hand there is VW, a multinational corporation, the

* Lene Kohl, Dr., Rechtsanwältin (German Attorney), Osborne Clarke, Berlin.
German Federal Statutes are available at <http://www.gesetze-im-internet.de> and Cases of the German Federal Court (Bundesgerichtshof – BGH) are available at <http://www.bundesgerichtshof.de>.

1 In the US, due to private class actions and suits by public authorities, a settlement with VW was reached within little more than nine months after the Environmental Protection Agency issued the first notice of violation on 18 September 2015.

largest car manufacturer in the world. On the other hand, millions of deceived consumers. It is in the nature of things that there is no level playing field (Section I.). While there are mechanisms to even the playing field between corporations and consumers, the legal system in Europe perpetuates the disadvantages of consumers (Section II.). The consequence is that many European consumers refrain from enforcing their rights (Section III.). To overcome this so-called 'rational disinterest'[2] in the VW emission scandal in Europe, claim bundling models have emerged in praxis and the legislator has started to act (Section IV.). As long as there is no real group litigation mechanism for redress, stipulated on a European level, however, consumers in Europe remain in a disadvantaged position.

I. THE INITIAL SETUP: NO LEVEL PLAYING FIELD

The initial setup in the VW emission scandal is the typical constellation 'repeat player versus one shotter' which the American law professor Marc Galanter had already described in the year 1974.[3][4] He characterised the repeat player as 'a unit which has had and anticipates repeated litigation, which has low stakes in the outcome of any one case, and which has the resources to pursue its long-run interests'.[5] The one shotter, on the other hand, 'a unit whose claims are too large (relative to his size) or too small (relative to the cost of remedies) to be managed routinely and rationally',[6] deals with the legal system only rarely.[7]

The structural predominance of the repeat player VW over the deceived consumers, each on his or her own a one shotter, is self-evident. The repeat player has numerous advantages from the outset: advance intelligence, expertise and access to specialists.[8] It enjoys economies of scale and has low start-up costs as well as opportunities to develop facilitative informal relations with institutional incumbents.[9] It must establish and maintain credibility as a combatant, can play the odds and for rules.[10]

2 'Gesetzentwurf der Bundesregierung zur Einführung einer zivilprozessualen Musterfeststellungsklage' (Draft law of the German Federal Government on the implementation of a civil procedure model declaratory action, explanatory memorandum) BT Drucks 19/2439, 14 (hereafter model declaratory action memorandum).

3 Marc Galanter, 'Why the "Haves" Come Out Ahead: Speculations on the Limits of Legal Change' (1974) 95 L&Soc'y Rev 95ff (hereafter Galanter, 'Speculations').

4 Jan Lampe, 'Legal Tech in Massenverfahren – Eine historische Chance für Verbraucher?' (2019) 3 Rethinking Law 34, 35 (hereafter Lampe, 'Legal Tech').

5 Galanter, 'Speculations' (n 3) 98.

6 Ibid, 98.

7 Ibid, 97.

8 Ibid, 98.

9 Ibid, 98ff.

10 Ibid, 99ff.

In addition, VW as the largest car manufacturer worldwide, has enormous financial means. Contrary to a single consumer, VW does not only have top-notch lawyers at hand, but is also able to engage experts with a long-established reputation in their fields as needed. In the emission scandal, VW has commissioned numerous expert opinions on every relevant topic to corroborate its position that European consumers cannot claim for damages. Quite often, these experts sow seeds of doubt in the public discussion by order of VW, where there is no room for doubt.[11] Well-respected law professors present their highly paid arguments in scientific journals, invoking a non-existent prevailing opinion in favour of VW or depicting a distorted image of the court practice in the VW emissions scandal, without unequivocally disclosing their commissioning by VW.[12] The influence on the public opinion and the courts, dealing with single actions for damages by individual consumers, is evident.

II. THE EUROPEAN LEGAL SYSTEM PERPETUATES THE DISADVANTAGES OF THE CONSUMER

While the US legal system contributes to evening this imbalance, the structural disadvantages of consumers vis-à-vis the repeat player VW are perpetuated in Europe due to

- the absence of European sanctions for the breach of European law (Section II.A.),
- the absence of a European collective redress mechanism (Section II.B.), and
- the absence of effective document discovery mechanisms (Section II.C.).

A. NO EUROPEAN SANCTIONS FOR THE BREACH OF EUROPEAN LAW

Throughout Europe, authorities, including the German Federal Motor Transport Authority Kraftfahrt-Bundesamt (KBA),[13] and courts, including the Federal Court of Justice (Bundesgerichtshof, BGH) in Germany,[14] have found VW to have violated European law, in particular article 5 (2) of Regulation (EC)

---

11 Michael Heese, 'Was der Dieselskandal über die Rechtsdurchsetzung, deren Protagonisten und die Funktion des Privatrechts verrät' [2019] Neue Zeitschrift für Verkehrsrecht 273 (hereafter Heese, 'Dieselskandal').

12 Ibid, 273, 276; Kristina Gnirke, 'Windige Helfer' *Der Spiegel* (Hamburg, 6 April 2019) 68, 69 (hereafter Gnirke, 'Windige Helfer').

13 KBA, Orders of 15 October and 17 November 2015.

14 BGH, Order of 8 January 2019, VIII ZR 225/17.

No 715/2007 of the European Parliament and of the Council of 20 June 2007 by developing and installing an illegal defeat device in 8.5 million vehicles in Europe. Nonetheless, there have not been any sanctions on a European level.

The responsibility for sanctioning infringements by manufacturers of the provisions of Regulation (EC) No 715/2007 is on the individual European Member States. According to article 13 (1), sentences 1 and 2 of Regulation (EC) No 715/2007, they are obliged to provide for effective, proportionate and dissuasive penalties and take all measures necessary to ensure they are implemented. However, the Member States responsible for the VW group type approvals, i.e. Germany, Luxemburg, Spain and the UK, have not taken actions against the manufacturers. The European Commission (EC) therefore initiated infringement procedures against these Member States as well as other Member States,[15] who failed to introduce penalties systems against car manufacturers in the first place.[16]

B. NO EUROPEAN COLLECTIVE REDRESS MECHANISM

There is no general European collective redress mechanism for the enforcement of claims following from the violation of European law. As a basic principle in most Member States, the consumers affected by the VW emissions scandal therefore need to pursue their rights individually. The consequence is tens of thousands of individual actions against the same company VW before thousands of judges and hundreds of courts throughout Europe leading to differing and often opposing decisions for one and the same infringement of European law.

This is not only totally ineffective and overwhelming for the courts. Also, VW can fully benefit from its position as repeat player, being able not only to establish a comprehensive pool of knowledge and experiences,[17] but also to trigger promising cases in order to produce favourable decisions and prevent the triggering of unpromising cases by settling and thus preventing unfavourable judgments which might have a signal effect for millions of other consumers.[18] This so-called 'Case Picking'[19] allows for VW to gain interpretive dominance, influence the public perception on the merits of consumer claims and the

15 Czech Republic, Greece and Lithuania.

16 European Commission, 'Car Emissions: Commission opens infringement procedures against 7 Member states for breach of EU rules' (press release IP/16/4214, 8 December 2016) <https://ec.europa.eu/commission/presscorner/detail/en/IP_16_4214>.

17 Lampe, 'Legal Tech' (n 4) 35.

18 Galanter, 'Speculations' (n 3) 101ff; Timo Gansel, 'Die Furcht vor amerikanischen Verhältnissen' (2019) 3 Rethinking Law 45 (hereafter Gansel, 'Die Furcht').

19 Catherine T Harris, Ralph A Peeples and Thomas B Metzloff, 'Does Being a Repeat Player Make a Difference? The Impact of Attorney Experience and Case Picking on the Outcome of Medical Malpractice Lawsuits' (3 July 2007) 2nd Annual Conference on Empirical Legal Studies, New York, 9–10 July 2007 <https://papers.ssrn.com/sol3/papers.cfm?abstract_id=998105##>.

chances of success in court, and thus prevent other consumers from enforcing their claims.[20] In fact, in order to prevent unfavourable decisions by Higher Courts and a judgment by the consumer-friendly European Court of Justice, which would be binding for all courts in Europe, VW is paying off individual consumers at the last minute before the courts can rule in their favour[21] or submit questions on the interpretation of the relevant European provisions to the European Court of Justice.[22]

C. NO EFFECTIVE DOCUMENT DISCOVERY MECHANISMS

Another factor favouring the predominance of the repeat player VW is the lack of effective document discovery mechanisms in most European countries. This has made it possible for VW to keep the details of what happened inside the company from the public for more than four years now. The internal investigation, commissioned by the VW supervisory board and conducted by the law firm Jones Day, is long over, but – in opposition to VW's initial announcement[23] – the public has not seen the results. The reason for the change of mind is presumably that the results incriminate VW managers up to the former chairman of the board of directors, who has been criminally indicted for fraud both in the US[24] and in Germany.[25] Nevertheless, in court, VW is still resorting to the statement that there is no indication that its board members had knowledge of the usage of an illegal defeat device in millions of vehicles. As the burden of proof for the tort is on the consumers claiming for compensation and there is no effective document discovery mechanism, this strategy has worked out in some courts.[26]

20 Lampe, 'Legal Tech' (n 4) 36.

21 Heese, 'Dieselskandal' (n 11) 275.

22 After the announcement of the Regional Court (Landgericht, LG) of Erfurt that it intended to submit questions to the ECJ in 22 comparable lawsuits of VW customers (LG Erfurt, Order of 25 March 2019, 8 O 1045/18), most of the actions were withdrawn due to last-minute settlements.

23 Volkswagen, 'Information der Volkswagen AG über den Stand der umfassenden Untersuchung im Zusammenhang mit der Diesel Thematik' (press release, 22 April 2016) <http://www.volkswagen-newsroom.com/de/pressemitteilungen/information-der-volkswagen-ag-ueber-den-stand-der-umfassenden-untersuchung-im-zusammenhang-mit-der-diesel-thematik-1898>.

24 US Department of Justice, 'Former CEO of Volkswagen AG charged with Conspiracy and Wire Fraud in Diesel Emissions Scandal' (press release, 3 May 2018) <http://www.justice.gov/opa/pr/former-ceo-volkswagen-ag-charged-conspiracy-and-wire-fraud-diesel-emissions-scandal>.

25 The public prosecutor's office Braunschweig, 'Anklage im Diesel-Skandal' (press release, 15 April 2019) <https://staatsanwaltschaft-braunschweig.niedersachsen.de/startseite/aktuelles/presseinformationen/anklage-im-diesel-skandal-176101.html>.

26 E.g. OLG Braunschweig, Judgment of 19 February 2019, 7 U 134/17. Recently, however, the BGH rejected this strategy and found VW to bear the so-called secondary burden of presentation (sekundäre Darlegungslast) and thus obliged to present details of its findings, BGH, Judgment of 25 May 2020, VI ZR 252/19.

III. THE CONSEQUENCE: RATIONAL DISINTEREST OF EUROPEAN CONSUMERS

The consequence of these deficits of the European legal system is that many European consumers refrain from enforcing their claims. The so-called 'rational disinterest' of consumers is particularly high, if the individual losses are low and/or the effort and cost of enforcement seems disproportional.[27]

In the VW emission scandal, both is often the case, due to VW's strategy to keep all information to itself, reject all consumer claims from the outset and conclude confidential settlements in many cases only in the second instance. In the meantime, the consumers drive around in their cars, mostly because they need to. As the BGH has found that the consumers' tort claims are reduced by a compensation for the usage of the vehicle,[28] VW's strategy pays off: the longer the enforcement takes, the less the consumer gets in many cases, or rather the more VW can keep. Thus, with the loser-pays rule prevailing in Europe, also the litigation cost risk for the consumer increases with time. Another cost risk for the consumer is that some courts regard it necessary to obtain expert evidence on the functioning of the defeat software, the software update to remove the defeat device and/or its effects on the vehicles' market value.[29] This is not only expensive, but also time-consuming, and a further obstacle for the consumer, who might be ordered to advance the expert costs in addition to the court fees, he or she needs to pay in advance in any event in order to sue VW for damages.

IV. POSSIBLE REMEDIES FOR EUROPEAN CONSUMERS

This rational disinterest of consumers can only be overcome by bundling claims of consumers.[30] In the absence of a collective redress mechanism, constructions to bundle claims have come up in practice, in particular through

- a Dutch Stichting (Section IV.A.) and
- assignment models (Section IV.B.).

---

27 Model declaratory action memorandum (n 2) 14.

28 BGH, Judgment of 25 May 2020, VI ZR 252/19. Against the deduction of a compensation for usage LG Augsburg, Judgment of 5 December 2018, 21 O 3267/17; LG Duisburg, Judgment of 16 May 2019, 8 O 106/18; LG Gera, Judgment of 16 April 2019, 3 O 566/18; LG Halle, Judgment of 5 March 2019, 5 O 109/18; LG Hannover, Judgment of 4 July 2019, 4 O 355/18; LG Limburg, Judgment of 12 June 2019, 1 O 447/18; LG Potsdam, Judgment of 29 May 2019, 6 O 76/19; Heese, 'Dieselskandal' (n 11) 274.

29 E.g. LG Berlin, Order of 19 October 2017, 14 O 142/17.

30 Model declaratory action memorandum (n 2) 14.

The German legislator has introduced the model declaratory action (Musterfeststellungsklage). It is doubtful, however, whether this instrument will help overcoming the rational disinterest of consumers (Section IV.C.).

Despite some deficits, the Directive on representative actions for the protection of the collective interests of consumers proposed by the European Commission in April 2018[31] which has gone through the European Parliament's first reading in March 2019[32] and has been adopted in a common position by the Council of the European Union in November 2019,[33] would certainly be an improvement for European consumers (Section IV.D.).

A. STICHTING

In the Netherlands, consumers affected by the VW emissions scandal have formed so-called Stichtings,[34] foundations established under Dutch law, which are able to seek a declaratory judgment before Dutch civil courts and negotiate a collective opt-out settlement (so-called WCAM settlement) with VW which can be declared binding by the Amsterdam Court of Appeal. The Stichting Volkswagen Car Claim has filed a representative action against VW on behalf of the 180,000 Dutch affected car owners with the Amsterdam District Court.[35] The proceedings have been split into three phases:

- phase 1 on the jurisdiction of the court, completed because VW has not objected;
- phase 2 in which all sorts of formal questions were discussed with oral pleadings on 7 October 2019, completed with a ruling of the Amsterdam District Court on 20 November 2019 declaring admissibility of the Stichting and ruling that all claims of the Stichting against VW are suitable for

31 Proposal for a Directive of the European Parliament and of the Council on representative actions for the protection of the collective interests of consumers, and repealing Directive 2009/22/EC [11 April 2018] COM(2018) 184 final (hereafter EC Directive proposal on representative actions for consumers).

32 Proposal for a Directive of the European Parliament and of the Council on representative actions for the protection of the collective interests of consumers, and repealing Directive 2009/22/EC – Texts Adopted by European Parliament in first reading [26 March 2019] P8_TA-PROV(2019)0222 (hereafter EP Directive proposal on representative actions for consumers).

33 Council of the European Union, 'Proposal for a Directive of the European Parliament and of the Council on representative actions for the protection of the collective interests of consumers, and repealing Directive 2009/22/EC – General Approach' [28 November 2019] 14600/19 (hereafter Council, 'General Approach – Directive proposal on representative actions for consumers').

34 E.g. Stichting Volkswagen Car Claim <http://www.stichtingvolkswagencarclaim.com>.

35 See Stichting Volkswagen Car Claim <http://www.stichtingvolkswagencarclaim.com/#faq>.

consideration in the collective action proceedings and will be assessed under Dutch law;
- phase 3 in which the merits are evaluated with a hearing taking place at the end of May 2020 and possibly a positive judgment to follow.[36]

However, as a positive judgment would only be declaratory, the individual consumers would still have to initiate subsequent procedures in order to get compensation. Also, a collective settlement can only be reached with the participation of VW. Thus, as long as VW is refusing negotiations,[37] a compensation for consumers cannot be achieved through the Stichting.

B. ASSIGNMENT MODEL

In various countries so-called assignment models, where the affected consumers assign their claims against VW to entities such as consumer associations, legal service providers or special-purpose vehicles, have been developed in practice in order to bundle consumer claims.

In Germany, the legal service provider myRight has filed several lawsuits claiming compensation for thousands of VW group customers from Germany, Switzerland and Slovenia who assigned their claims against VW to myRight for the purpose of collection. While the Supreme Court of Austria (Oberster Gerichtshof, OGH) found the assignment of claims for collection purposes to be admissible under Austrian law already in 2005, if the basis for the claims and the factual and legal questions involved are substantially similar,[38] the admissibility of the assignment model under German Law has been discussed controversially among German scholars. Some of them have expressed that the myRight assignment model conflicts with the German Act on Out-of-Court Legal Services (Rechtsdienstleistungsgesetz, RDG). It is telling that, although assignments to legal service providers have been utilised in German courts before, this discussion only came up with the use in the VW emissions scandal.[39] What is usually not mentioned in the respective articles is that they are based on legal opinions the authors prepared by order and for account of VW.[40] On 27 November 2019, the German Federal Court BGH has found that the

36 See Stichting Volkswagen Car Claim <jttp://www.stichtingvolkswagencarclaim.com/progress-process>.

37 According to Stichting Volkswagen Car Claim, VW and the other respondents 'have not entered in discussion with the foundation', <http://www.stichtingvolkswagencarclaim.com/progress-process>.

38 OGH, Order of 12 July 2005, 4 Ob 116/05w.

39 Gnirke, 'Windige Helfer' (n 12) 69.

40 Ibid, 69.

assignment of claims for collection purposes is in principle admissible under German law.[41] Although the BGH decision did not directly concern the use of the assignment model in the context of the VW emission scandal[42] and the BGH has made it clear that an assignment may conflict with the RDG and thus be void in a case with different circumstances, the BGH has rejected many of the arguments brought forward by German scholars on behalf of VW.

C. MODEL DECLARATORY ACTION (MUSTERFESTSTELLUNGSKLAGE)

On 1 November 2018, the model declaratory action was implemented in Germany in order to overcome the rational disinterest of consumers.[43] The German legislator predicted the filing of 450 model declaratory actions per year.[44] However, within the first year after the commencement of the Law on the implementation of a civil procedure model declaratory action, only six of such actions were brought,[45] two of which have already been found inadmissible.[46] The reason for this low number is that only certain qualified consumer protection associations such as the Federation of German Consumer Organisations (Verbraucherzentrale Bundesverband, vzbv) are competent for filing[47] which eschew the huge efforts and high financial risks.[48] Whether the model declaratory action will provide customers noticeable benefits is thus, and also due to the other deficits of this instrument,[49] most doubtful.

Also, the model declaratory action filed by vzbv in cooperation with the ADAC on 1 November 2018 with the OLG Braunschweig on behalf of consumers

41 BGH, Judgment of 27 November 2019, VIII ZR 285/18.

42 The case decided by the BGH in its judgment of 27 November 2019, VIII ZR 285/18, concerned the legal service provider Lexfox who operates the online rent calculator <http://www.wenigermiete.de> and *inter alia* enforces assigned claims based on the rent control (Mietpreisbremse) introduced in many German cities since 2015.

43 Model declaratory action memorandum (n 2) 14.

44 Ibid, 19.

45 Bundesamt für Justiz, 'Öffentliche Bekanntmachungen im Klageregister' <http://www.bundesjustizamt.de/DE/Themen/Buergerdienste/Klageregister/Bekanntmachungen/Klagen_node.html>.

46 OLG Braunschweig, Order of 12 December 2018, 4 MK 2/18; OLG Stuttgart, Judgment of 20 March 2019, 6 MK 1/18.

47 S 606 (1) of the German Code of Civil Procedure (Zivilprozessordnung, ZPO) in conjunction with s 3 of the Injunctive Relief Act (Gesetz über Unterlassungsklagen bei Verbraucherrechts- und anderen Verstößen, UKlG).

48 Gansel, 'Die Furcht' (n 18) 46.

49 See Heese, 'Dieselskandal' (n 11) 275. In particular, as the model declaratory action does only lead to a declaratory judgment, consumers still have to file individual actions for performance.

affected by the VW emission scandal,[50] has not proven to overcome the rational disinterest of VW customers. The German Federal Office of Justice, where consumers must register until the day before the beginning of the court hearing in order to be bound by a future declaratory judgment, recorded only around 430,000 registrations until the first court hearing on 30 September 2019[51] while, in Germany alone, 2.5 million vehicles are affected according to VW. Furthermore, from the experience in the dismissed model declaratory action against the Mercedes Benz Bank,[52] where only 140 out of 600 registered consumers fell under the aims of the action,[53] it can be assumed that the number of consumers eligible to participate is much lower than the number of registrations.

The vzbv model declaratory action has at least ended in rather short time with an out-of-court settlement on 28 February 2020.[54] As a consequence, around 260,000 of the 430,000 registered consumers are supposed to have received settlement offers from VW providing for minor compensation payments between 1,350 € and 6,257 €.[55] The consumers were able to accept the offer until 30 April 2020 or can alternatively pursue their claims in individual proceedings. The date was no coincidence: Only 5 days later, the BGH for the first time heard a case of a VW customer claiming for direct damages against VW, which resulted in a positive decision for consumers on 25 May 2020.[56]

D. THE PROPOSED DIRECTIVE ON REPRESENTATIVE ACTIONS FOR THE PROTECTION OF THE COLLECTIVE INTERESTS OF CONSUMERS

The position of European consumers would certainly be improved with a coming into force of the proposed Directive on representative actions for consumers, requiring all Member States to allow representative actions against certain

---

50 OLG Braunschweig, Order of 23 November 2018, 4 MK 1/18.

51 Vzbv, 'Musterklage gegen VW – Gericht drängt auf schnelle Lösung' (18 November 2019) <http://www.verbraucherzentrale.de/wissen/vertraege-reklamation/kundenrechte/musterklage-gegen-vw-gericht-draengt-auf-schnelle-loesung-29738>.

52 OLG Stuttgart, Judgment of 20 March 2019, 6 MK 1/18.

53 Among the people who registered for the model declaratory action against Mercedes Benz Bank were *inter alia* VW drivers, Marcus Jung 'Windhundrennen' *Frankfurter Allgemeine Zeitung Einspruch* (Frankfurt, 21 March 2019) <https://einspruch.faz.net/recht-des-tages/2019-03-21/7dbbddad68643aec54c603e2b57b12eb/?GEPC=s5>.

54 Vzbv, 'VW-Klage: Fragen und Antworten zum Vergleich zwischen Volkswagen und dem vzbv' (Q&A, 3 March 2020) <http://www.verbraucherzentrale.de/sites/default/files/2020-03/20-03-03_vzbv_faq_vergleich_vw.pdf>.

55 Vzbv, 'Vergleich zwischen vzbv und Volkswagen steht: Bis 30. April entscheiden!' (20 April 2020) <http://www.verbraucherzentrale.de/wissen/vertraege-reklamation/kundenrechte/vergleich-zwischen-vzbv-und-volkswagen-steht-bis-30-april-entscheiden-29738>.

56 BGH, Judgment of 25 May 2020, VI ZR 252/19, NJW 2020, 1962.

domestic or cross-border infringements of EU law protecting the collective interests of consumers in various areas, such as data protection, financial services, travel and tourism, energy, telecommunications, environment and health, although the provisions on the type approval of vehicles, violated by VW, are not covered.[57] Contrary to the German model declaratory action, the EC's Directive proposal enables representative actions claiming actual measures for redress, such as compensation, repair, replacement, price reduction, contract termination and reimbursement of the price paid for consumers, leaving it to the Member States whether or not to require consumers to opt in.[58] The explicit opt in would in any event be required from individuals who are not habitually resident in the Member State where the action occurs, according to the amended version adopted by the European Parliament[59] and the common position of the European Council.[60]

The Directive proposal provides for disclosure of evidence under certain conditions, in particular in the version after the European Parliament's first reading, national courts dealing with an action for damages shall be empowered to order the disclosure of evidence containing relevant information.[61] Also very positive is the projected suspension effect of the submission of a representative action for limitation periods applicable to any redress actions for the consumers concerned.[62]

The proposed Directive could fundamentally change the enforcement of European consumer rights, provided that the prospected actions for redress will be actually brought in practice. However, in light of the hesitant use of the German model declaratory action, this remains doubtful, as long as only limited qualified non-profit entities, designated by the Member States according to narrow criteria, shall have a right of action under strict obligations regarding the funding.[63]

---

57 EC Directive proposal on representative actions for consumers (n 31), explanatory memorandum sub 1. last bullet.

58 Art 5 (3), 6 (1) of EC Directive proposal on representative actions for consumers (n 31).

59 Art 6 (1a) of EP Directive proposal on representative actions for consumers (n 32).

60 Art 5b (3) of Council, 'General Approach – Directive proposal on representative actions for consumers' (n 33).

61 Art 13 (1b) of EP Directive proposal on representative actions for consumers (n 32).

62 Art 11 of EC Directive proposal on representative actions for consumers (n 31). According to art 11 of EP Directive proposal on representative actions for consumers (n 32), the representative action would even suspend limitation periods for all individuals concerned.

63 Arts 4, 7 of EP Directive proposal on representative actions for consumers (n 32). According to the common position of the Council, such strict obligations would apply only for cross-border representative actions and not necessarily for domestic representative actions for which Member States shall be entitled to designate qualified entities also on an ad hoc basis, art 4ff of Council, 'General Approach – Directive proposal on representative actions for consumers' (n 33).

A QUALIFIED ENTITIES COMMENT ON CONSUMER LAW ENFORCEMENT

Jutta Gurkmann*

I. INTRODUCTION

Before the Volkswagen emission scandal occurred, never had the discussion about consumer law enforcement in mass harm cases been as lively but also as wide-ranging as it is currently. It does not only affect Germany or the EU. It seems as if all over the world legal experts query their legal systems. For decades, the work of consumer associations was more or less disregarded by law firms. Since the declaratory model action (*Musterfeststellungsklage*) entered into force, Germany has been assailed with a veritable contest for 'customers'. Advertising messages meant to convince the consumers concerned to assign their claims, to engage a specific lawyer or to resort to a third-party funder are in many cases questionable: advertisements promising 100 per cent reimbursement within a very short time and without any risk, press conferences calling consumers to leave the Musterfeststellungsklage as this would certainly take years before coming to a result. The whole truth is that nobody could know at that stage what the outcome of the Musterfeststellungsklage would be and when it would end.

Unfortunately, the *modus operandi* of some players could have a counterproductive effect on the further development of legal instruments,

* Jutta Gurkmann, Head of Consumer Policy Division, Federation of German Consumer Organisations (Verbraucherzentrale Bundesverband e.V.).
German Federal Statutes are available at <http://www.gesetze-im-internet.de> and Cases of the German Federal Court (*Bundesgerichtshof* – BGH) are available at <http://www.bundesgerichtshof.de>.

which had just accelerated after decades of stagnation. Yet, there is more than enough work to do and the means the different players offer complement each other. Before explaining this complementarity, it is useful to explore the origin, the substance and the shortcomings of the enforcement rights of consumer organisations.

II. THE LEGAL STANDING OF CONSUMER ORGANISATIONS IN GERMANY

In Germany, individual consumers cannot file for injunctions under the unfair competition act. Since 1965, their interests have been represented by so-called qualified entities, which have the right to launch proceedings. Organisations applying for the inclusion in the official list of qualified entities must satisfy the legal prerequisites and be able to guarantee proper performance of the task. One prerequisite is that the organisation has qualified staff able to advise consumers. The organisation must also have sufficient financial resources. In the case of consumer organisations such as the consumer associations and vzbv, which receive public funding, it is assumed that they satisfy the necessary prerequisites for the right to take action.

The enforcement rights of consumer organisations in Germany have been extended over the last decades. Currently, they are entitled to take actions for:

- cessation and desistance as set out in section 8 of the UWG (*Gesetz gegen den unlauteren Wettbewerb* – Unfair Competition Act) with regard to unfair commercial practices;
- cessation and desistance as set out in section 1 of the UKlaG (*Unterlassungsklagengesetz* – Injunction Act) with regard to unfair contract terms;
- cessation and desistance as set out in section 2 of the UKlaG with regard to regulations for the protection of consumers;
- the disgorgement of profits as set out in section 10 of the UWG;
- recovery claim as set out in section 79 paragraph 2 sentence 3 of the ZPO (*Zivilprozessordnung* – Code of Civil Procedure);
- since 2015, consumer organisations can also file actions for the breach of data protection rules.

The purposes of enforcement by consumer organisations are various: in the first instance, consumer organisations contribute to a fair and functioning market which can only exist when all market participants respect the relevant rules. This market-shakeout is in the interest of consumers and competitors. The instruments usually applied in this field of activity are warnings and (if a cease and desist declaration is not signed) actions for injunctions. In the vast majority this procedure leads to quick and also cheap results as the costs for a (justified) warning add up to just around €250.

Furthermore, with around 1,000 lawsuits each year, vzbv and the consumer associations are helping the development of jurisprudence in the field of consumer law, reviewing current legislation with regard to its practicability and hence close the gap between concepts and commercial reality. Since 1985, vzbv and the consumer associations brought several lawsuits to the Federal Court of Justice (*Bundesgerichtshof* – BGH) and/or the European Court of Justice (ECJ), amongst them.

In 1987, the Federal Court of Justice decided about an advance payment clause in tourist travel contracts: if a travel organiser's customer is not insured against the travel organiser's risk of insolvency the latter may not request the full price of the trip to be paid at the moment of handing over ordinary travel documents to the customer, ahead of the start of the trip.[1] This decision by the Federal Court of Justice was one of the ground-breaking rulings on travel law and it influenced German and European legislation.

In 1993, the Federal Court of Justice ruled on banks' pricing policies: banks are not allowed to charge an extra fee when customers pay cash into or withdraw cash from their own account at the counter.[2] The Court held that any claim for payment by the bank is satisfied by the cash-in and that, in such cases, the creditor cannot demand a separate fee for accepting cash. In cases of cash withdrawal, the bank is simply fulfilling its legal obligation to refund the money once paid into the account and must thus not charge an additional fee either.

In its decision from 1994 and further judgments from 1995, the Federal Court of Justice ruled that general terms and conditions establishing a contract duration of ten years are to be considered void.[3] It thereby ended discussions about whether or not long-term contract duration clauses in private liability insurances, insurances on contents and accident insurances were acceptable. The court considered ten-year duration clauses to represent a significant burden for policy holders as they limit consumers' possibilities to conclude new contracts. Policy holders are also not in a position to adapt the contract duration to circumstances already present or foreseeable at the time the contract is being concluded. Even more importantly, policy holders had no possibility of applying normal market behaviour (shop for the best offer) after concluding such a contract. This in turns leads to a restriction of competition.

---

1 BGH, Judgment of 12 March 1987, VII ZR 37/86, NJW 1987, 1931.

2 BGH, Judgment of 30 November 1993, XI ZR 80/93, NJW 1984, 313 = VuR 1994, 7.

3 BGH, Judgment of 13 July 1994, V ZR 107/93, NJW 1994, 2693; BGH, Judgment of 22 February 1995, IV ZR 44/94, NJW 1995, 1289.

With its decisions on telemarketing in 1999, the Federal Court of Justice gave priority to the protection of privacy over the profit of market actors.[4] When opening a bank account, customers gave their consent to being contacted by the bank and its partners for advertising purposes as stated in the form's general terms and conditions. The Court held the given consent to be legally void. Telephone advertising severely affects the called person's privacy, which is protected by the constitution. The Court considered the company's interests to advertise their products to be legitimate but came to the conclusion that, in view of the large variety of advertising methods available, it is not necessary to use those that are particularly intrusive in terms of privacy. Explicit consent is hence required and cannot be given through contract terms. Nowadays, the Unfair Competition Act stipulates that telephone advertising must only take place after prior explicit consent. To date, the act does not contain any prescription in terms of which form this consent ought to take.

The Federal Court of Justice ruled in 2002 that banks must not give incorrect information about an account's balance to their customers on an ATM.[5] Such practices constitute unfair competition and can also be misleading. The consumer must be able to see that he may have sums already booked on his account that are not yet available without paying interest on a debit balance.

In 2008, the Federal Court of Justice stated that traders are not allowed to demand compensation for use when replacing faulty goods within the legal guarantee period.[6] In this specific case the enamel coat flaked off a faulty oven 17 months after purchase. Since it was not possible to repair the oven, it had to be replaced by a new one. The German Federal Court of Justice referred the case to the Court of Justice of the European Union (ECJ) which then decided that, in accordance with the EU Directive on Certain Aspects of the Sale of Consumer Goods and Associated Guarantees (1999/44/EC), the goods must be brought into conformity free of charge.[7] Therefore, no compensation can be demanded for the use of a faulty product. The decision resulted in the amendment of the relevant legal provision in the German Civil Code.

An airline may only demand a fee for using a credit card for online reservations if it also offers a well-established method of payment free of charge. This meant that previous practices of the low-cost airline in question was not legal. The airline had charged its customers a fee of four euros per passenger one-way when tickets were purchased using a credit card. A fee of €1.50 was applied when using a debit card. Customers were given no opportunity to pay

---

4 BGH, Judgment of 16 March 1999, XI ZR 76/98.

5 BGH, Judgment of 27 June 2002, I ZR 86/00, GRUR 2002, 1093; BGH, Judgment of 11 January 2007, I ZR 87/04.

6 BGH, Judgment of 26 November 2008, VIII ZR 200/05.

7 ECJ, C-404/06 *Quelle AG v Bundesverband der Verbraucherzentralen und Verbraucherverbände* [17 April 2008] ECR 2008 I-02685.

for their ticket without incurring additional costs. Payment 'free of charge' was only possible with a little used Visa Electron card, only available for an annual fee of €40 to €100. According to the Federal Court of Justice, this payment arrangement discriminated consumers in an unacceptable manner.[8] They must be able to comply with their legal obligation to pay without the opposite party demanding a separate charge for it. Furthermore, it must be possible to pay via a widely used method that does not put undue burden on the consumer.

If a travel agency offers additional services against payment while offering flights, it must comply with EU regulations when giving a quote for air fares online. Costs for additional services must be stated right at the beginning of each reservation process. Travel cancellation insurance must not be preselected. In this specific case, a travel agency had preselected a travel cancellation insurance for €9.00 on its website under the heading 'Your current travel costs'. Customers had to actively deselect this if they did not want the service. Such opt-out arrangements are no longer permitted according to EU Regulation on Common Rules for the Operation of Air Service in the Community (EC) No 1008/2008 which came into force in September 2008. In its decision, the Court of Justice of the European Union also pointed out that travel agencies must comply with these strict EU rules just as well as airlines when offering flights online.[9] Until then, there was disagreement whether the regulation was binding on airlines only.

In 2014 the Federal Court of Justice decided that embedding advertising into computer games with links pointing to ancillary pay-services (in-app purchases) directed at children is unlawful.[10] 'Grab this opportunity and give your armour and weapons that certain something.' This solicitation to purchase, directed at children, advertised accessories on the website of a computer role-playing game. Clicking the link opened a new website where various accessories were offered for sale. The Federal Court of Justice prohibited this. vzbv had complained that directly soliciting children to purchasing is unlawful according to the appendix to the Unfair Competition Act.

Food labels, design and advertising must not create the illusion that they contain a certain ingredient when the ingredient is not present and when that fact can only be found out by looking at the list of ingredients. A tea producer advertised a children's fruit tea by placing raspberries and vanilla on the front of the packaging. Furthermore, the labels 'fruit tea with natural aroma' and 'only natural ingredients' were placed in a prominent position on the front of the package. However, the tea contained neither raspberry nor vanilla. In fact, the tea contained no natural parts or aromas of these plants. This was stated

8 BGH, Judgment of 20 May 2010, Xa ZR 68/09.

9 ECJ, C-112/11 *ebookers.com v Bundesverband der Verbraucherzentralen und Verbraucherverbände* [19 July 2012] ECLI:EU:C:2012:487.

10 BGH, Judgment of 19 September 2014, I ZR 34/12.

in the small print containing the list of ingredients on the rear of the package. After the Federal Court of Justice submitted the case to the Court of Justice of the European Union, the latter ruled that even a correct and complete list of ingredients cannot sufficiently rebalance an incorrect or misleading impression created by the rest of the packaging.[11]

The breach of rules on data protection is another focus of vzbv within the last years. In its Planet49 case,[12] vzbv seeks to clarify whether the use of third party tracking cookies without informed consent is complying with current legislation: A highly important judgment by the Court of Justice of the European Union lately held that the consent to the storage of or access to information in the form of cookies installed on a website user's terminal equipment is not validly constituted if given by way of a pre-checked checkbox, irrespective of whether or not the information in question is personal data. Furthermore, the Court made clear that the information that the service provider must give to an internet user includes the duration of the operation of cookies and whether or not third parties may have access to those cookies. On 28 May 2020, the Federal Court of Justice decided that the German Telemedia Act must be interpreted in conformity with the E-Privacy directive meaning that consent must be given through active confirmation by the user.

On the very same day, the BGH forwarded on of vzbv's cases against Facebook (Az. I ZR 186/17) to the ECJ. Hence, the court did not issue a final decision based on the ECJ's decision in the FashionID case.[13] This case is not only concerning the interpretation of data protection law, but also our legal standing in data protection rights.

III. A NEW INSTRUMENT FOR MASS DAMAGES

Since actions for injunction are aimed at rectifying legal transactions for the future, this instrument reaches its limits when consumers suffer damages from unfair commercial practices or other breaches of consumer law. Before the model declaratory action entered into force on 1 November 2018, consumer organisations could only resort to recovery actions in order to get consumers their money back. Consumers could therefore cede their claims to the consumer organisation so that it was able to bring a bundle of claims to court. The obtained money was then paid to the respective consumer.

---

11 ECJ, C-195/14 *Bundesverband der Verbraucherzentralen und Verbraucherverbände v Teekanne GmbH & Co. KG* [4 July 2015] ECLI:EU:C:2015:361.

12 ECJ, C-673/17 *Verbraucherzentrale Bundesverband e.V. v Planet49 GmbH* [1 October 2019] ECLI:EU:C:2019:801.

13 ECJ, C-40/17 *Fashion ID GmbH & Co. KG v Verbraucherzentrale Nordrhein-Westfalen e.V.* [29 July 2019] ECLI:EU:C:2019:629.

Practical experience has shown that this instrument is not suitable for bundling a number of small sums in one claim. Organising recovery claims for a large number of consumers with regard to dispersed damages is very complex: the plaintiff has to come to an individual agreement with each and every consumer and must determine the amount of the claim individually or provide supporting documents. These efforts bear no relation to the results. And even if the case is won, only consumers represented in the litigation benefit from the result. Others would end up with nothing or their claims have reached their period of limitation.

For small claims this frequently results in consumers abstaining from putting in a claim for compensation. As the disgorgement of profits as set out in section 10 of the UWG is subject of legal prerequisites that are hard to fulfil, companies can then keep these profits even though they acted against the law.

Vzbv lobbied for more than ten years for an instrument offering consumers easier access to justice than the already established instruments. Since the average threshold experts have identified as being the limit value for going to court individually is between €1,500 and €2,000, the main application field was meant to be mass damages caused by unfair commercial practices or the use of unfair contract terms. The main effects of this new instrument should especially be an improvement on the interruption of the limitation period and a broader effect of judgments. The Musterfeststellungsklage was then a first step on national level when it became obvious during the Volkswagen scandal that the overwhelming majority of concerned consumers did not go to court.

Alas, the legislator has set the threshold for the Musterfeststellungsklage very high. The number of organisations authorised to file such an action is very limited. Furthermore, the liability situation of the associations and their lawyers is completely unclear. It cannot be ruled out that – in the event of faulty conduct of proceedings – the organisations themselves will have to compensate consumers for any damage inflicted.

Other legal regulations also make it difficult to reach settlements. Section 611 of the ZPO allows the parties to the action to reach a settlement in favour of the consumers who have registered. One of the prerequisites for a settlement to be effective is that all of these consumers have to be informed about the settlement by means of a letter. The consumers then have the possibility to drop out within one month after receiving the letter. If 30 per cent of the consumers or more reject the settlement, it will not be effected. The court has to check whether the number of rejections amounts to less than that percentage. Posting these letters is by itself an enormous challenge for the court in mass proceedings (almost 400,000 consumers participated in the lawsuit against VW), not to mention the task of checking whether less than 30 per cent have signed out. These circumstances stand in the way of the legislator's wish to enable a quick and easy settlement of the dispute. It is also problematic that even applicants who obviously do not belong to the group of entitled consumers must be counted when determining the quorum. If, for example, a sufficient amount of people has joined the action against Volkswagen who do not own a car at all, their signing out would also render the settlement void. All these deficiencies will have to be remedied by the legislator and led to the parties' conclusion that only an out-of-court settlement would be adapted to find a quicker solution for the consumers concerned. At the end of February 2020, vzbv and Volkswagen signed an agreement in which Volkswagen committed itself to offer consumers fulfilling certain criteria a settlement contract and to pay a compensation depending on the car model and the age of the car. This last factor reflects that most Higher Regional Courts deduced a compensation for use when condemning Volkswagen to compensate consumers' damages. This jurisdiction was confirmed by the Federal Court of Justice in its judgment of 25 May 2020. vzbv agreed to withdraw its action as soon as the consumers would have received the settlement agreements. In a press release from late April 2020, Volkswagen informed the public that out of approximately 262,000 entitled consumers 235,000 had accepted Volkswagen's offer. In order to assess this preliminary result, it is important to keep in mind that the register comprised approximately 320,000 valid entries and that two groups of cases were excluded from the settlement as they also would not have benefitted from a court decision: Consumers having purchased their cars after the end of 2016 would have to proof individually that they did not know about the scandal when purchasing the car. In cross-border cases, the court would have had to decide in each and every case the individually applicable law as the Musterfeststellungsklage is based on German law.

Even though the Musterfeststellungsklage could in this case not lead to a satisfying result for every consumer affected, it is a milestone in the field of collective redress in Germany. With this instrument, consumer organisations have the opportunity to clarify fundamental legal and factual questions in court, thus giving large numbers of consumers the possibility to establish their claims. Plus, the Musterfeststellungsklage ensures that the consumers' claims will not become statute-barred as long as the proceedings last.

Possible enhancements might follow within the next months when EU institutions will decide about the content of a directive on representative actions allowing qualified entities to seek redress, such as compensation, replacement or repair, on behalf of a group of consumers that have been harmed by an illegal commercial practice.

IV. FURTHER DEVELOPMENTS

Currently, the debate on a further improvement of our redress mechanisms is very much focused on the question whether qualified entities are better suited for obtaining redress for consumers or if law firms are. And the answer should be: they both are!

Market-driven redress instruments will probably only work for cases in which the damages are important enough to guarantee sufficient profit for the law firm and/or the litigation funder behind it. For smaller damages providers of legal services offer an easy and convenient way to assert legal claims through legal tech. Naturally, consumers have to pay for the service between 15 and 30 per cent of the claim, but only if the case is won. And also for these providers, the case has to be adapted for an automated processing. Unfortunately, the awareness level regarding the excellent and free of charge services of ADR bodies like the Insurance Ombudsman Association (Versicherungsombudsmann) or the söp (Schlichtungsstelle für den öffentlichen Personenverkehr e.V.) is still far too little.

For consumers suffering a less important damage or not willing to pay for such a service, a state under the rule of law must ensure that an appropriately comfortable redress instrument is at the consumers' disposal bearing in mind that according to German law a creditor's claim comprises also the costs of legal enforcement.

SECURITIES LITIGATION AGAINST VW AND PORSCHE

The 10 Billion Euro Marathon Walk

Maximilian Weiss*

I. INTRODUCTION

The focus of this chapter is to share experiences made with the securities litigation of investors against Volkswagen AG ('VW') and Porsche Automobil Holding SE ('PSE') in Germany. The following is only a snapshot and shall illustrate a few key issues of a complex case. The general procedural background regarding model case proceedings is explained (Section II.) and how Germany has become the

* Maximilian Weiss, LL.M. (Northwestern), Rechtsanwalt (German Attorney), TILP Litigation Rechtsanwaltsgesellschaft mbH.

forum of choice (Section III) before details of the VW/PSE securities litigation are touched upon, namely the procedural history (Section IV.A), the most relevant factual and legal issues of the case (Section IV.B) and latest developments (Section V). In view of the experiences made with the VW securities litigation to date[1] the chapter ends with conclusions on the case and the enforcement of capital markets law in general (Section VI).

II. KapMuG: THE GERMAN DEVICE FOR MASS PROCEEDINGS

Germany's procedural device for collective redress in capital markets law matters, the Capital Markets Model Case Act (*Kapitalanleger-Musterverfahrensgesetz* – KapMuG),[2] entered into force in 2005, was amended in 2012 and was originally prompted by the Deutsche Telekom case with 17,000 claims filed by investors[3] – a scenario that the German courts were unable to cope with at that time. The KapMuG was hence specifically enacted to streamline mass securities and other financial market-related claims in one single proceeding.[4] For a KapMuG proceeding a minimum of ten financial market claims have to be brought by individual claimants in the Regional Court (*Landgericht* – LG), alleging substantially the same facts, known as *Lebenssachverhalt*. If a defendant or a plaintiff applies for the establishment of a model case, the Regional Court shall publicly announce the application for the establishment of the model case pursuant to section 3(2) of the KapMuG in a so-called Complaint Registry. If ten such admissible applications have been announced in total and within six months after the first announcement, the Regional Court shall then, pursuant to section 6(1) of the KapMuG, refer the matter to the Higher Regional Court (*Oberlandesgericht* – OLG) for the establishment of a model case. The Higher Regional Court's task is to provide a resolution of common questions of fact and of law (so-called 'establishment objectives' or *Feststellungsziele*) in the model case proceeding, yet excluding any individual questions such as the proof of

---

1 June 2020.

2 For an English translation see <http://www.gesetze-im-internet.de/englisch_kapmug/>.

3 On the Telekom case see Andreas Tilp and Thomas Roth, 'The German Capital Market Model Proceedings Act as Illustrated by the Example of the Frankfurt Deutsche Telekom Claims' in Willem van Boom and Gerhard Wagner (eds), *Mass Torts in Europe: Cases and Reflections* (De Gruyter 2014) 131 (hereafter Tilp and Roth, 'German Capital Market Model Proceedings').

4 See the 'Gesetzentwurf der Bundesregierung zur Einführung von Kapitalanleger-Musterverfahren (2005)' (Draft of the Federal Government – Act on the Introduction of Capital Markets Model Case Proceedings) BT-Drucks 15/5091, 17 <http://dip21.bundestag.de/dip21/btd/15/050/1505091.pdf> (hereafter 'Gesetzentwurf Kapitalanleger-Musterverfahren').

transactions, individual losses or causation between the omitted disclosure of capital market information and an investor's decision to purchase the stock. In view of the model case proceeding, the Regional Court(s) order to stay the pending individual proceedings[5] and the plaintiffs in the individual proceedings become parties to the model case. The Higher Regional Court then appoints a model case plaintiff while all other plaintiffs, whose proceedings have also been ordered to stay, can participate in the model case proceedings as interested parties. The Higher Regional Court's ruling on the questions of fact and of law are binding for the Regional Courts and the ruling hence (ideally) pre-determines the outcome of the individual lawsuits in a way that questions common to all plaintiffs are resolved. When the Regional Courts take up the individual proceedings again, they only have to deal with a few individual questions related to each of the individual plaintiffs, while the Higher Regional Court's ruling on the establishment objectives has a binding effect.[6]

III. THE FORUM AND THE PLAINTIFFS

The disclosure of the VW emissions scandal on 18 September 2015 and VW's ad hoc announcement on 22 September 2015 marked the beginning of the biggest proceedings in the history of German securities litigation:[7] until 31 December 2018 thousands of investors filed lawsuits against VW and PSE in Germany. While there are no official numbers available, it can be estimated that at least 1,000 institutional and 2,000 retail investors have filed complaints. The claims in dispute amount to about €10 billion, which is 100 times the size of the Deutsche Telekom case.[8] The sizeable amount is not only due to the fact that VW and PSE shares underwent a massive wipeout in market capitalisation after the disclosure,[9] but also a result of the fact that institutional investors from all over the world assert their claims in German courts,[10] a quite remarkable difference compared to the Deutsche Telekom case.

5 Pursuant to s 8(1) of the KapMuG.

6 Pursuant to s 22 of the KapMuG.

7 For a list and brief description of other KapMuG cases see Christopher Hodges and Stefaan Voet, *Delivering Collective Redress: New Technologies* (Hart 2018) 84ff.

8 In the Deutsche Telekom case 17,000 investors filed complaints, but the average claims value of €5,900 was much lower, hence leading to an aggregate claims value of (only) €100 million. Institutional investors were not involved in the litigation, see Tilp and Roth, 'German Capital Market Model Proceedings' (n 3) 131–32.

9 The market value loss of VW ordinary and VW preferred shares after the first couple of weeks of the discovery of the emissions scandal came to around €40 billion.

10 Another example for a case mainly driven by institutional investors under the KapMuG umbrella and with claims totaling €1 billion is the Hypo Real Estate case, see OLG München, Order of 15 December 2014, Kap 3/10.

The fact that institutional investors choose to litigate in German courts is a more recent phenomenon and has nothing to do with the KapMuG:[11] in the past such securities fraud cases would have been brought and settled (rather than tried) in the US due to its much more plaintiff-friendly environment, including features such as discovery devices, the 'American Rule',[12] the opportunity to go to (jury) trial and the opt-out class action procedure, hence creating more risk for defendants and incentivising them to settle cases with merits – corresponding to the author's view of the VW emissions case – quickly. Yet, the US Supreme Court ruled in 2010 *in re Morrison*[13] that US securities laws do not apply to foreign-traded shares, practically blocking off US securities class actions against companies listed on foreign exchanges.[14] By cutting back the US securities laws' extraterritorial reach, *Morrison* changed the securities litigation landscape not only in the US, but also elsewhere: Without *Morrison* aggrieved institutional VW/PSE investors would have asserted their claims in the US[15] and not in Germany.[16]

IV. THE VW/PSE SECURITIES LITIGATION

A. THE PROCEDURAL HISTORY

1. *The Braunschweig Proceedings and Model Case*

The first investor lawsuit in Germany after the VW emissions scandal became known to the public was filed in October 2015 in the Regional Court of Braunschweig against VW. The complaint included an application made by the plaintiff for an order to refer the matter to the Higher Regional Court and – by doing so – to establish a KapMuG model case. Since then many more investors filed lawsuits in Braunschweig against VW and on 14 March 2016 a first group

11 The legislator misbelieved that the enactment of the KapMuG may attract investors to litigate in Germany rather than in other forums, see 'Gesetzentwurf Kapitalanleger-Musterverfahren' (n. 4) 16ff.

12 As opposed to the English 'loser pays rule', under the 'American rule' each party bears its own legal costs.

13 *Morrison v National Australia Bank Ltd* 561 U.S. 247 (2010).

14 Except for certain types of American Depositary Receipts (ADRs) traded in the US market.

15 This has happened for purchases of VW American Depositary Receipts (ADRs).

16 In some countries it was tried to establish international jurisdiction but rejected by the courts. For Ontario (Canada) see *Leon v Volkswagen AG* 2018, ONSC 4265 (CanLII), for Austria see OGH, Judgment of 7 July 2017, 6 Ob 18/17s. For Québec (Canada) though, see *Chandler v Volkswagen Aktiengesellschaft* 2018 QCCS 2270 (CanLII), where the court's jurisdiction was established – so far – for the 'authorisation stage' of the opt-out class action for residents of Québec, who invested in Volkswagen securities.

of 278 institutional investors filed a joint complaint with claims totalling €3.3 billion. On 5 August 2016 the Regional Court of Braunschweig issued an order referring the matter of investor claims in connection with the VW emissions scandal to the Higher Regional Court of Braunschweig,[17] paving the way for the model case. The Regional Court subsequently ordered to stay most of the then pending proceedings, while some others are still pending and not yet ordered to be stayed. Another wave of lawsuits reaching billions of Euros in claims followed in September 2016, while this wave was not yet the end.[18]

On 8 March 2017 the Higher Regional Court of Braunschweig appointed the model case plaintiff,[19] an institutional investor from Germany with the highest claimed loss of all plaintiffs[20] and represented by the law firm TILP. On 4 August 2017, the model case plaintiff submitted the initial complaint for the model case proceeding, which comprised 305 pages and 163 annexes. While most plaintiff law firms involved in the model case are passive and do not contribute to the proceeding by means of submitting briefs or by participating in the oral hearings,[21] a few law firms are creative. These active law firms submitted their first statements on matters of fact and law on 15 December 2017. Four law firms contributed altogether another 509 pages and 57 annexes. Hereupon, on 28 February 2018, the model case defendant VW submitted its statement of defence in response to all briefs that had been submitted so far by the active plaintiff law firms, which comprised of 693 pages along with 123 annexes and including several lengthy expert opinions on issues of law. On 15 June 2018 the Higher Regional Court ordered that PSE is a party to the model case, i.e. the model case defendant no 2 alongside VW as claims against PSE are also affected by the proceedings against VW.[22] However, the Higher Regional Court is of the opinion that the model case is only to resolve questions with regard to VW's liability, not PSE's, which is why the court denied applications made to amend the establishment objectives concerning PSE's liability.

The first four days of oral hearings before the Higher Regional Court took place on 10/11/17 September and 26 November 2018. As it joined the model

17 LG Braunschweig, Order of 5 August 2016, 5 OH 62/16 (hereafter LG Braunschweig).

18 Most investors had filed lawsuits before or on 19 September 2016 due to uncertainties regarding the limitation period for certain claims. Yet, the filing of further lawsuits kept accumulating and ended on 31 December 2018, since any claim filed after this date would be undoubtedly time-barred.

19 OLG Braunschweig, Order of 8 March 2017, 3 Kap 1/16.

20 For the determining criteria regarding the model case plaintiff appointment see Axel Halfmeier, 'Auswahl und Funktion des Musterklägers im Kapitalanleger-Musterverfahren' [2016] Zeitschrift für Wirtschaftsrecht 1705.

21 The absence of many lawyers of the plaintiffs' bar is a phenomenon that is typical for such mass proceedings in Germany, as noted for the Deutsche Telekom case by Tilp and Roth, 'German Capital Market Model Proceedings' (n 3) 131ff.

22 OLG Braunschweig, Order of 15 June 2018, Kap 1/16.

case late, PSE submitted its own statement of defence on 21 February 2019, and by doing so adding another 297 pages with 63 annexes to the court records. The oral hearings continued on 25 March, 1 July, 16 December 2019 and 9 March 2020. At present the court has not heard any witnesses yet, but only discussed legal issues with the parties and shared its preliminary views on matters of procedural and substantive law.

To date, the parties keep constantly submitting briefs. These also include applications made by both plaintiffs and defendants to add establishment objectives to the existing ones, even though the original order of the Regional Court to refer the matter to the Higher Regional Court already contained a considerable number of 193 establishment objectives[23] – which may further illustrate how complex the case is.

2. *The Stuttgart Proceedings and Model Case*

Further investor lawsuits have been filed by over 100 institutional investors and more than 200 other investors in Stuttgart against PSE, where it is headquartered. Their total claim volume amounts to approx. €1 billion. The allegations made by the plaintiffs are similar to those in the Braunschweig proceedings concerning VW, i.e. it is alleged that PSE failed to inform the capital markets about the use of defeat devices in cars produced by its subsidiaries, namely VW and Porsche AG.

The Regional Court of Stuttgart issued two separate orders to refer the matter to the Higher Regional Court so as to provide a forum for the common questions of fact and law regarding PSE's liability.[24] Both orders have been declared inadmissible by the Higher Regional Court of Stuttgart,[25] while one of the Higher Regional Court's decisions has been appealed[26] and is currently pending before the Federal Court of Justice (*Bundesgerichtshof* – BGH).[27] It remains to be seen if a model case against PSE focusing on PSE's liability will take place soon. If so, the question will be if this second model case will be ordered to be stayed until the decision in the first model case is final and if this second model case will take place in Stuttgart or in Braunschweig. If it takes place in Braunschweig, the decision needs to be made on whether oral hearings will be held in parallel to the first Braunschweig model case or if the proceedings will be consolidated.

---

23 LG Braunschweig (n 17).

24 LG Stuttgart, Order of 28 February 2017, 22 AR 1/17; LG Stuttgart, Order of 6 December 2017, 22 AR 2/17 Kap.

25 OLG Stuttgart, Order of 27 March 2019, 20 Kap 2/17; OLG Stuttgart, Order of 27 March 2019, 20 Kap 3/17; OLG Stuttgart, Order of 27 March 2019, 20 Kap 4/17. The court is of the opinion that, in view of the model case proceeding in Braunschweig a further model case proceeding would be inadmissible pursuant to s 7(1) of the KapMuG.

26 OLG Stuttgart, Order of 27 March 2019, 20 Kap 2/17.

27 BGH, Order of 5 February 2019, II ZB 10/19.

It is possible that investors who invested in PSE shares and who filed against its parent entity VW and PSE may have to await the outcome of the model case proceeding in Braunschweig before they will have to litigate in yet another model case proceeding against PSE. Either way, at this time the centre stage of the VW/PSE actions is the Higher Regional Court of Braunschweig.

3. *Discovery in the US*

Besides the proceedings in Germany institutional investors represented by TILP in the Braunschweig model case proceedings filed a discovery assistance request pursuant to 28 U.S.C. §1782 ('ss 1782'). In a nutshell, section 1782 provides a tool for an interested party in a foreign proceeding outside the US to obtain evidence in the US for use in proceedings outside the US before a 'foreign tribunal' through depositions and documents production. Furthermore, it should be noted that the party from which one seeks to obtain evidence does not have to be a party to the foreign proceeding. The section 1782 request was filed on 20 April 2017 in the Third Circuit District Court of New Jersey against VW's US subsidiary Volkswagen Group of America, Inc ('VwGoA'), seeking the production of documents for use in the German securities litigation against VW and PSE. After the applicants and VwGoA agreed on a protective order, the Third Circuit District Court of New Jersey so-ordered a stipulated confidentiality order. Following this, on 30 May 2018 VwGoA made a first production of documents. The review is ongoing.

B. FACTUAL AND LEGAL ISSUES IN THE KAPMUG PROCEEDINGS

The VW/PSE securities litigation in Germany is based on the alleged failure of VW and PSE to inform the capital markets about the use of defeat devices. The damage period ranges from purchases made on 6 June 2008 (first implementation of inadmissible defeat devices) until 18 September 2015 (when the emissions scandal became known to the public). The claims arise from a variety of statutes establishing an issuer's liability on the secondary market.[28] In the VW/PSE proceedings the claims are based on sections 37b and 37c (old version)[29] of the

28 For an overview see Dirk A Verse, 'Germany: Liability for Incorrect Capital Market Information' in Pierre-Henri Conac and Martin Gelter (eds), *Global Securities Litigation and Enforcement* (Cambridge University Press 2019) 363ff.

29 In essence, s 37c of the WpHG (old version) concerns claims based on an issuer's misrepresentation by disclosing incorrect inside information to the capital market, while s 37b of the WpHG (old version) concerns claims based on an issuer's omission to disclose inside information to the capital market as soon as possible.

German Securities Trading Act (*Wertpapierhandelsgesetz* – WpHG),[30] alleging the failure to disclose inside information, and on section 823(2) of the German Civil Code (*Bürgerliches Gesetzbuch* – BGB) in conjunction with a number of protective statutes, namely section 331 of the German Commercial Code (*Handelsgesetzbuch* – HGB),[31] section 400 of the German Stock Corporation Act (*Aktiengesetz* – AktG)[32] and sections 37v and 37w of the WpHG (old versions), altogether basically alleging the issuance of wrong and misleading financial statements. Finally, the claims are based on section 826 of the BGB, alleging intentional damage in a manner 'contrary to public policy'.

The factual and legal issues that play a role and are being disputed in the VW/PSE actions are numerous. Hence only few bullet points are named here that are of importance and to which the Braunschweig Higher Regional Court has already given a 'preliminary opinion'[33] in the oral hearings that have taken place to date.

1. *Claims under Section 37b(1) No 1 of the WpHG (Old Version)/Section 97(1) No 1 of the WpHG (New Version)*

A very promising claim can be brought under section 37b(1) no 1 of the WpHG,[34] pursuant to which investors who acquired an issuer's financial instruments during the disinformation period and who held the instruments until the truth was disclosed can claim damages. The Federal Court of Justice held in a landmark decision[35] that investors may then choose for which kind of damage they want compensation.

The investor can claim inflation damages, i.e. compensation based on the difference between the inflated price at which the investor actually purchased and the hypothetical value of the stock, had the inside information at the time of the acquisition been known to the markets. The damage hence amounts to the inflated stock price.

---

30 For an English translation see <http://www.bafin.de/SharedDocs/Veroeffentlichungen/EN/Aufsichtsrecht/Gesetz/WpHG_en.html>.

31 For an English translation see <http://www.gesetze-im-internet.de/englisch_hgb/index.html>.

32 For an English translation see <http://www.gesetze-im-internet.de/englisch_aktg/index.html>.

33 The preliminary opinions given by the court to the parties in the oral hearings are preliminary in nature. The court can change its view and is not bound in any way to change its opinion during the course of the proceedings. The views given are not court orders, nor judgments and cannot be appealed.

34 Since 3 January 2018, s 37b of the WpHG (old version) and s 37c of the WpHG (old version) have been removed and replaced by s 97 and s 98 of the WpHG, both of which literally correspond to the former. Hereafter only s 37b and 37c of the WpHG are referred to, as only these old versions are applicable to the VW/PSE case.

35 BGH, Judgment of 13 December 2011, XI ZR 51/10 – IKB.

Alternatively, the investor can claim rescission damages, i.e. he can claim for the difference between the purchase price and the sales price or – if the shares are still held – claim for the purchase price in exchange for the shares. If a plaintiff is awarded rescission damages, he will be put in the financial position as if he had never purchased the shares.

A major difference between these types of damages is that for the inflation damages the investor only has to prove loss causation, i.e. he only has to establish causation between the harmful event and the economic loss.[36] For rescission damages, instead, the investor must prove that his decision to purchase the securities was based on the issuer's failure to disclose the inside information, i.e. that he would not have purchased the shares if he had known about the undisclosed information. As a result, it is easier for an investor to be compensated for inflation damages than for rescission damages.

Furthermore, while the liability standard under section 37b of the WpHG is gross negligence, section 37b(2) of the WpHG orders a reversal of the burden of proof in a way that gross negligence is presumed. So, for an issuer to avoid liability he would have to prove that its non-disclosure of inside information was neither intentional nor the result of gross negligence.

According to the opinion of the court, investors may base their claims on section 37b of the WpHG for share purchases dating back to as far as 10 July 2012,[37] while claims based on purchases made in spring 2014 and after are considered the most promising of all.[38]

2. *Attribution of Knowledge*

Of utmost importance to the case is, who in the companies VW and PSE had knowledge of the use of defeat devices – and when. The defendants aver that the duty of the issuer to inform the capital markets is to be fulfilled by the issuer's legal representatives, the management board and – from this standpoint – further aver that the management board of the issuer can be liable for a tortious action only if the board itself has positive knowledge of the relevant facts, since without its own positive knowledge of the information in question, the management board would not be able to comply with the standard directive of having to publish inside information to the capital market 'without undue delay'.[39]

---

36 Ibid.

37 The specific date 10 July 2012 has to do with a matter of law, the statute of limitations (see Section IV.B.3.).

38 Spring 2014 is important because it saw the ICCT study and following investigations by the EPA and CARB, increasing the chance that the emissions manipulations be detected and which the court considers to be inside information.

39 Pursuant to s 15 of the WpHG (old version) and also the German language version of art 17 of the Market Abuse Regulation (MAR) inside information is to be disclosed 'without undue delay' (*unverzüglich*) as opposed to the English language version of art 17 of the MAR ('as soon as possible').

Furthermore, the defendants are of the opinion that liability under section 826 of the BGB and section 37b of the WpHG due to the breach of the issuer's obligation to disclose inside information can only be fulfilled if there is an information gap between the issuer's management board and the capital market. The line of defence is that the boards of VW and PSE were clueless about the use of defeat devices and that the attribution of certain employees' knowledge to the board would not be allowed. The concept of the 'attribution of knowledge' (*Wissenszurechnung*) is not new to German jurisprudence,[40] but unknown to other legal environments, where for example doctrines such as *respondeat superior* provide for a clearer judicial definition.[41] After the emissions scandal was revealed, a wave of papers from legal scholars[42] fuelled the debates around this issue. Against the background that Martin Winterkorn was the Chairman of the Management Boards of both VW and its majority shareholder PSE between 25 November 2009 and 23 September 2015 (which is almost congruent with the span of the alleged disinformation period), questions about the attribution of knowledge within a group of companies are concerned as well.

The Higher Regional Court of Braunschweig took a preliminary position in saying that certain individuals employed at VW below the board level, supervisors in charge of engine development for an operational unit of VW or all of VW, were to be considered so-called 'other constitutionally appointed representatives' (*andere verfassungsmäßig berufene Vertreter*) of VW.[43] And as such, knowledge from their part, the court concluded, can be attributed to VW. In this respect, the court agrees with the plaintiffs' view on this matter. The Statement of Facts of the Plea Agreement that ended the US criminal proceeding[44] shed light on their roles. Before this background, the assertion made by plaintiffs that these supervisors were aware of the use of defeat devices was left uncontested by VW.

3. *The Statute of Limitations*

Questions with regard to the statute of limitations for damage claims pursuant to sections 37b and 37c of the WpHG also play a significant role. One reason is that on 10 July 2015 a new act came into force,[45] which led to a repeal of the special statute of limitations provisions of sections 37b(4) and 37c(4) of the

---

40 BGH, Judgment of 2 February 1996, V ZR 239/94.

41 For a comparative overview see Gerhard Wagner, 'Wissenszurechnung: Rechtsvergleichende und rechtsökonomische Grundlagen' (2017) 181 Zeitschrift für das gesamte Handels- und Wirtschaftsrecht 203ff.

42 See Alexander Sajnovits, 'Ad-hoc-Publizität und Wissenszurechnung' [2016] Wertpapier-Mitteilungen 765ff.

43 Namely Friedrich Eichler, Jens Hadler, Rudolf Krebs and Heinz-Jakob Neußer.

44 *United States v Volkswagen AG* Nr. 16-cr-20394-SFC (E.D. Mich.).

45 Protection Act for Retail Investors (Kleinanlegerschutzgesetz), Bundesgesetzblatt I 2015, 1114.

WpHG, practically extending the limitation period from one year to three years. In view of the fact, though, that the legislator had not provided a transitional provision governing claims that expired before the new act came into force, it was uncertain if the new or the old limitations period applies.[46] The preliminary opinion of the Higher Regional Court on this issue is that the new limitation period applies to all such claims which at the time of the new law entering into force had not yet expired under the old law. It was good news for investors, since some of them filed claims a year after the disclosure or later (until 31 December 2018), which could have been too late under the previous limitations period. On the other hand, for any purchases made before 10 July 2012, the court's preliminary opinion is that claims based on sections 37b and 37c of the WpHG were time-barred by 10 July 2015 under the old statute of limitations provisions, i.e. even before the emissions scandal was revealed in September 2015.

4. *The 'Early Period' and Section 826 of the BGB*

Section 826 of the BGB is the general 'catch-all' residual provision of German tort law and covers – seen from a common law perspective – more of a wide range of torts what would elsewhere be different kinds of torts.

In the VW/PSE actions section 826 of the BGB is relevant for claims arising from purchases made before 10 July 2012. The reason is that claims under the WpHG for purchases made before 10 July 2012 were potentially[47] statute-barred when the emissions scandal came to light. Claims under section 826 of the BGB, instead, were definitely not statute-barred for the entire alleged disinformation period, reaching back to 8 June 2008. Plaintiffs are hence well advised to also establish liability under tort law other than the specific causes of action under sections 37b, 37c of the WpHG when it comes to the 'early period', i.e. purchases made between 8 June 2008 and 10 July 2012.

Establishing liability under section 826 of the BGB requires a plaintiff to prove that the defendant acted 'in a manner contrary to public policy'. This is to be decided based on the vague term of *boni mores*, which is why the precise scope of section 826 of the BGB is largely shaped by case law.

While the requirements are relatively difficult to meet in practice, wrong or misleading communication towards the capital markets can be such an act 'in a manner contrary to public policy'.[48] Further, the liability for section 826 of the

46 Alexander Druckenbrodt, 'Die Streichung der Sonderverjährungsvorschriften im WpHG – wirklich ein Schutz von Kleinanlegern' [2015] NJW 3749ff; Andreas Tilp and Maximilian Weiss, 'Verjährung von Schadensersatzansprüchen wegen der Verletzung von Ad-hoc-Pflichten' [2016] Wertpapier-Mitteilungen 914ff.

47 Plaintiffs and defendants hold differing views in this matter.

48 Thomas MJ Möllers and Franz C Leisch in Heribert Hirte and Thomas MJ Möllers (eds), *Kölner Kommentar zum WpHG* (2nd edn, Carl Heymanns Verlag 2014) §§37b, 37c paras 436ff.

BGB standard is intent and – other than it is governed in sections 37b(2) and 37c(2) of the WpHG – the burden of proof is not reversed.

The Higher Regional Court of Braunschweig is of the preliminary opinion that in the VW emissions scandal liability of VW pursuant to section 826 of the BGB comes into consideration. However, the court explained that the plaintiffs will have to provide further facts, namely to substantiate that VW acted with its statements 'in a manner contrary to public policy' towards investors, not car buyers. Furthermore, in German legal literature it has been discussed, if under section 826 of the BGB an investor must prove transaction causation even if the investor claims only inflation (and not rescission) damages.[49] In this regard the Higher Regional Court of Braunschweig explained in the oral hearings that the causation standard for claims brought under section 826 of the BGB should be exactly the same as with the WpHG claims, i.e. that an investor only has to prove transaction causation if he claims rescission damages, while for inflation damages it shall be sufficient for the investor to prove loss causation.

V. TAILWIND FROM THE FEDERAL COURT OF JUSTICE

On 25 May 2020, the Federal Court of Justice handed down a landmark decision that awarded an individual consumer damages for buying a Volkswagen diesel car.[50] The court found that VW violated section 826 of the BGB. VW was ordered to reimburse the owner the buying price of the car less compensation for the kilometers travelled against the return of the vehicle. The decision itself and the reasoning given by the court creates massive tailwind for the investor lawsuits, where the claims, as explained above, are based on a violation of section 826 of the BGB, too.

No less important is that the court held that the plaintiff substantiated the facts about the knowledge of the board and other constitutionally appointed representatives, which triggered the application of the principles of the 'secondary burden of proof' (*sekundäre Darlegungslast*). The court held that VW did not substantiate its pleading with regard to the knowledge of employees well enough. Therefore, the court further held that the declarations to the facts made by the plaintiff are to be deemed acknowledged pursuant to section 138(3) of the Code of Civil Procedure (*Zivilprozessordnung* – ZPO). Based on this, the court declared that the board and further employees had knowledge about the use of defeat devices and that their knowledge was to be attributed to the legal entity VW.

---

49 Ibid, paras 477ff.

50 BGH, Judgment of 25 May 2020, VI ZR 252/19, NJW 2020, 1962.

The Higher Regional Court of Braunschweig has not yet had the chance to explain its current standpoint in view of the Federal Court of Justice's judgment, which is technically not prejudicial. The next oral hearings in the KapMuG proceeding are scheduled for 8 and 9 September 2020.

VI. FINAL REMARKS

While these remarks are final, a final ruling is not in sight yet.[51] It cannot be ruled out that the VW/PSE actions will keep judges, attorneys and legal scholars busy for many years to come, which is why this litigation is a 'marathon walk'. Even though the resolution will take a long time, the silver lining is that the rulings to be handed down will inevitably be landmark decisions and enrich the body of case law and thus promote legal clarity and legal certainty for the future.

One has no doubts that the German courts will award compensation to the aggrieved VW/PSE investors. The preliminary views given by the Higher Regional Court of Braunschweig as well as the BGH judgment in the consumer case are promising. The question rather is, when and to which date within the alleged disinformation period investors can recover their losses stemming from purchases in VW and PSE stock. The future will tell.

The fact that institutional investors have stepped into the ring ensures that plaintiffs can fight with defendants on a level playing field in terms of financial resources. With retail investors alone plaintiff law firms would not be able to adequately fund 'extracurricular' (but necessary) activities such as discovery requests in the US or hire technical, economic and legal experts – as big corporate defendants extensively do.

Private enforcement against corporate defendants can only be effective, if sufficient financial resources and incentives are available. A workable framework for the handling of mass fraud cases must enable plaintiff law firms and/or consumer associations to fight at eye level with defendants.

Finally, difficulties in gathering evidence and a few legal issues related to this (such as the concept of the attribution of knowledge) would not play as much of a role in the VW/PSE actions if German civil procedure provided powerful discovery tools. Discovery is a game changer and needs to be firmly embedded into German civil procedural law. This would almost certainly shorten the lengthy duration of such proceedings.[52]

---

51 It should be noted that Model case rulings of the Higher Regional Courts are appealable on points of law pursuant to s 20(1) of the KapMuG – and in practice they are almost always appealed.

52 While the securities litigation in Germany continues, the ADR securities class action in the US has been settled *In re Volkswagen "Clean Diesel" Marketing, Sales Practices, and Products Liability Litigation*, MDL No 2672 CRB (JSC) (Judgment) (N.D. Cal. 10 May 2019).

PART V

INTRADISCIPLINARY ANALYSIS AND REFORM RECOMMENDATIONS

THE DIESEL EMISSIONS SCANDAL – PERSPECTIVES OF CONSUMER LAW AND CAPITAL MARKETS LAW ENFORCEMENT

An Intradisciplinary Analysis

Beate GSELL* and Thomas M.J. MÖLLERS**

---

* Beate Gsell, Dr., Professor, Ludwig-Maximilians-Universität Munich, Chair of Civil Law, Civil Procedure, European Private Law and Procedure; Judge at Munich Higher Regional Court (OLG München).

** Thomas M.J. Möllers, Dr. Professor, University of Augsburg, Chair of Civil Law, Commercial Law, European Law, International Private Law and Comparative Law, Jean-Monnet-Chair *ad personam*.

I. THE ENFORCEMENT OF CONSUMER LAW AND CAPITAL MARKETS LAW IN THE DIESEL EMISSIONS SCANDAL

A. A HETEROGENEOUS PICTURE OF ENFORCEMENT

Looking at the ways of law enforcement in the diesel emissions scandal, but also at its intensity and speed, huge differences between the various countries examined in this book become apparent: In the US 'VW was hit from every angle':[1] In a 'concert of government and consumer claims' violations of all possible regulations such as consumer and commercial law, environmental standards as well as rules governing misleading advertisement etc. were prosecuted.[2] Within a few months a settlement was negotiated between private claimants from all over the US and VW. Even criminal law aspects were addressed.[3] Questions of capital markets law regarding the Volkswagen bonds have also been settled with

1 See above Amy J Schmitz, 'Enforcing Consumer and Capital Markets Law in the United States' in this book Section V (hereafter Schmitz, 'US').

2 See above Schmitz, 'US' (n 1) Section II.

3 *United States v Volkswagen AG*, Case 16-CR-20394 (E.D. Mich.); see above Maximilian Weiss, 'Securities Litigation against VW and Porsche: The 10 Billion Euro Marathon Walk' in this

the SEC.[4] But not only private claimants but above all state authorities reacted astonishingly quickly at federal and state level.[5]

Wheels turn slower in Europe. Also, within Europe a variety of different instruments of law enforcement are actually used, such as individual and collective civil actions, including forms of hybrid enforcement whereby public authorities bring consumer claims before civil courts, as well as regulatory and administrative sanctions along with criminal prosecution.[6] In Germany the diesel emissions scandal even gave rise to the introduction of a new collective redress instrument, that is the model declaratory action (*Musterfeststellungsklage*).[7] Yet, the picture within Europe is very heterogenous and an overall assessment shows that so far individual and collective redress claims within Europe faced significant difficulties both with regard to substantive and procedural law and that the intensity and severity of the measures taken, and sanctions imposed is significantly lower than in the US.[8] It is particularly striking in comparison with the US, but also with other countries such as Australia[9] and Brazil,[10] that there is still no collective redress instrument on the European Union level that would enable aggrieved consumers let alone capital investors to assert their claims for damages in a bundled manner through one single claimant as

book Section III. (hereafter Weiss, 'Securities Litigation against VW and Porsche'); see above Schmitz, 'US' (n 1) 27ff.

4 The ADR securities class action in the US has been settled: *In re: Volkswagen "Clean Diesel" Marketing, Sales Practices, and Products Liability Litigation MDL*, No. 2672 CRB (JSC) (Judgment) (N.D. Cal. 10 May 2019); see above Schmitz, 'US' (n 1) Section III.B.; see above Weiss, 'Securities Litigation against VW and Porsche' (n 3) fn 51. In principle, however, there is only responsibility if the company has listed its own shares, see *Morrison v National Australia Bank Ltd* (2010) 561 U.S. 247. The position is similar in other states, see above Weiss, 'Securities Litigation against VW and Porsche' (n 3) fn 16.

5 Schmitz, 'US' (n 1) Section III.A.

6 See the country chapters above as well as Tanja Domej and Patrick Honegger-Müntener, 'Enforcing Consumer Law in Europe and Beyond: Similarities and Differences' in this book Section I. passim (hereafter Domej and Honegger-Müntener, 'Consumer Law in Europe'). In Germany, criminal investigations have so far been initiated against the former Chairs of the management boards of Volkswagen AG (Winterkorn) and Audi AG (Stadler), but the opening of criminal proceedings is still pending, see Martin Hesse and Alexander Preker, 'Dieselskandal. Die Strafakten der Autobosse' *Der Spiegel* (Hamburg, 31 July 2019) <http://www.spiegel.de/wirtschaft/unternehmen/diesel-affaere-die-strafakten-der-autobosse-a-1279809.html>.

7 See ss 606ff of the German Code of Civil Procedure (*Zivilprozessordnung – ZPO*) as amended by the Act on the Introduction of a Civil Procedural Model Declaratory Action (*Gesetz zur Einführung einer zivilprozessualen Musterfeststellungsklage*) of 12 July 2018, BGBl 2018 I, 1151 and above Caroline Meller-Hannich, 'Enforcing Consumer and Capital Markets Law in Germany' in this book Section I.B.1.d (hereafter Meller-Hannich, 'Germany').

8 See the conclusions drawn by Domej and Honegger-Müntener, 'Consumer Law in Europe' (n 6) Section IV. as well as the individual country chapters above.

9 See above Peter Cashman, 'Enforcing Consumer and Capital Markets Law in Australia' in this book Section II. (hereafter Cashman, 'Australia').

10 See above Claudia Lima Marques, 'Enforcing Consumer and Capital Markets Law in Brazil' in this book Sections II.B. and III.A (hereafter Marques, 'Brazil').

representative. However, in April 2018 the European Commission launched a proposal for a Directive on representative actions for the protection of the collective interests of consumers[11] and this proposal is remarkable because, unlike the earlier Directive 2009/22/EC,[12] it is not limited to injunctions but provides for the entitlement of consumer associations as 'qualified entities' to bring representative actions seeking measures eliminating the continuing effects of the infringement of consumer law such as, *inter alia*, compensation, repair, replacement, price reduction, contract termination or reimbursement of the price paid.[13] The proposal has just been politically adopted in the trilogue procedure by the European Commission (EC), the Council of the European Union and the European Parliament.[14]

Thus, most Member States of the European Union have yet to receive rulings on the diesel emissions scandal from the highest courts and it is uncertain whether the Court of Justice of the European Union (ECJ) will comment on the decisions under consumer law or capital markets law in the future. In Germany, at least a settlement was recently reached in the newly introduced model declaratory proceedings against Volkswagen AG[15] to the benefit of about 262,500 qualified consumers who joined the proceedings on good grounds, which obliges Volkswagen AG to pay compensation sums of between €1,350 to €6,257 to each consumer depending on the vehicle concerned.[16] Furthermore, the German Federal Court of Justice (BGH) finally handed down a first seminal decision against Volkswagen in an individual action, stating that Volkswagen acted unconscionably and awarding a used car buyer damages in the form of a rescission of the sales contract. However, the purchase price is only to be

---

11 Proposal for a Directive of the European Parliament and of the Council on representative actions for the protection of the collective interests of consumers, and repealing Directive 2009/22/EC [11 April 2018] COM(2018) 184 final, 2018/0089(COD) (hereafter Proposal for a Directive on representative actions, COM(2018) 184 final).

12 Directive 2009/22/EC of the European Parliament and of the Council of 23 April 2009 on injunctions for the protection of consumers' interests [2009] OJ L110/30.

13 See art 5(3) in conjunction with art 6(1) subpara 1 of the Proposal for a Directive on representative actions, COM(2018) 184 final (n 11).

14 Endorsement of 30 June 2020 (ST-9223/2020). For the course of the legislative process, see <https://eur-lex.europa.eu/legal-content/DE/HIS/?uri=COM:2018:0184:FIN>.

15 The action was filed by the Bundesverband der Verbraucherzentralen und Verbraucherverbände on 26 November 2018 at the Higher Regional Court of Braunschweig (OLG Braunschweig) – 4 MK 1/18 and more than 400,000 consumers enrolled to the proceedings; for details see above Jutta Gurkmann, 'A Qualified Entities Comment on Consumer Law enforcement' in this book Section III. (hereafter Gurkmann, 'Consumer Law Enforcement') as well as <http://www.bundesjustizamt.de/DE/Themen/Buergerdienste/Klageregister/Klagen/201802/KlagRE_2_2018.html>.

16 For the pertinent press releases of both parties see <http://www.vzbv.de/pressemitteilung/vzbv-und-vw-erzielen-vergleich-fuer-betrogene-kaeufer>, as well as <https://vergleich.volkswagen.de/de.html>. It is reported that 90% of the affected consumers have accepted the settlement offers.

reimbursed less compensation for the kilometres travelled by the buyer with the car[17].

Considering that in Germany buyers of about 2.8 million cars are affected by the diesel emissions scandal[18] this means, however, that the majority of buyers will continue to be left without compensation.

Also, the outlook in Europe under capital markets law is only partly optimistic. Since Volkswagen shares were admitted to official stock exchanges only in Germany, foreign courts have regularly declined jurisdiction over the matter.[19] Claims for damages under capital markets law also differ considerably from one Member State to another: conditions of entitlement to claim cover everything from simple negligence to intent.[20] In Germany, the bundling of legal claims under the German Capital Markets Model Case Act (*Kapitalanleger-Musterverfahrensgesetz* – KapMuG) has so far proved only partially successful in other proceedings[21] and the Higher Regional Court (OLG) of Braunschweig has not yet reached a decision in the Volkswagen KapMuG case on the failure to make an ad hoc announcement.[22] The German Federal Court of Justice (BGH) or the Court of Justice of the European Union will review decisions. It will therefore be a long time before a final and legally binding decision is reached.

As far as public enforcement is concerned, in several Member States of the European Union public authorities were rather reluctant in the diesel emissions scandal to take action against Volkswagen[23] even though it is well known that Volkswagen had violated provisions of environmental, civil and consumer law as well as competition and capital markets law. The pertinent European secondary legislation such as, among others,[24] Regulation (EC) No 715/2007

---

17 See BGH, Judgment of 25 May 2020, VI ZR 252/19, NJW 2020, 1962 and a comment by Beate Gsell, Frankfurter Allgemeine Zeitung (Frankfurt, 27 May 2020) 16.

18 For details see, e.g. the information given by Stiftung Warentest under <http://www.test.de/Abgasskandal-4918330-0/>.

19 See Section I.A. n 4ff above.

20 For an analysis, see above Rüdiger Veil, 'Private Enforcement in European Capital Markets Law – Perspectives for Reform – The Example of the Obligation to Disclose Inside Information' in this book Sections I., II. (hereafter Veil, 'Private Enforcement in European Capital Markets Law').

21 Kapitalanleger-Musterverfahrensgesetz (German Capital Markets Model Case Act) of 16 August 2005, BGBl I/2437; Reform of 19 October 2012, BGBl I/2182. For an overview of the criticism of the German Capital Markets Model Case Act (KapMuG), see Thomas MJ Möllers and Franz C Leisch, in Thomas MJ Möllers and Heribert Hirte (eds), *Kölner Kommentar zum WpHG* (2nd edn, Carl Heymanns Verlag 2014) §§37b, c mn 523ff; more positively Klaus Rotter, '14 Jahre KapMuG – Ein etabliertes Instrument zur Bewältigung von Massenschäden am Kapitalmarkt' [2019] VuR 283ff.

22 See above Weiss, 'Securities Litigation against VW and Porsche' (n 3) passim.

23 See for the UK John Sorabji, 'Enforcing Consumer and Capital Markets Law in England and Wales' in this book Section I.A. who explains the UK Government's reluctance to take action against Volkswagen with the intention 'to await developments, and the conclusion of investigations, in Germany by relevant German authorities'.

24 See also above Domej and Honegger-Müntener, 'Consumer Law in Europe' (n 6) Section II.A with regard to art 13 of the Directive 2005/29/EC of the European Parliament and of the

on type approval of motor vehicles (Euro 5 and Euro 6) which aims to ensure a 'high level of environmental protection'[25] requires Member States to provide for 'effective, proportionate and dissuasive' penalties applicable for infringement of the respective European provisions and to 'take all measures necessary to ensure that they are implemented'.[26] However, since Germany, Italy, Luxembourg and the UK have not properly implemented these provisions, the Commission is now taking the matter to the European Court.[27] Yet, in Germany at least the public prosecutor's office has so far imposed fines on Volkswagen AG, Audi AG, and Porsche AG for the violation of 'supervisory responsibilities', calculated in such a way that the unlawfully obtained profits were disgorged[28] and in addition each company had to pay €5 million.[29]

Council of 11 May 2005 concerning unfair business-to-consumer commercial practices in the internal market and amending Council Directive 84/450/EEC, Directives 97/7/EC, 98/27/EC and 2002/65/EC of the European Parliament and of the Council and Regulation (EC) No 2006/2004 of the European Parliament and of the Council [2005] OJ L149/22 (hereafter Unfair Commercial Practices Directive 2005/29/EC) and art 24(1) of Directive 2011/83/EU of the European Parliament and of the Council of 25 October 2011 on consumer rights, amending Council Directive 93/13/EEC and Directive 1999/44/EC of the European Parliament and of the Council and repealing Council Directive 85/577/EEC and Directive 97/7/EC of the European Parliament and of the Council [2011] OJ L304/22 (hereafter Consumer Rights Directive 2011/83/EU); see with regard to such penalties also art 9(4) (h) Regulation (EU) 2017/2394 of the European Parliament and of the Council of 12 December 2017 on cooperation between national authorities responsible for the enforcement of consumer protection laws and repealing Regulation (EC) No 2006/2004 [2017] OJ L345/1.

25 See recital 1.

26 See art 13 (1) of Regulation (EC) No 715/2007 of the European Parliament and of the Council of 20 June 2007 on type approval of motor vehicles with respect to emissions from light passenger and commercial vehicles (Euro 5 and Euro 6) and on access to vehicle repair and maintenance information [2007] OJ L171/1; see also arts 30 and 46 of Directive 2007/46/EC of the European Parliament and of the Council of 5 September 2007 establishing a framework for the approval of motor vehicles and their trailers, and of systems, components and separate technical units intended for such vehicles (Framework Directive) [2007] OJ L263/1.

27 European Commission, 'Air quality: Commission takes action to protect citizens from air pollution' (*Press Release*, 17 May 2018) <https://ec.europa.eu/commission/presscorner/detail/en/IP_18_3450>; 'EU-Kommission verklagt Deutschland: Scheuer findet ein Detail „zutiefst realitätsfern"' (*Merkur*, 17 May 2018) <http://www.merkur.de/politik/eu-kommission-klage-deutschland-diesel-skandal-luft-zr-9877270.html>. See also Lene Kohl, 'Practitioner Comment on Consumer Law Enforcement in Europe' in this book Section II.A (hereafter Kohl, 'Practitioner Comment').

28 According to s 17(4) of the German Act on Regulatory Offences (*Gesetz über Ordnungswidrigkeiten* – OWiG) fines shall exceed the economic benefit that the offender has derived from the administrative offence.

29 Thus for VW the total amount of the fine was €1 billion, see Staatsanwaltschaft Braunschweig, 'VW muss Bußgeld zahlen' (*Press Release*, 13 June 2018) <https://staatsanwaltschaft-braunschweig.niedersachsen.de/startseite/aktuelles/presseinformationen/vw-muss-bussgeld-zahlen-174880.html>; for Audi the total amount war €800 million, 'Audi zahlt 800 Millionen Euro Bußgeld' (*Zeit Online*, 16 October 2018) <http://www.zeit.de/mobilitaet/2018-10/dieselskandal-audi-zahlt-800-millionen-euro-bussgeld> and for Porsche the total amount was €535 million.

Against this background it does not come as a surprise that just recently it has been alleged in public media by the Federal Office responsible for vehicle registration (*Kraftfahrtbundesamt*) that the German Federal Ministry of Transport has been too hesitant in investigating the possible use of manipulative software in older Euro 4 diesel vehicles, and that therefore a prescription of claims of injured parties is imminent.[30]

And also, as regards the public enforcement of European consumer law as well as European rules on unfair commercial practices[31] the respective public authorities in the Member States are developed very differently and endowed with varying degrees of financial and other resources and consequently not in all Member States such authorities do operate very powerfully.[32] However, it should be noted that the European legislature has just recently enacted the 'New Deal for Consumers' Omnibus Directive (EU) 2019/2161 on a better enforcement and modernisation of Union consumer protection rules, dating from 27 November 2019[33] and thus taken desirable steps to improve enforcement of consumer law through penalties, in particular by imposing the obligations on the Member States to introduce fines for infringements of the respective European law by companies at a level that is at least 4 per cent of the trader's annual turnover in the Member State or Member States concerned.[34]

30 See with regard to Josef Streule and Lisa Wieschniok, 'Beim Audi-Skandal droht Verjährung' (*Tagesschau*, 8 December 2019) <http://www.tagesschau.de/investigativ/br-recherche/kba-verzoegerung-aufklaerung-101.html>.

31 For an analysis of the situation with regard to European competition law, see Thomas MJ Möllers and Andreas Heinemann (eds), *The Enforcement of Competition Law in Europe* (Cambridge University Press 2007) 361ff (hereafter Möllers and Heinemann, *Enforcement of Competition Law*).

32 See above the overall assessment by Domej and Honegger-Müntener, 'Consumer Law in Europe' (n 6) Section II.A. that 'fines for breaches of consumer protection law do not seem to be very effective, as far as can be judged on the basis of the national reports'; see also recital 5 of the recently enacted Directive (EU) 2019/2161 (see immediately below before and with the next note): 'Current national rules on penalties differ significantly across the Union. In particular, not all Member States ensure that effective, proportionate and dissuasive fines can be imposed on traders responsible for widespread infringements or widespread infringements with a Union dimension.'

33 See Directive (EU) 2019/2161 of the European Parliament and of the Council of 27 November 2019 amending Council Directive 93/13/EEC and Directives 98/6/EC, 2005/29/EC and 2011/83/EU of the European Parliament and of the Council as regards the better enforcement and modernisation of Union consumer protection rules [2019] OJ L328/7 (hereafter Consumer Omnibus Directive (EU) 2019/2161).

34 See art 3 (6) of the Consumer Omnibus Directive (EU) 2019/2161 (n 33) for the new art 13(3) of the Unfair Commercial Practices Directive 2005/29/EC (n 24); see art 4(13) of the Consumer Omnibus Directive (EU) 2019/2161 (n 33) for the new art 24 (3) of the Consumer Rights Directive 2011/83/EU (n 24); furthermore Council Directive 93/13/EEC of 5 April 1993 on unfair terms in consumer contracts [1993] OJ L95/29 has been added to the list of European Consumer Law Directives for which infringements are to be sanctioned by such penalties has been enlarged, see art 1(4) of the Consumer Omnibus Directive (EU) 2019/2161 (n 33) for the new art 8b of Directive 93/13/EEC on unfair terms in consumer

The Omnibus Directive (EU) 2019/2161 has yet to be transposed into national law.[35]

B. BETWEEN OVER-ENFORCEMENT AND UNDER-ENFORCEMENT

As far as the assessment of this heterogeneous finding is concerned, this also turns out – unsurprisingly – to be heterogeneous, and in this respect the diesel emissions scandal illustrates very clearly what is already generally known and has been discussed for a considerable time: on the one hand, rapid and drastic measures, such as those taken in the US in particular, can be regarded as particularly efficient in deterring the violation of consumer and capital markets law.[36] Yet, the extent to which and to whose benefit such a 'punishment' of an unlawfully acting company may go, whether or not it is appropriate, for example, that settlement proceeds from Volkswagen in the US serve to finance electric buses for US cities[37] is obviously open to disparate assessments.

Thus, on the other hand and in particular with regard to the US the allegation of over-enforcement and abusive litigation is often made, which is considered being fuelled by the famous 'toxic cocktail' of various elements of substantive and procedural law, such as punitive damages,[38] the American rule for attorneys' fees as well as the admissibility of contingency fees, jury trial, extensive discovery burdens and modest pleading standards.[39] It is alleged that class actions are brought primarily in the interest of lawyers[40] and that the deterrent potential of

contracts. Penalties at such a level are already stated by art 83(4)–(6) of Regulation (EU) 2016/679 of 27 April 2016 on the protection of natural persons with regard to the processing of personal data and on the free movement of such data (General Data Protection Regulation – GDPR) [2016] OJ L119/1.

35 The directive must be implemented into national law of the Member States by 28 November 2021 and applied by 28 May 2022, art 7 of the Consumer Omnibus Directive (EU) 2019/2161 (n 33).

36 In detail, see Alexander F Peter, 'Warum die Initiative » Law – Made in Germany « bislang zum Scheitern verurteilt ist' [2011] JZ 939ff; Domej and Honegger-Müntener, 'Consumer Law in Europe' (n 6) Section III.A.6.

37 For details see <https://uspirg.org/sites/pirg/files/reports/National%20-%20Paying%20for%20Electric%20Buses.pdf>.

38 See *Cooper Industries, Inc v Leatherman Tool Group, Inc*, 532 U.S. 424, 432 (2001): '[punitive damages], which have been described as "quasi-criminal", [...] operate as "private fines" intended to punish the defendant and to deter future wrongdoing'; see also *BMW of North America, Inc v Ira Gore, Jr*, 517 U.S. 559, 568 (1996): 'Punitive damages may properly be imposed to further a State's legitimate interests in punishing unlawful conduct and deterring its repetition.' On punitive damages see further Thomas MJ Möllers, *Legal Methods* (Beck-Hart Publishing-Nomos 2020) ch 5 mn 145 (hereafter Möllers, *Legal Methods*).

39 See above the differentiated analysis of Domej and Honegger-Müntener, 'Consumer Law in Europe' (n 6) Sections III.A.2., 6. and 7. and IV. with further references.

40 Insinuated by Schmitz, 'US' (n 1) Introduction see above.

the high costs resulting from loss of a case often forces the (presumed) perpetrator of the damage to *settle* against his will instead of giving him the opportunity to defend himself adequately in a necessarily time-consuming trial.[41] And indeed, with payments of more than US$26 billion agreed by Volkswagen, it is rather obvious that it is no longer just about compensating damages or skimming illicitly gained profits.[42]

Certain incentives to conclude a settlement cannot be rejected per se, precisely because they can serve to provide efficient compensation to a large number of victims. But excessive economic pressure imposed on the (presumed) perpetrator to yield to a speedy settlement and to accept the payment of large sums of money as punitive damages is particularly problematic under the aspect of the presumption of innocence, which, e.g. in Germany, as an expression of the principle of the rule of law, has constitutional status.[43] Furthermore, from a European perspective it may be considered incompatible with the principle of proportionality, which also derives from the rule of law and prohibits excessive state sanctions.[44]

If one further attempts to analyse the European situation and to explain why, in the VW diesel emissions scandal, the measures against Volkswagen have so far been significantly more tentative than in the US, *Domej and Honegger-Müntener*[45] pinpoint the reasons for this hesitancy in the enforcing of consumer law by way of collective redress very well, when emphasising that 'the European legislature does not have a coherent vision of collective redress' and that 'the

41 Insinuated by Schmitz, 'US' (n 1) Introduction see above.

42 In the past, motor vehicle manufacturers were exposed to product liability lawsuits, which ultimately led to relatively manageable claims for damages because the conditions for punitive damages were not met. See *Lee v Volkswagen of America, Inc*, 688 P.2d 1283 (Okla. 1984); *MacDonald v General Motors Corp*, 784 F.Supp. 486 (M.D. Tenn. 1992); *Kudlacek v Fiat S.p.A.*, 244 Neb. 822 (Neb. 1994). The VW diesel scandal has at least not resulted in immediate deaths. They were probably prosecuted for their years of covering up and denying the defeat technology to the US authorities. For the facts, see Schmitz, 'US' (n 1) Section I.

43 As expressed by BVerfG, Order of 26 March 1987, 2 BvR 589/79, BVerfGE 74, 358, 370 – Unschuldsvermutung; the presumption of innocence and the right to defence are also guaranteed by art 6(2) and (3) of the European Convention on Human Rights as well as by art 48 of the Charter of Fundamental Rights of the EU.

44 See in particular art 9(4) last sentence and art 12 sentence 1 of Regulation (EU) 2017/2394 on cooperation between national authorities responsible for the enforcement of consumer protection laws of 12 December 2017 [2017] OJ L345/1 where like in other European secondary legislation it is stipulated that measures of enforcement and in particular penalties imposed on companies for the violation of European Union law shall be proportionate. This principle originally is derived from the case law of the German Federal Constitutional Court (*Bundesverfassungsgericht – BVerfG*), see Fernand Schockweiler, 'Die richterliche Kontrollfunktion: Umfang und Grenzen in Bezug auf den Europäischen Gerichtshof' [1995] EuR 191, 200; the principle of proportionality was set out in ECJ, C-292/97 *Karlsson and Others* [13 April 2000] ECR 2000 I-02737 at [45]; ECJ, C-5/88 *Wachauf v Bundesamt für Ernährung und Forstwirtschaft* [13 July 1989] ECR 1989 2609 at [18]; Paul Craig and Gráinne de Búrca, *EU Law* (6th edn, Oxford University Press 2015) 551; Möllers, *Legal Methods* (n 38) ch 10 mn 70ff.

45 See above Domej and Honegger-Müntener, 'Consumer Law in Europe' (n 6) Section IV.

reason probably is not that the individual actors have no such vision. They just have very different, and often irreconcilable, visions of what the collective redress landscape should look like and indeed, whether there should be such a landscape at all'.

Accordingly, there is already disagreement about the appropriate level of enforcement and as to whether consumer rights are violated at all and whether enforcement in the interest of consumers is therefore desirable when environmental standards are violated by car manufacturers and public health aspects are concerned, while economic loss to the individual consumer might perhaps be difficult to prove.[46]

Furthermore, the European discussion on collective redress appears still to be dominated to a considerable extent by the intention to avoid abusive litigation. The scepticism towards elements of the US system, such as the opt-out mechanism, is not always well substantiated, let alone sufficiently questioned and this often makes a sober analysis of the pros and cons of the various models established in the respective countries,[47] including European countries,[48] more difficult.[49] The fear of abusive litigation is often accompanied by a great reluctance towards contingency fees and third-party funding,[50] while at the same time entities entitled to bring court actions for the benefit of consumers are manifestly lacking sufficient financial resources for doing so on a larger scale.[51]

---

46 See above Domej and Honegger-Müntener, 'Consumer Law in Europe' (n 6) Section I. with further references and with reference in n 7 to ECJ, C-240/09 *Lesoochranárske zoskupenie VLK v Ministerstvo životného prostredia Slovenskej republiky* [8 March 2011] ECR I-01255 at [44ff]: see also above Marques, 'Brazil' (n 10) Section II.B. who explains that in Brazil collective redress mechanisms are not only aiming at the protection of homogeneous individual interests or rights collective interests or rights as well as diffuse rights in the sense of trans-individual rights of an indivisible nature.

47 See for the advantages of the Australian system above Cashman 'Australia' (n 9) passim.

48 See above with regard to opt out-elements of collective redress mechanisms for damages within Europe with regard to Denmark Anders Schäfer, 'Enforcing Consumer and Capital Markets Law in Denmark' in this book Section I.C.3.a.ii. (hereafter Schäfer, 'Denmark'); Willem van Boom and Charlotte Pavillon, 'Enforcing Consumer and Capital Markets Law in The Netherlands' in this book Section II.A. (hereafter van Boom and Pavillon, 'Netherlands') and Portugal, Henrique Sousa Antunes, 'Enforcing Consumer and Capital Markets Law in Portugal' in this book Section II.A.1.a) and for a comprehensive analysis Domej and Honegger-Müntener, 'Consumer Law in Europe' (n 6) Section III.A.2.

49 See above Domej and Honegger-Müntener, 'Consumer Law in Europe' (n 6) Section III.A.2. are right to complain that the discussion about abusive litigation is 'largely based on rhetorics and anecdotal evidence'.

50 See above Domej and Honegger-Müntener, 'Consumer Law in Europe' (n 6) Section III.A.6.: 'The rules on third-party funding of collective actions have been and will presumably remain a central battleground in the European collective redress debate'.

51 See for problems of funding collective actions to the benefit of consumers above Schäfer, 'Denmark' (n 48) Section IV. with regard to class actions initiated by the Danish Consumer Ombudsman; Emmanuel Jeuland, 'Enforcing Consumer and Capital Markets Law in France' in this book Section I.C.4., with regard to the French 'action de groupe', introduced in 2014

The lacking consensus within Europe as to the desirable level of law enforcement and as to its preferable instruments is accompanied by difficulties arising from substantive law. Insofar as the imposition of damages is considered being limited to the only purpose of compensating the losses suffered by the victims, consequently, the exact amount of the respective individual damage and its causation by the allegedly unlawful act is to be established and proved.[52] However, such requirements of establishing and proving the respective individual damage are not only likely to increase the individual victim's so-called 'rational apathy' towards possible court actions but can also considerably aggravate the procedural burden on the respective courts and make the court procedures cumbersome and time-consuming.[53]

While recognising that the prevention of abusive litigation is legitimate, that the right of alleged perpetrators to an effective defence is indispensable and that the appropriate judicial handling of complex issues requires considerable time, the overall experience of the diesel emissions scandal and, more specifically, the fact that the vast majority of European purchasers of affected diesel vehicles, as well as capital investors, have not (yet) received compensation, nevertheless suggest that there is a law enforcement deficit in Europe.

It can therefore be concluded that the challenge for legislatures in Europe, and above all for the European Union legislature, is to find ways to a higher level of law enforcement by providing an effective mix of public and private enforcement instruments which overcome under-enforcement to the detriment of the individual victims and the public interest in the respect of the law, but at the same time avoid over-enforcement to the detriment of (alleged) perpetrators. And this challenge is all the greater because, in an effort to strike an appropriate balance between conflicting enforcement and defence interests, not a single model can be identified as an undisputed panacea and as clearly superior.

---

by the 'loi Hamon' under which only 14 associations are authorised to bring a group action (action de groupe), and an association may bring only one action at a time.

52 See for the controversial discussion in Germany on the extent to which buyers of diesel vehicles suffered damages caused by Volkswagen and on the extent benefits of use can be credited to mitigate damages on the one hand Michael Heese, 'Nutzungsentschädigung zugunsten der Hersteller manipulierter Diesel-Kraftfahrzeuge?' [2019] VuR 123–29 and on the other hand Thomas Riehm, 'Deliktischer Schadensersatz in den „Diesel-Abgas-Fällen"' [2019] NJW 1105–11.

53 That is why, for example, the recommendation of the procedural law department of the 72th Deutscher Juristentag in Leipzig 2018 (German Jurists Forum), *de lege ferenda* in the context of a new group action to be introduced, to permit liquidated damages in order to enable as many victims as possible to be compensated and at the same time make the procedure more efficient, makes perfect sense, see Ständige Deputation des Deutschen Juristentages (ed), *Verhandlungen des 72. Deutschen Juristentages Leipzig 2018, Vol II/1* (CH Beck 2019) K 75 recommendation no 31.

II. THE WAY FORWARD

In the following, based on the experiences with the diesel emissions scandal gathered in this book and by evaluating the relevant regulations and instruments in other fields of law, such as competition law in particular, some specific suggestions for the European Union legislature will be recommended in order to improve consumer and capital markets law enforcement in the future. First, it will be discussed to what extent activity at European level is desirable in the European multi-level system (A). Then, the strengthening of private enforcement (B) and public enforcement (C) should be discussed as well as the interplay of public enforcement, collective actions and private individual actions (D) and finally, the question of how to improve law enforcement within the company itself (E) is particularly interesting. In an intradisciplinary comparison, it will be established that European competition law can often show the way forward in search of a balanced middle way between over-enforcement and under-enforcement.

A. THE NECESSITY OF (FURTHER) INTERVENTION AT EUROPEAN LEVEL

The subsidiarity principle of article 5(3) of the TEU allows European Union intervention only to the extent that European institutions are better placed to act than the individual Members. The Volkswagen scandal very clearly raises the question as to which legislative and executive measures are desirable or even needed at the European level.

1. *Further Legal Harmonisation of Enforcement Instruments*

European harmonisation of enforcement instruments can be justified by the purpose of ensuring a level playing field, that is to avoid a race to the bottom and the respective forum shopping with claimants picking the most advantageous jurisdiction.[54] These considerations are clearly reflected in the recitals of the EU-Antitrust Damages Directive 2014/104/EU:[55] it aims to create legal certainty by avoiding forum shopping.[56] These considerations also apply to consumer protection and capital markets law.

---

54 See above van Boom and Pavillon, 'The Netherlands' (n 48) Section III.B.2; Petra Leupold, 'Enforcing Consumer Law in Austria' in this book Section IV.B.

55 Directive 2014/104/EU of the European Parliament and of the Council of 26 November 2014 on certain rules governing actions for damages under national law for infringements of the competition law provisions of the Member States and of the European Union [2014] OJ L349/1 (hereafter Antitrust Damages Directive 2014/104/EU).

56 Recitals 7 and 9 of the Antitrust Damages Directive 2014/104/EU (n 55) are Instructive, see above Veil, 'Private Enforcement in European Capital Markets Law' (n 20) Section IV.A.

In the authors' view, the measures advocated below,[57] and in particular a European harmonisation of the contours of private claims for damages and their enforcement including the already initiated introduction of a representative action for damages,[58] should therefore be regulated in their main features at European level. However, where, in view of the differences between the Member States, no consensus can be achieved in the legislative process on individual points or where it is simply unclear which way is best, opening clauses, which allow for heterogeneous national solutions are useful in order to achieve European solutions at all and to spur competition between the Member States, in which best practice might become apparent.[59]

2. *Subsidiary European Power of Intervention Desirable where Member States do not Take Sufficient Action*

European executive intervention should be possible where the individual Member States and their respective public authorities are too weak or unwilling to take action against violations of European Union law. As mentioned above,[60] the authorities of some Member States have been reluctant to take action against car manufacturers in the diesel emissions scandal. Similar examples of allegedly unlawful practices by companies which do not always entail sufficiently resolute intervention by Member States include the activities of international groups in the field of antitrust law;[61] and in capital markets law, the trading of globally operating rating companies[62] or participants in the capital markets who use inadmissible short sell attacks to exploit cross-border gaps.[63]

As far as Member States are under an obligation to provide for 'effective, proportionate and dissuasive' penalties against the violation of European Union law by companies[64] consideration should be given to granting the European

57 See below Sections B. to E.

58 See above Section I.A. with n 11.

59 The idea of a competition of legal orders is being developed by Charles M Tibout, 'A Pure Theory of Local Expenditures' (1956) 64 J Pol Econ 416 ff; Albert Breton, 'Towards a Theory of Competitive Federalism' (1987) 3 Europ J Pol Econ 263 ff; Eva-Maria Kieninger, *Wettbewerb der Privatrechtsordnungen im Europäischen Binnenmarkt* (Mohr Siebeck 2002); Anne-Christin Mittwoch, *Vollharmonisierung und Europäisches Privatrecht* (De Gruyter 2013) 194 ff.

60 See above under Section I.A.

61 Arts 101, 102 of the Treaty on the Functioning of the European Union (TFEU) [2012] OJ C326/47.

62 Thomas MJ Möllers, 'Regulation and Liability of Credit Rating Agencies – A More Efficient European Law?' (2014) 10 ECFR 333–63.

63 This would require *de lege ferenda* a more European dimension – such as the competence of ESMA or the Directorate General for Capital Markets, Thomas MJ Möllers, 'Market Manipulation Through Short Selling Attacks and Misleading Financial Analysis' (2020) 53 The International Lawyer 91–126.

64 See already above under Section I.A. and with n 23, 25 and 33.

Commission a subsidiary competence to investigate and to take direct action against the injuring party – at least in the event that a Member State does not investigate the respective (alleged) infringement but remains inactive over a considerable period of time.

B. STRENGTHENING PRIVATE ENFORCEMENT

In the following, some relevant aspects of substantive and procedural law will be highlighted in order to show how the private enforcement of consumer law and capital markets law, which on the one hand aims at enforcing the respective private rights, but which on the other hand also serves the public interest of achieving the greatest possible respect for the applicable legal norms, could be strengthened.

1. A European Right to Damages: The Antitrust Damages Directive 2014/104/EU as a Model

In the field of antitrust law it was the ECJ which first acknowledged that 'the full effectiveness of Article 85 of the Treaty [now: art 101 TFEU] and, in particular, the practical effect of the prohibition laid down in Article 85(1) would be put at risk if it were not open to any individual to claim damages for loss caused to him by a contract or by conduct liable to restrict or distort competition.'[65] Today, however, this right to full compensation of harm is codified in the Antitrust Damages Directive 2014/104/EU.[66] By way of contrast, a private victim's right to damages is still mostly left to the autonomy of the Member States in the fields of consumer law and capital markets law:[67] As to consumer law neither the old Consumer Sales Directive 1999/44/EC[68] nor its successor, the recently enacted new Sales of Goods Directive (EU) 2019/771[69] cover a right to damages.

65 See ECJ, C-453/99 *Courage Ltd v Bernard Crehan and Bernard Crehan v Courage Ltd and Others* [20 September 2001] 2001 I-06297 at [26]; see also ECJ, Joined Cases C-295/04 to C-298/04 *Vincenzo Manfredi and Others v Lloyd Adriatico Assicurazioni SpA and Others* [13 July 2006] 2006 I-06619 at [61].

66 See art 3 'Right to full compensation' of the Antitrust Damages Directive 2014/104/EU (n 55).

67 See already above Section A.I. with n 19.

68 Directive 1999/44/EC of 25 May 1999 on certain aspects of the sale of consumer goods and associated guarantees [1999] OJ L171/12.

69 Cf art 3(6) of the Directive (EU) 2019/771 of the European Parliament and of the Council of 20 May 2019 on certain aspects concerning contracts for the sale of goods, amending Regulation (EU) 2017/2394 and Directive 2009/22/EC, and repealing Directive 1999/44/EC [2019] OJ L136/28; cf the criticism by Gsell with regard to the Commission's proposal COM(2015) 635 final, 'Europäischer Richtlinien-Entwurf für vollharmonisierte Mängelrechte beim Verbraucherkauf – Da capo bis zum Happy End?' (2018) ZEuP 501–06. The twin Directive from the same date, i.e. Directive (EU) 2019/770 on certain aspects concerning contracts

And thus, in the diesel emissions scandal not only the damage claims of the consumer-buyers of vehicles featuring manipulative software are governed by tort law, but also contractual damage claims fall within the autonomy of the Member States. Under Italian law there is already the possibility that the consumer can sue for damages if the enterprise violated unfair competition law.[70] In Lithuania two public authorities are responsible for sanctioning violations of unfair competition laws.[71] However, in the wake of the diesel emissions scandal, just recently some progress has been made in this respect with the adoption of the 'New Deal for Consumers' Omnibus Directive (EU) 2019/2161 on a better enforcement and modernisation of Union consumer protection rules:[72] The new Directive amends Directive 2005/29/EC on unfair business-to-consumer commercial practices[73] by a provision according to which 'consumers harmed by unfair commercial practices, shall have access to proportionate and effective remedies, including compensation for damage suffered by the consumer'.[74] Such a European right to damages certainly would have been of help to consumer-buyers of diesel vehicles if it had been in force at the time the manipulated vehicles were sold, and all the more so since, for example, the prevailing opinion in German unfair competition law has so far rejected an individual consumer's right to damages.[75] It may also become important in view of the proposed Directive on representative actions for the protection of the collective interests of consumers,[76] since the scope of this Proposal is limited to the infringement of European law.[77] Collective actions for the mere infringement of the autonomous

for the supply of digital content and digital services [2010] OJ L136/1 does not contain provisions on damages either, see Beate Gsell, in Reiner Schulze and Dirk Staudenmayer (eds), *EU Digital Law* (Beck-Hart Publishing-Nomos 2020) comments on art 14 of Dir (EU) 2019/770 mn. 79ff (forthcoming).

70 See the case presented above by Marcello Gaboardi, 'Enforcing Consumer and Capital Markets Law in Italy' in this book Section I., fn 4ff.

71 See above Egidija Tamošiūnienė and Remigijus Jokubauskas, 'Enforcing Consumer and Capital Markets Law in Lithuania' in this book Section I.A.

72 See Consumer Omnibus Directive (EU) 2019/2161 (n 33).

73 See Unfair Commercial Practices Directive 2005/29/EC (n 24).

74 See art 3(5) of the Consumer Omnibus Directive (EU) 2019/2161 (n 33) for the new art 11a(1) of the Unfair Commercial Practices Directive 2005/29/EC (n 24) and already Beate Gsell, 'Das Ende der Zurückhaltung' [2018] (Issue 18) NJW-aktuell Editorial 3.

75 See, e.g. Helmut Köhler and others (eds), *Gesetz gegen den unlauteren Wettbewerb: UWG* (38th edn, CH Beck 2020) §1 mn 39, §9 mn 1.10, with further references which, however, are not very convincing in assuming that the legal situation will not change significantly as a result of the new art 11a(1) of the Unfair Commercial Practices Directive 2005/29/EC (n 24). Cf opposing opinion and a protective clause supporting *Rolf Sack*, 'Folgeverträge unlauteren Wettbewerbs' [2004] GRUR 625, 630; Thomas MJ Möllers and Andreas Heinemann, *The Enforcement of Competition Law in Europe* (Cambridge University Press 2007) 278ff; see also with regard to injunctions above Gurkmann, 'Consumer Law Enforcement' (n 15) Section II.

76 See n 11.

77 See art 2(1) in conjunction with Annex I of the Proposal for a Directive on representative actions, COM(2018) 184 final (n 11); art 2(1) of the Proposal for a Directive as amended by

law of the Member States such as, e.g. provisions of purely national tort law are therefore beyond the scope of the proposed Directive.

Yet, in the area of capital markets law the European legislature has mainly harmonised only supervisory law, whilst it is highly controversial whether further private law claims result from the *effet utile* of the respective European Law.[78]

The authors consider that, following the model of antitrust law, the enforcement of European consumer law and European capital markets law by way of private damage claims should be strengthened and therefore the European legislature should enact further European Damages Directives which provide for the right to full compensation under private law in the event of a violation of European consumer law or European capital markets law and which regulate the modalities of the enforcement of such damage claims.[79]

As regards the extent of damages provided for by the Antitrust Damages Directive 2014/104/EU, article 3(1) grants the right to full compensation, whereas, however, art 3(3) explicitly excludes overcompensation by way of punitive damages or multiple or other types of damages.[80] While the European courts do concede that damages under antitrust law have a preventive effect,[81] the Antitrust Damages Directive 2014/104/EU is unfortunately silent on this issue and the aforementioned article 3(3) rather points in the negative direction.[82] However, in academic literature there is a strong view

the Council of the European Union, 'Proposal for a Directive of the European Parliament and of the Council on representative actions for the protection of the collective interests of consumers, and repealing Directive 2009/22/EC – General Approach' [28 November 2019] 14600/19 (hereafter Council, 'General Approach – Directive proposal on representative actions for consumers'), at least clarifies that infringements of provisions of national law, which transpose the respective European law shall fall within the scope of the proposed Directive.

78 See above Veil, 'Private Enforcement in European Capital Markets Law' (n 20) Section I. with reference, though to the few provisions granting investors claims for damages such as art 35a of the CRA on the liability of credit rating agencies.

79 See already Thomas MJ Möllers and Franz C Leisch, in Thomas MJ Möllers and Heribert Hirte (eds), *Kölner Kommentar zum WpHG* (2nd edn, Carl Heymanns Verlag 2014) §§37b, c mn 77–84 with further references; Veil, 'Private Enforcement in European Capital Markets Law' (n 20) Section IV.B.2. with regard to liability for damages under private law for all disclosure obligations provided by European Law. Differing view Malte Wundenberg, 'Perspektiven der privaten Rechtsdurchsetzung im europäischen Kapitalmarktrecht' [2015] ZGR 124, 159 (hereafter Wundenberg, 'Perspektiven der privaten Rechtsdurchsetzung').

80 See also recitals 12 and 13 of the Antitrust Damages Directive 2014/104/EU (n 55).

81 CFI, T-329/01 *Archer Daniels Midland v Commission of the European Communities* [27 September 2006] ECR 2006 II-03255 at [140]. It is critical that this does not expressly mention the Antitrust Damages Directive 2014/104/EU (n 55), Veil, 'Private Enforcement in European Capital Markets Law' (n 20) Section IV.B.2.

82 See however s 33a(3) sentence 2 of the GWB (*Gesetz gegen Wettbewerbsbeschränkungen* – German Act against Restraints of Competition) according to which any profit made by the company as a result of the infringement is taken into account in calculating damage. See also ss 34 and 34a of the GWB for a right of the cartel authority and of associations to skim off profits and see also for a similar provision s 10 of the UWG (*Gesetz gegen den unlauteren Wettbewerb* – German Act Against Unfair Competition).

in favour of a general right to a skimming off of profits *de lege ferenda*.[83] This should also open up the discussion as to whether private law seeks to have a preventive or deterrent effect.[84] Experience shows particularly in the case of dispersed damage with very small individual losses the injured party hardly ever overcomes his rational apathy and brings an individual action.[85] The combination of a right to the skimming off of unlawfully gained profits with its procedural enforcement by way of a collective action that does not require the opt-in of the concerned victims of the infringement could be an effective enforcement mechanism.

2. *Collective Actions for Redress Measures*

a) The Proposed European Directive on Representative Actions as a Positive Development

Although, as the country chapters in this book have shown, Europe lacks a coherent vision of collective redress,[86] the bundling of similar claims into a single action, led by a single representative as claimant, is highly desirable for a number of reasons in order to strengthen effective as well as efficient enforcement of the law. These reasons are all well known.[87] Rational apathy often prevents consumers and investors from launching legal actions, which is why, especially in the case of dispersed damages, there is often no enforcement at all if collective actions are not available.[88] In addition, it also serves the general interests of procedural economy and the consistency of jurisprudence if a single collective action is brought instead of many individual actions. And

---

[83] For a new s 251(3) of the BGB (*Bürgerliches Gesetzbuch* – German Civil Code) *de lege ferenda*, Gerhard Wagner, *Neue Perspektiven im Schadensersatzrecht – Kommerzialisierung, Strafschadensersatz, Kollektivschaden, Gutachten A zum 66. Deutschen Juristentag* (CH Beck 2006) A 97.

[84] See in detail Peter Müller, *Punitives Damages und deutsches Schadenersatzrecht* (De Gruyter 2000); Michael Heese, 'Was der Dieselskandal über die Rechtsdurchsetzung, deren Protagonisten und die Funktion des Privatrechts verrät' [2019] NZV 273, 278; Veil, 'Private Enforcement in European Capital Markets Law' (n 20) Section V.

[85] See Astrid Stadler, 'Die Umsetzung der Kommissionsempfehlung zum kollektiven Rechtsschutz' [2015] Zeitschrift für die gesamte Privatrechtswissenschaft 61, 81 with further references; for the necessary strengthening of collective redress, see below Section B.2.

[86] See already above Section B. before and with n 44.

[87] For a detailed review see, for example, the report prepared for the 72nd German Jurists Forum in Leipzig 2018 (72. Deutscher Juristentag Leipzig) by Caroline Meller-Hannich, *Sammelklagen, Gruppenklagen, Verbandsklagen – Bedarf es neuer Instrumente des kollektiven Rechtsschutzes im Zivilprozess?, Gutachten A zum 72. Deutschen Juristentag* (CH Beck 2018) A 9ff; for a very compact analysis see Beate Gsell, Caroline Meller-Hannich and Astrid Stadler, 'Musterfeststellungsklagen in Verbrauchersachen' [2016] (Issue 5) NJW-aktuell 14–15.

[88] In detail, see above Kohl, 'Practitioner Comment' (n 27) Introduction.

last but not least, the principle of due process and more precisely the procedural equality of arms is jeopardised when an individual consumer or investor who brings his action only once faces a large company that is involved in thousands of similar legal proceedings.

In Germany where to date no collective action for compensatory relief has been introduced,[89] the need for bundling[90] is also proven by assignment models which have emerged in practice but which often present the courts with major challenges due to the lack of adapted procedural rules and which are also controversially judged because they function on the basis of pro rata success fees and professional litigation funders benefit from them.[91]

It is therefore highly positive that a European proposal for an EU Directive on representative actions is finally on the table, which by way of contrast to Directive 2009/22/EC[92] is no longer confined to injunctive relief but also covers compensatory relief.[93]

b) Questionable Rules on Standing and Funding

It is not intended to reassess the Proposal in its entirety here;[94] rather, only two aspects which are crucial for the success of all collective redress instruments but

---

89 The German Capital Markets Model Case Proceedings (*Kapitalanleger-Musterverfahren*) and the Civil Procedural Model Declaratory Action (*Musterfeststellungsklage*) (n 7) are confined to declaratory relief and therefore, even in the event of a successful outcome of the respective collective action, the injured party must subsequently enforce her individual claim by way of individual actions, see Gurkmann, 'Consumer Law Enforcement' (n 15) Section IV; however, consumer associations under German law were and are permitted to have claims assigned to them by consumers and then to bring these assigned claims to court. Yet this way of claim bundling has proven to be cumbersome, see Gurkmann, 'Consumer Law Enforcement' (n 15) Section III.

90 A combining of filed cases like the one carried out in the diesel emissions scandal by the Judicial Panel on Multidistrict Litigation (JPML), see Schmitz, 'US' (n 1) Section II.A. with fn 57, has no equivalent in German civil procedure law. Therefore, many thousands of individual actions for damages related to the diesel emissions scandal are currently pending, see, e.g. Elmar Streyl, 'Massen vor Gericht' [2019] (Issue 37) NJW Editorial who reports 64,000 individual lawsuits, about 600 of them at the Regional Court of Krefeld alone, one of the smallest regional courts in North Rhine-Westphalia.

91 For the legal admissibility of such assignment models, see BGH, Judgment of 27 November 2019, VIII ZR 285/18, [2020] NJW 208 – admissibility of legal tech providers strengthened.

92 See n 12.

93 See already above under Section I.A.; art 5b of Council, 'General Approach – Directive proposal on representative actions for consumers' (n 77) and above Domej and Honegger-Müntener, 'Consumer Law in Europe' (n 6) Section III.A.

94 For various relevant aspects of the proposal see above the review by Domej and Honegger-Müntener, 'Consumer Law in Europe' (n 6) Sections III.A. and B.; see also Tanja Domej, 'Die geplante EU-Verbandsklagenrichtlinie – Sisyphos vor dem Gipfelsieg?' [2019] ZEuP 446–71.

very controversial within Europe and which are moreover interrelated should be discussed, those are the issues of who will have standing to bring the proposed representative actions and how they will be funded.

It has previously been explained above[95] that in Europe the fear of abusive litigation is sometimes very strongly emphasised and that accordingly in some countries there is a great reluctance to use commercial models of litigation funding which holds particularly true with regard to the use of contingency fees and the involvement of professional litigation funders.

At the same time, it is obvious that considerable financial resources are required in order to successfully bring collective actions. This is all the more true when the defendants are large, internationally operating companies such as Volkswagen in the diesel emissions scandal, which are prepared to spend considerable sums of money on legal representation and favourable expert opinions on the legal situation in order to defend themselves against such actions. It must therefore be stated quite clearly: if the entities with standing to bring collective actions do not have sufficient financial and organisational resources to level those of the companies typically sued, there is a risk of procedural imbalance and, in the worst case, a situation in which such collective actions can hardly ever be brought (successfully) due to lack of funds.[96]

Thus, according to media reports, Volkswagen, in connection with the lawsuits brought against it in the diesel emissions scandal before German courts, has not only commissioned litigation lawyers, but also two dozen expert opinions on legal issues.[97] It seems inconceivable that, e.g. the Bundesverband der Verbraucherzentralen und Verbraucherverbände that is the consumer association, which brought the model declaratory action against Volkswagen in Germany on the claimant side, has comparable resources.[98] Furthermore, in Germany, there is already speculation as to whether lawyers in the future will be found to represent the interests of the claimant consumer associations in model declaratory actions: Since the amount in dispute is capped by law,[99] the respective lawyers would only have been entitled to a few thousand euros in fees in the case of the model declaratory action against VW, if the lawsuit had been terminated

---

95 See above Section I.B. with n 46 to 50 and Weiss, 'Securities Litigation against VW and Porsche' (n 3) Section V: 'The fact that institutional investors have stepped into the ring ensures that plaintiffs fight with defendants on a level playing field in terms of financial resources.'

96 See already above under Section B. before and with n 51 with examples for such a lack of funds from the country chapters collected in this book.

97 See for a respective press report Volker Votsmeier, 'VW und die Wissenschaft: Unklare Verhältnisse bei der Aufklärung des Dieselskandals' *Handelsblatt* (Düsseldorf, 6 November 2019) <http://www.handelsblatt.com/unternehmen/industrie/abgasaffaere-vw-und-die-wissenschaft-unklare-verhaeltnisse-bei-der-aufklaerung-des-dieselskandals/25191942.html?ticket=ST-958291-7q1FZbJqjVtH0aSNchEF-ap2>.

98 See above n 15.

99 According to s 48(2) sentence 2 of the *Gerichtskostengesetz* (German Court Fees Act) they amount to a maximum of €250,000.

by declaratory judgment, even though hundreds of thousands of consumers had enrolled to the proceedings.[100] It is therefore not surprising that the law firm in question apparently insisted on an exorbitantly higher fee during the settlement negotiations, which allegedly caused the negotiations to fail temporarily at a first attempt before they were successfully concluded after all.[101]

Against this background it is doubtful whether the rules on standing and funding in the European proposal for a Directive on representative actions[102] can really ensure that the entities with standing to bring representative actions will be sufficiently powerful. For, on the one hand, only entities with a non-profit-making character shall be entitled to bring a representative action.[103] But on the other hand the proposed Directive does not regulate the way in which these entities obtain funds to finance the representative actions[104] and furthermore the obligation of the Member States to assist these entities, as contained in the original draft, has been greatly weakened in the Council's General Approach.[105]

It is therefore to be feared that, when the Directive enters into force, in Member States which are reluctant to accept third-party funding, the entities entitled to bring a representative action will not have sufficient resources to establish a genuine level playing field with powerful companies as opposing parties. It would have been preferable for the proposed Directive to prevent such

---

100 See already above n 15.

101 See for this development of the model declaratory action against VW the interview with Volker Römermann who counselled the claimants' lawyers on the fees, conducted by Pia Lorenz, 'Eine Zumutung für Anwälte' (*Legal Tribune Online*, 5 March 2020) <http://www.lto.de/recht/juristen/b/kosten-anwalt-vergleich-musterfeststellungsklage-vw-goa-gebuehren/>.

102 See n 11.

103 See art 4(1)(c) of the Proposal for a Directive on representative actions, COM(2018) 184 final (n 11) and art 4a (3)(c) of Council, 'General Approach – Directive proposal on representative actions for consumers' (n 77).

104 Art 7 of the Proposal for a Directive on representative actions, COM(2018) 184 final (n 11) on funding which contained above all in the first para a duty to disclose the source of the funds used at an early stage of the action and in the second para prohibited a third-party funding the action to influence decisions of the claimant qualified entity was deleted in the further legislative procedure; according to the amended version of the proposal Member States' courts or public authorities are entitled to examine whether a qualified entity bringing a cross-border representative action for redress is funded by a third party having an economic interest in the outcome of a specific cross-border representative action and, if this is the case, reject the legal capacity of the qualified entity for the purpose of that action, see art 4b(3) subpara 2 and recital 11 and 10 of Council, 'General Approach – Directive proposal on representative actions for consumers' (n 77).

105 See art 15(1) of the Proposal for a Directive on representative actions, COM(2018) 184 final (n 11) on the one hand and art 15(1) of Council, 'General Approach – Directive proposal on representative actions for consumers' (n 77). According to the latter version of the proposed Directive the Member States must only avoid that procedural costs related to representative actions 'become insurmountable obstacles' for the respective qualified entities and concrete measures of support such as 'limiting applicable court or administrative fees, granting them access to legal aid where necessary, or by providing them with public funding for this purpose' are no longer explicitly listed in the provision itself but only in recital 39 which, however, emphasises that 'Member States should not be required to finance representative actions'.

a scenario through concrete rules on funding, for example by stipulating that a claimant entity in the event of the success of a representative action for redress should be entitled to retain part of the amount of damages to be paid by the defendant as an incentive and for the financing of future actions.[106]

3. *Information Rights and Corresponding Duties to Disclose Evidence*

Individual private as well as collective actions alleging infringements by companies, are often characterised by an information asymmetry.[107] Relevant evidence necessary to prove the prerequisites of a claim is often in the hands of the opponent or third parties, including authorities who have previously investigated the infringement. The effectiveness of law enforcement therefore depends to a large degree on the extent to which the opposing party, but also third parties and in particular public authorities, are obliged to inform the plaintiff or the court dealing with the case.[108] Thus, to this day, Volkswagen AG is withholding relevant information on the diesel emissions scandal. Although the Management Board had promised to do so, access to the results of the internal investigation carried out by the law firm Jones Day has not been granted.[109]

---

106 See also art 6(3)(b) of the Proposal for a Directive on representative actions, COM(2018) 184 final (n 11), according to which the redress sought by way of a representative action in the event of dispersed damage 'shall be directed to a public purpose serving the collective interests of consumers'. However, in the Council, 'General Approach – Directive proposal on representative actions for consumers' (n 77) the respective provision is no longer contained; see also Meller-Hannich, 'Germany' (n 7) Section I.A.3; 72. Deutscher Juristentag, 'Beschlüsse – Sammelklagen, Gruppenklage, Verbandsklagen –Bedarf es neuer Instrumente des kollektiven Rechtsschutzes im Zivilprozess?' (72. Deutscher Juristentag, Leipzig, September 2018) paras 12 and 14 <http://www.djt.de/fileadmin/downloads/72/Beschluesse_gesamt_final.pdf>. In contrast the reform of the German Capital Markets Model Case Act (n 21) increased the compensation for claimants, cf s 41a of the *Rechtsanwaltsvergütungsgesetz* (RVG – German Act on the Remuneration of Lawyers).

107 For the information asymmetry in competition law litigation see, e.g. recital 15 of the Antitrust Damages Directive 2014/104/EU (n 55); for a comparative analysis with regard to state aid law see Ferdinand Wollenschläger and Wolfgang Wurmnest, 'Comparative Analysis and the Way Forward' in Ferdinand Wollenschläger, Wolfgang Wurmnest and Thomas MJ Möllers (eds), *Private Enforcement of European Competition and State Aid Law. Current Challenges and the Way Forward* (Wolters Kluwer 2020) 378ff (hereafter Wollenschläger and Wurmnest, 'Comparative Analysis and the Way Forward'); see also above Domej and Honegger-Müntener, 'Consumer Law in Europe' (n 6) Section III.A.7: 'Information asymmetry is likely to be a regular feature of consumer disputes.'

108 See also above Weiss, 'Securities Litigation against VW and Porsche' (n 3) Section IV.B.4; Kohl, 'Practitioner Comment' (n 27) Section IV.D.

109 See above Kohl, 'Practitioner Comment' (n 27) Section II.C. However, at least the German Federal Constitutional Court came to the conclusion that a search of the offices of the law firm Jones Day in Munich and the seizure of documents relating to the 'VW diesel scandal' by the public prosecutor's office in order to access the results of the Jones Day law firm did not constitute an infringement of the fundamental rights of Volkswagen, BVerfG, Order of 27 June 2018, 2 BvR 1405/17 and 2 BvR 1780/17, [2018] NJW 2385.

In order to improve the enforcement of capital markets law and consumer law, it therefore makes sense to further harmonise the (possible) claimant's rights to information vis-à-vis the opposing party and third parties and the corresponding disclosure duties in relation to alleged violations of European law. This should include the strengthening of information rights against public authorities and the respective disclosure duties in order to facilitate the exploitation of relevant information gathered by public authorities in the course of their investigations and actions. However, it must be borne in mind that there is a complex situation with conflicting legitimate interests that need to be balanced out in a differentiated way. On the one hand, the respective procedural rules must be designed in such a way that effective law enforcement is possible, while on the other hand mere 'fishing expeditions' must be avoided and public and private interests of confidentiality and of secrecy, in particular professional and business secrecy must be taken into account.[110]

Article 15(3) subsection 1 of the TFEU gives a basic right of information against European authorities.[111] If injured parties decide to bring an action under antitrust law on the basis of a Commission decision, on the basis of article 2(1) of the Regulation (EC) No 1049/2001,[112] they may request access to documents drawn up, received and held by the Commission itself. However, article 4 of Regulation (EC) No 1049/2001 provides for numerous exceptions where access may be refused.[113] The ECJ considers a blanket refusal of access to be inadmissible and requires the Commission to carry out a 'concrete, individual assessment' of

110 See also the comparative analysis by Domej and Honegger-Müntener, 'Consumer Law in Europe' (n 6) Section III.A.7.

111 Furthermore art 41(2)(b) of the Charter of Fundamental Rights of the EU on the 'Right to good administration' guarantees 'the right of every person to have access to his or her file, while respecting the legitimate interests of confidentiality and of professional and business secrecy'. On the national level see for Germany the Freedom of Information Act (*Informationsfreiheitsgesetz* – IFG) which in s 1 grants a general right of access to information vis-à-vis the federal authorities, which, however, may refuse to provide information under the conditions specified in s 3. The details remain highly controversial, see BVerwG, Judgment of 24 May 2011, 7 C 6.10, [2011] ZIP 1313, case note by Thomas MJ Möllers and Charis Niedorf [2011] EWiR 569f; ECJ, C-140/13 *Altmann and Others v Bundesanstalt für Finanzdienstleistungsaufsicht* [12 November 2014] ECLI:EU:C:2014:2362 at [42]: professional secrecy as a limit; further ECJ, C-15/16 *Bundesanstalt für Finanzdienstleistungsaufsicht v Ewald Baumeister* [19 June 2018] ECLI:EU:C:2018:464 at [46]; similar rights to information against public authorities also exist at the level of the individual federal states, see, e.g. the general right to information as laid down in art 36 of the Bavarian Data Protection Act.

112 Regulation (EC) No 1049/2001 of the European Parliament and of the Council of 30 May 2001 regarding public access to European Parliament, Council and Commission documents [2001] OJ L145/43 (hereafter Transparency Regulation (EC) No 1049/2001).

113 Access may be denied where this is necessary to protect the public interest, privacy or the integrity of the individual. The protection of court proceedings and business interests may also justify a refusal for information, art 4(2) of the Transparency Regulation (EC) No 1049/2001 (n 112).

the content of the documents referred to in the request.[114] Recently, however, the Court has defined the claim narrowly.[115]

A remarkably elaborate regime of duties of the opposing party and third parties to disclose evidence in proceedings relating to an action for damages extending to the disclosure of evidence included in the file of a competition authority, is laid down in articles 5 and 6 of the Antitrust Damages Directive 2014/104/EU[116] which codify the case law of the European Union courts and are underpinned by various fundamental principles including the principle of proportionality and the principle of transparency.[117] This regime could certainly serve as a source of inspiration for considerations *de lege ferenda* in other areas of law such as capital market law and consumer law on how to balance the respective conflicting interests and to provide for appropriate procedural safeguards.

By way of contrast, the Proposal for a Directive on representative actions[118] only contains a vague provision under the heading 'Evidence' which exclusively deals with information in the control of the defendant and does not say anything about the obligations of public authorities or other third parties to provide relevant information: the respective 'court or administrative authority may order, in accordance with national procedural rules', that relevant 'evidence be presented by the defendant, subject to the applicable Union and national rules on confidentiality'.[119] In contrast, the amended version of the Proposal includes information under the control of third parties and makes the order for presentation of information subject to an additional proportionality requirement.[120] However, by mostly referring back to national law the provision cannot serve as a suitable model for a general harmonisation of information rights and corresponding disclosure duties. Moreover, the provision is too narrow in that it only covers collective actions, although information asymmetry also affects individual court actions.[121]

---

114 CFI, T-2/03 *Verein für Konsumenteninformation v Commission of the European Communities* [13 April 2005] ECR 2005 II-01121 at [74], [114].

115 ECJ, C-365/12 P *European Commission v EnBW Energie Baden-Württemberg AG* [27 February 2014] ECLI:EU:C:2014:112 at [100ff].

116 See n 54; for the interplay of the respective provisions with the Transparency Regulation (EC) No 1049/2001 (n 112) see the last sentence of recital 20 of the Antitrust Damages Directive 2014/104/EU (n 55): 'This Directive should be without prejudice to such rules and practices under Regulation (EC) No 1049/2001'; for the transposition into German law see ss 33g and 89c GWB (n 82).

117 For a detailed analysis see Anca D Chirita, 'The Disclosure of Evidence Under the "Antitrust Damages" Directive 2014/104/EU' in Vesna Tomljenović and others (eds), *EU Competition and State Aid Rules – Public and Private Enforcement* (Springer 2017) 147–73 <https://papers.ssrn.com/sol3/papers.cfm?abstract_id=2800910>.

118 See n 11.

119 Art 13 of the Proposal for a Directive on representative actions, COM(2018) 184 final (n 11).

120 See art 13 of Council, 'General Approach – Directive proposal on representative actions for consumers' (n 77); critical Domej and Honegger-Müntener, 'Consumer Law in Europe' (n 6) Section III.A.7.

121 See above Domej and Honegger-Müntener, 'Consumer Law in Europe' (n 6) Section III.A.7.

C. STRENGTHENING ENFORCEMENT BY PUBLIC AUTHORITIES

1. *Fines as Suitable Penalties*

Powerful public authorities are needed above all when it is doubtful whether private legal mechanisms are sufficient – for example, because there is no negotiating balance between the parties.[122] As in competition law, fines should generally focus on the sanctioning of the company rather than on the punishment of individual employees.[123] Criminal proceedings often come too late to act as a deterrent. The fines imposed on VW in Germany[124] and, above all, the fact that the unlawfully obtained profits were disgorged[125] must be regarded as an entirely positive development.

As regards the European level, the considerable increase in the amount of fines against companies violating European Union law as introduced by the 'New Deal for Consumers' Omnibus Directive (EU) 2019/2161[126] is also to be welcomed and it would be desirable for the enforcement of consumer law and capital markets law in general to be safeguarded by correspondingly deterrent fines. A further example of a tightening of sanctions is to be noted in the area of European market abuse law, where the Market Abuse Regulation (MAR)[127] and the Market Abuse Directive (CRIM-MAD)[128] have

---

122 See above Kohl, 'Practitioner Comment' (n 27) Introduction and above n 94.

123 In order to catch up internationally, Germany should introduce criminal liability for companies, see for the recent development the Draft Law on Combating Corporate Crime (*Referentenentwurf eines Gesetzes zur Bekämpfung der Unternehmenskriminalität*) issued by the German Federal Ministry of Justice and Consumer Protection (*Bundesministeriums der Justiz und für Verbraucherschutz*) on 15 August 2019 and for the controversial discussion on this draft law, e.g. the news article Elisa Hoven and Michael Kubiciel, 'Verbandssanktionsgesetz – Eine kleine Revolution im Strafrecht' *Frankfurter Allgemeine Zeitung* (Frankfurt, 6 November 2019) <http://www.faz.net/aktuell/politik/staat-und-recht/verbandssanktionengesetz-eine-kleine-revolution-im-strafrecht-16471979.html>, see also Wissenschaftlicher Dienst des Deutschen Bundestags, 'Eine Übersicht zum Unternehmensstrafrecht in einzelnen Mitgliedstaaten der Europäischen Union' (WD 7-3000-070/17, 28 June 2017) <http://www.bundestag.de/resource/blob/539400/9f7fe461015429dc5f71c4c3d2816704/wd-7-070-17-pdf-data.pdf>. On this Martin Henssler and others, 'Kölner Entwurf eines Verbandssanktionengesetzes' (2017) <http://www.verbandsstrafrecht.jura.uni-koeln.de/sites/fg_verbandsstrafrecht/user_upload/Koelner_Entwurf_eines_Verbandssanktionengesetzes__2017.pdf>.

124 See above under Section I.A. with n 27ff.

125 See above under Section I.A. with n 27ff.

126 See above under Section I.A. with n 32 and 33.

127 Regulation (EU) No 596/2014 of the European Parliament and of the Council of 16 April 2014 on market abuse (market abuse regulation) and repealing Directive 2003/6/EC of the European Parliament and of the Council and Commission Directives 2003/124/EC, 2003/125/EC and 2004/72/EC [2014] OJ L173/1 (hereafter MAR).

128 Directive 2014/57/EU of the European Parliament and of the Council of 16 April 2014 on criminal sanctions for market abuse (Market Abuse Directive – CRIM-MAD) [2014]

significantly increased the framework of sanctions and fines for insider dealing and market manipulation.[129]

However, as regards the use of the proceeds from such fines by the respective Member State or other public entity, consideration should be given to linking it *de lege ferenda* to the purposes of the pertinent legal provisions infringed. This should prevent the sums in question from ending up in the general budgets. Thus, for example, in Germany the fine against Volkswagen AG was payable to the federal state of Lower Saxony, which allegedly used it to renovate hospitals and finance a fast internet and universities.[130] In contrast, the use of the proceeds from a VW settlement in the US for the compensation of buyers of diesel vehicles and for the financing of electric buses, served the purposes of the violated legal provisions, i.e. consumer protection law and environmental law. Applied to Europe, the proposed solution would have meant that more than €2 billion in fines from Volkswagen AG, Porsche AG and Audi AG[131] would have been disposable to compensate (at least to some extent) injured consumers and investors, and to provide financial support to cities in their efforts to promote clean air.[132]

Against this background article 14(3) of the Proposal for a Directive on representative actions[133] which states that the collective interests of consumers should be taken into account in the allocation of the proceeds of fines for non-compliance with the final decisions issued within the representative action therefore deserves approval.[134] Unfortunately, at the current stage of the

---

OJ L173/179; on art 8f of Directive 2014/57/EU, see Petra Buck-Heeb, *Kapitalmarktrecht* (10th edn, CF Müller 2019) paras 440ff.

129 See also 81(4) of the GWB (n 82), s 120(18) of the WpHG (Wertpapierhandelsgesetz – German Securities Trading Act).

130 'Klimaschutz und Kliniken – dafür gibt Niedersachsen VWs Diesel-Milliarde aus' (*Manager Magazin*, 20 July 2019) <http://www.manager-magazin.de/unternehmen/autoindustrie/volkswagen-niedersachsen-hat-vws-abgas-bussgeld-vollstaendig-verplant-a-1278259.html>. If, on the one hand, the Minister-President of Lower Saxony, as a member of the Supervisory Board of Volkswagen AG, violates his supervisory duties, the perpetrator receives the amount that should actually benefit the victims. Regarding the obligation of the Supervisory Board to assert claims for damages against the members of the Board of Management, see Marcus Lutter, 'Wann klagt der VW-Aufsichtsrat?' *Frankfurter Allgemeine Zeitung* (Frankfurt am Main, 2 November 2016) 18.

131 See above under Section I.A with n 28.

132 A corresponding political demand is also made with regard to the German OWiG (*Ordnungswidrigkeitengesetz* – Act on Regulatory Offences), see Oliver Luksic (Member of German Parliament) and Wilfried Bausback (Bavarian Justice Minister) in 'Wohin fließen die Strafzahlungen aus dem Dieselskandal?' (*Deutschlandfunk*, 28 Oktober 2018) <http://www.deutschlandfunk.de/nachgefragt-wohin-fliessen-die-strafzahlungen-aus-dem.2852.de.html?dram:article_id=431290>. Instead, however, the German Government has promised a sum of €1 billion from the general federal budget for clean air in large cities.

133 See above n 11.

134 Art 14(3) of the Proposal for a Directive on representative actions, COM(2018) 184 final (n 11).

legislative process, this provision has been removed from the Proposal for a Directive on representative actions.[135]

In the Republic of China, the ordinary consumer quite often uses a kind of shaming, giving the consumer the chance to discuss emotionally defects of a product in the public.[136] In European law, the legal instrument of shaming exists, for example regulated by the MAR; here the principle of proportionality applies.[137]

2. *Monitoring as a Means of Checking Companies*

The concept of monitoring is used in the US and has also been used in the diesel emissions scandal.[138] Thereby, in the event of a legal violation by a European company it is agreed with the US authorities that it would be monitored for several years whether companies had optimised their own compliance systems in such a way that a legal violation could be largely ruled out in the future.[139] As part of a settlement, European companies are often involuntarily forced to such a compliance with US law. Whether such measures are compatible with German company law is not yet clear. A European solution would certainly be desirable here, to ensure that such monitoring is in line with European legal principles.[140]

D. STRENGTHENING THE INTERPLAY OF PUBLIC ENFORCEMENT, COLLECTIVE ACTIONS AND PRIVATE INDIVIDUAL ACTIONS

In the following, suggestions are made on how the findings gathered in the course of public enforcement can be better used for subsequent individual or collective actions for damages. In cartel cases, private damages actions are usually

---

135 See above Council, 'General Approach – Directive proposal on representative actions for consumers' (n 77).

136 Tong Zhang, 'Enforcing Consumer Law in China' in this book Section II.A.1.c) fn 23.

137 Art 34 of the MAR (n 127). Cf the relevance in the earlier section Möllers, 'Efficiency as a Standard in Capital Markets Law – The Application of Empirical and Economic Arguments for the Justification of Civil, Criminal and Administrative Law Sanctions' (2009) 20 EBLR 243, 255ff.

138 See with regard to Volkswagen above Schmitz, 'US' (n 1) Section II.C.

139 See Jürgen Wessing, 'Internal Investigations – Interne Ermittlungen im Unternehmen' in Christoph E Hauschka, Klaus Moosmayer and Thomas Lösler (eds), *Corporate Compliance* (3rd edn, CH Beck 2016) para 46; Gregor Bachmann, 'Interne Ermittlungen ohne Grenzen?' (2016) 180 ZHR 563ff.

140 Klaus Hopt, 'Interne Untersuchungen, Whistleblowing und externes Monitoring' [2020] ZGR (forthcoming).

brought as follow-on actions that is in the aftermath of decisions of competition authorities imposing penalties on the respective companies.[141] Therefore, the Antitrust Damages Directive 2014/104/EU in particular provides for mechanisms to facilitate the use of the outcome of public authority proceedings for subsequent civil actions.[142] Thus, with regard to the interplay between public and private enforcement, it is once again antitrust law that can serve as a seminal model, which should be followed for enforcement in other areas of law such as consumer and capital markets law.[143] And furthermore, such mechanisms can also be made useful for the interplay between collective actions and individual private actions for damages.

1. *Suspension or Interruption of Limitation Periods*

a) Suspension or Interruption of Limitation Periods as a Result of Public Authority Intervention

If private claimants cannot await the outcome of public authority proceedings because of the impending statute of limitation, then the results of such public authority proceedings cannot be reliably used for subsequent private actions for damages. That is why according to article 10(4) of the Antitrust Damages Directive 2014/104/EU,[144] the limitation period is suspended or interrupted until at least one year after the ending of competition authority proceedings which have been taken 'in respect of an infringement of competition law to which the action for damages relates'. Hence, for example in Germany, injured parties benefit under section 33h(6) sentence 1 of the Act Against Restraints of Competition (GWB) from such a suspension of the limitation period if the *Bundeskartellamt* (German Competition Authority), the EU Commission or the competition authority of another Member State initiates antitrust proceedings: injured parties can therefore await the investigations of the supervisory

141 See recital 26 of the Antitrust Damages Directive' 2014/104/EU (n 55).

142 In detail Ferdinand Wollenschläger, Wolfgang Wurmnest and Thomas MJ Möllers (eds), *Private Enforcement of European Competition and State Aid Law. Current Challenges and the Way Forward* (Wolters Kluwer 2020) passim.

143 Already discussed in Thomas MJ Möllers and Bernhard Pregler, 'Zivilrechtliche Rechtsdurchsetzung und kollektiver Rechtschutz im Wirtschaftsrecht' (2012) 176 ZHR, 144ff, translated as Thomas MJ Möllers and Bernhard Pregler, 'Civil Law Enforcement and Collective Redress in Economic Law – A comparison between collective redress actions in competition, antitrust, company and capital markets law' [2013] Europa e diritto privato 27–74 (hereafter Möllers and Pregler, 'Zivilrechtliche Rechtsdurchsetzung'); approving Wundenberg, 'Perspektiven der privaten Rechtsdurchsetzung' (n 79) 124ff; Philipp Maume, 'Staatliche Rechtsdurchsetzung im deutschen Kapitalmarkrecht: eine kritische Bestandsaufnahme' (2016) 180 ZHR 358ff.

144 Antitrust Damages Directive 2014/104/EU (n 55).

authorities before bringing an action, without suffering any legal disadvantage as a result.[145] This also makes sense in terms of procedural economy because it avoids a double deployment of resources for fact-finding by avoiding an early investigation of facts by civil courts, which have to be investigated by public authorities anyway.

In contrast, neither in consumer law nor in capital markets law has a similar European regime of suspension of limitation periods by public authorities' investigations been introduced so far.[146] Thus, for example, in Germany, neither the German Capital Markets Model Case Act (KapMuG)[147] nor the provisions on the civil procedural model declaratory action (*Musterfeststellungsklage*)[148] provide for such a suspension or interruption of limitation periods resulting from related public authorities proceedings.[149]

De lege ferenda, however, the European legislator should ensure in a more general manner that public authorities' investigations of infringements of European law suspend the limitation period for related private actions for damages so as to make the findings of such public proceedings usable for subsequent private actions.

b) Suspension or Interruption of Limitation Periods as a Result of Collective Actions

Individual private enforcement can also be facilitated by allowing the individual claimant to await the outcome of a collective action and this holds particularly true with regard to actions for injunctive or declaratory relief.[150] The country chapters collected in this book have revealed considerable differences as to the effects of collective actions on limitation periods applicable to individual claims.[151] Therefore, it means a step forward when article 11 of the Proposal for a Directive on representative actions[152] states that 'the submission of a

---

145 See Bundesregierung, 'Entwurf eines Siebten Gesetzes zur Änderung des Gesetzes gegen Wettbewerbsbeschränkungen' [12 August 2004] BT-Drucks 15/3640, 55 <http://dip21.bundestag.de/doc/btd/15/036/1503640.pdf>.

146 But see with regard to the effect of collective actions on the prescription of individual claims below under b).

147 See above Section I.A. with n 11.

148 See above Section I.A. with n 7.

149 On this demand already, see Möllers and Pregler, 'Zivilrechtliche Rechtsdurchsetzung' (n 143) 155. It would have been conceivable, for example, that administrative fines would have been levied in Germany by the Federal Motor Vehicle Office (*Kraftfahrt-Bundesamt – KBA*) (regarding the diesel software) and BaFin (for the failure to make an ad hoc announcement).

150 See the comparative analysis of this aspect by Domej and Honegger-Müntener, 'Consumer Law in Europe' (n 6) Section III.A.4.

151 See the various country chapters above as well as the comparative analysis of this aspect by Domej and Honegger-Müntener, 'Consumer Law in Europe' (n 6) Section III.A.4.

152 See above n 11.

representative action [...] shall have the effect of suspending or interrupting limitation periods applicable to any redress actions for the consumers concerned'.

Furthermore, in the revised Proposal it is clarified that such a suspending or interrupting effect is not only induced by representative actions for redress measures, but also by representative actions for injunctive relief.[153] However, according to the revised Proposal this suspensive or interruptive effect works only to the benefit of 'consumers concerned by the action'[154] whereas the original Proposal extended it to 'the consumers concerned'.[155] If this modification of wording is intended to mean that only consumers shall benefit who previously opted in to the representative action or who have not opted out,[156] then this makes sense on the one hand, as it creates an incentive for an opt in and thus for overcoming individual rational apathy. On the other hand, there is no possibility for those who prefer to bring only an individual action to await the outcome of the collective action for reasons of better assessment of the litigation risk, and this can lead, especially in the case of mass damages with higher individual amounts of damage, to the courts having to deal with a large number of individual actions, which might prove pointless for the injured parties due to a later unfavourable outcome of the collective proceedings.

2. *Binding Effect of the Findings of an Infringement on (Other) Court Proceedings*

a) Binding Effect of the Findings of an Infringement by a National Competition Authority or by a Review Court under the Damages Directive 2014/104/EU

A second linkage between public and private enforcement, which again, on the one hand may facilitate the latter and on the other hand may help to avoid the double deployment of public resources, is the imposition of a binding effect of the finding of an infringement which had been established by a public authority or a court on a subsequent private action.[157]

Once again, the Antitrust Damages Directive 2014/104/EU can serve as a model here, when stating in article 9(1) that 'an infringement of competition law found by a final decision of a national competition authority or by a review court

153 See art 11 sentence 1 of Council, 'General Approach – Directive proposal on representative actions for consumers' (n 77).

154 See art 11 sentences 1 and 2 of Council, 'General Approach – Directive proposal on representative actions for consumers' (n 77). See also Meller-Hannich, 'Germany' (n 7) Sections II.A. and III.F.; Domej and Honegger-Müntener, 'Consumer Law in Europe' (n 6) Section III.A.4.

155 See art 11 of the original Proposal for a Directive on representative actions, COM(2018) 184 final (n 11).

156 This is how the amendment is understood by Domej and Honegger-Müntener, 'Consumer Law in Europe' (n 6) Section III.A.4.

157 On this already Möllers and Pregler, 'Zivilrechtliche Rechtsdurchsetzung' (n 143) 154ff.

is deemed to be irrefutably established for the purposes of an action for damages brought before their national courts under Article 101 or 102 TFEU or under national competition law'. Such a mechanism is not without problems, because on the one hand it limits the independence of civil courts and on the other hand it raises the question of how a civil court should proceed in cases where the respective public authority's decisions have been taken on a factual basis which would be insufficient in civil proceedings, or where the respective decision is manifestly illegal.[158] Even so, it certainly is a considerable relief to the claimant, since in the course of the action for damages there is no longer any need to prove the harmful act and the illegality.[159] However, in view of the aforementioned difficulties, a binding effect could not be ordered to such a far-reaching extent in all cases by the Antitrust Damages Directive 2014/104/EU. Instead, due to the lack of harmonisation of national administrative proceedings according to article 9(2) of the Antitrust Damages Directive 2014/104/EU the binding effect is less extensive in cross-border cases:[160] Member States are only required to grant final decisions taken in another Member State at least the status of 'prima facie evidence' in damage proceedings before their courts.

b) Binding Effect of Findings under the Proposal for a Directive on Representative Actions

In the light of the Antitrust Damages Directive 2014/104/EU, it seems appropriate for the European legislature to consider attributing a certain binding effect to administrative or judicial decisions which establish an infringement of rights in the area of capital markets law or consumer law by a company, for subsequent civil actions for damages. This should at least apply if the respective administrative or judicial proceedings comply with certain European minimum standards for establishing the facts and ensuring a fair procedure.

Against this background it does not come as a surprise that article 10(1) and (2) of the Proposal for a Directive on representative actions[161] follow the model of article 9(1) and (2) of the Antitrust Damages Directive 2014/104/EU and provide for a similarly binding effect by stating that 'an infringement

---

158 For both aspects see Wollenschläger and Wurmnest, 'Comparative Analysis and the Ways forward' (n 107) 363ff.

159 In this respect, see the information provided by the European Commission, 'Antitrust: Commission fines producers of CRT glass €128 million in fourth cartel settlement' (*Press Release*, IP/11/1214, 19 October 2011) <https://ec.europa.eu/commission/presscorner/detail/en/IP_11_1214>; see also Kurt L Ritter, in Ulrich Immenga and Ernst-Joachim Mestmäcker (eds), *Wettbewerbsrecht* (6th edn, CH Beck 2019) art 30 VerfVO mn 1. But there still has to be established causation and the damage.

160 Wollenschläger and Wurmnest, 'Comparative Analysis and the Ways Forward' (n 107) 362ff.

161 See n 11.

harming collective interests of consumers established in a final decision of an administrative authority or a court [...] is deemed as irrefutably establishing the existence of that infringement for the purposes of any other actions seeking redress before their national courts against the same trader for the same infringement', whereas in cross-border cases the respective binding effect is limited to 'a rebuttable presumption'.[162] Furthermore article 10(3) of the Proposal for a Directive on representative actions[163] stipulates that a final declaratory decision issued in the procedure of representative action provided for by the proposed Directive 'is deemed as irrefutably establishing the liability of the trader towards the harmed consumers by an infringement for the purposes of any actions seeking redress before their national courts against the same trader for that infringement.'

However, particularly in view of concerns about the independence of the judiciary,[164] the binding effect as laid down in article 10(1) and (2) of the original Proposal has been weakened in the last version of the proposal: accordingly, Member States only shall ensure that the respective final decision can be used as evidence of the existence of the respective infringement 'in accordance with national law on evaluation of evidence'.[165] This modification is acceptable as long as there is no guarantee that all procedures in the Member States where such findings are made meet sufficiently harmonised standards.

Moreover, the rule on the binding effect of declaratory decisions in article 10(3) of the original Proposal has been dropped in its entirety. On the one hand, this is understandable because collective actions for a declaratory judgment with opt-in mechanisms, as permitted by the proposed Directive, become unattractive if all consumers, including those who have not joined, benefit from the outcome of the proceedings (free-riding problem).[166] On the other hand, however, it is regrettable that not all subsequent individual actions for damages are facilitated by a binding effect of the respective declaratory judgment which also means that the respective courts are burdened with the effort of a new finding of the relevant facts.[167]

---

162 See for a critical assessment Domej and Honegger-Müntener, 'Consumer Law in Europe' (n 6) Section III.A.5.

163 See n 11.

164 See recital 33 of Council, 'General Approach – Directive proposal on representative actions for consumers' (n 77).

165 See art 10 of Council, 'General Approach – Directive proposal on representative actions for consumers' (n 77).

166 This is rightly emphasised by Domej and Honegger-Müntener, 'Consumer Law in Europe' (n 6) Section III.A.5.

167 As far as legal issues are concerned, however, even legally non-binding decisions will often have a strong factual effect on the following individual actions, see with regard to this aspect Domej and Honegger-Müntener, 'Consumer Law in Europe' (n 6) Section III.A.5.

E. STRENGTHENING THE INTERNAL MONITORING OF THE COMPANIES

1. *Compliance Duties of the Management Board*

The solutions proposed so far all carry one disadvantage: As long as public authorities or private individuals ignore an infringement, it cannot be stopped or punished. The informational deficit of authorities and private persons is immanent with non-public and secret internal company information. Conversely, the company knows the internal company information best, and it is to this extent an information monopolist.[168] There are two conceivable ways of compensating for this system-immanent disadvantage that authorities and private claimants have. In recent decades, internal and external monitoring has been massively tightened. Originally, German company law provided for the monitoring of internal corporate conduct in addition to controlling, auditing and risk management by the supervisory board and auditors.[169] In the meantime, extensive compliance systems have been added.[170] For years, Volkswagen had promoted these systems as a global leader; in retrospect, it is clear that its system had clearly failed.[171]

To leave the structures of a compliance system subject to the business-judgement rule at the discretion of the Management Board[172] seems too general. Volkswagen claims that only a few people had knowledge of the defeat software. Here, it should not be possible to allow the board to simply rely on a lack of

---

168 On this term, see Thomas M J Möllers and Franz C Leisch, 'Haftung von Vorständen gegenüber Anlegern wegen fehlerhafter Ad-hoc-Meldungen nach §826 BGB' [2001] WM 1648, 1654; approving Oliver Rieckers, 'Haftung des Vorstands für fehlerhafte Ad-hoc-Meldungen de lege lata und de lege ferenda' [2002] BB 1213, 1217; Rüdiger Krause, 'Ad-hoc-Publizität und haftungsrechtlicher Anlegerschutz' [2002] ZGR 799, 823.

169 Cf the relevant ss 107 para 3 sentence 2, 111 of the German Stock Corporation Code (AktG) and ss 321ff German Commercial Code (*Handelsgesetzbuch – HGB*).

170 Cf No A.2 German Corporate Governance Kodex (DCGK). The introduction of a compliance codex is based on art 20 of Directive 2013/34/EU of the European Parliament and of the Council of 26 June 2013 on the annual financial statements, consolidated financial statements and related reports of certain types of undertakings, amending Directive 2006/43/EC of the European Parliament and of the Council and repealing Council Directives 78/660/EEC and 83/349/EEC [2013] OJ L182/19. Cf Thomas M J Möllers, 'Europäisches Gesellschafts- und Unternehmensrecht' in Reiner Schulze, Stefan Kadelbach and André Janssen (eds), *Handbuch Europarecht* (4th edn, Nomos 2020) §18 mn 76ff (forthcoming).

171 Sönke Iwersen and others, 'Wie die Kontrolle bei VW versagte' *Handelsblatt* (Düsseldorf, 7 February 2019) <http://www.handelsblatt.com/unternehmen/industrie/dieselskandal-wie-die-kontrolle-bei-vw-versagte/23955944.html?ticket=ST-38473556-Oa0VQjh5jp1TH5dZ735m-ap2>. This could be remedied by the monitoring previously described.

172 See Barbara Grunewald, 'Informationen als Grundlage der Leitung und Überwachung' [2020] ZGR (forthcoming).

knowledge. Rather, one will have to ask to what extent important information carriers in a company have been monitored and the corresponding knowledge has been passed on. For this reason, the compliance structures must be further substantiated and thus made legally binding, so that the knowledge of individual persons can also be attributed to the management board and thus to the legal entities.[173] If the management board stipulates compliance with strict emission values, it must satisfy itself in detail that the development department is achieving them. Finally, whistleblowing should be considered as an appropriate means of disclosing scandals to the management board or the public. Here too, there are examples from European competition law, which cleverly uses the findings of game theory such as the prisoner dilemma.[174]

2. *Penalties and Incentives*

Penalties and incentives should be combined to enforce the companies' obligations. Since the WorldCom and Enron scandals, under European law the Chief Executive Officer (CEO) and the Chief Financial Officer (CFO) have to make a statement of responsibility regarding the accuracy of the annual financial statements;[175] and the liability of auditors has also been made much more stringent. Now, the CEO, the CFO and the auditor can be sued for damages if their statement had been incorrect.[176] It is possible that a personal 'compliance statement' from the Chief Legal Officer can further increase the effectiveness of the compliance system. Moreover, the increase in fines in antitrust and capital

---

173 Such persons can be identified from the insider lists of art 18 of the MAR (n 127). This may include the head of the development department, for example. On the view of OLG Braunschweig to regard employees of the development department as appointed representatives, see Weiss, 'Securities Litigation against VW and Porsche' (n 3) fn 43.

174 For example, a leniency scheme ('Bonusregelung') under which only the first cartel member to uncover the cartel remains unpunished, Bundeskartellamt (German Federal Cartel Office), 'Bekanntmachung Nr. 9/2006 über den Erlass und die Reduktion von Geldbußen in Kartellsachen – Bonusregelung' (7 March 2006) <http://www.bundeskartellamt.de/SharedDocs/Publikation/DE/Bekanntmachungen/Bekanntmachung%20-%20Bonusregelung.pdf?__blob=publicationFile&v=7>; 'Commission Notice on Immunity from fines and reduction of fines in cartel cases' (2006/C 298/11) [8 December 2006] OJ C298/17.

175 Cf. The annual accounting oath is based on art 4(2) of Directive 2004/109/EC of the European Parliament and of the Council of 15 December 2004 on the harmonisation of transparency requirements in relation to information about issuers whose securities are admitted to trading on a regulated market and amending Directive 2001/34/EC [2004] OJ L390/38. On the introduction of s 264(2) sentence 3 of the German Commercial Code (HGB), s 289(1) sentence 5 of the HGB and the comparable situation under US law after the Sarbanes-Oxley Act, see Thomas M J Möllers, 'Creating standards in a global financial market – the Sarbanes-Oxley Act and other activities: what Europeans and Americans could and should learn from each other' (2007) 4 ECFR 173ff.

176 S 264 para 2 sentence 3 of the Commercial Code (HGB) in conjunction with s 823 para 2 of the Civil Code (BGB) and s 323 para 1 sentence 3 of the Commercial Code (HGB).

markets law[177] already has the effect that companies have a vested interest in uncovering infringements. Conversely, it should have the effect of reducing penalties or fines for the company if it has set up a compliance system that has failed in the specific individual case but is fundamentally effective. Here, other legal systems seem to be more advanced than the case law of the ECJ, which does not yet provide for a privileged treatment of the injuring party for the establishment of an effective compliance system.[178] Finally, US authorities are offering whistle-blowers the prospect of high premiums.[179] This incentive can also help to identify infringements.

---

177 See Section II.B.1 above.

178 Rejecting the compliance defence under European competition law, see CFI, T-279/02 *Degussa AG v Commission of the European Communities* [5 April 2006] ECR 2006 II-00897 at [350]; CFI, T-352/94 *Mo Och Domsjö AB v Commission of the European Communities* [14 May 1998] ECR 1998 II-01989 at [419]; in contrast favoured by the US, France, the UK, Canada, Brazil and Spain. On this, see Alexander Eufinger, 'Berücksichtigung von Compliance-Programmen bei der Bußgeldbemessung – Vorbild USA?' [2016] Corporate Compliance Zeitschrift 209ff.

179 This can be up to 30 per cent of the fine levied by the authorities, see s 21F(b)(1) of the SEA; on this Silvelyn Wrase and Christoph Fabritius, 'Prämien für Hinweisgeber bei Kartellverstößen?' [2011] Corporate Compliance Zeitschrift 69, 70ff.

KEY SOURCE BIBLIOGRAPHY*

Afferni G, '"Opt-In" Class Actions in Italy: Why are they Failing?' [2016] JETL 82.

Alderman RM and Pridgen D, *Consumer Protection and the Law* (2019–2020 edn, Thomson Reuters 2019).

Alexander C, Schadensersatz und Abschöpfung im Lauterkeits- und Kartellrecht – Privatrechtliche Sanktionsinstrumente zum Schutz individueller und überindividueller Interessen im Wettbewerb (Mohr Siebeck 2010).

Assmann HD, Schneider UH and Mülbert PO (eds), *Wertpapierhandelsrecht, Kommentar* (7th edn, Otto Schmidt 2019).

Bartlett J, Naranjo M and Plungis J, 'Guide to the Volkswagen Emissions Recall' (*Consumer Reports*, 23 October 2017) <http://www.consumerreports.org/cro/cars/guide-to-the-volkswagen-dieselgate-emissions-recall->.

Belli C (ed), *Le azioni collettive in Italia. Profili teorici e applicativi* (Cedam 2017).

Benjamin AHV, Marques CL and Miragem B, *Comentários ao Código de Defesa do Consumidor* (6th edn, Revista dos Tribunais 2019).

Berry D and others, *Blackstone's Guide to the Consumer Rights Act 2015* (Oxford University Press 2016).

Bien F, 'Die neue französische Action de groupe der Verbraucherschutzverbände' [2014] Neue Zeitschrift für Kartellrecht 507.

Bontje M, 'Eerste Nederlandse boete voor Volkswagen AG inzake "manipulatiesoftware": de software wordt als oneerlijke handelspraktijk aangemerkt door de ACM' (2018) 21 Bedrijfsjuridische berichten 68.

Bridge M, *Benjamin's Sale of Goods* (Sweet & Maxwell 2017).

Bruns J, 'Vorteilsanrechnung beim Schadensersatz für abgasmanipulierte Diesel-Fahrzeuge' [2019] NJW 801.

Cashman P, *Class Action Law and Practice* (The Federation Press 2007).

Cassano G and others (eds), *Concorrenza, mercato e diritto dei consumatori* (UTET 2018).

Conac PH, 'Vers des class actions en matière boursière en Europe et en France?' [2018] Revue des Sociétés 472.

Consolo C and Zuffi B, *L'azione di classe ex art. 140-bis cod. cons.* (Cedam 2012).

Daujotas R, 'Grupės ieškinys lietuvoje – praktinės įgyvendinimo problemos' (2016) 101 Teisė 29.

de la Brosse J, 'Dieselgate: la justice française déboute des clients de Volkswagen' *L'Express* (Paris, 27 April 2016) <http://lexpansion.lexpress.fr/actualite-economique/dieselgate-la-justice-francaise-deboute-des-clients-volkswagen_1786835.html>.

* Only the most important works on the Diesel Emissions Scandal and the enforcement of consumer and capital market law have been included in this bibliography. Further references can be found in the footnotes of the respective chapters.

Domej T, 'Einheitlicher kollektiver Rechtsschutz in Europa?' (2012) 125 ZZP 421.

—— 'Die geplante EU-Verbandsklagenrichtlinie – Sisyphos vor dem Gipfelsieg?' [2019] ZEuP 447.

Dybus C and Lemmen J, '"Dieselgate" and Consumer Law: Repercussions of the Volkswagen Scandal in the Netherlands' [2017] Journal of European Consumer and Market Law 91.

Ewing J, *Faster, Higher, Farther: How One of the World's Largest Automakers Committed a Massive and Stunning Fraud* (WW Norton & Company 2018).

Fang Ying, 'On the Organization System of Consumers' Right and Interests Protection: A Perspective of "State-Society" Cooperation Governance' (2018) 2 Journal of Guangzhou University (Social Science Edition) 62.

Federal Trade Commission, 'Volkswagen Group of America Inc.' <http://www.ftc.gov/enforcement/cases-proceedings/162-3006/volkswagen-group-america-inc>.

Fidler P, 'Private Enforcement – Rechtstheorie und Rechtswirklichkeit im Wettbewerbs- und Kapitalmarktrecht' [2018] JBl 81 (Part 1) and 152 (Part 2).

Franzolin CJ and Vieira LK, 'Emissões de poluentes em veículos e empresas transnacionais: a tutela ambiental na sociedade de consumo e os desafios no cenário internacional' (2019) 121 Revista de Direito do Consumidor 459.

Frazão A, *Direito da Concorrência: pressupostos e perspectivas* (Saraiva 2017).

Fuchs A (ed), *Wertpapierhandelsgesetz (WpHG), Kommentar* (2nd edn, CH Beck 2016).

Gambino AM (ed), *Rimedi e tecniche di protezione dei consumatori* (Giappichelli 2011).

Golden J and Burn L (eds), *The Capital Markets Law Journal* (Oxford Journals).

Grave D, Adams K and Betts J, *Class Actions in Australia* (2nd edn, Lawbook Co/Thomson Reuters 2012).

Grave D and Mould H (eds), *25 Years of Class Actions in Australia: 1992–2017* (Ross Parsons Centre 2017).

Grinover AP and others, *Código de Defesa do Consumidor Comentado pelos Autores do Anteprojeto* (11th edn, Forense Universitária 2017).

Harsagi V and van Rhee CH (eds), *Multi-Party Redress Mechanisms in Europe: Squeaking Mice?* (Intersentia 2014).

Heese M, 'Nutzungsentschädigung zugunsten der Hersteller manipulierter Diesel-Kraftfahrzeuge?' [2019] VuR 257.

—— 'Was der Dieselskandal über die Rechtsdurchsetzung, deren Protagonisten und die Funktion des Privatrechts verrät' [2019] NZV 273.

Hellgardt A, *Kapitalmarktdeliktsrecht* (Mohr Siebeck 2008).

Hensler DR and others, *Class Action Dilemmas* (RAND Institute 2000).

Herlin-Karnell E and Ryder N, *Market Manipulation and Insider Trading: Regulatory Challenges in the United States of America, the European Union and the United Kingdom* (Hart Publishing 2018).

Hertz K, 'Gruppesøgsmål' in Bang-Pedersen UR and others (eds), *Retsplejeloven – 100 år* (Djøf Forlag 2019) 441.

Hess B, 'Massenklagen und Managerhaftung' in Krieger G and Schneider UH (eds), *Handbuch Managerhaftung* (3rd edn, Otto Schmidt 2017).

Hirte H and Möllers TMJ (eds), *Kölner Kommentar zum WpHG* (2nd edn, Carl Heymanns 2014).

Ihrig HC, 'Wissenszurechnung im Kapitalmarktrecht – untersucht anhand der Pflicht zur Ad-hoc-Publizität gemäß Art. 17 MAR' [2017] ZHR 381.

Jung P (ed), *Die private Durchsetzung von öffentlichem Wirtschaftsrecht* (Mohr Siebeck 2018) 129.

Kalss S and Oppitz M, 'Insiderhandel und Kursmanipulation – Sanktionen' [2011] RdW 575.

Keske S, Renda A and Van den Bergh R, 'Financing and group litigation' in Tuil M and Visscher L (eds), *New Trends in Financing Civil Litigation in Europe* (Edward Elgar 2010) 57.

Klauser A, 'Alpine, VW und noch immer keine echte österreichische Sammelklage' [2015] Zeitschrift für Verbraucherrecht 182.

Klöhn L (ed), *Marktmissbrauchsverordnung, Kommentar* (CH Beck 2018).

Koch H, *Verbraucherprozessrecht – Verfahrensrechtliche Gewährleistung des Verbraucherschutzes* (2nd edn, Nomos 2019).

Kodek G, 'Die „Sammelklage" nach österreichischem Recht – Ein neues prozeßrechtliches Institut auf dem Prüfstand' [2004] BankArchiv 615.

—— 'Groß- und Massenverfahren de lege lata und de lege ferenda' in Neumayr M (ed), *Beschleunigung von Zivil- und Strafverfahren – Zwischen Richtigkeitsgewähr, Fairness und Effizienz* (Manz 2014) 1.

Lange S, *Das begrenzte Gruppenverfahren* (Mohr Siebeck 2012).

Legg M and McInnes R, *Australian Annotated Class Action Legislation* (2nd edn, Lexis Nexis 2018).

Lego Andersen E, 'Gruppesøgsmål' in Backhausen P and others (eds), *Proceduren* (4th edn, Djøf Forlag 2019) 1135.

Lein E, Fairgrieve D, Otero Crespo M and Smith V (eds), *Collective Redress in Europe – Why and How?* (British Institute of International and Comparative Law 2015).

Leupold P, 'Enforcing Consumer Rights: Collective Redress in Austria and the European Union' [2019] Journal of European Consumer and Market Law 121.

—— 'Kollektiver Rechtsschutz: Österreich und Deutschland im Vergleich' [2019] ecolex 564.

Linhart K and Finazzi Agrò E, 'Kollektiver Rechtsschutz in Italien: Die italienische „azione di classe"' [2013] RIW 443.

Lomnicka E and Powell J, *Encyclopedia of Financial Services Law* (Sweet & Maxwell 2019).

Mandard S, 'Dieselgate: D'un côté les gens meurent, et de l'autre, la justice pénale est silencieuse' *Le Monde* (Paris, 17 September 2018) <http://www.lemonde.fr/pollution/article/2018/09/17/dieselgate-d-un-cote-les-gens-meurent-et-de-l-autre-la-justice-penale-est-silencieuse_5356187_1652666.html>.

Mansel HP, Dauner-Lieb B and Henssler M (eds), *Zugang zum Recht: Europäische und US-amerikanische Wege der privaten Rechtsdurchsetzung* (Nomos 2008).

Marchetti P and others (eds), *Commentario alla riforma delle società* (EGEA and Giuffrè 2005).

Marques CL, *Contratos no Código de Defesa do Consumidor: o novo regime das relações contratuais* (9th edn, Revista dos Tribunais 2019).

Meller-Hannich C, 'Sammelklagen, Gruppenklagen, Verbandsklagen – Bedarf es neuer Instrumente des kollektiven Rechtsschutzes im Zivilprozess? Gutachten A zum 72.

Deutschen Juristentag' in *Verhandlungen des 72. Deutschen Juristentags – Leipzig 2018, Band I, Gutachten, Teil A–G* (CH Beck 2018).

Micklitz HW and Saumier G (eds), *Enforcement and Effectiveness of Consumer Law* (Springer 2018).

Mikalonienė L, 'Subsidiari akcininko atsakomybė' (2010) 76 Teisė 176.

Miragem B, *Curso de Direito do Consumidor* (8th edn, Revista dos Tribunais 2019).

Moalem D, Hedegaard Thomsen H and Rosenbaum T, 'Om prospektansvaret i dansk ret – efter Højesterets dom i bankTrelleborg-sagen' [2013] Erhvervsjuridisk Tidsskrift 153.

Möllers TMJ, 'Zur methodischen Arbeit mit allgemeinen Rechtsprinzipien – aufgezeigt an Beispielen aus dem europäischen Kapitalmarktrecht' in Siekmann H and others (eds), *Festschrift für Theodor Baums zum siebzigsten Geburtstag* (Mohr Siebeck 2017) 805.

Møgelvang-Hansen P, 'Forbrugerret og erhvervsret: to sider af samme sag' in Juridisk Institut, *Julebog 2000* (Jurist og Økonomiforbundets Forlag 2000) 207.

Morabito V, 'An Evidence-Based Approach to Class Action Reform in Australia: Common Fund Orders, Funding Fees and Reimbursement Payments' (January 2019) <https://ssrn.com/abstract=3326303>.

—— 'An Evidence-Based Approach to Class Action Reform in Australia: Closed Class Actions, Open Class Actions and Access to Justice' (October 2018) <https://ssrn.com/abstract=3272089>.

—— 'An Evidence-Based Approach to Class Action Reform in Australia: Competing Class Actions and Comparative Perspectives on the Volume of Class Action Litigation in Australia' (11 July 2018) <https://ssrn.com/abstract=3212527>.

—— 'An Empirical Study of Australia's Class Action Regimes: The First Twenty-Five Years of Class Actions in Australia' (Fifth Report, July 2017) <http://ssrn.com/abstract=3005901>.

—— 'An Empirical Study of Australia's Class Action Regimes: Facts and Figures on Twenty-Four Years of Class Actions in Australia' (Fourth Report, August 2016) <http://ssrn.com/abstract=2815777>.

—— 'An Empirical Study of Australia's Class Action Regimes: Class Action Facts and Figures – Five Years Later' (Third Report, November 2014) <http://ssrn.com/abstract=2523275>.

—— 'An Empirical Study of Australia's Class Action Regimes: Litigation Funders, Competing Class Actions, Opt Out Rates, Victorian Class Actions and Class Representatives' (Second Report, September 2010) <http://globalclassactions.stanford.edu/sites/default/files/documents/Vince%20Morabito%202nd%20Report.pdf>.

—— 'An Empirical Study of Australia's Class Action Regimes: Class Action Facts and Figures' (First Report, December 2009) <http://globalclassactions.stanford.edu/sites/default/files/documents/Australia_Empirical_Morabito_2009_Dec.pdf>.

Mozetic AM, 'Collective redress: a case for opt-out class actions in England and Wales' (2016) 35 CJQ 29.

Mulheron R, 'The Case for an Opt-out Class Action for European Member States: A Legal and Empirical Analysis' (2009) 15 ColumJEurL 409.

Nascimento Rodrigues S, *A Protecção dos Investidores em Valores Mobiliários* (Coimbra 2001).

Nekrošius V and others 'Grupės ieškinys kaip civilinio proceso spartinimo priemonė' (2016) 98 Teisė 16.

Neuer L, 'Scandale Volkswagen: faut-il engager une action de groupe?' *Le Point* (Paris, 13 November 2015) <http://www.lepoint.fr/editos-du-point/laurence-neuer/scandale-volkswagen-faut-il-engager-une-action-de-groupe-12-11-2015-1980911_56.php>.

Oberhammer P, 'Kollektiver Rechtsschutz bei Anlegerklagen' in Kalss S and Oberhammer P (eds), *Anlegeransprüche – kapitalmarktrechtliche und prozessuale Fragen* (Manz 2015) 73.

Passinhas S, '"Dieselgate" and Consumer Law: Repercussions of the Volkswagen scandal in Portugal' [2017] Journal of European Consumer and Market Law 42.

Pavillon CMDS, 'Leent het materiële privaatrecht zich voor de afwikkeling van massaschade? Een onderzoek naar de veralgemeniseerde toepassing van het aansprakelijkheids- en schadevergoedingsrecht in het pre-WAMCA-tijdperk' [2019] RMTh 163.

Pfeiffer R, *Defesa da Concorrência e Bem-Estar do Consumidor* (Revista dos Tribunais 2015).

Pinto Monteiro A, Passinhas S and Guimarães MR, 'Enforcement and Effectiveness of Consumer Law in Portugal: Filling the Gap Between the Law on the Books and the Law in Action' in Micklitz HW and Saumier G (eds), *Enforcement and Effectiveness of Consumer Law* (Springer 2018) 457.

Podszun R, Busch C and Henning-Bodewig F, 'Consumer Law in Germany: A Shift to Public Enforcement' [2019] Journal of European Consumer and Market Law 75.

Posocco L, 'French Report' in Frigessi di Rattalma M (ed), *The Dieselgate, A Legal Perspective* (Springer 2017) 3.

Riehm T, '"Dieselgate" und das Deliktsrecht' [2016] DAR 12.

Römermann V and Günther T, 'Legal Tech als berufsrechtliche Herausforderung – Zulässige Rechtsdurchsuchung mit Prozessfinanzierung und Erfolgshonorar' [2019] NJW 551.

Schacherreiter J, 'VW Dieselgate – Rechtsdurchsetzung betroffener Fahrzeughalter in Österreich gegen den Hersteller' in Leupold P (ed), *Forum Verbraucherrecht 2018* (Facultas 2019) 37.

Schaumburg-Müller P and Werlauff E, 'Efter Trelleborg – om emittentselskabets eget prospektansvar' [2013] Ugeskrift for Retsvaesen 198.

Scholl B, 'Die Musterfeststellungsklage nach §§606 ff. ZPO: Eine kritische Würdigung mit Bezügen zum französischen, niederländischen und US-amerikanischen Recht' [2019] Zeitschrift für die gesamte Privatrechtswissenschaft 317.

Shen Zhenyi, 'The Volkswagen Emissions Scandal Continues' (2016) 7 Prosecutorial View 57.

Skorupskas V, 'Privataus asmens teisė į žalos, atsiradusios dėl piktnaudžiavimo dominuojančia padėtimi ir kartelinių susitarimų, atlyginimą skirtingose valstybėse' (2015) 22(2) Jurisprudencija 318.

Spitzer M, 'Kollektivinteressen im Zivilprozess' in Kietaibl C, Mosler R and Pacic H (eds), *Gedenkschrift Robert Rebhahn* (Manz 2019) 573.

Stadler A, 'Kollektiver Rechtsschutz bei Anlegermassenschäden' in Lehmann M and Zetzsche D (eds), *Grenzüberschreitende Finanzdienstleistungen* (Mohr Siebeck 2018) 519.

—— 'Stand und Perspektiven der kollektiven Rechtsdurchsetzung in Deutschland und Europa' in Jung P (ed), *Die private Durchsetzung von öffentlichem Wirtschaftsrecht* (Mohr Siebeck 2018) 129.

Tamošiūnienė E and Terebeiza, Ž, 'Problems inherent in the abstract nature of general distribution rule of the burden of proof in civil proceedings' (2013) 9(22) European Scientific Journal 317.

Terryn E and Verbiest P, 'De herziene CPC-verordening als oplossing voor grensoverschrijdend consumentenleed?' [2018] Tijdschrift voor Consumentenrecht & handelspraktijken 6.

Thaler C, *Sanktionen bei Marktmissbrauch: Marktmanipulation, Insiderhandel und Ad-hoc-Publizität* (Manz 2014).

Thelen M, 'Schlechte Post in eigener Sache: Die Pflicht des Emittenten zur Ad-hoc-Mitteilung potentieller Gesetzesverstöße' [2018] ZHR 62.

Tillema I, *Entrepreneurial Mass Litigation: Balancing the Building Blocks* (Eleven International Publishing 2019).

—— 'Exclusieve en concurrerende belangenbehartigers: balanceren op glad ijs?' [2018] Ars Aequi 476.

Tolksdorf K, '„Sammelklagen" von registrierten Inkassodienstleistern – eine unzulässige Erscheinungsform des kollektiven Rechtsschutzes?' [2019] ZIP 1401.

Tzankova I, 'Funding of Mass Disputes: Lessons From the Netherlands' (2012) 8 Journal of Law, Economics & Policy 549.

van Boom WH and Pavillon CMDS, 'The Netherlands takes collective redress to a next level. An introduction to the Collective Redress of Mass Damages Act 2019' [2019] Zeitschrift für Verbraucherrecht 4.

van Lück K, 'Kaufrechtliche Ansprüche des Käufers im Diesel-Abgasskandal' [2019] VuR 8.

United States District Court – Northern District of California, 'In re: Volkswagen "Clean Diesel" MDL' <http://www.cand.uscourts.gov/judges/breyer-charles-r-crb/in-re-volkswagen-clean-diesel-mdl/>.

United States Environmental Protection Agency, 'Volkswagen Light Duty Diesel Vehicle Violations for Model Years 2009–2016' <http://www.epa.gov/vw>.

Veil R, 'Europäisches Insiderrecht 2.0 – Konzeption und Grundsatzfragen der Reform durch MAR und CRIM-MAD' [2014] Zeitschrift für Bankrecht und Bankwirtschaft 85.

—— '§14 Insider Dealing' in Veil R (ed), *European Capital Markets Law* (2nd edn, Bloomsbury 2017) 189.

Wald A, 'A evolução do mercado de capitais no Brasil (1998–2008)' (2008) 41 Revista de Direito Bancário e do Mercado de Capitais 9.

Wei Jinqiao, 'Why doesn't anyone in China Care about the Volkswagen Emissions Scandal?' <http://www.sohu.com/a/37104667_122189>.

Wolf C and Wink T, '§31 Private Haftung' in Meyer A, Veil R and Rönnau T (eds), *Handbuch zum Marktmissbrauchsrecht* (CH Beck 2018) 695.

Xia Xiaoxiong, 'The Three Types of Interest harmed by the Volkswagen Emissions Scandal' *Economic Information Daily* (Beijing, 25 May 2016) 6.

Yang Qin, 'The Development of Chinese Legislations for Protection of Consumer in Sixty Years' (2009) 6 Journal of Guizhou University (Social Sciences) 38.

Yang Xiande, 'Litigation Process Relating to the Volkswagen Emissions Scandal in the US' *Procuratorate Daily* (Beijing, 1 August 2017) 3.

INDEX

D

ABOUT THE EDITORS

Prof. Dr. Beate Gsell holds the Chair of Civil Law, Civil Procedure, European Private Law and Procedure at the Ludwig-Maximilians-Universität Munich (LMU), Germany. She is also a Judge at the Munich Higher Regional Court (OLG München) and member of the management board of the Munich Center for Dispute Resolution (MuCDR). She was appointed a permanent member of the Jean-Monnet-Centre of Excellence on European Integration (INspiRE) at the University of Augsburg. Her research focuses on the system of civil law and its doctrinal coherence including the specific methodological challenges of the multi-level system within the European Union. Within this field, she is particularly interested in the areas of the law of obligations as well as consumer law. Her research is also concerned with (European) civil procedural law, with a particular focus on the enforcement of consumer rights and consumer redress.

Prof. Dr. Thomas M.J. Möllers holds the Chair of Civil Law, Commercial Law, European Law, International Private Law and Comparative Law, Jean-Monnet-Chair ad personam at the University of Augsburg, Germany. He is the coordinator of the EU-funded Jean-Monnet-Centre of Excellence on European Integration – Rule of Law and Enforcement (INspiRE) and founder of Caplaw, a database on German and European Economic Law (www.caplaw.eu). He is Managing Director of the Augsburg Centre for European Legal Studies (CELOS). His research focuses on European law and European economic law. Through an intradisciplinary approach at the interface between (European) contract and tort law, capital markets law and company law, he contributes to new insights to improve law enforcement. Within this framework, his current research focuses in particular on questions of legal methods.